Glenn Arthur Pierce

NAMING RITES

A Biographical History of North American Team Names

with a complete index

Providing some surprising and curious historical account of the origins and creation stories for those collective names by which the professional and collegiate actors in game and sport are recognized by faithful devotees of same.

Ken & Darlene: Thanks! Enjoy!

"History must be this or it is nothing."
Ralph Waldo Emerson

Naming rites: a biographical history of North American team names
International Standard Book Number: ISBN 978-1497545328
First Commercial Printing: September 2014
All content copyright © 2014 by Glenn Arthur Pierce.

For faith in this first print edition and select matters else, the author thanks the Pierce family, the metaphorical and literal button pushers in the Gorgievski family, Tim Green, Bill Littlefield, Mark L. Ford, all hands at SE/BOS, the hundreds of college archivists and athletic department representatives who took our inquiries seriously, and the helpful staff at the Stevens Memorial Library (North Andover, Massachusetts), especially the late Karen Bellaire, whose sneaky suspicion that something was up could not be rewarded in a timely manner. Deserving of a more general appreciation are Prof. George H. Bailey at NECC, Superhoney, Francis W. Cleary, Anthony John Verrino, and E. Stephen Foster of the Brooklyn Public Library.

Contents

Washingtons | Dream | Breakers | Violets

"San Francisco **49ers**."

For decades, middle school teachers have used that phrase to associate a historic event (the Gold Rush) with both a time (1849) and a place (northern California). The present volume humbly suggests that the creation stories for many of your favorite professional and college athletic team names can similarly serve as unwitting historical markers.

At one time teams were identified only with their home cities. Checking the box score from the October 4, 1899 "paper of record"—the *New York Times*—we see that **New Yorks** lost to **Bostons** while **Brooklyns** and **Washingtons** split a double-header.[1] Until World War I, baseball cards were usually stamped with nothing more specific than "TY COBB, Detroit Americans" or "WAGNER, PITTSBURGH." None mentioned **Giants**, **Red Stockings**, **Dodgers**, **Senators**, **Tigers**, or **Pirates**, but sportswriters would soon be coloring reports with such descriptors. Modern fans who wish to comment on "the **Bulls**" rather than "the Chicago Professional Sports Limited Partnership" (their legal name) can understand why. And being named after an old enterprise called the Philadelphia Athletic Club, it's reasonable to ask if the Oakland **Athletics** even have a nickname.

Any veteran of junior high school already appreciates that the nicknames one gives oneself—The Dominator, Magic Hands, Mr. Smooth—rarely resemble those assigned by contemporaries ... Peter Pushover, Butterfingers, Doc Dufus. Thus, the first team at any given college (often footballers) were all too willing to draw attention to the otherness of their competition, making **Parsons** of seminarians, **Rebels** of Southern students, **Teachers** of those trained for such, and **Aggies** or **Mechanics** of A&M attendees. In rare cases, such intended insults as "**Tar Heels**" and "**Boilermakers**" become the identities most cherished at and most quickly associated with their sponsoring institutions.

In fact, "New nicknames, especially when applied to a school, team or group are apt to appear ill-fitting, but they take on polish with constant usage, and are mellowed, aged and honored with time."[2] So said a prescient Fred Pettijohn in 1947 at the start of an illustrious career in Florida journalism. He was addressing the lack of intimacy in the awkward new team tag at Florida State: **Seminoles** ... proving that even the best-loved athletic names can seem unlikely at inception. Or as Nova Scotia author Thomas Chandler Haliburton said of personal nicknames in 1853, "The most ridiculous are the most adhesive." But just try to slip a nonstandard moniker past the watchdogs on today's University Panel for Nickname and Mascot Review. You'd be tarred and feathered for nominating anything so silly as "**Tar Heels**" or "**Hokies**."

When colleges search for new athletic representation, they're likely to launder the decision-making process through outside marketing firms that deliver such extraordinary *new* identities as **Wolves**, **Red Hawks**, or **Storm**. After such an instance of in-the-box thinking has overwhelmed one of our liberal institutions, the team name often arrives fully formed with accompanying emblems, plush mascot costumes, and strictly specified web colors. The attending copyright and trademark protections further divorce the moniker from any historical definition of *nickname*—that which is a casual alternate to a formal or legal name.

If a modern sportswriter called the **Yankees** the "Big Apple **Nine**," we would recognize the intended informality, but problems occur when one such casual reference on microfilm is unearthed decades later by a well-intended researcher. Its subsequent repetition by generations of writers obscures the single-source trail and makes fact of fleeting fancy. In the absence of other samples, who can say whether the team nickname used by a lone knight of the keyboard was or wasn't the one most widely accepted in his day? We mention this to write ourselves a huge blank check in discussing the earliest nicknames; few teams thought to officialize such designations until the post-World War I period.

The WNBA Atlanta **Dream** (est. 2008) explained their name with platitudes about civic pride, core values, and the transcendent power of sport.[3] In other words, "**Dream**" doesn't mean a darned thing in Georgia that it doesn't mean everywhere else, so the **Dream** wakes us to the realization that any Golden Age of Team Naming is behind us. Most honest persons would admit that **Rebels** or **Redskins** are more intriguing than either **Panthers** or **Professionals** in the same way a serial arsonist is more interesting than a habitual jaywalker. Understanding those objections to the former, we wouldn't pick on the **Dream** or what vaguely named teams may come, who—as shall be shown—are simply reacting to the not necessarily bad march of human progress.

Provided with the year-end standings for every sports leagues since 1871, the proverbial visiting alien couldn't be blamed for thinking North America has been occupied almost exclusively by animal predators, Indian warriors, and white, Protestant, male pioneers, all seemingly preoccupied with their sock color. (Blame not the author if persons of other experiences are underrepresented herein.) Still, the identities of our athletic teams—like our surnames, our languages, our physical attributes, our religions—are our history hiding in plain sight. Every backstory doesn't pan out as well as that of San Fran's **49ers**,[4] but modest scrutiny does yield surprises.

· · ·

Like every book about history, this is a book *of* history, reflecting its own place and time. Publication comes at the end of a revisionist wave that put to rest many **Redskins** and **Crusaders**, and with exhibition matches and a few regular-season games being played on other shores, major league sports in the early twenty-first century appear poised for intercontinental expansion, something to broaden the scope of this already too-hefty volume. We're also sure the backstories for future-named teams will be available to any person with even modest web surfing skills.

This wouldn't be much of a history book if we ignored teams of the past. As proved by the Colorado **Rockies**, Milwaukee **Brewers**, New York **Mets**, Ottawa **Senators**, Washington **Nationals**, and Winnipeg **Jets**, old names can be dusted off after generations of neglect.

Witness the unbreakable staying power of "**Breakers**." Football's Boston **Breakers** of 1983 were named after Atlantic waves along New England shores. Those USFLers moved to the Gulf Coast the next year as New Orleans **Breakers**. For their last season, they were Oregon's 1985 Portland **Breakers**, an allusion to

Pacific swells. (Up in Washington State, junior hockey's 1977-named Seattle **Breakers** were just then becoming **Thunderbirds**.) Sixteen years later came the WUSA Boston **Breakers** (2001–03). When the women's soccer returned as the WPS in 2009, Bostonians were again **Breakers**.

That's just one example of a nickname's cross-sport shelf-life. To those still skeptical we offer the 1933 NFL, in which four of the teams had the same name as their established baseball neighbors: Brooklyn **Dodgers**, Cincinnati **Reds**, New York **Giants**, and Pittsburgh **Pirates**. Two of the remaining names complemented those of their baseball landlords: Chicago's **Bears** were mature versions of Wrigley's **Cubs** while the Boston **Redskins** (now in D.C.) borrowed an introductory syllable from Fenway Park's **Red Sox**. In fact, the 'Skins had already been the NFL's Boston **Braves**, renting Braves Field from a baseball club of that name for the season previous.

Readers may have already come across broadcasts of "retro nights" or "classic weekends" in which pros wear throwback uniforms. Increasingly media-savvy fans realize that such events are geared primarily toward apparel sales, but they might yet appreciate explanations as to why their Washington **Wizards** are wearing the Chicago **Zephyrs**' tank tops. And we wouldn't want to ignore those vintage *base ball* clubs of gentlemen amateurs who keep history alive through some monikers as old as the mid-nineteenth century rules they use.

• • •

We must at once make a distinction between mascots and nicknames. *Mascotte* is French slang that describes a sorcerer or charm. In Edmond Audran's 1880 French operetta *La Mascotte*, a young protagonist brings luck to her village. After that piece's 1882 translation, *mascot* was applied in English to a person or animal associated with good fortune, so mascots can either accompany or graphically represent sports teams.

Athletes that once adopted live ruminant or equine or bovine mascots often found themselves labeled **Rams** or **Chargers** or **Bulls** (especially at agricultural colleges). Among the most popular team names by far, "**Bulldogs**" was almost always drawn from the sideline-roaming canine companions of old-time college footballers.[5] The inverse can also be true. Many **Saints** have represented Catholic colleges at which St. Bernard mascots (p. 205) showed up much later.

Athletic rivals of New York University are often flummoxed: Are NYU jocks **Violets** or **Bobcats**? Having long ago taken their color from flowering violets in the adjacent Washington Square Park, NYU's **Violets** are often incorrectly called **Bobcats**. It began in 1984 when a cat cartoon was used to acclimate students to the Bobst Library's digitized book register—the *BOB*-st *CAT*-alog. A costumed bobcat soon turned up at athletic contests. Yogi Berra said, "You can observe a lot just by watching," but even attentive fans can't deduce the real nickname from the stands; like many schools, NYU puts only "NYU" on uniforms.

Athletic mascots are so correspondent to college life that many colleges maintain them even in the absence of varsity teams,[6] and some of the new breed of for-profit colleges use such iconographical devices to create a sense of the *real* college experience for online students never cooled by the shadow of the Old Main. Compare that to Virginia's Hollins University, where the green and gold have competed for decades without a nickname, an irregularity that has yet to visit disaster upon their Roanoke campus.

• • •

Some ground rules.

This book is organized neither alphabetically nor by league, division, sport, or region. The chapters aim to stitch together team names to reveal interlocking histories, with some teams having cross-narrative appeal (especially those that have changed names or home cities over time). You'll need the index to track all references to a given team. A modest effort has been made to reward cover-to-cover reading, but we won't sweat it if the index proves to be a catalyst to aimless wandering during timeouts and commercial breaks.

Some historical details, alternate creation myths, former team names, and troublesome nuances are buried in endnotes. Those persons with a great interest in a particular team or historic event should look therein.

Colleges constantly evolve into universities or move their athletic programs into more prestigious conferences, often simultaneously adopting a less intimate moniker. Minor league teams come and go so fast that it's impossible even on a monthly basis to track them. Leagues of independent baseball, indoor football, and women's football are so particularly volatile that we've often identified their members simply as "minor league" or "semi-pro," and the various circuits and tiers within junior hockey have been reduced to "junior hockey."

In requesting that students and alumni donate everyday objects and anecdotes relevant to campus life and traditions, archivists at Taylor University in Upland, Indiana conceded that a lack of such diligence in the past means they don't know why their own teams are **Trojans** or why they wear purple and gold.[7] Ditto for the University of Arkansas at Little Rock, where archivists have traced the first mention of their own **Trojans** to a 1930 edition of the college paper, but they know nothing of why that name was deemed relevant.[8] You might be an impassioned fan of **Warriors** or **Eagles**, but the absence of any profound nicknaming story may explain their omission herein.

As much as we enjoy the names of some collegiate intramural teams, they've been left out because they operate without the endorsement of institutional administrators and athletic directors. We therefore apologize to (among others) the athletic supporters of the Rhode Island School of Design's **Nads** (crying "Go Nads!" since 1961) or University of Northern Colorado's **Fighting Whities**, mixed-race players who cheekily inverted the Native American mascot controversy in 2002.

For dates, we've used the abbreviations BCE (Before the Common Era) and CE (Common Era), with midfield being Year 0 on the Western calendar. The years of operation assigned to teams indicate seasons played and not necessarily dates founded.

Keeping North American custom, "hockey" refers to ice hockey. Only when necessary, we've identified the similar (and much older) grassbound game as "field hockey."

Redhawks | Savages | Warriors | Redskins

During the last ice age, much of the world's ocean water was locked up in glaciers and polar ice caps. Sea levels dropped so much that human hunters were able to chase game from Asia to Alaska on a land bridge. They then followed the warmth of the sun and settled from southern Canada to Patagonia. After some centuries, hundreds of distinct cultural groups were evident.

To consider those peoples only through their relationships to sports imagery would be unforgivably disrespectful … except that such a treatment is entirely consistent with that for all other actors in this volume.

• • •

The University of North Carolina at Pembroke was founded in 1887 to educate the native Croatan people of Robeson County. Members of any tribe could attend after 1945, justifying UNCP's adoption of "**Braves**" the next year. (Non-Indians have attended only since 1953.) According to Pembroke's chancellor emeritus, Joseph B. Oxendine:

The use of American Indian names, symbols, or traditions by non-Indians is not in and of itself offensive. […] However, there are at least two troublesome aspects to this issue. First, Indians have usually not been involved in the name selection process, and secondly, the manner of their portrayal often has been offensive.[1]

It's been said that athletic **Indians**, **Redskins**, or **Savages** and their mascots serve to define Native Americans only in terms of a historical *otherness*. Author Fergus Bordewich succinctly describes the collective failure to appreciate Indians in any way that transcends that unrelenting otherness: "as if a culture that is literally saturated with allusions to fictional Indians had no interest in living Indians at all."[2] Amerindians are themselves divided about those sporting motifs. Are proud traditions affirmed and honored by **Brave** and **Warrior** lineups? Or have cornball versions of cherished ancestors and sacred ceremonies been co-opted to entertain the skybox-dwelling descendents of the oppressor?

A debate about whether such imagery indicates reverence or identity theft went national when the 1995 World Series had the Cleveland **Indians** facing the Atlanta **Braves**. The former display one of the most clearly racist mascots left in sports (the daffy Chief Wahoo), while fans of the latter practiced the Tomahawk chop, a robotic hacking motion some Indians found mocking.[3] A year later, the United Methodist Church encouraged its schools to reexamine their team identities in a "call for repentance for the Church's role in the dehumanization and colonization of our Native American sisters and brothers." Oklahoma City University had traded **Methodists** and **Goldbugs** for **Chiefs** back in 1945 but responded to the UMC request in 1999 with **Stars**, after night skies on the prairie.

Since its founding in 1968, the American Indian Movement has been trying to get Indian-themed teams to more properly honor their eponyms. Similar efforts are supported by the National Congress of American Indians (est. 1944). In 2001 the U.S. Commission on Civil Rights called for an "end to the use of Native

American images and team names by non-Native schools." The report—which lacked regulatory muscle—pointed out that team names and mascots that employ stereotypical Amerindian themes potentially violate antidiscrimination laws.

A report the next year by the NCAA's Minority Opportunities and Interests Committee recommended that member colleges reexamine their own Native American imagery. The organization set out in 2005 to prohibit colleges and universities from employing any such themes that were "abusive or hostile" on racial or ethnic grounds. A paper to that effect specifically challenged eighteen institutions to investigate nicknames referential to Native Americans, and it established dates after which colleges would be barred from either showing up at NCAA competitions with Indian-emblazoned uniforms or hosting NCAA events.[4]

In light of their institutional history, UNC-Pembroke's **Braves** weren't on the watch list, an exemption the NCAA hoped would exhibit its respect for thoughtful appeals. Along with protests from some of "the eighteen"[5] came quick changes:

- The Midwestern State University **Indians** (Wichita Falls, Texas) probably referred to the county's Caddo people. They became **Mustangs** in fall 2005.
- The Carthage [Ill.] High School **Blue Boys** were named for their blue jerseys. They once played students from nearby Carthage College, who were **Red Men** for distinction. A one-word version—***Redmen***—went to Kenosha, Wisconsin when CC moved in 1962, and that identity became associated with Indian motifs. That imagery was gone by 2006 and the **Redmen** reverted to **Red Men** while **Lady Reds** remained,[6] modifications that satisfied the NCAA.
- The University of West Georgia swapped **Braves** for **Wolves** in 2006. The Carrollton school is in the former territory of Lower Creek Indians.

• • •

Newfoundland's Beothuks were no longer a distinct people by the early 1800s. Their habit of covering their bodies and possessions with oxide-rich soil had been noticed by white explorers and fishermen who may have called them "redskins" for the first time. Memorial University of Newfoundland in St. John's had **Beothuks** until 1989 but has since referenced coastal ospreys through **Sea-Hawks**.

In fact, teams abandoning Indian imagery often embrace winged raptors. We again quote Joe Oxendine (a Lumbee Indian): "The tradition of the hawk goes back centuries for local Native Americans."[7] He was speaking at the 1999 unveiling for a bronze statue of the hawk mascot that his own UNC-Pembroke **Braves** had adopted in 1992. Other **Braves** and **Indians** became **Hawks** outright:

- Chowan University (Murfreesboro, N.C.) presented its **Hawks** in 2006 to get off the NCAA list but maintained the hawk feather that had been associated with past **Braves**. Both the university and the Chowan River are namesakes of the Chowanoke people who were among the great Algonquian tribes of North Carolina. They battled the English colonists in the Virginia Colony but were pretty much done in by European diseases and were among the first natives to be confined to reservations.
- The Catawba Trail was part of the Great Indian Warpath from Georgia to Niagara Falls. It crossed Pennsylvania's future county of Indiana and the town of Indiana, the home of Indiana University of Pennsylvania. IUP teams became

Indians in 1928. Citing the red-tailed hawks (*Buteo jamaicensis*) near campus, the crimson and gray became the **Crimson Hawks** in 2006. Their hawk mascot is named Norm to allude to the **Normalites** that used to represent that normal (teachers') college.

- North Carolina's Catawba people are at the southern end of the Catawba Trail, and other namesakes include the Catawba River and Rowan County's Catawba College (which was in Catawba County from 1851 to 1925). The Catawba College **Indians** became **Catawba Indians** in 2006. Back in Catawba County, students at Catawba Valley Community College voted to ditch their land-locked **Buccaneers** in spring 2014. The red, white, and black were thereafter **Red Hawks**, with a red-tailed hawk mascot.
- Dickinson [N.D.] State University's **Savages** became **Blue Hawks** in 1973, a change likely welcomed by the area's Siouan people.
- Montclair [N.J.] State University started out innocently with the red-and-white **Big Red** in the 1920s before making the nearly inevitable transition to **Indians** through cartoon mascots. Montclair State's women came to be **Squaws**, which is complicated because etymologists can't decide if *squaw* is an Algonquian word for a woman or a derogatory reference to her anatomy (making for few **Squaws** squads today). Since 1989, MSU has kept **Red Hawks**. Not far from MSU's campus is the New Jersey Audubon Society's Montclair Hawk Watch, an outlook from which one can spot raptors against the New York City skyline.
- In historical Iroquois country, the Hartwick College **Warriors** (Oneonta, N.Y.) dropped Indian mascots to become Hartwick **Hawks** in 1994.
- The best-known of the Puget Sound Indians was the Duwamish-Suquamish chief *Si'ahl* or *Sealth* or—to whites—*Seattle*. He was once remembered by the Seattle University **Chieftains**, recast as **Redhawks** in 2000.[8]
- Martin Methodist College (Pulaski, Tenn.) swapped its **Indians** for **Redhawks** in 2002.
- A Christian seminary in Rochester, New York became Roberts Wesleyan College in 1949 and formed a basketball team of **Raiders**. They were named after desert raiders in the Old Testament (those that bullied the Israelites and those Israelites that retaliated), but they never had mascots to convey that. By the 1960s, drawings of Indians were associated with the **Raiders**, who were firmly in old Seneca country. In the 1980s the **Raider** became a cavalryman, but RWC entered the NCAA Division II in fall 2012 as **Redhawks**.[9]
- Teams under coach Red Martin at Ripon [Wis.] College were "Red's Men" or **Redmen** in the late '20s, although the latter may have already been an alternate to "**Crimson and White**." To escape the inevitable Indian themes, they tried to pass the parsed "**Red Men**" and "**Lady Reds**" forms in 1990 and then simply "**Red**" in 1991, finally settling as—*spoiler alert!*—**Red Hawks** in 1994.[10]

• • •

As long as the above list is, it doesn't include those **Hawks** discussed elsewhere, including the Miami University **RedHawks** (ex-**Redskins**), Southeast Missouri State **Redhawks** (ex-**Indians**), Lake Michigan College **Red Hawks** (ex-**Indians**),

Northeastern State **Riverhawks** (ex-**Redmen**), and UMass-Lowell **River Hawks** (formerly **Chiefs** and **Indians**).

It also ignores variations like "**Warhawks.**" For example, the University of Louisiana at Monroe had **Indians** at its 1931 founding because the Ouachita River basin was the home of Choctaws and Caddos. ULM got off the NCAA list in 2006 by launching **Warhawks**. They now have a red-shouldered hawk (*Buteo lineatus*) mascot, but the moniker actually salutes pilots of the Curtiss P-40 *Warhawk*. That was the signature aircraft of the American Volunteer Group, which attacked Japanese positions from bases in China during World War II. More famous as "Flying Tigers," they'd been assembled by Lt. Gen. Claire Chennault, whose boyhood was spent in northeast Louisiana.

Chennault had developed revolutionary flying and pursuit tactics in the 1930s at Maxwell Field in Montgomery, Alabama, so the **Warhawks** at Auburn University–Montgomery recall those same pilots. (AUM hosted **Senators** until spring 2011, as Montgomery is the state capital.)

The Detroit **Tigers** moved their spring training camp to Lakeland, Florida in 1934. Their Lakeland **Tiger** affiliates were summer residents from 1963 onward. Lakeland's aeronautics school trained thousands of new combat fliers for World War II. Because some ended up in Chennault's command, the Lakelanders were extended to *Flying* **Tigers** in 2007.

When McMurry University opened at Abilene, Texas in 1923, its president was Methodist educator James W. Hunt, whose dad had been a doctor on the Kaw Indian reservation. It was for those people that Hunt named McMurry's **Indians**. To get off the infamous NCAA list, administrators decided (somewhat indignantly) to forgo any nickname in 2006, playing only as "McMurry" for five years until teams became **War Hawks** in spring 2011. In 1960 the school formed a cooperative educational program with the nearby Dyess Air Force Base. Lt. Col. William Dyess was shot down in World War II and escaped a Japanese P.O.W. camp in the Philippines to become the first man to detail the horrors of the Bataan Death March. Echoing the transition at UL-Monroe, Dyess's aircraft was a P-40 *Warhawk*.

• • •

"**Eagles**" is the most familiar team name in college sport[11] and another common choice for teams dropping Indian connections. In summer 1967, Eastern Washington University's trustees overruled many students and alums to change its **Savages** to **Eagles**. Evansville's University of Southern Indiana recast **Chiefs** as (**Screaming**) **Eagles** in 1989. The **Eagles** at the University of Wisconsin–La Crosse are former **Indians** (1937–89), possibly because the Indian game lacrosse was first observed by Frenchmen at the place they called *Prairie La Crosse*.[12]

Across the state, Milwaukee's blue-and-gold Marquette University **Warriors** were **Golden Eagles** by 1994. It takes a couple of hours to drive south to Illinois Valley Community College (Oglesby, Ill.), where **Apaches** became **Eagles** in 2001, acknowledging that Athabascan speakers of the Southwest didn't have homelands on the Great Lakes. Husson College in Bangor replaced **Braves** with **Eagles** in 2005. (Presumably, central Maine's Penobscot people were the **Braves** in question.) Other **Eagles** in this pattern (that are discussed elsewhere) are at Eastern Michigan (ex-**Hurons**) and Juniata College (ex-**Indians**).

There's a good reason **Eagles** and **Hawks** often replace **Indians**, **Redmen**, and **Chiefs**. In the United States, only members of federally recognized tribes can possess feathers or other parts of certain raptors. Even then, a license is required and the display of such relics is restricted to religious and spiritual ceremonies. That Eagle Feather Law aims to protect the bald eagle, golden eagle, and the red-tailed hawk, so newly named **Eagles** and **RedHawks** don't stray as far as they might from Native American totems.

• • •

Getting the "**Red**" out of "**Red Raiders**" was a late-century fashion:

- Southern Oregon University in Ashland shortened **Red Raiders** to **Raiders** and dropped all Native American notions in 1980 in favor of "Raider," who was … *wait for it* … a red-tailed hawk.
- The Central Lakes College **Red Raiders** (Brainerd, Minnesota) switched to **Raiders** in 1989.
- Shippensburg University of Pennsylvania is locked in the Cumberland valley, but because it is affectionately "the Ship" the **Red Raiders** were able to drop the adjective in 1993 and switch to pirate raiders. (City founder Edward Shippen was a Quaker Loyalist and an original trustee at both Princeton and Penn.)
- Colgate University (p. 98) fielded its first **Red Raiders** in 1932, but they too were **Raiders** by 2001.[13]

• • •

The **Warrior** at Michigan's Rochester College "changed from an Indian theme to a Christian **Warrior** in 1997."[14] When classes began in fall 1960 at California State University–Stanislaus, its **Warriors** in gold, green, and "Indian red" were intended to "perpetuate for many decades the role of the Indian in the history of the Old West,"[15] but in 1999 those Indian mascots yielded to a "warrior hawk." That proved to be an intermediate step when CSUS turned to Greco-Roman foot soldiers in 2005. This too is a trend. Many Indian-themed **Warrior** teams avoided controversy by swapping mascots near the turn of the twenty-first century:

- Milwaukee's Wisconsin Lutheran College **Warriors** replaced Native American emblems in 2005 with the visored helmet of a knight.[16]
- Southern Wesleyan University (Central, S.C.) is on former Cherokee land. Its **Warriors** traded their crossed Indian arrows for a knight in 2012.
- In the 1940s the NBA's Philadelphia **Warriors** posted silly-looking Indian emblems. As California's Golden State **Warriors**, they created a spandex-wrapped comic book hero named Thunder in 1997. (Golden State fans felt their thunder had been stolen in 2008 by the new Oklahoma City **Thunder**.)
- St. Louis Community College's Meramec campus dumped **Warriors** for alliterative "Meramec **Magic**" in 2000. All of the STLCC campuses confederated their teams as **Archers** in 2011, referring to that memorial to westward expansion, St. Lou's Gateway Arch (previously cited by WPSL St. Louis **Archers**, 2004–05).

- The Hendrix College **Warriors** (Conway, Ark.) traded Indian heads for warrior shields in 2001. When alternate imagery of an ancient warrior was introduced in 2007, Hendrix took pains to indicate his ethnic ambiguity. But with his two-tone face paint and his light-colored hair fluttering in the winds of war, that advancing broadswordsman looks like a prototypical Gaelic barbarian to us.
- In 1947 war veterans on the G.I. Bill composed 60 percent of the first all-male class at Merrimack College (North Andover, Mass.) (Coeducation came in 1950.) MC's paper was the *Warrior* and **Warriors** soon occupied a Quonset hut gym. They traded Indian head profiles for classical warriors in 2003.[17]
- Also in 1947 the first classes at El Camino College (Torrance, Calif.) were held in some modified Air Force barracks. Its **Warriors** had arrowhead emblems through 2009, but ECC jocks no longer use mascots or logos.
- Corban University's **Warriors** (Salem, Ore.) had Indian mascots until arming with gladiator swords and shields in 2003.
- The **Teachers** and **Peds** at one Minnesota teachers' college became **Warriors** in the 1930s. As Winona State University, they dropped their Indian for a classical warrior in 2005.
- A columnist for the East Stroudsburg [Pa.] University newspaper decided in 1932: "This writer in the future is going to refer to the [**Red and Black**] as the **Warriors**."[18] Corresponding Indian imagery lasted until 1995, so there was no mascot until a student in a bear suit and gladiator armor—"Burgy"—became the face of Stroudsburg athletics in 2010.
- Eastern Connecticut State University stripped its maroon-and-blue **Warriors** of their Indian head in the 1990s. Then a blue bobcat represented Eastern (as in "eastern bobcat," *Lynx rufus rufus*) until the Willimantic school's **Warriors** got behind a gladiator shield in 2009.

• • •

Another undeniable trend has broken the horizon:
- The Simpson College **Redmen** and **Lady Reds** corresponded to the name of their Indianola, Iowa campus. In 1992 they rode out as a (singular) **Storm**.
- St. John's University (Queens, N.Y.) upgraded its cardinal-colored **Redmen** (and its women's basketball **Express**) to a **Red Storm** in 1994.
- The last collegiate **Redskins** were those at Southern Nazarene University in Bethany, Oklahoma. They became a **Crimson Storm** in 1998.
- Also in '98, the Chemeketa Community College **Chiefs** (Salem, Ore.) turned into a **Storm**.
- Southeastern Oklahoma State University's **Savages** became a **Savage Storm** in May 2006, an immediate effect of their inclusion on the NCAA list.
- The **Redmen** and **Redwomen** at the University of Rio Grande (Rio Grande, Ohio) are a **Red Storm** as of 2008.
- The Keuka College **Warriors** (Keuka Park, N.Y.) became a **Storm** in 2000 but switched to a **Wolfpack** in August 2014.

In 2010, Macon State College made a **Blue Storm** of its first intercollegiate teams since 1997 (the old **Mustangs**). That **Storm** lasted until MSC merged in 2013 with Macon's Middle Georgia College to become Middle Georgia State College. The combined institution sallied forth with (mounted) **Knights**, combining the **Blue Storm's** mustang mascot with MGC's **Warrior** history.

• • •

Even ignoring the red make-up worn by Beothuks, American Indians generally had more richly colored skin than Europeans, and it's entirely possible that "red men" or "redskins" were innocently developed as differentiators by either the newly arrived "white men" or the natives themselves.

Expanding white settlement into Indian lands, however, inevitably created animosity that gave "redskin" a requisite contemptuousness. Nearly every major dictionary now says the word is either a pejorative or offensive slang, and it's been a good long while since any white person has felt comfortable greeting a given Native American with "Hey Redskin!" ... which is perhaps the simplest way to appreciate the problem presented by the *R-* word.

Athletes have been running from "**Redskins**" for decades. (The yearbook for the Oklahoma State **Cowboys** was the *Redskin* until it ceased publication in 1991.) The NFL Washington **Redskins** (p. 25) are exceptions, being steadfast in their particular manner of honoring Indians.

Some **Red Men** or **Redmen** claim innocence through their historical use of crimson uniforms, saying the Indian motifs with which they later became inde- liberately associated should not preclude the continued use of said identity. But "redmen" resonates in the collective cultural memory only because of the Native Americans; if the association between "redmen" and Indians is only coincidental, our league chronicles should be crowded with objectively labeled **Greenmen**, **Bluemen**, and **Goldmen**, but such instances are rare at best. And we need not address the etymology of *redskin* to know how long a team of **Whiteskins**, **Yellowskins**, or **Blackskins** would last today, even if said athletic moniker had been derived from the shirt color.

Mohawks | Salukis | Seminoles | Chippewas | Illini

The Eastern Woodland people lived in the forests south and east of the Great Lakes. They subsisted by hunting, fishing, and planting, with buckskin clothes and footwear being natural byproducts of game hunting.

The Five Nations of the Iroquois (Mohawks, Oneidas, Onondagas, Cayugas, and Senecas) were the dominant Woodlanders below Lake Ontario. They and the Hurons have been playing lacrosse for 800 years, sometimes with hundreds of players per side. Their descendents in New York and Ontario have been competing internationally as **Iroquois Nationals** since 1983, even traveling to some overseas tournaments on Haudenosaunee (Iroquois) passports. Canada's first MML team, the 2009-founded Toronto **Nationals**, hoped to attract stars from both the **Iroquois Nationals** and Canada's *national* team. They've been forty miles south as Hamilton **Nationals** since 2011. Using the tagline "Two nations, one team," their emblem includes both the Canadian maple leaf and the Hiawatha wampum belt that is symbolic of Five Nations unity.

Junior hockey's Toronto **Nationals** of the early 1970s were the *Seneca* **Nationals** in later years (1976–80), recalling members of the westernmost Iroquois nation whose alliance with Britain brought them to Ontario after the American Revolution. The Seneca Nation's namesake is Greater Toronto's Seneca College, at which Indian-themed **Braves** (men) and **Scouts** (women) gave way to the **Sting** in 1999. Senior box lacrosse's Six Nations **Chiefs** (est. 1993) play in the Iroquois Lacrosse Arena (Six Nations, Ont.), as do the junior-level Six Nations **Arrows**.[1]

The easternmost Iroquois were the *Kanienkehaka* (people of the flint). They were called "Mohawks" by Narragansett Bay enemies to whom *Mohowawog* describes a cannibal in the Algonquian language. A string of **Mohawk Giants** represented the Mohawk River town of Schenectady (*Skahnéhtati* is a Mohawk description for a place beyond the pines), the most famous being among the top independent black baseballers in the early teens and again in the 1930s. The Massachusetts College of Liberal Arts in North Adams dropped its **Mohawks** for **Trailblazers** in 2002, both derived from the Mohawk Trail. That's the name that New York's state highway 2—an old Indian trail—assumes when it crosses into Massachusetts to pass right in front of MCLA's front door.

• • •

From southern Saskatchewan to Florida, Eastern Woodlanders built flat-topped earthen mounds at the centers of farming villages. Those could be burial plots, shrines, or (less often) defensive ramparts. Some surviving mounds are state parks at which the decline of their builders around the time of European contact is being investigated. Southwestern College keeps **Moundbuilders** in Winfield, Kansas.

Some moundbuilders created animal-shaped earthworks, especially the Effigy Mounds people of the western Great Lakes, the likely ancestors of the Ho-Chunk (Winnebago) people. In the 1830s white pioneers in Wisconsin found mounds that are now on the Beloit College campus. The most famous is Turtle Mound, inspired by the snappers in nearby Turtle Creek. The city's minor league baseball players have been Beloit **Snappers** since 1995.

Earthworks along Ohio's Scioto River are indicative of the Hopewell culture, a term applied indiscriminately to Woodlanders whose huge trade network was the Hopewell exchange system. (The type site at Chillicothe is the former farm of the [white] Hopewell family.) The Scioto Valley town of Circleville is in fact built atop ancient circular Hopewell earthworks. Ohio Christian University in "Roundtown" has **Trailblazers** that owe to the vast system of footpaths, but many of its settlers would have arrived via Zane's Trace, a frontier trail that puts **Tracers** at Ohio University–Zanesville (p. 229) sixty miles away.

A frontier minister saw weathered Indian mounds near the confluence of the Mississippi and Ohio Rivers and thought things looked enough like pyramids along the Nile to call it Goshen (after Egypt's Land of Goshen from the Bible). Soon all of southern Illinois was "Little Egypt,"[2] and an 1818-founded city was named Cairo after Egypt's largest city—locally, "*kay*-row." It was home to minor league Cairo **Egyptians** for most baseball seasons from 1903 to 1950.

In 1852 enterprising businessmen put a town fifty miles north of Cairo and called it Carbondale. (The Illinois Central would soon pass through, and carbon-based coal is the fuel for a steam engine's boiler.) The rail town did prosper and the school that became Southern Illinois University opened there in 1869. Its paper has been the *Daily Egyptian* since 1916, but SIU's maroon-and-white **Maroons** weren't called **Salukis** until 1951. The saluki was hieroglyphically validated as the hunting dog of pharaohs with the discovery of Tutankhamun's tomb in 1922. In fact, the canine "King Tut" who was the school's mascot in the early 1950s will rest eternally beneath a pyramid-shaped stone in front of Saluki Stadium until some British guy in a pith helmet decides to dig him up.[3]

Down the Mississippi a piece is Memphis, named for the capital of Egypt's Old Kingdom. Greater Memphis is home to the campuses of Southwest Tennessee Community College, where **Saluqis** better resemble *Saluq*, the name of the ancient town in Yemen at which the saluki breed probably originated. Baseball's Memphis **Egyptians** (1901–08) were in the Southern Association, and indoor football's Memphis **Pharaohs** (1995–96) played in the city's 32-story Pyramid Arena, one of the largest pyramids outside Egypt.[4]

In 1960, Southeastern Illinois College opened at Harrisburg, forty miles east of SIU's **Salukis**. There's a sphinx on the SIC shield and campus streets are Sahara and Egyptian Drives. SIC's **Falcons** and feathered mascots may at first seem to not fit that theme, but they are the acknowledged namesakes of Horus, the Egyptian sky god. You've probably seen hieroglyphs of Horus countless times; he has the body of a man and the oversized head of a falcon.

The Egyptians used salukis to hunt rabbits and hares on open terrain. That oldest form of dog racing ("coursing") was later a rage in Renaissance England. In fact, English greyhounds—today's track dogs—were long thought to be descended from salukis (but modern DNA evidence suggests otherwise). By the mid-1800s greyhounds were all over Missouri and Kansas to rid fields of rabbits, and the first coursing event in the U.S. was held in Kansas in 1886. You'll still find top greyhound breeders in that region, and teams of **Greyhounds** represent both Kansas's Fort Scott Community College and Missouri's Moberly Area Community College.

Greyhound is derived from *grighund*, the origin of which is in the grey area between Norse and Old English words for a hound. So a priest at Assumption College (Worcester, Mass.) had no problem calling his Catholic school's speedy blue-and-white basketballers **Greyhounds** in 1933. That was soon official, even with the old colors. In fact, grey greyhounds are like many steel-colored dogs in that "blue" describes them.

• • •

Eastern Mississippi's Nanih Waiya mound complex is the legendary birthplace of the Choctaw Indians, farming people from modern Mississippi and western Alabama.[5] Because the Choctaws had allied with the French during the Colonial Wars, they weren't at home in their own homeland after the English won the Mississippi's eastern bank.

President Jefferson wanted all natives moved across the Mississippi as early as 1803. That plan accelerated with the 1828 election of Indian fighter Andrew Jackson to the presidency. Mexico still held the deserts, so the Oklahoma Territory was the southwesternmost United States and a seemingly convenient place to deposit the natives of the Southeast and Old Northwest. "Indian *Schmindian*" the Euro-Americans must have thought as they moved the Eastern Woodlanders onto those plains long occupied and understood by people with whom they shared no cultural history.

Under threat of military action, a few Choctaw elders signed the 1830 Treaty of Dancing Rabbit Creek near Nanih Waiya. That facilitated a twenty-year relocation of the Choctaw Nation of Red People to the Indian Territory, named with the Choctaw (Muskogean) words *okla* (red) and *humma* (people). The headquarters for the Choctaw Nation of Oklahoma are in Durant, a city later shared with the Southeastern Oklahoma State University **Savages**. They changed to a less offensive **Savage Storm** in 2006.[6]

The Dancing Rabbit Creek treaty allowed some natives to stay as the Mississippi Band of Choctaw, but even most of them would be cheated out of land, and they endured white settlement and animosity. By 1900 most Choctaws were poor sharecroppers, but livelihoods have improved since the 1970s through campaigns to attract industry and by federal rulings in the 1990s that allow sovereign Indian nations to open gambling casinos. Most Mississippi Band members now live on reservations in east-central Mississippi, which isn't too far east of the Mississippi College **Choctaws** in Clinton.

One of the largest Indian mounds is Emerald Mound near Natchez, Mississippi, built by the Natchez people. The Gulf Coast Frenchmen and Choctaws destroyed the Natchez as a cohesive tribe by 1740, but the Natchez Trace remains the 400-mile road from Natchez to Nashville. Near the start of the Trace is Alcorn State University (Lorman, Miss.). Its basketball **Scalping Braves** caused offense when they played at Wisconsin in 1993, and the **Badgers** consequently refused to schedule games against foes employing Indian imagery except for conference rivals and tournament opponents. (Fellow Big 10-ers at Iowa followed suit, which is a little ironic because UI's **Hawkeyes** are to some degree named after a Sauk chief, Black Hawk [p. 136].) The "**Scalping**" bit and the attending tomahawk emblem were quickly gone, but Alcorn retains **Braves**.

A pocket of Siouan speakers in the western Carolinas and Virginia are connected to the moundbuilders through their traditional pottery, although the depth of the relationship isn't clear. The meaning and origin of *Catawba* is also unknown, but it applies to those who called themselves *Iswa*, "river people." The NCAA executive committee opposed the vagueness of the **Indians** at Catawba College (Salisbury, N.C.), so in 2006 Catawba teams agreed to go forward only as "Catawba College **Catawba Indians**," providing they maintain the endorsement of the Catawba Nation.[7]

• • •

White settlers called the Eastern Woodlanders of the Southeast (Cherokees, Choctaws, Chickasaws, Creeks, Seminoles) the Five Civilized Tribes. Indications of civilization apparently include their settlement of permanent villages, their election of officials, and their ownership of slaves.

The Seminoles were a communion of Lower Creeks and escaped slaves from Georgia and Alabama who found refuge in Spanish Florida. In fact, *Seminole* is from the Muskogee (Creek) words *simanó-li* and the Spanish *cimarrón*. Both mean "runaway" and were applied to natives who'd escaped from bondage or been expelled from their tribes. They later took in African slaves who'd escaped Southern plantations or revolted in the Caribbean. The parallel French word is *maronage*. Anglicized as *maroon*, it resonates in eastern Kentucky, where slaves escaping on the Underground Railroad likely made their last stops before crossing into the North. Eastern Kentucky University came to its "**Maroons**" honestly through reddish-brown uniforms, but when African American students arrived on the Richmond campus in 1963, EKU president Robert Martin quietly made teams **Colonels** (see p. 134), reportedly having been made aware of the ambiguity of "maroons."[8]

After the War of 1812, Gen. Andrew Jackson went into Spanish Florida to round up escaped slaves and Britain's former Indian allies. His victory in the First Seminole War (1817–18) put many Indians onto reservations. Jackson exceeded his orders by seizing Spanish forts in West Florida. That convinced Ferdinand VII that his hold on the area was untenable, and Spain ceded it to the U.S. in 1821 to cancel a debt. A central capital under territorial governor Jackson was set up at the Seminole village of Tallahassee ("old fields" in Muskogee), which is now the home of the Florida State University **Seminoles**.[9] Seminole State College of Florida in Sanford has **Raiders**, but raptor mascots steer intuition away from Indian raiders.

After he became president, Jackson signed the first Indian Removal Act of 1830, sending the Indians of the Southeast to the center of the future state of Oklahoma (which freed up northern Georgia for America's first gold rush). A Second Seminole War (1835–42) erupted when warriors under Chief Osceola resisted the deportation. After that, only the few hundred Seminoles that were hunkered down in the Everglades remained a threat,[10] so Fort Myers was built to protect white settlers in 1850. Indeed, Indian raids were common when the Third Seminole War broke out in 1855. After the surrender and removal of the most troublesome band in 1858, other Seminoles kept low profiles in the wilderness. Their ancestors in southern Florida call themselves "unconquered people," the only eastern Indians to have successfully resisted the Federal removal. Florida Gulf Coast University is in modern Fort Myers. Its blue-and-green **Eagles** don't reveal a lot of history, but their eagle mascot Azul refers to the Spanish period, as *azul* is the Spanish word for "blue."

Northeastern Georgia's Yonah Mountain is in the southernmost Blue Ridge Mountains. Its profile justified the **Mountaineers** at Truett-McConnell College in Cleveland. Wishing to be representable by animal mascots, they became **Great Danes** and female **Danettes** in 1966. With *yonah* being the Cherokee (Iroquoian) for a bear, TMC moved easily to **Bears** squads in 2004.

The historical Cherokee lands include the Blue Ridge's Smoky Mountains, which split North and South Carolina. Newberry is in the latter. Its Newberry College **Indians** played until spring 2008, retiring that identity after failing to find agreement with the NCAA. Nicknameless for a spell, the Newberrians became **Wolves** in mid-2010.

• • •

The Cherokees and Choctaws fought their trans-Mississippi relocation and even won in the U.S. Supreme Court in 1832. But Georgia—in an example of states' rights issues—didn't abide the decision. Even President Jackson ignored the ruling and sent in federal troops to collect the natives.

One internment camp was on the Tennessee River at Moccasin Bend (named for its Indian slipper shape), adjacent to the transportation hub of Chattanooga. The University of Tennessee at Chattanooga kept **Moccasins** until the Chattanooga InterTribal Association asked that Indian motifs be dropped in late 1996. UTC was lucky, though. By shortening **Moccasins** to **Mocs**—most people called them that anyway—teams could recognize the state bird, the mockingbird (*Mimus polyglottos*).[11]

After their lockdown at Moccasin Bend and other Tennessee Valley sites, many Indians were marched overland during the harsh winter of 1838/39. The Cherokees called it *Nunna daul Tsuny*, "Trail of Tears," because one quarter of their nation (some 4,000 people) died en route to Oklahoma. Southeastern Missouri's Trail of Tears State Park is the resting place for one Cherokee victim, "Princess" Otahki, once remembered by female **Otahkians** at nearby Southeast Missouri State University in Springfield. Men's teams were **Indians** for eight decades, but all SEMO teams became **Redhawks** in 2004.

The Trail of Tears ended at the new Cherokee capital at Tahlequah, Oklahoma (now the Cherokee County seat). The Cherokee Female Seminary that opened there in 1851 is today's (coed) Northeastern State University. With a higher percentage of full-time Amerindian students than any other four-year college, NSU was somewhat sensitive when its **Redmen** and **Lady Reds** were scrutinized, but all teams at the Illinois River campus became **Riverhawks** in 2007.

A corresponding Cherokee Male Seminary also opened in 1851 at Tahlequah, but it closed in 1898 because the Feds wanted to assimilate Native Americans into mainstream society and open tribal lands to white settlement. To educate Indians with Christian values, the Male Seminary's superintendent, A.C. Bacone, opened

Tahlequah's Indian University in 1880 with help from the Baptists' Home Missionary Society. Five years later it moved to Muskogee, the administrative center for the relocated Five Civilized Tribes. The **Warriors** at the renamed Bacone College get behind a cross-emblazoned Indian brave's shield.

• • •

The Algonquian-speaking Ojibwas, Odawas, and Potawatomis had a common history north and east of Lake Huron until about 1500. Migration sent the Ojibwas to northern Michigan and Minnesota and the Potawatomis into southern Michigan. The new arrivals competed with the *Meskwaki* (Fox) and the Sioux for planting fields, hunting grounds, and fishing spots. The Lake Michigan College **Indians** in Benton Harbor, Michigan were the Potawatomis' acknowledged namesakes until becoming **Red Hawks** in April 2012, embracing the red-tailed hawk so revered by the Pokagon Band of Potawatomi.

In the mid-1700s the Ojibwas got French rifles through Odawa traders and drove the Sioux from Minnesota and forced the Fox into defensive confederations with Sauks. The Ojibwas also elbowed the powerful Iroquois out of Michigan's mitten to claim dominion over land from Ohio to Saskatchewan, the largest swath ever controlled by a single tribe. Ojibwas—Anglicized as "Chippewas"—worked with Frenchmen during the colonial wars, with Pontiac during his rebellion of the 1760s, and with the English during the Revolution and the War of 1812. After Britain's defeat in 1815, the Ojibwas were moved onto reservations. The Chippewa River runs through their old territory, including Mt. Pleasant, the city where Central Michigan University keeps **Chippewas.**[12]

The Ojibwas' cousins were the *Odawas* (traders). Ottawa is their namesake Canadian capital in their easternmost ancestral homelands. Many stateside Ottawas were relocated to reservations in an 1833 treaty, so there's another Ottawa in Kansas, where Baptists opened a school for Ottawa children in 1865. Ottawa University has had **Braves** since 1924. Unfortunately, the institution's founding turned out to be a bit of an instrument for relieving Ottawas of their real estate, a situation historian William Unrau called "an unusual example of church and government collusion in appropriating Indian land, under the guise of educational advancement."[13]

• • •

Iroquoian Mohawks had good trade relations with the Hudson Valley Dutch and they offered to run such a near-monopoly for the French in 1641, but Frenchmen had never gotten along with the Iroquois and were reluctant to alienate their Huron-Wyandot partners. With the Hudson watershed trapped out, the Iroquois tried to eliminate the competition by attacking Huron villages north of the St. Lawrence and Lake Ontario in the Beaver Wars of the 1640s. As a result, most Hurons had fled to the Ohio Valley and southeast Michigan by 1700.

Many Huron descendants are now in eastern Kansas and Oklahoma, having been removed from the Midwest in the 1840s. But Eastern Michigan University in Ypsilanti remains bounded on the north by the Huron River, as attested by **Hurons** teams between 1929 and 1991. The former normal school had **Normalites** before then and **Eagles** after, having dropped Indian images.

Several related tribes in the upper Mississippi and Illinois River valleys were collectively the *Hileni* or *Illini*, their Algonquian words for "superior men" from which Frenchmen rendered *Illinois*. European diseases killed thousands of Illini in the first half of the 1600s, but mutual anti-Iroquois sentiments made the Illini France's military and commercial partners. After France gave up ground in the colonial wars, the Illini faced their numerous Indian enemies alone. They ceased being the region's dominant natives, and internal conflicts would put Illini warriors on both sides in the Revolution.

By the 1803 Louisiana Purchase, only a relative few Illini remained in southern Illinois and Missouri. In 1867 even they were moved to Oklahoma, where their descendents are the Peoria and Kaskaskia tribes. That same year the University of Illinois was founded at Urbana-Champaign, where athletes are **Fighting Illini**. In 2006 the NCAA approved the continued use of that moniker when it accepted UI's claim that it refers to all Illinoisans. But a fictitious Chief Illiniwek had represented UI since first appearing at a halftime show in 1926. For decades he was the chief offender to folks opposed to Indian mascots. Defenders pointed to the authentic Sioux design of the costume that the chief started wearing in 1982, confusing (if not insulting) anyone who knew that the culturally distinct Sioux and Illini are historical enemies. The chief was retired in February 2007.[14]

Single-A baseball's Peoria **Chiefs** (1984–) play in an Illinois city named for the Peoria band of the Illini. That city's Bradley University is the former Bradley Polytechnic Institute, where **Techs** and **Techmen** yielded to **Braves** in 1937. (They dumped Indian emblems in 1989.)[15]

Having old alliances with Britain, the Maumee (Miami) people of western Ohio and northern Indiana were driven to Kansas reservations with little sympathy in the 1840s. Their rights were combined with those of the culturally and linguistically similar Peorias and Kaskaskias, so they were part of the subsequent 1867 removal to Oklahoma. The Maumees give their name to the Little and Great Miami Rivers in southwestern Ohio and therefore indirectly to Miami University at Oxford. Jocks at "Miami of Ohio" were **Redskins** by about 1930, but they responded to a request for change from Oklahoma's Maumee people and became **RedHawks** in 1997.[16]

Wisconsin's western shore of Lake Michigan was a home to the Chippewa, Menominee, Ottawa, Potawatomi, and Winnebago people until its cession to the U.S. in the 1830s and '40s. The Sheboygan **Redskins** (est. 1938) were a good NBL team that joined the BAA/NBA for the 1949/50 season, long before that team name was a political hot [redskin] potato.

Aztecs | Zias | Apaches | Fighting Sioux

The people who called themselves *Mexica* claimed to be from the mythical land of *Aztlán*. They gave Uto-Aztecan languages to many Indians in the Great Basin and Southwest, but the word *Aztec* usually applies only to their Mexica ancestors.

The Aztec capital at Tenochtitlan was Mexico's cultural and political power-base after 1400 CE. There they practiced advanced arts and engineering, but neighbors more likely took notice of the Aztec habit of tearing out and presenting the still-beating hearts of war prisoners for sacrifice, often to the god of the sun and war, Huitzilopochtli. In one myth he transforms into a white eagle to represent the Aztec homeland. *Águilas Blancas* (white eagles) play American football at Mexico City's *Instituto Politécnico Nacional*.[1]

Hernán Cortés left Spanish Cuba in 1519 to relieve Mexico of mineral riches. He allied himself with the natives most fearful of heart abstraction and waged bloody war on Aztecs for two years, unwittingly deploying European diseases as his most effective weapon. Cortés built atop Tenochtitlan's ruins and renamed it Mexico City after those he'd wiped out.

Other visitors would also soon be destroying native cultures only to name cities, rivers, and sports teams in their honor. But these aim to be more reverent:

- Texas has hosted soccer's Austin **Aztex** since 2008. The Comanches are the Uto-Aztecan people most closely associated with the region.
- Many fans of the L.A. **Aztecs** (NASL, 1974–81) were Mexican-American.
- The Pimas of south-central Arizona and northern Mexico speak Uto-Aztecan *O'odham*, so Tucson's Pima [County] Community College has **Aztecs**. *Jego* ("*jug*-oh") is the O'odham word for a strong dust storm before a downpour. Pima County's Tohono O'odham Community College (in Sells) first presented **Jegos** in mid-2011.
- Some Uto-Aztecans migrated to California between Death Valley and San Diego Bay. Athletes at San Diego State Teachers College (now San Diego State University) replaced **Staters** and **Professors** with **Aztecs** in 1925.[2]
- In Mexico proper, *Aztecas representan la Universidad de las Américas en Cholula, Puebla*.
- Just after the defeat of the Aztecs, the Virgin Mary reportedly appeared on Mexico City's Tepeyac Hill. Franciscan *fraires* (friars) spotted an opportunity to graft the characteristics of the Aztec goddess Tonantzin onto that "Virgin of Guadalupe" and built Mexico's most sacred shrine. A mile away are the **Frailes** of American football at the *Universidad del Tepeyac*.

The Uto-Aztecan Hopis and Zunis from the Four Corners area are the Aztecs' descendants. By 900 CE they were making clay homes that the Spaniards called *adobe* (mud brick) in villages called *pueblos* (towns). At northern New Mexico's Zia Pueblo, the Zia sun symbol was first seen. (It's been on the state flag since 1925.) **Zias** teams of women represent Eastern New Mexico University in Portales, but ENMU's men are **Greyhounds**, owing to their swiftness. (ENMU's women were **Greyhoundettes** until 1981.)

Traders along Colorado's Arkansas River recalled the adobe style when they named one mudbrick post Fort Pueblo. That town of Pueblo is north and east of the Pueblos' homelands, but "Pueblo **Indians**" would have sounded familiar anyway. (Several such sides were in baseball's Western League between 1900 and 1912.) Colorado State University–Pueblo traded **Indians** for **ThunderWolves** in 1995. The WL Pueblo **Braves** (1931–33) recognized that Ute and Apache warriors attacked Fort Pueblo in 1854, leaving most whites uninterested in settling the area until the Colorado Gold Rush of 1859 (p. 271).

• • •

Often allied against the Spanish with the Pueblos were nomadic Apache and Navajo tribes. Both speak the Athabascan-Apachean languages derived from their common ancestors of the Alaskan interior who'd dropped down into the Southwest by around 1100 BCE. There are **Apaches** at Tyler Junior College in Tyler, Texas and Cochise College in Douglas, Arizona. The latter—in the Apache State's Cochise County—is named for the Apache chief Cochise, who fought white encroachment into Apache homelands from 1861 to 1871.

Navajos fought federal armies in the Mexican-American and Civil Wars. The 9,000 Navajos who surrendered in the latter endured the Long Walk of 1864, a 300-mile forced winter migration to internment camps along eastern New Mexico's Pecos River. An 1868 treaty returned some ancestral lands as reservations (mostly in northeast Arizona), but the Indians had to walk back. Exactly a century later, Navajo Community College opened in Tsaile, Arizona. Because Athabascan speakers call themselves *Diné* (people), NCC is now Diné College. Its **Warriors** embrace the spirit of Navajo braves. Diné is the oldest of thirty-plus colleges in the American Indian Higher Education Consortium, and elsewhere in the Navajo Nation is a newer such institution, Navajo Technical College (Crownpoint, N.M.). Smack between NTC and Diné is the Navajo Nation Zoo, which rescues the injured and abandoned red-tailed hawks and golden eagles that are so celebrated by Navajo people. With similar reverence, NTC teams are **Sky Hawks**.

• • •

For generations before European contact, Plains Indians drove bison herds over cliffs to maintain their supply of meat, hides, bone tools, and fuel (dung and grease fat). Noting that bison had long provided for regional natives, the founders of Shawnee's Oklahoma Baptist University named their campus Bison Hill in 1906, hoping that grads would likewise "meet the needs of the world."[3] OBU's **Baptists** were therefore **Bison** after 1918.

The hunting got easier as European horses and guns were gained in trade, and former agricultural Sioux, Cheyenne, Crow, and Pawnee people started migrating with the great herds. In the 1700s, the ancestors of the Confederated Salish and Kootenai Tribes of Idaho and Montana became bison hunters. Salish Kootenai College (Pablo, Mont.) on the Flathead Reservation backs **Bison**.

The French heard the Chippewas and Ottawas call their adversaries *Nadouessioux* (little snakes), shortly shortened to *Sioux*. Exhibiting an opposing bias, Siouan speakers call themselves "friends" in their different dialects: *Nakota* to the Yankton, *Dakota* to the Santee, and *Lakota* to the largest Sioux band, the Tetons. In North Dakota's old Teton territory are the **Tetons** of Williston State College.

Several incarnations of Sioux City **Soos** ("Siouxs," 1903–60) played minor league ball[4] in an Iowa city that's hosted minor league Sioux City **Indians** (1914–19) and Morningside College's **Maroon Chiefs**, both named for the Yanktons. Morningsiders became **Mustangs** to escape that association in 1988, but the last wild mustangs of the Northern Plains that descended from Indian ponies are in fact often called Nokota (variant of *Nakota*) horses. South Dakota's University of Sioux Falls switched **Braves** to **Cougars** in 1978.

The **Farmers** and **Aggies** at the Fargo agricultural college that's now North Dakota State University became **Bison** in 1919. In 1894 a great football rivalry had started with the University of North Dakota **Flickertails** (a nickname for prairie squirrels) from Grand Forks.[5] In the 1930s, UND jocks became the **Fighting Sioux**, so games against the **Bison** metaphorically revived the buffalo hunts.[6] The rivalry ended in 2003 when the **Bison** left the division. In 2011, UND retired "**Fighting Sioux**" after decades of painful controversy, and teams were known simply as "North Dakota." We doubt the athletic identity that will be unveiled some time after 2014 will invite controversy.[7]

• • •

The plural of *bison* is *bison*, observed above by the **Bison** from SKC and NDSU. However, several colleges do field **Bisons**, including Winnipeg's University of Manitoba.[8] That's not necessarily incorrect. Once *Bison* describes an athlete, it can assume all of the benefits pursuant to its proper-noun station; the first letter is capitalized while the regular plural simply adds the -*s*. An invitation from Mr. and Mrs. Foot—for example—is signed "The Foots," not "The Feet." This is the noun-to-proper noun transition that excuses **Maple Leafs** and **Forest Citys**.[9]

That gives some comfort to those Miami **Marlins** fans who think the plural of *marlin* is *marlin*. It is, but *marlins* is a perfectly acceptable form (in some dictionaries, the preferred one). We blame the zero-plural, a morphological wild card that allows words that look singular to act all in-your-face plural-y. Outdoorsmen use it to "bag some marlin" or to "track down bear," and some writers refer to a "village of 700 Eskimo" or the "removal of the Cherokee." (We mostly do not.)

In the opposite scenario, a high draft pick might be welcomed as "the newest **Wolf**," but that noun is really a back-formation from the established team name, **Wolves**. A small but growing number of names in the singular don't help; it's not practical to call a Miamian "a **Heat**" or an Alabaman "a **Crimson Tide**." And a lone **Red** or **White** *Sock* would be little use to anybody (especially the Foots).

"Buffalo" is so stubbornly applied to the American bison (*Bovidae: Bison bison*) that it's barely considered wrong anymore. In a strict sense, though, buffaloes are found only in Africa and Asia as respective Cape buffalo (*Bovidae: Syncerus caffer*) and water buffalo (*Bovidae: Bovinae bubalus*).[10] Unlike the *bison*-or-*bisons* quandary, you can't screw up "more than one buffalo"; *buffaloes, buffalos,* and *buffalo* are all accepted plurals. Most colleges on historical bison turf use the preferred form, "**Buffaloes**," as seen at West Texas A&M in Canyon, Arkansas Baptist College in Little Rock, and the University of Colorado in Boulder.

Totems | Seahawks | Kermodes | Thunderbirds

Coastal Indians from the Columbia River to Alaska use totem poles to tell ancient stories or to display clan membership. Washington State's last pro hockey players were in fact minor league Seattle **Totems** (1958–75).

Modest poles were traditionally carved with stone, bone, flint or shell, but the magnificent ones that became hallmarks of the Pacific Northwest weren't possible until steel tools and axes were gained in trade from the Russians, and later the British and Americans.

• ••

Totem poles reflect local traditions, so the spiritual roles of totem animals differ among the area's indigenous peoples. Take these explanations as general:

- **Ravens**: The raven is a clever trickster in many regional myths. The NLL's Vancouver **Ravens** played lacrosse in British Columbia from 2002 to 2004.

- **Eagles**: A hooked beak distinguishes a totem eagle from a raven. The eagle represents the heavens, strength, and leadership, or it can assume the form of a human dancer. The Lummi people of northwest Washington run Bellingham's Northwest Indian College and its **Eagles**. An hour up I-5 is the lower Fraser River valley, the homeland of the Kwantlen people of the Coast Salish. In 1981 their descendents approved the use of their tribal name by a new tech school in Surrey called Kwantlen Polytechnic University. Its athletes are also **Eagles**.

- **Seawolves**: Different folks along the coastal British Columbia–Alaska border have their own tales of sea creatures with both wolfish and fishy features. The mascot for **Seawolves** at the University of Alaska at Anchorage is the half-wolf, half–killer whale that the Haida people call *Wasgo*. UAA teams had been **Sourdoughs** until 1977. Miners became identified with sourdough bread during California's Gold Rush, in which packets of sourdough (starter bread) around the neck marked experienced miners. (In fact, Sourdough Sam remains the San Francisco **49ers**' mascot.) The practice went north with the Alaska Gold Rush of the 1890s, and that state's old-timers are still called sourdoughs.

- **Thunderbirds**: Thunderbirds are mystical protectors and harbingers of storms. The Vancouver campus of the University of British Columbia hosts a marvelous museum of totem poles and **Thunderbird** athletes. (The UBC women were **Thunderettes** until 1982.) Junior hockey's 1985-named Seattle **Thunderbirds** are fifteen miles north of Highline College's **Thunderbirds** (Des Moines, Wash.). Cascade College (Portland, Ore.) had teams of **Thunderbirds** until it closed in 2009.

- **Falcons**: The emblems for most of the above teams are drawn with the clean formlines carried over from the carving process. (The killer whale of the NHL Vancouver **Canucks** is an excellent example, with the orca totem symbolizing size and power.) In fact, totem figures are so stylized that it's tough to tell eagles from falcons. Seattle Pacific University and Langara College in Vancouver both field **Falcons**, which represent birth and leadership.

- **Seahawks**: The United States Commissioner of Education in Alaska, Andrew Thompson, had graduated from a Colorado normal school in 1897. Under circumstances that were never that clear, Thompson ended up in a position to donate a beautiful fifteen-foot Tlingit totem pole to the Greeley campus in 1914. The grizzly on top turned **Teachers** into **Bears** at the University of Northern Colorado in the mid-1920s. Congress's 1990 Native American Graves Protection and Repatriation Act let native people reclaim ancestral remains and archeological treasures from museums, so Totem Teddy was returned to the *Teikweidi* (bear) clan of the Tlingits at Angoon, Alaska in 2002.

• ••

The word *totem* had been carried west after being derived from the Ojibwa-Algonquian form *ododam/odoodeman*, which refers to family or clan kinship. That proves that Amerindian clans outside the Pacific Northwest can be identified with symbolic animal totems. They just don't necessarily carve them on poles.

   In fact, the thunderbird is widely revered among Native Americans from the Great Lakes, the Great Plains, and the Southwest. Large birds predict thunder and lightning simply because their ample wingspans let them float ceaselessly on updrafts created by the instability of approaching storms. Sioux, Caddo, and Ojibwa people administer United Tribes Technical College in Bismarck, North Dakota and its **Thunderbird** teams. The Southern Utah University **Broncos** in Cedar City changed into **Thunderbirds** in 1961.[1]

• ••

The kermode black bear (*Ursus americanus kermodei*) is found only in the rain-forests of British Columbia's central and northern coasts. Most kermodes look like other black bears, but a genetic variation gives about 10 percent of the population white or soft cream coats. To First Nations people, that ghostly "spirit bear" demands reverence. South of the kermode's range, the only collegiate **Kermodes** represent Quest University Canada in Squamish, B.C.

• ••

The indigenous Pacific Islanders of Hawaii are *kanaka maoli* (true people). The mascot for Honolulu's triple-A Hawaii **Islanders** (1961–87) on Oahu was a native warrior from the time of Kamehameha I. He was the first ruler of the Kingdom of Hawaii in 1795.

   Local families thought the essence of a deceased member could be become manifest in a divine power animal, or *aumakua*. Kamehameha's guardian along those lines was *pueo*, Hawaii's short-eared owl (*Asio flammeus*) subspecies. The other top *aumakua* token is *mano* (the shark). **Sea Warriors** at Hawaii Pacific University on Honolulu Harbor used to have shark mascots, but they became **Sharks** in mid-2014 out of expressed reverence for *mano*.

Indians | Little Giants | Bulldogs | Braves

In 1879 the Carlisle Indian Industrial School opened in abandoned Army barracks at Carlisle, Pennsylvania. Its **Indians** seem to demand no more explanation than would Italian soccer players called **Italians**, but even here there's irony; the concession made by "**Indians**" contradicted Carlisle's plan to strip young students of their native identity and assimilate them into mainstream society, best expressed by Carlisle founder Richard H. Pratt: "Kill the Indian, save the man." A veteran of the Civil War and Indian Wars, Col. Pratt's institution was one in the mode of those he understood best, a military academy at which students were dressed and addressed as "Cadets."

In 1884, Kansas Congressman Dudley Haskell helped start the Indian Industrial Training School in Lawrence that's now Haskell Indian Nations University. Hundreds of Indian industrial schools operated between the 1880s and 1930s, but "only two attained significant acclaim in the area of athletics. […] Athletes were actively recruited to Carlisle and Haskell in the belief that a prominent sport program would reflect well on the institution."[1]

Carlisle closed in 1918 after Congress looked into the "laxity in the academic program [and] overemphasis on athletics"[2] (among other concerns). Thereafter, Haskell alone—the "New Carlisle of the West"—would draw most of the superior Amerindian talent to its **Fighting Indians**, and the American Indian Athletic Hall of Fame opened on the HINU campus in 1972.

• • •

James Francis Thorpe discovered football at Haskell but left for Carlisle in 1904. His career took off when Glenn "Pop" Warner returned for his second coaching stint there in 1907. Thorpe played multiple positions, excelling as runner and placekicker. He and Warner got famous while turning a profit for Carlisle during a great 1911 season. Thorpe even won gold in the new pentathlon and decathlon events at the 1912 Olympics. When it was revealed the next year that he'd played semi-pro baseball in 1909 and 1910, the Olympic overseers stripped his amateur status and medals (restored in 1982). Thorpe could now play for pay, but with pro football still unsteady, he joined New York's 1913 baseball **Giants**. Hired largely for his Olympic fame, he continued being distracted by football and joined the Ohio League's Canton **Bulldogs** in 1915, just a week after they'd defeated the Altoona **Indians** (or **Ex-Carlisles**), a line stocked with Thorpe's former Carlisle mates.[3]

In 1920, the year after Thorpe left baseball's bigs for good, **Bulldogs** owner Ralph Hay held meetings in his Canton auto showroom to create the American Professional Football Association (APFA, soon the NFL). Thorpe became the symbolic president of the circuit and the player-coach for Hay's own **Bulldogs**.

Jim and Chippewa teammate Joe Guyon (future pro Hall of Famers) went to the APFA Cleveland **Tigers** in 1921, promptly making them Cleveland **Indians** (echoing local baseballers). Thorpe was injured in game two and sat out the rest, with the **Indians** folding at season's end.[4]

Thorpe's athletic prowess makes a strong case for hybrid vigor. Raised on a Sac-Fox reservation in the Indian Territory, he characterized himself as an American Airedale,[5] referencing his Irish-Sac-Fox-French-Potawatomi blood. English Airedale terriers have the mixed blood of otterhounds and several big terriers, resulting in an extremely smart and vigorous canine. Thorpe would have known of Airedales through his hunting partner, breeder Walter Lingo, who enjoyed hanging with celebs. Lingo assembled the only all-Native American team in pro sports history in 1922, with Thorpe as head coach and recruiter for the NFL's "Jim Thorpe's Oorang **Indians**." They were based at LaRue, the Ohio home of Lingo's Oorang Kennel and the smallest-ever APFA/NFL home city.[6] Having convinced himself that Indians and Airedales were kindred spirits in some kind of touchy-feely new-age symbiosis, Lingo had his players wear native dress while ushering his dogs around in the middle of **Indians** games, which many sports historians cite as the dawn of the halftime show. (Going 4-16 over two seasons, the Oorang **Indians** folded after 1923.)

• • •

Other Carlislians made excellent coaches. Omaha Indian Francis Cayou was an 1896 Carlisle grad who improved the football program at Indiana's Wabash College from 1904 to 1907. In his first season, players acquitted themselves well even while losing to much larger intrastate rivals like Indiana, Notre Dame, and Purdue, and Cayou was heard to congratulate his "little giants" by a reporter for the *Indianapolis News*. That gave the Crawfordsville school its **Little Giants**.

The first footballers at Washington State's aggie and tech school in Pullman were **Farmers**, changing to **Indians** somewhere during the coaching tenures of former Carlisle players Frank Shively (1898–99), William Henry Dietz (1915–17), and Gus Welch (1919–22). During Welch's first season at what became Washington State University, his **Indians** tore up Cal's **Golden Bears** by a score of 14-0. A Bay Area illustrator drew the Washingtonians as grizzly-pestering cougars. With momentum from the cartoon, "**Cougars**" was firmly in place when former Carlisle **Indian** Al Exendine took over in 1923.

The aforementioned "Lone Star" Dietz was Thorpe's best blocker in Carlisle's famous 1911 lineup. Then he was head coach at Washington State (1915–17),[7] Purdue (1921), Louisiana Tech (1922–23), Wyoming (1924–26), and Haskell (1929–32). In 1933, Dietz took over the NFL Boston **Braves**, who'd been established in the '32 season at Braves Field (the home of National League baseball's **Braves**). But owner George Preston Marshall was already moving his year-old crew a mile east to Fenway Park as Boston **Redskins**. That name maintained the **Braves**' Indian theme and recognized the heritage of Coach Dietz as he reported it. (More on that in a second.) But one certainly notices the repetition of the *Red-* prefix from Fenway's **Sox**.

Disgusted with the low turnout for his winning Boston team, Marshall moved them to his hometown as Washington **Redskins** for 1937 and was immediately the first NFL owner to fund a large college-style pep band. Musical director Barnee Breeskin wrote "Hail to the Redskins" in '38 for the NFL's southernmost team, and the lyric "Fight for Old D.C." was changed to "Fight for Old Dixie" from 1959 to '61. That was one of Marshall's subtle tactics for keeping the South in his own NFL pocket, as was blocking the admission of the Dallas **Cowboys** to the league. But Breeskin split with Marshall and sold the rights to "Hail" to a lawyer for would-be Dallas owner Clint Murchison. That meant Murchison was able to trade the **Redskins'** own fight song back to Marshall as part of the agreement that let the **Cowboys** into the NFL in 1960.

• • •

The etymology of *redskin* actually isn't that clear, but almost every modern dictionary says it's offensive or derogatory. Unrelenting pressure on the Washington **Redskins** to change their name during the 2013 season meant that every conversation about them either started or ended with thoughts about the moniker, all the more because the team (bought by Dan Snyder in 1999) met high pre-season expectations with a craptacular 3-13 record that left folks with little else to talk about.[8] A cascade of journalists, newspapers, and websites then stated that they could get along just fine in the future by referring to Snyder's side simply as the "Washington D.C. NFL team."

And it's not like the capital's franchise can lean on a proud history of race sensitivity. Its original players were called **Braves** only for having leased the grounds of baseball's Boston **Braves**—themselves named by some Tammany Hall political operatives who'd co-opted Indian honorifics. (See p. 222.) They became **Redskins** in supposed honor of Dietz, who back in 1920 had been very publicly sentenced to a month in the joint after pleading no contest to charges that he'd assumed his Native American identity only to avoid the Great War draft.[9] (Native Americans couldn't serve until they gained full citizenship in 1924.) The John F. Kennedy administration had to leverage the **Redskins'** lease at a year-old federally owned bowl (later Robert F. Kennedy Stadium) to integrate the team for 1962 because Marshall had theretofore refused to sign a single African American to the last all-white NFL team, saying, "We'll start signing Negroes when the Harlem **Globetrotters** start signing whites." He died in 1969, leaving much of his fortune to a youth charity so long as none was applied to "any purpose which supports or employs the principle of racial integration in any form."

In June 2014 the team's "**Redskins**" trademark was canceled by the U.S. Patent and Trademark Office on the basis that derogatory terms cannot enjoy such protection. That alone can't force the team to pick a new name, but—assuming the ruling stands after the lengthy appeals process—anyone will be able to stamp "**Redskins**" on their line of foam fingers or beer koozies … a loss of exclusivity that represents some deep green to your neighborhood sports mogul and the other revenue-sharing owners in his league.

Lacking much curiosity as to whether those inconvenient truths put the **Redskins** on the wrong side of history, the defenders of the nickname (and there are plenty) almost universally counter each of the above points with a single word: "tradition." Team officials continue to wonder aloud how anyone could see their name and imagery as anything other than a respectful charity and benevolence. If the team survives the pressure, though, it will be the first to have done so, making for an odds-on bet that a child near you will someday ask if we really followed major league **Redskins** well into the twenty-first century.

Bisons | Bills | Sabres | Zephyrs

Sixty-million bison roamed the American plains before the Civil War. The railroads of the 1860s paid bison hunters to feed their workers, but that finished off the great herds only when it was compounded by sport killing, itself part of a plan to make the Plains Indians more manageable by destroying the object central to their culture and economy.

"Buffalo" Bill Cody got his nickname by shooting thousands of big shaggies for the Kansas Pacific Railway (which would become a branch of the transcontinental Union Pacific Railroad in 1880). Many whites first saw real Indians when *Buffalo Bill's Wild West* toured nationally and in Europe starting in 1883. That's how the tepees and headdresses of the Plains tribes became the boilerplate for recognizable Indianness,[1] a circumstance that often burdens east coast **Indians** with geographically misplaced attributes.

A 1947 fan poll changed the AAFC Buffalo **Bisons** (1946) to **Bills** to remember Buffalo Bill. The 1950 AAFC-NFL merger sent those players to Cleveland's **Browns**, but "Buffalo **Bills**" returned with a 1960 AFL team, now in the NFL.[2] The redundancy of Buffalo's many **Bisons** seems to have bothered few:

- There were Buffalo **Bisons** in baseball's NL (1879–85) and PL (1890), and minor league **Bisons** have played nearly continuously since 1886.
- The NFL fielded Buffalo **Bisons** from 1924 to 1929.[3]
- The **Bisons** that played in the 1926/27 ABL were remnants of basketball's legendary Buffalo **Germans.**
- Buffalo **Bisons** skated in the AHL from 1940 to 1970.

Expressly to gain distinction from those listed above, the University at Buffalo put its own **Bisons** out to pasture in 1930 to favor another bovine brand—**Bulls.** (In 1997 the UB women became **Bulls** too, having been **Royals** and **Lady Blues** from colors of royal blue and white.) When NHLers arrived in 1970, they understandably didn't want anything **Bison-** or **Buffalo-**related, but they came pretty close as **Sabres**. That exhibits rapier wit for a team that scoots around on *blades*. *Sabre* is also a variant spelling of *saber*, the sword that has served for centuries as a symbol for cavalry units, like those who fought the bison-hunting Indians on the Great Plains after the Civil War. The city of Buffalo's subconscious connection to the Plains persistently results in Wild West names for sports teams, like the NLL Buffalo **Bandits** (1992–). They and their cowboy mascot are tied to the **Sabres'** ownership group.

Of course, understanding how an eastern municipality got named *Buffalo* to begin with would explain most of these Nickel City's team names. We've thus far avoided that question because … we don't know the answer. The city was named for nearby Buffalo Creek, which only helps if we discover its origin. French missionaries supposedly called the magnificent Falls of the Niagara *la beau fleuve* (beautiful river). Say "*beau fleuve*" three times fast to see how Anglo tongues rendered "buffalo." But that story isn't in the historical record until the 1860s, around the same time that *boeuf à l'eau* (ox at the water) is suggested as the name of a local pasture. A Seneca named Buffalo may have lived near the creek, or early white settlers could have carried "Buffalo Creek" west from Pennsylvania, where a so-named stream feeds the Juniata.[4]

• • •

Collis P. Huntington was the principal backer of the Central Pacific Railroad. Immediately after the Civil War, he planned a deep-water port to which his Chesapeake and Ohio Railroad could export Ohio Valley coal. He chose Newport News, where Virginia's James River empties into Chesapeake Bay.[5] That city is the namesake of Capt. Christopher Newport, who'd brought England's first permanent New World colonists to Jamestown in 1607. The Newz is home to Christopher Newport University's **Captains** and their Captain Chris mascot. The huge ship-building and repair shop that Huntington opened in 1886 is now across the strait from the world's biggest naval base at Norfolk. Both Newport News and Norfolk have launched athletic **Shipbuilders**, **Builders**, and **Admirals**.

• • •

Bridges over wild rivers made rail service between Chicago and western frontiers possible by the early 1880s. Things got even more exciting in the 1930s with the advent of diesel-powered Zephyr trains. Named for the Greek god of the west wind, the streamlined Zephyr was famous after making the thousand-mile run from Denver to Chicago's 1934 World's Fair in thirteen hours. Chicago and Denver have therefore both hosted pro **Zephyrs**, including the triple-A Denver **Zephyrs** (1985–93) and the NBA Chicago **Zephyrs** (1962/63). The latter had been Chicago **Packers** the year before, but Windy City fans hardly knew those **Zephs** before they blew out of town to become the Baltimore **Bullets** and then the Washington **Wizards**.[6] The emblem for minor league hockey's Chicago **Express** (2011/12) was a diesel-powered bullet train.

• • •

The transcontinental line was completed in May 1869 when the Central Pacific (coming east from Sacramento) met the Union Pacific (out of Omaha) in northern Utah. People expected one of two golden spikes to secure the final tie, but those nails were only ceremonial. One is in a museum at Stanford (funded by CPR bigshot Leland Stanford, Sr.) and the other is long lost. Salt Lake has a long history of Utah **Golden Spikers** in minor and club sports. Back at the Union Pacific's hometown, some minor league baseballers were Omaha **Golden Spikes** from 1999 to 2001.

Vandals | Celtics | Paladins | Lutes

During Europe's Iron Age, linguistically similar warrior tribes dominated the lands north of the Alps. Their Chieftains led family clans whose power was based on an ability to produce tools and armor and a willingness to use them in battle. Crawling west after 600 BCE, they introduced their metal-making technologies to those they invaded.

The Greeks called those troublemakers *Keltoi* or *Galatai* (others). Roman variations included *Celtae* and *Gallia*. To us they're *Celts* or *Gauls*.

The Celts crossed the Alps to invade northern Italy around 400 BCE, nudging the once powerful Etruscan city-states onto the road toward irrelevance. Within a decade they'd handed Rome its first taste of barbarism. But the Romans would recover, finish off the Etruscans, and forge an empire. The Celts retreated across the Alps, but revenge was exacted centuries later when Roman general Julius Caesar divided and conquered the Celtic tribes in the land of Gaul (roughly modern France).

During those Gallic Wars from 58 to 51 BCE, Caesar stopped by the island of Great Britain to check in on its Celtic *Britons* to dissuade them from assisting their Continental cousins. Approaching Britain's coast, Roman legionnaires would have described Dover's chalky White Cliffs with the Latin word for white, *albus*. *Albion*, therefore, is a Latinized description of Britain, so Albion College's **Britons** (and their medieval warrior Brit) are a bit redundant. (Both Albion, Michigan and its seminary were founded in the 1830s by Methodist settlers from Albion, New York.)

Caesar's military successes made him Rome's dictator,[1] but Romans would wait nearly a century before reinvading Britannia. That's when the most troublesome Celtic tribes were pushed to the hinterlands of Ireland, Scotland, Wales, and Cornwall. It's precisely because those places exceeded Rome's reach that distinct Celtic and Gaelic cultures could thrive in them.

• • •

Rome's empire peaked near the end of the second century CE, but soon it could hardly contain itself. Civil wars and political rivalries destabilized the western part of the empire and created loopholes through which nomadic gangs from the north and east could slip. The Roman emperor Constantine avoided those hordes in 330 by moving his capital a thousand miles east to Byzantium and modestly renaming it Constantinople. His earlier big play had been a 313 edict that declared toleration within the empire for Christianity, which had theretofore been an inconsequential religious sect.

After his death, Constantine's huge empire split into more manageable halves with a western emperor at Rome and an eastern emperor at Constantinople. In 394 the emperor of the east, Theodosius I, capitalized on political struggles in the west to reunite the empire. He banned pagan celebrations (ending the thousand-year run of the Olympic Games) to favor Christianity, as emperors increasingly put the influence of Rome behind what was later the *Roman* Catholic Church.

Soon, the barbarians' aggression coincided with their retreat from an even greater threat. The Huns were ruthless Central Asian warriors whose horsemen and archers raided both halves of the Roman Empire. The Hun invasions of the late 1300s provide background for the legend of Ursula, a Christian British princess who was leading a band of virgins home from Rome when they found the city of Cologne-on-Rhine overrun with Huns. After Ursula refused to marry the Hun chieftain, she and her maidens were massacred. In 1535, Italian nuns started the Company of Saint Ursula to foster the education of girls and unmarried women. The Ursulines founded Ursuline College in 1871 at Cleveland, Ohio, but it's now ten miles east of there at Pepper Pike. Its **Arrows** athletes aim directly toward the martyrdom of Ursula and company at the hands of Hun archers.

The vicious Hun Attila terrified Europe after 441, forcing other barbarians into alliances of convenience with Rome. Knocking on Rome's door in 452, Attila was persuaded to spare the Eternal City by Pope Leo the Great. (The starving and sick Huns probably grabbed the excuse to avoid a fight.) St. Leo, Florida and its St. Leo University are both namesakes of Mr. the Great. As Leo had guarded Rome's doors—and because a *leo* is a Latin lion—concrete lions guarded the Catholic academy's gate during its prep school years, leading to teams of **Lions**.[2]

Already unfriendly toward Rome, the Vandals were an Eastern Germanic tribe on the run from Huns. In 406 they crossed a frozen Rhine to invade Roman Gaul. Fighting through an early Frankish kingdom, the Vandals crossed the Pyrenees in 409 to establish the kingdom of Vandalusia (now Andalusia, Spain), but they were soon muscled out by Visigoths, the area's dominant barbarians who were fresh off a sack of Rome. The Vandals took Roman camps in North Africa in 429 and their marines backtracked to capture a lightly defended Rome in 455. Thanks to Attila, St. Leo was practiced in sweet-talking barbarians at his gate, and he gained assurance that Roman lives would be spared while the Vandals plundered the city. The havoc, therefore, was relatively controlled (in fifth century terms), so we've maligned the victors by using *vandalism* to describe the senseless destruction of property. The Vandals' influence fizzled after a Byzantine fleet conquered their North African ports in 533.

For repeatedly laying waste to opponents in 1917, the basketball players at the University of Idaho (in Moscow) were called **Vandals**. (The nickname was made official in 1921.) In 1968 former **Vandal** halfback Gene Bates became the first athletic director at Washington's Walla Walla Community College, where he's believed to have mapped his alma mater's fighting spirit and black and gold colors onto newly named **Warriors**.[3]

• • •

Problems in post-Roman northern Britannia came from some people that Rome had never even dared conquer, the Picts and Scots. The power vacuum was also noticed by some allied tribes from Europe's Jutland Peninsula, who were always raiding north European shores. Those Angles, Saxons, Jutes, and Frisians crossed the North Sea to invade Britain, where their common Germanicism got them forever filed under "Anglo-Saxons."

When Romanized Britons asked the empire for a little help with their Pictish, Scottish, and Anglo-Saxon issues in 410, they were told to run their own defense;

the legions were going home to counter the Visigoths' already-mentioned sack of Rome. The guy who stepped up was one King Arthur, about whom we know little because the centuries of warfare in post-imperial Europe weren't ideal for record keeping (ergo the "Dark Ages").

Excalibur is the sword that represented Arthur's sovereignty. It's on the coat-of-arms for the city of Peterborough as a salute to the veterans of the War of 1812 whose service was rewarded with land grants in Ontario. P'bro's Trent University **Excalibur** (always singular) pulled the team identity from there.

Whether Arthur was a Celtic chieftain, a Romanized Briton, or some mythical Gaelic hero, his cause was doomed because the Anglo-Saxons conquered what was thereafter *Angle-land* (England). Following precedent, the Celts remained on Britannia's outskirts.

The first newspaper at the Oneonta State Normal School was the *Pen-Dragon* in 1928. Its quill-wielding serpent emblem was a pun; the word *pendragon*—head dragon—often describes the late Celtic-British kings, especially Arthur's father, uncle, and self. The *Pen-Dragon* called Oneonta's red-and-white basketballers **Dragons** in 1938. All squads were **Red Dragons** by the time it became SUNY College at Oneonta in 1948.[4] This got the attention of upstate rivals at SUNY Cortland, who'd already been **Red Dragons** since 1933, based on their own red and white. (Cortland's soccer players were **Red Mules** for decades.)

• • •

For centuries, the people in Celtic Britain applied "Celts," "Gaels," and "Gauls" only to Continental ancestors, but nationalistic revivals would make "Celtic" and "Gaelic" romantic descriptions for those things respectively Irish and Scottish.

After 1900 famous Irish authors and dramatists who wrote in English with a distinct Celtic-Irish lyricism contributed to Ireland's wider Celtic Revival. Soon "Celtic" described the Irish on both sides of the Atlantic, including American athletes of presumed Irish blood. For example, Carlow University's gold-and-purple **Celtics** acknowledge the 1929 founding of that Catholic women's college in Pittsburgh by the Sisters of Mercy from Carlow, Ireland.

After 1845 ports in New York and Boston accepted large numbers of Irish immigrants who were escaping mid-century famines and the limits on economic opportunity set by Ireland's English overlords. Irish descendant Frank McCormack assembled basketball's New York **Celtics** before World War I, and players re-convened afterward as ***Original* Celtics**.[5] Home court was New York's Central Opera House, but fame came in the 1920s through long barnstorming tours.

In Beantown, two pro teams set the Irish tone in the 1930s. The AFL Boston **Shamrocks** (1936–37) and ASL Boston **Celtics** (1933–41) had players of Hibernian stock. That city's BAA/NBA franchise, however, would represent a bit of a watershed. Until World War II it was unusual to adopt nicknames that didn't jibe with the players' own ethnicities, but owner Walter Brown decided to acknowledge both his host city's large Irish population and the late New York team with *Boston* **Celtics** (est. 1946), even though they were heavy with Jewish talent (as were most BAA rosters).

• • •

Written works by Robert Burns and Sir Walter Scott drove the Scottish Enlightenment. That infusion of Gaelicness into the late–eighteenth-century literature of a people long at odds with England gave Scots a strong nationalistic identity. In fact, *Gael* and *Gaelic* came to English as references to Scottish Highlanders, but *Gaelic* is now embraced by all Scots as part of their identity, as indicated by the **Golden Gaels** at Queen's University (Kingston, Ont.), which was chartered in 1841 by Queen Victoria on behalf of the Church of Scotland.

In 563 the Irish monk Columba tried to fortify Pictish Christianity from a monastic foothold off of Scotland's northwest coast, the Isle of Iona. Iona College (New Rochelle, N.Y.), has St. Columba's wheel cross on the seal and **Gaels** sports sides. The Catholic fraternity that opened the school was the Congregation of Christian Brothers, a teaching order founded in Ireland in 1802.

Different "Christian Brothers"—the Lasallians—assumed control of Saint Mary's College of California (in Moraga) in 1868. Bay Area sports editor Pat Frayne called SMC's Catholic footballers the **Galloping Gaels** in 1926. (They later got a mounted Irish-Gaelic warrior mascot.) At that time, *Catholic* and *Irish* were becoming increasingly interchangeable, circumstances that had already given **Fighting Irish** teams to Notre Dame.[6]

• • •

King Clovis led a confederation of Germanic Franks westward from the Rhine and ejected the last Roman governor of Gaul in 486 CE. Within a decade, Clovis converted to Catholicism on behalf of all Franks to unify his hordes and facilitate alliances with Romans, Byzantines, and those Gauls already Romanized. Clovis's newfound Christian purity became symbolized by the *fleur-de-lis* (lily flower), adopted by subsequent Frankish (then *French*) kingdoms. In French-founded cities, *la fleur* shows up on the shoulder patches for the New Orleans **Saints**, Quebec **Nordiques**, and **Impact de Montréal**.

The partitioning of power to family princes after Clovis's death fractured his grand kingdom, but Charles Martel came to power in 714 and reunited the Franks across *Francia*. Then he saved Continental Christianity by hammering a Muslim army from Iberia in 732. Still, Martel is overshadowed by a grandson named Charles le Magne (or *Charlemagne*, "Charles the Great"), who squelched his and Rome's enemies to control much of Central Europe. Because that restored some abstract version of the old Western Empire, the pope crowned Charlemagne the first Holy Roman Emperor in 800.

Charlemagne called the knights of his inner circle "paladins," comparing himself to the first Christian emperor Constantine, whose original paladins guarded the palace (*palatio*) on Rome's Palatine Hill. The principalities under Charlemagne's paladins included east-central Bavaria and the land west of the mid-Rhine, the respective Upper and Lower *Palatinates*.

England's Charles I created a New World palatinate of his own in 1632 and called it *Terra Maria* (Maria Land) for his French-Catholic queen, Henrietta Maria. An intended refuge for English Catholics, *Maryland* was administered by George Calvert, the Catholic lord of Ireland's Baltimore Manor. He soon died, and his son Cecil ran the project as the 2nd Lord Baltimore. The family's estate title was attached to modern Maryland's biggest city in 1729 and later to the NA's

Baltimore **Lord Baltimores** (1872–74). They lacked an imaginative moniker but were good enough in baseball terms to run the Charm City's other NA team out of business. Those 1873 Baltimore **Marylands**—another wickedly clever name—went 0-6 as the shortest-lived franchise in major league history.

The alliterative Cecil College **Seahawks** (North East, Md.) are in Cecil County, named for the same Cecil Calvert. The College of Southern Maryland (La Plata) is in Charles County, named for Cecil's own son Charles (Lord B. III). His namesake was Charlie, a red-shouldered hawk that frequented campus enough in the mid-1970s to make CSM teams **Hawks**.

King Charles II was enough impressed with his father's Maryland experiment to cut the southern Virginia Colony off as the Carolina Palatinate in 1663, giving jurisdiction to a few of his own paladin-esque nobles, eight Lords Proprietor who had remained with the royal Cavalier faction during England's Civil Wars (p. 69). The words *Carolinian* and *Carolingian* were already descriptions of the dynasty of Charles Martel and Charlemagne as derived from the Latin form of "Charles" (*Carolus*), and they occasionally apply to palatinate-loving English kings named Charles, so it was probably only a matter of time before jocks at one Carolina college or another were called **Paladins**. A reporter gave that distinction to the basketball players from Furman University (Greenville, S.C.) in the 1930s. That Baptist-founded school's baseball **Hornets** and football **Purple Hurricanes** were also **Paladins** by 1961.

After World War II the Royal Military College of Canada (Kingston, Ont.) presented cadet-athletes called **Redmen**, named for their scarlet dress uniforms. A 1997 shift toward racial and gender neutrality made them **Paladins**. That name for Constantine's guards could certainly apply to teams at any military academy, but a delicious coincidence—or perhaps a slick in-joke—put the ice hockey **Paladins** into Constantine Arena, which had been named in 1960 for a recently deceased former commandant of "Canada's West Point," Maj. Gen. Charles Francis Constantine.

Saxons | Student Princes | Vikings | Saints

For ages, the Scandinavian countries were separate and syndicated Viking kingdoms. A first-born son inherited the family estate while his little brothers sought their bounties along northern European coasts. From the late eighth to mid-eleventh centuries, Vikings raided at will and forged a trade network among the ports they conquered.

The Viking Age in Britain began with violent attacks on coastal monasteries and continued inland. The invaders wouldn't face serious resistance until the time of Alfred the Great, who ruled Wessex (West Saxon), the last intact Anglo-Saxon kingdom. Instead of paying the traditional tribute to the Vikings, Alfred fought his foes and forced them into an 878 treaty that divided England between the Danes north of the Thames River and his own Anglo-Saxon-Jute confederacy.

In the early 1800s, some land in western New York was settled by Seventh Day Baptists. (They'd split from English Baptists decades earlier.) To those pioneers the area resembled Alfred's Wessex, so they named it Alfred. Alfred University was founded there in 1836, with **Purple** athletes redubbed **Saxons** in 1928. With the university's support, a state aggie school was put adjacent to the campus in 1908. It's now Alfred State College, whereat **Pioneers** recall the same early settlers.

• • •

After Alfred's death, his family's House of Wessex would rule an early version of England under their wyvern battle flag. A wyvern is a two-legged dragon-serpent that can still be seen around former Anglo-Saxon kingdoms like Worcestershire. Its namesake Massachusetts city—Worcester—keeps **Wyverns** at Quinsigamond Community College.

Alfred's famously ill-advised descendant Ethelred II executed all Danes in England in 1002 to start decades of war with and occupation by Denmark. The early-1066 death of Ethelred's son King Edward the Confessor brought claimants out of the woodwork. The last was crushed in October by William of Normandy, thereafter "the Conqueror." He ruled the Anglo-Saxon confederation of Alfred's heirs, concluding both Saxon rule in Britain and its Viking Age.

Despite recent Christian kings like Olaf I, most Norwegians observed Norse paganism. But Norway's Olaf Haraldsson turned Christian during his time in Britain, and Saxon-Nordic relations got tangled up enough to make him Ethelred's Viking ally during the Danish wars. Haraldsson's own 1015 invasion of Norway freed it from the Danes' rule precisely because the Danish army was traipsing around England. As King Olaf II, Haraldsson forced Christianity upon his homeland and installed Norwegian commoners in positions of state.

Norway's newly displaced Danish lords raised an army that drove Olaf into Russia in 1028. He died reinvading Norway and was instantly celebrated as a patriot and his nation's patron saint. One memorial is St. Olaf College (Northfield, Minn.), founded by Norwegian Lutherans in 1874. Its **Oles** ("*oh*-lees") are shortened *Olefites*, an old nickname for students.[1]

• • •

Visiting Rome in 1510, the German monk Martin Luther saw a lot of emphasis on ceremony and little on biblical truth. He also met the influential mistresses and illegitimate children of supposedly celibate popes and cardinals, men he found far more allegiant to their noble families than to the one true Church.

Guided by *Sola Scriptura* (scripture alone), Prof. Luther couldn't see how the Church had drawn seven sacramental practices out of a Bible that listed only two (baptism and communion). His thinking held great sway at the University of Wittenberg, the first German college to be "founded without the permission of [Catholic] Church authorities."[2] It had opened in 1502 under Saxony's intellectually curious Catholic elector, Frederick the Wise.

Luther made the Plays of the Millennium reel in 1517 by posting his scathing critique of Catholic practices at a Wittenberg church. European nationalism was then on the rise, and folks in the German Holy Roman States and Spanish Netherlands took Luther's talking points to their Catholic overlords, protestations collectively called the Protestant Reformation. Christendom would thereafter comprise two major camps, Catholics and Protestants, with early subscribers to the latter called "Lutherans." Springfield, Ohio's own Wittenberg University (est. 1845) fielded **Fighting Lutheran** footballers in the 1890s that were alternately **Tigers** in the early 1920s and permanently so after World War II. The latter name avoids deep history, but Ezra the **Tiger** does recall the institution's founding Lutheran preacher, Ezra Keller.

The Church sought Luther's arrest in 1521, so he hid for months at Wartburg Castle. His Wartburg alias was Knight George, so it's not shocking that Wartburg College (a Lutheran institution in Waverly, Iowa) posts **Knights**.[3] The same history explains the **Knights** at Martin Luther College in New Ulm, Minnesota, founded in the 1850s by immigrants from Bavaria's staunchly Protestant city of [old] Ulm. The **Kingsmen** (men) and **Regals** (women) at California Lutheran University in Thousand Oaks have knight mascots.

During Luther's exile, his cohort Philipp Melanchthon continued to guide U. Wittenberg toward reform. The House of Habsburg's Catholics feared that the Protestant outbreak would weaken any Christian resolve against impending Turkish invasions, so Charles V of Spain didn't punish the Lutherans; he told them to write up something he could examine at his breakfast nook. Melanchthon therefore set down the fundamental principles of the new faith in 1530's *Augsburg Confession*. Its namesake is Augsburg College in Minneapolis, where newly assembled **Auggies** were named in the mid-1920s to contrast with the many **Aggies** of that era's A&M schools (p.160).

• • •

After Luther's death in 1546, Melanchthon backed off pure Lutheranism to consider the ideas of John Calvin, a French-born Protestant in Swiss Geneva. Whatever sympathies Calvin's followers ("Calvinists," "Calvinites," or "Reformers") shared with the Lutherans didn't keep their respective ministers from arguing bitterly over sacramental and iconographical technicalities.

Melanchthon mentored many at Wittenberg who became A-list Reformers themselves. His teacher's pet was Zacharias Baer, whose name when Latinized was *Zacharias Ursinus* (*ursus* being Latin for "bear"). German Reformers opened Ursinus College at Collegeville, Pennsylvania in 1870, naturally fielding **Bears**.

Ursinus was a famous and well-traveled Reformer, eventually landing a position at *der Universität Heidelberg*, where Calvinists and Lutherans were continuing their unlikely theological food fight. To end the squabbling, the Rhineland's Reformer prince, Frederick the Pious, asked for a Calvinist creed he could spread out on the living room floor to compare to the Lutherans' *Augsburg Confession*. That *Heidelberg Catechism* of 1563 (largely authored by Ursinus) standardized Reformed doctrine and started to shift the nerve center of Calvinism northward from Geneva. As historian Diarmaid MacCulloch describes it, "Heidelberg saw itself as a second and better Wittenberg, a German university that would complete the half-finished Reformation of the Lutherans."[4] Frederick would continue mapping Reform onto north-central Europe until his death in 1576, but a Lutheran-leaning son succeeded him and moved Calvinists like Ursinus to the Heidelberg bench.

The aforementioned school at Heidelberg (est. 1386) is Germany's oldest university. It was a training ground for both Reformers and prototypical Renaissance princes. German Reformers founded a new Heidelberg University in Tiffin, Ohio in 1850. Its public relations guy referred to teams as **Fighting Student Princes** after seeing a poster for MGM's 1927 film *The Student Prince in Old Heidelberg*. But folks had a habit of calling them "the **Berg**" and both names are now official, although the women have always favored "the **Berg**" over either "**Lady Student Princes**" or "**Student Princesses**."

In 1580, Lutherans spread their papers all over the driveway and picked out a definitive greatest hits collection that included ancient Christian texts, the writings of Luther and Melanchthon, and the *Augsburg Confession*. The single volume was *Concordia* (Book of Concord), so there are nearly a dozen Lutheran institutions in North America named Concordia *Something-or-other*, not all of which have profoundly Lutheranistic team names. Examples of the arbitrary include the Concordia University of Alberta **Thunder** (Edmonton), Concordia University **Cavaliers** (Portland, Ore.), Concordia University Wisconsin **Falcons** (Mequon), Concordia University Ann Arbor **Cardinals** (Mich.), and Concordia College–Selma **Hornets** (Ala.). Concordia University Irvine (Calif.) has **Eagles**, but at least its feathered mascot is Marty, after Martin Luther.

Protestantism really stuck in northern Europe. Sweden, Norway, and Finland were all officially Lutheran by 1600. But there wasn't any separation of church and state; churchmen kept the public records and levied high taxes.

• • •

The Vikings were probably the first Europeans in the Americas, but they abandoned their short-lived villages on the shores of Canada before 1000 CE. Then the Nordics lost interest in the newly found land.

For about 900 years.

The U.S. government always had trouble creating a bill to distribute western farmlands because Southern senators would block any such action out of fear that the new agrarian states would favor abolition. (See p. 142.) When secession rendered that opposition moot, the Congress passed the Homestead Act of 1862.

Immigrants and Americans alike set out for the growing farm and timber industries of the Great Lakes, where Indian treaties had recently secured new lands.[5]

In the century before the Homestead Act, populations in Scandinavia doubled at the same time innovation was cutting factory jobs. Norway's poor were increasingly alienated by oligarchic governance. Denmark's loss of farmland to Prussia after an 1864 war came with the threat of the German military draft. Sweden's "starvation years" owed to crop failures in the late 1860s. These are the immigration theorist's "push factors," circumstances that drive people from their homeland. Folks in motion are destined for places with coincident "pull factors," and Scandinavians went to America for a taste of democracy, freely available land, and religious tolerance.

Letters home invited other Nordics to the Midwest. Most were members of the state-sponsored church, and stateside Scandinavian Lutherans united under the Augustana Synod of 1860 (from the *Augsburg Confession's* Latin name, *Confessio Augustana*). Their learning institutions often flaunted the "Augustana" bit. Examples include Augustana University of Alberta (in Camrose) and two schools called Augustana College, one in Rock Island, Illinois and one in Sioux Falls, South Dakota.[6] All three Augustanas sponsor **Vikings**, presumably based on liberally applied algebraic rules of transitive equivalence: $a = b$ and $a = c$, therefore $c = b$. That is, the Vikings were Scandinavians and Scandinavians are Lutherans … so Lutherans are undoubtedly **Vikings**. One should consider also that a Scandinavian pan-nationalism—a "Viking Revival"—was peaking just when so many Nordic Lutherans were arriving in the U.S. and opening colleges:

- After 1872 the Northern Pacific Railway brought many Norwegians to Minnesota's Red River Valley where they opened (*another*) Concordia College in 1891. Its **Lutherans** or (of course) **Vikings** were outside downtown Moorhead, so they were called **Corncobs** and finally **Cobbers** in the 1930s. "Fear the ear!" they say.

- In Blair, Nebraska, **Vikings** represented Dana College, which was founded in 1884 by Danish Lutherans and closed in 2010. *Dana* is a poetic term for Denmark that comes from *Danu*, a goddess of ancient Continental Celts.

- More **Vikings** are in Des Moines, Iowa, where Danish Lutherans started Grand View University in 1896.

- Swedish Lutherans founded Chicago's North Park University in 1885, where **Vikings** play.

- Norwegian Lutherans in Minnesota started Mankato's Bethany Lutheran College in 1927. Its **Vikings** (named in 1947) surely noticed when the neighboring NFL Minnesota **Vikings** co-opted that identity in 1961.

- In 1962, Nebraska's Midland Lutheran College in Fremont absorbed Luther College in Wahoo. The merger kept MLC's **Warriors** and sank LC's **Vikings**. When MLC became Midland University in 2010, **Warrior** mascots made the switch from Indians and Spartans to unmistakable Vikings.

- Lindsborg, Kansas is called "Little Sweden" because it was founded by Swedish Lutherans in 1869. They started Bethany College in 1881, where Viking mascots accompany the **Swedes**.

- Norwegian Lutherans founded Luther College in Decorah, Iowa in 1861. Its **Norse** athletes are served by warrior mascots with Viking helmets.
- Swedes and Norwegians were among the first white settlers at Willmar, Minnesota, where the mascot for the Ridgewater College **Warriors** is a Viking.

In 1593 the Church of Sweden became officially Lutheran by subscribing to the Augsburg Confession at the city of Uppsala. For the three-hundredth anniversary (1893), Swedish Lutherans opened Brooklyn's Upsala [*sic*] College to avoid shipping their children off to Lutheran colleges in the Midwest.[7] Upsala moved to Manhattan the next year and to East Orange, New Jersey in 1898, where it hosted **Vikings** until closing in 1995.

• • •

North Dakota's Valley City State University is a public school (not a former Lutheran seminary), but it has **Vikings** to reflect the local ethnic heritage. Like other immigrant groups, Nordics would continue to move west, with the Pacific Northwest being particularly attractive to lumberjacks and fishermen perhaps pining for the Scandinavian fjords. **Viking** teams represent Oregon's Portland State University, Western Washington University (Bellingham), and Big Bend Community College (Moses Lake, Wash.). It's a short sail to their Scandinavian cousins in British Columbia, where the University of Victoria's **Vikings** and **Vikettes** were degendered and abbreviated to "Victoria **Vikes**" in the mid-1990s. But not all Lutheran-backed schools keep **Viking** crews:

- Lutheran Swedes founded a college at St. Peter, Minnesota in 1862 and named it after Sweden's Protestant hero of the Thirty Years' War, King Gustaf Adolph the Great. Sports teams at Gustavus Adolphus College are **Golden Gusties**, with a lion mascot indicating Gustavus's "Lion of the North" nickname.[8]
- The Pacific Lutheran University **Lutes** (Tacoma, Wash.) are abridged Lutherans, although their knight mascots recall earlier **Gladiators** and **Knights**.
- You might see the "Lutheran **Lutes**" alliteration in the "Muhlenberg **Mules**" from Muhlenberg College (Allentown, Pa.). That school is named for the progressive "patriarch of American Lutheranism," Henry Melchior Muhlenberg (1711–87), but its **Mules** point to the mule towpaths of the Lehigh Canal.[9]
- In 1830, Lutherans founded Capital University in Bexley, Ohio. Its **Fighting Lutherans** changed to **Crusaders** in 1963.

The 1880s brought Finns to the copper mines and timber forests of Michigan's Upper Peninsula. Coming first from the Norwegian fishing ports and mines to which they'd already migrated for work, large numbers sailed from Finland proper as word spread about America. In 1896, Hancock, Michigan got the only Finnish-founded college outside of Finland. *Suomi* is what Finns call their own country, and the Lutherans' Suomi College became Finlandia University in 2000. Its **Lions** refer to the lion rampant on Finland's coat of arms.[10]

• • •

A Swedish farmer in central Minnesota found a Nordic-language message carved on a large rock in 1898. His own translation told of Norwegian Vikings who—contrary to all recorded history—traveled just so far inland in 1362. People have long argued about the Kensington Runestone, but it made "Minnesota **Vikings**" a somewhat obvious name for Minneapolis's 1961 NFL expansion franchise. The Heavener Runestone (also subject to scrutiny) is in a park near Poteau, Oklahoma, where Carl Albert State College's **Trojans** became **Vikings** in 1991.

In 1903, Norwegians started Waldorf Lutheran College in Forest City, Iowa, the seat of Winnebago County. Students selected the "**Warriors**" ID in 1934 to reference the Ho-Chunk (Winnebago) people.[11] Today's Waldorf College doesn't use Indian mascots, having switched at some point to a horned helmet. That headgear is popularly associated with Viking raiders, but incorrectly so. The wings and horns slapped on the brain buckets for so many **Viking** teams are similarly wrong-headed because such ornamentation was probably originated by and should be primarily associated with those tireless Iron Age metallurgists, the Celts. Even then, the decoration would likely have been for ceremonial purposes only, exacting no advantage toward invasion or warfare. Nonetheless, mistaken artists have given Vikings such lids in poems, paintings, and operas since the nineteenth century.

Ohioans at Cleveland State University who'd attended the city's St. Joseph High School are suspected of having stuffed the ballot box with SJHS's "**Vikings**" nick in a 1965 vote. CSU's mascot is Magnus, after the several Kings Magnus ("the great") that ruled eleventh- and twelfth-century Norway and Sweden.

• • •

Before the 1906 baseball season, Pennsylvania's Lancaster **Maroons** became **Red Roses** and remained so until 1961. That compared them to their opening day foes across the Susquehanna, the York **White Roses** (1894–1969). Lancaster and York are named for the English cities that clashed in the Wars of the Roses, which set the red rose battle flag of Lancaster against the white rose of York starting in 1455. Henry Tudor was on the Lancastrian team, but when he ascended the post-war throne in 1485 as Henry VII, he married a cute Yorkie to forge a dynasty behind the red-*and*-white Tudor Rose.

The king died in 1509, but his son reignites our discussion of the Protestant Reformation. Henry VIII took Martin Luther to task in his *Defence of the Seven Sacraments*, and an appreciative Pope Leo X made him *Fidei Defensor* (Defender of the Faith) in 1521. That Latin title is still attached to British monarchs, but you don't have to be an English regent to put *F.D.* on your stationery; **Defenders** play on both sides of the ball at Christian colleges, including Dordt College (Sioux Center, Iowa) and Baptist Bible College (Clarks Summit, Pa.).

Two decades of marriage to Catherine of Aragon produced no male heir, so Henry feared his death would start new wars of succession. As a Catholic, he needed papal permission to divorce the Spanish princess to marry his new squeeze Anne Boleyn. New pope Clement VII, however, was heavily invested in the king's wedlock; he didn't want to upset Charles V, the Catholic monarch of Spain who was both the Holy Roman Emperor *and* Mrs. VIII's own nephew. The papacy also had its hands full with the Protestant uprising, so Henry's Lord Chancellor, Cardinal Thomas Wolsey, was unable to fast-track the annulment in Rome. When Wolsey died, Henry installed a lay chancellor to speed things up. Sir

Thomas More (the likely ghost author of Henry's aforementioned *Defence*) got the job, but he liked neither the king's motives nor his methods and he refused to press the "Great Matter." With Ms. Boleyn pregnant, an enraged Henry pushed the 1534 Act of Supremacy through Parliament, making England's monarch—not the Pope—the head of the new Anglican Church. (Theretofore, *Ecclesia Anglicana* had simply been a geographical designation for Rome's English domain.) Unbound from the Catholic red tape, the annulment was rubber-stamped by the new archbishop of Canterbury, staunch Protestant Thomas Cranmer.

Bishop John Fisher of Rochester had joined More's opposition to the annulment, so Henry threw him in the Tower. Pope Paul III elevated the aging cleric to Cardinal in a bit of gamesmanship, but Fisher and More were beheaded in mid-1535 anyway and canonized in tandem in 1935. The College of Saints John Fisher & Thomas More in Fort Worth, Texas didn't field intercollegiate teams before closing in 2014, but the Cardinal of Rochester is the sole namesake at St. John Fisher College in Rochester, New York, a Catholic school opened in 1948 that now presents **Cardinals**.[12] Cardinal Fisher's contemporary is remembered by **Saints** for all seasons at Thomas More College (Crestview Hills, Ky.).[13] The Thomas More College of Liberal Arts in Merrimack, New Hampshire is not affiliated with the TMC in Kentucky, but its fall Mud Bowl of bygone days was a pickup football match between **Saints** and **Sinners**.

Having broken with Catholic Europe, some folks in England detected the onset of capital-*R* reform, but the Anglicans were not really Protestants because they'd slid out from under the Church of Rome's control without dumping its rituals. Those Reformers who wanted to wipe the church of all things "popish"— thus *purifying* it—were the Puritans. Their influence was felt as token changes by Henry's Protestant heirs made Anglicanism somewhat distinct from the old faith, but London's monarchs would pretty much steer a *Via Media* (middle way) between Catholics and Calvinists until England's Civil Wars of the 1640s (p. 69).

• • •

The **Saints** at the College of St. Joseph (Rutland, Vt.) and Maryville University (St. Louis) are indebted to their respective Catholic institutions' eponyms, Saints Joseph and Mary. Named for unspecified Catholic do-gooders are the **Saints** at Holy Cross College (South Bend, Ind.) and Presentation College (Aberdeen, S.D.). The female **Saints** (and male **Cavaliers**) at St. Mary of the Plains College in Dodge City, Kansas shut down when their school did in 1992.

Protestants don't pray through saints, claiming unmediated access to Jesus, so they don't find persons canonized by the Vatican in post-Reformation times to necessarily be more saintly than other worthy Christians. Older Protestant denominations (like Lutherans and Anglicans) might open churches or colleges named for saints that predate the split with Rome, and a few **Saints** do serve some Christian-but-not-Catholic colleges, including Hillsdale Free Will Baptist College (Moore, Okla.) and the non-denominational Limestone College (Gaffney, S.C.). Secular **Saints** are at the publicly funded St. Clair College (Windsor, Ont.), named after nearby Lake St. Clair.

Renegades | Fighting Squirrels | Griffins | Gothic Knights

William the Conqueror fought out in front of the Norman-French invasion force he landed in southern England in 1066. (p. 34). Taking advantage of a relatively new option in helmetry—the visor—William bared his head in battle to quell rumors that he'd been killed. Like hockey players who limit turnovers by passing to their own colors, knights would soon avoid such confusion on the battlefield through a formalized system of identifying heraldry, although plenty of historians insist that this was simply a point of vanity: "Hey! … Check out my nifty fightin' smock!"

A mounted knight's heraldic title and other accoutrements—flag, shield, and coat of arms—were handed down the generations. The notable exceptions were "black knights," independent warriors whose place outside the feudal hierarchy left them without sanctioned colors. Because those anonymous and unaffiliated knights could rock the whole system, there are many times more black knights in romantic fictions than recorded histories. West Point famously fields **Black Knights** (p. 186). California's black-and-red Bakersfield College **Renegades** have had the same mascot since 1937, one such "renegade knight."

The Latin root *renegare* means "deny," and during the Crusades *renegade* was applied to traitors, usually Christian knights who'd turned Muslim. Columbia College Chicago is an arts and media academy with campus buildings scattered about the South Loop. It is therefore unlike any conventional college, which is exactly what club-level **Renegades** intend to suggest.[1]

• • •

Heraldry quickly became a conspicuous exhibition of good blood. When family trees couldn't be traced to European nobles, well-off North Americans often adopted the emblemry of like-named clans from what may or may not have even been their own Old Country. It is an artifact of heraldry that we impulsively approve colors and seals (or military-esque *shields*) for clubs, commonwealths, corporations, and colleges:

- A Presbyterian female seminary in Staunton, Virginia was renamed for sitting president Mary Baldwin in 1895. The Mary Baldwin College seal is topped off by a squirrel sejant that was purportedly copied from Britain's Baldwin family. In BMC's library, the critter appears again on a 1901 stained-glass window, a memorial to Ms. Baldwin. BMC athletes are **Fighting Squirrels**.

- There are three wolves on the seal at Pennsylvania's Grove City College. That Christian college usually fielded **Grovers** or **Crimson** jocks, sometimes with wolf mascots. Ignoring that wolves have little in common with ferocious weasels, GCC made teams **Wolverines** in the 1940s.[2]

- Purple-and-gold **Purple Panthers** at Boston's Emerson College became **Lions** in 1968 to match the lion on its (old) coat of arms.[3]

- The relationship between **Ravens** on the field and ravens on the shield at Carleton University is chronologically inverted. The Ottawa school's black-clad footballers were first called **Ravens** in the 1948 campus news. The largest members of the *Corvus* (crow) genus wouldn't appear on the Carleton coat of arms until four decades later.[4]

• • •

Thanks largely to alliteration, Grossmont College (El Cajon, Calif.) has a griffin seal and **Griffins** teams. In fact, the griffin is the beast that most often leaps from the college seal to football helmets. The half-lion/half-eagle griffin has appeared in lore from North Africa and the East for millennia, and it runs rampant through European heraldry via its Christian association (p. 107). Its wings associate the griffin with the sun and, therefore, enlightenment, so **Griffins** represent many colleges with lofty ambitions.

Wildcat athletics at Johnson & Wales University (Providence, R.I.) were dropped in the early 1970s. They joined NCAA Division III in 1995 as **Griffins**, referencing the griffin atop the JWU seal. The **Wildcats** returned through a student vote in 1998, just after some attentive person noticed that the griffin was actually the dragon of St. George, which JWU associates with the family crest of its co-founder from 1914, Gertrude I. Johnson.[5]

Because griffins guarded gold stashes in the ancient Middle East, this protector of "the treasure of knowledge" became the symbol of St. Joseph [Mo.] Junior College in 1915. Using a French spelling, the *Griffon* yearbook and **Griffons** teams soon followed. The board of regents tried and failed to change that to something closer to the Greek/Latin *gryphons* when SJJC became Missouri Western State College in 1969.[6] (It's now Missouri Western State University.)

Looking for just such a link to classicism, the nameless teams at Sarah Lawrence College (Bronxville, N.Y.) became **Gryphons** in 1998.[7] The sometimes-*y* version is also at Ontario's University of Guelph, where the architectural highlight is Johnston Hall's Collegiate Gothic tower, a medieval touch that got **Aggies** and **Redmen** replaced with **Gryphons** in 1968.

MacEwan University in Edmonton is named for respected author and educator J.W. Grant MacEwan (1902–2000). His grandparents were Highland immigrants to Canada, so the griffin from the MacEwan family arms is supposed to explain those on GMU's emblem and its **Griffin** sides. But according to Lyon Court—the keepers of Scottish heraldry—the MacEwans have *undifferenced* arms, which means the clan is recognized without any heraldic association with a particular chieftain, so it's hard to find the ancestral griffin that GMU cites.

In fact, there's no such thing as a *family* coat or arms a *family* crest. According to the official registry for English, Welsh, and Irish heraldry (The College of Arms), arms can be associated only with specific entitled men and their direct male heirs. Any claim to same by their cousins or by folks with coincidentally comparable surnames is a bit of a latter-day hoodwink.

For example, several of Britain's Read, Reade, and Rede families have used griffin symbols, but many more have not. Still, Reed College sponsors **Griffins** based on what are fancied to be *the* family arms of Oregon steamboat baron Simeon Gannett Reed, whose bequest established the Portland school in 1908. Franklin Pierce University in Rindge is named for the only New Hampshire–born American president. Its athletic **Ravens** are said to be from the three ravens on some version of arms from England's Peirce/Pierce family.

Philadelphia's Chestnut Hill College was founded in 1924 by the Sisters of Saint Joseph, a Jesuit order started by the French Bishop of Le Puy in 1650. The bishop's griffin symbol is on the CHC seal, and **Griffins** defend a campus full of buildings that imitate various Medieval and Renaissance styles. The Fontbonne Hall dorm is named for Jeanne Fontbonne (1759–1843), who'd reassembled the Sisters of St. Joe after the French Revolution. Another of her namesakes is Fontbonne University in St. Louis, originally a school for women (now coed) that the sisters founded upon Mother Fontbonne's instructions in 1836. The same griffin of Le Puy inspires FU's own **Griffins**.

Strongly associated with battle arms, heraldic beasts often appear at military schools. Indeed, the griffin on the coat of arms at Wentworth Military Academy (Lexington, Mo.) was explicitly ignored when a nickname was chosen to favor "better known and more ferocious" winged beasts from European heraldry: **Dragons**.[8]

• • •

As already noted for **Griffins** or **Griffons**, campus buildings in European styles can bring on **Knights** teams. This is most true for Collegiate Gothic architecture. It copies the Victorian Gothic style at England's Universities of Oxford and Cambridge, which itself was a revival of the Continent's medieval Gothic style:

- Blue-and-maize **Knights** at the Congregationalist-founded Carleton College (Northfield, Minn.) match the English Gothic style of Skinner Memorial Chapel and other campus buildings, but "Carleton **Knights**" also inescapably resembles "Carletonites."
- Built in the 1930s to suggest Collegiate Gothicism, Welles and Sturges Halls are iconic buildings at SUNY Geneseo that suit SUNY-G's **Blue Knights**.
- Hepburn Hall was the original building at New Jersey City University (Jersey City). Its Gothic tower inspired past **Gothics** and present **Gothic Knights**. (They'd been **Crows** until 1954.)
- From NJCU, go fifty miles up the Hudson to West Point, where the United States Military Academy has its own adjective—Military Gothic—for prominent campus buildings. USMA's **Black Knights** suit that theme as well as that of renegade medieval warriors discussed above.
- In the 1870s monks opened a school for Pottawatomie children near Konawa, Oklahoma. It evolved into St. Gregory's University in Shawnee, where the Tudor-Gothic architecture effected athletic **Knights**. But they're now **Cavaliers**, from the Anglicized version of *chevalier*, the French word for a knight that commemorates SGU's founding by French Benedictines.[9]

• • •

The defining characteristic of Gothic architecture is the pointed arch, the steepness of which reduced horizontal thrust to make possible buildings both tall and elegant in medieval times. The portal between the Moody Bible Institute campus and Chicago's LaSalle Boulevard is the Gothic arch of Crowell Hall, which makes MBI's teams **Archers**.

Dolphins | Wolfpack | X-Men | Musketeers

Ignatius of Loyola was born in 1491, the year before Spain captured the Moors' last Iberian foothold after eight centuries of occupation. The Catholic kingdom immediately expelled Sephardic (Iberian) Jews and would soon be suspicious of those Lutherans and Calvinists called Protestants. That pro-Catholic–anti-everybody-else mood rubbed off on Ignatius, who founded the Society of Jesus at Paris in 1534 to spread the gospel.

The Holy Mother Church didn't just stand there and let the Lutheran-Calvinist team swing away; it launched its own Counter-Reformation to clarify doctrine in the face of Protestant faultfinding. Seeing Catholic zeal in the sons of Loyola, Pope Paul III recognized the Society of Jesus in 1540 and scattered its members across Asia, South America, and New France (Canada). Their Protestant critics called them "Jesuits" for employing the savior's name a little too earnestly—think "Jesus freak"—but the Society eventually embraced the nickname.

Saint Ignatius founded the world's first Jesuit college on the island of Sicily in 1548, the University of Messina. Down the coast is Siracusa, where the bishop's seal was a dolphin. It's the "king of fishes" and Christ's first disciples were fishermen, so the dolphin is an ancient symbol for Jesus or his followers (p. 107).[1] In New York State the dolphin is repeated on the arms of the Diocese of Syracuse (ol' Siracusa's namesake), which backed the establishment of the Jesuits' land-locked Le Moyne College in the 1940s. It too presents **Dolphins**.[2]

In 1545, Paul III convened the Counter-Reformation's main event, the Council of Trent. Its bishops met sporadically until 1563, so it was a later pope (Pius IV) who installed his own Medici family nephew, Milan's Archbishop Charles Borromeo, to close the late innings at Trent. Charles guided the council toward the *Catechism of Trent*, a manual for cutting clerical corruption. Also putting Borromeo in the fast lane to sainthood were his efforts to stem the German-Swiss Calvinist tide. Exactly three centuries after his 1610 canonization, Borromeo's newly founded memorial was Mount Saint Charles College (Helena, Mont.). It was renamed for its founder, Bishop John Patrick Carroll in 1932, but Carroll College's **Fighting Saints** recall the original eponym.

A personal protégé of Borromeo and the Medicis was Aloysius, an Italian who renounced his House of Gonzaga entitlements to enter Jesuit training. He died in 1591 at age 21 while providing aid in a famine. His namesake, Gonzaga College (Spokane, Wash.), was opened by Italian Jesuits in 1887. By the time it became Gonzaga University in 1912, its **Blue and White** were being called the **Fighting Irish**, aiming to be the "Notre Dame of the West." (Several ND grads were on the coaching staff.) Gonzaga got a new nickname after footballers fought like bulldogs in a 1921 game,[3] but you're just as likely to encounter the "Zags" sobriquet as you are the official "**Bulldogs**." GU bears some responsibility for the confusion by periodically emblazoning the **Bulldogs**' uniforms with "Zags."

Loyola University Maryland put up **Irish** and **Jesuits** in the 1920s. When they took colors of green and grey in 1927, proactive students made **Greyhounds** of their footballers.[4] Dog racing as a gambling sport was just becoming popular, and the representation was suitably athletic for all future teams.

The Jesuits' Loyola College in southwestern L.A. was also named after Ignatius, and "**Lions**" was a contraction of its earlier **Loyolans**. The all-male institute absorbed the four-year program of the all-female Marymount College in 1973, but Loyola Marymount University jocks remain **Lions**. As for Marymount, its two-year school had evolved into a four-year by 2010. Its **Mariners** indicate the waters surrounding their campus on the Palos Verdes Peninsula.

• • •

The ancestral Loyola arms include a cauldron symbol of hospitality offset by two wolves rampant. That's repeated on the seal at the Jesuit-founded Loyola University New Orleans, home of the **Wolfpack**.

The same cauldron and wolves are on the seal at the University of Scranton, where the mascot for the royal purple-and-white is Iggy (as in Ignatius) the Royal Wolf. The 1888-founded institute wasn't under Jesuit control until 1942. It was originally St. Thomas College, whereat football **Tommies** and **Tomcats** remembered the thirteenth-century Dominican priest St. Thomas Aquinas. STC became the University of Scranton in 1938 and made its teams **Royals** in 1946.

The same imagery on the university emblem gives a wolf mascot named Lobo to the **Blue Streaks** at the Jesuits' John Carroll University (p. 212).

A modernized version of the Loyolan arms are on the shield at Loyola University of Chicago. The lupine mascot for LU is Lu Wolf because a *loup* ("lou") is a French wolf, but the Jesuit school's **Maroon and Gold** footballers became **Ramblers** after completing an exhaustive road schedule in 1926.

• • •

Ignatius's initial handful of followers included Father Francis Xavier. That first Jesuit missionary spread the faith to India and Japan. At his namesake school, St. Francis Xavier University (Antigonish, N.S.), one jock's mother stitched an *X* on his rugby sweater in 1901, leading to StFX's **X-Men** and eventual **X-Women**.[5]

In 1831 the first Bishop of Cincinnati, Edward Fenwick, started the Athenaeum, the first Catholic college beyond the Alleghenies. Fenwick was a Dominican, but he placed the academy under the spiritual patronage of St. Xavier[6] and let the faculty implement the Jesuits' *Ratio Studiorum*, a late Renaissance "plan of studies" for liberal arts. Fully administering the Ohio institution by 1840, Jesuits renamed it Xavier College (today's Xavier University). In 1925, XC lit professor Father Francis Finn (also a famous author of boys' books) successfully suggested illuminating the Jesuits' French origins with **Musketeers**. *Musketeer* and *French* have been inextricably linked since the 1846 English publication of *The Three Musketeers*, a magazine serial by Frenchman Alexandre Dumas about guards in the court of Louis XIII. (The name of XU's mascot is that of Dumas's protagonist, D'Artagnan.) In fact, *three* and *musketeers* are so connected through Dumas's stories that the Sioux City **Musketeers** were named in 1972 just to attract junior hockey fans from *three* neighboring states, Iowa, Nebraska, and South Dakota.

Tar Heels | Shockers | Cornhuskers | Billikens | Brewers

Martin Luther's Protestant reforms (p. 35) continued to take hold in the German states after his 1546 death. In the 1555 Peace of Augsburg, the Holy Roman Emperor Charles V let German princes choose a non-Catholic religion, inevitably Protestant Lutheranism. But the up-and-coming Calvinist Reformers would yet fight their own battles for self-rule and religious freedom from H.R.E. overlords.

Dutch Calvinists moved first. In 1568, William I of Orange invaded Catholic Spain's Low Countries to start the Eighty Years War, in which Spain's Armada was hassled by ragtag Dutch privateers called *Watergeuzen*—sea beggars. That puts **Sea Beggars** at Providence Christian College (Pasadena, Calif.), which opened with a Reformed perspective in 2005.

A 1648 treaty concluded both the Eighty and Thirty Years' Wars. The latter started in 1618 when other Central Europeans decided to buck Catholic authority. Calvinists now had the kind of toleration from Catholics that Lutherans had enjoyed for decades, but large swaths of Europe—especially German states—lay ruined. Most of America's few Germans had theretofore been indentured servants. That changed during the wars when the Dutch put settlements between the Delaware and Connecticut Rivers. Rhinelanders and Palatinates appreciated that Peter Minuit, the director-general of "New Netherland," was a Huguenot Rhinelander who spoke Low German. Other Palatinates (like Quakers and Mennonites, who were neither Lutheran nor Reformed) accepted William Penn's invitation to northwest Philadelphia's Germantown neighborhood in 1683.

Europe's ceaseless wars were increasing demand on Scandinavia's high-grade naval stores, a collective term for tar, pitch, turpentine, and rosin from pine trees. (It also covers wooden byproducts like masts and boards.) Long before hitters improved their bat grip with pine tar, it was a sealant for planks and ropes. Waterproof sails and hatch coverings were sewn out of tar-treated canvas, *tarpaulin.* (You've seen the tarp during rain delays). Deck hands rubbed tar on their clothes and faces for insulation, making "Jack Tar" a nickname for sailors. Eastern Canada's largest port hosts rugby's Halifax **Tars** (est. 2009). When World War I left Florida's Rollins College with only ten male students, its women noticed the "tars" assigned to Navy training vessels on Lake Virginia next to their Winter Park campus.[1] After the war, male students were stuck with "Tars," and **Blue and Gold** athletes were soon **Tars**.

Parliament's Naval Stores Act of 1705 determined that Britain would develop its own naval stores to counter wartime price-jacking by Swedish and Russian tar monopolies. With English assistance, Germans escaping their impoverished and war-torn homelands were shipped out. Three-thousand went to the Hudson Valley in 1709 to secure naval stores but failed when the yield of the area's white pine proved poor.

The Germans were frankly neither trained nor inclined toward the task, and many moved west to start planting farms in unspoiled country (which was all they'd been asking London for). When the longleaf pine of the Carolina Colonies turned out to be ideal for naval stores production, "tar boilers" set to cooking and draining oleoresins from felled trees to collect in trenches. Truly, the sneakers that touch such pitch are defiled, and North Carolinians ever since have been "tar heels," like Chapel Hill's famous University of North Carolina **Tar Heels**.[2]

• • •

Devastating famines after 1846 left Europeans mad, hungry, and looking to make scapegoats of monarchs. From 1848 to '52 independent rebellions tried to unseat the sovereign lords of France, Italy, Austria, and some German states. Those Revolutions of 1848 failed because urban liberals couldn't instill a passion for progressivism in rural areas, and many leading rebels skipped to North America.

Germans were already plentiful in southwestern Illinois, but by 1848 they composed 90 percent of Belleville, nicknamed "Dutch Town" (from the word *Deutsche*, "German"). Athletes at Belleville's Southwestern Illinois College were **Dutchmen** until becoming a **Blue Storm** in 2000.

Presbyterian "Forty-Eighters" in New Jersey trained German-speaking ministers at Newark's German Theological Seminary (est. 1867). It's now Bloomfield College in Bloomfield, where **Deacons** became **Bears** in mid-2014.

French liberals of the late 1860s were still clinging to the ideals of '48 and wanted to flaunt democracy in the face of their imperial ruler, Napoleon III (r. 1852–70), so they planned a gift for their "sister republic." The Statue of Liberty would commemorate the centennial of the Declaration of Independence in 1876, but it took so long to raise funds and build the modern colossus that it didn't go up in New York Harbor until 1886. Lady Liberty is on the jerseys of the WNBA New York **Liberty**, having long ago been reinterpreted to represent the hopes of immigrants.

• • •

Germans added the failed Revolutions of 1848 to the reasons they were ready for a fresh start. Jobs and land were scarce as industrialization packed German cities. There were high taxes and feudal inheritance codes that benefitted only first-born sons, and there was Otto von Bismarck's ever-present army draft. (Only after Bismarck united Prussia with surrounding German-language states in 1871 did a country called Germany exist.) Many set out for the established German-speaking settlements in America, but they also made for the rapidly expanding West.

Many Rhinelanders and Palatinates who'd suffered in Europe's Seven Years' War (1756–63) went to Russia, where the newly crowned empress was a German-born princess who had married her way to power. Catherine the Great invited Germans (largely Mennonites, Baptists, Catholics, and Lutherans) to fields near the Volga River and Black Sea that had just been gained from the Turks. Those "Volga Germans" and "Black Sea Germans" would give wheat to Russian cities and get a good deal of autonomy, but those privileges began evaporating a century later, just when railways were offering land along the tracks through Kansas. Pacifist Mennonites were upset when the exemption from Russia's military draft got yanked in 1874, so to the American Plains they brought Turkey red winter wheat, a hardy crossbreed from southern Ukraine.

Until then, American wheat farming had been pretty hit-or-miss, but Mennonite know-how made Kansas the Wheat State. Football players at Wichita State

University spent vacations putting harvested wheat in tepee-shaped stacks to dry, a process called shocking. Teams were **Wheatshockers** by 1904, shortened to **Shockers** decades ago. After wheat is shocked it's threshed—beaten—to remove it from the chaff. In the 1960s, gray-maroon **Graymaroons** became **Threshers** at Newton's Bethel College, founded by Kansas Mennonites in 1893.[3]

Above Kansas is Nebraska, another immigrant magnet of the era. "Cornhusker State" reflects its farming history, but that's not why University of Nebraska athletes have been **Cornhuskers** since 1902. It's the other way 'round; football at Lincoln's land-grant college is so popular that the state's official nickname became "Cornhusker State" as a tribute in 1945, ousting "Planter State."[4] Corn is no longer husked by hand, but most Nebraskans are self-identified Cornhuskers.

• • •

John R. Bender was born to a town of Black Sea Germans at Sutton, Nebraska. In the middle of his *five* seasons at Nebraska (eligibility rules have changed), they became **Cornhuskers**. He coached Washington State's **Indians** (1906–07, 1912–14) but was running the **Blue and White** at the Jesuits' Saint Louis University (1910–11) when a Missouri sportswriter said he bore an uncanny resemblance to a Billiken. This was at the height of Billikenmania, when hundreds of thousands of such impish statuettes were gifted as good-luck tokens. (Designed by a Kansas City art teacher, seated Billikens have upturned feet, pointed heads, squinted eyes, and wide smiles.) SLU's boys were thereafter Bender's **Billikens**.

Bender coached at various places during the era in which fans were coming to expect clever team identifiers, so new nicknames perpetually popped up in his wake. Arriving at Kansas State Agricultural College (now Kansas State University) in 1915, Bender recast **Aggies** as **Wildcats**. He left after that season to coach Tennessee's (already-named) **Volunteers** until 1920, and his Kansans became **Farmers**, but "Wildcats" was revived in 1920 by new Kansas State coach Charles Bachman (just off a year at the helm of those **Wildcats** at Northwestern). A few months before his unexpected death in 1927 at age 45, Bender started coaching tennis at the new Houston Junior College. Washington Staters had been **Indians** during Bender's time there, but he transferred their contemporary "Cougars" name to the school that's been the University of Houston since 1934.[5]

Basketball coach Bob Stairs watched Houston's **Cougars** claw into the Final Four in 1967 and '68 and decided that same metaphor applied to his scarlet-and-white Clark University **Scarlets** (Worcester, Mass.), thereafter **Cougars**.[6]

• • •

From a loose confederation of principalities, Germans didn't have overseas colonies, so their destinations were scattered. Many Mennonites went to South and Central America or Canada. Their white Russian seed wasn't amenable to Manitoba's southern prairies, but they made the red fife grain (which has Baltic roots) the top seed in the region, where farming became a leading industry. Brandon is the heart of Manitoba's agricultural area, as indicated by hockey's senior Brandon **Wheat Cities** (1903–23) and junior **Wheat Kings** (1936–).

During and after the American Revolution, the Mennonites' pacifism sent many from Pennsylvania Dutch Country to German settlements in Canada.

Ontario's Conestogo River has been the (misspelled) namesake of Pennsylvania's Conestoga River since the Mennonite resettlement. Conestoga College is the (not-misspelled) institution in modern Kitchener's Conestogo neighborhood, but CC's **Condors** are purely alliterative.

Mennonites take a literal view of the teachings of Jesus, especially those in his Sermon on the Mount that advance pacifism and exemplary living: "You are the light of the world [...] let your light shine before men, that they may see your good deeds" (Matthew 5:14–16). That should shed light on Canadian Mennonite University's **Blazers** (Winnipeg) and Steinbach Bible College's **Flames** (Steinbach). Both are Mennonite schools in Manitoba. Another Mennonite school drawn to the flame is Omaha's Grace University. It fields **Royals**, but GU's emblem is a torch with an open book. The Mennonites' Fresno Pacific University puts rays of light on its shield and **Sunbirds** on its field. Mentioned elsewhere, Virginia's Eastern Mennonite University and Indiana's Goshen College have **(Runnin')** **Royals** and **Maple Leafs** respectively, but EMU too has a sun seal and Goshen repeats the book-lamp motif.[7]

• • •

America's first beers were dark, top-fermenting ales and stouts in the British tradition. A major stateside ale maker was Matthew Vassar, born of England but resettled on the Hudson. His money started Vassar College (Poughkeepsie, N.Y.) in 1861. It's been coed since 1969, but the Main Building hints at Vassar's days as a women's college; ample corridors anticipated ladies rushing to class in hoop skirts. A bogus story says those broad halls were intended to accommodate the rolling of beer kegs in case circumstances forced the building's conversion to a brewery, but VC's **Brewers** more faithfully indicate the founder's occupation.

Boiled during brewing, beer was more healthy for medieval Europeans than was water. Output was seasonal because beer spoils in heat, but Bavarians kept kegs in icy caves to create a slow, bottom-fermenting yeast. Their new brew was called lager (from the German *lagern*: "to store"). A middle-aged Matthew Vassar would have detected a sea change when the speedy clipper ships of the 1840s allowed lager yeast to survive Atlantic crossings. Newly arrived Germans set up so many tap houses that pale lager is now the default American brew. Beer gardens were especially plentiful at the corners of the German Triangle: Cincinnati, St. Louis, and Milwaukee.

In 1929, German soccer players in Wisconsin started **Fussball Club Bayern** (Bavarian Football Club), today's NPSL Milwaukee **Bavarians**. The Sisters of St. Francis arrived at Milwaukee in 1849 expressly to minister to its German population. In 1937 they started Cardinal Stritch University, where burgundy-and-gray **Red Devils** turned to **Crusaders** in 1983. They were finally **Wolves** in 2001, which refers to the legend of St. Francis and the Wolf, in which Francis of Assisi (c. 1181–1226) talked some sense into a wolf that had been terrorizing the Italian town of Gubbio. In fact, "Gubi" is the furry mascot for the **Gray Wolves** at the Franciscans' Lourdes University (Sylvania, Ohio), and that same story applies to Bona Wolf, the mascot for **Bonnies** jocks at the Franciscans' St. Bonaventure University (Allegheny, N.Y.).

The Great Fire of 1871 destroyed Chicago's German breweries at exactly the moment that refrigerated rail cars were coming of age, and the city never caught up with beer barons in St. Louis (Busch, Anheuser) and Milwaukee (Schlitz, Pabst, Miller). The latter's baseballers have made the most of their "Beer City" nickname. Milwaukee **Brewers** were in the UA (1884) and AA (1891). Different **Brewers** were part of the (minor) Western League's transition to the major AL in 1901, but they were St. Louis **Browns** the next year (and Baltimore **Orioles** since 1954). The next **Brewers** (1902–53) were in a minor AA, playing through when Prohibition closed city breweries. Today's **Brewers** started AL play in 1970 and moved to the NL to balance MLB expansion in 1998.

• • •

The Erie Canal ended at Buffalo, an industrial boom town that drew Central European immigrants to grain and steel mills hydroelectrically powered by the Niagara River.[8] Fred Burkhardt was the Naismith disciple who introduced basketball to Buffalo's East Side Germans. By 1895 his best boys were accepting challenges as Buffalo **Germans**.[9] After the Y's **Germans** crossed the street to represent the Fraternal Order of Orioles in 1905, they barnstormed their way to 111 straight victories in 1907 and '08. Their Oriole Hall court allowed them to pass as Buffalo **Orioles** during the Great War[10] because Prohibitionism and its (not accidental) toll on brewers fed on anti-German sentiment, motivating many Americans to conceal their *Deutschtum* (Germanness) for the war years.

In 1925, German Lutherans assumed the administration of Valparaiso University (Valparaiso, Ind.). Teams became **Uhlans** in 1931 after the smartly dressed Uhlan chargers of nineteenth-century Prussian cavalry units. Choosing to avoid such Germanic pageantry during World War II, VU teams became **Crusaders** in 1942, fitting the original plan to instill attendees with Christian values.

In 1922, "Wolfpack" was applied to rabid fans of the North Carolina State University **Red Terrors**, and athletes too were soon a **Wolfpack**. Raleigh's one-time land-grant college (previously fielding **Aggies**, **Farmers**, **Mechanics**, and **Techs**) realized new growth and prestige during the two-decade chancellorship of J.W. Harrelson. He wanted to drop "**Wolfpack**" after World War II because "wolfpacks" of German U-boats had ripped apart Allied shipping convoys. (At least three U-boats sunk by the U.S. are just off North Carolina's coast.) But howling from NCSU's student body drowned out any call for change.

Two grandsons of Queen Victoria, England's George V and German Kaiser Wilhelm II, faced off during the Great War. The king wasn't sure that the Saxe-Coburg-Gotha surname of his German grandfather Prince Albert was cool with his British subjects, so family members were suddenly *Windsors* in 1917. Their thousand-year-old residence at Windsor Castle was already remembered in the name of an Ontario town settled by Loyalists after the American Revolution. In 1962, several colleges came together as the University of Windsor. That name demanded sporting regality, so teams became **Lancers**. More **Lancers** are at Loyalist College in Belleville, also in Loyalist Ontario.

One can see the irony then, in the **Lancers** at Lenoir Community College in Kinston, North Carolina. Locals dropped the *g* from the middle of *Kingston* right after the Revolution to be rid of any suggestion of monarchicalism.

SPHAs | Jewels | Hakoah | Maccabees

At its height, the Roman Empire controlled a bold ring around the Mediterranean, so its administrators in remote Judea had a tough time balancing Roman law and ancient traditions. Non-Romans who threatened the peace were crucified. (The routine execution of one trouble-making Jewish preacher named Jesus bore consequences not immediately apparent.) Jews led a series of failed revolts after 66 CE and even sought full independence in the revolt of 132. To emphasize their ultimate victory, the Romans destroyed Jerusalem's Temple in 135 and scattered the Jews, a Diaspora yielding two major cultural groups: *Ashkenazi* and *Sephardi,* respective Hebrew descriptions for Rhineland and Iberian Jews.

Ashkenazis were in Central Europe by the 300s, but the sailing was never smooth. They were slaughtered as the first "infidels" encountered by the Crusader armies (p. 207). The Black Death of the mid-1300s was fallaciously attributed to the poisoning of wells by Jews. And Jews were the perceived enemies of both camps in wars between Catholics and Protestants. An eighteenth- and nineteenth-century liberalism loosened restrictions on German Jews just as a Reform movement within Judaism was easing assimilation into the mainstream. Jews therefore often emigrated at the same time, for the same reasons, and to the same places as other Germans.

Earning interest on loans had long been a Christian sin, so the banking biz was left to Jews in cities across Europe. When the Industrial Revolution kicked in, Continental Jewish families like the Rothschilds were positioned to become influential financiers and merchants. An urban people in Europe by circumstance, Jews were more likely than other Germans to settle in the cities of America.

Requiring only a hoop and a ball, basketball is conducive to tight city spaces. A contemporary proof is the stateside domination in that sport by black players. The Great Migration to northern factories (p. 177) would so transform a former agricultural slave class that "urban" and "inner-city" are now circumlocutions for "African American." But because the first pro basketball leagues banned black players, they were flush with young Jewish talent from the big cities.

The mostly Jewish team at Philadelphia's Southern High School won three city titles starting in 1914.[1] Star player Eddie Gottlieb persuaded the South Philadelphia Hebrew Association to buy uniforms for a semi-pro side of key SHS player-grads.[2] In 1921 the S.P.H.A. ("spä") stopped sponsoring the **SPHAs**, so players opened a sporting goods store and dressed themselves.[3] After his 1925 retirement from playing, Gottlieb coached the **SPHAs** to eleven Eastern League and ABL championships. With *S-P-H-A* spelled in Hebrew letters across their chests, they were alternately **"Hebrews"** but occasionally "Philadelphia **Warriors**," especially in the late '20s when they featured some gentiles.[4]

Like many from the ABL talent pool, Gottlieb went to the new BAA in 1946 to coach new Philadelphia **Warriors** (today's NBA Golden State **Warriors**).[5] Treated less seriously were the **SPHAs**, who became the frustrated foils to the Harlem **Globetrotters**.[6] In 1950, Gottlieb sold the **SPHAs** to Red Klotz, a former

SPHA and Baltimore **Bullet** who in '53 made them the Washington **Generals** out of respect for the new U.S. president, World War II general Dwight Eisenhower.

Four Jewish kids from city blacktops represented one of N.Y.C.'s Catholic enterprises, St. John's University. As four-fifths of the **Red Men's** "Wonder Five" of 1929, they had a .900 winning percentage before being bounced from school in 1931 for talking with bookies.[7] Turning pro as independents and then ABLers, they barely disguised their ethnicity as New York **Jewels** (1934–43).

Hungarian-born Jew Max Rosenblum was a sports promoter in northern Ohio whose Cleveland **Rosenblums** won the first ABL crown in 1926 with player-coach Honey Russell and the "Heavenly Twins," Barney Sedran and Marty Friedman, each one a New York–born Jew and future Hall of Famer. When the ABL champs of 1927 and '28, the **Original Celtics**, temporarily folded, Max snapped up future inductees Joe Lapchick and Dutch Dehnert. The reconfigured Rosenblum's [**Original**] **Celtics** won the next two league titles.

• • •

In the 1920s the Austrian capital had Europe's third-largest Jewish population, represented by SC **Hakoah** Vienna—*hakoah* being Hebrew for "strength." That club had powerhouse swimming, water polo, and wrestling squads and followed its 1925 Austrian soccer championship with a ten-game U.S. exhibition tour. Some **Hakoahs** stayed around to join the ASL's New York **Giants** or Brooklyn **Wanderers**,[8] and by 1929 there were enough stateside ex-**Hakoahs** to assemble the ASL Brooklyn **Hakoah**. They merged with the Eastern Soccer League's New York **Hakoah** to form the ASL's **Hakoah All-Stars** (1930–32).[9]

Many Jews went to New York State after the Erie Canal opened in 1832 and especially after the Revolutions of 1848 (p. 47). The Rochester **Centrals** were mostly Jewish chums from a Central Avenue high school who got together in around 1905.[10] They displayed that name in the ABL from 1925 to 1931.

Jews fled Eastern Europe after anti-Semitism ramped up in the 1880s. Newly arrived Rabbis in New York established *yeshivas*, places of Talmudic study. Yeshiva University opened in 1927 for secular and religious learning, but its **Maccabees** (or **Macs**) athletes emphasize the latter. The apocryphal books of the Maccabees record the valor of the five Maccabeus brothers who defended Israel against the Hellenization campaign of Syrian-Greeks from 170 to 121 BCE.[11]

Russian immigrant Joseph Krauskopf graduated in the first class at Cincinnati's Hebrew Union College (no teams) in 1883 and became a prominent Reform Jew in the Midwest before leading a large Philadelphia temple. As Russian Jews continued to fill port cities, Dr. Krauskopf became increasingly concerned with urban squalor. To reconnect to a pastoral life, he founded the National Farm School in Doylestown (north of Philly) in 1896, "primarily with the needs of young Jewish men in mind, [although] he insisted the school be open to boys of all faiths and backgrounds."[12] The Farm School is today's Delaware Valley College, but **Aggies** indicate the original intent.

Patroons | Flying Dutchmen | Pride | Kazoos

Giovanni da Verrazano was a Florentine working for France to find the Northwest Passage to Asia. In 1524 his was the first ship through the narrow strait in New York harbor where his namesake bridge now staples Staten Island to Brooklyn. Just west of that span, the College of Staten Island was founded in 1976. Its **Dolphins** are named for Verrazano's ship *La Dauphine*.[1]

Renaissance works influenced by the Roman poet Virgil would likely have familiarized Verrazano with *Arkadia*, a region of natural splendor in ancient Greece. Verrazano called the mid-Atlantic coast's forests "Arcadia," and French map makers later stamped "*L'Acadie*" on shores from northern Maine to the Maritimes. The city at the heavy end of Long Island was once a rustic village deemed analogous to *Arkadia*, presumably explaining the ABL Brooklyn **Arcadians** (1925–27), or at least their gym, Arcadia Hall.[2]

You can still experience some of Brooklyn's pastoral past at Prospect Park, farmland morphed into a meadowed landscape by Olmsted and Vaux after their work at Central Park. Many independents of the 1920s were simply "**Pros**," but basketball's MBL Brooklyn **Pros** (1920–25) actually represented an abbreviation of "Prospect [Park] **Big Five**."[3]

• • •

The French never occupied Verrazano's new harbor, so English captain Henry Hudson claimed his namesake valley during his search for Asia in 1609 while in the employ of the Dutch East India Company. A new *West* India Company settled *Nieu Nederlandt* with trappers and farmers to limit English expansion after the Pilgrims stepped off at Plymouth Rock in 1620. (In fact, the Hudson-Champlain Valley remains the pronounced geographic interruption between *New* England and the other states.) The Dutch established Fort Orange, a Hudsonside fur post, in 1624. That same year they took root on lower Manhattan Island (soon New Amsterdam).[4] Kiliaen Van Rensselaer was a West India Company director and a major player in the fur trade. When the Dutch partially privatized their American farming and trapping operations in 1630, Rensselaer became the "first *patroon*" (Dutch for *patron* or *employer*), a kind of semi-feudal landlord. Tribute payments to the House of Orange put *Kolonie Rensselaerswyck* under the tacit protection of Fort Orange, a later home for minor league basketball Albany **Patroons** (1982–92, 2005–09).

The Protestant English and Dutch allied against Catholics in the Thirty Years' War. When that ended in 1648, the spice and tea routes of the weakened Portuguese and Spanish were up for grabs. With England distracted by its civil war (p. 69), the Dutch took over the Eastern trade. Britain tried to handicap Dutch merchants by barring foreign ships from its ports, starting the Anglo-Dutch Wars (1652–74). At the end of those naval battles, England got New Netherland from New Amsterdam to Fort Orange, later New York City and Albany, respectively.

Suddenly under the same English king, colonial Dutch and Yankee families began settling each others' turf. Dutch themes are still apparent across the former

Nieu Nederlandt. The great-great-great-grandson of "the first patron" was U.S. Congressman Stephen Van Rensselaer III, whose inheritance financed Troy's Rensselaer Polytechnic Institute in 1824, the first civilian technical college in the country. RPI's **Cherry and White** became **Engineers** in the early 1920s. Administrators later worried that the nick suggested a curriculum of exclusively geeky studies, so in the mid-1990s they tried switching to "**Red Hawks**." Students and alumni protested, so **Engineers** and **Red Hawks** now share a campus, making Rensselaer one of the few schools with monikers that vary by sport.[5]

• • •

In 1680, Netherlandish people founded Orangetown up the Hudson from Manhattan. Its hamlet of Sparkill ("spruce creek" in Dutch) is the home of St. Thomas Aquinas College, whose **Spartans** of Sparkill are purely alliterative.

Northwest of Albany, Dutch Reformers ran the Schenectady Academy from 1785 to '94. The next year, trustees of various faiths avoided the sectarianism of the colonial colleges by getting a state charter for the country's first nondenominational one. The academic union's new name was Union College, but that is somewhat undermined by **Dutch** and **Dutchwomen** jocks.

A neighborhood in Dutch *Breukelen* is Bushwick, from *Boswijck*, "little town in the woods." The Brooklyn **Bushwicks** (1917–51) were integrated semi-pro baseballers who shared Dexter Park with independent football's Brooklyn **Bushwicks** of the 1920s and '30s. More of Long Island's rustic history is revealed by baseball's semipro Glendale **Farmers**, who played at Farmers Oval in Queens for decades before it became an auto track in 1938. East of Brooklyn is Hempstead, where Dutch descendent William S. Hofstra lived in his "Netherlands" mansion. The estate is now Hofstra University, where male lions on the seal were from the Dutch arms of Orange-Nassau. One lion became a female in 1988. The next year, boosters started the Pride Club and "**Pride**" (the term for a lion pack) became an instant alternate for Hofstra's **Flying Dutchmen**, **Dutchmen**, and **Dutch**. As of 2005, **Pride** was the single official nickname. Kate Hofstra's will had established the university in her late husband's name in 1935, so HU's lion mascots are Kate and Willy. Hofstra probably chose "**Pride**" over "**Lions**" because Nassau Community College—right next door—had already taken **Lions** from the lion rampant on the orange-and-blue Nassau County seal, also copied from the Dutch arms.

• • •

Louis Bonaparte was Holland's first king in 1806. After the final defeat of big brother Napoleon in 1815, the Congress of Vienna created the United Kingdom of the Netherlands (Holland, the Low Countries, Belgium, and Luxembourg). Its king, William I, believed France and Austria would not so easily forfeit the Southern Netherlands and solidified his realm by taking over Dutch churches in 1816. That transition was smoothed a secularism already infiltrating Reformed congregations, but it bugged orthodox ministers in the north, especially at the historically Protestant Leiden University. Clinging to conservative Calvinism, they executed an *Afscheiding* (secession) from the state church in 1834.

Population explosions and increased industrialization were already driving emigration, but "Seceders" had the added burden of having offended their king.

So Rev. H.P. Scholte led his party to a new settlement in 1847, Pella, Iowa. A leading historian of Dutch immigration, Robert P. Swierenga, says: "The intense and focused migration of the minority Seceders […] gave them a strong presence in the Midwest that was disproportionate to their numbers."[6] For instance, assimilation in Pella was quick after various other Christians arrived, but Netherlandish themes are plainly evident in the town's architecture, Tulip Festival, and Central College **Dutch**.

A few months after Scholte founded Pella, his Leiden U. chum Albertus Van Raalte led fifty Seceders to a new Michigan *kolonie* sentimentally given the name Holland. (W.S. Hofstra was born there in 1861, later earning his fortune in Midwestern timber.) The Pioneer School opened in 1851, which Rev. Van Raalte called his "anchor of hope" (Hebrews 6:18–19). As Hope College, it presents **Flying Dutchmen** and **Flying Dutch** (women).[7]

A party headed for Van Raalte's Holland in 1850 was within fifty miles of the finish line when cholera killed seven of their number and got the rest quarantined at Kalamazoo. They stayed as the town's first permanent Dutch settlers. Archivists at Kalamazoo College think their colors may have been suggested by a turn-of-the-century dean who graduated Princeton and repeated its orange and white. Those colors could have effected athletic **Hornets**, but a few older alums remember their guys *stinging* the opposition. Another story attributes "**Hornets**" to the swarm of buzzing kazoos in the bleachers, supported by the "Kazoo" nickname for both the city and the college. In fact, baseball history is sprinkled with Kalamazoo **Kazoos**.

The Midwest's strict Dutch Calvinists were shocked when Rev. Van Raalte joined his Holland *kolonie* to the more liberal Reformed Church of America in 1850. (Van Raalte wanted to raise funds for Hope College from RCA congregations in the east[8] and forge connections with the Reformed seminary at Rutgers.)[9] Van Raalte's new tangent created concern within Michigan's Dutch Triangle, for which Holland, Kalamazoo, and Grand Rapids are the vertices. This caused a conservative Grand Rapids church to split off in 1857 to become the first congregation in today's Christian Reformed Church. In 1876 the CRC founded G-Rap's Calvin College, where "Calvin **Knights**" was derived from "**Calvinites**" in 1926.

• • •

In the Netherlands, the wood from plentiful poplar trees has an easy workability that belies its durability. That makes shoes of carved poplar practical in soggy fields, explaining these traditions:

- The Holland **Wooden Shoes** (1910–11) and Holland **Carvers** (1965–68) were minor league baseballers in Holland, Michigan.
- Also in Michigan's Dutch Triangle, the prize for winning the annual football game between the Hope College **Flying Dutchmen** and Kalamazoo College **Hornets** is a pair of carved wooden shoes. Another such trophy is awarded in the cross-Michigan rivalry between the Wayne State **Warriors** and the Grand Valley State **Lakers**.
- Back in the Hudson-Mohawk Region, the Union College **Dutch** play the RPI **Engineers** (p. 54) for football's Dutchman's Shoes.

Voyageurs | *Freemen* | *Beavers* | *Sea Otters*

France opened Europe's first New World fur post at the mouth of Quebec's Saguenay River in 1599. Local Francophones have self-identified as *saguenéens* ever since, as do junior hockey's *Les* **Saguenéens** *de Chicoutimi* (est. 1973).

French *voyageurs* (travelers) were guides and relentless paddlers who learned to navigate the wilderness in birch-bark canoes from the First Nations people with whom their operations would become integrated. The voyageur work ethic is a great model for athletes because they were small, but hard-bodied. (Larger men would have consumed space intended for pelts and trade goods.) Those who trapped on Ontario's lakes and rivers between the Ottawa River and the Great Lakes are recalled by North Bay **Trappers** (several junior and minor league hockey sides since 1961) and Sudbury's Laurentian University **Voyageurs** and **Lady Vees**.[1] Voyageurs set their paddling cadence to song, like the famous *Alouette* (skylark), recalled by three separate CFL Montreal **Alouettes** from 1946 to the present.[2]

International Falls is a Rainy River fur post between Minnesota and Ontario. It's the closest city to Voyageurs National Park, so the Rainy River Community College **Voyageurs** are reminders of Minnesota's frontier Frenchmen.[3] The state motto, *L'Etoile du Nord*—the star of the north—is another. Bloomington's Minnesota **North Stars** joined the NHL in 1967 and moved from the North Star State to the Lone Star State before the 1993/94 season, where they were shortened to [Dallas] **Stars**.

The English word often substituted for *voyageur* is *wanderer*, as with the amateur Montreal **Wanderers** (est. 1903), who evolved into an inaugural franchise in both the NHA and NHL, appealing largely to their bilingual city's Anglophones. (Some say **"Wanderers"** suggested a willingness to wander around to defend their five Stanley Cups.) Winnipeg's Norwood **Wanderers** won soccer's first two national challenge cups in 1913 and 1914.[4]

> The fur trade brought white trappers to western Montana, but that's not how minor league baseball's Great Falls **Voyagers** got named in 2008. A 16-second home movie of two unidentified flying objects was recorded at G'Falls in 1950. Hundreds of local sightings of intergalactic voyagers have been reported since.[5]

• • •

Back in 1534 the land north of the St. Lawrence River had been claimed for France by Jacques Cartier, in whose journals the Iroquois word for a village—*kanata*—is the first record of a "canada." (In fact, the Ottawa **Senators** play in Kanata, Ontario, a suburb of their eponymous capital.)

Britain got Canada in the 1763 victory that ended the French and Indian Wars, and Charles II chartered England's Hudson's Bay Company in 1670, giving to it half of Canada. British subjects then flooded to Canada, especially enterprising Scots who were always seeking opportunity in the colonies. Young voyageur James McGill was among the new Scot-Quebecers on the Great Lakes frontier in 1766, but he was running the business end out of Montreal within a decade. Even successful independents like McGill got squeezed by the royal HBC monopoly, so his and eight other operations confederated as the North West Company in 1779.

• • •

The NWC's French-Canadian traders decided to out-hustle HBC agents in the wilderness. Because the HBC men tended their fires and simply waited for the Indians to show up with the goods, the English never fostered those relationships to the degree that the French had, explaining both the Indian alliances with the French in the colonial wars and the reason French remained the language of the fur trade long after Britain won Canada.

The NWC voyageurs were called *engages* to indicate the terms of engagement they'd signed with the company. When those contracts expired, the *engagés* leveraged their experience toward their own profit as *hommes libre* (free men), doing temp work for any company. The best-connected among them were the *Métis*, first identified by that name in the fur-rich Red River basin.

The original *Métis* (roughly "mixed blood" in French) were the children of French voyageurs and Cree or Ojibwa women, but their Anglo blood increased in proportion to the arrival of Britons. The Red River town of Otterburne, Manitoba is in the former *Métis* territory, verified by the **Freemen** and **Lady Freemen** at its Providence University College.

The *Métis* traded fur and pemmican along the Red and Assiniboine Rivers. The NWC and HBC built forts at their confluence in 1809 and 1812 respectively, setting the roots for modern Winnipeg. The city's French Quarter annually hosts Western Canada's largest winter carnival, *le Festival du Voyageur*. The same block is home to the **Voyageurs** of the French-language *Université de Saint-Boniface*.

The villages of the *Métis* eventually ran to the Pacific. Other Indians they met called them *Zoch*, which was a swipe at the common French name *Jacques*. In the Dakota Territory, the *Métis* called one watercourse the *Riviere Aux Jacques*.[6] Because *Jacques* and *James* have the same Latin root—*Jacobus*—the river is now the James and on its bank is the city of Jamestown, North Dakota, which irreverent locals call "Jimtown." In fact, the stream is the "Jim River" and the University of Jamestown athletes of both sexes are **Jimmies**.

In the forests of Alberta, the NWC's Fort Saskatchewan and the HBC's Fort Edmonton were the first white settlements at Edmonton when they opened in 1795. (Refer to the junior hockey Fort Saskatchewan **Traders** [est. 1976] and the minor league baseball Edmonton **Trappers** [1981–2004].) In short order, both companies moved northeast with posts at Lac La Biche, where *le portage la biche* was the ground track between the Churchill and Athabasca-Mackenzie River basins. Paddlers from the *Métis* villages that arose thereabout explain the Portage College **Voyageurs**. In fact, we still use the French word *portage* (to carry) to describe canoe hauling.

Fur men used a nine-mile Chippewa footpath—*le grand portage*—to cut around gorges and falls near the Lake Superior mouth of the Pigeon River. In the 1780s the NWC started a great summer rendezvous for voyageurs, agents, and Indians at Grand Portage. Rookie voyageurs from Montreal who showed up with company-issued rations of corn, peas, and pork were derided as *mangeurs de lard* (pork eaters) by their partners who lived year-round in the wilderness. Those more experienced voyageurs were the *hivernants* (winterers) or *hommes du Nord* (Northmen). Toronto **Northmen** were set to commence play in the WFL's inaugural 1974 season, but last-minute intervention by Canada's government blocked the WFL from CFL markets. The **Northmen** went down to Tennessee as the Memphis **Southmen**, with their polar bear symbol transformed into a brown bear in a sphinx position (a nod to Memphis's eponymous Egyptian city). The graphic inspired "**Grizzlies**" as an informal alternate to "**Southmen**." In fact, it was as Memphis **Grizzlies** that they tried and failed to enter the NFL after the WFL's 1975 collapse.

Today's Memphis **Grizzlies** are different Canadian transplants who (like Toronto's **Northmen**) never played under their originally intended name. The new NBA team in B.C. in 1995 wanted to be Vancouver **Mounties**, but the Royal Canadian Mounted Police didn't want that association with a private enterprise. (No such protests had been raised when different Vancouver **Mounties** played PCL baseball from 1956 to '69.) They revived the name of a 1941-only CFL team, playing six unprofitable seasons as Vancouver **Grizzlies** before becoming Tennessee's Memphis **Grizzlies** in 2001.

> SUNY Canton used to indicate its close proximity to the international border through **Northmen** teams, but they became gender-neutral **Northstars** in 1995. They're now "Canton **Kangaroos**," having *jumped* (their joke, not ours) from two- to four-year athletic programs in 2007.

• • •

A 1795 Anglo-American treaty reasserted U.S. ownership of the Old Northwest, which had been contested since the Revolution. That gave the Yanks undisputed control of Grand Portage (now in northeasternmost Minnesota), so the North West Company moved its men—the "Nor'Westers"—north to British Ontario's *Baie de Tonnaire* (Thunder Bay), where Lakehead University now stands in the shadow of the Nor'Wester Mountains. Its teams were once **Nor'Westers**, but since 2001 they've been **Thunderwolves**.

Real estate would prove more profitable than fur for Montreal's richest man, and James McGill's 1813 will left cash and land sufficient to establish Quebec's premier English-language college. McGill University's shield copies the three martlets (mythical heraldic birds) from Scotland's McGill/MacGill family crest. The red-and-white shield inspires McGill's male **Redmen** and female **Martlets**, although baseball's **Redbirds** combine those features.

Simon Fraser was the top NWC agent beyond the Rockies by 1805, often exploring B.C.'s longest river, now the Fraser. Simon Fraser University was founded near its mouth at Burnaby in 1965. The Fraser family roots are evident through SFU's Centre for Scottish Studies and its **Clan** teams. When Mr. Fraser retired in 1818, the HBC's aggressive effort to catch up with the NWC was creating a sort of mini-civil war. The fur stopped flying only when the companies consolidated in 1821 as a larger Hudson's Bay Company (with current mall stores called The Bay).

• • •

Trappers collected bear, fox, and otter coats, but *Castor canadensis* could have single-handedly driven the fur trade, which is seen as we track these sporting **Beavers** from east to west:

- The year they had their first New World settlement at Jamestown (1607), the English established trade with the Abenakis on Maine's Kennebec River. That watershed still sees **Beavers** at the University of Maine–Farmington.

- The Massachusetts Bay Colony didn't sink a lot of agents deep into forests, but business was good as Indians from Connecticut and Maine brought in their beaver skins. Beavers are freshwater critters, so you have to follow the Charles River inland from Boston Harbor to see them. In fact, the Babson College **Beavers** are fifteen miles upstream at Wellesley.

- The beaver became New York's state animal in 1975, recalling the Dutch and English trappers in Manhattan and along the Hudson. German-born John Jacob Astor had a humble N.Y.C. fur shop in 1786, but his Pacific Fur Company made him America's richest man by his 1848 death. City College of New York is a den for **Beavers**.[7]

- *Castor canadensis* was the symbol for Quebec's junior hockey Sherbrooke **Castors** (1969–82, 1998–2003), who Anglophones called **Beavers**. Moving west, a beaver is atop the coat of arms for the city that hosted the Continental Football League's Montreal **Beavers** (1966–67).

- Moving south to Lake Champlain, Burlington's Champlain College canceled its varsity **Beavers** in 2002, but some club teams remain **Beavers**. (The same city has Vermont **Voyageurs** [est. 2010] of box lacrosse.)

- Trappers from France used Ohio Valley forts to forge Indian alliances and keep English colonials on the coast. Ohio's Bluffton University **Beavers** are in the Maumee River watershed.

- The **Beavers** at Minnesota's Bemidji State University recall trappers in the "Land of Ten-Thousand Lakes."

- On the lower Missouri watershed, Iowa's Buena Vista County is a place of historically good trapping, but Buena Vista University's **Beavers** in Storm Lake got tagged through a nickname for students: "BV-ers."

- French trappers from Montreal or Louisiana went west by following the Arkansas watershed, including both forks of the Ninnescah River. The southern fork is in south-central Kansas, home of the Pratt [County] Community College **Beavers**.

- Canada's Souris River swings south to snare North Dakota's city of Minot and its Minot State University **Beavers**. The Souris valley was targeted by early beaver men and mapped in 1797 by "North America's greatest geographer," the NWC's David Thompson.

- The NWC wanted Thompson's party to explore the length of the Columbia and establish a Pacific post at its mouth, but arriving there in July 1811 they learned that J.J. Astor's men had already founded Astoria. The NWC bought Astor out in 1813 and merged with the HBC in 1821. Three years later, the huge monopoly set up Fort Vancouver at the top of the Willamette Valley (now Vancouver, Washington). That was just over the Columbia from the future site of

Oregon's most populous city, where a nearly continuous string of Portland **Beavers** have played minor league hardball since 1906.

- In the Beaver State's Willamette Valley, a land-grant university at Corvallis fielded **Aggies** and **Orangemen**, but they've been the Oregon State University **Beavers** since about 1916.
- By 1830, HBC men were using the Indians' Siskiyou Trail to cross the hills between the Willamette Valley and California's Central Valley. The abundant trapping opportunities near the confluence of the Sacramento and American Rivers gave **Beavers** to Sacramento's American River College.

• • •

The beavers back east were quickly trapped out, so the Iroquois launched the Beaver Wars (1650–1700) to get control of the Indian side of the French trade. Pushing as far west as the Mississippi, the Iroquois completely rearranged the tribal map of the Midwest.

Blackburn College (Carlinville, Ill.) is next to Beaver Dam State Park, but we don't have to account for wildlife, the state park, or the southwesternmost battles of the Beaver Wars to explain its **Battlin' Beavers**. Blackburn is in the Work College Consortium, seven small colleges at which student labor counts toward tuition. Beavers are the oft-recognized symbols for such industriousness.

There are **Beavers** at Los Angeles Trade-Technical College and Pasadena's California Institute of Technology, or "Caltech." Those L.A. County schools are south of better trapping regions, but the imagery is appropriate for tech schools because the beaver is "nature's engineer"; by felling trees and building dams and canals, beavers purposefully manipulate their environment more than any non-human species. The assiduous beaver is embraced often at techs that don't necessarily field **Beaver** teams, as is the case with the beaver mascot—colloquially "the rat"—for the Massachusetts Institute of Technology **Engineers** (Cambridge).

• • •

Wyoming usually hosted the Rocky Mountain Rendezvous, an annual market and meetup. According to T.A. Larson—"Mr. Wyoming History"—the fur trade was "nearly the entire economy of Wyoming for many years. And all the white actors on the Wyoming stage before 1840, with very few exceptions, were connected with the fur trade."[8] The Rendezvous spanned the last years of the beaver trade (1825–40), so the famous trappers in attendance would soon switch to careers as guides for Oregon Trail pioneers. There are still Wyoming **Trappers** at Powell's Northwest College, or "NWC"—the initials of the North West Company.

• • •

Without invitation, Europeans invaded territories long held by indigenous peoples to exploit fur-bearing animals. Their monarch established a fur monopoly, which relied on the cooperation of the natives, who—in turn—came to require the newcomers' iron tools and liquor even as European diseases reduced their numbers. Forts and trading posts were established along key waterways, often by subjects from the fringes of the invading empire. Then natural resources like lumber and minerals were harvested from conquered lands. The original inhabitants invariably suffered as the newcomers crossed the continent to the Pacific.

That's the story of the Russians in Asia.

After losing their own battles with the czars, nomadic Eastern Slavs called Cossacks served as peasant-soldiers on the vanguard of Russian imperialism. They crossed the Urals in the 1500s to conquer Turkic and Mongolian peoples for Russia and continued east to manage the trade of Siberian beaver, sable, and fox furs that were so necessary in pre-electric heat Europe.[9] Cossacks and Russians trapped their way to the North Pacific and Arctic coasts to find the world's thickest fur on the sea otter. Having all but depleted coastal otters by 1760, they crossed to Alaska to hunt seals. By 1799 they were running the czar-chartered Russian-American Company. Alexander Baranof established RAC headquarters at Sitka (on the rock now called Baranof Island) after violently ejecting its Tlingit inhabitants.

When Russia sold Alaska to the U.S. in 1867, a Presbyterian minister arrived to educate Tlingit and white children, but he introduced Siberian reindeer too. Sitka's college was renamed Sheldon Jackson College after his death in 1910. Until closing in 2007, SJC teams were **Golden Seals**.

A graduate of Princeton's seminary, Sheldon Jackson had already been the leading Presbyterian missionary in the West. He founded the Salt Lake Collegiate Institute in Utah in 1875, a secondary school established by Protestants to minister to those white pioneers who might otherwise be tempted by Mormonism. SLCI became Sheldon Jackson College in 1897 and was Westminster College by 1902. Its purple-and-gold **Purps** became **Fighting Parsons** in 1920 after Rev. Jackson, but since 1999 they've been **Griffins** (Christian symbolism on p. 107).

• • •

Russians got all the way down to modern Sonoma County, where they built Fort Ross (*Rossiya/Russia*) as a base for hunting fur, growing wheat for Alaskan posts, and trading with California's Spanish missions. The **Cossacks** at Sonoma State University (Rohnert Park) came under fire because Cossack troops had a historical hand in the heavy persecution of Ukrainian Jews, so SSU made teams **Seawolves** in 2002. *The Sea Wolf* is Jack London's 1904 novel about northern Pacific seal hunters written while he lived in the Sonoma Valley. Also, SSU is the custodian of some of London's important papers, and his family estate is the nearby Jack London State Historic Park.

With the end of *The Sea Wolf* comes a rescue by a vessel in the U.S. Revenue Cutter Service, a resolution inspired by real events. The Scottish-built *Bear* had set sail as a Canadian sealer in 1874 but was purchased by the U.S. in 1884 and sent immediately to aid an Arctic rescue (the infamous Greely Expedition). The next year the *Bear* was a floating federal office building and courthouse in the Bering Sea, but it also rescued stranded whalers and transported Sheldon Jackson's relocated reindeer. The new Coast Guard absorbed the Cutter Service (and the *Bear*) in 1915. The *Bear* reprised its days as a sealer in the 1930 film version of *The Sea Wolf*, four years after the U.S. Coast Guard Academy (New London, Conn.) named its **Bears** for both the Guard's most famous cutter and a live bear mascot, *Objee*—whose very presence some cadets found *objectionable*.

• • •

Beavers and sea otters were hunted to near extinction by about 1800 and 1850, respectively, although research and orphan adoption programs at the Monterey Bay Aquarium are fighting the good fight to save the latter. Five miles up the coast, the city of Seaside hosts the CSU Monterey Bay **Sea Otters**. The depletion of the sea otter should have sent prices sky high, but fur values were actually dropping in the wake of a style that caught on after 1840, the cheaper silk hat. With no further use for its California posts, Russia sold them to settler John Sutter in 1841. In 1867 they signed over Alaska to the U.S. at a bargain price to keep it from Britain, against whom Russia was engaged in a global war of imperial expansionism.

In fact, when Britain was moving regular troops from Canada to such exotic destinations as India and the Crimea in its effort to control half the world in the 1850s, defensive militias had to be raised from the general population. One such large company was in Brampton, Ontario, where citizen-soldiers would make disproportionate sacrifices through two world wars and beyond. The name and olive sweaters of junior hockey's Brampton **Battalion** (est. 1998) celebrated the military tradition. Since the 2013/14 season they've been up on Ontario's Lake Nipissing as the North Bay **Battalion**, fitting their new home at North Bay Memorial Gardens, named in 1955 for locals killed in the world wars. (The ice is shared with Nipissing University's skating **Lakers**.)

Canadiens | Maple Leafs | VooDoo | Lakers

The French tried poking through North America to Asia as early as 1523, but serious settlement didn't begin until New France's first governor, Samuel de Champlain, established trading posts in the Acadian Maritimes, Quebec City, and Montreal after 1604. St. Lambert, Quebec looks across the St. Lawrence to Montreal, and the sword emblem for its Champlain College **Cavaliers** is much like the one the knight-cavalier-musketeer Champlain probably wielded.

Native Americans got along better with the nomadic paddlers and trappers of New France than with the families of *New* England who were turning forests into farms. The Frenchmen's alliances and trade relations with Algonquian-speaking Ottawas and Iroquois-speaking Hurons were strong, but Champlain made a bad first impression on other Iroquois people, who would remain hostile.

Quebec's frontiersmen got some company in 1617 when French farming families started arriving. Following an ancient feudal model, those *habitants* (inhabitants) worked under the stewardship of a lord who bound his duty to the French crown while *les habitants* quietly tended to their farming. The *Université du Québec a Montréal* presents **Citadins**, "city dwellers" in French, a distinguishment from Quebec's ruralist *habitants*.

Headline writers starting calling the Montreal **Canadiens** "Habs" around 1924 after New York **Rangers** owner Tex Rickard repeated a false rumor that the *C-H* logo represented *Canadien habitants*. In fact, *H* stands for … "hockey." The franchise was established for the 1910 NHA season as *Club Athletique Canadien* and only adopted their familiar *C-H* upon becoming *le Club de Hockey le Canadien* in 1917. English speakers in other leagues had excluded Francophone players, so the new NHA wanted to exploit the niche market for a quality French-Canadian side.[1] *Canadien*-with-an-*e* was a self-reference for Quebec's French speakers (a role now satisfied by *Québécois*), so "**Canadiens**" intended to mark their arrival at the game's highest level.[2] Across Montreal is the French-language *Collège Ahuntsic* (est. 1967), where *Indiens* mirror a familiar local spelling.[3]

The Protestant Victorians barred Canadian Catholics from their social and athletic clubs, so the French-Canadians and immigrant Irish were thrown together by their religion. The French learned hockey from the Irish at parochial secondary schools (in Canada, "colleges") that usually had Anglophonic and Francophonic halves. The 1893 lacrosse world championship at Chicago's World's Fair was won by Montreal's Shamrock Amateur Athletic Association, which would soon assemble the first hockey team with French talent by combining players from the Jesuits' *Collège Sainte-Marie* and its sister institution, the (all-Irish) Loyola College. As Montreal **Shamrocks** they won five Stanley Cup challenges between 1899 and 1900.[4]

Owing to French, English, Scottish, and Irish citizens, Montreal took the Latin motto *Concordia salus* (salvation through harmony) in 1833, explaining its CFL Montreal **Concordes** (1982–85) and its Concordia University **Concordians**, who arbitrarily became **Stingers** in 1975, a name just getting major league exposure through the WHA Cincinnati **Stingers** (p. 427).

• • •

The **Canadiens** made Montreal's Forum famous, but it wasn't even built for them, compelling us to explain the birth of the NHL.

The amateur Eastern Canadian Hockey Association transitioned to a more stable professional Canadian Hockey Association just to get rid of the Montreal **Wanderers**. (Those four-time Stanley Cup champs were moving to the Montreal Arena, which other owners deemed too small for meaningful profit sharing.) The CHA rejected the application of Ontario's Renfrew **Creamery Kings** (named for the rich agriculture of the Ottawa Valley), so team owner J. Ambrose O'Brien started his own seven-team National Hockey Association. Starting play in January 1910, the NHA included the rebuffed **Creamery Kings** and **Wanderers** and the brand-new **Canadiens**. Renfrew's **C-Kings** signed superstar brothers Lester and Frank Patrick for a whopping $5,000 and became **Millionaires** (although that's also informed by Renfrew's silver mine magnates, including O'Brien's own father).[5]

The NHA was the most stable pro circuit to date but still had problems during the 1916/17 campaign. It lost its first-half darlings when the entire Toronto **228th Battalion** (Canadian army fusiliers) shipped out for Great War duty. An even larger threat was Toronto **Blueshirts** owner Eddie Livingston, who was thought a selfish bully by other owners who formed their own National Hockey League. (They insisted Livingstone hadn't been booted; his NHA team had simply not been invited to the NHL.) That first 1917/18 NHL season included a Toronto squad with a roster suspiciously similar to that of the **Blueshirts**. They were at Mutual Street's new Arena Gardens as shrewdly labeled **Torontos** (or **Arenas**).[6] In 1919 they were recast as **St. Patricks** for the famous Christianizer of Ireland's Celtic tribes.[7] Former UT **Varsity Blues** hockey coach Conn Smythe bought the ailing **St. Pats** in 1927 and made them **Maple Leafs**. The maple leaf had been an unofficial symbol of Canada for generations, as an insignia for fighting forces and on provincial coats of arms. In fact there were already Toronto **Maple Leafs** in baseball's International League, and the Guelph **Maple Leafs** were renowned semi-pro baseballists in the Ontario of the 1870s. (The leaf finally made it onto the Canadian flag in 1965.)

The **Wanderers** played four games in the brand-new NHL then folded when their rink burned down. When the city's Forum opened in 1924, it hosted a new NHL side of English speakers, the Montreal **Maroons**. Their fascination with color was reminiscent of the "Redbands" nickname the **Wanderers** had gotten from the fat stripe around their sweaters. Only in 1926 were the **Maroons** joined at *le Forum* by the Mount Royal Arena's **Canadiens**, who've been supported by both Montrealers and *Montréalais* since the **Maroons** folded in 1938.

• • •

Jesuit priests traveled with New France's explorers, trappers, and *habitants* to spread Christianity to the natives. The most famous was Jacques Marquette, who befriended the Ottawas and the Illinois, although religious conversions were few.

The Algonquian-speaking Ojibwas told Father Marquette that a *misi sipi* (great river) might yet lead to China.

Marquette is joined at the historical hip to Louis Joliet, a Quebec-born, Jesuit-trained explorer and hydrographer. In 1673 the duo left Marquette's Mackinac mission to prove that the Great Lakes could connect to the Gulf of Mexico via the Mississippi watershed. From Green Bay, their small band of French paddlers got their two canoes to the Mississippi and eventually found the mouth of another large stream where they met the folks their Algonquian acquaintances called the *Arkansas* (down river people), who called themselves *Ugahxpa* (Quapaw) in their Siouan tongue, but the area was also home to Caddo, Tunica, and Osage peoples. Any could have inspired the **Indians** that represented Jonesboro's Arkansas State University after 1931 (although its Chief Big Track mascot memorializes an Osage leader of the early 1800s named *Cashesegra*: "large track"). Under pressure from Native American groups and the NCAA in 2008, A-State traded **Indians** for **Red Wolves**, after the *Canis lupus rufus* of the south-central and southeastern states.[8] (Red wolves are smaller than grey wolves and bigger than coyotes, and may be a hybrid thereof.)

When Marquette and Joliet learned the river would lead to the Gulf Coast outposts of their Spanish enemies, they turned around, eventually banging a right onto the Illinois. That valley's Kaskaskia-Illini people (who Marquette thought would make swell Christians) guided the party to the one-mile *Portage de Checagou* (a Franco-Algonquian contrivance for "portage over stinky ground"), which linked the Des Plaines and Checagou Rivers. Back at Green Bay in late September, Father Marquette stayed while Joliet continued to Quebec. But Marquette's small party returned to the Kaskaskias in late 1674 to be the first white men known to have wintered near *Checagou* (Chicago). Illness had been slowing the priest, and he died on Lake Michigan's eastern shore in the spring. Jesuits in Milwaukee remembered Father Marquette two centuries later with Marquette University. The **Warrior** teams that made a connection between Marquette and his intended aboriginal converts first took the field in 1954 (which many believe is less than coincidentally the year after the Milwaukee **Braves** arrived from Boston). The **Warriors'** Indian mascots were eventually scrutinized, so they became **Golden Eagles** in 1994.[9]

• • •

The next big bat off New France's bench was Robert de la Salle, who in 1678 launched the ten-ton schooner *Frontenac*, named for the governor general of New France. As an emphatic promoter of the Great Lakes fur trade, Count Frontenac founded many posts, including Fort Frontenac where Lake Ontario empties into the St. Lawrence at modern Kingston, Ontario. Many minor league and junior hockey teams have been Kingston **Frontenacs**. St. Lawrence College is just downriver in Brockville (but still in Frontenac County). Its **Schooners** recall a long history of Lake Ontario vessels in the same class as the *Frontenac*, which quickly busted up on some rocks.

The undeterred La Salle went on to finish a fifty-ton barque, but the fur-laden *Griffon* vanished on its maiden voyage. The Jesuit-trained La Salle had launched *Le Griffon* near Buffalo's Lasalle [*sic*] Park, three miles from the Jesuit-founded

Canisius College. Both that ship and the griffin's nobility in ancient folklore (p. 42) were cited when the *Canisian* campus newspaper reappeared as the *Griffin* on September 29, 1933. The same issue announced that the blue-and-gold teams would thenceforth be **Griffins**.[10] They're now **Golden Griffins**.

With fifty persons in six canoes (half voyageurs and half Indians) La Salle descended the Illinois and Mississippi Rivers all the way to the Gulf in 1682. He called the bigger river and its drainage basin *La Louisiane*, claiming it (and its Indians) for Louis XIV. La Salle again departed France in 1684, this time to sail up the Mississippi from the Gulf with four ships and 300 men. That he never found the muddy river mouth wasn't even the bad news. One ship fell to Spanish privateers, one ran aground, one wrecked in a storm, and one was turned back by a disgruntled crew. The remaining company wandered the Gulf Coast looking for the Mississippi on foot, but mutineers killed La Salle in Texas in 1687.

One might assume the La Salle University **Explorers** are named for Sieur de la Salle, but *misnamed* for him is more like it. The ink slinger who first called athletes **Explorers** in 1931 was probably either confused or careless. The Phila-delphia school was opened in 1863 by the De La Salle Christian Brothers, an educational order founded in 1681 by a different Frenchman, John Baptist de la Salle (1651–1719),[11] the patron saint of teachers. The like-named explorer never got anywhere near Philly. Nonetheless, the French musketeer that has accom-panied the **Explorers** since the 1950s is La Salle's mustached, sword-wielding clone. (He was a space explorer from 1962 to '72, following the Army's 1958 launch of an artificial satellite, the first in the Explorers program.)

• • •

Unlike La Salle, Pierre le Moyne d'Iberville found the mouth of the Mississippi from the Gulf of Mexico. In 1699 he sailed upstream past a crimson pole that Choctaws called *istrouma* (red stick), indicating a hunting boundary for lower-Mississippi Indians. A French red stick is *un bâton rouge*, so minor league Baton Rouge **Red Sticks** and **Redsticks** of the past are redundant. (Compare them to the Montreal **Royales**—or **Royals**—in several sports: "Mount Royal **Royals**.")

Captain Iberville and his brother Jean-Baptiste le Moyne de Bienville set up the Louisiana capital at Mobile (now in Alabama) in 1702. Iberville died of fever during Queen Anne's War, so Bienville assumed the governorship and founded New Orleans 100 miles up the Mississippi in 1718. It is the city that's usually identified with Mardi Gras celebrations, but it was probably at Mobile that the holiday was first celebrated in North America by French Catholics.

The *Voudou* rituals practiced by sugar plantation slaves on French Hispaniola merged their West African religions with their masters' Catholicism. Noticing that slaves greatly outnumbered their French masters, Voodoo priests led a revolt (1791–1804) that effected an independent black Haiti and sent the island's French aristocracy to New Orleans, sometimes with slave property in tow. Voodoo con-tinued there in secret, but when France sold Louisiana to the U.S. in 1803, the doctors of Voodoo emerged from the shadows and into the city's cultural fabric.

For almost two centuries, charitable *krewes* (crews) have driven Mardi Gras balls and parades in Mobile and New Orleans. Krewe members are called *Mystics* or *Mystiks* from voodoo's African mysticism component. Mobile is the "Mother of Mystics," and various minor leagues have seen stickhandling Mobile **Mysticks** (1995–2002), D-league hoop's Mobile **Revelers** (2001–03), and indoor football's Mobile **Wizards** (2002). Voodoo dolls have become recognized instruments of revenge and the New Orleans **Voodoo Dolls** (2001) were female footballers. Lady dancers of that name accompany Arena Football's 2004-named New Orleans **VooDoo**. Southern Blacks brought their traditions north, giving Memphis voodoo shops in the Beale Street neighborhood's "black magic district." **Magicians** still perform for the city's historically black LeMoyne-Owen College.

Omahans wanted some family-friendly fun for their 1895 state fair, so they sent businessmen south to borrow floats from the New Orleans Mardi Gras parade. On the train back, those guys formed a civic organization to emulate the krewes they'd seen. They would be Knights of Ak-Sar-Ben, which is actually a bass-ackwards spelling of *Nebraska*. (Hilarious.) Decades later, those Knights sponsored minor league hockey's Ak-Sar-Ben **Knights** (1939–42), based at Omaha's Ak-Sar-Ben Arena.[12]

• • •

Even when they didn't sink like the *Frontenac* and the *Griffon*, ships that were built on the Great Lakes had to stay on the Great Lakes; there was no link to the Atlantic until the St. Lawrence Seaway opened in 1959. Modern "lakers" are long and thin to exactly meet the specifications of the Seaway's interlake canal locks, but "lakers" also refers to crewmen on those vessels.

The massive Soo Locks are the gates between Superior and the other Great Lakes. Blocks from those locks are the Lake Superior State University **Lakers** (Sault Ste. Marie, Mich., **Hornets** until 1967). Lake Michigan's shores host the **Lakers** of Roosevelt University (Chicago) and Grand Valley State University (Allendale, Mich.). On Lake Erie are the **Lakers** of Mercyhurst University (Erie, Pa.) and Lakeland [County] Community College (Ohio). The **Teachers** at the Oswego Normal School—now SUNY Oswego—long ago became (**Great**) **Lakers**, being inches from Lake Ontario. Lake-Sumter State College serves Florida's Lake and Sumter Counties. Its **Lakers** started 2013 as the only **Lake Hawks** in college sports. The point is, you can trust our general explanation: **Lake-** teams play near lakes.

With one profound exception.

The most famous **Lakers** were basketballers in Minnesota, a state-name derived from the Siouan words for sky-colored (cloudy) water. Minnesota has 200 miles of shore along Lake Superior, but the many inland lakes that were dug by retreating glaciers are what make it the Land of Ten-Thousand Lakes. Its largest city is surrounded by lakes and the Mississippi River runs through it, so Sioux and Greek forms combine to make *Minneapolis*—"city of water." Jeweler Morris Winston owned the money-losing Detroit **Gems**, so he sold them to Minnesotans who made them Minneapolis **Lakers** for the 1947/48 NBL season. They moved again to southern California in 1960 as Los Angeles **Lakers**, nested against the world's largest ocean.

Scots | Cavaliers | Mountaineers | Fighting Irish

Collegiate **Scots** and **Highlanders** are usually named for Scots-Irish pioneers, hardscrabble folks who stood in stark contrast to those courtiers remembered by the **Cavalier**, **Knight**, and **Lancer** athletes across the former Virginia Colony. To know why huge numbers of Scots-Irish settled the Appalachian backcountry and why "Cavalier" describes Virginia's plantation class, one must understand the relationship of those two camps back on the British Isles. Which'll take a little doing.

• • •

England's last Tudor monarch, Elizabeth I, died in 1603. Her House of Stuart cousin, James VI of Scotland, became James I of England. He was raised by Calvinists handlers but nonetheless used the Tudors' Anglican bishops to politically unify his United Kingdom of Great Britain (as the English-Scottish realm was suddenly named). But the Church of Scotland had been on a fixed Presbyterian path ever since John Knox's return from Geneva in 1559, so Scots resisted being force-fed Anglicanism by James and his son Charles I. The Presbyterians' pledge to keep Scotland's liturgy free of "popish" episcopacy—the *National Covenant* of 1638—set up the Bishops' Wars between Charles and the Scottish "Covenanters."

> Reformed Presbyters opened a school at Beaver Falls, Pennsylvania in 1838, naming it Geneva College after the Swiss base of Calvinism. Recalling the 1638 *Covenant*, its teams were **Covenanters** (or **Covies**) until switching to **Golden Tornadoes** in the mid-twentieth century.[1] Pasadena, California's Covenant College was founded and named with a Reformed Calvinist direction in 1955. The school and its **Scots** have been in Lookout Mountain, Georgia since 1964.

In the Bishops' Wars, Covenanters waved their famous Blue Banner battle flag, and Scots embraced the blue-and-white cross of St. Andrew even after eschewing most other Catholic devotions. The blue remains favored by Presbyterian colleges, giving blue-and-white **Blue Jays** to Westminster College in Fulton, Missouri in 1903. Thomas Wentworth, Earl of Strafford, was an advisor to Charles I who tried to raise an Irish-Catholic army to fight the Scots. He forced Scottish-blooded Protestants in Ulster Province (more on them in a minute) to disown the Covenant of 1638. With a treasury insufficient to rebuff the Covenanters, Charles recalled the long-dormant Parliament to authorize wartime taxes. Once the House of Commons was seated, however, its newly elected Puritans were willing to discuss only the recent despotism of king and court, and they went after Wentworth for his Irish actions. He was beheaded in May 1641.

> Arioch Wentworth died in 1903, leaving his marble and real estate fortune to start a Boston industrial school the next year. The Wentworth Institute of Technology shield now comprises the chevron and three leopard faces from the Earl of Strafford's Wentworth family arms. Its **Technicians** transitioned to **Leopards** around 1950.

• • •

Irish Catholics had been watching Protestant power in both England and Ireland growing and rebelled five months after Wentworth's execution, killing thousands of English-backed Protestants on northern plantations. Charles thought his Protestant government would readily fight the Catholic rebels, but Parliament demanded control of any new army, lest those troops be turned on them. Charles burst into the House of Commons to arrest its leaders in January 1642, but the targeted ministers had been warned and were absent. Having overplayed his hand, the king fled London. Within months, the Crown's royalists would be fighting the Protestant armies of Parliament in the First English Civil War.

Nobles in the king's army were called Cavaliers by their less entitled foes. They were characterized as having fine garments, flowing hair, and snobbish attitudes. In turn, the gentlemen-Cavaliers derisively called the Parliamentarians "Roundheads" because they cropped their bangs like Pete Rose.

With the war going well, Puritan churchmen released the 1646 *Westminster Confession of Faith*, a Calvinist document that standardized Presbyterian worship (and gave name to the aforementioned Westminster College). The Scots captured Charles in 1647 and surrendered him to the English, but he escaped and was actually able to employ Scottish support by guaranteeing to empower Presbyterians once he regained control. (The Scots could be so turned because Parliament's Congregationalists had reneged on similar promises.) Scots fought emphatically for their new ally in a Second Civil War, but Charles was captured again in mid-1648, this time executed for high treason in early '49.

> Johnson County Community College in Kansas first fielded **Cavaliers** in 1983. In 2012 the new mustached **Cavalier** mascot Jean Claude appeared. That name sounds a little French, but at least it conforms to JCCC's initials. In fact, one could mistake Jean Claude for a French musketeer (p. 45), but the college took the liberty to invent a yarn (using the always iffy "legend has it" syntax) in which an unnamed former history professor lost an ancestor's English cavalier sword in the nearby woods, retroactively explaining all **Cavalier** traditions.[2]

Many Cavaliers escaped suspicion and capture by fleeing to the plantation colonies. That's why **Cavaliers** and **Knights** play all over the Southeast. But don't take our word for it. Refer to the first frame of a famous film about the fall of the antebellum South: "There was a land of Cavaliers and Cotton Fields called the Old South. Here in this pretty world, Gallantry took its last bow. Here was the last ever to be seen of Knights and their Ladies Fair, of Master and of Slave [...] a Civilization gone with the wind."[3] Charlottesville's University of Virginia keeps **Cavaliers**.[4] The **Highland Cavaliers** at a UVa branch school, the College at Wise, are derived from both the parent institution's teams and the mountains of southwestern Virginia.[5]

• • •

The victorious Roundhead generals hand picked the Parliament of 1653, called the "blew [*sic*] stocking Parliament" because its modestly attired Presbyterians wore cheap blue wool socks (instead of more fashionable black silk). Consequently, "old blue stocking Presbyterian" became a self-description for Scots with conservative Calvinist values, giving Presbyterian academies another reason to bend toward the blue. Footballers at a Presbyterian college in Clinton, South Carolina that's actually called "Presbyterian College" donned blue socks in 1915, ensuring that some smarty-pants reporter would call them **Blue Stockings**. For once, "**Stockings**" didn't shrink to "**Sox**"; PC's **Blue Hose** have been socking it to opponents since 1954.[6]

Parliament gave near-dictatorial power to former M.P. Oliver Cromwell, lately revealed as a superior military leader. He divided England among his generals, crushed the Irish Rebellion, and rebuffed invasion in the Third English Civil War (1650–51), in which Covenanters got behind the late king's son, the would-be Charles II. Cromwell died suddenly in 1658 in a country tired of militarism and extreme Puritanism. A sudden nostalgia for a stable monarchy and Anglican worship led a newly elected Parliament to invite back the exiled Charles II in 1660.

The new king fostered the political rise of enough sympathizers that the legislature that sat from 1661 to 1667 is recorded as the Cavalier Parliament. Charles set southern Virginia aside as the Province of *Carolina* (Latin for "Charles") in 1663 and placed it under the care of eight loyal Cavaliers, the Lords Proprietor.[7] The **Cavaliers** at Montreat College (Montreat, N.C.) ignore that the institution has always been administered by Presbyterians, the very people opposed to the Cavalier factions at the outbreak of war.

• • •

Cavalier and *cavalry* come from *caballarius*, a Latin-language horseman. Aloof Cavaliers saw themselves in the tradition of knighted horsemen, although a familiarity with horses didn't seem to be a prerequisite. Tons of **Cavaliers**, **Knights**, **Regals**, and **Royals** celebrate this regal tradition, as do **Chargers** (royal cavalry units) and **Lancers** (mounted knights). You'll find those nicknames nearly everywhere, but they're disproportionately abundant in regions with a historical loyalty to the English crown, especially southern Ontario and the former massive Virginia Colony.[8] A single example of knight/lancer/royal/cavalier/charger imagery in Virginia is provided by the Longwood University **Lancers** at Farmville. Their medieval knight with a lance predated the unit he was intended to commemorate, the Queen's Own Lancers (a cavalry serving Britain's royals only since 1759), so L-wood's jouster was replaced in 2006 by an equine charger named Elwood.

Colonial borders ran perpetually westward under British kings (although they skipped over Dutch New York). To comply with the 1787 Northwest Ordinance, Connecticut gave up claims to Pennsylvania's Erie Triangle in 1792 but held on to a "Western Reserve" wilderness (now northeast Ohio). In 1795 that tract was sold to Connecticut Land Company speculators to fund public education. CLC surveyors named a site after their Yale-educated crew chief, Moses Cleaveland, but it was "Cleveland" after a vowel was dropped to fit in an 1831 headline. Cavalier sympathies would have been lost on the many Yankee Puritans who settled there after the War of 1812, so the NBA's Cleveland **Cavaliers** are justified only by a pleasing repetition of vowels and consonants.

Cleveland's Case Institute of Technology and Western Reserve University merged in 1967 as Case Western Reserve University, echoing Connecticut's Western Reserve. (CIT founder Leonard Case, Jr. was the son of an influential CLC agent.) For no stupendous reason, CWRU teams are **Spartans**, but before the merger, Case Tech hosted **Scientists** and also **Rough-Riders** during the tenure of Athletic Director Ray Ride (1931–55).

• • •

English monarchs had wanted to rule Scotland since the Norman Invasion, so England's Edward I invaded in 1296. Opposition came from Scottish heroes William "Braveheart" Wallace and Robert the Bruce, the latter outlasting old Edward to gain Scottish independence in 1328. But life along the English-Scottish border had been disintegrating for centuries. The perpetual comings and goings of armies had relieved locals of their crops, their livestock, and (eventually) their principles. Raiding, robbing, and rustling were common as Scottish Lowlanders came to resemble medieval organized crime families. Those "Border reivers" were romanticized in hundreds of folk ballads, but it was a hard life for which no informed person would long.[9]

> Scots-Irish pioneers applied "reivers" to riverboat robbers on the Missouri River frontier. **Reivers** at Iowa Western Community College (Council Bluffs) have Caribbean pirate mascots, but the word's roots are in that bandit history.[10]

Nobles in Northumberland built Alnwick Castle in 1096 to contain Scottish armies and reivers. Its copy is Grey Towers Castle, an 1893 estate home in Glenside, Pennsylvania. When it became the heart of the Beaver College campus in 1928, regal athletic representation was called for, so teams became **Knights**. Beaver was renamed Arcadia University after an idyllic region in Greece (p. 53) when it attained university status in 2001.[11]

Tudor and Stuart regimes long feared that Europe's Catholic powers would establish invasion bases in Ireland, especially in the north, where the most vexing Gaelic patriots lived. In the "Plantation of Ulster," King James I put thousands of subjects in six northern counties after 1609, many of whom were Presbyterians leaving Scotland's troubled borderlands to lease quality farmland from their king of Scottish birth. Those rents, however, jacked skyward upon expiration and the Ulster-Presbyterians found themselves being treated much like the Native Irish … restricted in terms of social mobility and unexpectedly forced to accept Anglican worship. Unspoiled North America beckoned, and there was an explosion of Protestant immigration from Ulster between a drought in 1717 and the American Revolution.

Those folks we call Scots-Irish came as indentured servants or on their own accounts. They arrived in disproportionate numbers at Pennsylvania aboard the ships of the Philadelphia-to-Ulster linen trade. Philly's fathers used the Scots-Irish settlers to create a buffer between themselves and the hostile Indians on the western frontier. That perfectly suited a people who'd negotiated the no-man's-land between England and its Highland enemies for centuries before serving as unwelcome Protestant occupiers in Ireland's north.

Many Presbyterian pioneers (and other arrivals from fractured German states) slipped down the Appalachian ridge on the Great Wagon Road. Those mountain-eers shared few sensibilities with Virginia's royalist Cavaliers, but the Anglican Church looked the other way while the colony's western edge opened to Scots-Irish settlers in the 1730s (again setting a screen against Indians). Already in the backcountry were hardy servants—many Scots-Irish—who'd either fulfilled indentures or been run off the plantations by the Cavaliers' new agro-economic model, the slave system. Backwoods descendants within sight of the Blue Ridge Highlands play as Radford University's Scottish-themed **Highlanders**. (RU's equestrians are **Redcoats**, from its red, navy, and forest green tartan.)

When America's Civil War came, the people of the hills naturally sided with the Union against the Cavaliers. (Teddy Roosevelt famously said America's Scots-Irish were "rightly called the Roundheads of the south.")[12] Virginia seceded in the spring of 1861, but mountaineers between the Alleghenies and the Ohio pulled a sort of counter-secession in October when a collection of western Virginia counties formed the Restored State of Virginia. Statehood for this *West* Virginia was finalized in 1863. The self-determining mindset was manifest in the state's official Latin motto in 1872, *Montani semper liberi*: "Mountaineers are always free." So the **Mountaineers** at Morgantown's West Virginia University speak more to pride than geography. (Those 'Eers were **Snakes** until 1905.) For a more literal in-state example, refer to West Liberty University's **Hilltoppers**.[13]

• • •

Appalachia's backcountry people were long concerned about their children's education. John G. Fee built a schoolhouse and church in 1855 on land donated by emancipationist Cassius Marcellus Clay, the son of a wealthy slave owner. (A descendant of the Clay plantation slaves was boxer Cassius Marcellus Clay, Jr., known as Muhammad Ali after his 1964 conversion to Islam.) Fee wanted his school for underprivileged eastern Kentuckians to be the South's first interracial college, but Berea College was just incorporating in 1859 when antiabolitionists ran Fee and company out of town. Immediately after the Civil War, Fee recruited a student body of mountain folk and ex-slaves. Berea still provides tuition-free education to its exclusively low-income attendees, including its **Mountaineers**.

Worried their children would seek education elsewhere, folks in north-central Pennsylvania's mountains opened a Mansfield seminary in 1857,[14] today's base camp for the Mansfield University of Pennsylvania **Mountaineers**

Frontiersman Daniel Boone was famous for blazing a wagon trail through the Cumberland Gap to facilitate trans-Appalachian travel. East of the Gap is his namesake town of Boone, North Carolina, where a school to train teachers for Blue Ridge Mountain children opened in 1899. It became Appalachian State University in 1967. The mascot for AppState's **Mountaineers** (informally the "Apps") is named Yosef. That's usually an east European form of *Joseph*, but here it accentuates the regional habit of doing things for *yerse'f*.

• • •

The Scots-Irish who made it down to the Southeast were "Crackers," from their practice of cracking either cattle whips or corn (to make whiskey).[15] Georgia, the Cracker State, had minor league baseball's Atlanta **Crackers** (1901–65). Between world wars their park hosted Atlanta **Black Crackers**.[16]

Major league recognition for western Pennsylvania's Scots-Irish came with the ABA's first champions, the Pittsburgh **Pipers** (1967–70),[17] a name to recall Scotland's national instrument, the bagpipe. (Alliteration with the city name and baseball's established **Pirates** helped.) Greater Pittsburgh's Scots-Irish had their high-profile moment during the Whiskey Rebellion. Scots had made Scotch

(Scottish whiskey) ever since fifth-century Irish monks introduced distilling, but Treasury Secretary Alexander Hamilton decided to test the young Constitution's powers with a 1791 federal tax on whiskey that hurt frontier operators. Attacks on tax collectors forced President Washington and his Revolutionary-era chief of staff (Hamilton again) to lead a huge army into western Pennsylvania in 1794. The Whiskey Rebellion was quickly abandoned, but continued taxation and regulation moved the whiskey stills into the backcountry where they steamed away for a century.

The repeal of Prohibition in 1933 failed to stop the production of cheap spirits, especially in hundreds of Southern counties that remained dry for the rest of the century. The cost of being collared had been high during Prohibition, so bootleggers souped up their cars to outrun John Law. It was inevitable that moonshiners would eventually test each others' rigs, and an acquired taste for speed had racers meeting with increased formality. The National Association for Stock Car Auto Racing evolved as a governing organization. (When NASCAR's first race was held at Charlotte in 1949, the fastest car was DQ'd for its suspension modified for bootlegging.) Greater Charlotte is still home for most NASCAR teams, and the Charlotte Motor Speedway opened in the Concord suburb in 1960. Trackside neighbors have included the ABA Carolina **Thunder** (2004/05) and indoor football's Carolina **Speed** (est. 2007). The checkered flag at every NASCAR finish line drapes minor league hockey's Charlotte **Checkers** (1956–77, 1993–).

Ten miles north of the track is the textile town of Kannapolis, the birthplace of legendary NASCAR "Intimidator" Dale Earnhardt. After the 2000 baseball season, Earnhardt bought into the single-A Piedmont **Boll Weevils** (named after Kannapolis's cotton-processing history). Dale was killed on the last lap of the 2001 Daytona 500 before the renamed Kannapolis **Intimidators** ever took the field. Like all NASCAR numbers, Dale's number 3 was assigned to an owner and cannot be retired in a driver's name. It is, however, permanently deactivated by the **Intimidators**.[18]

• • •

With Presbyterianism being the Scottish form of Calvinism, athletic representatives for Presbyterian-founded colleges are pre-qualified as **Scots**:
• Presbyterians founded Ohio's College of Wooster in the 1860s. The campus news turned the **Presbyterians** or **Presbyterian Steamrollers** into more folksy **Scots** in the 1920s. Taking postgraduate classes at Penn in summer 1950, Wooster football coach Phil Shipe was entranced by the grind-it-out play of the eventual NL champs, the "Fightin' **Phils**." Shipe made his Woosterians the **Fighting Scots**,[19] joined later by **Lady Scots**.
• The 1819-founded Presbyterian seminary at Maryville, Tennessee is today's Maryville College, with **Lady Scots** and **Fighting Scots**.
• In 1928, **Bulldogs** changed to **Fighting Scots** at Monmouth [Ill.] College, a school founded by Scottish Presbyterian pioneers in 1853.
• **Scots** sides serve Macalester College at St. Paul, founded by prominent Minnesota Presbyterians in 1874 and named for its benefactor in the east, Scottish-born Philadelphia merchant Charles Macalester.

- A Highland Festival at the Presbyterians' Alma [Mich.] College marks the end of summer. Alma is nicknamed "Scotland U.S.A.," so teams are **Scots**.
- Little Rock appliance dealer Frank Lyon was a lifelong Presbyterian whose generosity toward Presbyterian-founded Arkansas College got that Batesville school renamed Lyon College in 1994.[20] Spring's Arkansas Scottish Festival isn't LC's only Scottish connection; former **Panthers** and **Highlanders** became **Scots** in the 1940s. (The women were **Pipers** until 2010.)
- Presbyterians opened the Decatur Female Seminary near Atlanta in 1889 with financing from industrialist George Washington Scott. It was renamed for Mr. Scott's Scots-Irish immigrant mom in 1906. Agnes Scott College's **Scotties** are represented by a Scottish terrier named Irvine (Mrs. Scott's middle name).
- Presbyterian Samuel Irvin started ministering to Iowa, Sac, and Fox Indians in the Kansas Territory around 1840. The town that later popped up was Highland, and Highland University evolved from Irvin's schoolhouse. That first college in Kansas is now Highland Community College, where **Scotties** (again with Scottie dogs) salute the school's Presbyterian roots and Scottish name.

Confederate colonel Jones S. Hamilton named his Jackson, Mississippi house "Belhaven" after his ancestral home in Scotland's borderlands. In 1894 (the year before it burned down), the house became a women's college under the Belhaven name. It formed a lasting association with the Presbyterian Church in 1910. Having gone coed in 1954, Belhaven College's **Clansmen** referred to Scottish Highland clans, but the Deep South school feared being confused with Klansmen of the Ku Klux variety, so in the 1980s they became **Blazers**, explained elsewhere as popular at Christian institutions (p. 105).

Three Presbyterian colleges folded during the Civil War but combined efforts in 1869 as Trinity University at Tehuacana, Texas. The school and its **Trinitonians** or **Presbyterians** moved to the booming cotton town of Waxahachie in 1902, where Detroit's **Tigers** held spring training from 1916 to 1918. Waxahachians embraced Ty Cobb and company, and the **Tigers** socialized with local players, even signing one Trinity prospect. The appreciative collegians immediately became **Tigers**, a name carried to a new San Antonio campus in 1942.[21]

• • •

There are places named *Cumberland* all over eastern North America, most named for the Duke of Cumberland. At the 1746 Battle of Culloden Moor in Scotland, the duke fought in the name of his father George II after the Stuart family's Young Pretender, Charles Edward Stuart, try to overthrow the Hanovers' rule of Britain. Cumberland defeated the Bonnie Prince in a half-hour then spent months brutally hunting down the remnants of the Highlander army. In Vineland, New Jersey, **Dukes** of Cumberland represent Cumberland County College.

Culloden broke forever the power of the clan chieftains, and London rubbed it in with the Dress Act, which prohibited Scots from displaying traditional Highland garb (kilt, shoulder-belt, plaid, etc.). The precedent for such humiliation had earlier been established by the 1716 Disarming Act, which stripped Scots of pistols, swords, "or other warlike weapon[s]." The bagpipe wasn't mentioned by name, but had already been "adjudged in the High Court to be an instrument of war."[22] The weapon the Highlanders would most reluctantly have forfeited was the *claidheamh mòr* ("great sword" in Gaelic). Anglicized as *claymore*, the broadsword is used repeatedly as the insignia for sporting **Scots** and **Highlanders** (and more explicitly by NFL Europe's Scottish **Claymores**, 1995–2004). Warriors with claymores represent Brewton-Parker College's **Barons** in Mount Vernon, Georgia, who reflect the state's rich history of Scottish immigration while recalling the Highlands' entitled feudal barons. (Those barons were disenfranchised by the Scottish Parliament only in 2004.)

The Dress Act was repealed in 1782, having squelched Highland traits except for cases that advanced the empire. (His Majesty's Scottish regiments got to keep their kilts and pipes.) An 1822 visit to Edinburgh by a kilted George IV and the romantic Scottish themes popularized by writers like Sir Walter Scott revitalized interest in a pastoral Highland culture that was subsequently accepted as typically Scottish by not only Gaelic Highlanders but by Lowlanders whose ancestors were Anglo-Saxons, Britons, and Normans.

In the Americas, this means Presbyterian colleges founded by the descendents of Protestant Lowlanders can (and do) lay a second-hand claim to **Highlanders** and **Pipers**. Also, rosters of **Scots** and **Scotties** at Presbyterian schools think but little of perpetuating an association with Celtic-Gaelic pipe bands and tartan pageantry, even though these are customs of Highlanders … people Lowlanders long considered to be barbaric foreigners. And if tartan colors had indicated anything it would have been one's home region and not one's family roots. The "tartan craze" came only after the royal visit, when opportunistic manufacturers first produced plaids in supposedly historical clan colors.

• • •

Ancient folks created modest rock piles to mark graves, trails, cliff edges, and mountain peaks, none of which can rule out some Neolithic traveler's existential itch to simply suggest, "You may be here now, but I was here before, as indicated by this modest rock pile." Because such modest rock piles are found across the Scottish Highlands, we call them *cairns*, from the Gaelic word for a modest rock pile, *carn*. Philadelphia Biblical University (Langhorne, Pa.) was renamed Cairn University in July 2012, having reinterpreted such modest rock piles to be silent witnesses to the faith of believers. To match the new Scottish theme, Cairn's **Crimson Eagles** became **Highlanders** and adopted crossed claymore emblems.

• • •

In 1809, Williamson Dunn's family became the first white settlers on a river bluff in the Indiana Territory. Dunn and other Scots-Irish elders opened the Hanover Presbyterian Church in 1820 and the associated Hanover College in 1827. A downhill view of the Ohio made teams **Hilltoppers**, but they've been **Panthers** since 1928.

The **Hilltoppers** were sometimes **Hillbillies** in the campus papers of athletic foes.[23] *Hillbilly* as applied to rural country folks hints at Scots-Irish ancestry because many Scottish border ballads had praised "Billy"—William of Orange—who ousted the Catholic James II from Britain's throne in 1688 then crushed James's Catholic army in Ireland. That 1690 Battle of the Boyne made Ulster safe for Protestant locals thereafter called "Orangemen." Minor league baseballers from Scots-Irish pioneer country have included the Vicksburg [Miss.] **Billies/Hill Billies** (1946–50) and Snow Hill [N.C.] **Billies** (1937–40).

• • •

Some Scottish-sounding jocks represent non-Presbyterian schools that happen to have had Scots-Irish students or benefactors. For instance, Methodists founded Jacksonville's Illinois Female Academy in 1846. It was renamed MacMurray College in 1930 for benefactor James E. MacMurray, a Chicago industrialist whose daughter attended. When a college for men was added in 1957, the planning commission wanted a Scottish-themed nickname to match the scarlet and navy colors that had already been taken from the MacMurray clan tartan. After considering Highland-ish names like "**Macmen**" and "**Clan**," MacMurray settled on "**Highlanders**."[24]

Edinboro University is a state school at which Indian-themed **Red Raiders** became **Fighting Scots** in the 1960s. Back in 1840, Scots-Irish pioneers named their Pennsylvania town after Scotland's capital, Edinburgh.

Ohio Valley University (Vienna, W.Va.) opened in 1960. Many descendents of Scots-Irish pioneers would have enrolled, but that doesn't explain its **Highlanders**. The moniker was influenced by the first president, who couldn't stop talking up his Christian "college on the hill." **Highlanders** later transitioned to **Fighting Scots**.[25]

Baptist John Calvin Gordon was a Scottish-born namesake of super-Protestant John Calvin. Relocated to Boston, Deacon Gordon sired A.J. Gordon, an influential churchman who founded a Boston missionary school in 1889, now Gordon College (Wenham, Mass.). **Fighting Scots** commemorate the Gordons' Scottish roots. Another Gordon College in Barnesville, Georgia is named for a Georgia-born Confederate general and U.S. senator, John B. Gordon. His Scottish blood changed **Generals** to **Highlanders** in the 1980s. (Neither Gordon College has Presbyterian backing.)

• • •

The institute most emphatically wearing a tartan on its sleeve is the University of California–Riverside. Its Pipe Band shows at sporting events, dorms are named for Scottish domains, and two athletic decorations—the Braveheart and Rob Roy Awards—commemorate Scottish heroes. The bear mascot (also "Braveheart") is distinguished from the sleuth of **Bears** and **Bruins** in the UC system by a tartan shawl. All this for a school claiming no Scottish-Highland-Celtic-Gaelic heritage; opened as the state-sponsored Citrus Experiment Station in 1907, UCR is the state university on the highest ground, next to the Box Springs Mountains (a.k.a. "the highlands"). **Highlander** teams date to 1954, with all Scottish traditions being derived therefrom.

UCR isn't the only institute on a hill that hosts **Highlanders** without referencing history. The New Jersey Institute of Technology's **Highlanders** are on Newark's University Heights. Houghton [N.Y.] College jocks were represented by a claymore-wielding Celtic warrior until switching to the lion rampant of Scotland's royal standard in 2006, but the best explanation for its **Highlanders** is the raised relief of the northernmost Allegheny Plateau. Southeast on the plateau is Misericordia University (Dallas, Pa.), a Catholic institution that had blue-and-gold **Highlanders** before changing to a "highland animal" (the *mountain* lion) by adopting "**Cougars**" in 1987.

• • •

Appalachian—o r "mountain" or "hillbilly"—music and Celtic music have many instruments in common because the Scots-Irish arrived with their fiddles and mandolins in hand. Then they incorporated the blues inflection and banjo licks from America's slave history into their art. (Guitars and washtub basses were added later.) Music fans rush to Nashville's Ryman Auditorium, the host site of the Grand Ole Opry radio program from 1943 to 1974. Dozens of local venues and studios make Nashville "Music City U.S.A." Its Music City Bowl is a college bowl game and local history is sprinkled with short-lived minor league Nashville **Rhythm** and Nashville **Noise** teams.

The "Nashville sound" owes to producers who upgraded country's honky-tonk character through lush pop arrangements in the 1950s and '60s. Baseball's Nashville **Sounds** (est. 1978) got a guitar-shaped scoreboard in 1993, and astonished praise for Nashville's many superb string pickers was doled out by the Lovin' Spoonful's rock-country crossover hit "Nashville Cats" in 1966, leading to indoor football's Nashville **Kats** (1997–2001, 2005–07).

• • •

The Great Wagon Road down the Appalachians resulted in one of the heaviest concentrations of Scots-Irish immigrants on the continent. In fact, Virginia's upper Shenandoah Valley was the "Irish Tract," indicating that *Irish* sufficiently described Presbyterian settlers from the Emerald Isle's north. Those same people wouldn't be described as Scots-Irish until the 1800s, the distinction becoming necessary when huge numbers of "Native" (Catholic) Irish immigrated during the famines of the 1840s.

There were so many stateside Native Irish by 1900 that American-born Protestants started using "Irish" and "Catholic" as synonyms. For example, teams at the Jesuits' Rockhurst University in Kansas City were **Catholics** and **Irish** before they were **Hawks** in the late 1920s.[26] The **Fighting Irish** at the country's pre-eminent Catholic college, Indiana's University of Notre Dame, are former **Catholics**, **Notre Damers**, and **Hoosiers**. Ignoring both Notre Dame's French name and its founding French priests, "**Fighting Irish**" first appeared on campus some time around 1919, gaining momentum soon after with a campus visit by Éamon de Valera, a high-profile American-born advocate of Irish republicanism. (That fight would pull most of Ireland out of the Kingdom of Great Britain and Ireland in 1922.) When ND alum Francis Wallace became a sportswriter in the New York of the 1920s, he was positioned to popularize the now-famous nickname.[27]

• • •

Notre Dame had employed the little-used forward pass to trounce Army (31-13) in 1913. From that day forward, defenses would have to worry about more than just the run. ND was suddenly playing a national schedule, with sportswriters calling them **Nomads** and **Ramblers**.[28]

The footballers from Saint Joseph's University became so identified with an airborne attack that they were passing as "**Hawks**" by 1929. The Philadelphia school has kept that handle even though its gridiron squad folded in 1939.[29]

Persistent passing by Ohio's University of Toledo against favored Carnegie Tech (p. 265) in 1923 made them **Rockets**, although they did lose the game.[30]

Returning to our discussion of Presbyterian schools, the **Fighting Presbies** from the College of Emporia [Kan.] are sometimes championed as the overlooked pioneers of the overhand forward pass. (C of E closed in 1974.)

• • •

Only on special occasions do ND's **Fighting Irish** wear the green that is most associated with the Emerald Isle. Otherwise, their blue and gold are the colors of the Virgin Mary, *notre dame* ("our lady" *en français*). Those same hues (or blue with white) are repeated by uncountable Catholic colleges and secondary schools, especially where *Mary* is in the name. Marymount ("mountain of Mary") University (Arlington, Va.) hosts blue-and-white **Saints**. Montreal's Marianopolis ("city of Mary") College has blue-and-white **Blue Demons**. Blue-and-gold **Lightning** teams show for St. Mary's University College (Calgary), where the motto is *In Lumine Tuo Videbimus Lumen* ("In your light we see light," Psalms 36:9). The College of Saint Mary (Omaha) keeps blue-gold **Flames**. Mount Senario College (Ladysmith, Wis.) opened to educate the Servants of Mary in 1930 but ended the run of its blue-and-gold **Fighting Saints** by closing in 2002. Mount Saint Mary College (Newburgh, N.Y.) adds black to its white-and-blue **Blue Knights**. Blue-and-gold **Knights** serve Marian University in Indianapolis. (In 1972 a different Catholic "Marian University" in Fond du Lac, Wisconsin arbitrarily fielded its first blue-and-white **Sabres**, as in saber-toothed cats.)

Saint Mary is very often "Our Lady of *Some Notable Geographical Feature*," making San Antonio's Our Lady of the Lake University and its blue-and-white **Saints** her namesakes. Likewise, *Mercyhurst* means "Our Lady of Mercy of the hurst (woods)," so the Mercyhurst University North East **Saints** are surrounded by state forests.

Mary's husband—and therefore the earthly father of Jesus—was St. Joseph, which puts blue-and-gold **Lions** at Mount St. Joseph University (Cincinnati). The University of Saint Joseph **Blue Jays** (West Hartford, Conn.) wear blue, gold, and white, as do the **Golden Eagles** at St. Joseph's College (Patchogue, N.Y.). SJC's Brooklyn campus has same-colored **Bears**.

Mary Frances Clarke, founder of the Sisters of Charity of the Blessed Virgin Mary, is the eponym for Clarke University in Dubuque, Iowa. It's convenient to our discussion that its institutional names from bygone days have included both "St. Mary's Female Academy" and "St. Joseph Academy." CU presents navy-and-gold **Crusaders**.

Conquistadors | *Razorbacks* | *Isotopes* | *Angels* | *Dons*

Hernando DeSoto was a Spanish *conquistador* (New World "conqueror") and the governor of Cuba. He's the co-eponym at Florida's Pasco-Hernando State College, where **Conquistadors** represent Pasco and Hernando Counties.

In 1539, DeSoto went to the mainland that Ponce de León had named *Pascua Florida* (flowery Easter) in 1513. Its natives told him that *El Dorado*—a city of gold—was to the west and that he and his men should *totally* keep moving. (Their reputation for slaughtering and enslaving Indians perhaps preceded them.) They were the first Europeans to see the Mississippi, probably near today's DeSoto Park in Memphis. The University of Memphis yearbook was the *DeSoto* from 1916 to 1996, and the mascot for indoor football's Memphis **Xplorers** (2001–06) wore the Conquistador's helmet and beard. The same sport's Rio Grande Valley **Dorados** ("golden ones," 2004–09) recalled the conquistadors' travels through their name, their golden temple emblem, and their base at Hidalgo, Texas (*hidalgo* being a Spanish nobleman). DeSoto died from fever near the Arkansas River in 1542, and only half of his 600 men made it to their Gulf Coast rescue.

While DeSoto was lost on the upper delta, fellow conquistador Francisco Coronado set out from Culiacán (a Mexican city hosting soccer's *Dorados de Sinaloa*). Hunting for *Cíbola* (seven cities of gold), Coronada ran a long slant route all the way to Kansas, but he had only the destruction of Pueblo villages to show for his pains. Dodge City Community College's **Conquistadors** are among the Kansas historical markers that trace his route.

• • •

DeSoto introduced European swine to the mainland from stock brought to the Caribbean by Columbus. Spanish and French colonizers kept importing Old World boars (*Sus scrofa*), which sometimes escaped or got traded inland to Indians. Omnivorous, adaptable, and reproductively inclined, feral versions of sharphaired "razorbacks" were soon plentiful in the South. After Hugo Bezdek's cardinal-and-white football **Cardinals** from Fayetteville's University of Arkansas were undefeated in 1909, Coach said they were as ferocious as those hogs. UA's consequent "**Razorbacks**" nickname was so popular that Arkansas (unofficially) became the "Razorback State."

New World pigs (the *Tayassuidae* family) are the razorback's only American cousins, ranging from northern Argentina to the Southwest. Peccaries are only about twenty inches high, but Spaniards compared their tusks to a light horseman's javelin. The determination and grit of *Javelinas* ("hav-ah-*lee*-nas") allow them to sometimes ward off jaguars. Emulating such tenacity, Texas A&M University–Kingsville (at about the northeastern limit of peccary habitat) has thrown forth **Javelinas** since its 1925 founding.

• • •

A settlement that sought recognition as a *villa* (established town) from Spain did not meet the required headcount, so residents fudged the numbers in their 1706 appeal to the Viceroy of New Spain, the Duke of Alburquerque [*sic*], saying, "It would be swell to name our humble 'hood after your Dukeness" [paraphrased]. That flattery made 'Burque the "Duke City," yielding a long line of minor league baseball Albuquerque **Dukes** (1915–2000). When the Calgary **Cannons** moved to central New Mexico in 2003, locals assumed they'd assume the "**Dukes**" title.

So what happened? Well, Homer Simpson happened. In the Fox TV series *The Simpsons*, the eponymous family follows baseball's Springfield **Isotopes**, named for the atomic power plant that employs half the town. (A definition of *isotope* in terms of relative subatomic masses can be found elsewhere. For us, "nuclear physics stuff" suffices.) In a 2001 episode, Homer stumbles into a plan to move the '**Topes** to Albuquerque. Enough *Simpsons* fans in New Mexico preferred the nuclear option that "Albuquerque **Isotopes**" easily beat out all comers (including "**Dukes**") in a team-naming contest.[1] But local history does make "**Isotopes**" a perfectly cromulent team name; Albuquerque's National Museum of Nuclear Science & History tells us that the world's first atomic weapons were designed and built in secret just north of the Duke City at Los Alamos Labs during World War II, and they were tested to the south at White Sands Missile Range.[2]

• • •

Albuquerque is near the end of *El Camino Real*, "the royal road" from Mexico City. In the 1920s the **Varsity** from the University of New Mexico at Albuquerque became **Lobos** (Spanish "wolves"). Backtracking toward Mexico, there are **Lobos** at Sul Ross State University in Alpine, Texas. In Saltillo, Mexico, **Lobos** represent the *Universidad Autónoma de Coahuila*. (The steely tone of the region's Mexican grey wolf, *Canis lupus baileyi*, is common to UNM's cherry-and-silver and Sul Ross's scarlet-and-grey **Lobos**.)

Presidios (forts), pueblos (towns), and Jesuit missions (churches) popped up across New Spain. Few Indians took to Christianity, so the conversion effort seemed to hinder production and conquest just when the Jesuits in Europe were coming to represent an old-world papacy that threatened absolute monarchies. When the Bourbon family's courts expelled Jesuits after 1759, Gaspar de Portolá was charged with deporting them from *Baja* (lower) *California*. That coincided with an order from Madrid to move into *Alta* (upper) *California* to dissuade Russians in Alaska from moving south. Gaspar's expedition named the Santa Ana River in 1769, and the riverside city of Santa Ana keeps **Dons** at its Santa Ana College. Both are Don Gaspar's namesakes, *Don* being a title of respect for Spanish gentlemen (think "Mister").

Among Gaspar's company was Junipero Serra, the Franciscan priest who'd execute Spain's gameplan in post-Jesuit California. Padre Serra established the mission of *San Diego de Alcalá* in 1769. That southwesternmost city in Alta California would later host the legendary PCL San Diego **Padres** (1936–57). The current NL team of that name came with 1969 expansion, and both have worn the padre brown of Franciscan habits.[3] Like most monks, Franciscans are also "friars," from the Latin *frater* (brother). So the **Padres**/*fathers* shared the city with the WTT San Diego **Friars**/*brothers* (1975–78). San Diego **Conquistadors** (ABA, 1972–75) also recalled the city's founding Spaniards.

San Diego was the first of nine missions started by Serra on Alta California's own *Camino Real*. The next was Monterey in 1770. It became the capital in 1777 and remained so throughout its Spanish-Mexican history. Monterey Peninsula College's **Lobos** should now seem expected, but grey wolves started disappearing from Alta California at around the time of its white settlement.

Serra founded the *Mission San Gabriel Arcángel* in the southern San Gabriel Valley in 1771. It never became a major city, but its spin-off did. In 1781, San Gabriel settlers built a sub-mission called *El Pueblo de Nuestra la Reina del Los Angeles* (the Town of Our Lady Queen of the Angels). Movie cowboy Gene Autry started a 1961 AL expansion team in the City of Angels and resurrected the name of past PCLers: Los Angeles **Angels**. They became *California* **Angels** late in the '65 season with plans to leave Dodger Stadium for the suburb of Anaheim. (Bilingual Angelenos already knew "the Los Angeles **Angels**" means "the-the angels-angels.") Another L.A. team with a Spanish name was the AAFC's Los Angeles **Dons** (1946–49), whose president was famous Italian-American actor Don Ameche. Anaheim **Amigos** (friends) played the 1967/68 ABA season. The WPS Los Angeles **Sol** (sun) shone only for 2009. CSU Los Angeles had **Diablos** (devils) until 1981, but they're now black-and-gold **Golden Eagles**.

Gaspar and Serra had gone straight to the Pacific and up the coast, but Conquistador Juan Bautista de Anza got to San Gabriel in 1774 with a shortcut that bypassed San Diego. He set up a presidio at San Francisco in March 1776, three months before Serra's priests established its mission. (The PCL **Mission Reds** were in the Mission District neighborhood from 1926 to '37.) In 1855, Spanish Jesuits started the University of San Francisco, where **Dons** were the **Grey Fog** until 1932, indicating the low clouds that are common to summer in the City. Across the Golden Gate Strait is Marin County, a placename from the word Spaniards had given the bay's Native American boatmen, *marinero*. It hosts **Mariners** at the College of Marin. You can also take the Bay Bridge from San Fran to the intended home of the Oakland **Señors** (sirs), AFLers that became **Raiders** just before taking the field in 1960.

Don Juan de Anza continued north through the Santa Clara Valley and named a creek after an Italian saint, Joseph of Cupertino. Today, Cupertino has **Dons** and **Lady Dons**[4] at the captain's namesake, De Anza College.

Serra founded the Santa Clara mission in 1777. The city is named for St. Clare of Assisi, as are its Mission College **Saints**. Nearby is Santa Clara University. The Jesuit school's **Broncos** are from Spanish descriptions for things rough or wild, which *rancheros* applied to an unbroken mustang.

The 1786 mission at Santa Barbara was the first of a dozen founded after Serra's 1784 death. It hosted soccer's **Real** Santa Barbara (1989–90), named for *El Camino Real*, but they invited comparison to Spain's famous **Real** Madrid. The NPSL **Real** San Jose (est. 2007), play near another mission, *Mission San José* (est. 1797), home of the California League San Jose **Missions** (1979–81).

• • •

"Mission Revival" refers to those modern buildings that imitate Spanish Califor- nia's colonial structures. There are nice examples in Riverside, including a retirement home to which California Baptist University moved in 1955. Athletic **Lancers** appeared almost immediately, keeping the colonial theme through the mounted Conquistador's weapon of choice.

Pequots | Stormy Petrels | Jeffs | Ragin' Cajuns

The words *Quinnipiac* and *Quinnehtukqut* were Algonquian variations for "long tidal river." Anglicized mangling turned those into *Connecticut*. Settlers in the new Connecticut colony of the 1630s hindered the Indians' trade with the Dutch and gave them devastating smallpox. The Pequot tribe rebelled, but the colonists had allied with the Pequots' historical enemies (Narragansetts and Mohegans) to win the 1637 Pequot War along the south New England coast.

That first real war between resettled Europeans and indigenous people scared English plantations into the 1643 Articles of Confederation of the United Colonies of New England, the first attempt at colonial unity in the Americas. The vindictive victors banned the word *Pequot*, even when used by the Pequots themselves, so the Pequot River village of Nameaug soon became New London on the renamed Thames. Mitchell College opened on Pequot Avenue in 1938, promptly fielding **Pequots**. To smooth their admission to NCAA Division III, they became **Mariners** in 2008 because New London has been a preferred mainland port on Long Island Sound since Revolutionary times.

Just after the Puritans' 1620 arrival at Plymouth, they joined in a treaty with *Ousamequin*, the *Massasoit* (great sachem) of the Pokanoket Wampanoag, who—along with *Squanto* of the Patuxet Wampanoag—famously helped colonists avoid starvation. Wampanoags would be neutral in the Pequot War, but their braves inspire jocks at Massasoit Community College and Blue Hills Regional Technical School, both backing **Warriors** and both in Canton, Massachusetts. In fact, the Wampanoag/Algonquian form *massachusett*—by the large hill—referred to those Blue Hills south of Boston.

Massasoit died in 1661. His son Metacom would come to battle colonists who called him Philip (after Philip II of Macedon, the father of Alexander the Great). In King Philip's War, Metacom's Indians tested the New England Confederation with some successes, including the burning of Springfield, Massachusetts by Agawams in October 1675, as recalled by a long string of minor league Springfield **Indians** in hockey (1926–94) and same-named baseballers (1937–39).[1] Springfield College dropped "**Chiefs**" and decided to go with "**Pride**" before the fall of 1998. (The city's **Indians** and **Chiefs** also recall America's first motorcycle maker, Indian, which built bikes in Springfield from 1901 to 1953. Its most popular models were the *Scout* and the *Chief*.)

A smaller Indian attack on Springfield five months later coincided with their victory at Providence, Rhode Island, where the quickly abandoned white settlement burned to the ground. (That city's Bryant University hosted **Indians** from the late 1800s until teams became **Bulldogs** in 1995.)[2] Over the summer of 1676, Philip's allies slowly surrendered, and the "king" himself was shot dead in August. New England's Indians could never again resist colonial expansion.

Weakened by disease, southern New England's Quinnipiac Indians had joined the colonists against the Pequots and then the Wampanoags. (Quinnipiacs called themselves *Eansketambawg* [original/true people].) In 1638 they were the first natives put on reservations, and they ceased being a distinct people by the mid-1800s. Quinnipiac warriors were remembered for decades by the Quinnipiac University **Braves** (Hamden, Conn.), but they've been **Bobcats** since 2002.

• • •

Confident in La Salle's 1682 claim to the Mississippi Valley, the French had wanted to use the West (the trans-Appalachian wilderness) and the Mississippi to connect its outposts in Canada and Louisiana. English speculators in Pennsylvania and Virginia disagreed and angered the French by trading with Ohio Valley Indians. In 1694, New York's colonial governors sent surveyor and Indian agent Arent Schuyler inland from New Jersey's coast to see if the French and Indians were cooperating in today's Passaic County. No trouble was found so Schuyler bought himself some farmland from the Lenapes and moved to the township of Wayne with several other families. After World War II, Wayne was still a quiet spot with a few historic homes, including that of the Schuylers, putting **Pioneers** at its William Paterson University.

To replace an Indian workforce dying of European diseases, French-allied Spain made Florida a safe house for escaped slaves in 1693. (Putting a big dent in Britain's plantation economy was a welcomed byproduct.) So King George II was already in a listenin' mood when Gen. James Oglethorpe suggested a new colony between the Protestant English in the Carolinas and Florida's Spanish Catholics. In 1732 the king chartered a new colony named Georgia out of royal vanity. Tasked by Parliament to investigate conditions in English jails, Oglethorpe thought incarcerated debtors could better serve his Highness as colonists, but the responsibility of shaping up the coastal boundary suddenly seemed too important to leave to malefactors, and few ex-prisoners were among the more than 100 passengers on Oglethorpe's 1733 crossing.

Sailors long considered the appearance of *Hydrobatidae* family seabirds to forecast bad weather, but Oglethorpe was encouraged on his voyage by the determined flight of a storm-petrel. Intrepid **Stormy Petrels** now represent Atlanta's Oglethorpe University, at which the Latin motto is *Nescit Cedere*: "He knows not how to yield."

Stopping at the mouth of the Savannah River, Oglethorpe's first dispatch reported the fearful attendance of cougars, rattlesnakes, bison, and crocodiles, but: "What is most troublesome, there, are flies and gnats, which are very numerous near the rivers." Sandflies (or greenhead horse flies, *Tabanus nigrovittatus*) have been ruining perfectly good beach days from Maine to Florida ever since. In the Southeast they're "sand gnats," as are some minor leaguers in Oglethorpe's city, the Savannah **Sand Gnats** (est. 1996).

As expected, there was quick trouble with Spaniards. Scottish marines charged by Oglethorpe to patrol for Spaniards and Indians found a natural port south of Savannah and settled it in 1738. Brunswick has since been a busy harbor and a dock for the College of Coastal Georgia's **Mariners**.

• • •

In later years, President George Washington would make Brunswick one of five official ports of entry, but for now—late 1753—that young officer was tasked by the Virginia Colony to chase the French from Ohio Country posts. He headed for the "Forks," the triangular piece of land at which the Allegheny and Monongahela Rivers meet to form the Ohio, but the French quickly scattered the Virginians and built Fort Duquesne, named for the governor-general of New France, the Marquis Duquesne.

Today, those Forks of the Ohio delineate downtown Pittsburgh's Golden Triangle, explaining both the WTT Pittsburgh **Triangles** (1974–76) and the three-sided background historically present in Pittsburgh **Penguin** emblems. Just east of the fork, German immigrants founded a Catholic college in 1878, one renamed Duquesne University in 1911 for the French marquis. Because marquises and dukes are largely indistinguishable to nobility-averse Americans, teams are the alliterative Duquesne **Dukes**. (Until the 1980s the women were **Duchesses**, and earlier footballers were sometimes **Iron Dukes**, owing to local steel plants.)

• • •

The actions at the Forks helped launch the last of four major wars that Britain fought against the French (and often the Spanish) and their Indian allies after 1689. These were usually battles for North American waterways and trade routes, although each was tied to wider conflicts in which Protestant Britons wanted to either check French-Catholic power or aid Continental allies in claiming European thrones. The last war, the French and Indian War (1754 to 1763), was the only one started in North America, but it spread to Europe, India, Africa, and the Philippines as the Seven Years War.

The F&I War would finally sort out ownership of Canada and the Ohio Valley (at least to Europeans). The French started well, but it turned out to be a war of attrition against Britain's deep bench. In the simultaneous Seven Years' War, British Prime Minister William Pitt split the defense by attacking France's Caribbean sugar plantations and forts in India, and his escalation of force in America yielded major victories. Two of Pitt's generals, James Wolfe and Jeffery Amherst, captured Louisbourg in Acadia in 1758 just as John Forbes's Highlanders were retaking Fort Duquesne to rename it Fort Pitt.

William Pitt was the Earl of Chatham, so Pittsburgh has a Chatham University. Its **Cougars** (named in 1995) are inevitably compared to the famous **Panthers** of the University of Pittsburgh down Fifth Avenue.[3] General Forbes's local namesake was Forbes Field, a past home for the **Pirates** (1909–71), **Steelers** (1933–63), Homestead **Grays** (1939–48), and Pitt's football **Panthers** (1909–24). The stadium grounds on Forbes Avenue are now occupied by Pitt classrooms.

Amherst spent the summer of '59 overrunning French posts in the Hudson-Champlain Valley but arrived too late to aid Wolfe's September conquest at Quebec. He did direct the force that took Montreal in October 1760, effectively ending hostilities just three weeks before his old king died. The 1763 Peace of Paris allowed the French to keep New Orleans while forfeiting Canada and all holdings east of the Mississippi. Britain also got Spanish Florida, and George II's grandson, George III, was suddenly running one of history's greatest empires.

The king's new trans-Ohio Indian subjects had been friendly toward transient Frenchmen, but the English looked more like conquerors as farms and forts popped up all over. Wolfe's mortal wound at Quebec gave military control of

British America to Lord Amherst, whose contempt for the "savages" trickled through his ranks. The inevitable Indian backlash was called Pontiac's Rebellion, named for the Ottawa leader and former French ally whose confederation of Great Lakes tribes attacked British strongholds in 1763. It's generally agreed that Amherst entertained the idea of letting Fort Pitt's soldiers give the Indians some smallpox-infected blankets, but it's not known if any such plan was executed. That puts the **Lord Jeffs** (and **Lady Jeffs**) at Amherst College (Amherst, Mass.) among the monikers some people find most objectionable. Pontiac's raid at Detroit failed, but a few forts were held briefly by collaborators. The rebellion fizzled out by fall 1764, but it had moved George III toward the Proclamation of 1763, which reserved those lands west of the Appalachians for Indian hunting grounds.

His majesty didn't wish to fund any future Indian wars.[4]

• • •

Being the coastal border of French and English claims, Acadian ports changed hands often in the colonial wars. In 1690 the Massachusetts fleet of Sir William Phips captured Port Royal, Nova Scotia, but his subsequent attack on Quebec was crushed. That enterprise had been expected to fund itself through any assets seized at Quebec, but Massachusetts was instead nearly bankrupted. Putting blame squarely on the victims, the colony dragged its feet for fifty years before rewarding the Phips veterans (or their heirs) with land grants on the upper Merrimack watershed called the Canada Townships. They were in the Province of New Hampshire, which would be part of Massachusetts until 1741.

Henniker was founded in 1740 as Township no. 6, so its New England College **Pilgrims** recall its Massachusetts-Puritan roots. In fact, an explicit association with Pilgrim Fathers down at Plymouth Plantation was made when a New Hampshire settlement incorporated as Plymouth in 1763. Plymouth State University's green-and-white **Green Guards** monitored the southern entrance to the White Mountains until becoming alliterative Plymouth **Panthers** in 1958.[5]

Phips's success at Port Royal proved inconsequential because captured posts were usually returned in the treaty that ended the war. The notable exception was a 1710 capture of Port Royal during Queen Anne's War, after which the *Nova Scotia* (New Scotland) sign that Britain had been trying to hang out front for a century was finally secure.

With few English boots on the ground, the Maritimes' French-Acadian fishing and farming villages continued in relative isolation. In 1710, Nova Scotia had 2,000 Acadian residents, but that quintupled before the outbreak of the French and Indian War in 1755. That's when British governors became concerned with potential pockets of French sympathy, forcing Acadians to swear loyalty to the British crown and renounce their (French) Catholicism. The refusal of those terms brought about the Acadian Expulsion, in which the British burned homes, stole livestock, and scattered families as indentured servants in other colonies.

Many Acadian refugees set out for the historically French port of New Orleans, unaware that Louis XV had secretly loaned Louisiana to Spain in 1762 when the war started going downhill. (He didn't want to forfeit that turf if the French ended up losing.) The Spanish accepted the bumped-up Catholic headcount to deter the Protestant English from expanding, but a century of isolation had made the Acadians' dialect unique, and even Louisiana's French thought they sounded a little weird. Spanish and Creole influences further corrupted the language to the point that *Acadian* itself became "Cajun."

With quality lots unavailable to them, the Cajuns took to the swamps and poor farmland west of New Orleans. Lafayette is the "capital of Acadiana," and the University of Louisiana at Lafayette's **Bulldogs** became **Ragin' Cajuns** in 1963, a nod to the many Acadian descendants in the student body.[6]

The Maritime plots that the Acadians had left usually went to Protestant Britons, Germans, and Scots, so today's Francophonic Nova Scotians are mostly descended from those who returned after France's 1763 defeat. They settled the outskirts that became the "French Shores" of Prince Edward Island, New Brunswick, and southwestern Nova Scotia.

The annual *Festival Acadien de Clare* started on Nova Scotia's French Shore in 1955 to observe the bicentennial of the deportation. Festivities spill over to the Church Point campus of *Université Sainte-Anne*, where the 1972-founded *Centre acadien* is a repository for Acadian documents, memorabilia, and genealogical records. Extramural teams were (informally) called **Acadians** before a 1989 move to conference play. Being the province's only Francophone university, *Sainte-Anne's* has a strong French immersion program, so administrators wanted a name spelled the same way in both French and English. "**Dragons**" fit that requirement and matched the romantic theme of the *Château* student center.[7]

Acadia University is in Wolfville, somewhat north of Nova Scotia's French Shore, but it wasn't founded or named by French-blooded *Acadiens*; Baptists who started the non-denominational institution in 1838 simply took the name from the Acadian region. Woodsmen felled trees to build the original College Hall, a legacy evinced by crossed axes on the school's coat of arms and by **Axemen** and **Axewomen**. (The latter were **Axettes** until 1997.)

Some of the few Acadians who'd followed the St. John River to refuge in French Quebec to avoid expulsion backtracked as part of the increased Acadian settlement of the upper valley in the 1780s. The fixing of the U.S.-Canadian border in 1839 turned the folks south of the St. John into Francophonic Americans. In 1878 a teacher training school opened on the Maine side of the river, largely to spread the English language across northern Aroostook County. It's now the University of Maine at Fort Kent, where teams of **Acadians** were changed to more menacing **Bengals** by an ambitious new coach in early 1960s.[8]

• • •

The Acadian Expulsion left Quebec with British North America's only significant Catholic population, and *les Québécois* were uncomfortable with their overseers. The 1774 Quebec Act let Francophones maintain their French legal codes and Catholic practices, which was appeasement enough that the Continental Congress was unable to enlist Quebec as a "Fourteenth Colony" when revolution broke out the next year.

Even so, the arrival of the Church of England was inevitable, and the first Anglican Bishop of Quebec arrived in 1793. Fifty years later, the third Bishop established Bishop's University at Lennoxville. "**Gators**" was proposed as the name for footballers in 1947. 'Twas a pun; Anglican bishops wore knee-length frocks, but respectability could be maintained simply by covering the legs with black sleeves, or *gaiters*. The school went for "**Gaiters**," although a reptilian gator—wearing gaiters—is now on the university badge.[9]

Quebec's first independence movement was sparked by Francophone liberals who mobilized militias during *Les rébellions de 1837 et de 1838*—the Patriots War. The British quickly quelled the unrest, but Francophones in the heart of Quebec remember that attempted sovereignty through *Patriotes* at *l'Université du Québec à Trois-Rivières*.

Troops from English-speaking Ontario went to stop the Quebec uprising, leaving local armories understaffed. A grass-roots army of poor farmers with *Patriote* sympathies saw a chance to take Toronto from its wealthy landlords, but armed Loyalists stopped that threat. Some retreating patriot militiamen ended up on Navy Island above Niagara Falls, and the British got the idea that the revolt was American-backed. There were several give-and-take raids on the border. The **Cannoneers** at Jefferson Community College (Watertown, N.Y.) commemorate the artillery units that were installed during that crisis at the nearby Madison Barracks on Lake Ontario. (In 1947 those barracks were absorbed by Watertown's Fort Drum, whose soldiers often attend JCC.) Quickly arriving at stalemate, the spirit of rebellion faded.

A new governor was sent to Canada to straighten things out. He was John Lambton, the first Earl of Durham. Among the reforms suggested in Lord Durham's 1838 report was a kind of Canadian self-government within the Empire (foreshadowing independence in 1867). Durham College (Oshawa, Ont.) and its men's and women's **Lords** are named for Lord Lambton, as is Ontario's Lambton County. Its largest city, Sarnia, became the site of Lambton College in Canada's centennial year, 1967, but Lambton's **Lions** are only alliterative.

Crimson | Tribe | Quakers | Tigers | Bruins

There were more than a few seminaries and secondary schools in Britain's thirteen American colonies. Most of those that got re-chartered as colleges did so only after the Revolution, so there were only nine actual colleges during the colonial period. We'll reveal the nickname creation story for each, with some inevitable straying from the basepath.

• • •

The first college in the colonies was underwritten in 1636 by clergyman John Harvard at Newtowne. Like most Massachusetts Bay ministers, Harvard had graduated from Emmanuel College, the Protestant seminary at Cambridge, England. Newtowne was in fact renamed Cambridge in 1637, two years before Harvard College became Harvard University.[1] It trained Puritan ministers domestically so they wouldn't have to be shipped over from Emmanuel. There was a lesser emphasis on creating Indian ministers to their own people.

In the nineteenth century Harvard teetered between official colors of crimson and magenta. At an 1858 regatta, rower Charles W. Eliot bought his fellow scullers red bandanas to keep the sweat from their eyes, but that same moisture darkened the cloth to the crimson color that the team would keep. The *Magenta* news became the famous *Harvard Crimson* in 1875 and all teams were officially recognized as the **Crimson** in 1910, the year after the retirement of Harvard's longest serving president (1869–1909), the same Charles W. Eliot.[2]

• • •

The first Puritans in Massachusetts were seeking a haven for folks at odds with England's state (Anglican) church, but the Virginia Company plantation at Jamestown had been a commercial venture tied to James I and his noble cronies since setting up in 1607. Anglican traditions, therefore, were part and parcel of doing business with the Crown colony's regal stockholders.

Already a Dutch prince, William (III) of Orange married English princess Mary Stuart. Then he ran her dad (England's last Catholic monarch, James II) out of power in the Glorious Revolution of 1688. The next year, an Act of Toleration made William and Mary's realm safe for all Christians, but it was in association with Virginia's Anglican Church that the second colonial college was chartered at Middle Plantation in 1693. Mary died from smallpox the next year and in 1699 the colonial capital shifted from Jamestown to Middle Plantation, which then became the king's namesake, Williamsburg. The College of William and Mary's charter established a program for creating Anglican ministers, educating local youths, and ensuring "that the Christian faith may be propagated amongst the Western Indians." The latter gave W&M its **Indians** in 1916, but the "**Tribe**" alternate had replaced it by the 1980s.[3]

The **Braves** at the Norfolk Division of the College of William and Mary were derived from its parent school's **Indians**. Seeking a unique identity in 1961, they became **Monarchs** to recognize the eponymous joint sovereigns. The next year brought true institutional independence, as the Norfolk Division became Old

Dominion College (Old Dominion University since 1969). Also sprouting from W&M was the Richmond Professional Institute, whereat the repetition of the older school's green and gold effected **Green Devils** and **Devilettes**. When RPI became independent in 1962, it got behind **Rams** in blue and gray to commemorate the centennial of the Civil War. RPI merged into the new Virginia Commonwealth University in 1968 and colors switched again to black and gold, but the **Rams** remained.

The Williamsburg that's in Kentucky isn't the namesake of King William. It instead honors a War of 1812 colonel, William Whitley. Nonetheless, locals set to mimic the bricks and columns at Virginia's Williamsburg, especially at two small institutes that merged into today's University of the Cumberlands in 1913. Its jocks of the early 1920s were maroon-and-white **Redhounds** and then **Indians** (recognizing regional Cherokees). In 2001 a new identity, **Patriots**, was intended to better complement the retro-colonial architecture.

Don't confuse Kentucky's University of the Cumberlands with Cumberland University, their Mid-South Conference opponents 100 miles away in Lebanon, Tennessee. CU's **Bulldogs** have no historically pertinent creation story.

• • •

Thomas Hooker avoided questions from English Anglicans about his Puritan sermons by taking the usual Puritan detour through Holland before turning up at Massachusetts Bay in 1633. Resisting the paternalism of Gov. John Winthrop and Boston pastor John Cotton, Hooker wanted to give Congregationalism back to the congregations in a new frontier colony. (This would also give Hooker's flock better farmland and enable the English to check Dutch expansion.) Hooker and Rev. Samuel Stone settled their followers on the fertile Connecticut floodplain in 1636 at Hartford, named for Stone's Hertfordshire birthplace.

In England's Hertfordshire, you can still visit Hatfield Forest, one of many medieval hunting grounds reserved for monarchs. Norman Forest Law seemed to give more rights to game animals (especially deer) than peasants. In fact, *Hertford* combines two Middle English words, *hert* (red deer stag) and *ford* (stream),[4] so a stag at a creek is on both the seal of Hertfordshire's namesake Connecticut city and the coat of arms for the Diocese of Hartford. In 1942 the diocese backed a Jesuit university at Fairfield. Fairfield University's deer-near-stream stamp and its (male and female) **Stags** maintain the Hartford connection, even though Fairfield shifted to the new Diocese of Bridgeport in 1953. The bishop of Bridgeport founded another college at Fairfield in 1963, Sacred Heart University. It has **Pioneers**, not because the Connecticut coast was among the first places to which New England puritans expanded, but because SHU was the first Catholic university in the U.S. staffed by the laity.

In 1638 more Puritans led by Rev. John Davenport established the New Haven Colony at the mouth of the Quinnipiac River. (A royal charter would combine New Haven with the Saybrook and River [Hartford] Colonies as the Connecticut Colony in 1662.) Part of Davenport's colonial dream was fulfilled three decades after his death when the Collegiate School was founded as a Calvinist seminary in 1701. That same year, Harvard turned from Puritan orthodoxy and toward enlightened ideas, pushing Boston's Congregationalist stalwart Increase Mather out of Harvard's presidency. Cotton Mather (Increase's son and John Cotton's grandson) was disheartened with the swing at Cambridge and decided to preserve the Collegiate School as a Calvinist stronghold.[5] Looking to raise capital for the institute's move from Old Saybrook to New Haven in 1716, Mather appealed to Elihu Yale, the Boston-born son of Welsh Puritans who'd made a fortune for London's East India Company. In a written *quid pro quo*, Mather told Mr. Yale that the third colonial college "might wear the name of Yale College [...] your munificence might easily obtain for you such a commemoration." Nowadays, Yale University teams are **Bulldogs**, after Handsome Dan,[6] the canine companion of 1890s footballers (and the first mascot for any college jocks), but the closer you get to New Haven the more likely you'll hear the "**Elis**" alternate, from Mr. *Elihu* Yale. "Yale blue" was officially adopted in 1894 after being worn for decades by the rowing crew.

Abraham Baldwin was the founding president of Franklin College at Athens, Georgia in 1798. The Yale grad, however, was soon consumed by duties as state legislator, so when the doors opened in 1801, the new president of what would soon be the University of Georgia was a fellow Yalie, Josiah Meigs. Echoes of the two Connecticut-born presidents' sympathies are evident in both UGA's Old College (an 1806 copy of Yale's oldest standing building) and its **Bulldogs**, although writers at the *Atlanta Journal* reportedly started using "**Bulldogs**" in 1920 just because it was better than nothing.

Mr. Baldwin is also the eponym at Abraham Baldwin Agricultural College (a UGA satellite in Tifton). Its aggie students are often found in its rodeo arena and stables or in the grandstands at **Golden Fillies** (women's) and **Golden Stallions** (men's) games.

• • •

In 1727, Scots-Irish minister William Tennent started training some Presbyterian preachers for the Middle Colonies in a small cabin north of Philadelphia. That "Log College" gave rise to a number of evangelical "New Side" Presbyterian ministers who embraced the revivalist fire then being stoked by Europe's Dutch Reformers. Log College grads—especially Tennent's son Gilbert—would become famous during the Great Awakening (p. 96), which included a scramble to create denominational seminaries in the late colonial period. New Siders were opposed by the more orthodox Presbyterians, ergo "Old Siders." A parallel split among Congregationalists yielded New Lights and Old Lights.

Barred from Harvard and Yale by Old Lights, New Siders in the Log College mold chartered their own academy in 1746, the College of New Jersey in Elizabeth, but it moved to Nassau Hall in Princeton in 1756. Because they were Calvinists, Presbyterians drew inspiration from Europe's first-team Protestant, Prince William of Orange-Nassau, for whom Princeton and Nassau Hall are both named. His family arms featured a lion rampant, so matching lions were placed on Nassau Hall's steps in 1879 (the same year their purported sculptor, Frédéric Bartholdi, started work on the Statue of Liberty). Thus, the oldest teams were **Lions**. The 1874 Saratoga Regatta was the first time the orange color of Dutch princes was used with black by "Old Nassau" teams. Footballers followed suit within a few years, making it inevitable that "**Tigers**" would overtake "**Lions**."[7] The transition was complete by about the time the College of New Jersey became

Princeton University in 1896, and Bartholdi's zinc lions finally yielded to bronze tigers by A. Phimister Proctor in 1911.

> The original College of New Jersey at Princeton has no ties to today's College of New Jersey in Trenton, and **Lions** at the latter aren't foils to Princeton's **Tigers** (or earlier **Lions**). It's simply the case that TCNJ players came back "like lions" in a 1929 basketball victory. (From the 1920s to the 1940s, the semi-pro and pro hoop teams south of Princeton included Trenton **Bengals** and **Tigers**.)

Before a 1904 game, Princeton's baseballers told their rivals at Pennsylvania State College that they'd fall prey to the **Tiger**. Thinking quickly, Penn State infielder Joe Mason recalled seeing a stuffed catamount on his own Nittany Valley campus in the town of State College. Mason told the Princetonians they'd be surprised by the "Nittany lion" that day. Indeed, Penn State struck an upset victory, and Mason's editorship of a campus magazine positioned him to make "**Nittany Lions**" standard by about 1907.[8] (PSC became Pennsylvania State University in 1953.)

• • •

Taking over a church-school project abandoned by Great Awakening preacher George Whitefield, a board of trustees led by Ben Franklin opened the Academy of Philadelphia in 1751. In a city controlled by the Quaker Assembly, the academy was backed by Anglicans who were "evidently anxious not to alienate Philadelphia's Quakers, and they made their new college officially nonsectarian."[9] That jibed with Franklin's idea for a new kind of American college ... one for practical, secular studies as opposed to theological deliberation. Nevertheless, its Anglican roots made the academy a presumed rallying point for Loyalists during the Revolution, so it was taken over by the state in 1779 and renamed the University of the State of Pennsylvania.[10] It changed again to the University of Pennsylvania when privatized in 1791. Designed in 1900, the university arms borrowed from those of the Penn and Franklin families, although the Quaker Mr. Penn "would most certainly have objected since the College was the stronghold of the Episcopal [Anglican] party."[11] Nonetheless, the historical local influence of the Society of Friends is verified by Penn's **Quakers**.

Usually identified with the Quaker City, Franklin was born in Boston. He died in 1790 and his will established a lending fund for entrepreneuring tradesmen. Trustees instead used the interest that the principal earned to open a Boston tech school (assisted by Andrew Carnegie) in 1908. We're less than stunned to find utility players called **Shockers** at the Benjamin Franklin Institute of Technology because their eponym famously experimented with electricity and was the first to apply *conductor, positive, negative, charge,* and *shock* to that science.

• • •

Despite any support his institution might have received from Congregationalist well-wishers like the Mathers, Timothy Cutler took a sudden turn toward Anglicanism in 1722 and was expelled from Yale's presidency. He and fellow Connecticut Congregationalist Samuel Johnson were reordained as Anglican ministers in England and reassigned to the colonies. Three decades later, Johnson was the first president of a new Anglican institution in New York. King's College received its royal charter from King George II in 1754 but closed in 1776 while G-III tried to foil the Revolution. It reopened after hostilities in 1784 as Columbia College. It moved uptown to become Columbia University in 1896. Somewhat surprisingly, the Hanover family's crown insignia and royal lion survived the transition. In 1910 the Student Board decided to accept the Alumni Association's suggestion for the lion being the official mascot (ergo, **Lions**), but some did say the American eagle might have been a more appropriate choice.[12] Colors of "Columbia blue" and white were adopted from a long-defunct literary society.

Probably noticing that Columbia had abandoned "King's College," Loyalists in Nova Scotia created their own University of King's College in 1798. Moved from Windsor to Halifax after a 1920 fire, its **Blue Devils** refer to their royal blue-and-white uniforms. At another NYC school, The King's College, the king is Jesus. It's blue-and-white **Lions** are aptly Christian (symbolism on p. 107) for a school founded in 1938 by radio and televangelism pioneer Percy Crawford.

The reflective silvery coat on the black bear of southeast Alaska's Glacier Bay region makes it the "blue bear," but Livingstone College's **Blue Bears** (Salisbury, N.C.) are named for a display of Columbia-blue and black. Likewise, the College of New Rochelle [N.Y.] drapes **Blue Angels** in Columbia-blue and white. When varsity lacrosse started at Baltimore's Johns Hopkins University in the 1890s, school colors of old gold and sable were uncomfortable reminders of their black-and-orange Princeton **Tiger** rivals. So new athletic colors of black and Columbia-blue wrapped **Black and Blue** sides, which by the early 1920s were **Blue Jays**, as *Jay* is short for *Johns*. (J-Hop retains gold and black academic colors.)[13] In the 1940s athletes from Dover's Delaware State College for Colored Students traveled on a run-down bus. That Columbia-blue ride—the "Blue Hornet"—put **Hornets** at today's Delaware State University. Columbia-blue with white and gold gave a **Gold Wave** to Shorter University (Rome, Ga.), which arbitrarily changed to **Hawks** in about 1960.

• • •

There are more casually named **Hawks** at Roger Williams University in Bristol, Rhode Island. After being booted from Massachusetts by Puritan fathers, Baptist minister Roger Williams founded the religiously tolerant Colony of Rhode Island in 1636. Its new seal featured an anchor, a Christian token for faith in rough seas (p. 107). The Ocean State flag repeats the design, so crews of **Anchormen** and **Anchorwomen** represent Providence's state-run Rhode Island College.

But RIC wasn't founded until 1854. The state's colonial-era college was the College of Rhode Island, opened at Warren by Baptists in 1765. In Providence since 1770, it was Brown University by 1804. Brown alumnus T.F. Green (a future governor and U.S. senator) was on the building committee for Brown's Rockefeller Hall. Tired of cartoons that matched up Yale's **Bulldog** or Princeton's **Tiger** against relatively wimpy Puritan mascots for Brown, Green mounted a grizzly head on one wall. When the building opened in 1904, a brown bear named Bruno ("brown one" in Old High German) accompanied teams that came to be **Bruins** by the 1930s. *Bruin* already means "brown bear" when its Middle Dutch origin is examined, so it was a short hop when Brown's **Bruins** became the Brown **Bears** in 1988.[14]

In 1992 the Boston **Bruins** started a farm team of Providence **Bruins**, so it was providential that Brown had just abandoned "**Bruins**." The brown/bruin bear species includes grizzlies and Kodiaks, so despite the alliterative **Bruins** at both Boston and Brown, nobody's ever seen wild brown bears east of the Mississippi. Still, Western New England University (Springfield, Mass.) is where gold-and-blue **Golden Bears** can be mistaken for California's extinct golden bear (p. 193). (The WNEU mascot is actually a different grizzly subspecies, the Kodiak.) A black bear (*Ursus americanus*) cub has accompanied **Black Bears** from the University of Maine at Orono since 1916, better reflecting New England's fauna.[15]

• • •

Like other denominations, the Dutch Reformed Church in America wanted to educate clergymen in the colonies rather than Europe. They got George III to charter a minister-training school in 1766 that opened as Queen's College at New Brunswick, New Jersey in 1771.[16] It fell on hard times and closed during the War of 1812. Through the generosity of Henry Rutgers (a Revolutionary colonel of Dutch descent), it reopened as Rutgers College in 1825. Still, the original name lived through **Queensmen**. Spirited students looked to display the orange of Dutch Nassau in 1869, but with red ribbons and pennant cloth much easier to come by, the **Queensmen** ended up scarlet. When the college became Rutgers University in 1924, a new red rooster mascot inspired a change to **Chanticleers**. Tired of listening to "Chicken!" chants, Rutgerites reverted to regality in the mid-1950s as **Scarlet Knights**.[17]

• • •

Congregationalist minister and 1733 Yale grad Eleazar Wheelock caught the Connecticut Valley's revivalist fever and became an animated preacher of the Great Awakening (p. 96). Inspired by his success in preparing a young Mohegan named Samson Occom for the ministry, Wheelock opened an Indian school at Lebanon, Connecticut. When the money ran out, Wheelock sent Occom and another minister on an 18-month British tour to get more. They returned in 1767 with sacks full, the major donor being William Legge, Secretary of State for the Colonies and Earl of Dartmouth. England's Hanover family king, George III, chartered Legge's namesake school in 1769 at Hanover in the Province of New Hampshire. Pine trees were cleared to make the central quad (The Green) north of Wheelock Street and forest green became the color in the 1860s. Owing to its early days as an Indian school, Dartmouth College teams became **Indians** in the 1920s.

That's the story, anyway. In reality, both Occom and Lord Dartmouth ended up feeling a bit snookered by Wheelock, who did start a modest Indian school at Hanover, apparently diverting funds "to found Dartmouth, not to create an Indian college, as myth would have it, but to get out of the Indian business by preparing white scholars for missions and the ministry."[18] Dartmouth claimed to return to its roots in 1972 with an ambitious Native American Program, which to some conflicted with the **Indians** and their stereotypical mascots. So teams transitioned to the **Big Green**, a historical alternate.

One Vermont newspaper called the jocks from the Johnson Normal School **Professors** in 1949. Students reacted quickly with a poll that made them **Indians**. Knowing that Dartmouth (100 miles away) had abandoned "**Indians**," administrators at the renamed Johnson State College were reexamining their own "Dartmouth green" and white **Indians** in the late 1980s. A new vote made teams **Badgers**. JSC biology professors were quick to indicate that those ferocious weasels never ranged so far east, but fans embraced the pound-for-pound fight of their underdog **Badgers**.[19]

The wearing of gold and Dartmouth green gave **Green Juggernaut**, **Green and Gold Waves**, and **Goldmen** athletes to St. Norbert College (De Pere, Wis.). Its intercollegiate program folded in 1926 but returned in 1929 with **Green Knights**. A faculty priest who'd attended West Point had recommended that name to resemble Army's **Black Knights** (p. 186).[20]

• • •

In respecting the oldest North American colleges, many universities have copied Harvard crimson, Yale blue, Columbia blue, or Dartmouth green. The paw of the orange-and-black Princeton **Tiger**, however, has left the most prints:

- Presbyterians founded Los Angeles's Occidental College in 1887. The self-described "Princeton of the West" hosts orange-and-black **Tigers**.
- Several schools proudly self-identify as the "Princeton of the South." Only Tennessee's University of the South in Sewanee (usually just "Sewanee") backs it up with **Tigers** (in purple and gold).
- Being established at the outbreak of Revolution in 1775, Hampden-Sydney College (Hampden-Sydney, Va.) took its garnet and grey colors from the militia uniforms of its first class of student-patriots. The board of trustees included Patrick Henry and Princeton man James Madison, and HSC's first two presidents were Presbyterian preachers and Princeton grads Samuel Stanhope Smith and John Blair Smith. The brothers consciously patterned their school on the "Log College model" of their alma mater, to which **Tigers** attest. (S.S. Smith was even a later Princeton president.)
- The year after the 1889 Oklahoma Land Rush, the Stillwater Congregational Church hosted the territory's land-grant college, Oklahoma Territorial A&M. Its first president was Princeton grad Robert J. Barker, who copycatted Old Nassau's colors and **Tigers**. But students stubbornly called teams **Aggies** or **Farmers**, leading to **A&M Cowboys** by the mid-1920s (eventually **Cowboys** matched by **Cowgirls**). But the orange and black are worn still at Stillwater's "Princeton of the Plains," the renamed Oklahoma State University.
- Ada, Oklahoma is one-hundred miles south of OSU. Opened in 1909, East Central University maintains both OSU's orange and black scheme and its discarded "**Tigers**" nickname.
- Virginian Woodrow Wilson was Princeton's president when he gave a 1905 speech at Marion [Ala.] Military Institute. The audience was so impressed that MMI's **Fighting Cadets** immediately became **Tigers** in Princeton's orange and black. (This was years before Wilson's presidency, 1913–21.)

- Pocatello's Idaho State University fielded **Bantams** after its 1901 founding. In 1917 a new athletic director made them **Tigers** after the (Bengal) **Tigers** at his alma mater, Princeton. They were **Bengals** by 1927 (their cat mascot is Benny Bengal), but the colors wouldn't catch up for decades; Idaho Staters wore the black and gold of the University of Idaho's **Vandals** until switching to black and orange in the early 1970s.[21]

- New England Congregationalists opened Colorado College in 1880. The Colorado Springs school was somewhat modeled on Ohio's Oberlin College, which New England Presbyterians had founded in 1833. But comparisons to the oldest Calvinist colleges were always welcome, probably leading to the copying of Princeton's **Tigers** in the late 1800s.

- The **Bengal Tigers** at Riverside [Calif.] City College took their name and orange and black colors from Princeton.[22] (They've dropped the "**Bengals**.")

- Presbyterian minister and Princeton grad Samuel Doak opened Tusculum College at Greeneville in 1794, which explains its claim to be the oldest institute of higher education in Tennessee and the first west of the Appalachians. Orange-and-black athletes have a natural right to be **Pioneers**.

- The Presbyterian-founded Waynesburg [Pa.] University has **Yellow Jackets**, even though they copy Princeton's orange and black.

- Presbyterian pioneers in Oregon founded Portland's Albany Collegiate Institute in 1867. Students chose to reuse Princeton's colors in 1891. Moving south of downtown in 1942, the school became Lewis & Clark College, which in 1946 swapped **Pirates** for **Pioneers** to celebrate its early days in the new location, its pioneer founders, and (to a lesser extent) the eponymous explorers. L&C's **Pioneers** do have a Newfoundland dog mascot—"Pio"—who resembles the one Meriwether Lewis brought on the entire crosscountry journey.

- Presbyterians in Kentucky founded the University of Pikeville to educate young mountain people in 1889. UPike teams flash Princeton's orange and black, but central Appalachian wildlife makes teams **Bears**.

Yeomen | Deacons | Battling Bishops | Blazers | Rams

To Protestant rulebook maker John Calvin, God's "unconditional election" had mapped out any given person's eternity, leaving individuals unable to transcend their own sinful natures. Late in life, theologian Jacobus Arminius questioned the inflexibility of this predestination doctrine as sold by the Dutch Reformed Church. The year after he died, the followers of Mr. Arminius—*Arminians*—presented the Remonstrance of 1610, five articles that summarized their precepts.

The Dutch state church convened the Synod of Dordt in 1618 to counter those five articles with Five Points of Calvinism. Each point reinforced the Reformers' predestinationism and dismissed the Arminians' arguments, so the Remonstrants were booted from the Dutch church. The Christian Reformed Church in America (which adheres to the Canons of Dordt) started Dordt College at Sioux Center, Iowa in 1955. Its **Defenders** protect home fields as emphatically as the Dordt synod defended ultra-Calvinism.

• • •

Churches and churchmen were few and far between for western New England's second- and third-generation pioneers. Far from Boston's Puritan watchdogs, they became susceptible to Arminianism, enlightened ideas, and plain ol' ecclesiastical laxity. Owing to the influential Calvinism of Rev. Jonathan Edwards, settlers in the Connecticut Valley were the first to experience a "Great Awakening," a late-colonial revival to shake pioneers from secular sleep. Calvinist ministers of that era traveled widely on horseback to assure frontier families that private Christian devotion could yield a close relationship to God even without formalized worship, although you still couldn't do much to save your own soul.[1]

The message of a *Second* Great Awakening (c. 1800–40) was that believers could validate or reject salvation, a free-will "conditional election" based on how Christian a life they led. Many on the seaboard found this Arminianist argument to be a lot more democratic than cold, hard Calvinism. The message moved inland as preachers of various denominations held huge camp meetings in Kentucky and Tennessee, undermining the influence of churchmen to the east (in this case, Virginia's Anglicans).

This Awakening's heaviest hitting revivalist was Charles Grandison Finney, within whom the Holy Spirit had been animated in 1821 by upstate New York's Presbyterian pastor George Washington Gale. (Finney's eventual rejection of his mentor's intellectual Calvinism was a bellwether of Awakening II themes.) Mr. Finney was the influential second president (1851–56) of Oberlin College, established in Ohio by New England Presbyterians to educate farmers in 1833. It was the first coeducational college in the U.S. and the first to accept African American students, so **Yeomen** and **Yeowomen** befit a school that has historically attracted industrious students with the motto "Learning and Labor." (A yeoman is a commoner or small-time farmer raised to respectability through his own diligence.)[2]

The aforementioned G.W. Gale was doing good work back upstate, having opened the Oneida [County] Manual Labor Institute in 1827. As already hinted at by Oberlin's black attendees, there was a Protestant surge toward abolitionism during the Second Awakening, and Oneida's interracial student body absorbed antislavery dogma while working off tuition with chores. Gale persuaded Calvinist associates to establish a similar institution for the western prairies. They founded Galesburg, Illinois in 1836, where the Knox Manual Labor College—now Knox College—opened the next year.

Humorist George Fitch graduated from Knox in 1897. His best-known stories were set at a fictional Siwash College, so similar to Fitch's alma mater that students were calling Knox "Old Siwash" by the 1920s. Knox's **Purple and Gold** were thereafter the **Siwash**.[3] By 1993 folks agreed that *siwash* was from the French *sauvage* (savage), so administrators switched to a name from a school tradition. In the spring Prairie Burn, students scorch fields to rid them of bushes and non-native plants that hinder the growth of tall grasses. Teams were re-baptized as "**Prairie Fire**," but they could have arrived there with a more poetic backstory. Religious revivals are often compared to prairie fires. In fact, that part of central and western New York State that included Mr. Gale's original Oneida school—the model for Knox—is famously remembered as the Burned-Over District, having been so consumed by the "revival fire" of the Second Great Awakening.

• • •

Denominational competition during the First Great Awakening had brought about the colonial colleges. Ironically the preachers sent forth by those very academies spearheaded Awakening 2.0, the core principals of which blurred denominational borders. Pioneers that had forfeited devotion to particular Calvinist sects might yet have remained eager for some churchin' up, and they became increasingly enamored with evangelical messengers—namely Baptists and Methodists—whose numbers rose dramatically.

The America of 1830 had only four Baptist colleges for training ministers. Three decades later, there were twenty-five (nearly one in every state),[4] with others to follow:

- Influential Georgia Baptist Jesse Mercer funded Penfield's Mercer Institute in 1833. It's now Mercer University in Macon, where club-level **Baptists** became varsity **Bears** in 1924.[5] Lake Russell (multi-sport coach of the 1920s and '30s) said the ursine comparison owed to a girl of 4 who saw the **Baptists** fighting like bears in 1914.[6] Other sources cite the first-ever meeting between Mercer and the University of Georgia in 1892, where Mercer's especially hairy players drove one wag to ask, "Whence cometh that bear?"[7]
- For ex-slaves in South Carolina, Baptists opened Benedict College on a former Columbia plantation in 1870. The purple-and-gold both practiced and preached as **Deacons** until becoming **Tigers** in 1938.
- Despite its name, Gainesville's 1878-founded Georgia Baptist Female Seminary was not formally a Baptist school. In 1900 it became Brenau College by combining the German verb *brennen* (burn) with the Latin noun *aurum* (gold). In fact, Brenau University's motto is "As Gold Refined By Fire" (Revelation 3:18), so gold with black make for **Golden Tigers**.

- In 1834, North Carolina Baptists founded Wake Forest University in Raleigh. (It moved to Winston-Salem in 1946.) WFU's gold and black were adopted in 1895 to match its existing **Tigers**. They were later **Baptists** or the **Old Gold and Black**. Their own "devilish" play in a 1923 football victory over the **Blue Devils** from nearby Trinity College (now Duke) made them **Demon Deacons**.[8]
- Baptist preacher J.A. Campbell opened the Buies Creek [N.C.] Academy in 1887. It's now Campbell University, where the **Campbellites** (and unexplained **Hornets**) became Campbell (**Fighting**) **Camels** in 1934.[9]
- Carson College and Newman College were Baptist academies for men and women in Jackson, Tennessee that merged in 1889. The Carson-Newman University **Fighting Parsons** became **Eagles** in 1931.
- William Colgate had the dough to endow a Baptist seminary in Hamilton, New York in 1824 even though his soap company wouldn't introduce its radical toothpaste tube until after his 1857 death. The Colgate University **Raiders** had been **Red Raiders** until dumping Indian themes in 2001. (Some say "**Red Raiders**" had been intended to compare them to their **Big Red** rivals at Cornell [p. 268].) A Colgate faction that failed to move the school to the Erie Canal boom town of Rochester set up a breakaway Baptist institution there in 1850. The dandelions on that first University of Rochester campus made "dandelion yellow" the school color in 1893, which yielded **Yellowjackets** in the 1920s. ("Rochester blue" was added in 1954.)
- John Howard died of typhus in a Ukrainian jail in 1790, but he was never convicted of a crime. England's top prison reformer had been inspecting lock-ups across Europe. The good Baptist gentleman's memorial was Howard College (est. 1841), which moved from Marion, Alabama to Birmingham in 1887. Howard's **Tigers** too much resembled those at Auburn, so they changed to **Baptist Bears**. In 1916 they switched again to **Crimson Bulldogs**, intending to eat meat from the bones of Birmingham-Southern's crosstown **Panthers**.[10] Howard College gained university status in 1965 as Samford University. (Insurance man and Baptist deacon Frank P. Samford was enough of a benefactor to provide an excuse to avoid confusion with D.C.'s extant "Howard University.") Samford retains **Bulldogs**.
- Soldier, Alabama Congressman, lawyer, and Baptist preacher R.E.B. Baylor found himself in the Republic of Texas. Judge Baylor became one of its Supreme Court justices and co-founder of Baylor University in Independence. (It's been in Waco since 1848.) Baylor's "**Bears**" nickname owes to an arbitrary 1914 student vote and not any amazing history. Its live ursine mascots, however, always bear the name "Judge."
- Baptist College (McMinnville, Ore.) became Linfield College in 1922 after a generous gift from the widow of Baptist minister G.F. Linfield. Its **Baptists** have been **Wildcats** since 1924, having displayed the fight of Pacific coast bobcats (*Lynx rufus fasciatus*).
- Baptists founded Bluefield, Virginia's Bluefield College in 1922. Its **Fighting Deacons** and **Ramblin' Reds** became **Ramblin' Rams** and finally just **Rams** in 2010 … the ram being a Christian symbol of sacrifice (p. 106).

- After playing Louisiana Tech in 1910, footballers from Ouachita Baptist University (Arkadelphia, Ark.) came home in bandages. They looked like the striped cat on a placard in a downtown clothing store, one that was "all patched up" in his Tiger brand suit.[11] They were **Tigers** from then on.
- These Baptist institutions back **Tigers** without much explanation: Champion Baptist College (Hot Springs, Ark.), Campbellsville [Ky.] University, East Texas Baptist College (Marshall), Georgetown [Ky.] College.[12]

William Carey co-founded the Baptist Missionary Society at Northamptonshire, England in 1792. Then the "father of the modern missionary movement" went on a Christianizing tour of India. He met American Congregationalists Adoniram and Ann Judson in Calcutta in 1812 and fostered their conversion to the Baptist faith. The British expelled American preachers during the War of 1812, so the Judsons went to Burma as America's first overseas missionaries while Carey got American Baptists to back them. Ann died in 1826, but her husband would learn that Judson College (Marion, Ala.) was named for her in 1838. His own namesake is Judson University (Elgin, Ill., est. 1963). Both Judsons present **Eagles** because that's the most common team name, especially at Christian schools (p. 107).

In fact, Baptist **Eagles** represent Faith Baptist Bible College (Ankeny, Iowa), Trinity Baptist College (Jacksonville, Fla.), West Coast Baptist College (Lancaster, Calif.), and Williams Baptist College (Walnut Ridge, Ark.). **Golden Eagles** play for the Baptists' Pensacola [Fla.] Christian College. Walking away from its **Comets** in 1994, the Baptist-founded Cornerstone University (Grand Rapids) explained **Golden Eagles** through Isaiah 40:31: "Those who wait for the Lord shall renew their strength, they shall mount up with wings like eagles, they shall run and not be weary." The Baptist College of Florida (Graceville) fielded **Eagles** for fall 2010, citing Isaiah through their own winged mascot Izzy.

As for Mr. Carey, his namesake is William Carey University (Hattiesburg, Miss.). It hosts **Crusaders**, as does the Baptist-run North Greenville University (Tigerville, S.C.). There are gold-and-royal-blue **Royals** at the Baptists' Bethel University (St. Paul), which is inching us toward our general explanation for Christian **Eagles**, **Crusaders**, and **Royals**. (Read on.)

• • •

John and Charles Wesley started a small spiritual group within the Anglican community at Oxford University in 1729. An unusually deliberate approach to worship got its members called Methodists. The brothers spoke directly to England's poor and imprisoned, bringing them into association with jail reformer James Oglethorpe. (See Oglethorpe University, p. 83.) They were active in Oglethorpe's colony of Georgia, as was fellow Methodist preacher George Whitefield.

Some Moravians went from German Saxony to Georgia in 1735 to minister to Indians. Their pacifism excluded them from the buffer colony's actions against Spanish Florida, and many Moravians returned to Europe. Whitefield was then a popular colonial preacher, inviting some of Georgia's Moravians to Quaker Pennsylvania where they founded two towns ten miles apart, Nazareth in 1740 and Bethlehem in 1741. Quickly, there were seminaries for men (Nazareth) and women (Bethlehem). The men moved to Bethlehem in 1858 and later played as

Moravian College's **Blue and Gray**, colors that got more animated when teams became **Greyhounds** in 1935. After two centuries of parallel development, Bethlehem's female seminary merged into Moravian in 1954.

The country's other Moravian-founded college was started in 1772 in Salem, North Carolina, a town established by Bethlemites eight years earlier. Salem College is still next to the historic district of Old Salem within Winston-Salem's modern limits. SC's **Spirits** reflect the Moravians' observed sanctity.

When John Wesley called for traveling preachers, a working-class English kid supposedly responded with words from Isaiah 6:8: "Then I heard the voice of the Lord saying, 'Whom shall I send, and who will go for us?' And I said, 'Here I am; send me!'" On American frontiers, the grown-up Francis Asbury would ride on horseback a quarter-million miles as the most famous "circuit rider" of the late Second Great Awakening. His namesake college, Asbury University (Wilmore, Ky.), backs purple-and-white **Eagles**, whose mascot Isaiah can be compared to the aforementioned Izzy at the Baptist College of Florida.

As subscribers to England's state religion, Anglicans were suspected Loyalists in the late colonial era. After George III lost the colonies, stateside Anglican Bishops couldn't maintain their oath to the crown, so a new source of clergymen was needed. With new bishops from the Scottish Episcopal Church, most American Anglicans switched to the Protestant Episcopal Church. Those clerics, however, couldn't arrive fast enough for Bishop of Ohio Philander Chase, who wanted to open an Episcopal seminary. Fundraising in England yielded generous donations from two Anglican benefactors, Lords Kenyon and Gambier. Either lord could have been the school's eponym, but Chase chose a middle path, opening Kenyon College in Knox County's newly named village of Gambier in 1828. The **Episcopalians** that once roamed Kenyon's gyms and Gothic halls are now **Lords** and **Ladies**.

John Wesley wanted his guys to pick up America's ministerial slack, but the Church of England refused to ordain Methodists as bishops. Asbury (the colonies' only Methodist minister during the Revolution) and the recently arrived Thomas Coke were nonetheless created bishop-like "Superintendents" in 1784, splitting American Methodists from the Anglican Communion and creating the Methodist Episcopal Church of America. Coke and Asbury eventually buckled to the "Bishop" designation and became eponyms for America's first Methodist academy, Cokesbury College in Abingdon, Maryland. It opened in 1787 and closed after a 1795 fire, too early to have methodically deduced team names. Asbury greeted the destruction with some relief, being unconvinced that seminary training could substitute for a divine call to minister. Nonetheless, Methodists would start many colleges during the Second Awakening:

- Indiana Asbury College opened in 1838 at Greencastle to memorialize Rev. Asbury but was renamed for industrialist benefactor Washington DePauw in 1884. Neither **"Fighting Parsons"** nor **"Old Gold"** was very intimidating, so Depauw University's black and gold colors yielded **Tigers** in 1918.
- Methodists founded a school at Lebanon, Illinois in 1828 on a campus donated by the first American-born Methodist bishop, William McKendree. McKendree

University's **Methodists** became **Bearcats** in the early 1900s for reasons seemingly forgotten.

- Wesleyan University (Middletown, Conn.) had cardinal-and-black **Fighting Methodists** until one footballer turned up for a 1932 practice with a red bird on his jacket. Teams have since been **Cardinals**.[13]

- Jacob Albright was born a German Lutheran in eastern Pennsylvania. He switched to Methodism and converted many German families to that faith after the Revolution. The bishop's namesake is the Methodist-run Albright College (Reading, Pa.), where **Lions** are typical representatives for Christian colleges (p. 107).

- Scholarly circuit-riding bishop John Emory died in 1835 when his carriage flipped near his Maryland home. The next year, Methodists chartered two new colleges in his name. Blue-and-gold footballers for Emory and Henry College (Emory, Va.) were **Wasps** after reporters saw them *swarm* all over Tennessee's **Volunteers** in 1921.[14] Georgia's Emory College at Oxford moved to Atlanta in 1915 as Emory University, leaving behind a feeder school called the Oxford College of Emory University. Today, both Oxford and the university have "Emory **Eagles**" that are alliterative only.[15]

- Ordained by Asbury, Martin Ruter became an influential minister. Intending to organize circuit riders and colleges in the new Republic of Texas, he fell ill and died there in 1838. Nonetheless, Rutersville College became the first Texas college in 1840. It and three other Methodist institutions merged at Georgetown in 1873 as Southwestern University. We don't know why its land-locked athletes became **Pirates** in 1914, but at least the mascot is Captain Ruter.

- Ohio Wesleyan University (Delaware, Ohio) was founded in 1842 to train frontier ministers. Its **Methodists** and **Red and Black** became **Battling Bishops** in 1925. The other **Battling Bishops** are at North Carolina Wesleyan College in Rocky Mount, which opened with Methodist backing in 1960. (The NCWC mascot is a mounted circuit rider.)

- In 1854, Methodists founded a college at Red Wing, Minnesota with a large gift from Bishop Leonidas Hamline. *The Pied Piper of Hamelin* is a folk tale from 1284, but better-known versions are from the 1800s. Despite the spelling discrepancy with *Hamelin*, the **Red and Grey** at Hamline University (in St. Paul since 1880) were ushered to their "**Pipers**" title in the early 1920s.[16]

- Methodist bishop O.C. Baker founded Baker University in Baldwin City, Kansas in 1858. Its football **Methodists** reportedly played like "wild cats" in 1890 against the neighboring Kansas **Jayhawks** (p. 143), but they were not officially **Wildcats** until the 1920s.[17]

- Methodists added a college component to their Wheaton, Illinois prep school in 1860. Then they formed a cooperative relationship with Congregationalists, even recruiting Knox College president Jonathan Blanchard to move cross-state to run things. Warren Wheaton (one of the town's founding brothers) donated a large chunk of land to today's Wheaton College. Reverend Blanchard's non-denominational school would earn a reputation for evangelical zeal, but its **Crusaders** would later come on too strong for some, so Wheaton retired it in

2000. (Some not-so-Christian acts by medieval Crusaders rendered the handle anachronistic in a world made smaller by the information age.) Citing biblical passages that compare God's awesome power to heavy weather, Wheatonites now clap for the **Thunder**.

- It's often reported that footballers at Northwestern University (Evanston, Ill.) were **Fighting Methodists**, but Larry LaTourette insists in his book about that program that the "sadly pedestrian nickname '**Northwesterners**' was used instead."[18] After the *Chicago Tribune* reported in 1924 that the University of Chicago **Maroons** encountered a "purple wall of wildcats," **Northwesterners** were **Wildcats**.[19]

- An 1898-founded Methodist seminary at Boaz, Alabama was funded by businessman John Snead. It was taken over by the state in 1935, but the **Parsons** named in the 1920s survived the transition to Snead State Community College.

- Buckhannon's West Virginia Wesleyan College has fielded **Methodists** and **Bobcats**, with the latter having gained dominance.

- Folks at Dakota Wesleyan University (Mitchell, S.D.) weren't happy putting up **Methodists** or **Fighting Deacons** against teams with animal identities and decided to have a new name for the 1923 homecoming game. Administrators and team reps met in chapel to elect the "**Tigers**" nickname.[20]

- Southern Methodist University presented **Parsons** soon after the school's founding in 1911, but by 1917 spirited play had made them **Mustangs**, which is appropriate in a cowboy town like Dallas.[21]

- A Methodist seminary in Barboursville, West Virginia was saved in 1900 by Morris Harvey's mining fortune, so it moved as Morris Harvey College to Charleston in 1935. It dropped the affiliation with Methodists in 1940 and became the University of Charleston in 1978. The **Golden Eagles** don't reveal much history, but the maroon-and-gold eagle mascot is MoHarv.

- Methodists started Winnipeg's Wesley College in 1886. It forged a bond with the Presbyterians' Manitoba College after Congregationalists, Methodists, and (most) Presbyterians merged into the United Church of Canada in 1925.[22] The complete union of Wesley and Manitoba in 1938 created United College, which is when respective **Wesleyans** and '**Tobas** were unified as **Uniteds**.[23] But an older Wesley nickname, "**Wesmen**," never fully vanished, maybe because it so resembles "Westman," the name for the census area immediately west of downtown Winnipeg. **Wesmen** and **Lady Wesmen** still represent the renamed University of Winnipeg.

- Wesley College in Florence, Mississippi (closed, 2010) had **Warriors** because alliteration is always an option. Other Methodist schools observing that convention include Wesley College's **Wolverines** (Dover, Del.) and Methodist University's **Monarchs** (Fayetteville, N.C.). Indiana Wesleyan University in Marion has **Wildcats** and a Wesley-the-Wildcat mascot.

John Wesley had famously opposed slavery, so there was a heated argument within Methodism when Georgia-born Bishop J.O. Andrew came to hold slaves through marriage. Southern congregations spun off as the Methodist Episcopal Church, South in 1844. Its leaders didn't think they were racist, but the MECS's paternalism was partly to blame when black Methodists broke away after the Civil War. The first bishop of that Colored Methodist Episcopal Church was ex-slave William H. Miles. He put the CME's Tennessee Annual Conference of 1878 at Jackson under the direction of (fifth) Bishop Isaac Lane, who pushed for a CME high school there (now Lane College) in 1882. Later that year the MECS and CME backed the Paine Institute in remembrance of newly deceased MECS co-founder Bishop Robert Paine, the biographer of William McKendree and the founding president of the Methodists' LaGrange Female Academy. The unique contributions of those men are concealed by some run-of-the-mill team names in Georgia: Andrew College **Fighting Tigers** (Cuthbert), Lane College **Dragons**, Paine College **Lions** (Augusta), and **Panthers** at the renamed LaGrange College (LaGrange). Miles College (Fairfield, Ala.) is a black Methodist school named for Bishop Miles that keeps purple-and-gold **Golden Bears**.[24]

• • •

Noted Christian historian Mark Noll says, "Where Congregationalists (Jonathan Edwards), Anglicans (George Whitefield), and Presbyterians (Gilbert Tennent) had spearheaded the first Awakening, Methodists, Baptists, and Disciples (Barton Stone and Alexander Campbell) rapidly came to dominate the second."[25] We've discussed the Baptists and Methodists. So who are Stone and Campbell?

They're the guys who fully embraced the Second Awakening's non-denominationalism by dissolving distinctions between Catholic, Protestant, and Orthodox doctrine with hopes that an explicit emphasis on New Testament teachings would reveal a single church of Jesus. Campbell's father had been a driving force in this Christian primitivism, and the son started the Buffalo Seminary in the family home on Buffalo Creek (Bethany, Va.) in 1818. As for Barton Stone, he was an active Presbyterian who'd been ordained in 1798 despite his sneaky feeling the *Westminster Confession* wasn't altogether in line with scripture. When Stone and Campbell met at Georgetown, Kentucky in 1824, they realized the congruence of their ideas and merged efforts. Congregations now within the "Stone-Campbell Restoration Movement" include those in the Christian Church (Disciples of Christ), the Churches of Christ, and the Independent Christian Churches, but we're satisfied to refer to their colleges and universities simply as "Restorationist" in nature.

The 1902-founded Atlantic Christian College (Wilson, N.C.) became Barton College to honor Mr. Stone in 1990, the only case we find where the eponym's Christian (first) name is the institutional name. Barton's **Bulldogs** are purely alliterative, although they'd replaced **Little Christians** in 1928.[26]

Alexander Campbell opened Bethany College in 1840, the oldest college in West Virginia. It's a mile west of his old home classroom, so Bethany's **Bison** subliminally refer to the old Buffalo Seminary on Buffalo Creek.

A different Buffalo Creek near a different Restorationist college gives name to its teams. Tennessee's Buffalo Creek Christian Church sponsored the Buffalo Institute in 1866. It was renamed Milligan College by President Josephus Hopwood when it was expanded in 1881. The school—also next to Buffalo Mountain—fields **Buffaloes**. (MC is the namesake of Dr. Hopwood's late friend, Dr. Robert Milligan, a Restorationist scholar-minister who taught at Campbell's Bethany College.) Hopwood left Milligan in 1903 to start Lynchburg [Va.] College. L-burg's hills are full of wasps, so **Hornets** replaced **Fighting Parsons** in 1919.

The Civil War challenged Alexander Campbell's Christian pacifism. His support for even gradual emancipation was with enough reluctance to alienate northern congregations. A few abolition-minded students were even bounced from Campbell's Bethany College in 1855, ending up in Indianapolis at the new North Western Christian University.[27] Financed by lawyer-abolitionist and Church of Christ member Ovid Butler, it was Butler University by 1877. Fans of Butler's **Christians** wanted to put memories of a miserable 1919 football season behind them, so the college paper prepared for a 1920 game against the Franklin College **Baptists** (p. 251) with a front-page cartoon of a bulldog tearing the pants off John the Baptist. The **Christians** lost that day, but Butler jocks have been **Bulldogs** since.[28]

Union General Francis Marion Drake was a Campbell family friend, post-war railroad magnate, Iowa governor, and founder of a Des Moines school that has been informally associated with the Disciples of Christ since its 1881 establishment. Drake University's **Ducks** and **Ganders** confirmed that a *drake* is a male mallard, but Coach John Griffith brought his bulldogs to football practices during his tenure (1908–15), making players **Bulldogs**.[29]

James W. Harding was a Kentucky preacher for the Church of Christ and a friend of Stone and Campbell. His son James A. Harding was the evangelist president of Nashville Bible College in 1891. NBC had been co-founded by Tennessean and fellow Restorationist David Lipscomb, and it is today's Lipscomb University. Two years after Harding's death, Restorationists opened Harding College (Morrilton, Ark.), but it's now Harding University in Searcy. For what chalks up to coincidence, Lipscomb and Harding both back **Bisons**.

Two schools for African Americans in west-central Mississippi that were chartered by Restorationist missionaries merged into Tougaloo College at Jackson in 1954. It has **Bulldogs** for no reason other than what must now be considered an affection for that nickname among Restoration institutions. (See Barton, Butler, and Drake.) In fact, Tougaloo grads opened Jarvis Christian College (Hawkins, Texas) in 1913, a home for … **Bulldogs**.[30] The Disciples of Christ founded Hiram [Ohio] College in 1850. Its **Terriers** stray from the **Bulldog** pattern, but even Hiramites got nicknamed in 1928 when a coach said his boys played like "a little bull terrier that holds on until the end."[31]

Students at Chapman University (Orange, Calif.) voted in **Panthers** over **Camels** in 1925. "**Camels**" would have effected alliteration with the school's Campbellite principles,[32] but the nicknames of the nearly 80 colleges founded in the Stone-Campbell tradition don't have creation stories that relate to their Christian roots. As usual, wild felines are common; Restorationist athletes include **Cougars** (College of Missouri in Columbia) and **Wildcats** (Abilene [Texas] Christian University and Culver-Stockton College, Canton, Mo.), and **Panthers** play at York [Neb.] College and Drury University (Springfield, Mo.).

In 1937 auto parts king George Pepperdine endowed the Church of Christ's George Pepperdine College in south-central Los Angeles. Pepperdine squads were **Waves** even though they were a few miles inland. The neighborhood experienced racial tensions in the 1960s, especially after hundreds of buildings were destroyed in the '65 Watts Riots (wherein protesters reacted to police actions against black motorists), so the school moved to Malibu in 1972, the year after becoming Pepperdine University. Ironically, "**Waves**" now fits better, as students can roll out of their dorm beds and right onto Pacific surfing beaches.

Some early followers of Barton Stone and a few churches in the northeast resisted specific key points of Campbellite doctrine within the Stone-Campbell Movement and didn't join the Disciples of Christ, instead forming their own "Christian Connexion" or simply "Christians." The college those Christians established at Yellow Springs, Ohio in 1850 without the Disciples' help was named after a Syrian city, for "it was in Antioch that the disciples [of Jesus] were first called *Christians*" (Acts 11:26). Antioch College's **Christians** were named to match the Connexion's intent "to be distinguished from the Disciples of Christians who established Hiram College."[33] The emphasis on athletics can be gleaned from an ironic local T-shirt: "Antioch College: No Football Since 1929."

• • •

Subscribing to both Restorationist and Methodist principles, the Church of God was founded at Anderson, Indiana in 1881 by Rev. D.S. Warner. His namesakes are Warner Pacific College (Portland, Ore.) and Warner University (Lake Wales, Fla.). We're about to reveal how WPC's **Knights** and WU's **Royals** (and their lion mascot) fit with Christian imagery.

• • •

Whereas so many denominational seminaries evolved into secular universities, Restoration Movement institutions tend to maintain their emphasis on biblical scholarship, so they're living laboratories for Christian-themed team names. The monikers for the following Restorationist colleges are explained in terms of Christian imagery, so look for the same athletic identities at uncountable historically Christian—but not necessarily Restorationist—schools:

Beacons, Blazers, Fire, Flames: The Restorationists' Mid-Atlantic Christian University (Elizabeth City, N.C.) had **Preachers** at its 1948 founding. They were **Flames** in the mid-1980s and **Mustangs** since 2009. "**Flames**" referred to a good Christian's internal spirit, or as Jesus puts it, "I am the light of the world: he that followeth me shall not walk in darkness, but shall have the light of life" (John 8:12). The Disciples of Christ's Northwest Christian College (Eugene, Ore.) applies that thinking to its **Beacons (Crusaders** until 2004).[34]

Preachers, Deacons, Parsons, Angels, Evangels: These titles for ministers were the first team names at many seminaries that became large universities. They now appear almost exclusively at small Bible institutes, including the following Restorationist schools. Nebraska Christian College in Norfolk hosts **Parsons**. The **Red Lions** at Lincoln [Ill.] Christian University are converted **Preachers** (men) and **Angels** (women). Angels are more ethereal agents of the Lord's word. In fact, *angel* is from the Greek *angelos* (messenger), so **Angels** are closely related to **Evangels** at a few Bible colleges. (*Evangelist* is a Greek-derived form describing the bringer of the gospel.) Find **Evangels** at Oklahoma City's Mid-America Christian University, which is backed by Anderson, Indiana's Church of God. Tennessee evangelist Ashley S. Johnson was inspired by Campbellite ideals to start Knoxville's Johnson University. In 2013 its female **Evangels** (and some **Spirits**) and male **Preachers** changed to **Royals** with a lion mascot. (The Christian symbolism of both is provided below.)

Ambassadors, Heralds: These aren't so different from **Deacons** and **Evangels**, except (being borrowed from the language of diplomacy) they remind seminarians to "make disciples of all nations" (Matthew 28:19). **Preachers** and **Angels** at Ozark Christian College (Joplin, Mo.) became **Ambassadors** in 1958. Athletes at Central Christian College of the Bible (Moberly, Mo.) executed their playbook as **Heralds** until 2007 but as **Saints** thereafter.

Saints: Central Christian's **Saints** (above) are anomalous. Sainted persons are those whose post-mortem miracles have been confirmed by the Catholic canonization process. In Restorationist, Protestant, or Mormon jargon, "saints" is applied more liberally to Christians in good standing. So a college named after a particular saint—or one backing athletic **Saints**—is often a Catholic one.

Rams: Southwestern Christian College (Terrell, Texas) is run by the Churches of Christ. It has **Rams**, as do many other Christian institutions, owing to the ram's role as a biblical symbol of sacrifice (Genesis 22, Numbers 6, Leviticus 5 and 9) and an allusion to Jesus as "good shepherd" to his flock.

Kingsmen, Monarchs, Regals, Regents, Royals: Teams with such names can indicate a student body that celebrates Jesus as divine power—a King of kings— to whom all mortal monarchs are subordinate. Hope International University's **Royals** (Fullerton, Calif.) are the Restorationists in this class.

Cavaliers, Knights, Lancers, Vanguards: Even while noting the distinction between a divine King of kings and earthly rulers, it's not beyond the realm of possibility that Christians would draw team names from regal protocols. The Restorationists' Kentucky Christian University (Grayson) and Crossroads College (Rochester, Minn.) both have **Knights**, but the same thinking applies to any number of courtly nicknames at other Christian colleges.

Chargers, Conquerors, Crusaders, Warriors: Ephesians 6:13–17 says to take "the whole armor of God [...] and put on the breastplate of righteousness [...] take the shield of faith [...] the helmet of salvation, and the sword of the Spirit." This is among the more explicit scriptural comparisons between warfare and gospel service. Athletes in the Stone-Campbell influence include **Crusaders** at Dallas Christian College, Great Lakes Christian College (Lansing, Mich.), and Manhattan [Kan.] Christian College. The Restorationist **Chargers** at Point University (East Point, Ga.) became **Eagles** in 2011. **Warriors** at both William Jessup University (San Jose, Calif.) and Rochester College (Rochester Hills, Mich.) fight for Restorationist institutions.

Soldiers: Crusading armies justified their efforts through the Second Epistle to Timothy (2:3): "Share in suffering as a good soldier of Christ Jesus." Two verses later (2:5) comes moral instruction for jocks: "An athlete is not crowned unless he competes according to the rules." Athletes serving the Restoration Movement's St. Louis Christian College (Florissant, Mo.) are **Soldiers**, but the centurion's helmet on the SLCC insignia can be disconcerting to those who know that Roman soldiers mocked Jesus in the hour before his execution.

Anchors, Dolphins: **Anchormen** and (women) **Anchors** were dug in at Puget Sound Christian College (Everett, Wash.) until that Restorationist school closed in 2007. But it's excuse enough to talk about **Anchors** at some other Christian schools. Hebrews 6:19 describes Christian hope as "an anchor of the soul, both sure and steadfast." The anchor represents Christian faith even in troubled waters. When the cross-like anchor is superimposed on the Christian symbol of the dolphin, it remembers the crucifixion to inspire **Anchor** and **Dolphin** athletes.

Lions: The Asiatic lion (*Panthera leo persica*) once ranged from Greece to India and across northern Africa. There are dozens of allusions to Palestine's lions in the Hebrew Bible, and the king of beasts represented Jesus in the medieval bestiary (an anthology of Christian allegories). Those same parables misreport that lions are born dead and "licked to life" by their mothers, taken to symbolize Jesus's resurrection. As already stated, Lincoln Christian's **Preachers** and **Angels** became **Red Lions** in 2009, but other Restorationist-backed schools embrace a little lion-ism. There are **Lions** at Patten University (Oakland, Calif.) and Freed-Hardeman University (Henderson, Tenn.), which opened in 1908 under the direction of Church of Christ preachers A.G. Freed and N.B. Hardeman. Warrior Crusaders of the eleventh-century might have encountered western Asia's last lions, which remained symbolic of valor and nobility for centuries, so **Monarchs**, **Regals**, and **Vanguards** often employ lion mascots.[35]

Eagles: Any Christian college's chapel is a natural gathering place. Its Bible often rests on an ornate eagle lectern, from which the word of God can be metaphorically spread on eagle's wings. The eagle also represents Christ's resurrection or his ascension to heaven thereafter. **Eagles** among Restoration Movement colleges are at Oklahoma Christian University (Oklahoma City), Midway [Ky.] College, and Faulkner University (Montgomery, Ala.). Ohio's Cincinnati Christian University has purple-and-gold **Golden Eagles**, but there are so many such teams in general that we can't explain the forty-plus Christian colleges with **Eagles** only in terms of biblical devotion; **Eagles** (and *Aguilas* in Mexico) appear all over the place for a variety of noble reasons.[36]

> Speaking of **Lions** and **Eagles**, their attributes are combined in griffins. A mythical griffin had a lion's body and an eagle's head, wings, and talons, thereby suggesting heavenly (divine) and earthly (human) ideals. But "**Griffins**" seems to be the only recurring team name for Christian schools that Restorationists missed, and it might not be accidental. Dante famously noted the griffin's dual nature in *Purgatorio* (Canto XXXI), which scholars take as an explicit reference to Jesus as God-man in the Holy Trinity. Trinitarianism is one of the few areas of friction between Misters Stone and Campbell, so it is certainly possible Restorationist colleges don't want to encourage further debate with **Griffins** teams.

• • •

The many new men's seminaries of the Second Great Awakening got educator Mary Lyon to notice that colleges for women were distinctly second-class. From productive frustration she created a curriculum comparable to those at the best men's schools and administered it to the inaugural class at Wheaton Female Seminary in Norton, Massachusetts in 1835. Ms. Lyon was ready to open her own Massachusetts school in 1837, South Hadley's Mount Holyoke Female Seminary. Today the **Lyons** at Wheaton College and Mount Holyoke College are remembrances of their common framer.[37]

According to their startup dates, those are two of the world's oldest women's colleges. But the Mount Holyoke and Wheaton seminaries didn't become colleges until years after their foundings (1888 and 1912 respectively), so some newer institutions have been granting college degrees exclusively to women for longer.[38]

For example, the Wesleyan College **Pioneers** (Macon, Ga.) represented the world's oldest degree-granting women's college, one chartered by Methodists in 1836 and opened in 1839. (Wesleyan made the alliterative switch to **Wolves** in fall 2013.) Elmira College was founded in 1855 as the first to grant women baccalaureate degrees equal to those at men's colleges (E.C.'s own description). Coed since 1969, teams are **Soaring Eagles** because cliffs in the Chemung Valley are conducive to flying gliders in several directions, making the city of Elmira, New York home to the National Soaring Museum.

Columbia University didn't go coed until 1983, but a partnership with the all-female Barnard College across Broadway goes back to 1900, meaning Columbia instructors and facilities had already been available to women for decades. Otherwise, Dartmouth and Harvard were the last Ivies to go coed in 1972.[39] Women's colleges that resisted that integration could have trouble recruiting. An 1869-founded Presbyterian school at Chambersburg, Pennsylvania operated successfully as the first women's college to have been endowed by a woman, Sarah Wilson. By its centennial, Wilson College's enrollment had reached an all-time high but dropped enough by 1979 that the Board of Trustees voted to close the doors.[40] Over a few short months, Wilson alumnae used legal maneuvering and dramatic fundraising to effect a recovery from an all-but-certain disintegration that is now commemorated by **Phoenix** teams (symbolism on p. 174). Faced with a later financial crisis, Wilson decided to go fully coed in fall 2013.

Monrovians | Railsplitters | Panthers | Golden Bulls

Quakers opened Philadelphia's Institute for Colored Youth in 1837. In 1902 it moved twenty-five miles west to the farm of Quaker settler George Cheyney. Pennsylvania's last gray wolves had recently disappeared, but the surrounding woods provide background for Cheyney University's **Wolves**.

The 1858 class valedictorian at ICY/Cheyney and its future administrator was educator and civil rights advocate O.V. Catto, who was gunned down on his way to a Philly voting booth in 1871. On the less heavy side, O.V. had managed and played infield for ICY's baseball team after 1867. Most of his teammates belonged to the Colored Knights of Pythias, which was one of many charitable fraternal organizations from the city's huge black population.

Catto's Philadelphia **Pythians** were among the earliest black teams anywhere and the first one banned from the top league of the day based on the color of its players. When rejecting them for the 1868 season, the National Association said the **Pythians** would create "in all probability some division of feeling, whereas, by excluding them no injury could result to anyone." One can hardly appreciate the scale of that insult to Catto, who'd just led a civil disobedience campaign to desegregate city streetcars.

The **Pythians'** intrastate black rivals included the Monrovia Base Ball Club of Harrisburg. Some **Monrovians** belonged to the American Colonization Society, an organization that sought to relocate former slaves to the new West African country of Liberia. That movement gained momentum during James Monroe's presidency (1817–25) because the former Virginia governor was happy to have the example of free blacks removed from the plantation states. Trans-Atlantic relocation began in 1822, and two years later the Liberian capital was renamed Monrovia (after the prez), explaining Harrisburg's **Monrovians**.[1]

Presbyterian minister John M. Dickey of the Colonization Society wanted to educate leaders for Liberia but failed to gain admission for black students at Princeton's seminary (his alma mater). Dickey and his wife Sarah Cresson instead opened an institute for black ministers in Pennsylvania's Chester County in 1854. In 1866—the year after President Lincoln's assassination—it was renamed Lincoln University. (As of 2013 it was *The* Lincoln University.) Owing to its provenance, LU is "the black Princeton," whereat orange-and-blue **Lions** are believed to be feline foils to Princeton's orange-and-black **Tigers**, although anagramists should spot *l-i-o-n* hiding sequentially within *Lincoln*.[2]

• • •

African American leadership at the top level would soon come to black institutes like Cheyney and Lincoln, but one Ohio school that opened in 1856 had the full participation of both white and black Methodist ministers from the get-go. The town and the academy were both named after William Wilberforce, a leading Member of Parliament who drove the banning of the slave trade across Britain's Empire. Like most **Bulldogs**, those representing Wilberforce University were named for hanging tough.

But if anyone had asked what the teams at his namesake university should be called, Mr. Wilberforce would likely have said, "Anything but **Bulldogs**, please." To him, the suppression of the slave trade was one of "two great objects" on his divinely inspired to-do list. The second was a Christian "reformation of manners," which was intended to address society's moral health. As such, he aimed to stop violence against animals by co-founding the Royal Society for the Prevention of Cruelty to Animals in 1824. He was particularly sickened by the sport of bull-baiting, in which fierce canines ripped the nose of a bovine until it died of either suffocation or blood loss. The ill-tempered beast bred for that purpose was the Old English Bulldogge. The O.E.B. is now genetically extinct, but its better-behaved, shorter-legged descendent is the mascot for uncountable teams.[3]

Another black college a few hundred feet away is Central State University. It's a much larger school, but it spun off from Wilberforce in 1947 as a teachers' and technical college. CSU explains its **Marauders** thus: "According to legend, marauders were African pirates who raided slave ships during the middle passage and freed fellow Africans from a life of bondage in the Americas."[4] That's less a "legend" than an improbable fiction; pirates of African blood—usually escaped slaves—are certainly among the historically overlooked sea-rovers (more than half of the crews of Blackbeard or the infamous Welshman "Black Bart" Roberts might have been black),[5] but any liberation of human cargo would have been incidental to other pirating ambitions and never the primary initiative. The historical record does not align with CSU's redemption narrative.

• • •

The first black colleges (like those above) were in the north. Things changed after the Civil War when the federal Freedmen's Bureau set out to provide basic services, employment, and education to former slaves. The Bureau often cooperated with denominational missionary societies, so it was in concert with Congregationalists that the Bureau's chief, O.O. Howard, founded a school at Washington D.C. in 1866, Howard University. He was also the eponym for the 1877-founded Howard School, today's Fayetteville [N.C.] State University. Howard and FSU have respective **Bisons** and **Broncos**, the lack of relevance for which will be explained shortly.

While Gen. Howard had been in command of the Army of the Tennessee, President Lincoln expressed to him his appreciation for the loyalty of the pro-Union mountain people in the eastern part of that state. (Secession had been spurred by planters farther west.) Howard saw a Tennessee college as Lincoln's living memorial and was on the board of directors when Lincoln Memorial University was chartered at Harrogate in 1897. LMU teams take Lincoln's own folksy nickname, **Railsplitters**.[6]

In 1867 the Freedmen's Bureau opened Saint Augustine's University in Raleigh, North Carolina. It was named for the saintly bishop of Hippo (354–430 CE). We were perplexed by SAU's transition from **Fighting Saints** to **Horses** some time in the late 1920s ... until it dawned on us that *hippo-* is a Greek prefix for all things horsey. In 1948 the more standard "**Falcons**" was jockeyed in, corresponding to a falconry bell on the school shield.

• • •

The schools above are a few of what were designated Historically Black Colleges and Universities by the Higher Education Act of 1965. HBCUs at the NCAA Division I level usually compete in the Mid-Eastern Athletic Conference or the Southwestern Athletic Conference. We will list the nicknames of their regular members, alleviating ourselves from examining all 100-plus HBCUs:

- **MEAC**: Bethune-Cookman **Wildcats** (Daytona Beach), Coppin State **Eagles** (Baltimore), Delaware State **Hornets**, Florida A&M **Rattlers**, Hampton **Pirates**, Howard **Bison**, Maryland–Eastern Shore **Hawks**, Morgan State **Bears**, Norfolk State **Spartans**, North Carolina A&T **Aggies**, North Carolina Central **Eagles** (Durham), South Carolina State **Bulldogs** (Orangeburg), and Winston-Salem [N.C.] State **Rams**.[7]

- **SWAC**: Alabama State **Hornets**,[8] Alabama A&M **Bulldogs** (Normal), Alcorn State **Braves**, Arkansas–Pine Bluff **Golden Lions**, Mississippi Valley State **Devils/Devilettes**, Prairie View A&M **Panthers**, Southern **Jaguars**, and **Tigers** at Grambling State, Texas Southern, and Jackson State.[9]

• • •

Their ancestors may have arrived against their will, but African Americans often have New World roots far deeper than Euro-American neighbors. This long, rich experience could have yielded nicknames more informed than those above, but the truth is that HBCUs tend to carry unsurprising nicknames by design, as explained by Patrick B. Miller, who often writes about sport and race in America:

*In adopting familiar team colors and nicknames, African-American students in the New South hoped to give their schools a prominent place on the collegiate map. Thus from the menagerie of ferocious mascots available to them, black collegians at Atlanta Baptist chose to become **Tigers**, while at Livingstone they adopted the nickname [**Blue**] **Bears**. Other schools distinguished themselves as the Lincoln **Lions**, Wiley **Wildcats**, and Howard **Bisons** [emphasis added].*[10]

Nicknames were often assigned by one's opponents in accord with some readily discernible otherness, and HBCUs preemptively and shrewdly adopted familiar monikers from the animal kingdom. (That also avoided the racially identifiable human mascots that would be expected to correspond to **Pioneer** or **Cowboys** teams.) But even with the gates of Miller's menagerie thrown wide open, nearly 10 percent of HBCUs present **Tigers**, an astonishingly high incidence.[11] HBCU **Tiger** dens include Benedict College (Columbia, S.C.), Saint Paul's College (Lawrenceville, Va., closed 2013), Edward Waters College (Jacksonville), Paul Quinn College (Dallas), Stillman College (Tuscaloosa, Ala.),[12] and the above-listed Jackson [Miss.] State University and Texas Southern University (Houston).

In *Plessy v. Ferguson* (1896), the U.S. Supreme Court upheld the states' rights to sustain "separate but equal" segregated public facilities. Coahoma County, Mississippi opened an agricultural high school for African American students in 1924 to conform to "separate but equal." In Texas, a junior college for whites (today's University of Houston) and a corresponding one for "Negroes" both opened at Houston in 1927. The latter hastily reorganized as Texas Southern University in 1947 to justify a new law school that could accept black students like Heman Sweatt, whose lawsuit cited the Fourteenth Amendment's equal protection clause after he was denied entry to the all-white law school at the University of Texas. Sweatt's 1950 victory in the Supreme Court set up the landmark 1954 decision in *Brown v. Board of Education*, wherein the court's majority said, "[Separate] facilities are inherently unequal" and have "no place in the field of public education." For all that history, Texas Southern and Coahoma Community College keep the **Tigers** theme, leading one to wonder why black student-athletes seem drawn to southern Asia's *Panthera tigris*.[13]

We'll explain. Alabama's Tuskegee Institute opened in 1881 with Hampton grad Booker T. Washington as president. He believed the descendents of slaves would be served best through training in the practical trades. That would effect the eventual assimilation of the broader society, one in which the vast majority of persons of all colors were still laborers. Washington's long game was famously at odds with black thinker W.E.B. Du Bois, who took "the Hampton-Tuskegee model" to task for holding back the "Talented Tenth" ... the 10 percent or so of African Americans who—once educated in the liberal arts—would be exemplary citizens, more quickly effecting an integrated and progressive society. Today Tuskegee University has crimson-and-gold **Golden Tigers** (male) and **Tigerettes** (female) for reasons no better than those above, but HBCUs created in the Tuskegee mold tend to repeat "**Tigers**," including Tennessee State University (Nashville), Voorhees College (Denmark, S.C.), St. Philip's College (San Antonio), and Grambling State.

Richard R. Wright tried balancing the agendas of Washington and Du Bois as the first president of an industrial college in Savannah, Georgia, but the scales tip toward Tuskegee in sport; Savannah State University keeps **Tigers**.[14]

Veterans of some U.S. Colored Infantry units from Missouri opened Jefferson City's Lincoln Institute in 1866. Clement Richardson left Tuskegee's faculty for Lincoln's presidency in 1918, changed the name to Lincoln University, and started Tuskegee-like training programs. LU's **Tigers** became **Blue Tigers** in 1974 to be distinct from the **Tigers** thirty miles away at U. Missouri, but that they're **Tigers** at all may owe to the 'Skegee connection.

The Atlanta Baptist College that Miller mentions is now Morehouse College, founded in 1867 and renamed in 1913 for Henry Morehouse of the American Baptist Home Mission Society. (In fact, "talented tenth" first appeared in an 1896 essay by Rev. Morehouse and spread among his ABHMS brethren before being picked up by Du Bois.)[15] Samuel Archer was the Morehouse president by 1931 and transferred to it the colors from his Baptist-founded alma mater, Colgate (p. 98). Colgate's **Raiders** wear—in fact, have always worn—maroon and white, despite past lives as *Red* **Raiders**, so Morehouse's teams are *Maroon* **Tigers**, except for track and field's *Flying* **Tigers**.

Two years before Baptists started the city's ABC/Morehouse, Restorationist Movement missionaries founded Atlanta University. The Methodists' prototype for their own freedmen's schools, Clark University, also opened in Atlanta in 1869. It was named after Bishop D.W. Clark of the Methodists' Freedman's Aid Society. Atlanta and Clark merged as Clark Atlanta University in 1988 and are now part of a virtual single campus of the Atlanta University Center Consortium, which includes Morehouse and the all-female Spelman College. The latter is the former Atlanta Baptist Female Seminary, founded in 1881. Its financial support from rich Baptist John D. Rockefeller passed through Rev. Morehouse of the ABHMS, which increasingly became the "conduit for Rockefeller's wholesale philanthropy in education."[16] Eventually the oldest HBCU for women was named for the abolitionist family of J.D.'s wife, Laura Spelman. Cats on the AUC block include Morehouse's **Maroon Tigers**, Clark Atlanta's **Panthers**, and Spelman's **Jaguars**.[17] There are **Cougars** eight miles away at another Atlanta HBCU, Carver College.

There are multiple **Panthers** at HBCUs too. They're at Virginia Union University (Richmond), Claflin University (Orangeburg, S.C.), Denmark [S.C.] Technical College, Philander Smith College (Little Rock, Ark.), Prairie View A&M, and Simmons College of Kentucky.[18] While the mascots for **Panthers** elsewhere are either tawny or melanistic (all black) in fairly equal percentages, those at the HBCUs are exclusively the latter.

The Scotia Seminary (Concord, N.C.) opened in 1867 as the first post-war HBCU for women. That "Mount Holyoke of the South" merged in 1930 with a fellow Presbyterian school, Alabama's Barber Memorial Institute. The saber-toothed mascots for Barber-Scotia College's **Sabers** fit the established **Tiger** pattern.[19] The Scotia Seminary originally complemented the all-male Presbyterian institute fifteen miles away at Charlotte, now Johnson C. Smith University. When JCSU's gold-and-navy footballers trounced Howard in the early 1920s, a reporter was perhaps drawing a bovine comparison to Howard's **Bisons** when he made them **Golden Bulls**.[20] (BSC and JCSU both went coed in 1954.)

• • •

The Baptist, Methodist, Presbyterian, and Restorationist preachers who'd come of age before the Civil War would align the core abolitionist message of the Second Great Awakening (p. 96) with their support for Reconstruction-era black colleges. In some cases, ministers and other administrators influenced the athletic identity:

- A former Methodist missionary to China, Bishop Isaac Wiley, founded the first HBCU west of the Mississippi in 1873 at Marshall, Texas. The seminary is now Wiley College, home of alliterative Wiley **Wildcats**.
- Behind the HBCU that opened at Nashville in 1866 were emphatic educator John Ogden and ministers Erastus Milo Cravath and Edward P. Smith. That first black college to attain university status is now Fisk University, named after Gen. Clinton B. Fisk of the Freedmen's Bureau (who'd made Nashville's barracks available for classrooms in 1865). Footballers during Rev. Cravath's presidency (1875–1900) were **Sons of Milo**,[21] but all teams are now **Bulldogs**.
- Dr. James H. Dillard was from a white slave-holding family but became a force for black education. Two New Orleans schools that he fostered merged into Dillard University in 1929. Its alliterative blue-and-white Dillard **Devils** have transitioned to **Bleu Devils**, a spelling that reflects the city's French history.
- In 1896, Seventh-day Adventists opened an industrial school in Huntsville, Alabama. More than most other HBCUs with denominational roots, Oakwood University maintains a decidedly Christian character, as indicated by teams of **Ambassadors**, a nickname now found only at smaller Bible colleges.

Buzz | *Sting* | *Utes* | *Runnin' Rebels*

Living in western New York's Burned-Over District, Joseph Smith would have sponged up any number of fervent Christian messages. When the 14-year-old went into the woods to pray for spiritual guidance in 1820, "personages" very similar to God and Jesus appeared to report that no Christian church was on quite the right track and it would be great if he could please start a new one. Assisted by angels, Smith found and translated some gold plates that had been compiled and edited by an ancient Native American prophet named Mormon into a new testament of Jesus, published in 1830 as the *Book of Mormon*.

Smith's "Mormon" followers called themselves Latter-day Saints, and LDS members wanted to convert Amerindians, whom their *Book* counted among the Lost Tribes of ancient Israel. That sat poorly with white neighbors, and Smith and company—*Mormons*—were forced westward from homes in New York, Ohio, and Missouri. Backtracking across the Mississippi to Nauvoo, Illinois in 1840, they built a temple, fielded a militia, and controlled local politics. There were scrapes between the Saints and other settlers, and Smith and his brother were held in connection with a mob's destruction of an anti-Mormon press in 1844. The jail at Carthage was overrun and the pair were slain in their cells.

Smith's successor Brigham Young led a wagon train of 15,000 Mormons out of the U.S. and into a desert nominally in Mexico's jurisdiction. They were the first to travel the Mormon Pioneer Trail, which a half-million people would take west before the 1869 completion of the transcontinental railroad. July 24 is Utah's Pioneer Day, commemorating the 1847 arrival of Young's party at the Great Salt Lake. Pioneers are remembered fondly on all frontiers, but in Utah there's special significance for those who suffered tremendous hardships on the Mormon Trail while hauling their belongings in handcarts during the late 1850s. On that first Pioneer Day, the Saints founded Deseret, now Salt Lake City.

Deseret is the name of the honeybee in the Book of Mormon (Ether 2:3). It symbolized the industry and diligence Mormons embrace as part of their pioneering spirit. Brigham Young's Beehive House was adorned with beehives, and those on the state flag suggest the Beehive State's Mormon history.[1] The first of baseball's several Salt Lake **Bees** appeared in the 1915 Pacific Coast League. PCL owner Joe "Buzz" Buzas moved a team to Salt Lake in 1994, where they were the bee-like **Buzz**. But Georgia Tech's **Yellow Jackets** had recently trademarked "Buzz the bee," so Buzas's **Buzz** became Salt Lake **Stingers** in 1998, recalling soccer's bee-themed Salt Lake **Sting** (APSL, 1990–91).

The point of going to Utah was to leave the U.S. for Mexican territory, but as soon as the Mormons got there the entire Southwest was forked over in the 1848 treaty that ended the Mexican-American War. The Mormons were petitioning Congress for annexation as the State of Deseret almost immediately because they thought statehood would likely give them more autonomy than would territorial status.

• • •

The Utes had been the dominant culture in the eastern Great Basin for a thousand years before the Mormon pioneers arrived. They were hunter-gatherers who moved with the seasons until they got Spanish horses in the mid-1600s. Then they raided livestock, sold Indian enemies into Spanish slavery, and became the West's first mounted bison hunters. Large Ute camps protected by war parties were the natives that Brigham Young and company found.

From the Utah Territory, the Ute-controlled San Luis Valley was east across the Rockies in the New Mexico Territory. (It would be in the new Colorado Territory in 1861.) A U.S. fort built there to guard against Ute attacks in 1852 was replaced in 1858 by nearby Fort Garland, just east of Alamosa's Adams State University. ASU's **Indians** became **Grizzlies** in 1996 to dissociate from a history of conflict.

The growing number of Mormons threatened Indian traditions, and the Saints fought a series of small wars against the Utes between 1853 and 1868, which started to put those natives on reservations. The U.S. Cavalry set up Fort Lewis in 1878 to monitor Utes in the Four Corners area and Federal agents tried to force the Utes to give up their horses and nomadism to become farming Christians, but the natives were uninterested and insulted. In September 1879, Utes massacred eleven federal Indian agents and ambushed a cavalry column, accelerating their defeat and confinement to reservations. Fort Lewis moved within Colorado from Pagosa Springs to Hesperus in 1880 to be closer to troublesome Utes. It was abandoned in 1891 and was later an Indian school and then Fort Lewis College (an A&M hosting **Aggies** and **Beavers**). It moved again to Durango and became a four-year college in the early 1960s. That's when athletes became **Raiders**, represented by a mounted Plains cavalryman. Retreating from that militarism in 1994, FLC fielded **Skyhawks**.

Across Colorado's northern border is Eastern Wyoming College in Torrington. In 1968 students wanted a new symbol that referred to cavalry troops because Fort Laramie was only twenty miles away. Learning that soldiers in the 6th Pennsylvania Cavalry of the Civil War had been outfitted with only lances—a spear-like weapon enjoying a post-Napoleonic revival—teams became **Lancers**.[2]

The isolated and self-reliant Mormons opened thirty-plus academies, some of which are now colleges. Brigham Young founded Salt Lake City's University of Deseret in 1850, but it's been the University of Utah since 1894. Like Utah itself, UU teams are named for the Great Basin's Utes; **Runnin' Utes** replaced **Runnin' Redskins** in 1972.[3] The Brigham Young Academy at Provo was spun off from the University of Deseret in 1876 and became Brigham Young University in 1903. Athletes were called **Cougars** in 1923, adopting puma cubs found near campus as mascots in 1925. A Salt Lake school founded by Latter-day Saints in 1886 is now LDS Business College. It once ran with **Saints**,[4] but no longer fields varsity teams.

• • •

Mormons recruited heavily in Wales, Scandinavia, and (especially) Denmark in the 1840s. Bishop Thomas E. Ricks led some converted Welsh and Scandinavian Mormons into the Idaho Territory in 1882. Midway along the new rail link between Salt Lake City and Montana's mining camps they founded Rexburg

(German for "Ricks fort").[5] The local academy was Ricks College until being incorporated as BYU-Idaho in 2001. Recalling the Scandinavian background of those first settlers, BYUI teams are **Vikings**.

Mormons founded Snow College in 1888 at Ephraim, another Scandinavian-heavy settlement in Utah. The 1924 **Ephraimites** wanted an animal to compare to BYU's **Cougars** (for which Snow is a two-year feeder school). They became **Badgers** because Utah is high-value habitat for one American badger subspecies, *Taxidea taxus jeffersonii*. Utah Mormons opened the Weber Stake Academy at Ogden in 1889. Wally "Wildcat" Morris was a **Weberite** footballer of the late 1920s, and the repetition of his own nickname explains Weber State University's alliterative **Wildcats**. (Weber State and Snow College transferred to state sponsorship in the early 1930s.)

To support Pacific Rim missionaries, Latter-day Saints opened an Oahu seminary in 1955. It's now BYU-Hawaii, where **Seasiders** are geographically (not historically) informed.

• • •

The Mormons' political presence in the western Utah Territory (now Nevada) meant little to ore diggers or miners on the trail to California. There were never enough resident miners to qualify for statehood, but the Union needed the area's silver and gold to finance the Civil War. Congress decided to accelerate Nevada's territorial status in 1862 and then its statehood two years later, thus the "Battle Born State."

By contrast, Utahns would wait three more decades for statehood despite the booming numbers of Mormons toward whom the Feds remained suspicious. Anticipating that cotton would be scarce after Southern secession, Brigham Young sent Saints to southwestern Utah to grow "white gold" in the new Virgin River town of St. George. In 1911 descendants of those "Dixie Mormons" started the St. George Stake Academy. The name was Dixie Junior College when the inevitable "**Rebels**" nickname was adopted in 1951. Joining the U-of-U system as Dixie State College of Utah in 2000 brought pressure to drop even a mild reference to Confederate history, so a student poll created a **Red Storm** in 2009.[6] The institutional name changed again to Dixie State University in spring 2013.

More geographically surprising **Rebels** are just 200 miles from St. George. At one time, Nevada Southern University was the Las Vegas satellite campus of the state-run University of Nevada. Because required courses were taken hundreds of miles away at the main Reno campus, NSU sought institutional independence. Students were particularly vocal in their *Rebel Yell* newspaper, a name educed from "Nevada *Southern*." (The original rebel yell was the battle cry of charging Confederates.) Naturally, jocks at the renamed University of Nevada, Las Vegas were **Rebels** when autonomy came in 1968. (Only male hoopsters are ***Runnin'*** **Rebels**.) UNLV's first mascot was the "rebel wolf" Beauregard. He poked fun at UN-Reno's **Wolfpack** and was the namesake of P.G.T. Beauregard, a famous Confederate general. Still, UNLV insists its gray-and-red, rifle toting, mustached rebel is a pioneer, not a Southern soldier.

Dutchmen | Keystones | Colonials | Shoremen

Traveling through Europe in the 1670s, English Quaker William Penn invited German Quakers and Mennonites (who were both too radical even for Continental Protestants) to his Pennsylvania colony. Some left the Catholic-dominated Holy Roman Empire to found Germantown, Pennsylvania in 1683.[1]

Some Mennonites back in Switzerland became disappointed with their less disciplined brethren. They created a conservative splinter church led by Jakob Amman—the *Amish*—in 1693. Many Amish would join their Mennonite cousins in Pennsylvania, Ohio, and Indiana. In the first, Germanic settlers were called Pennsylvania Dutch because *Dutch* is a corruption of *Deutsche* ("*doy*-cha"), the German word for "German."[2] In 1866, German Methodists founded Lebanon Valley College at Annville (in Pennsylvania Dutch Country), at which male and female **Flying Dutchmen** tolerate the mistaken identity.[3] York [County] College in southwestern Dutch Country shunned its **Flying Dutchmen** and female **Dutcherettes** to back **Spartans** around 1970 to be less exclusive … or at least equally non-inclusive of YCP's mostly non-Peloponnesian student body.

In a barn raising, an Amish community comes together to build one neighbor's barn in a single day. The Atlantic League's Lancaster **Barnstormers** in central Amish country refer to both Amish barns and the barnstorming ways of past independent teams. In fact, they'd been **Road Warriors** until 2004 because they'd struggled financially while looking for a permanent home.

Realizing that their kids might enroll in another denomination's college, Mennonites started their own. The first was at Elkhart, Indiana in 1894, but it moved twelve miles to Goshen in 1903. Goshen College's **Maple Leafs** reflect their burg's "Maple City" tag (although *Acer* genus trees cover much of the U.S. and Canada). Fundamentalists saw too much liberal thinking at Goshen College, and intra-Mennonite arguing closed it for the 1923/24 academic year. That's when some Mennonites back east determined that their 1917-founded Eastern Mennonite University in Harrisonburg, Virginia would be more conservative stronghold for the faith. A lion named HeRM—His Royal Majesty—is the mascot for EMU's **Royals** because both royal themes (p. 106) and lions (p. 107) show up regularly at Christian colleges.

• • •

A wedge-shaped stone at the center of an arch distributes weight evenly throughout. When Georgia became the thirteenth English-founded colony in 1732, Pennsylvania was the middle—or "keystone"—colony, jamming the Keystone State with **Keystone** teams.[4] Keystone College in La Plume was still a high school when the dominant pitcher of the early twentieth century graduated in 1898. Most of Christy Mathewson's career was with New York's **Giants**, commemorated by Keystone's own **Giants**. Staying in state, Matty had played college sports at Lewisburg's Bucknell University, where he's buried in a cemetery next to Christy Mathewson–Memorial Stadium (co-named for BU's war vets). L-Burg is in the Buffalo Valley, where some of the last eastern herds were seen until about 1800, and Bucknellians chose to be **Bison** in 1923, noting that rivals at nearby Penn State had taken its **Nittany Lions** (p. 91) from the Nittany Valley years earlier.

• • •

Colonials play throughout England's former seaboard colonies. In fact, *Colonial* refers to English colonial furniture and architecture, ignoring the significant North American settlements of the French, Spanish, and Dutch:

- Columbian College in the District of Columbia was founded in 1821. When it became The George Washington University in 1904, it traded blue and orange for the buff and blue of Continental Army uniforms. GWU fielded the **Buff and Blue**, but footballers of the 1920s were **Hatchetmen**, **Axemen**, or **Crummen** under Coach Harry Crum. (The campus news was already the *Hatchet*, referring to a youthful Master Washington coming clean about taking out Dad's cherry tree.) G-Dub finally presented **Colonials** in 1926.[5]
- Georgia College is in Milledgeville, named after John Milledge, a Patriot veteran, Georgia governor, and Congressman. (He donated the land for the University of Georgia.) GC's **Colonials** became **Bobcats** in 1998.
- Western Connecticut State University's **Colonials** are in Danbury, an important Continental Army supply depot sacked by Brits in April 1777.
- The Community College of Philadelphia puts **Colonials** in a former colonial capital that was also the largest city in the Thirteen Colonies.
- Long Island's Stony Brook University switched its **Patriots** for **Seawolves** when moving to Division I in 1994.[6] In 2006, Stony Brook took over the Long Island campus of Southampton College, which had just closed and ended the run of its own **Colonials**.[7]

• • •

Built in 1745, Fort Massachusetts protected Berkshire pioneers from French-sponsored Indian raids. Commander Ephraim Williams was killed in the French and Indian War in a 1755 advance on Lake George, but he'd left land and money for a college near his fort "provided Said township fall within the jurisdiction of the Province of Massachusetts Bay." Why the qualification? Because conflicting edicts from Georges II and III had poorly defined the borders between New York and New England, so Fort Massachusetts had been built as much to keep an eye on New York's Hudson River land barons as to defend against Frenchmen and Indians. Williams College did open in 1791, and Ephraim Williams is fondly remembered by **Ephs** ("eefs").[8]

Fort Massachusetts also watched for French and Abenaki raiders in the "green mountain" (*vert mont* in French)[9] space between the Connecticut and Hudson-Champlain Valleys. In 1761, New Englanders founded Bennington in southwest Vermont, ten miles north of Williamstown. That city's frontier spirit is evident in its Southern Vermont College **Mountaineers** and (club-level) Bennington College **Pioneers**. Choosing a color was easy for **Green Knights** at Randolph's Vermont Technical College (smack amid the Green Mountains) or the hunter-green (and yellow) **Eagles** at Poultney's Green Mountain College.

Especially concerned that the Dutch patroon system along the Hudson threatened New England's family farms were Ethan and Ira Allen, Connecticut brothers speculating on Vermont lands. In the 1770s, Ethan led the paramilitary Green Mountain Boys to keep Yorker expansion in check. The GMBs met at Bennington's Catamount Tavern, where a stuffed mountain lion faced New York, so the panther (or catamount) is a Vermont motif that justifies Middlebury's Middlebury College **Panthers** and Burlington's University of Vermont **Catamounts**.[10] But this was a clash of cultures, not armies. The path to a Yorker-Yankee war was interrupted by Revolution, during which the scruffy Green Mountain Boys transitioned to a well-regarded Patriot militia.

• • •

Facing huge war debts, British Prime Minister William Pitt wanted colonials to defray the costs of their own past defense through a 1765 tax on printed paper. When Pitt's economic minister, Charles Townshend, suggested colonists should be content with that Stamp Act, he discovered opposition within Parliament. A veteran of the North American wars, Isaac Barré, took the floor to predict a tax rebellion by colonial "Sons of Liberty." Adopting the words of Barré, Patriots bent on Stamp Act repeal formed Sons of Liberty chapters in Boston and New York and effected the statute's cancellation, but it was replaced by the 1767 Townshend Duties, taxes on British imports to fund colonial government. Two years later, Susquehanna Valley colonists renamed their Pennsylvania town Wilkes-Barre after Col. Barré and his vocal ally in Parliament, John Wilkes. Its Wilkes University named for John has **Colonels** named for Isaac.

Philadelphia lawyer John Dickinson authored a series of popular essays about the Townshend Duties that encouraged a boycott of British goods. He was also a representative at the Continental Congress and Constitutional Convention. During his Pennsylvania governorship (1782–85), Dickinson College opened in Carlisle (the first college chartered after the 1783 Treaty of Paris). With all this rich history, DC takes its nickname from a football game … a *loss* nonetheless. A reporter made **Red Devils** of DC's **Red and White** after they were edged (7-6) by George Washington's heavily favored **Colonials** in 1930.[11]

• • •

Britain's failing East India Company had a tea surplus in 1773, so the crown helped out with an exclusive and exceptionally low tea tax. Colonial merchants had been navigating the gray between good business and Patriot passion, but many turned to the rebel cause after their smuggled Dutch tea ending up costing more than the royal monopoly's legal stock. The Sons of Liberty foreshadowed a history of cheaply attired mascots in December when they superficially disguised themselves as Mohawks, boarded the EIC's *Dartmouth*, and chucked its chests into Boston Harbor. The NASL's New England **Tea Men** (1978–80) shared a regional prefix and a Foxboro address with the New England **Patriots**.[12]

Similar demonstrations went on for months. The "tea party" most resembling Boston's was at Chestertown, Maryland in May 1774. When hostilities ended, that port hosted America's first post-war college (est. 1782). General Washington himself was the main benefactor and eponym for Washington College, where **Shoremen** and **Shorewomen** are abridged longshoremen. The former royal port of entry has a long history of dockworkers, but "Shoremen" also describe the other residents on Chesapeake Bay's "Eastern Shore."[13]

Patriots | Minutemen | 76ers | Diplomats

Britain's Boston Port Act closed that harbor in June 1774. It was the first of the Intolerable Acts, reactions to the Boston Tea Party that confirmed the King's intention to keep his thumb down. That fueled Patriotism in those colonies that feared they might next attract royal attention, and new colonial conventions sent delegates to a Continental Congress in Philadelphia in September, where reps could voice grievances about taxes and other policies.

Independence was on the minds of few attendees, but things would heat up over the winter. In March 1775, Patrick Henry told the Virginia Convention that troops should be mobilized to rebuff British invasions. His introduction addressed those who thought war was still avoidable: "No man thinks more highly than I do of the patriotism [of those] who have just addressed the House." His conclusion was more dramatic: "[A]s for me, give me liberty, or give me death!"[1] At Martinsville—the seat of Virginia's Henry County—Patrick Henry Community College hosts red-white-and-blue **Patriots**.

Within days of Henry's speech, Boston's British occupiers learned that colonists had gathered weapons and gunpowder to their west at Concord, the seat of the illegal Massachusetts Provincial Congress led by John Hancock (a trader who turned smuggler to avoid taxes). Late on April 18, a heavy British detail set off to seize Hancock, Sons of Liberty leader Sam Adams, and the munitions, but midnight riders spread the word and the Redcoats were intercepted by about eighty riflemen on the Lexington Green before dawn. After the shooting started, eight militiamen were dead and ten were wounded, with the rest fleeing into the woods. With two wounded, the British continued to Concord to destroy the few on-hand supplies. The Redcoats were harassed all along the twenty-mile retreat to Boston as militiamen popped up from behind trees and rocks, the first actions by volunteer militias whose ability to mobilize quickly made them "Minutemen." **Minutemen** and **Minutewomen** still work the clock at the University of Massachusetts in Amherst.[2] The Bay State celebrates Patriot's Day each April 19 (or the closest Monday) with the Boston Marathon, the world's oldest annual twenty-six-miler.

When Boston got an AFL franchise in 1960, a fan poll made them Boston **Patriots**. Moving south to Foxboro after their first NFL season in 1970, they were officially set to be Bay State **Patriots**, but by the '71 kickoff the new field (closer to Rhode Island's capital than that of Massachusetts) made them *New England* **Patriots**. The stadium is now shared with the MLS New England **Revolution**. Boston Baptist College runs its own **Revolution**.

• • •

The Crown never firmed up colonial borders, and Vermonters wanted war to give Patriots control of the Hudson-Champlain Valley. Three weeks after Lexington and Concord, Ethan Allen's Green Mountain Boys joined a Connecticut militia under Benedict Arnold (not yet the traitor who'd try to forfeit West Point) to take Fort Ticonderoga. That was done without a shot fired because news of events in

Boston hadn't reached the unprepared garrison. Fort Ti was a critical chokepoint, but the immediately intriguing detail was the capture of its fifty-nine cannons.

That same day, a *Second* Continental Congress first convened in Philadelphia (meeting at various spots for the next fourteen years). It funded a new Continental Army on June 14, too late to help at the Battle of Bunker Hill three days later, wherein Brits paid dearly to gain some high ground on Boston Harbor. George Washington got command of the army on July 3 but didn't have the firepower to eject the King's men from Boston. When winter's snows came, Washington had Col. Henry Knox drag Ticonderoga's cannons 300 miles on ox sleds to Boston. Their overnight emplacement on Dorchester Heights effected the evacuation of the city by a shocked British fleet on March 17, 1776. Ten-thousand Redcoats and a thousand Loyalist families quickly sailed for the safety of Nova Scotia, an evacuation at cannonpoint that validates the MLL Boston **Cannons** (est. 2001).

Exiting the harbor, the British blew up colonial America's oldest lighthouse. Boston Light was rebuilt right after the war and is now amid a string of historic lighthouses that are seen from the Dorchester playing fields of UMass Boston's **Beacons**. Also, the state capitol is on Beacon Hill, named for an old Puritan signal fire. Beacon Street runs southwest from there to crazily merge with other major thoroughfares at Kenmore Square near Fenway Park, which hosted Boston **Beacons** during the first NASL season, 1968.

• • •

Planter George Mason was an opponent of British taxes and the primary author of both the Virginia Declaration of Rights and that state's constitution. (The former was a model for Jefferson's Declaration of Independence three weeks later.) Mason was also a fierce champion of individual liberties and abolition. Today, he lends name and spirit to the **Patriots** at Fairfax's George Mason University. (Until 1968 they were **Chargers** and **Marauders**.)

Back in 1751, Philly printer Ben Franklin had written that the royal policy of shipping convicts to the colonies should be answered by unleashing American rattlesnakes in Britain. The serpent appeared again three years later when Franklin invented the American political cartoon, but the reptile had by then been cut into pieces to represent colonies that died in isolation rather than thrive in confederation. With calls for independence, Franklin's rattler became a symbol for both colonial unity and resistance (appearing on the famous "Don't Tread On Me" battle flag). Old Ben's snake is the emblem for the MLS Philadelphia **Union**, a franchise awarded to the city in 2010 after years of lobbying by boosters called S.O.B.s (*Sons of Ben*).

Members of the Second Continental Congress signed the Declaration of Independence in July 1776, as the NBA Philadelphia **76ers** (or **Sixers**) remind us.[3] To mark the Declaration's one-hundredth birthday, Philly hosted the 1876 Centennial Exhibition, America's first world's fair, putting Philadelphia **Centennials** in baseball's 1875 NA. It was pretty obvious the European textiles outclassed those produced domestically, so locals opened a school to catch up. Basketballers at that Philadelphia College of Textiles & Science were later **Weavers**, an obvious reference to cloth production and a more subtle one to a revered full-court passing drill, the *weave*. In late 1958 the folksy sounding **Weavers** became **Rams** because sheep provide wool for textile processing. PCTS has been Philadelphia University since 1999.[4]

The Centennial spirit also gave life to a story that the grandson of Betsy Ross was telling, that she'd designed the American flag. There'd actually been several similar flags floating around, but Ms. Ross may have been responsible for giving each of its thirteen stars their five points ('stead of six). Philly's Betsy Ross House is in the neighborhood where she did her needling (although it may not be her actual townhouse). The patriotic design effected the Philadelphia **Stars** of Negro league baseball (1933–52) and the USFL (1983–84).

A century later Hartford had the NASL Hartford/Connecticut **Bicentennials** (1975–77) and ASL Connecticut **Yankees** (1975–78). The latter name is maintained by Norwalk's 1975-founded rugby club and also refers to Mark Twain's 1889 novel *A Connecticut Yankee in King Arthur's Court.*[5]

Philadelphia is known as the birthplace of the nation, the birthplace of liberty, the birthplace of freedom … and it has club names to match. The emblem of the WFL Philadelphia **Bell** (1974–75) was the Liberty Bell, which hung at the State House ("Independence Hall") during the Revolution. Tennis superstar Billie Jean King was the player-coach of the 1974-founded WTT Philadelphia **Freedoms**.[6] Local WPS reps were the Philadelphia **Independence** (2010–11).

• • •

With Britain's Indian allies raiding frontier settlements, Ohio Company surveyor George Rogers Clark convinced Virginia's commonwealth governor, Patrick Henry, to fund the defense of trans-Appalachian Virginia, "Kentucky." In fact, Washington County is Kentucky's oldest, founded in 1776 and named for the general on whom hopes were fixed. The county seat of Springfield has **Patriots** at St. Catharine College.

Clark's volunteers followed the Ohio from Fort Pitt to the Falls of the Ohio (now Louisville) in 1778. Preparing to shoot those rapids on a June morning, the party got spooked by a solar eclipse, but Clark convinced them it was a good omen and they continued. "Eclipse" still appears around the Falls City, in the names of more than a few businesses. The Louisville **Eclipse** (1882–84) at Eclipse Park were in baseball's AA.[7] (They were Louisville **Colonels** [p. 134] after that and were in the NL from 1892 to '99.)

Clark's capture of several major British forts ensured Patriot control of the Old Northwest for the war's duration and beyond. A major artery in the original 1830 grid plan for that region's biggest city would be his namesake, and North Clark Street's Chicago **Cubs** named a new bear mascot "Clark" in 2014.

Across the river from Louisville are some Ohio lands that were reserved in 1781 for veteran officers by an appreciative Virginia Assembly. New Albany is one city in "Clark's Grant" at which Indiana University Southeast replaced its club-level **Cougars** in 1971 with intercollegiate **Grenadiers**, named for Britain's forward assault troops in the colonial and Revolutionary Wars.[8]

• • •

In 1777, Britain wanted to end rebellion in the north by taking the Hudson Valley to isolate New England. The plan had several royal armies converging at Albany and marching east. From Canada, Gen. John Burgoyne's regulars, Hessians, Indians, and Tories retook Ticonderoga on July 6. The British army of Lt. Col. Barry St. Leger moved southeast from Fort Oswego and laid siege to Fort Stanwix (now Rome, N.Y.) on August 3. Three days later, Gen. Nicholas Herkimer and his Patriot relief column got within a few miles of reinforcing the fort when they were ambushed by the Loyalist-Iroquois army of Chief Joseph Brant. Among the first wounded, Herkimer propped himself against a beech tree to direct the battle. It was a clear British victory, but Patriots from Fort Stanwix had scattered St. Leger's Seneca allies, permanently denting Britain's alliance with Indians. Herkimer would die of his wounds, but everlasting monuments include Herkimer, New York and its Herkimer County Community College **Generals**.

Running low, Burgoyne sent 800 men to seize munitions at Bennington, but 1,500 militiamen under Bunker Hill hero Gen. John Stark smashed the enemy west of town on August 16.[9] Ignoring his losses and a lack of force cohesion, Burgoyne pushed toward Albany while Sir John Vaughan's army came up the Hudson. To keep Ulster County Patriots from resupplying Washington, Vaughan burned Kingston to the ground on October 16. The evacuation cost Kingston its new station as New York capital. (Kingston hosts a satellite campus of SUNY Ulster, but the **Senators** that commemorate the county's former state assembly are at the main campus five miles away in Stone Ridge.)[10] Meeting resistance, Vaughan retreated to New York, and Burgoyne was stopped at Saratoga County by Gen. Horatio Gates. Separate long engagements on September 19 and October 7 forced Burgoyne to surrender of his 6,000 surviving men on October 17 to a colonial army that had swelled to 20,000.

Victory at Saratoga was followed in June 1778 by the Battle of Monmouth in New Jersey, at which Washington forced Sir Henry Clinton's retreat. That longest one-day battle of the war was inconsequential and the last one between large armies in the north. Frontier skirmishes did continue that summer as Iroquois-Tory bands terrorized whites in north-central Pennsylvania. In a particularly brutal moment on June 10, twelve settlers were massacred at Lycoming Creek in today's Williamsport, where the Lycoming College **Warriors** dropped fifty-year-old Indian imagery in 2005. (Lycoming is a corruption of the Lenape phrase *Legaui-hanne* [sandy stream], but Lycoming's **Warriors** adopted a wolf mascot named *Lycos* in fall 2013 because *lycos* is a Greek "wolf.") Then Loyalists and Iroquois torched a thousand homes and methodically slaughtered dozens of captives in eastern Pennsylvania in July's Battle of Wyoming.

In mid-1779, Washington sent Gen. John Sullivan's army from the Wyoming Valley to the Finger Lakes with instructions that the Six Nations camps "not be merely overrun but destroyed." As Sullivan burned forty villages, braves in northwestern Pennsylvania rushed east to resist him, allowing Fort Pitt commander Daniel Brodhead to rip away at the lightly guarded heart of Seneca Nation. One skirmish disintegrated when Senecas lost their footing while pursuing Brodhead across a Pennsylvania stream north of Fort Pitt. Legend says Senecas thereafter called the place *Wechachochapohka*: "slippery rock." A town of that name is now the site of Slippery Rock University, where **Rockets** became the **Rock** in 2000.

• • •

In the late 1700s, European princes could still draft peasants into military service. With royal German ancestors, George III could raise troops from the Holy Roman states, especially through imperial cousins in Hesse-Cassel, so *Hessian* was indiscriminately applied to Germanic soldiers. The king's comfort with his Teutonic roots is evinced by his queen-consort, Charlotte of Mecklenburg-Strelitz, for whom Charlotte (in North Carolina's Mecklenburg County) was named in 1768. Queen City teams that pay their respects are the Queens University of Charlotte **Royals** and Charlotte's Carolina **Queens** (tackle football, est. 2005).

After the war, Hessian John Reed stayed in a German farming community near Charlotte. His yard became America's first gold mine in 1803. In 1946 the G.I. Bill funded the opening of North Carolina's Charlotte Center. (The night school for veterans would eventually field **Owls**.) Municipal leaders saved the institution after the state dropped its support in 1949. The renamed University of North Carolina at Charlotte (or "Charlotte") later chose to have **49ers** to commemorate the year of its survival, but there are obvious allusions to Reed's gold mine through UNCC's pickaxe emblem and "Gold Rush" homecoming week. North Carolina remained the biggest gold-producing state until being surpassed by California in 1849. In fact, having been established in 1946, San Francisco's NFL franchise had already made familiar the link between athletic **49ers** and gold-mining areas.

Unlike reluctant peasant draftees, European nobles actively sought military commands. When interviewed at Paris, a Baron Freidrich von Steuben oversold his Prussian army experience to American diplomat Ben Franklin, who recommended him to Washington. Steuben got command of the ragtag Continental Army at Valley Forge west of Philadelphia. Starting in February 1778, Steuben trained his troops hard and turned them into a disciplined army by spring. Within five miles of that camp are Phoenixville's University of Valley Forge **Patriots**.

• • •

By spring 1780, Gen. Clinton had taken the ports of Savannah and Charleston for the British, who wanted to capitalize on perceived Loyalist sympathies in the southern colonies. Returning to New York, Clinton left Lt. Gen. Charles Cornwallis to hold only that which had been gained. Charleston was the worst Patriot defeat of the war, making Gen. Francis Marion's guerrilla band the largest rebel force in South Carolina.

His ability to hide in backcountry bogs after hitting British lines got Marion called "Swamp Fox" by his English nemesis Lt. Col. Banastre Tarleton. Marion's South Carolina namesakes have included the Francis Marion University **Patriots** (Florence) and indoor football's Charleston **Swamp Foxes** (2000–03).

Marion could only harass the British, not expel them, so the Continentals sent Saratoga hero Gen. Horatio Gates into South Carolina. When he and Cornwallis met early on August 16 at Camden, the British regulars scared the wits out of the Virginia and Carolina militias. Those were soldiers by neither occupation nor inclination; they were just farmers with rifles who started sprinting before any serious fighting began. Nearly two thirds of the Patriot force turned tail in the Camden engagement, the rest being routed by the King's army. Gates's own person was seen fleeing the Camden field, so Washington replaced him with trusted West Point commander Maj. Gen. Nathanael Greene.

With momentum from Camden, Cornwallis moved up into North Carolina. Still expecting Loyalist support, he instead found Charlotte to be a "hornet's nest of rebellion." When his army decided to pillage a farm, a few armed farmers resisted, but it was a swarm of disturbed bees that put both sides into retreat. Minor league baseball's Charlotte **Hornets** (1901–73) and the WFL Charlotte **Hornets** (1974–75) were sporting reminders of both the Battle of the Bees and Cornwallis's comparison. NBA expansion created new Charlotte **Hornets** in 1988 and eventually the corresponding WNBA Charlotte **Sting** (1997–2006).[11] Lacking a new arena deal, the men moved to Louisiana as New Orleans **Hornets** in 2002. They became **Pelicans** after the 2012/13 season,[12] which allowed Charlotte's NBA-ers to reclaim "**Hornets**" for the 2014/15 campaign.

Virginian Thomas Sumter was a guerilla swamp fighter who won several Patriot victories in the fall 1780. Sumter's moxie earned him the nickname "Gamecock," the probable seed for **Gamecocks** at the University of South Carolina in Columbia (midway between Sumter National Forest and Sumter County).

Cornwallis still though he'd make it to British-held Pennsylvania. Greene sent Daniel Morgan's Patriot force to distract the British with swamp fox tactics, and Cornwallis diverted Tarleton's Tories to counter. Morgan's rifles had taken pot shots at the Redcoats to start things at Saratoga, but he abandoned his hit-and-run instincts to stake out a position in a pasture called Hannah's Cowpens. Knowing the British had seen the militia retreat at Camden, Morgan set a trap, telling his rifles to fire a couple of volleys at officers before withdrawing like scared marsh rabbits. In reality, they would fall back to join successive lines of concealed Continentals. On game day (January 17, 1781), the play ran just the way Morgan had chalked it up. Tarleton's boys jumped offside to chase the snipers but found themselves surrounded by regulars with cavalry support. Tarleton managed to escape, but his army surrendered within an hour, leaving 100 dead and 700 taken prisoner (compared to about a dozen Patriot fatalities). The contributions of South Carolina's Spartan Riles were remembered when the Cowpens field was renamed the Spartanburg District in 1785. The University of South Carolina–Spartanburg used to celebrate Morgan's false retreat with its **Runnin' Rifles**, but they became **Spartans** when the school was renamed USC Upstate in 2004.

• • •

After Cowpens, Cornwallis tried avoiding guerillas by traveling fast and light. Buying time for Greene and Morgan to regroup, Patriot officer William Lee Davidson was killed stalling Cornwallis at the Catawba River in February 1781. Of Scots-Irish heritage, the Davidson family quickly buried the general at a nearby Presbyterian church to prevent desecration of his body by the enemy. Davidson's namesakes include the nearby North Carolina town of Davidson and its Davidson College, which opened in 1837 on land from the general's son. Appreciating its Presbyterian backers, DC had **Presbyterians** and **Preachers**, but they scraped their way to enough football victories in 1917 to be called **Wildcats** in the sports pages.

In March, Greene conceded Guilford Courthouse in a costly victory for Cornwallis. Greensboro, North Carolina encompasses the battlefield. It's named after the general, as were minor league hockey's Greensboro **Generals** (1959–77 and

1999–2004). The spirit of Revolution was also celebrated by baseball's Greensboro **Patriots** (several franchises between 1911 and 1968) and indoor football's Greensboro **Revolution** (2006–07).

Cornwallis headed for Virginia's Yorktown Peninsula to dig in and wait for the Royal Navy to sail up from Charleston. Then he could resupply or evacuate by sea. Rather than forfeit tar supplies to the enemy, Patriot swamp fighters are said to have dumped it into eastern North Carolina's Tar River. The British boots that became gummy from crossing the Tar are sometimes cited in explaining UNC's **Tar Heels**, but scholars are skeptical.

• • •

After the stunning Saratoga victory, Paris-based Ben Franklin had persuaded France to aid in the war against their British foes. When France recognized an independent U.S. in February 1778, Franklin was the first U.S. diplomat on foreign soil. In fact, athletic **Diplomats** represent a college for which he is the co-eponym. Franklin and Marshall College (Lancaster, Pa.) was the result of the 1853 merger of two neighboring German Protestant institutions, Franklin College (endowed by Ben F. in 1787) and Marshall College, named at its 1836 founding for the Supreme Court's recently deceased chief justice, John Marshall.[13] Like Franklin, Judge Marshall was no diplomatic slouch, having been instrumental in both the rise of Federalism and some touchy international negotiations (notably the XYZ Affair).

At Yorktown, French officers took over the game. Rear Admiral De Grasse defeated the Royal Navy sailing north while Washington and French Generals Marquis de Lafayette and Count Rochambeau sealed off the peninsula. Cornwallis surrendered to Washington on October 19, 1781, ending hostilities.[14]

The Treaty of Paris wouldn't actually be signed for another two years, so only in late 1783 did Washington dismiss his troops at Somerset County. The general and his men had moved many times from encampments at Morristown, Princeton, Trenton, and Monmouth, which is why New Jersey says it's the Crossroads of the Revolution. After wintering at Morristown, the Continentals moved to the Middlebrook Encampment in Bridgewater Township in June 1777. The near-disaster at Valley Forge followed that winter, and troops returned to Middlebrook in late 1778. Just four miles north of there are the Atlantic League's Somerset **Patriots**.

All those armies traipsing around should have explained the USFL New Jersey **Generals** (1983–85). But New Jersey had been hosting New York's **Giants** since 1976 and **Jets** since '84 at its Meadowlands Sports Complex in East Rutherford and finally wanted a state-named team. So—*and we're not making this up*—the "New Jersey **Generals**" were vaguely historical by design. That is, *general*. In fact, the team's five-star insignia actively dismissed Revolutionary times because the Army had no such rank until World War II.[15]

• • •

Robert Morris was among the colonies' wealthiest men when he signed the Declaration of Independence and the Constitution. He was the business-minded Pennsylvania Quaker that kept the Continental Army solvent by borrowing from colonial merchants and Frenchmen (using his tobacco fortune to plug the gaps). Robert Morris University (Moon Township, Pa.) celebrates his patriotism with the *Minuteman* weekly news, *Patriot* yearbook, and athletic **Colonials**.

From 1781 to '84, Morris was the country's Superintendent of Finance, but the U.S. mint he'd suggested didn't open in Philadelphia until 1792. It's been putting the bald eagle on its biggest coins since 1795, so it is Morris's association with either the patriot spirit or the dollar bill—"the eagle"—that puts **Eagles** at a different Robert Morris University in Chicago. (The **Eagles** meet the **Colonials** from the other RMU only in hockey.)

With Robert Morris's encouragement, Senecas gathered at a massive riverside oak to sign away their land beyond the Genesee in the 1797 Treaty of Big Tree. The spot is now Geneseo, where SUNY Geneseo once fielded **Indians** or **Big Trees**,[16] which became **Blue Knights** in the 1950s. Morris transferred those lots to Dutch bankers in the Holland Land Company. The HLC office in Genesee County's new seat at Batavia (a Latin name for the Netherlands) profited from settlers that were anxious to till the fertile soil, which is the dirty little story behind minor league baseball's 1998-named Batavia **Muckdogs**. Morris was actually ruined by his Holland deals, spending four of his last eight years in debtor's prison.

• • •

Alexander Hamilton was Morris's hand-picked successor for the renamed office of Secretary of the Treasury. Hamilton was also a trustee and the eponym for an academy for white and Oneida children in Clinton, New York. He asked drill-master Baron von Steuben to lay the cornerstone for the school in 1794. Hamilton's time as chief of staff for Washington's Continental Army justifies **Continentals** at various Hamilton College venues, including the gridiron on Steuben Field.

Ohio Valley Indians were resistant to the former colonists' post-war expansion, so white forts went up to protect federal surveyors. Fort Steuben was built in 1786 and named for the aforementioned baron. Steubenville, Ohio still has **Barons** at the Franciscan University of Steubenville.

New York's Corning Community College has had **Barons** since the late 1960s. In part, those Steuben County athletes salute the same Gen. Steuben, but a more immediate influence was the Royal Guardsmen's huge 1966 novelty hit "Snoopy vs. the Red Baron," which detailed comic dogfights between cartoonist Charles Schulz's famous pooch and his imaginary flying nemesis.[17] Also named during the 1966/67 academic year were the **Barons** of Ohio State University at Lima, but our dogged pursuit of rumors could not verify that they too were named for Snoopy's nemesis.[18]

Mossbacks | Jubilees | Thunder | Carabins

Captain Robert Rogers's frontier regiment of New York and New England colonists countered Indian attacks in the Seven Years' War. Unlike British Redcoats, those Queen's Rangers had green uniforms for identification and camouflage. In many actions, Rogers's Rangers banded together with the Jersey Blues, the continent's oldest militia force (formed at Piscataway, New Jersey in 1673). "Blues" is proudly retained by a state National Guard unit and by blue-and-red **Jersey Blues** at Lincroft's Brookdale Community College.

To fight on Britain's side in the Revolution, Rogers reassembled the Queens Rangers from Loyalists in New Yorkers and Virginia. Unable to replicate earlier successes, he was replaced by Lt. Gen. John Graves Simcoe in 1777. Many of the Rangers would go north with other post-war Loyalists, and Simcoe himself was the first lieutenant-governor of Upper Canada (west of the Ottawa River and above the Great Lakes). He gave generous terms of settlement to Loyalists and veterans. In 1793, Rangers built Fort York at a spot the Mohawks and French called *Toronto*. That explains the **Rangers** that have played for generations at all levels in Ontario. Members of the Berlin-based Western Football Association acquitted themselves well on an 1888 tour of Britain. That Team Canada of soccer was well-stocked with Berlin **Rangers**, collected almost exclusively from graduates from Berlin High School's own **Rangers**. The current junior hockey Kitchener **Rangers** are coincidentally a farm club of the New York **Rangers**. (We'll soon return to Berlin and Kitchener.)

• • •

The Caribs that were native to north-coastal South America and the Lesser Antilles give name to the Caribbean Sea and **Caribs** at Nassau's College of the Bahamas. Some Caribs intermarried with marooned and escaped slaves and then emphatically resisted British rule, sometimes fighting black soldiers from neighboring islands who'd been lured into the empire's Loyal Black Rangers.

During the American Revolution, some Loyalist brought their slaves with them to Canada. Other slaves would be persuaded by Britain to fight that war for their own freedom, sometimes in (the unfortunately designated) "Lord Dunmore's Ethiopian Regiment." Black Loyalists later established towns in the Maritimes, joined after 1796 by black Maroons who were removed from Jamaica for resisting colonization. Black Canadians composed a "Coloured Corps" under former Senagalese slave Richard Pierpont (a member of Butler's Rangers during the Revolution). They fought on the Niagara Frontier in the War of 1812, the same war that saw many stateside slave families escape to British warships before making homes around Halifax.

Like Francophones, eastern Canada's persons of African descent were shut out of the early Anglo-Canadian hockey leagues. They created the Colored Hockey League, the dates for which are generally 1900 to 1920, but it was a less formal challenge circuit for a broader period. The CHL's Truro **Victorias**, Amherst **Royals**, and Halifax **Stanleys** (named for Governor General Frederick Stanley) were typically imperial, but a name that commemorated black soldiers belonged to the only CHLers outside Nova Scotia, the West End **Rangers** from the boggy west side of Charlottetown, P.E.I.

The CHL Hammonds Plains **Mossbacks** (West Halifax) knew that escapees on the Underground Railroad would have observed that moss grows on the damp (north) sides of trees and rocks. They kept the moss at their backs en route to a new life in Canada. (Escaping to the northern U.S. would have been insufficient after the 1850 Fugitive Slave Law required the return of all such property within U.S. borders.)

Greek mathematician Archimedes supposedly cried "Eureka!" ("Found it!") when he made deductions about volume by watching his body displace his bath water (c. 265 BCE). Miners yell the same when they make a strike. Nova Scotia has a long history of harvesting gold, coal, gypsum, salt, and building stones, so one might guess the CHL Halifax **Eurekas** were miners. But in their book about black Maritime hockey—*Black Ice*—authors George and Darril Fosty report that those teams were run by their community's black Baptist churches, with the Bible being consulted as a rule book; what Halifax's **Eurekas** had *found* was God.[1]

Across Halifax Harbor were the CHL Dartmouth **Jubilees**, noting biblical guidelines for freeing slaves in the year of jubilee, every fiftieth year. (White neighbors might have assumed they were respecting Queen Victoria's Golden Jubilee of 1887.)[2] The Seaview African Baptist Church was in Africville, the black Halifax neighborhood behind the CHL's turn-of-the-century Africville **Sea-Sides** and later the Africville **Brown Bombers** (1932–36).

• • •

The Revolution was a de facto civil war between Britain and its own colonies, so taking sides had been tough on everyone. Crown-friendly colonials who moved to Upper Canada before the "Treaty of Separation in the year 1783" were dubbed "United Empire Loyalists," the descendents of whom may stamp *U.E.L.* on personal effects. Quakers were particularly ambiguous because their doctrinal pacifism had been born of the English Civil Wars (p. 69), and many colonial Friends had family in Britain. Quakers and Mennonites were historically exempt from military service, and they refused to pay wartime taxes. In fact, the Pennsylvania Assembly's Quaker majority had resigned or refused to run again rather than support the colonial wars, leaving a new legislature to fine or imprison pacifists.

Most of Pennsylvania's "Peace Churches" managed to restructure allegiances for post-war life, but many went to Nova Scotia and Upper Canada at Simcoe's invitation. Some of Pennsylvania's isolationist Mennonites saw a chance to create a German farming community in Ontario's Grand River valley. Their "Dutch" (*Deutsche*) nickname followed them. In fact, Berlin **Dutchmen** played every season in the Ontario Professional Hockey League (1907–11), the first major pro circuit (in which five of seven teams were **Professionals** or **Pros**). Minor league hockey's Kitchener **Flying Dutchmen** (1928–30) were followed by senior Kitchener **Dutchmen** (1947–60), now a name for juniors. Minor league Kitchener-Waterloo **Dutchmen** skated for Canada at the 1956 and 1960 Olympics.[3]

You've probably noticed that German people and **Ranger** or **Dutchmen** teams congregate in Berlin and Kitchener. In fact, they're the same place. In September 1916, during the anti-German feeling of World War I, the town that Mennonites had named for Germany's greatest city was renamed for the 1st Earl of Kitchener, a British military hero who'd died that summer when his armored cruiser exploded after hitting mines dropped by German U-boats.

• • •

Mohawk leader *Thayendanegea* ("Joseph Brant" to whites) was educated by and connected to the British. Brant's irregular force in New York (Loyalist farmers and Iroquois) was shut down by the 1779 Sullivan Expedition, and he removed to British Canada after the war to be the steward of Brant's Ford on the Grand River (near Berlin), which later hosted pro hockey Brantford **Indians** (1907–11, 1929–30). The Grand River banks had been reserved for Iroquois allies who'd lost New York hunting grounds in the war, but Mennonite settlement occurred after Brant concluded that cash from the sale of those lots (through U.E.L. speculators) would better benefit Indians. East of Brantford is today's city of Hamilton, also settled by Loyalists in the post-war period. The dominant Iroquois tribe gives a name to its Mohawk College. Mohawk's decades-old "Mo the Hawk" mountain hawk represents **Mountaineers**, while **Hawks** at Mohawk Valley Community College (Rome, N.Y.) named their own flying mascot "Mo" in 2012.

Hamilton's Mohawk Sports Park hosted rugby's Niagara **Thunder** (2004–10). "Niagara" is from the Iroquois *ongiara*: "thundering water." From there it's sixty miles to Niagara County Community College's **Thunderwolves** (Sanborn, N.Y.). Junior hockey's Niagara Falls **Thunder** (1988–96) had the same problem of redundancy, but they've had other funky names. They were Hamilton/St. Catharines **Fincups** (1974–78), after owners with the surnames Finochio and Cupido. They were Brantford **Alexanders** until 1984, after Alexander Graham Bell, the famed inventor who lived in Brantford of the 1870s.

• • •

As suggested above by the Kitchener-Waterloo **Dutchmen**, the two Ontario cities are adjacent. Waterloo was named by Mennonites in 1916, the year after English and Russian armies handed Napoleon final defeat at the Battle of Waterloo in Belgium. The University of Waterloo seemed to subliminally commemorate that decisive battle with **Warriors** in 1960, but their mascots have always been of the classical variety.⁴

Bethel University (McKenzie, Tenn.) teams showed aggression in "battle" during the Great War era and got the nickname Napoleon's soldiers had given him, *le petit Caporal*. Bethel's (**Little**) **Corporals** became **Wildcats** some time after World War II.⁵ Those French armies had referred to battlefield surgeons bent on amputation as *les carabins*, "saw-bones." Quebec's *Université de Montréal* opened in 1878 to teach theology, law, and medicine, the latter leading to athletic **Carabins**.

Warhawks | Volunteers | Colonels | Blackhawks

George Rogers Clark captured several British posts (notably Forts Kaskaskia and Vincennes) and therefore the Old Northwest in the Revolution. After the war, however, a Western Confederacy of Indians south of the Great Lakes tried to stop the new country's trans-Ohio expansion. Having disbanded the Continental Army, President Washington sent in a big militia, which the Indians smashed in October 1790 near the largest Miami village, *Kekionga*.

Miami chief Little Turtle and Shawnee chief Blue Jacket would continue hassling militias over the next year, so the U.S.'s first standing army was entrusted to Gen. Anthony Wayne, who ended the Northwest Indian War at the 1794 Battle of Fallen Timbers. Little Turtle and Blue Jacket signed a treaty that surrendered much of the Ohio Country. Wayne then built Fort Wayne up the Maumee River from Kekionga, so Indiana's (redundant-sounding) NA Fort Wayne **Kekiongas** won the first-ever major league game against Cleveland's **Forest City** (May 4, 1871) but folded in mid-season.[1]

Wayne's recklessness in battle made him "Mad Anthony," as alluded to by the NBA D-league's Fort Wayne **Mad Ants** (est. 2007). The **Warriors** at that city's Indiana Institute of Technology once had Indian mascots but changed to Roman legionnaires in 2005.[2]

• • •

The Indiana Territory was cut out from the Northwest Territory in 1800 with the governorship going to Wayne's lieutenant (and future president) William Henry Harrison. He established a capital at Vincennes and named Indiana's pioneer college Jefferson Academy for his president. It was incorporated as Vincennes University in 1806 and now fields **Trailblazers**. Harrison's post was a key point of contact between Jefferson and an expedition led by a couple of Army captains named Meriwether Lewis and William Clark, which further informs "**Trailblazers**." In fact, Clark was the younger brother of the aforementioned George Rogers Clark, hero of the Battle of Vincennes.

Jefferson had tasked L&C's thirty-three–man Corps of Discovery to figure out what he'd gotten in the 1803 Louisiana Purchase by finding a navigable water route to the western ocean. On May 14, 1804, their three boats pushed off from St. Louis, which is barely south of Lewis & Clark Community College in Godfrey, Illinois. Its **Trailblazers** are only partly named after the trailblazing eponyms; Godfrey is also on the Goshen Trail, the main Indian road across southern Illinois.

Lewis and Clark stopped for three days in June at the confluence of the Missouri and Kaw Rivers, where Kansas City **Explorers** (est. 2000) play WTT tennis. Moving up the Missouri, Sgt. Charles Floyd became the only person on the treacherous trip to expire (probably from appendicitis). He's buried at Floyd's Bluff near modern Sioux City, home of Iowa's minor league Sioux City **Explorers** (est. 1993) at Lewis and Clark Park.

• • •

In their journals, Lewis and Clark noted many new animal species. On September 14, 1804, Clark made the first scientific observations of the white-tailed jack-rabbit (*Lepus townsendii*), mistaking it for the European hare (*Lepus europaeus*). That was in south-central South Dakota, a short hop west of the South Dakota State University **Jackrabbits** (named in 1907) in Brookings. Still in the area four days later, Clark scribbled that he'd finally "killed a prarie [*sic*] wolf" or coyote. Until then, the Corps had heard yelping but hadn't seen *Canis latrans* (barking dog), but the official state animal now inspires Vermillion's University of South Dakota **Coyotes**. More prairie wolves were spotted in October in modern Idaho. Caldwell's College of Idaho keeps **Coyotes**, owing some to the repeated sounds in "C-of-I **Coyotes**." A three-syllable approach is closest to *la pronunciación original del "coyote" en español*, but as you move north the *-e* becomes silent, as inferred from the "**Yotes**" alternate for **Coyotes** at either C-of-I or USD.

In late winter the Corps camped with the Mandans and Hidatsas in central North Dakota. Spring came, and the Indians pointed out large tracks, warning that the wilderness ahead had a huge beast prone to post-hibernation crankiness. When Lewis shot and killed a "brown or yellow bear" in April, white men got their first close inspection of a grizzly (*Ursus arctos horribilis*). They decided to be more cautious in subsequent encounters, the vast majority of which were in Montana, where the grizzly is now the state animal and the face of two programs. The **Bruins** that haunted Missoula's University of Montana officially became the **Grizzlies** in 1923. (The **Lady Griz** arrived later.) Rocky Mountain College in Billings has **Battlin' Bears** and **Lady Bears**.

The cruelest part of the journey was getting to Idaho from Montana by cros-sing the Bitterroot Mountains. Sliding down those slopes in fall 1805, the Corps was saved from starvation by Snake Valley natives who called themselves *Nimi-ipuu* (people). We know them by the exonym assigned earlier by French trappers who'd seen a few regional Indians put bones in their nostrils, thus *nez percé* (pierced nose). That wasn't actually something the Nez Perce did, but the Corps's French guides perpetuated the mistake. The seat of modern Idaho's Nez Perce County is Lewis's namesake, Lewiston, where Lewis-Clark State College drop-ped Indian motifs in 1969, struggling to find appropriate **Warrior** mascots since.[3] The Snake River (or the Lewis River) separates Lewiston from Clark's namesake city, Clarkston, Washington. Its Walla Walla Community College also supports mascot-less **Warriors**.

• • •

The Corps of Discovery never intended to settle permanently along their route, doing more *exploring* than *pioneering*. Near the Oregon end of their journey is Portland's Lewis & Clark College, where **Pioneers** recall the frontier Presbyteri-ans who founded the school in 1867, not the exploring duo. In fact, "**Pioneers**" was the top choice in a 1970 fan poll for Portland's new NBA team, but that was canceled to avoid confusion with the city's LCC **Pioneers**. "Portland **Trail Blazers**" was instead favored to remember all trail guides to and within the Oregon Country.

Across the Columbia from Portland is Vancouver, Washington, the seat of Clark County and home of Clark College (both named for Clark), but there is no team name linked to the great journey. In the early 1930s, Kool cigarettes started using one of the first cartoon mascots to push product, a classy penguin named Willie. Somebody put up a Willie poster and cut a hole through his mouth and right into the wall so he could hold a butt. The smoking penguin soon brought about Clark's **Penguins**.[4]

Lewis and Clark's trip lasted until September 1806, starting and ending near the city at which the French had signed over Louisiana in 1804. The centennial celebration in 1904 was the St. Louis World's Fair. Its amusement strip—the "Pike"—ran through the city's Washington University. Jocks were once **Pikers**. That can describe stingy gamblers, so a 1925 student vote made them **Bears**.

• • •

The Shawnee warrior Tecumseh had refused to sign the 1795 treaty after the Battle of Fallen Timbers because he thought it was a few more yards gained on the ground toward the taking of all Indian lands (skepticism that seemed to be verified by the 1803 Louisiana Purchase). Trying to solidify some resistance among native peoples from the Great Lakes to the Gulf Coast, Tecumseh returned from an Alabama recruiting trip in January 1812 to learn that Harrison had overrun his brother in November's Battle of Tippecanoe. This allowed Gen. Isaac Brock (the military commander of Upper Canada) to win Tecumseh over by promising the Indians stewardship of their tribal lands after British victory came in some future war.

The War of 1812 did unfold, with origins all tangled up in the wars between Britain and Napoleon's France, along with a web of global maritime restrictions that had taken effect after 1800. The U.S. tried to stay neutral but took exception when Britain blocked American ships from French ports and boarded them to impress defectors into the Royal Navy. (Some royal sailors had indeed jumped to higher paying American ships, but they were rarely those accused.)

Frontier Congressmen who feared that British Canada wanted some of the Northwest Territory argued for taking Canada preemptively. (An attack on Britain was simply impractical.) The Senate's most famous "War Hawks" were Henry Clay of Kentucky and John C. Calhoun of South Carolina, the latter of whom is recalled by the Calhoun Community College **Warhawks** (Decatur, Ala.). President James Madison declared war in June 1812, and Gen. William Hull crossed from Fort Detroit to Canada in July. That left other positions unprotected and Indian warriors aided British victories at Fort Michilimackinac and Fort Dearborn (now Chicago). Hull retreated to Detroit but surrendered to Tecumseh and Brock on August 16.

Directed by Stephen Van Rensselaer III (the future founder of RPI, p. 54), one militia crossed the Niagara River to Ontario in October to attack British batteries at Queenston Heights. General Brock was brazenly leading a counterattack when he was felled, expiring only after telling his men to keep charging. In fact, *Surgite!* (Push on!) was his supposed last command and the Latin motto at Brock University in nearby St. Catharines. Brock's **Badgers** might seem only alliterative, but *brock* is actually a chiefly British alternate to *badger*.[5]

• • •

In 1812 the British had 800 ships. The Yanks had 50. So Congress hired privateers to target British ships and slip blockades. Their vessels were nimble schooners and packet ships built on Chesapeake Bay that had been historically favored
by slave traders and smugglers. "Baltimore clippers" harassed enough commercial vessels to force the Brits to waste warships on escort duties. Basketball had
the ABL Baltimore **Clippers** (1939–41), but from 1946 to 1981 there were Baltimore **Clippers** in every minor hockey league you can name,[6] followed in that
sport by Baltimore **Skipjacks** (1981–93). In fact, the oyster harvester's shallow-
draft sailboat is actually Maryland's state boat, as commemorated by Chesapeake
College's **Skipjacks** in Wy Mills. (The past name for the University of Maryland,
Baltimore County yearbook is the *Skipjack*.)

The Creeks (Muscogees) of the Southeast fought on all sides in 1812, having
been stuck between British, American, and Spanish forces and fractured by civil
wars over their own changing traditions. Small skirmishes between British-armed
Creeks and U.S. militias escalated to the massacre of 500 Americans and mixed-
blood Creeks at Fort Mims (north of Mobile Bay) in July 1813. Tennessee governor Willie G. Blount's call for militias to wreak vengeance was met with an
overwhelming response. Tennesseans have served willingly in every war, but this
moment most informs the state nickname (although "Volunteer State" wouldn't
be so expressed until the Mexican-American War). Back in 1794, the legislature
of the Southwest Territory (now Tennessee) had chartered Knoxville's Blount
College, named for sitting territorial governor, William Blount. He's Willie G.'s
older half-brother, but it's the younger man's call to arms that ultimately put
Volunteers and **Lady Vols** at the school into which Blount College evolved, the
University of Tennessee.[7]

The U.S. took control of Lake Erie in September 1813. Weeks later, Harrison
won the Battle of the Thames in southwest Ontario. Both Tecumseh and his
dream of Indian solidarity died that day, and he's naturally more revered in
Canada than the States (especially in Ontario's Loyalist communities). The town
of Tecumseh hosted junior hockey **Chiefs** (2001–08), and London **Tecumsehs**
have appeared in various sports for a century.

Principle to the Thames victory were thousands of volunteer Kentuckians
under Gov. Isaac Shelby, who made every man in his command an honorary
Colonel of Kentucky. In 1819, Shelby was the first chairman of Danville's Centre
College. Word leaked in 1917 that Centre's football **Colonels** were invoking
spiritual aid before games, being **Praying Colonels** thereafter.

By then, honorary colonels were common in Kentucky, serving first as
governor-appointed ceremonial guards and then good-will ambassadors. Athletic
Colonels represent Richmond's Eastern Kentucky University, and Louisville
hosted the ABA Kentucky **Colonels** (1967–78). The name of the major league
Louisville **Colonels** (AA, 1885–91; NL, 1892–99) was copied by numerous
minor leaguers and blackball's **Black Colonels**. Theoretically, the NFL Louisville
Colonels (1926) were a revived version of Louisville **Brecks**, but they played all
games on the road from their base at Chicago.[8]

Ceremonial colonelcies are so strongly associated with Southern culture that Curry College in Milton, Massachusetts has **Colonels** simply because eponym Samuel Silas Curry was from Tennessee.[9]

• • •

After the loss at the Thames, Quebecers prepared for invasion by volunteering for light militias called *voltigeurs* (riflemen). Those French-Canadians and their Mohawk cohorts were instrumental in turning back American advances in the fall of 1813, service recognized by a modern regiment (*Les Voltigeurs de Québec*, est. 1862) and junior hockey's *Voltigeurs de Drummondville* (est. 1982).

Because Britain and Spain were Napoleon-era allies, the U.S. feared the Brits would establish ports in Spanish Florida. Georgia militias invaded Florida several times in that Patriot War, even building Fort Mitchell in the Ocala Forest as the capital of a Republic of East Florida in early 1814. The Patriot cause was abandoned when Seminoles killed the post commander in May, but **Patriots** replaced **Rebels** at Ocala's College of Central Florida in 1969.

The British methodically attacked the seaboard in 1814. Burning Washington, D.C. was but a sidebar in the ultimate plan to destroy the "pirate's nest" of Baltimore clippers. That required sailing right past Fort McHenry's guns, so the British started a twenty-five-hour bombardment early on September 13. By the light of dawn, the American flag signaled that the fort had held. Lawyer Francis Scott Key watched the attack from a British warship while negotiating a prisoner release. His quickly scribbled lyrics to an old English drinking song (*yup!*) appeared in a Baltimore newspaper. You'll hear it if you get to the game on time; "The Star-Spangled Banner" became the National Anthem in 1931. Key's tune inspired the WTT Baltimore **Banners** (1974), but we can't attribute the name of the 1985 USFL Baltimore **Stars** to broad stripes and such; they'd already been Philadelphia **Stars** for two seasons. But Key's Maryland hometown has hosted minor league baseball's Frederick **Keys** since 1989, and "rockets' red glare [and] bombs bursting in air" inspired Charm City lacrosse teams, the MISL Baltimore **Blast** (1980–92, 1998–) and NLL Baltimore **Thunder** (1987–99).[10] The Atlanta **Braves'** Homer the **Brave** is a baseball-headed mascot that alludes to the phrase that concludes each of Key's verses, "home of the brave."

In late summer 1814, Sir John Coape Sherbrooke took Maine's Penobscot River valley and held it for Britain through the war. Customs fees collected during the occupation were used to start Halifax's Dalhousie University when they returned to Nova Scotia. Dal's **Tigers** were named arbitrarily, but *Volontaires* (volunteers) at *Cégep de Sherbrooke* (Sherbrooke, Que.) do remember Lt. Gen. Sherbrooke's men.

A decisive battle usually comes at the end of a war, but news was so slow that the War of 1812's largest battle happened on January 8, 1815—*after* the Treaty of Ghent was signed. Andrew Jackson's overtime victory at the Battle of New Orleans was impressive but changed nothing in the *status quo ante bellum* treaty. The Jacksons in Mississippi and Tennessee were named for the general in 1821 and '22 respectively, and both have had Jackson **Generals** in minor league baseball (Mississippi: 1991–99; Tennessee: 1935–54; 2012–).

Because Isaac Brock and *les voltigeurs* rebuffed several invasions, Canadians claim victory in the War of 1812. Even so, by beating the point spread against the British Empire, America announced itself as a player of value.

> Like many stateside 1812 veterans, Benjamin Crowley was given land across the Mississippi in 1821. The Crowleys were among the first of many Kentucky-bred families that would move to the Arkansas ridge. Ben is buried in the Shilo Cemetery (affectionately the "pioneer cemetery") at Crowley's Ridge State Park, six miles west of the Crowley's Ridge College **Pioneers** in Paragould.

• • •

The Sauk war chief *Makataimeshekiakiak* (Black Hawk) was a British ally in the War of 1812. After losing an 1814 battle to the chief, Maj. Zachary Taylor built Fort Johnson on the Mississippi River. It was quickly abandoned, but the Federals erected a nearby trading post called Fort Edwards (present-day Warsaw, Illinois). In 1822 the improvement of the thirty-five-mile road from the fort to Quincy fell on frontiersman John Wood, a later Illinois governor (1860–61) and eponym for Quincy's John Wood Community College, where **Trail Blazers** salute his path-finding acumen. Because posts like Edwards cut the Sauk off from their fall hunting grounds, Black Hawk remained a problem. His Sauk-Fox-Kickapoo confederacy was fighting Illinois militias by May 1832, but Gen. Winfield Scott's army ended the Black Hawk War in August. It was the last native resistance in Illinois, Iowa, and Wisconsin, and the Indians gave up the Mississippi-side Black Hawk Purchase (eastern Iowa). Its Southeastern Community College's West Burlington campus retained "**Blackhawks**" in 2002 while moving from Native American imagery to dark-colored raptors—that is, *black hawks*.[11]

The 1825 opening of the Erie Canal and 1832 end to the Black Hawk War synergistically increased white settlement in Illinois, and the NHL Chicago **Blackhawks** are indirectly named after the chief whose very defeat spurred the rapid growth of their Second City. Chicagoan Frederic McLaughlin had been a Great War major in the 86th Blackhawk division, named after *Makataimesheki-akiak*. In 1926 he used his family coffee fortune to buy the Portland **Rosebuds** of the dying PCHA,[12] quickly naming them Chicago **Black Hawks** after that fighting unit. In 1986 the one-word form—"**Blackhawks**"—was adopted.[13] Like SSC, the team unveiled a black bird mascot (Tommy Hawk) in 2000.

The NBL/NBA Tri-Cities **Blackhawks** (Moline, Ill., 1946–51) were in former Sauk territory. They've since been Milwaukee **Hawks** (1951–55), St. Louis **Hawks** (1955–68), and Atlanta **Hawks**. The Tri-Cities (Moline, Davenport, Iowa, and Rock Island, Ill.) have been the Quad Cities since Bettendorff, Iowa became a manufacturing center after World War II, putting **Braves** at Black Hawk College–Quad Cities. Its sister school in Kewanee, BHC-East, has (mascotless) **Warriors**.

Illinois's McHenry County is named after Black Hawk War veteran Maj. William McHenry, a pioneer whose surname reveals his Scots-Irish roots. McHenry County College in Crystal Lake presents **Fighting Scots**.

Privateers | Buccaneers | Corsairs | Leathernecks

Piracy has caused problems since ancient times. Water thieves on the high seas go by a variety of names, and there are loads of waterfront **Privateer**, **Buccaneer**, **Pirate**, or **Corsair** crews. Those terms are often interchanged, so we're determined to appreciate them in their distinct geohistorical contexts, but be aware that your favored side might not have been so etymologically judicious.

• • •

A sailing privateer contracts his services to one political power or another in wartime. With a broadly written commission, privateers target the ships of their sponsors' enemies then split the booty with the government of record.

With ports from Florida to Mexico, Spain's galleons sailed away with sugar, rum, cocoa, gold, silver, and gems from the conquered Aztecs and Incas while bringing back African slaves. Those "treasure ships" tempted Dutch, French, and (especially) English privateers. When European wars ended, non-uniformed naval combatants often had trouble adapting their plunder-specific skill set to polite society. Privateers were then likely to swashbuckle toward their own benefit, completing the transition to pirates.

In 1493 the Vatican gave the West Indies to Spain, but trespassing French and English hunters kept tracking down feral cattle in northern Hispaniola to supply hides and tallow to Dutch traders. Their base was Tortuga, an inhospitable isle Spain had ignored, and these confirmed rogues and ruffians inevitably targeted Spanish vessels. Tortuga's raiders had seen the region's native Arawaks roast goats over open coal pits on wooden racks called *bukans* (or *boucans*).[1] European *buccaneers* applied that method to beef and pork, cooking "from the beard to the tail" (*de la barbe à la queue*, "barbecue"). On the nearby island of St. Thomas, **Buccaneers** and **Lady Bucs** represent the University of the Virgin Islands.

Being a Spanish sailor, José Gaspar was an unlikely buccaneer, but he seized a Spanish vessel in 1783 and became a real threat to other Spanish captains. There's no record of "Gasparilla" until around 1900, and much of his story steers a little too conveniently toward the origins for west Florida place names. Nonetheless, the mutinous buccaneer has been honored since 1904 by Tampa's biggest annual party, the Gasparilla Pirate Festival. He's also the influence for the MLS Tampa Bay **Mutiny** (1996–2001) and NFL Tampa Bay **Buccaneers** (est. 1976).

Elsewhere along Florida's Gulf Coast, Edison State College (Fort Myers) became Florida SouthWestern State College in mid-2014, saying its **Buccaneers** (1963–97) would be relaunched in fall 2015. Spain's colonial port at Pensacola was oft-targeted by English rovers, putting **Pirates** at Pensacola State College.

Buccaneers could have represented the Tampa Bay **Bandits** (USFL, 1983–85), but their mascot was a cowboy outlaw. Robbers of just such countenance were known to steal cattle from west Florida pioneers. Former FSU halfback and ridiculously famous movie star Burt Reynolds was a team co-owner still riding high on *Smokey and the Bandit* (the most successful film of 1977 after *Star Wars*, it was), giving impetus to "**Bandits**."

The logotype for the NASL Tampa Bay **Rowdies** is in a Victorian style (technically an Antique or Gothic variation of the Tuscan typeface) that's associated with the signage and "WANTED" posters of the Wild West.

• • •

Jean Lafitte attacked Spanish galleons from bases in Louisiana's Barataria Bay. Lafitte claimed that his corsair license from Cartagena made him a privateer, but that was a weak argument because Colombia enjoyed neither independence from Spain nor international recognition. Lafitte and his brother Pierre delivered smuggled goods and slaves to eager customers in New Orleans. In fact, "Lafitte" is the alligator mascot for **Privateers** at the University of New Orleans. The city also hosted ABA New Orleans **Buccaneers** (1967–70). Moving north, minor league baseballers (1904–10) and CFLers (1994–95) in Louisiana have both been Shreveport **Pirates**.

After Lafitte assisted Andrew Jackson at the Battle of New Orleans, President Madison pardoned his band of sailors, but Lafitte resumed raids from Galveston Island (then in New Spain) in 1817.[2] His slave trading took on new importance, often run out of the port of Lake Charles (home of indoor football's Louisiana **Swashbucklers** since 2005). Spain ceded Florida to the U.S. in February 1819, and President Monroe's State of the Union address that December promised a global crackdown on the "spirit of piracy." The Navy thus chased Lafitte from Galveston to obscurity in 1821.

That same mop-up operation forced the pirate Henri "Black" Caesar from behind the barrier islands of Florida's Biscayne Bay and into permanent hiding. Of mixed blood, Caesar may have turned pirate after the 1804 slave revolt in his native Haiti (although his biography is largely tied to the unsustainable Gaspar legend). A different "Black Caesar" from a century earlier—an escaped slave—was a rover of that same bay. Either Black Caesar or any of the scores of plunderers along that coast inspire Barry University's **Buccaneers** and **Lady Bucs** in Miami Shores.

• • •

Suffering a mid-life crisis, Barbados planter Stede Bonnet left a comfy life for the thrill of piracy in 1717. The "Gentleman Pirate" immediately violated the pirate code by *paying for* his flagship. His sometime partner was Blackbeard, an ex-privateer for Queen Anne who used Bonnet's ship in a blockade of Charleston Harbor, holding the city for a week until he got "a chest of medicines" as ransom (even though colonial Charlestonites had often welcomed Spanish gold with few questions asked). The South Carolina authorities apprehended Bonnet and hanged him in Charleston in December 1718, part of the freebooting history that keeps **Buccaneers** on deck at Charleston Southern University.

Blackbeard too was feeling the heat and maintained hideouts among the Outer Banks, where Pamlico Sound's shallow waters afforded protection from naval squadrons. Virginia's colonial governor got fed up watching Blackbeard get a free pass from authorities in North Carolina. From Hampton, he dispatched shallow-draft sloops that tracked down Blackbeard and killed him near Ocracoke Island (three weeks before Bonnet's execution). The villain's hairy head was brought back and displayed as a warning, but would-be sea spoilers are plainly visible at Hampton's annual Blackbeard Festival or its seaside Hampton University, where **Seasiders** became **Pirates** in 1933. Up the Tar River from Pamlico Sound is East Carolina University (Greenville, N.C.), whose **Pirates** date to its days as a teachers' college in the 1930s. That black-bearded **Pirates** replaced ECU's **Teachers** is more than apt; Blackbeard's real name was Edward Teach.[3]

• • •

Fifty miles north of Georgia's Blackbeard Island is the state's largest port, where one Captain Flint "died of rum at Savannah." The fictional Mr. Flint's lost loot was coveted by every character in Robert Louis Stevenson's *Treasure Island*, so Savannah still hosts **Pirates** at Armstrong State University. The 1883 novel set the template for romantic piracy by standardizing peg-legged captains, shoulder-perched parrots, X-marked spots, and shivered timbers ... so blame Stevenson when half the people at your Halloween party have the same costume or when the mascots for **Pirates**, **Privateers**, **Marauders**, and **Raiders** are indistinguishable. When such buccaneering images—or "buccaneer" itself—show up in places other than the Caribbean or coastal Southeast, they're out of home waters.

Stevenson's English pirates threatened to haul each other over the keel, but *kielhalen* was actually a Dutch practice of towing a sailor from port to starboard along the barnacle-encrusted hull. The brutal punishment was rarely used by Brits, so it's Stevenson again who makes keelhauling typical of piratic melo-drama. The California Maritime Academy **Keelhaulers** in Vallejo indicate that students that hold acquaintance with the waves are pulled toward pirate imagery.[4] Other examples include the Massachusetts Maritime Academy **Buccaneers** on Buzzards Bay and the SUNY Maritime College **Privateers** in the Bronx. Some sailing academies have less menacing imagery, but there's almost always a nautical theme. All hands are **Mariners** at Maine Maritime Academy (Castine) and the United States Merchant Marine Academy (King's Point, N.Y.).

His notes reveal that Stevenson's book was inspired by California's northern coast, which the Scotsman first saw after following an American lady there from France. They spent their 1880 honeymoon in a nearby wilderness (Robert Louis Stevenson State Park) and the 1934 movie version of *Treasure Island* was shot on those shores. If you take the Bay Bridge from Oakland, you can look down on a Treasure Island in San Francisco Bay, an artificial isle created in 1939. The bridge dumps you off near Frisco's old Barbary Coast, which in Gold Rush days was the place to find gamblers, prostitutes, and hoodlums. The name of the neighborhood was a comparison to the unrestrained behavior of North Africa's Barbary pirates. (We'll get to them.) The buccaneer-themed AFL/NFL Oakland **Raiders** (est. 1960) conform to these Bay Area landmarks, even in the absence of a local pirate history.[5] Orange Coast College in Costa Mesa and Palo Verde College in Blythe are two-year schools with California **Pirates**, as are Ventura College and Porterville College (in their eponymous cities). Students at the Golden State's Modesto Junior College had been slogging through the mud of late winter in 1927 when they accepted the suggestion in on the editorial page that "**Pirates**" could be appropriately applied to teams if fans considered the "marine condition of the campus."[6]

• • •

The Milwaukee School of Engineering's **Engineers** were **Pats** by the 1980s (after St. Patrick, the Patron saint of engineers).[7] For a 1982 photo, MSOE's hoop team dressed up as Dr. Henry Walton "Indiana" Jones from Steven Spielberg's 1981 film *Raiders of the Lost Ark*. Teams were soon **Raiders**, but switched to buccaneer iconography in 1993.[8]

With a similar plan, the mascot for **Raiders** Michigan's Grand Rapids Community College was once a soldier from the Civil War era. (Michiganders well-removed from those battlefields nonetheless served the Union in admirable numbers.) In 2001, GRCC went with a cartoon raccoon named Raider because masked coons are "night raiders," but his tomb raiders' clothing and fedora hat make comparisons to Indiana Jones inescapable.

• • •

Corsairs in Coastal California are at Santa Monica College and Eureka's College of the Redwoods. *Corsaire* is French for "pirate." It came to English via the Ottoman Empire's Muslim rovers. Those North African corsairs had attacked European ships since the Crusades and were still at it when thirteen colonies banded together as the young United States. With no navy of consequence and with individual new states unable to afford their own squadrons, the U.S. paid Barbary States millions in "protection money" for its merchant ships.

Corsairs at the University of Massachusetts–Dartmouth are validated by a campus on Buzzards Bay, but they're actually named after a different maritime marauder. Having flown the Navy's Vought F4U *Corsair* fighter in the Pacific during World War II, school president Joseph Driscoll shot down his student's election of "**Vikings**" (another ocean-themed name) in the 1960s. This was the beginning of Driscoll's troubles, as he soon clashed with students and faculty opposed to the Vietnam War. He resigned in 1971 after altercations with the university's board,[9] but **Corsairs** remain, their backstory obscured by pirate mascots.

• • •

The Articles of Confederation that were ratified in 1781 didn't allow Congress to raise taxes for a national defense.[10] Those who wanted to bend the Articles toward a stronger central government were called the Federalists. Attempts to amend the Articles at Philadelphia evolved into a total rewrite that effected a new Constitution that was adopted by Congress in fall 1787. Arguing for its subsequent ratification were *The Federalist Papers*, eighty-five columns in New York papers in 1787 and '88. The anonymous authors were James Madison (the "Father of the Constitution"), Alexander Hamilton (of Washington's wartime staff), and John Jay (Washington's Secretary of State). The required ninth state ratified the Constitution in mid-1788, and the first Congress on its terms sat at New York in March 1789. Pressure from Southerners moved it back to Philly the next year with an agreement to create "Federal City" on the Potomac. The site was instead called Washington D.C., where Washington **Federals** played two USFL seasons (1983, 1984).

Federalism's big shots were well rewarded. Future president Madison sat for Virginia in the House of Representatives. (It and the Senate composed the new Constitution's bicameral legislature.) President Washington made Hamilton the

first Secretary of the Treasury and picked Jay as the Chief Justice for the top—
"Supreme"—court of the new federal judiciary.

Jay is the eponym of New York City's John Jay College of Criminal Justice,
where **Bloodhounds** are as relentless as those canines that hunt down offenders
by their scents. Brooklyn's Jay Street—another John Jay namesake—is where the
Fighting Blue Jays represented the Polytechnic Institute of New York. New
York University absorbed Poly in 2008 and replaced its blue and gray with purple
and green (closer to NYU's violet and white),[11] but NYU-Poly's **Jays** have
understandably maintained their blue duds.

The federal powers of the Constitution let Congress build a navy, so at the
outbreak of the First Barbary War in 1801, U.S. Navy captains—especially
Stephen Decatur—had success against North African pirates. American Marines
led a mercenary army from Egypt into the Battle of Derna and forced the Muslim
Pasha's surrender. Decatur also served in the War of 1812, a conflict that so preoccupied the U.S. that African rovers were able to resume raiding unchecked.
When the war ended in 1815, a Second Barbary War erupted, one in which
Decatur helped end the corsair threat for good. During either Barbary War,
Decatur's vessel would have flown the large blue ensign of a commodore, or flag
officer. (Commodore wasn't an official rank until the Civil War, but a naval
squadron's commander had historically assumed that role.) Decatur, Illinois was
named for the captain three years after his 1820 dueling death, and his pennant
color was chosen to represent the city's new Millikin University in 1903, setting
the tone for MU's **Big Blue**.[12]

That 1805 Battle of Derna on the shores of Tripoli was a defining moment for
the U.S. Marines. Having already sported high stock collars for decades (either to
keep heads upright or to provide light armor in close combat), it wasn't until the
early Barbary Wars that other sailors started calling Marines "leathernecks." In
1926 former Marine colonel Ray "Rock" Hanson arrived in Macomb to become
the athletic director and multi-sport coach of the Western Illinois University
Fighting Teachers. The Navy let Hanson apply "**Leathernecks**" and the associated bulldog symbol to his teams because he'd been decorated for his own Great
War service.[13] Western's women were the **Westerwinds**, but they too were
Leathernecks by 2009.

• • •

Pizza millionaire, committed Catholic, and former Detroit **Tigers** owner Tom
Monaghan founded Ave Maria University at Naples, Florida in 2003. He cited his
own Marine experience of the 1950s when he grafted Corps imagery onto school
teams. Like Western Illinois's **Leathernecks**, AMU uses the Marine bulldog, in
this case to represent **Gyrenes** jocks. After World War I, Navy sailors started
comparing their own Marine infantrymen to the Army's G.I.s. This gave the
Leathernecks another nickname: "G.I.-rines" or "Gyrenes."

Jayhawks | Bluejays | Ichabods | Scouts

The University of Missouri **Tigers** and University of Kansas **Jayhawks** are three hours apart on I-70, but their team names share in a bloody regional history.

• • •

Believing that any new federal compact would give states with large populations proportionate representation, tiny Rhode Island skipped a 1787 Philadelphia convention. Six pro-slavery states and six against created the new Constitution's bicameral legislature, which did award population-based numbers of seats in its House of Representatives. But every state got two seats in the Senate, where Southerners killed all antislavery bills with tie votes. New states were admitted thereafter in balanced pairs for and against slavery. Folks in the two states created by the 1854 Kansas-Nebraska Act, however, would determine their own slave-holding status through popular vote. It was a given that the more northern of the two, Nebraska, would go slave-free, so it all came down to Kansas.

Folks immediately started crossing the Missouri River from Council Bluffs, Iowa. A July 4 picnic on one river bluff (now Capitol Hill) celebrated the opening of the Nebraska Territory and the founding of Omaha. Edward and John Creighton were successful telegraph men with ambitions for the region. Edward and his wife died, leaving brother John to run their endowment for the hilltop's college. Creighton University's blue-and-white **Hilltoppers** became **Bluejays** in 1924.

The Massachusetts Emigrant Aid Company settled many Yankee abolitionists in Kansas to vote down slavery, but they couldn't outnumber the slave-holding Missourians who slipped over the border to vote fraudulently. That's why abolitionists called the pro-slavery representatives elected in 1855 the "Bogus Legislature." The first new Kansas town incorporated by that body was Olathe in 1857, explaining the **Pioneers** at its MidAmerica Nazarene University.

In 1855 abolitionists and "free soilers" (farmers opposed to the plantation system) created their own Kansas legislature at Topeka. When an antislavery settlement at Lawrence was destroyed by Missouri "border ruffians" the next year there were few injuries, but a counter-raid by abolitionist zealot John Brown killed five Missourians. Border battles between Kansas "Jayhawkers" and Missouri "Bushwhackers" ended only when the admission of two free states—Minnesota and Oregon in 1858 and '59—broke the Senate balance.

Years of guerilla warfare in "Bleeding Kansas" created many outlaw gangs, and the Civil War would re-ignite old feelings, with Bushwhackers raiding abolitionist and Union compounds. Infamous Bushwhackers included Bloody Bill Anderson and Confederate army captain William Quantrill. (In 1862, Quantrill sacked Olathe, which was already tilted toward antislavery sympathies.) On the Union side, the 7th Kansas Cavalry—Colonel Jennison's Jayhawkers—used its military cover to attack Missourians with Southern sympathies.

The college town of Columbia remained a pocket of Union sentiment within Missouri. When Columbians heard that Anderson was in the area, they fortified their defenses. The Bushwhackers never showed up, perhaps having received report of the "Missouri tigers" in Columbia's militias. They've been remembered by **Tigers** at its University of Missouri since 1892.[1] One mile north is Columbia College "of Missouri," where **Cougars** ensure distinction from the **Tigers** at MU and the **Lions** at the Columbia University in New York … both institutions that had previously been named "Columbia College."

Massachusetts textiler Amos A. Lawrence was a major backer of the Emigrant Aid Company.[2] He's the eponym of Lawrence, Kansas, where University of Kansas teams are **Jayhawks**. Imaginary jayhawks combine two birds common to North America; the blue jay (*Cyanocitta cristata*) is adamantly territorial while the sparrow hawk (*Accipiter nisus*) is a small but effective hunter.

> It's not known whether the blue-and-gold **Bluejays** at Tabor College in Hillsboro, Kansas meant to emphasize the *jay-* from *jayhawk*. In Fayette, Missouri, an eagle that fought off a party of blue jays in 1914 was nursed back to health by students to be the mascot at the school that's now Central Methodist University.[3] That fall, Central handed a 53–0 loss to some intrastate rivals, the Westminster College **Blue Jays** (p. 68). CMU's footballers were **Eagles** thereafter.[4]

Another Massachusetts industrialist was a deacon and a passionate abolitionist. In 1868, Worcester's steel-wire magnate Ichabod Washburn made a gift to Lincoln College, a Topeka school for newly arrived New Englanders. Washburn died that same year effecting its renaming to Washburn University. Athletes came to be **Ichabods**. (The women had been **Lady Blues** until the 2013/14 school year because WU had taken its blue and white from Mr. Washburn's fellow Congregationalists at Yale.)

• • •

William A. Lewis crossed the border in 1913, leaving a teaching position at North Missouri Normal School (now Truman State) for the presidency of a normal school in Hays, Kansas. The stadium for the Fort Hays State University **Fighting Tigers** is Lewis Field, named for the guy believed to have mapped the name and colors of U. Missouri's black-and-gold **Tigers** onto FHSU's **Normals**.[5] In 1923, former Mizzou basketball star Dan Stark also went to Kansas to coach for two decades at Cowley College. Stark also named his players **Tigers** after his alma mater and gave them colors of orange and black.[6]

A new seat for Franklin County, Missouri was chosen in 1825. The town was named Union, to suggest a union of centralized county responsibilities. Nonetheless, athletes at the town's East Central College enjoyed a bit of irony as "Union **Rebels**" for decades, becoming **Falcons** in 2008.

Just over the Missouri River from Kansas, minor league hockey's Kansas City **Mohawks** got named by adding their state abbreviation (Mo.) to the back half of Kansas's "Jayhawks." A 1974 NHL expansion team were also to be **Mohawks**, but Chicago's **Blackhawks** protested the similarity. (A more informed objection might have been that Mohawks of the eastern Great Lakes have no history in the Midwest.) The new players were instead Kansas City **Scouts**, after Cyrus Dallin's sculpture of a mounted Sioux scout, which had been unveiled in the city's Penn Valley Park in 1915. (The **Scouts** were later Colorado **Rockies** and New Jersey **Devils**.) The statue is also only a half-mile from **Scouts** at the city's Metropolitan Community College–Penn Valley.

Blue Boys | Blue Jackets | Bullets | Presidents

The 1820 Missouri Compromise banned new slave territories above Missouri's southern border, but that was traded away in 1854 by Sen. Stephen Douglas, who supported the Kansas-Nebraska Act to buy Southern backing of a new transcontinental railway that would run west from his state's biggest city, Chicago.

For potentially expanding slavery, Douglas—a Democrat—motivated some northerners to form the antislavery Republican party. Its rising star was former Whig Congressman Abraham Lincoln, who argued seven debates against Douglas in 1858. Back then, whichever man most impressed Illinois's state legislators would be elected to the Senate. Douglas kept his office, but the newly famous Lincoln went on a speaking tour that helped him earn his party's nomination for the presidency in May 1860.

The states of Kentucky, Indiana, and Illinois have all preserved Lincoln family log cabins that are connected by the Lincoln Heritage Trail. The Lincoln Trail College **Statesmen** are in Robinson, Illinois.

Deeply introspective and intelligent, Lincoln had no secondary education (not uncommon at the time). He read enough law books to pass Illinois's bar exam in 1836, but he could still play Joe Average. Frontier plots were likely surrounded by split-rail fences, and a Republican-spun yarn had a young Honest Abe making fences for Midwestern neighbors, so it is altogether fitting and proper that there are **Railsplitters** at Lincoln Memorial University in Harrogate, Tennessee[1] and **Loggers** at Lincoln Land Community College in Springfield, Illinois.

The Republicans got their man elected in November. Six weeks later, South Carolina seceded from "the compact entitled *The Constitution of the United States of America*." Jefferson Davis of Mississippi had opposed the disunion, but when his state seceded in January 1861, he resigned his Senate seat. By Lincoln's March inauguration, there were seven states convening at Montgomery, Alabama as the Confederate States of America, electing Davis as their president.

Erskine College in Due West once fielded **Seceders**, but not because South Carolina was the first state to leave the Union. Erskine was founded in 1839 by the Associate Reformed Presbyterian Church, also called the "Seceder Church" because they'd followed Rev. Ebenezer Erskine in walking away from Scotland's less conservative Calvinists in 1733. In a 1929 game at Furman, the **Seceders**' passing game impressed the longtime sports editor of the *Greenville News*, Carter "Scoop" Latimer, who called them the **Flying Fleet**.

South Carolina demanded all U.S. property within its borders. The Confederates surrounded Charleston Harbor's Fort Sumter, making failures of Northern efforts to re-supply it. Early on April 12, Charleston's batteries fired the opening volleys of the American Civil War. (Refer to the USL Charleston **Battery**, est. 1993.) Thirty-four hours later, Sumter was in Southern hands and the Confederacy would soon peak at eleven member states. Now Davis determined to show the North a real fight, as conveyed by the Jefferson Davis Community College **Warhawks** (Brewton, Ala.).

• • •

In the war's first land battle on June 3, the Union took control of the Baltimore and Ohio Railroad at Philippi, Virginia. (By war's end, it was in the breakaway state of West Virginia. See p. 72.) That puts **Battlers** at Philippi's Alderson-Broaddus University, but the event is often called the Philippi Races owing to the swiftness of the Confederate retreat. The Union expected the entire rebellion to be so easily foiled, but the South bounced back with a major July victory near Bull Run Creek in Manassas, Virginia.[2]

Southern Illinois had strong Southern roots owing to many resettled planters (and their slaves) who'd crossed the Ohio from Virginia and the Carolinas. Like many Illinoisans, Col. John Logan's loyalties were challenged by secession, but he joined with the Union in time to fight at Manassas. Returning home as a trenchant Union advocate, Logan raised the 31st Illinois Volunteer Infantry and did much to solidify Illinois's Union sympathies. He rose to major-general while his volunteers' bravery was widely reported. The **Volunteers** at Carterville's John A. Logan College are memorials to the 31st.

North of there, students at Jacksonville's Illinois College felt no such ambiguity going into war. The frontier school had been founded in 1829 by the "Yale Band," seven Yale graduates who'd helped start Congregationalist-backed Midwestern colleges like Grinnell, Knox, and Beloit. To central Illinois they'd carried both their New England sensibilities and Yale's blue and white. Most students enlisted as blue-jacketed Union soldiers, "blue boys," and after the war they remained **Blue Boys**, later joined by **Lady Blues**. Blue had been the traditional color of soldiers from all states, but with confusion caused by gray-jacketed militiamen on both sides at Bull Run, some standardization was required. Union boys for the most part wore blue thereafter and Confederates donned the cadet gray of Southern military institutions like VMI and the Citadel.

Over 300,000 Ohioans joined the Union effort, probably because they were separated from the enemy state of highest influence, Virginia, by only the Ohio River. (There wasn't yet a *West* Virginia.) Two of the three famous Ohio-bred generals—Sherman, Grant, and Hayes—were later presidents. The downtown area of the capital is dotted with war monuments and cannons, and it's where you find the NHL's Columbus **Blue Jackets** (est. 2000).[3]

• • •

There were huge fights in valleys from coastal Virginia to western Tennessee in the months after Manassas. Upon the South's second Bull Run victory in August 1862, Robert E. Lee's Army of Northern Virginia set for Washington. He was stopped in Maryland by Gen. George McClellan at September's Battle of Antietam. In that bloodiest one-day battle in U.S. history, McClellan let slip a chance to destroy Lee. Lincoln used his commander-in-chief powers to both strip McClellan's command and issue the Emancipation Proclamation, freeing Southern slaves "as a fit and necessary war measure."

Lee enjoyed momentum from another Virginia victory at Chancellorsville in May 1863, but Ulysses S. Grant soon had Vicksburg, Mississippi's batteries under siege. Taking the Confederate Gibraltar would let the Yanks control the Mississippi and split the Confederacy. Lee tried to lure Union troops from Vicksburg and break Northern resolve with a bold move into Pennsylvania, and the

Blue and the Grey fought at Gettysburg over the first three days of July. Lee set up HQ on Seminary Ridge (the site of the country's oldest Lutheran seminary), from which he hoped to direct the battle, but some tactical errors forced a Confederate withdrawal. Southern forces would neither mount such a grand attack nor move a large army so far north again.

For the next two months thousands of casualties were cared for at the seminary that was associated with the Lutheran school. It was renamed Gettysburg College in 1921. Bullet holes on walls around town and GC's **Bullets** are testaments to the largest and bloodiest battle ever fought in North America.

Grant's six-week siege did capture Vicksburg on July 4 (the day after victory at Gettysburg). Like other Civil War battlefields, Vicksburg is strewn with monuments to men on both sides. Perched atop the Wisconsin memorial is a bronze likeness of Old Abe, the war eagle who survived more than thirty battles with Wisconsin's 8th Infantry: the "Screaming Eagle Regiment." Additional monuments to Wisconsin's volunteers are the **Eagles** (and *Screaming Eagles* band) at the University of Wisconsin–La Crosse.[4]

Wisconsin's 101st reserve infantry formed after World War I behind the Screaming Eagle patch. That insignia and nickname have been adopted and maintained by the Army's 101st Airborne. Paratroopers of the 101st who trained at Georgia's Camp Taccoa in 1942 were the subjects of the 2001 HBO miniseries *Band of Brothers*. Respecting those warriors, the **Eagles** at Toccoa Falls College became **Screaming Eagles** before the 2014/2015 year.

The Union army of William Rosecrans spent the summer of '63 pushing Braxton Bragg's Army of Tennessee around their eponymous state. When Bragg was ejected from the rail hub at Chattanooga, Federals saw nothing between themselves and the Georgia coast, a path that would bisect enemy forces. Rosecrans pursued Bragg into Georgia, but Southern regiments handed him a brutal September defeat at Chickamauga Creek. Rosecrans backtracked to Chattanooga, but Bragg's occupation of the surrounding high ground had him locked down. Grant arrived from Vicksburg and was soon joined by armies under William Tecumseh Sherman and Thomas Hooker. In fall's Chattanooga Campaign, those Federals drove the rebels from Missionary Ridge and Lookout Mountain. The latter is described by the Creek word *Chattanooga* (pointed rock), and a series of Chattanooga **Lookouts** have played minor league ball since 1885, joined in the 1920s by black baseball's **Black Lookouts**.

John Hunt Morgan commanded the Confederates' 2nd Kentucky Cavalry. From camps in Tennessee, "Morgan's Raiders" had cut up Union supply lines in Kentucky in 1862. Against Bragg's orders, Morgan crossed the Ohio on July 8, 1863 for a two-week campaign of looting and destruction in Indiana and Ohio that he thought would pull Federals from Gettysburg, Vicksburg, and Chattanooga. Pressing farther north than any other Confederate force, the Great Raid boosted Southern morale, but a different Kentucky Cavalry led by the Union's Col. Frank Wolford chased Morgan to his July 26 capture in eastern Ohio. Morgan usually managed to strike Columbia, Kentucky on his trips across the Cumberland, and several historical markers trace the route of Morgan's Raiders, including the **Blue Raiders** at Columbia's Lindsey Wilson College[5] (only a five-minute walk to the grave of Morgan's captor, Wolford).

• • •

By 1864, Union generals in the Southeast were breaking enemy supply lines and recruiting slaves to the infantry. Florida's largest Civil War battle, the Battle of Olustee, pushed Union troops back to Jacksonville on February 20. Confederates wounded in those events went by rail to a mansion-turned-hospital in Madison that's now part of North Florida Community College. Its **Sentinels** refer to soldiers on guard duty. In fact, at the dedication for an Olustee memorial in 1912, U.S. Senator Duncan Fletcher said the granite cross "stands sentinel […] over the field where the Confederate soldier won admission to the temple of fame."

Illinoisans were still arguing about which side they were on. On March 28, antiwar Democrats upset with "the Republicans' war" got into a gunfight with Illinois volunteers on furlough in Charleston and nine men were killed. In 1905, Charleston's Eastern Illinois University would adopt colors to foster post-war unity, but its **Blue and Gray** became more animated **Panthers** in 1930.

That March, Grant got command of the entire Union effort. For the rest of '64 he would try to block logistics support for Lee from either Georgia or Virginia's Shenandoah Valley. In June, Lee's army dug in at Petersburg, a rail hub just south of the capital at Richmond from which he hoped resupply would be possible.

After a September victory in the valley, the Army of the Shenandoah under Chattanooga hero Philip Sheridan systematically destroyed anything that could bolster Southern forces. (Sheridan County Wyoming and its Sheridan College are named for the general, as are the latter's **Generals**.)[6] Chattanooga had indeed proved to be the "Gateway to the South," and while Sheridan was occupied in the Valley Campaign, Sherman lit a path to the railyards and munitions depots at Atlanta, which he captured on September 2. Finally confident that victory was forthcoming, Northerners reelected President Lincoln in November over his Democratic challenger, old foe George McClellan.

As with "The Burning"—Sheridan's scorched earth approach in the Shenandoah—Atlanta was subjected to a plan for destroying the South's ability and will to engage, a new concept called "total war." Sherman burned Atlanta in November before moving his 62,000 men on a March to the Sea, a 250-mile track of destruction that reached Savannah on December 10.

The Federals had held Middle Tennessee since 1862, but after Atlanta the Confederates wanted to take Nashville back and snatch its Union supplies. The Southern advance, however, was decidedly crushed in the last major fight in the Western Theater. One posh Union command post during the Battle of Nashville was an Italianate plantation home called Belmont. Some of the estate's barns and slave quarters were destroyed to build defenses, but the antebellum mansion survives as the centerpiece for Belmont University, where **Rebels** and **Rebelettes** dropped Confederate themes in 1995 to become **Bruins**.

In early 1865, Sherman turned north toward Lee's last great Confederate army. The devastation continued as they crossed South Carolina, the state blamed for driving secession. Columbia burned to the ground in coincidence with Sherman's arrival on February 17, although who got the cotton bales burning and why are debated. (Columbians would likely have destroyed anything Sherman could use.) Sherman's actions were recalled by hockey's NHL Atlanta **Flames** (1972–80, now in Calgary) and the minor league Columbia **Inferno** (est. 2001), whose cartoon Dalmatian seems less serious than that dark history.

> Sherman's March dipped below Anderson, South Carolina, where the Anderson University **Rebels** (named in 1963) became arbitrarily named **Trojans** in 1970. Valdosta State University is in south-central Georgia, too far south to have been in the way of Sherman's torches, so we don't know why its teams became **Blazers** in 1973, but they too had been **Rebels** before.

Late in the war, man-for-man losses favored the heavily populated North, but the clock would run as long as Lee was entrenched at Petersburg. After his lines were nearly broken in an April 1 attack by Sheridan, Lee abandoned Petersburg and spent a week trying to reach the remnants of Joseph Johnston's North Carolina army, but Sheridan's cavalry blocked every retreat. Lee surrendered to Grant on April 9.

Sherman had sent a large Union cavalry under Brig. Gen. James H. Wilson across Alabama to the Georgia border to destroy Southern arsenals, foundries, and supplies. Wilson's victory over Lt. Gen. Nathan Bedford Forrest at the Battle of Columbus [Georgia] is considered the war's last battle. The first teams at its Columbus College (est. 1958) were **Rebels**. African American students arrived in 1964, and in 1970, Thomas Y. Whitley—the founding president of the school that's now Columbus State University—said, "I'm here to tell you … [from] this day on our mascot will not be called **Rebel**." He handed off to a panel of students and administrators who came back with "**Cougars**."[7]

Johnston laid down arms to Sherman at Durham on April 26. Game over.

• • •

From its North African colony of Algeria, France had recruited Arab Zouaves for militias. Their fearlessness in battle and the stripes on their baggy pants got them called "Tigers." Early in America's Civil War, one New Orleans rifle company adopted Zouave-style uniforms as "Tigers." Every man in the parent battalion was soon considered a "Louisiana Tiger," followed by Louisiana infantries under Lee and then Louisianans in other theaters. Some would undoubtedly have attended Pineville's Louisiana State Seminary of Learning & Military Academy. It's now in Baton Rouge as Louisiana State University, which first presented **Fightin' Tigers** in 1896 to salute the many veteran sons of the state.

The NASL Indy **Eleven** (est. 2014) could simply indicate the number of soccer players per side, but they in fact intend to commemorate Indianapolis's 11th Indiana Infantry Regiment, famously called "Colonel Wallace's Zouaves" during the War Between the States.

Despite the pervasive belief that Detroit's American Leaguers were named for the stripes on their stockings, author Richard Bak has found a relationship between those **Tigers** and their city's own famed Civil War unit. In 1893 west coast businessman George Vanderbeck moved his California League players to Michigan to join Ban Johnson's reorganized Western League. Vanderbeck predicted that his boys would be "the cream of the league," making for Detroit **Creams**.[8] Soon, though, they were **Tigers** from a nickname the Detroit Light

Guard carried after serving with distinction in the Civil War. By around 1900 the team had adopted the Guard's tiger mark, and the unit's band played at home games.[9]

• • •

Reuben Millsaps distinguished himself in Tennessee during the war. In 1892 the Confederate major and fellow Methodists financed a college, the home of Millsaps College's **Majors** (Jackson, Miss.). Confederate veterans are remembered by other college teams in the Deep South:

- General Francis Tillou Nicholls lost an arm and a foot in separate 1862 battles. He was a later governor of Louisiana and the eponymous person for a Thibodaux junior college within the LSU system that opened in 1948. But don't expect **Generals** at today's Nicholls State University. In its early years, the institution had a strong ROTC program, so the NSU **Colonels** recognize the highest ROTC rank, that of cadet colonel.

- The University of Mississippi at Oxford keeps **Rebels**, although the nickname for the institution is just as famous as that of its teams. "Ole Miss" at first seems an innocent abbreviation, but that's what slaves called the wife of their white master (Ole Massa), so "Ole Miss" is considered by some to be no more progressive than "**Rebels**."[10]

- The teachers' college in Hattiesburg was renamed Mississippi Southern College in 1940, just when **Tigers**, **Normalites**, and **Yellow Jackets** were becoming **Confederates**. Two years later, they were the Mississippi Southern **Southerners**, represented by General Nat, a caricature of Lt. Gen. Nathan Bedford Forrest (antebellum slave trader, Confederate general, and post-war leader in the Ku Klux Klan). MSC became the University of Southern Mississippi in 1962, adopting "**Golden Eagles**" in '72. Mississippi's "Eagle State" nickname owes to the territory's adoption of an eagle seal in 1798.

In 1934, Robert E. Lee High School (Baytown, Texas) started sharing space with the new Lee College. By 1951 the college had its own campus, with scarlet-and-gray **Runnin' Rebels** and **Lady Rebels**.

As the superintendent of the military academy at West Point from 1852 to 1855, Lee had fostered the educations of many officers who would serve both sides in the war. Immediately after its conclusion, he returned to education as the president of Washington College in Lexington, Virginia, named for its first major benefactor, Gen. George Washington (Lee's own step-grandfather-in-law). Lee diversified and expanded the curriculum and was buried on campus after his 1870 death. The next year, the school became Washington and Lee University, where **Generals** recall both Virginia-born soldiers.

A Washington College in Washington, Pennsylvania had the common problem of struggling to find enrollees during the Civil War, so in 1865 it absorbed another Presbyterian school, Jefferson College in nearby Canonsburg. Renamed for the first and third chief execs, Washington and Jefferson College keeps **Presidents** for four-year undergrad terms.

Longhorns | Broncos | Mavericks | Sooners

To have meat and milk on their New World adventures, the Spaniards brought their livestock with them. Only the hardiest cattle, sheep, goats, and swine were picked for the long voyage. With Conquistador-lords served by indigenous farm-hands, the Southwest's Spanish mission ranches came to operate in the model of European fiefdoms.

When the Mexican War of Independence (1810–21) cut ties with Spain, the Spanish friars—agents of the crown—fled their mission posts, leaving horses and cattle to multiply unchecked on Texas grasslands. Andalusian cattle were already sturdy hybrids of Iberian breeds, but after Anglo settlers mingled them among Scottish Angus and English Herefords, an even tougher crossbreed came forth: the Texas Longhorn. The newspaper editor at the University of Texas at Austin branded varsity teams "**Longhorns**," which UT officially adopted in 1906. The Texas College **Steers** and **Lady Steers** in Tyler are *both* named after the castrated Longhorn raised for beef, as were the Jasper **Steers**, a black baseball team from that East Texas cattle and lumber town.

Longhorn mascots in Texas aren't always tied to **Longhorn** teams. The NFL Houston **Texans** (est. 1999) and MLS **FC** Dallas (est. 2006) have well-horned bovine mascots. The AHL San Antonio **Rampage** (est. 2002) skate in an auditorium that has long hosted livestock shows. As their charging Longhorn mascot reveals, the specific rampage to be worried about is a stampede. In fact, *estampida* is one of many ranching terms from Spanish: *rodear* (encircle) becomes "rodeo"; *la reata* (the rope) evolves to "lariat"; and *rancho* becomes "ranch." Gilroy, California is at the center of the old Spanish-Mexican *Rancho San Ysidro*, a cattle, horse, and sheep ranch. Its Gavilan College has **Rams**.

So why all the Spanish? Unable to fund the colonial-era infrastructure in the 1830s, Mexico City secularized the missions, thereby creating large-scale operations on which both the habits and lexicon of North American ranching evolved. Cow herders were *vaqueros*, literally "cow-men/boys." With a two-century head start, vaqueros mentored the cowboys that followed:

- California has **Vaqueros** at both Santa Barbara City College and Glendale Community College.
- *La Fiesta de los Vaqueros* (est. 1925) is Tucson's annual rodeo. It's an hour's drive from Coolidge, where Central Arizona College follows proper grammatical gender with respective male and female **Vaqueros** and **Vaqueras**.
- Puerto Rico was Spain's fortified gateway to the Caribbean, but its rich history of agriculture leads to **Vaqueros** and **Vaqueras** at *la Universidad de Puerto Rico de Bayamón* and the neighboring *Vaqueros de Bayamón* (est. 1930) of the island's top pro basketball league.
- In Spanish, a *v* can sound to Anglophones like a soft-*b*, meaning attempts at "*vaqueros*" might yield "buckaroos." Minor league hockey in Oregon has twice seen Portland **Buckaroos** (1928–41 and 1960–75).

• • •

North American horses disappeared about 10,000 years ago. The Conquistadors reintroduced an Iberian-Moorish stock, but some escaped from Spanish or Indian camps to form feral bands. Vaqueros applied the Spanish word *mesteño* (stray) to those wild horses. "Mustangs" would be rounded up whenever cattlemen needed quick, smart cow ponies, and there are **Mustangs** all over the Great West. New Mexico examples include the University of the Southwest in Hobbs and Western New Mexico University in Silver City. In Texas they're at SMU (p. 102) and Midwestern State (p. 6). The Master's College **Mustangs** romp around a former Spanish/Mexican estate in Santa Clarita, California.[1]

Spaniards may have anchored north of their usual shipping routes to meet with Tuscarora allies, or they might have gotten blown there by hurricanes. Either way, horses escaped, survived shipwrecks, or were abandoned on North Carolina's Outer Banks. The Mid-Atlantic Christian University **Mustangs** in Elizabeth City are named for surviving bands of feral Banker Horses. Similarly, a story at the University of Alabama in Huntsville has a grand stallion escaping from Conquistadors to make frequent ghostly appearances thereafter in the azure morning mists. That explains UAH's **Chargers** and their Charger Blue equine mascot.[2]

Bronco is Spanish for "untamed" or "wild." Determined cowboys that rounded up free-range mustangs couldn't just hop on; inuring broncos to the saddle took a gutsy horse breaker who'd hang on 'til the animal embraced futility or got plumb tuckered out. Still, it could take a week to bust a resolute bronco. As you'd guess, jocks out West are those most likely to be **Broncos** or **Broncbusters**. Edinburg's University of Texas–Pan American hosts **Broncs** while Edmond's University of Central Oklahoma busts out the "**Bronchos**" alternate.[3]

The *pinto* (paint) is a spotted mustang. Plains tribes liked its natural camouflage,[4] and baseballers at Chillicothe, Ohio wanted to accentuate the front part of their new *Frontier* League as Chillicothe **Paints** (1993–2008). They had a multicolored pony mascot, but **Paints** were especially at home in Chilli, where Paint Street is the main drag near Paint Creek.

• • •

Spain's former colonial plots are full of **Toros** (bulls), **Toreros** (bullfighters), and **Matadors** (killers [of bulls]). Bullfighting never caught on in North America like it had in South and Central America, but there are **Toros** at California State University–Dominguez Hills in Carson, part of the vast 1769 estate grant to Juan Jose Dominguez. That veteran of Spanish exploration in California founded the presidio at San Diego, near the **Toreros** at the University of San Diego (**Pioneers** until 1961). The **Matadors** at Lubbock's Texas Tech University were intended to match the Spanish influence of campus buildings. TTU's traditional matador colors of scarlet and black led to **Red Raiders**, first unmasked in 1936.[5] Arizona Western College keeps **Matadors** at Yuma, where Conquistadors established a town in 1540 at an ancient Colorado River crossing.

• • •

Los gaúchos were the bodacious cowboys of the South American pampas who had Iberian and Indian blood. They were folk heroes for supporting revolts against Spain's colonial rule. With the release of the 1927 Douglas Fairbanks movie *The Gaucho* (set in the Andes), the term was firmly in the American lexicon. Its Romance-language etymology is unclear, but the word *gaúcho* seems to have slipped from Portugal's Brazil colony to Spain's outposts.

In 1934, the **Roadrunners** at the University of California–Santa Barbara became **Gauchos**, adding a bit of Iberian flair to the city founded as Alta California's tenth Spanish mission in 1786. More **Gauchos** saddle up at Saddleback College in Mission Viejo, the ranching territory around the seventh mission (Mission San Juan Capistrano, est. 1776). The Glendale Community College **Gauchos** are close to Arizona's historic Sahuaro Ranch.[6] *Gaúcho* is a masculine noun, but the women at these schools are **Gauchos** also. The feminine plural, *Gaúchas*, is rarely used as a name for women's teams because it describes the domestically inclined common-law wives of *los gauchos*.

· · ·

Before the Civil War, Texas cattle were driven to California gold fields and Gulf Coast ports. The latter route was retraced by cattleman John McNeese in 1873 when he drove a drought-stricken herd to a quick sale in New Orleans. McNeese then settled in southwest Louisiana and became a prominent educator. A school founded with support from local ranchers in 1839 is base camp for the McNeese State University **Cowboys** and **Cowgirls**.

The Civil War slowed the laying of track to the West and stopped new lines to the South, making it impossible to get beef cattle to northern markets where the price might jump tenfold. But post-war rail laying was fast and furious, and by 1867 the Union Pacific had a railhead at the old stage coach stop of Abilene, Kansas. Enterprising businessmen wanted to drive Texas Longhorns from the Rio Grande up to Abilene on the Chisholm Trail so they could be railed to the new stockyards and slaughterhouses at Kansas City and Chicago, which would make beef nearly as available as pork. Chicago was soon the "slaughterhouse to the world," but there would be packing plants across the Midwest, especially after refrigerated boxcars became widely used in the 1870s. The NBL's Chicago **Packers** played in the International Amphitheater, which was next to (and owned by) the city's huge Union Stock Yards. (In Chicago for the 1961/62 season, the **Packers** were the first in a long line of teams that evolved into the Washington **Wizards**.) Chicago **Bulls** of an earlier ear—a 1926 AFL team—had played on a Comiskey Park gridiron.

Known locally for All-American play at Northwestern and then professionally with the NBL Chicago **American Gears**, Dick Klein tried and failed to keep the **Packers** in town, but he was a force behind a new syndicate (including the family of famous sausage packer Oscar Mayer) that secured the Amphitheater's new NBA tenants for the 1966/67 season and beyond, the Chicago **Bulls**.[7]

Chicago's Armour Institute of Technology was founded in 1893 by meat-packing giant Philip D. Armour. AIT's scarlet-and-grey **Packers** and **Techawks** transitioned to **Scarlet Hawks** in the mid-1930s,[8] carrying that name through the 1939 merger that created the Illinois Institute of Technology. Another packing town with easy access to Lake Michigan is 200 miles north of Chicago at Green Bay. That's where Earl "Curly" Lambeau persuaded bosses at Indian Packing to back a company football team. Lambeau's 1918 **Indians** were soon **Packers**, a name that could be kept after Indian sold out to Acme Packing the next year. The

Acme **Packers** joined the 1921 APFA/NFL but got kicked out at season's end for having enlisted collegians. After exhibiting genuine contrition, Lambeau received a 1922 NFL charter for the Big Bay **Blues**. That name was to distance them from recent disgrace, but fans would have none of it and the Green Bay **Packers** have been packing the house since.[9]

• • •

Before cattle drives, calves were branded to indicate ownership. Texas land speculator Sam Maverick branded lazily, possibly because he got into the game reluctantly after accepting a herd as a debt repayment. Maverick sold those interests in 1856 in a deal that included all unmarked cattle on the range. When new owners stamped those unbranded cattle—"Mavericks"—their neighbors retaliated in kind to create a legal nightmare. Just north of Sam Maverick's old Matagorda Bay ranchlands is Houston, past home of the ABA Houston **Mavericks** (1967–69).

The University of Nebraska at Omaha also hosts **Mavericks** or "O-Mavs" (former **Indians**, 1935–71). Colorado Mesa University started as a Grand Junction junior college in 1925. Because it competed for respect, students, and athletes with established state institutions, the "unclaimed strays" on its rosters were **Mavericks**.[10] Teams at a Tonkawa, Oklahoma prep school in the 1920s were isolated in that they had no conference affiliation, so they were the first **Mavericks** at today's Northern Oklahoma College.[11]

The University of Texas at Arlington has derived team names in any number of ways. As Grubbs Vocational College, it was in the Texas A&M system from 1917 to 1921. Early Grubbers were **Grubbers** or **Shorthorns**. The latter hooked them to their **Longhorn** rivals at UT-Austin. The -*horn* suffix even led briefly to **Hornets**. They were **Junior Aggies** in relation to Texas A&M's **Aggies** (1923–49) then blue-and-white **Blue Riders**. Those Southerners elected to be **Rebels** in 1951. A stampede of ballots in the late '60s brought about Arlington **Aardvarks**, the **Rebels** (again), and finally **Mavericks** in 1971.[12] Nine years later, UTA would protest the naming of the new NBA Dallas **Mavericks** twenty miles down I-30, but that went nowhere because fanatical legal efforts to protect sporting brands (pun intended) weren't yet in vogue. The NBA **Maverick** owners also included Oklahoman James Garner, who played cowboy gambler Bret Maverick in the TV series *Maverick* from 1957 to 1962.

Maverick now describes a nonconformist type. If a person can be a maverick, so too can a horse. At least, that's what we guess from those **Mavericks** that use and have used mustang mascots instead of bovines, including the aforementioned Dallas NBA team and Texas-Arlington jocks.

• • •

Location, timing, and good planning created a huge cattle market in the "City of Kansas." The first rail bridge over the Missouri River was there after 1869 and its stockyards opened two years later, allowing ranchers to auction off herds rather than accept the railroads' cheap price. Kansas City **Cowboys** played in baseball's UA (1884, alternately "**Unions**"), NL (1886), and AA (1888–89). Different Kansas City **Cowboys** (1902–03) in a revived AA would become **Blues** (1904–54), a timeline reversed by NFL Kansas City **Blues** (1924) that became **Cowboys** (1925–26). The NASL had Kansas City **Spurs** (1968–70). One of the largest livestock, horse, and rodeo shows in the country—the American Royal—has been held every fall since 1899. The Royal is the best explanation for the longest-lived Negro league team, the Kansas City **Monarchs** (1920–65).[13] The AL Kansas City **Royals** (est. 1969) are named after the town's biggest annual party (and to a lesser degree the late **Monarchs**). Their royal blue uniforms remember the above-mentioned **Blues**.

The new Texas and Pacific Railroad's tracks ran west out of Longview, but the Panic of 1873 (p. 237) stopped them at Dallas, which consequently became a major rail head and in 1960 the home of the NFL Dallas **Cowboys**. When the rails continued west in 1881, North-central Texas ranchers steered them toward the pastures at Buffalo Gap. That burgeoning cattle town was renamed Abilene after the same-named Kansas stop. Its **Cowboys** and **Cowgirls** represent Hardin-Simmons University.

Texas **Wranglers** are at Odessa College and Cisco College, and there were Austin **Wranglers** (2004–08) of indoor football. *Wrangler* is from the Spanish *caballerango*, "horse ranger." He's the cowboy in charge of the *remuda* (change of horses), a group of mustangs from which drovers select fresh mounts.

• • •

Everywhere the Longhorns went, other cattle tipped over dead. Few suspected that "Texas fever" owed to diseased ticks carried by the immune Longhorns. Brahman (or Brahma) bulls were known to tolerate heat and insect-borne diseases in their native India, so they came to America for crossbreeding. This did effect a fever-resistant hybrid, and the late 1800s saw Brahmans on ranches from the Gulf Coast to California. In 1982 green-and-gold **Golden Brahmans** at Tampa's University of South Florida shortened to **Bulls** (even the women).

Jacksonville is an old cattle crossing on the St. Johns River (until 1822 it was called Cowford), so the USFL Jacksonville **Bulls** (1984–85) were named for both that history and team owner Fred Bullard. Los Angeles's Pierce College opened as an agricultural school, so its El Rancho Drive bisects a working farm and leads to fields for **Brahmas**. When South Park College (Beaumont, Texas) became Lamar College in 1932, red-and-white **Brahmas** changed to **Cardinals**. (It's now Lamar University.) Minor league hockey's Texas **Brahmas** were established in 1997 as Fort Worth **Brahmas**.

• • •

Texas Fever closed the borders of Missouri and eastern Kansas to Texas drovers, who started looping their herds around Kansas on the Goodnight-Loving Trail in 1866, the same year gold miner and cattleman Nelson Story drove 3,000 Long-horns through western Kansas and up the Bozeman Trail to Montana's mining camps. Bison grasslands could obviously support huge herds, and ranching became a major industry. The Goodnight-Loving ended at the Union Pacific's new Wyoming stockyards. The Cowboy State adopted its familiar Bucking Horse and Rider emblem in 1918, and the state now works with the University of Wyoming to license its use. Established at the UP stop in Laramie in 1886, UW would have had many real cowboys among students, and teams were already **Cowboys** before 1900, joined later by **Cowgirls**.

Whether or not one was a rustler (cattle thief) in Wyoming's Powder River valley was a matter of perspective. Most Wyoming cowboys ended up working for the large cattle operations that were run out of Cheyenne with money from back east and Britain (indicating the speed with which the independent cowboy hero of myth became a tiny cog in the big business machine). Through an 1884 Maverick Law, the corporations claimed all of the unbranded calves on the range. When angry homesteaders started grabbing strays to get back to even, the cattle barons launched an intimidation campaign. Their hired guns murdered several accused rustlers in 1892, and it took the U.S. Cavalry to end that Johnson County War, a chapter that puts **Rustlers** at Riverton's Central Wyoming College.

• • •

The 1872 Dominions Land Act opened the Canadian West for white pioneers. A new militaristic and administrative force was planned to manage the Indians of the prairies and effect some sense of order. After the U.S. Cavalry cracked down on traders who sold the Indians whiskey in the late 1860s, Montana traffickers went to Canada to sell to the Prairie People of the North West Territories, the anything-goes "Whoop-up" country. Montana hunters who'd lost horses to thievery in 1873 crossed the border and massacred two-dozen Assiniboine (Nakota) Indians whom circumstance had made suspicious to their liquored-up attackers.

Ottawa's outraged governors accelerated the creation of their new mounted rifle force, the North West Mounted Police. "Mounties" quickly closed the white men's whiskey forts and restored some order. Pioneer Leaguers three miles east of Lethbridge's Fort Whoop-Up National Historic Site were Lethbridge **Mounties** (1992–95). Heavy artillery would have been impractical in pursuit of bootleggers, but baseball's PCL Calgary **Cannons** (1985–2002) were named for whatever few artillery pieces the Mounties managed to drag to remote western forts.

The Mounties needed nourishment themselves, but treaties with Canada's First Nations obligated the government to provide beef to reservations after the bison disappeared. The Mountie post of Fort Calgary had been founded in 1875 on a fertile plain near Kicking Horse Pass, through which it was decided the Canadian Pacific should run, and Calgary was Canada's "Cow Town" nearly upon the arrival of the first train in 1883. Hockey's WHA Calgary **Cowboys** (1975–77) and junior Calgary **Wranglers** (1977–87) were at the Stampede Corral, a rodeo hall built in 1950 for one of the world's great annual cowboy competitions, the Calgary Stampede. Its bronco-busting competition gave name to rugby's Calgary **Bronks** (1935–40). They reassembled after World War II under the name today's CFL fans recognize: Calgary **Stampeders** (a moniker already used by Corral-based minor league hockeyists between 1938 and 1972). Rugby has Calgary **Mavericks** (est. 1960).

To further Alberta's agronomy, Canada's Department of Agriculture started opening various Demonstration Farms in 1913. Two such institutes at Vermilion and Olds became Lakeland College and Olds College, which now host **Rustlers** and **Broncos**, respectively.

• • •

Ichabod Washburn's Massachusetts factory made piano wire and skirt hoops. He died soon after wiring $25,000 into the endowment for Kansas's Lincoln College, now Washburn University (p. 143). His company later became the leading manufacturer of modern barbed wire, used by homesteaders and railways to prevent bovine trespass. When blizzards in the early 1880s froze thousands of strays in their tracks, some angry drovers blamed the "devil's rope" for blocking migration to warmer climes and hacked right through. Laws to end fence-cutting brought out hard feelings and vigilantes (Spanish for "watchmen"). Refer to arena football's Dallas **Vigilantes** (2010–11) and the barbed wire emblem of the MLL Denver **Outlaws** (est. 2006).

The wire was just one factor that closed the open ranges. Kansas extended its quarantine laws westward across the state in 1885, but the arrival of railroads at the cow towns would itself have rendered the great drives moot. By 1879 the Santa Fe Railroad was running as far as the old New Mexico trail stop at Las Vegas. It boomed into a ranching and trade center and was one of the wilder Wild West towns. Greater Las Vegas was a set for uncountable Westerns, and its New Mexico Highlands University keeps **Cowboys** and **Cowgirls**.

The railroad also changed everything when it arrived at Round Rock, Texas in 1876, even moving the city center from Old Town to a trackside New Town. There's a locomotive emblem for minor league baseball's Round Rock **Express**, named in 2004 after being bought by Texan Nolan Ryan. (His Hall of Fame fastball was the "Ryan Express," from the 1965 Fox film *Von Ryan's Express*, in which wartime Allies escape a German prison camp by train.) Similarly, the farm economy in Texas's Collin County didn't take off until the iron horse arrived in 1872. Its Collin College **Express** became **Cougars** in 2007.

From the huge number of movies and novels they gave us, you'd scarcely guess the cattle drives were all jammed between the end of the Civil War and the arrival of the railroads at nearly every ranching center twenty years later. Still, the trail rider is the definitive Western hero, as celebrated by Western Texas College's **Westerners** in Snyder, represented by cow handlers in ten-gallon hats.[14]

• • •

In the post-bison West, federal agents paid top prices to buy beef for Army posts and reservations in Oklahoma's Indian Territory. Cherokees leased Oklahoma grasslands to drovers who paused to fatten up cattle destined for boxcars, a cowhand heritage indicated by **Cowboys** and **Cowgirls** at Oklahoma State University and **Drovers** at Chickasha's University of Science and Arts of Oklahoma.

Farmers and would-be ranchers from Kansas and points east coveted a piece of the Oklahoma action, as did ex-slaves seeking fresh starts. The Army spent years chasing those pro-expansionist "Boomers" from the territory, but Boomer pressure finally opened Oklahoma to new settlement. When the starting gun went off at noon on April 22, 1889, boomers raced toward 160-acre parcels on a first-come, first-take basis. Oklahoma City—a small train stop that morning—had a population of 10,000 by sundown.

The more anxious Boomers who created a legal nightmare by jumping the gun and camping overnight in the territory were soon "Sooners," and **Sooners** teams replaced **Boomers** and **Rough Riders** in 1908 at the University of Oklahoma in

Norman. Most Oklahomans consider themselves Sooner-born and Sooner-bred, and they've celebrated for decades with clubs and societies of "Eighty-Niners." The minor league baseballers who followed the Oklahoma City **Indians** (1918–57) were Oklahoma City **89ers** (1962–96), now the **RedHawks**.

> The Outlaws who rustled cattle and robbed prairie stage coaches on the Chisholm Trail feared the lawmen in the Kansas cow towns and the Rangers in Texas, but in between was the lawless Indian Territory: Oklahoma. The USFL's Oklahoma **Outlaws** (1984, Tulsa) recalled that bandit past, later merging with the Arizona **Wranglers** in Phoenix as Arizona **Outlaws**. All over the West are **Rustlers**, **Wranglers**, **Outlaws**, and **Bandits** as neighbors to **Cowboys** and **Mustangs**.

• • •

Along with cattle, Texas's Spanish-Mexican missions raised sheep, a tradition continued by Anglos after Texas independence. Texas Wesleyan University keeps **Rams** and **Lady Rams** in Fort Worth, a one-time stagecoach hub near the start of the Chisholm Trail. It grew into a monster rail center and the biggest stock trading town in Texas after the arrival of the Texas and Pacific in 1876.[15] **Rams** and **Lady Rams** are at Austin's Huston-Tillotson College. Like Tex-Wes, HTU can explain its **Rams** through either the ranching history or the school's Methodist founding because the ram represents Christian sacrifice, strength, or leadership.[16]

San Angelo was a West Texas town near the start of the Goodnight-Loving Trail. When the Santa Fe Railroad arrived in 1888, it became a livestock and wool boom town, putting **Rams** and **Rambelles** at Angelo State University. The San Angelo Stock Show and Rodeo has been held annually since 1932, explaining minor league baseball's San Angelo **Colts** (est. 2000).

Cattle and sheep operations south of the Rio Grande were always productive, but—same ol' story—the real money came with the railroads in the late 1800s. Mexico's *Instituto Tecnológico y de Estudios Superiores de Monterrey* ("Monterrey Tech") hosts ***Borregos Salvajes*** (wild sheep).

Charles Goodnight started the Texas Panhandle's first ranch in 1876. His bison were shipped to zoos all over, and the injection of three Goodnight bulls at Yellowstone in 1902 probably helped save its herds. Mr. Goodnight founded Goodnight College in Goodnight in 1898. Its *Buffalo* yearbook appeared in 1916,[17] but GC closed the next year owing to competition from colleges nearby, notably West Texas A&M University in Canyon. In fact, when that school held a 1921 assembly to pick a mascot, one of Goodnight's old ranch hands told an exciting story about roping a bison at the site of WTAMU's original building. Students immediately embraced "**Buffaloes**"[18] and were then able to procure a live bison mascot from the octogenarian Charles Goodnight.

• • •

White settlement of the Midwest exploded after the 1825 opening of the Erie Canal and the 1832 victory in the Black Hawk War (p. 136). After easterners and immigrants cleared forests, Michigan was an agricultural powerhouse. Its non-Indian population jumped from 30,000 to 200,000 in the 1830s, and the next decade saw new rail lines to Chicago, making it inevitable that western Michigan would be cattle country. The 1899 Grand Rapids **Rustlers** (today's Cleveland **Indians**) were cowboy-themed *Western* Leaguers. South of Grand Rapids, the

Western-ness of Kalamazoo's *Western* Michigan University may have brought about its **Broncos**. (Until 1939, WMU teams on Prospect Hill were **Hilltoppers**.) We would suggest the same for the University of *Western* Ontario's **Mustangs**, but they too have a supporting history. A nineteenth-century immigration boom created many Ontario farms on which cowhands built herds from British breeds.

• • •

Many "59ers" of Colorado's Pikes Peak Gold Rush were "go-backers" as early as 1860. This left only the hardiest settlers at Denver, which had become just a rest stop on the Goodnight-Loving Trail. Frontier folk were the first attendees at the Methodists' Colorado Seminary in 1864. The struggling school closed from 1868 until reopening as the University of Denver in 1880. **Fighting Parsons** referred to the seminarians, but those who rode out the tough times have been remembered by **Pioneers** since 1925.

The seminary had been founded by territorial governor John Evans, who secured the Denver Pacific link up to Cheyenne by 1870.[19] Denver City's head-count of 5,000 had increased twentyfold in twenty years as it became a huge rail stop, cattle market, and banking center. The 1921 Midwest Baseball League included Denver **Broncos**, but readers are likely more familiar with NFLers who've ridden that name since the 1960 AFL season. Both **Broncos** followed the 1920 unveiling of A. Phimister Proctor's famous "Bucking Bronco" bronze at Denver's Civic Center.

Cattle from the Willamette Valley backtracked on the Oregon Trail to feed miners during a gold rush that started in northern Idaho 1860. Activity refocused on the Boise River Basin by 1862, and Boise town became a supply center for tools and agricultural products.[20] Within a decade, ranches would be welcoming Texas Longhorns. Idaho's ranch hands and sports fans accuse the NFL's Denverites of appropriating the name (and soon enough the colors) of Boise State University, which has kept orange-and-blue **Broncos** since its founding in 1932.

• • •

The Midwest is ideal for corn farming, but crops require shipping, whereas "pork on the hoof" transports itself. Never romanticized like the later cattle drives, the great hog drives through Indiana and Ohio were usually destined for Cincinnati. Canals connected Cincy to Lake Erie by 1833, facilitating the shipment of pork to eastern cities. Before refrigeration, salt kept meat from spoiling, and Cincinnati was near West Virginia's salt mines. Its slaughterhouses were prototypes for those at Chicago and Kansas City, effecting Cincy's "Porkopolis" nickname.

The 1869 Cincinnati **Red Stockings** were baseball's first salaried team, but their core moved to Boston to play in the new NA in 1871. Pork packer Josiah Keck returned pro ball to the city with the new National League in 1876. His players were **Porkopolitans**, but playing in the **Red Stockings**' former ballpark, they soon had the old moniker. "Cincinnati **Red Stockings**" continued to come and go in several leagues,[21] but when the 1882-founded **Red Stocking** nine jumped from the AA to the NL in 1890, they became today's **Reds**.

Spartans | Aggies | Hokies | Boilermakers | Keydets

In a fertile valley on Greece's Peloponnesus, the Spartans were at the height of their power between 600 and 200 BCE. Trouble from other city-states could come at any time, so Sparta turned all energies toward sustainable agriculture and combat preparedness. Boys trained for soldiering and girls hit the gym to ensure the birthing of healthy soldiers. (Slaves did everything else.) Unsurprisingly, Sparta's buff athletes dominated the first two centuries of Olympic competition, which began in 776 BCE.[1]

Militant Sparta and newly democratic Athens were among the allied city-states that fended off invasions in the name of the Persian king Darius I after 500 BCE. The first invasion was stopped by an unlikely Athenian win on the plain of Marathon in 490 BCE. A messenger who supposedly ran back to Athens used his last mortal breath to report the victory. (That twenty-six mile route was retraced for the first modern Olympics in 1896, and it's the standard measure for modern "marathons.")

Darius died and his son Xerxes decided to reinvade Greece in 480 BCE. Capturing Athens by land would require bringing the Persian army through the narrow pass at Thermopylae, so the Greeks sat waiting. During the battle, the spectacularly outnumbered Greeks accepted the looming defeat and excused most of their force, leaving a thousand men—notably 300 Spartans—in the channel to fight to the death. That bought time for Athenians to escape their city.

The Spartan king who led the 300 and was himself killed is history's most famous *Leonidas*, meaning "son of the lion" or "lion-like." That wouldn't matter to us, except that **Lions** at Texas A&M University–Commerce are named for the educator who founded it in 1889, William Leonidas Mayo.

Their never-surrender attitude during the 1931/32 basketball season got the **Blue and White** (occasionally **Bulldogs**) at Iowa's University of Dubuque called **Spartans**, with other sports following suit after 1933.[2] The first male basketballers at the recently all-women's University of North Carolina–Greensboro settled on "**Spartans**" in 1967 to exhibit a masculine courage. For refusing to cancel matches in all kinds of crazy weather, the highly competitive athletes at the all-female D'Youville College (Buffalo, N.Y.) were called **Spartans** in the 1920s. Their sport was croquet.[3] (DYC went coed in 1971.)

A self-sufficiency that is gained through the denial of comforts and amenities is still called a "Spartan existence." One Depression-era example left the faculty and students at a two-year-old junior college in Florida to do much of the heavy lifting to convert the empty and abandoned Tampa Bay Hotel to classrooms and labs in 1933. The results were impressive enough to foster its immediate transition to the University of Tampa, a story of perseverance that some say explain its **Spartans**.[4] That brings us to 1963, when students at the year-old junior college that's now Trinity Western University (Langley, B.C.) "were looking for a name for their athletic teams. [They] didn't have a lot of facilities [or] plushness, and perhaps [the] name **Spartans** came out of that."[5]

The navy of Athens finally defeated the Persians in 479 BCE. Sparta came to resent the ensuing era of Athenian hegemony and the two cities were enemies when the Peloponnesian Wars broke out in 431 BCE. Sparta's warriors expected to make quick work of the democratic theorists and poetry-reading pansies to their north, but Athens had built a powerful navy to protect its trade routes, so twenty-seven years passed before the Spartan victory.

The fight and fitness of Spartan citizens have inspired too many **Spartan** teams to list; military trainees, students of the classics, unyielding athletes, and schools that follow Sparta's example of public education can all justify their **Spartans**.[6]

In 1855, Michigan chartered the nation's first agricultural college on fields east of Lansing. The legislature sold surrounding acreage to fund the new Agricultural College of the State of Michigan. When it became the Michigan State College of Agriculture and Applied Science in 1925, students voted to change **Aggies** to **Staters**. Sports editor George Alderton at the *Lansing State Journal* didn't see the vim in that, and he rifled through the ballots to find "**Spartans**." We don't know why that suggestion had been made, which is too bad because the East Lansing school—now Michigan State University—could have made a pretty good claim to "**Spartans**." Persons familiar with the history of agricultural colleges might have known that the Michigan school had been the model for a federal program of similarly funded "land-grant institutions." When arguing for such academies in 1858, Sen. Justin Morrill of Vermont singled out Michigan's institute as a "successful experiment" just before comparing the obligation of states to educate their citizen-patriots with the social model of ancient Sparta.[7]

• • •

Before the Civil War, Southern senators resisted westward expansion, fearing that reps from new free states would vote down slavery. That became moot when Southern states seceded from the Union. Without that opposition, Congress signed three 1862 acts into law, the Homestead Act, the Pacific Railway Act, and the hinted-at Morrill Land Grant Colleges Act, all of which encouraged settlement in western territories on government terms.

The Morrill Act gave each state federal land to sell to fund engineering, agricultural, and teaching colleges "without excluding other scientific or classical studies." A few states—like Michigan—had already chartered land-grant tech schools, but this was the first such national incentive. Most colleges with *A&M* in the name were originally land-grants, and many are now state universities with diverse curricula. **Aggies** or **Engineers** were apt for schools that emphasized either the *A* (agricultural) or the *M* (mechanical) respectively. In Cambridge, the Massachusetts Institute of Technology is one of the few Morrill beneficiaries that maintains **Engineers**. As for **Aggies**, there are still bushels. New Mexico State University in Las Cruces (the former New Mexico A&M) has **Aggies**. (NMSU's women were **Roadrunners** until 2000.) **Aggies** at Logan's Utah State University (est. 1888) reveal the former Agricultural College of Utah. **Aggies** at the University of California–Davis represent a school set up in 1905 to assume the A&M responsibilities of UC-Berkley. In the late 1940s, **Aggies** officially replaced the

Farmers at Texas Agricultural and Mechanical University ("Texas A&M"), established at College Station in 1876.

• • •

Former and current teams indicate the land-grant roots of other schools:

- The first new school established through the Morrill Act was Kansas State Agricultural College in 1863. Turn-of-the-century teams at the Manhattan school—now Kansas State University—were **Aggies** and briefly **Farmers** until settling as **Wildcats** in 1920.

- The John Tarleton Agricultural College at Stephenville was pulled into the Texas A&M system in 1917, immediately bringing about **Little Aggies**. They were **Plowboys** in the 1920s, but male **Texans** and female **TexAnns** since 1961.[8] J-TAC became Tarleton State University in 1973.

- The men are **Bulldogs** at Ruston's Louisiana Tech University, but Tech's A&M pedigree is promulgated through **Lady Techsters**. They were **Lady Bulldogs** until basketball coach Sonja Hogg protested that a "lady dog is a bitch" in 1973.[9]

- In 1919 the Jonesboro agricultural school's football **Aggies** (now Arkansas State's **Red Wolves**) had sewn up the state championship before playing their game against different **Aggies** from Arkansas Tech University in Russellville. Tech's unexpected victory made them **Wonder Boys** in the Little Rock press. In 1976, Tech's **Wonder Girls/Wonderettes** used their forest green and old gold to become **Golden Suns**.[10]

- Mississippi A&M was chartered in 1878. It became Mississippi State College in 1932 and switched its dark-red **Aggies** to **Maroons**. Just a couple of years after becoming Mississippi State University in 1958, tenacious teams were **Bulldogs** for good, an alternate ID that had been around for half a century owing to live English bulldog mascots.

- Techs with successful agriculture programs include California Polytechnic State University (in San Luis Obispo) and its spin-off, Cal Poly Pomona. Teams are **Mustangs** and **Broncos**, respectively.

- When Blacksburg's 1872-founded Virginia A&M College became Virginia Polytechnic Institute in 1896, senior O.M. Stull submitted a football cheer that began: "Hoki, hoki, hoki, hy!" Stull admitted it didn't mean much; it was just hard to ignore. Nonetheless, **Techmen** and **Techs** at "Virginia Tech" were **Hokies** thereafter.[11]

As generous as the Morrill Act was, it took a gift of land and money from local businessman John Purdue to start Indiana's land-grant college at West Lafayette in 1874. Some of Purdue University's football rivals were twenty-five miles south at Wabash College, a Crawfordsville school that still self-identifies as "a liberal arts college for men." When the 1889 Wabashers fell to Purdue, their fans and reporters resorted to name calling. Names like "**Blacksmiths**" and "**Boilermakers**" were intended to draw attention to the technical and (by implication) less enlightened backgrounds of Purdue students.[12] Those were also veiled accusations that tradesmen were playing for PU on Saturdays. "**Boilermakers**" is now riveted to Purdue teams, and it was for persevering against Big 10 competition (like Purdue) that Wabash College jocks became **Little Giants** in 1904.

> Every A&M wasn't a public institution. Some states invested A&M funds at existing private colleges like M.I.T. and Cornell. The former is one of the techs to have been heavily influenced by the systems-based manual training schools in Russia and Scandinavia. Having seen those principles applied in American secondary schools, businessman and Wisconsin state senator James H. Stout endowed the Stout Manual Training School in Menomonie, which opened in 1891. Its **Manuals** or **Trainers** or **Blues** played in the facilities that Mr. Stout generously built at today's University of Wisconsin–Stout, but after 1931 they were blue-and-white **Blue Devils,** possibly drawn from preexistent intramural **Daredevils.**[13]

• • •

Even after the 1862 Morrill Act expanded educational opportunities, it was clear that black Americans were being left out. A Second Morrill Act in 1890 dictated that land-grant bills would either fund integrated institutions or create separate schools for African Americans, and many of the Historically Black Colleges and Universities—"the 1890s"—were founded. Of more than 100 HBCUs, only the North Carolina Agricultural & Technical State University (Greensboro) retains **Aggies**.

The University of The District of Columbia was the amalgamation of several regional teachers' colleges and tech institutes, so it's both an HBCU and the only urban land-grant. The flaming torch on its shield is metaphorically passed to succeeding generations of students, so red-and-yellow jocks are **Firebirds**.

• • •

Some state and private aggie and tech schools were not Morrill beneficiaries and are therefore not officially land-grants, but they might keep **Aggies**. That's the case at Goodwell's Oklahoma Panhandle State University, founded in 1909 as the Pan-Handle Agricultural Institute. Cameron State [High] School of Agriculture (Lawton, Okla.) became a college in 1927, now the home of the Cameron University **Aggies**. **Fighting Tigers** at SUNY College of Agriculture and Technology at Cobleskill were **Aggies** until the 1960s.

• • •

Engineers represent Worcester Polytechnic Institute, founded in 1865 by two local metal industrialists, John Boynton and Ichabod Washburn of Washburn University's **Ichabods** (p. 143). The first president of WPI was educator and engineer Charles O. Thompson. He left Massachusetts in 1882 to be the first president of Rose Polytechnic Institute (Terre Haute, Ind.). It had been established by railroad man Chauncey Rose to create engineers for his projects, but subsequent support from the Hulman family made it the Rose-Hulman Institute of Technology by 1971. WPI and RHIT are among the relatively small number of private technical colleges that have a little A&M-ism displayed by gym rats:

- Like other normal schools, Tri-State Normal College (Angola, Indiana) was founded to educate teachers, but the engineering school that opened in 1902 earned a great rep. **Engineers** became alliterative Tri-State **Trojans** in 1967 but were **Thunder** after 1990. (It's been Trine University since 2008.)

- In 1865, Pennsylvania industrialist Asa Packer financed a new engineering college at Bethlehem. Lehigh University teams were **Engineers** (a not-very-accidental reference to the locomotive engineers for Packer's Lehigh Valley Railroad), but they've been **Mountain Hawks** since 1995.
- The 1888-founded Williamson Free School of Mechanical Trades (Media, Pa.) is a junior trade college with **Mechanics** jocks.
- The **Techmen** at the Rochester [N.Y.] Institute of Technology went undefeated in the 1955/56 basketball season, which effected an identity in line with their ferocity: **Tigers**. (RIT's Bengal mascot is Ritchie ... *RIT*-chie.)

• • •

It's a state tech that's hosted **Blacksmiths** and **Engineers**, but Atlanta's Georgia Institute of Technology didn't get federal land-grant funds. Its **Ramblin' Wreck** ("from Georgia Tech") has two influences: [1] The cars that Tech students fixed up for developing South American countries in the 1920s were relative wrecks; [2] Tech's 1890 footballers were on a train that derailed.[14] GT teams are alternately **Yellow Jackets** from their jersey color, while swimmers and divers splash around as less official **Aqua Jackets**.

Georgia Tech's regents wanted to address post–World War II industries and opened a two-year tech ten miles away at Chamblee, where the newspaper was the *Southern Technical Institute News Gazette* ... the "STING." That eventually put **Hornets** at Southern Polytechnic State University (which moved to Marietta in 1958). SPSU was absorbed by Kennesaw State University (and its **Owls**) after the 2013/14 school year.

• • •

Rams—male sheep—are the recognized leaders of their respective flocks, so they've been symbolic of harvests and fertility since ancient Egypt. At the risk of putting the reader to sleep, our sheep-count includes these institutions, all founded as agricultural colleges and represented by male and female **Rams** (even though *Lady* **Rams** are zoological impossibilities):

- Nova Scotia Agricultural College in Bible Hill fielded **Rams** in 1980. They've represented the Agricultural Campus of Dalhousie University since 2012.
- Kingston's University of Rhode Island is the state's 1892-founded A&M. The mascot for its 1923-named **Runnin' Rams** is Rhody the Ram.
- The Agricultural College of Colorado was founded at Fort Collins in 1870. In the 1940s, **Aggies** adopted a live bighorn ram mascot named CAM, an acronym for the school's new name, Colorado A&M. Teams at the renamed Colorado State University followed as **Rams** in 1957.
- The **Rams** at Farmingdale State College recall days as the State Institute of Applied Agriculture on Long Island. (They were sometimes the "New York **Aggies**" in press accounts until the 1940s.)
- Albany State University was founded as the Albany Bible and Manual Training Institute in 1903 before being taken over by the state of Georgia as the Normal and Agricultural College in 1917, so either Christian symbolism (p. 106) or aggie training can explain its **Rams**.

• • •

Team names sometimes serve to indicate a specific skill:

- Apothecaries-to-be at the St. Louis College of Pharmacy fill and refill the goal as **Euts** ("utes"), from *eutectic*, a chemistry term for the lowest common melting point of fused materials.
- The **Penmen** and **Lady Penmen** at Manchester's Southern New Hampshire University recall its days as the College of Accounting and Commerce.
- Tiffin [Ohio] University's reputation as an excellent business school gave it **Bookkeepers**, but they divested themselves of that identity in the 1930s to become **Dragons** for reasons not known.[15]
- The Culinary Institute of America (Hyde Park, N.Y.) cooks up **Steel** teams to suggest kitchen cutlery.
- Would-be tradesmen were called **Traders** at Thaddeus Stevens College of Technology (Lancaster, Pa.) until becoming **Bulldogs** in the 1990s.
- When G.L. Archer founded Boston's Suffolk [County] Law school in 1906, one passionate instructor was his older brother Hiram. He remained a trustee until his 1966 death, having seen Suffolk University's **Judges** (or **Royals**) become **Rams** (from Hi-*ram*) in 1950.

• • •

Many of North America's thousand-plus state- and province-funded community colleges are technical institutes:

- Edison Community College (Piqua, Ohio) is a two-year tech named for the prolific inventor Thomas Edison. Its teams are **Chargers** because their eponym controlled the flow of *charged* particles to make electric light bulbs economical and safe.
- The court should be absolutely dry before engaging in contact sports against the **Surge** from Ohio's Cincinnati State Technical & Community College.
- Broome County, New York's Broome Community College was founded as the Institute of Applied Arts and Sciences in 1946. BCC spiked its **Technicats** in 1949 to favor more standard **Hornets**.[16]

• • •

Senator Morrill's act had been conceived in the heat of civil war, in which even some West Point–trained officers had performed poorly, so the new law encouraged its beneficiary institutions to train reserve officers. The precedent for military training alongside college classes at civilian institutions had been set in 1819 at the American Literary, Scientific and Military Academy at Norwich, Vermont. "Morrill was a friend and neighbor of Norwich founder Alden Partridge and was particularly impressed with the level of preparation and competence of Norwich graduates serving in the Union army."[17] Capt. Partridge had also been superintendent of West Point, which for years after its 1802 founding was the country's only true technical college,[18] and he created the model for the Morrill Act's Reserve Officer Training Corps (ROTC) program at what is now Norwich University (est. 1819). The required cavalry training made athletes **Horsemen**, but its current cadet-athletes are **Cadet** athletes. (The school remained "Norwich" even after an 1866 fire forced an intra-Vermont move from Norwich to Northfield.)

Other schools soon followed the Norwich model. The Virginia Military Institute was founded at Lexington's state arsenal in 1839. VMI had **Flying Squadron** jocks, but they've mostly been **Keydets** since the 1930s, probably an exaggeration of the way Southerners say "cadet." Charleston's 1842-founded Citadel (officially "The Citadel, the Military College of South Carolina") keeps **Bulldogs**. Citadel grads were disproportionately present in Charleston's small police force in the mid-1850s, during which they were nicknamed "Paddy Miles's Bull Dogs" after Mayor William Porcher Miles. This may be the root of the team name.[19]

The A&M College of Kentucky was a Morrill beneficiary with a highly regarded Cadet Corps program. Its combined armory-gymnasium was shared by cadets and **Cadets**. A 1902 football victory over Illinois caused the institute's commandant to say his **Cadets** "fought like wildcats," forever putting **Wildcats** at the school called the University of Kentucky since 1916.[20]

• • •

Norwich, The Citadel, and VMI are half of the six Senior Military Colleges. The rest are military-style academies within larger land-grant universities:

- North Georgia College and State University in Dahlonega was an SMC with **Cadets** until the basketball team's St. Bernard mascot (p. 205) made them **Saints** in the 1970s. The 2013 merger of NGCSU (and its SMC program) with Gainesville State College created the University of North Georgia. A student vote renamed the consolidated teams **Nighthawks**.[21]
- A car full of SMC cadets from Texas A&M hit a dog in 1931. They took her back to the **Aggies'** campus for nursing, but she didn't perk up until she heard the next day's reveille (the bugle blower's wake-up call). She was the first in TAMU's string of canine mascots named Reveille.
- Virginia Tech is an SMC, so ROTC cadets run the game ball around their stadium for 100 miles during **Hokie** homecoming week, and real cannon fire gets fans going at games.

The U.S. also funds five Junior Military Colleges, but they lean toward less dramatic nicknames. The New Mexico Military Institute (Roswell) runs out **Broncos** because it was once a school for cavalrymen. Georgia Military College is in Milledgeville, which is named for UGA founder John Milledge, so the school that was founded as part of the UGA system copies the one-time parent school's **Bulldogs**. MJC jocks discussed elsewhere are Wentworth Military Academy's **Dragons** and Marion Military Institute's **Tigers**. Valley Forge Military College (Wayne, Pa.) relies on both the assonance and consonance between "Forge" and "**Trojans**."

Normals | Profs | Owls | Nighthawks

Horace Mann developed a regiment for teacher training in Massachusetts. From his nineteenth-century perspective, Mann favored the maternal instincts of female teachers, and his normal-school model paved the way for the large-scale entry of women into higher education. *Normal* in this sense is from the Latin *normalis*, meaning in accordance with an established model, so normal-trained teachers gave instruction in the manner in which they'd received it.

Mann opened the country's first normal at Lexington in 1839, but it's been in Framingham since 1853. If any institution warrants a scholarly athletic identity, this would be it, but a Framingham State University jock is a **Ram**, from f-RAM-ingham. Another of Mann's Massachusetts normals became Bridgewater State University, but there's no explaining its **Bears** either, except that *B-e-a-r* can be found in "Bridgewater." (In fact, the ursine mascot is named Bristaco, from *Bri*-dgewater *sta*-te *co*-llege.)

The Father of American Education's methods moved outside Massachusetts, and some normals in the Midwest later shared campus space with the land-grant colleges (a scenario anticipated by the Morrill Act, p. 160). Like the land-grants, many normals are now well-known universities.

Profs ("professors") represent New Jersey's former Glassboro Normal School, Rowan University. Theirs is the team name that most explicitly reveals a normal school past. But wherever teams were once **Normals**, **Normalites**, or **Teachers**— or if Normal Street bisects a town named Normal—the local U is probably a former teachers' college:

- Illinois State University (ex–Illinois State Normal U.) is in the town of Normal, halfway between Chicago and St. Louis. Its cardinal-and-white **Teachers** became **Redbirds** in 1923 and adopted the state bird (northern cardinal) as the emblem, but they were careful not to be **Cardinals** to avoid being confused with St. Lou's major league baseballers.[1]
- The Eau Claire State Normal School backed **Normals** or **Normalites**. Early in the four-decade tenure of multi-sport coach Bill Zorn (1928–68), they were sometime **Zornmen** or **Golden Zornadoes**,[2] but usually **Blue and Gold** at today's University of Wisconsin–Eau Claire. The current **Blugolds** were first mentioned in a 1935 edition of the campus paper.
- The Maryland normal school at Towson had **Profs**, **Teachers**, and **Schoolmasters** (sometimes **Indians** or **Golden Knights**). They alliterated their way to "Towson **Tigers**" in the year before the school became Towson State College in 1963. (It's now Towson State University.)
- Statesboro's A&M school switched emphasis to teacher training in 1924. When it became Georgia Southern College in 1959, the **Professors** didn't represent all students, so they became **Eagles**. (GSC is now Georgia Southern University.)[3]
- Brockport State Normal School fielded **Normals**, but students at the renamed College at Brockport ("SUNY Brockport") voted to make them green-and-gold

Golden Eagles when intercollegiate football started under Coach Robert Ellsworth Boozer in 1947. In fact, the eagle mascot is "Ellsworth."

- Oshkosh's normal had **Normals** and **Normalites** in the late 1800s, but "**Titans**" would later be arbitrarily applied at the University of Wisconsin–Oshkosh.
- Troy University was as an Alabama teachers' college at Troy, so early teams were **Normals** and **Teachers**. The **Red Wave** first seen in 1932 was derived from Alabama's **Crimson Tide** (p. 266) up at Tuscaloosa, but the school tired of that comparison and moved to alliterative "Troy **Trojans**" in 1973.
- Students at Eastern State Teachers College (Madison, S.D., now Dakota State University) wanted reporters to stop calling teams **Teachers** in 1928. (Some forgotten yearbooks have them as "the **Normal**" or "**N Men**"). A name-the-team contest brought forth **Trojans**,[4] joined later by **Lady Ts**.
- The **Golden Rams** at West Chester University of Pennsylvania were formerly the State Teachers College **Teachers**.
- The Marquette normal school that's become Northern Michigan University fielded **Teachers**, **Normalites**, **Northerners**, and **Upstaters**. In 1935 basketball coach C.B. Hedgcock started running a man-to-man defense with his underclassmen while putting more experienced players in a zone. These were "cubs" and "cats" respectively, explaining **Wildcats** thereafter.[5]
- The West Tennessee Normal School was founded in 1912 with colors that represented a unified North and South, evinced by its **Blue and Grey** athletes. "We fight like Tigers!" was a 1914 cheer that made them **Tigers** for a while. "**Teachers**" and "**Tutors**" were preferred through the 1920s and most of the 1930s until the **Tigers** returned for good at what we call the University of Memphis.
- SUNY Fredonia is the former normal where the blue-and-white **Normalites** became **Blue Devils** in 1936.
- A 1922 student vote at the normal in Denton switched its **Normals** to **Eagles**. Later the forest-green uniforms at today's University of North Texas effected their transition to the **Mean Green** (although eagle mascots remain).[6]
- Fairmont [W. Va.] State University expanded its post-war curriculum, swapping **Fighting Teachers** for **Fighting Falcons** in 1947.[7]
- An education in education was among the practical programs offered by the Clarkson Memorial College of Technology in Potsdam, New York, where the **Teachers**[8] are now the Clarkson University **Golden Knights**.
- The 1913 Athletic Constitution for the Glenville, West Virginia normal school (now Glenville State College) put a *G* on athletic sweaters, yielding unofficial **Normal Boys** and **G-Men**. When the *Glenville Pathfinder* called them **Pioneers** in the late 1920s, the campus yearbook and newspaper followed.[9] (Gilmer County's first white pioneers were veterans of the War of 1812 who'd received local land grants.)
- In 1866 the cornerstone was set for the Kutztown normal that's now Kutztown University of Pennsylvania. Teams were **Teachers** then a **Golden Avalanche**, rumbling down from Normal Hill for road games. They've been **Golden Bears** since 1961, but the KU bear mascot is named Avalanche.

- The college for teachers at Emporia, Kansas presented **Yaps** in the 1930s. Students were apparently bothered by the non-stop yapping of their instructors. The unique moniker was put aside in around 1933 when the yellow and black became **Yellow Jackets**. Reporters casually substituted "**Hornets**," which now applies to all athletes at Emporia State University.[10]
- The normal at Bowling Green, Ohio backed **Normals**, **Teachers**, and **Pedagogues**. In 1927 an alum at the local *Sentinel-Tribune* who'd been reading up on falconry suggested falcon mascots for the orange and brown. The **Falcons** at today's Bowling Green State University suspect Cleveland's AAFC/NFL team to their east of appropriating their colors for the first **Browns** in 1946.
- Middle Tennessee State University opened in 1911 as Murfreesboro's normal. Its teams were **Normalites**, **Teachers**, and **Pedagogues** until fans of Colgate's **Red Raiders** (p. 98) campaigned to make them **Blue Raiders** in 1934.

• • •

As for the BGSU and MTSU **Pedagogues** ("child leaders" in Romance language), that word applies to teachers who conform to formalized, regimented instruction. It describes normal school grads precisely, so athletes on those campuses were often **Pedagogues** or **Peds**:

- Shortly after the New York State College for Teachers became the University at Albany in 1962, its **Pedagogues** (and their Pedwin the penguin) were replaced by **Great Danes**, based on a cultural predisposition that huge, muscular canines are somehow more athletically inspiring than academic instructors.
- Gold-and-purple teams at a Cedar Falls teachers' college (now the University of Northern Iowa) hated being **Pedagogs** or **Teachers**. A 1931 contest in the campus paper yielded something with more bite: (**Purple**) **Panthers**.
- **Pedagogues** represented a teachers' college in Cleveland, Mississippi. Today's Delta State University continues to appreciate its public sponsorship through **Statesmen** and **Lady Statesmen**.[11]
- The University of Wisconsin–Milwaukee ran out green-and-white **Normals** (1896–1927) then **Green Gulls** (referring to Great Lakes birds). Later nicknames tracked color changes; the red and white became **Cardinals** in 1956, but they've been black-and-gold **Panthers** since 1965.[12]
- California's San Jose State University has the oldest founding date—1862—of any CSU school. The former normal's **Teachers**, **Pedagogues**, and **Normalites** lasted until becoming something more normal in 1924: **Spartans**.[13]
- A Tennessee normal opened at Johnson City in 1911. A 1935 student vote turned **Teachers** into **Buccaneers**. The nearest pirate waters are 500 miles from East Tennessee State University, but the moniker may owe to whomever named a stream in the region's spooky limestone caverns "Pirate Creek."
- The *Pedagogian* at a Peru, Nebraska teachers' college (now Peru State College) usually called teams **Teachers**. That paper's editor made them more intimidating **Bobcats** in 1921.[14]
- Minnesota State University at Mankato is a former state normal where **Peds** were **Indians** after 1935, then they got hooked on the repetition of letters in "Mankato **Mavericks**" in 1977.

- A 1930 fire consumed Old Main Hall at Moorhead State Teachers College (now Minnesota State University Moorhead), giving the student body excuse to exchange **Peds** for **Dragons**.
- In Duluth, yet another Minnesota normal had **Peds** until 1933 and **Bulldogs** thereafter, the identity maintained at the University of Minnesota–Duluth.

• • •

An 1886-founded Chicago institution that developed radical ideas for early childhood education became the much-copied National College of Education. It's now National-Louis University, where **Eagles** allude to that *national* symbol. Otherwise, team names at former normals don't always have a supporting history:

- The New Britain normal that's now Central Connecticut State University is the state's oldest public college. Its **Blue Devils** are explained only through blue-and-white uniforms.
- Ellensburg's 1892-founded state normal is now Central Washington University. We know the year teams became **Wildcats** (1926), but not the reason.
- A Montana state normal opened at Dillon in 1893. Previous nicknames are unknown, but today's University of Montana–Western keeps **Bulldogs**.
- Two formal normals that explain their **Vikings** through their famous ports are Elizabeth City [N.C.] State University and Salem [Mass.] State University.
- Kids at the normal school that became the University of Wisconsin–River Falls elected to replace their **Red and White** with **Falcons** in fall 1931, based on that flyer's admirable attributes.[15]

• • •

Rowan University's **Profs** (p. 166) have an owl mascot named Whoo RU (whoo are you?). That's apt representation for any college because owls have come to indicate braininess through their association with the Greek goddess of wisdom and learning, Athena.

A giant concrete owl over the doorway of the academic building at William Woods University (Fulton, Mo.) gave name to its **Owls** and *Green Owl* campus paper. Craving attention from WWU's all-female student body, enrollees at the all-male Westminster College would travel ten blocks to paint the owl forest green. Aficionados of rivalry-based vandalism remain puzzled as to why those trespassers splashed around WWU's green instead of the blue that explains Westminster's own **Blue Jays** (p. 68).[16]

Owls on the seals of Rice University (Houston) and Bryn Mawr [Pa.] College are explicitly those of Ms. Athena, and both schools in fact back **Owls**. When an institution has a normal school past, **Owl** athletes are even more likely present:

- In 1838, Horace Mann founded a Massachusetts normal at Barre that moved to Westfield in 1844, explaining Westfield State University's **Owls**.
- Southern Connecticut State University grew out of New Haven's 1893-founded normal, as its **Owls** suggest.
- The Keene State University **Owls** represent a former New Hampshire normal (est. 1909).
- The **Owls** at the University of Maine at Presque Isle indicate its 1903 founding as a state normal.

Some ex-**Owls** are more famous under later names. Arizona State University evolved out of Tempe's normal (est. 1885). Its teams were first **Normals** or **Owls** and then **Bulldogs**. They've been **Sun Devils** since 1946, the decade after travel agencies started using "Valley of the Sun" to describe the Phoenix-Tempe area (thus, the NBA Phoenix **Suns**, est. 1968). Alabama's Jacksonville State University has roots as an 1883 normal. Its early teams put an aggressive spin on things as **Eagle Owls**. (The Eurasian eagle owl, *Bubo bubo*, is the largest owl.) In 1946 the war veterans on the hoop squad wanted something with a little more fight and switched to **Gamecocks**.

• • •

People active after sunset are "night owls" or "nighthawks," after two groups of raptors with excellent low-light vision. We can't list all institutions with night-school roots (or similarly purposed community and junior colleges) that keep **Owls** or **Nighthawks**,[17] but these have evolved into four-year programs:

- In the early 1960s, Gov. Carl Sanders "pledged to place a public college within commuting distance of virtually every person"[18] in Georgia. One was Kennesaw Junior College, which opened in 1966. It fielded **Golden Owls** in the early 1980s that were **Fighting Owls** by '86. They're now simply **Owls** at Kennesaw State University.

- Georgia State University opened in 1913 as a business school. Night classes made for **Owls**, but they were **Ramblers** (for reasons unknown) in 1947 and **Panthers** after 1955. The downtown Atlanta campus is ten miles from some of the GSU playing fields in an Atlanta neighborhood with the coincidentally historical name of Panthersville.

- In 1884, Rev. Russell Conwell started using the basement of his Baptist temple to informally educated North Philadelphia workmen at night. There would soon be a college charter, but those original "night owls" are remembered by Temple University's **Owls**.

- Thomas University (Thomasville, Ga.) has **Night Hawks**. It was founded as a junior college in 1954, but has since been a community college (1976), a four-year college (1988), and a university (2000).

- **Nighthawks** represent Newbury College, a former junior college in Brookline, Massachusetts.

- Monmouth Junior College (West Long Branch, N.J.) had teams of **Nighthawks** to honor "the night-only schedule."[19] They were **Hawks** when daytime classes started in 1956 at what is now Monmouth University.

Trojans | Titans | Olympics | Orange | Phoenix

The West's fascination with all things Greek comes through Rome, which added Greece to its empire in 146 BCE. The Romans absorbed the cultural peculiarities of their domains rather than extinguish them, so Greek forms were mimicked across the empire. *Classical* is the word we use to describe old Greco-Roman things.

Before the A&Ms and normals emphasized practical education, the study of "liberal arts" was only for the privileged elite. In fact, *liber* (free) indicated intellectual pursuits that befit men of leisure, not men of trades. Post-Renaissance students of classical philosophy, literature, mathematics, and arts have examined Greek and Latin (Roman) texts for centuries. That yields any number of Greek- or Roman-themed team names. Whereas **Vikings**, **Celtics**, or **Dutch** often indicate regional immigration trends, **Spartans**, **Titans**, **Trojans**, and **Gladiators** occur even in the absence of Greek and Italian laborers who wouldn't arrive in significant numbers until the twentieth century. Had they come earlier, we might follow many more **Centurions** and **Apollos** at the expense of **Wildcats** and **Eagles**.

American educators often named new college towns from classical history and literature, sometimes creating pairings with a maximum of redundancy. (Refer to Troy University's **Trojans**, p. 167.) But there are plenty of **Trojans** and **Spartans**, if only to indicate a learned student body.

Because the University of Southern California had been affiliated with John Wesley's Methodist church from its 1880 founding until 1952, its athletes were **Wesleyans** and **Fighting Methodists**. Owen Bird of the *Los Angeles Times* called USC athletes **Trojans** in 1912 because they fought to the bitter end, an unintended imitation of those citizens of Troy whose bravery couldn't stave off Greek invaders in the Trojan War (c. 1200 BCE). Collegians would have encountered that near-mythical war in Homer's *Iliad* and *Odyssey*, and USC's ladies are the **Women of Troy**, the name of a 415 BCE Greek play by Euripides that chronicles the many troubles endured by royal Trojan women at the hands of Greek captors.

Many suitors called on Helen of Troy, the alluring daughter of Zeus whose face launched a thousand warships to start the Trojan War. **Helenas** therefore appeared beside male **Trojans** at Calgary's Southern Alberta Institute of Technology after World War II, but by 1988 they too were **Trojans**.

Portsmouth, Ohio's high school had good footballing **Trojans**. In the 1920s, graduates formed the semi-pro Portsmouth **Spartans**, a name to classically match the junior **Trojans**.[1] The **Spartans** joined the NFL in 1930 but moved to Detroit for 1934. They decided to avoid confusion with the **Spartans** over at Michigan State by becoming **Lions**, a bit of felinity borrowed from baseball's **Tigers**.[2]

There was another **Trojans**-to-**Spartans** evolution at Norfolk State University. As "Norfolk Division," it had been a branch of Virginia State University. Its **Baby Trojans** echoed VSU's own arbitrarily named **Trojans**. When developing its own identity in 1952, Norfolk's "lesser" **Trojans** became **Spartans**. (Norfolk State did become independent of VSU in 1969.)[3]

W. Barron Hilton probably called his 1960 AFLers "Los Angeles **Chargers**" because the USC bugle call for a **Trojan** *"CHAAARGE!"* had filled their stadium since the 1940s. (Hilton's hotel company had just introduced one of the first credit cards, so some say "**Chargers**" encouraged spending sprees, a story to which historians extend little credit.) Different Memorial Coliseum tenants—the NFL's established Los Angeles **Rams**—were more formidable obstacles to creating an AFL fanbase, so San Diego sports editor Jack Murphy talked Hilton into bolting south with his blueshirts for 1961. As *San Diego* **Chargers**, they merged into the NFL in 1970.[4]

• • •

Titans were giants in Greek myths. Led by Cronus, they overthrew their father Uranus for control of the universe, so titanic imagery is something athletes might embrace. "You can't coach height" is an old hoop adage, but John Lawther at Westminster College (New Wilmington, Pa.) forced the other guy to coach around height in 1926 by benching his veterans and running a zone D of tall underclassmen. A reporter called them "towering titans," now simply **Titans**.[5]

Nashville opened many prestigious centers of learning after the Civil War. Its State Capitol is an excellent example of Greek Revival architecture. Downtown, there's a full-size replica of Greece's most famous building, the Parthenon. Many antebellum homes in central Tennessee were built in the neo-classical style. Why are we telling you this? Because each helps to make Nashville the "Athens of the South." It's only natural the city's NFL Tennessee **Titans** wear a Greek mask.[6]

In February 1959 the U.S. Air Force tested its first multistage intercontinental ballistic missile—the huge Titan I—at Cape Canaveral, Florida. Just across the Indian River Lagoon, Brevard [County] Junior College (now Eastern Florida State College) opened the next year. Its SpaceTEC program would train a bunch of aerospace technicians that were eligible **Titans**.

California's Orange County State College opened as a **Titan** base seven months after the Titan I's maiden flight. Coincidence? The archives aren't clear. It's just as likely the **Titans** were classical foils to USC's **Trojans** a few miles away. The OCSC **Titans** were without mascots until jokesters advertised an Inter-collegiate Elephant Race in 1962. Surprisingly, mounts showed up from as far away as Harvard and England's Oxford University. Tuffy the Titan was the host entrant, giving pachyderm mascots to what is now California State University–Fullerton.

A 1969 election at Indiana University–South Bend launched its **Titans**. There's no documented connection to Titan missiles, but one seems likely because the same vote brought in colors of white and "Air Force blue." After only one year, IUSB switched to the red and white to more closely match other schools in the IU system, but **Titans** remain.[7]

Illinois Wesleyan University teams in Bloomington were **Green and Whites** (or **GAWs**) until becoming **Titans** for reasons unrecorded in 1928.[8]

• • •

In a literally *classic* case of comeuppancey, the Titans of myth were vanquished by Cronus's own son Zeus of the next-generation Olympian gods, which included the sea god Poseidon and his merman son Triton. Most athletic **Tritons** are in port cities, as is the case at the University of California–San Diego, Eckerd

College (St. Petersburg, Fla.), and Edmonds Community College (Lynnwood, Wash.). In 1966, **Rivermen** and **Riverwomen** appeared at the University of Missouri–St. Louis (as did the river-themed *Current* student news). Mostly owing to gender specificity, those nicks were abandoned in favor of "**Tritons**" in 2007.

To honor Zeus, the Greeks held the Olympic Games at Olympia every four years from 776 BCE until Rome outlawed non-Christian festivals in 394 CE. That inspired many **Olympic** teams or stadiums called Olympic Park even before European aristocrats jump-started the modern games in 1896.[9]

Montreal's 1967 World's Fair—"Expo '67"—gave a name to baseball's 1969 expansion Montreal **Expos**. Quebec's largest city soon earned another international party, the 1976 Summer Olympics. In anticipation, a 1971 NASL team was called the Montreal **Olympique,** but they lasted only until '73. Greater Ottawa's 1970-founded QJHL Hull **Festivals** became **Olympiques** in '76. Hull is now part of Gatineau, so they've been Gatineau **Olympiques** since 2003.

Adolph Rupp's Kentucky **Wildcats** beat Baylor University's **Bears** for the 1948 NCAA championship. But UK's "Fabulous Five" was edged out at the Olympic trials by Bud Browning's Phillips **66ers**, an Oklahoma AAU squad. At the London Games, co-coaches Browning and Rupp won gold simply by substituting Kentucky's starting five for that of the **66ers**. In an unprecedented move, the Kentuckians joined the NBA as a virtual unit after repeating as NCAA champs in 1949. They replaced the NBA Indianapolis **Jets** as Indianapolis **Olympians**.

Scandal broke in 1951 when some **Olympians** turned out to be among the many players who'd toyed with point spreads during their late college years. The NBA banned those **Olympians** for life and their Indy team was dissolved after the 1952/53 season. The big winners were the pros; being up front about player salaries and having new access to arenas previously booked up with collegiate doubleheaders (notably Madison Square Garden), the NBA started to thrive.

• • •

When upstate New York's Military Tract was diced up and distributed to war veterans in the 1790s, a post-Revolutionary embrace of Athenian aesthetics and Roman republicanism were apparent in townships that were named for people and places that seem to have been pulled from John Dryden's popular translation of Plutarch's *Lives of the Noble Grecians and Romans*.[10] Historians generally say those names were given by the well-read land-board secretary, Robert Harpur, a trustee and former math professor at King's College (later Columbia University).

The trend started when the village of Vanderheyden was renamed Troy in 1789. Its NLers were among many Troy **Trojans** (1879–82), a theme paralleled by Rome **Romans**, turn-of-the-century baseballers in the New York State League.

In 1820 citizens in one upstate burg wanted to take the name of a powerful Peloponnesian city-state, Corinth. When the postmaster discovered that Saratoga County already had a Corinth, he suggested the name of Sicily's Siracusa (another salt-producing city). Syracuse University opened there in 1871 with unintimidating colors of pink and pea-green. In 1890 the 'Cuse switched to a single hue inspired by fruit: the Golden Apples of Hesperides. Stealing said apples from Zeus's fruit bowl had been among the Twelve Labors of Hercules. Not to compare apples and oranges, but a literal translation of *golden apple* from Greek or Latin describes an orange, so SU's golden color skews to the red.

Even with orange as the color of their dress (blue was added to their silks later as an unofficial accent), it took a while for Syracusans to arrive at their "**Orange**" label. A 1928 hoax in the campus paper reported that excavations for a new college building had yielded evidence for "The Saltine Warrior, Big Chief Bill Orange," immediately making athletes **Warriors**. Their Indian mascots were later at odds with the university's historically healthy relations with the area's Onondagas, so SU dropped the name in the mid-1970s to favor the longtime alternates **Orangemen** and **Orangewomen**, both sliced to **Orange** in 2004.[11]

Buffalo State College's orange-and-gray **Orange** and **Orangemen** risked being confused with Syracuse, so basketballers changed to **Billies** from 1951 to '59, nicely filling the bill between the 1949 demise of the AAFC Buffalo **Bills** and the 1960 arrival of the AFL/NFL **Bills**. By 1969 all BSC teams were tigertoned **Bengals**.[12]

Triple Cities College of Syracuse University opened in 1946 to serve World War II vets in the Binghamton–Endicott–Johnson City area. Old Colonial Hall, the main building in Endicott, led to **Colonials**. TCC parted with SU in 1950 to join the new State University of New York (SUNY) system. It moved to Binghamton as Harpur College (after the abovementioned Robert Harpur) and is now Binghamton University.[13] Students grew to dislike "**Colonials**," so teams became (historically barren but alliterative) Binghamton **Bearcats** in 1999.

• • •

The phoenix in Egyptian and Greek mythology was depicted as a peacock, heron, or crane that ignites in its nest before rising from the ashes to realize another 500-year lifetime. To the ancients, this was illustrative of the daily cycle of sunrise and sunset. Christians see the life-death-rebirth cycle and the purported incorruptibility of the peafowl's flesh as having parallels with the resurrection of Jesus. Anyway, such tales yield pretty cool nicknames:

- Colors of white and peacock blue were somewhat arbitrarily chosen to represent Upper Iowa University in the 1890s. Mustering behind those shades, students in Fayette called themselves "peacocks" long before athletes did, but jocks have been proud to be **Peacocks** since about 1920.[14]

- Its enrollment dwindled during World War I, so Saint Peter's University (Jersey City, N.J.) closed. When the Jesuits reopened it in 1930, one dean suggested that a phoenix-ish name would celebrate that reemergence.[15] SPU deserves compliments for its complementary male **Peacocks** and female **Peahens**.

- Athletes at Elon [N.C.] University became **Fightin' Christians** in 1921 to expressly contrast with their **Quaker** rivals from Guilford College (p. 220).[16] Elon quickly snapped back after a bad 1923 fire, but it didn't have **Phoenix** squads to commemorate that recovery until 2000.

- The literal description of the phoenix is "fire bird," making redundant the name an Arizona's PCL Phoenix **Firebirds** (1986–97).

- Tackle football's 2001-founded Philadelphia **Liberty Belles** split after the 2002 season. Some women remained **Belles** while others returned from disintegration as the **Phoenix**. The latter moved into a league that already had a Carolina **Phoenix** team in Greensboro, so they became Philadelphia **Firebirds**.

> Kirtland's warbler (*Dendroica kirtlandii*) looks nothing like a phoenix, but it's a *firebird* because it nests in Jack Pine forests that pop up only after forest fires. The warbler's namesake is Kirtland Community College (Roscommon, Mich.), where the **Firebirds** have a winged mascot named Sparky.

The phoenix's rebirth is associated with the dawn. As the sun rises, so does your thermometer's mercury. These facts give us the Phoenix **Suns** and **Mercury**, Arizona's NBA-WNBA tandem. (They're also paired in celestial terms, Mercury being the closest planet to our sun.) Arizona's largest city grew after white settlers used the Salt River for irrigation. Two millennia earlier, the Hohokam people (the probable ancestors of southern Arizona's later tribes) also managed their desert environment with canals. The state capital, therefore, isn't called Phoenix because it's hot as a burning bird but because it's reborn from the ruins of the Indian village. Phoenix's Mesa suburb was home to the Mesa Community College **HoKams** until "**Thunderbirds**" was adopted from Indian myths in 1974.

• • •

In ancient Greek medicine, Aries the ram ruled the head and brain, qualifying him for Ryerson University's coat of arms. The Toronto school with the Latin motto *Mente et Artifici* (with mind and skill) keeps **Rams**.

• • •

The Greek words *meter* (mother) and *polis* (city) yield *metropolis* and *metropolitan*, words so common that *metro-* now describes city things, not maternal ones. Any city can declare its metropolitanism, and the biggest of American cities often does, as exhibited by New York's **Mets** ("metropolitans" abridged). The MLS **MetroStars** (1996–2005) played in various New Jersey stadiums (sometimes identifying with the metropolitan region as the "New York–New Jersey" **Metro-Stars**). Red Bull energy drink bought the **M'Stars** in early 2006 and made them **Red Bull** New York. The Austrian company had bought Salzburg's beloved first-division club the year before and renamed it **Red Bull** Salzburg. (Corporate ownership of a major North American team hadn't been so transparent since the industrial Midwest's football and basketball leagues of the 1940s.)

The Greek *kosmos* (world) and *polites* (citizen) lead to *cosmopolitan*, which describes a city of international persons. The NASL New York **Cosmos** (1971–84) played in an immigrant city with a roster of international talent.[17] New **Cosmos** were New York entrants in the 2013 NASL.

Havana's *Los **Guerreros** Metropolitanos* (metropolitan warriors) are top-flight Cuban baseballers assembled in 1974 from the downtown area of the island's biggest city. "**Metros**" distinguishes them from their more successful Cuban National League rivals, *Los **Leones** de Industriales* (est. 1961). Those "industrial lions" (also *Los **Azules***: "the blues") are a collection of players from factories on the city's fringes. The state assigns Cuban players to regional squads, so teams are often identified accordingly. Therefore, these teams are usually called *Metropolitanos* and *Industriales* (instead of **Guerreros** and **Leones**) by fans.

Creoles | Jazz | Blues | Soul

In our introduction we took pains to say that team names drawn from the human history of North America almost always refer to Indians (however unflattering) or white male pioneers. An exception is forced by the undeniable impact African American musical traditions have had domestically and abroad.

• • •

The offspring of entitled European-born persons in Spain's colonial West Indies were called *criollos*.[1] From that, Louisiana's French called their New World kids *creoles*. Then—as with *yankee*—the definition of *creole* branched out. After the 1803 Louisiana Purchase, any native-born Louisianan could self-identify as a *creole* to contrast with the newly arrived Anglos. And it was about then that mixed-race *gens de couleur libre* (free people of color) were first called black Creoles. Those were often the offspring of European men and female slaves, but Afro-Carib-Franco-Iberian blood in any relative percentages could yield *creoles*.

Being professionally, socially, and culturally adept, the black Creoles seemed to have a destiny apart from their black neighbors. The luckiest were even sent by their white fathers to take studies in France that might have included musical training. With historical pride attached to the word, black minor leaguers in New Orleans were **Creoles** during the first half of the twentieth century.

Post-Reconstruction segregation would reclassify Louisiana's black Creoles simply as black. For all of their refined habits, they would endure the same hardships as ex-slaves. Their formal training gave some Creoles a familiarity with classical music, syncopated marches, and ragtime, and they'd worked up the technical chops to execute them. When former plantation slaves taught them West African rhythms and improvised folk forms—work songs, blues, gospel hymns— New Orleans started bustling with a new sound that would be called *jazz*. The place to check it out was the red-light district's Victorian parlors, where soon-famous musicians provided background music for drinking, dancing, and whatever else was going on.

The Gulf port was a dumping ground for surplus equipment when the Civil and Spanish-American Wars ended, so by 1900 anybody in N'awlins who wanted a military band instrument could get one. The city became a breeding ground for horn players like Buddy Bolden, King Oliver, Louis Armstrong, Sidney Bechet, and Kid Ory, as remembered by minor league hockey's New Orleans **Brass** (1997–2002).

New Orleans announced the name of a new NFL team on November 1, 1966, which residents of the historically Catholic city recognize as All Saints' Day (an everyone-gets-a-trophy feast day for the thousands of martyrs for whom a 365-day calendar is not sufficient). The next fall, the New Orleans **Saints** strode in to Tulane Stadium to the sound of the Dixieland jazz tune "When the Saints Go Marching In."[2]

• • •

World War I required that soldiers and sailors be at their stations and not laid up with social diseases, so the New Orleans *jass* houses (brothels) were shut down. Out-of-work musicians traveled north, bringing a new music to audiences that called it *jass* or *jazz* for the first time. The NBA's Utah **Jazz** don't have a *bad* name, just a geographically inappropriate one. The franchise started out aptly enough as New Orleans **Jazz** in 1974. To say the Beehive State lacks a profound African American musical tradition is an understatement, but it's hosted the **Jazz** since their move to Salt Lake City in 1979.

During the war, factories stopped hiring foreign workers, so the musicians' northward trek was part of the former slave class's Great Migration to industrial cities. A first stop was often up the Delta at Memphis, where Alabama-born cornetist W.C. Handy was a major player on Beale Street. In 1912 he was the first to use blues forms in a popular published song with "The Memphis Blues." Semi-pro rugby players are the Memphis **Blues** R.F.C. (est. 1968), and minor league baseball's Memphis **Blues** (1968–76) had an eighth-note logo.

Memphis is where the blues, jazz, and gospel that were moving north inter-sected with the bluegrass and mountain music from the east. If any one spot gave birth to rhythm-and-blues and rock 'n roll, it's Memphis, as argued by the Memphis **Rockers** (1990–92) of the World Basketball League (1988–92, a pro minor league for players under 6'7").

In the late 1940s, Memphis had the country's first radio station programmed for black audiences. The next decade saw the city's Sun Records introduce some insanely popular white country-rockabilly-blues artists. By 1959, the music that was pouring out of the black neighborhood called Soulsville was being captured and released by Stax Records. Hi Records cut rockabilly and soul sides through-out the 1960s and 1970s. Irrespective of the target audience, the production of music in Memphis was largely an integrated affair. The former ABA **Pros** and **Tams** (p. 337) were the Memphis **Sounds** during the 1975/76 session, having been named when the group that tried (and failed) to buy them included Stax's top artist-producer Isaac Hayes.

Business leaders in western Tennessee applied for NFL expansion rights in 1993. Their Memphis **Hound Dogs** were named after Elvis Presley's 1956 Sun smash, "Hound Dog." The Presley estate pulled its investment when the NFL dis-missed the bid, so they played as the CFL's Memphis **Mad Dogs** for 1995. A later team played the 2000/01 ABA season as Memphis **Houn'Dawgs**.

• • •

The American Jazz Museum and the Negro Leagues Baseball Museum both stand on a corner near 18th and Vine, which was the heart of Kansas City's vibrant black neighborhood after World War I. For decades, ensembles filled local halls with the up-tempo, riff-based sound of "jump blues." The practitioners of K.C.'s swinging style included Jay McShann, Bennie Moten, Jimmy Rushing, and Joe Turner. Taking it all in was McShann's young altoist Charlie "Yardbird" Parker, soon to be listed among the jazz immortals for pioneering the harmonically advanced and pyrotechnic bebop style. But Bird did reveal his swinging soul on more moderately paced classics like 1951's "K.C. Blues."

Citing this history, it would be convenient if the many past Kansas City **Blues** teams had saluted these musical traditions, but that's not the case. The Western League's Kansas City **Blues** (1898–1900)[3] predated the city's unique sound by decades and were therefore named directly after their blue unis. (They were later Washington **Senators** [1901–60] and then today's Minnesota **Twins**.) Various K.C. teams have since been **Blues**, including more baseball minor leaguers (1904–54) and a 1924 NFL team. Finally in 1967 came minor league hockey's Kansas City **Blues**, who had an eighth-note emblem, which surely owed to city's musical heritage … ? Nope. Those **Blues** were named after their NHL parent club in St. Louis.

But now we're getting somewhere. St. Louey would be a musical hotbed on par with Memphis after African Americans flooded into its factories. Chuck Berry and Miles Davis are favorite sons; Scott Joplin became the king of ragtime after arriving from Texas; and in 1914 old friend W.C. Handy penned what is likely the most recorded blues song ever, "St. Louis Blues." So the NHL's St. Louis **Blues** were indeed named during the 1967 expansion to trumpet the city's home-grown sound.

• • •

Newspaper ads in the *Chicago Defender* lured black Southerners north to the end of the Illinois Central line. King Oliver, Jelly Roll Morton, and Louis Armstrong were among the transplanted New Orleanians playing the jazz that white north-erners called Dixieland. (It would heavily influence Chicago-bred players like Benny Goodman and Lionel Hampton.)

As the full force of the Great Migration hit the Windy City, it got harder to hear acoustic string instruments over the crowds and ever-larger ensembles in clubs. The "Chicago blues" style is therefore associated with the amplified hum and sustain of the modern electric guitar as played by sons of Mississippi like Elmore James, Muddy Waters, and Bo Diddley. Chicago is also rich in the gospel tradition thanks to Georgia-born Thomas Dorsey and New Orleanian Mahalia Jackson.

Having somehow overlooked those contributions, Continental Basketball League players were Chicago **Rockers** (1994–96). Worse still, a press release by the 2006-only ABA Chicago **Rockstars** declared, "New York, L.A., Atlanta, and Houston have had their turn. It is time for Chicago to stand up and take its place as music's powerhouse." Then some recent (but not necessarily historically sig-nificant) acts were cited as justification. Finally a short-lived MISL side was called Chicago **Soul** FC (2012/13) in remembrance of the gospel-edged "Chicago soul" sound of the 1960s, exemplified by Lou Rawls, Sam Cooke, Jackie Wilson, Curtis Mayfield, and the Staple Singers.

• • •

Because the auto plants in the Motor City—"Mo' Town"—were migration mag-nets, the black population of Detroit boomed. The Motown sound is identified with a single label, Motown Records, started in 1960 by Berry Gordy, whose parents left Georgia for Michigan in the 1920s. Detroit's Motown **Jammers** joined the 2004 ABA, but they couldn't keep hanging on even through that season. Back in Gordy's home state, rap and rhythm and blues musicians were fashioning Atlanta as "the new Motown." From 2001 to 2003, Georgia's WUSA side was the Atlanta **Beat**. Like many in that league, the **Beat** picked up again in 2010 and 2011 when the WPS resurrected its A-town presence.[4]

Philadelphia's slaves were often domestic servants, as indicated by basketball's Philadelphia **Colonial Maids**, a successful black women's team of the early 1930s. Its famously abolitionist Quaker population had made Philly a major stop on the Underground Railroad before the twentieth century brought tons of black Americans to Pennsylvania mills, mines, and docks. Against that backdrop, many black vocal groups popped up in 1960s Philly. Early in the next decade, Philadelphia International Records rivaled Motown by backing up singers (like the Spinners, O'Jays, and Blue Notes) with ambitious arrangements to produce the velvety smooth "Philly soul" sound. Coming up alongside Philly's black groups were some of white guys who copied the style of Motown groups like the Temptations. Those Temptones (being attendees at Temple University) included Daryl and John, who as Hall and Oates would become leaders of "blue-eyed soul," a term black Philadelphia DJ Georgie Woods used to describe white singers in that tradition. When Arena Football's Philadelphia **Soul** appeared in 2004, hard rocker and R&B fan Jon Bon Jovi was a majority owner.

Post-war America's white population generally ignored the contributions of black musicians, so rhythm-and-blues recordings ("race records") were marketed to black consumers. Those same songs received mainstream airplay only after being covered by white performers like Pat Boone, Georgia Gibbs, or the Crew-Cuts. Nobody wanted to be the first white DJ to play R&B sides, so Cleveland's Alan Freed spun the original black versions as "rock & roll." It was Freed's coinage more than any locally grown form that made his city the "home of rock & roll," but it was enough to justify both the groundbreaking for Cleveland's Rock and Roll Hall of Fame in 1993 and the WNBA Cleveland **Rockers** (1997–2003).

• • •

Boston's Berklee College of Music is famous for jazz studies. Students there spend most waking hours practicing mixolydian scales or seeing what fun can be had by flipping the 3rds and 7ths in substitute dominant chords, but a few find time for hockey as club-level **Ice Cats**.[5] They're named for Berklee's hepcat mascot Mingus, named after the eccentric bassist whose big-sounding small ensembles merged blues and jazz forms for multiple post-war decades. The other major contribution made by Charles Mingus to Western civilization was his *CATalog*, a how-to pamphlet that chronicled the toilet training of his cat Nightlife.

• • •

Gene Simmons and Paul Stanley were original members of the legendary New York rock band Kiss and the most visible co-owners of an Arena Football team that launched near their new California homes in 2014, the Los Angeles **Kiss**.

Brown Dodgers | American Giants | Globetrotters | Zulus

Black baseballers of different eras are casually called "Negro leaguers," but the first professional Negro National League wasn't formed at Kansas City until 1920. Subsequent black leagues experienced various degrees of success and lots of volatility. Players jumped often among squads only slightly faster than those same teams switched leagues, cities, or monikers, so forgive us for not always strictly assigning league affiliations or years of operation to the teams that follow.

• • •

Some say black baseball's 1902 Indianapolis **ABCs** were named for their sponsor, the American Brewing Company, but Paul Debono's book on the club calls any company sponsorship "minimal and short-lived." At any rate, no such relationship was possible after the brewery closed in 1917, three years before the **ABCs** entered the NNL.[1] Compounding the confusion, the **ABCs** merged in 1939 with Atlanta's **Black Crackers**—different "A.B.C.s"[2]—who shared the field of the 1903-founded (white) Atlanta **Crackers**. This makes the **Black Crackers** indicative of a baseball trend; many black squads simply slapped *Black* or *Brown* in front of a familiar moniker. Refer to Brooklyn's **Brown Dodgers**, New York's **Black Yankees**, and Washington's **Black Senators**. (Using irony to buck this trend were the Denver **White Elephants**, usually Colorado's best black baseballers between 1915 and 1935.)

Multi-racial Cuban players often barnstormed the country as **Havanans, All Cubans**, or **Cuban Stars**. A few African Americans pretended to be from the Caribbean's largest island and passed as "**Cubans**" because Cubans weren't barred from the major leagues (although some prospects were ignored for having particularly dark skin). Florida native Alessandro Pompez was the Cuban-American owner of the New York **Cubans** (1939–50) and the **Cuban Stars East** (1916–33), the latter being regionally distinct from the unaffiliated **Cuban Stars West** (1907–32).

• • •

Members of a religious colony called the Israelite House of David settled at Benton Harbor, Michigan in 1903. While waiting on the glorious return of their lord Jesus Christ, they put together the **House of David** baseball team. Citing Leviticus 19:27, the HOD men didn't cut their hair or trim their beards. The curiosity they aroused and their polished skills brought them national fame through matches against other great barnstormers, often the black clubs. You might even see the HOD listed among Negro League records of the day without any sense of irony. The **HOD** had traveling basketballers too. (A 1930 split in the Michigan colony turned the **HOD** teams into **City of David** teams.)

Exploiting the **HOD's** fame was the Minneapolis **Colored House of David**. Blackball promoter Syd Pollock then absurdly advanced the cross-pollination of team names with the **Cuban House of David**. In the clownin' tradition (p. 183), those black and Latino players wore ridiculous beards that mocked the original **HOD**.

• • •

In the 1920s, the Crawford Avenue recreation center in Pittsburgh's Hill District sponsored a sandlot team called Crawford **Giants**, later Pittsburgh **Crawfords**. In 1930 those successful independents were purchased by numbers runner Gus Greenlee, who owned the Crawford Grill jazz club. As noted baseball historian G. Edward White points out, black teams were often "controlled by entrepreneurs in the numbers business. In 1937, for example, the **Crawfords**, the [Homestead] **Grays**, the New York **Black Yankees**, the Washington **Elite Giants**, the Philadelphia **Stars**, and the Newark **Eagles** were owned by numbers operators" [emphasis added].[3] Greenlee himself initiated a second NNL in 1933. With a roster of Hall of Famers Cool Papa Bell, Oscar Charleston, Josh Gibson, William "Judy" Johnson, and Satchel Paige, the **Crawfords** that won the 1935 and '36 NNL championships are counted among the game's all-time great sides without qualification.[4]

• • •

Like any league, there were **Tigers**, **Eagles**, and **Athletics** in their midst, but one trend is hard to ignore. About half the teams in the first NNL (1920–31) and the rival Eastern Colored League (1923–28) were **Giants** of one manner or another. They were named after either the first black pro team (the **Cuban Giants**) or the early century's dominant major leaguers in New York. For example, the Nashville **Elite Giants**, Pittsburgh **Crawford Giants**, and Philadelphia **Giants** are some of the clubs for which Satchel Paige pitched … *in just 1931.*

The ECL had been formed by breakaway NNL teams in 1923. The Hilldale Athletic Club (est. 1910) from the black Hilldale neighborhood of Philadelphia's Darby borough won the first three ECL titles behind third baseman Judy Johnson. The **Hilldales** were later the Darby **Daisies** (owing to daisy-covered Hilldale Park) and sometimes—of course—Hilldale **Giants**.

Black sides often needed advertisers to pick up their travel expenses. The Page Fence **Giants** toured in the 1890s to promote a Michigan barbed-wire company. In 1899 some disbanded Page Fencers formed the Chicago **Columbian Giants**, bankrolled by a black fraternity, the Columbia Club.

A few black-owned businesses sponsored neighborhood clubs that became nationally known. The New York **Gorhams** were black players named in 1886 for Alexander Gorham's Manhattan tavern.[5] The Brooklyn **Royal Giants** (1905–42) were paid by the Royal Café.

Frank Leland and W.S. Peters started the Chicago **Giants** in 1887. They were **Union Giants** after absorbing the Chicago **Unions** in 1901, and then the **Leland Giants** in 1905.[6] When Leland fell out with manager (and NNL founder) Rube Foster in 1910, the team remained **Leland Giants**, but the better players went to Foster's new Chicago **American Giants**, who won the first three NNL championships and often outdrew the city's major leaguers. Ample coverage in the nation's preeminent black newspaper, the *Chicago Defender*, justified their national ("**American**") moniker. The NNL played only one season beyond Foster's death in December 1930, but his team survived in different leagues until 1952 as Cole's **American Giants** under South Side businessman Robert A. Cole.

• • •

The stream of black literature, art, music, and political thought coming out of
New York's Harlem neighborhood between World War I and the Depression was
unparalleled in American history. To single out W.E.B. Du Bois, Langston
Hughes, Duke Ellington, or Aaron Douglas as giants of the Harlem Renaissance
is to dismiss the long list of thinkers and creative types who contributed to the
movement. Harlem landmarks of the era included the Apollo Theater, the Savoy
Ballroom, and the Renaissance Casino.

The Casino's dance floor was the home court of the first professional black
basketball team in 1923, the **Renaissance Five**.[7] The **Rens** followed their 112-7
season in 1939 by winning the *Chicago Herald-American's* inaugural World Professional Basketball Tournament. (That meeting of black and white barnstormers
was the semi-official world championship until 1948.) The Washington **Bears**
that won the 1943 tourney—*and all of their other games that year*—were really
the **Rens**, having been confined to weekend games in D.C. by wartime travel
restrictions.[8] In the midst of the 1948/49 season, the **Rens** went to Ohio to complete the NBL schedule of the disintegrated Detroit **Vagabond Kings**[9] as Dayton
Rens. That made them "the only all-black franchise in the history of major league
sports,"[10] but the NBL disbanded after that season.

• • •

In early 1928 the strong hoop team from the South Side's Wendell Phillips High
School transitioned to a Negro American Legion squad. Then they represented
Chicago's Savoy Ballroom (named and modeled for its New York sister) as the
Savoy **Big Five**. Forward Tommy Brookins split with management later that year
and led some of the **Five's** core players to the Legion armory as Chicago **Globe
Trotters**.[11]

In 1929, Chicagoan Abe Saperstein (the son of Jewish immigrants) went from
being the **Globe Trotters'** matchmaker to their coach, manager, and lone bench
player (at all of 5'3").[12] Believing Midwesterners might not be that impressed with
players coming "all the way from Chicago," Saperstein renamed them "New York
Harlem **Globe Trotters**." Any confusion with Harlem's **Rens** was probably the
intention.[13] (The **Globetrotters**—eventually one word—wouldn't play a "home"
game near New York's Harlem River for four decades.) Widely known for court
foolery, the **Trotters'** legacy as a legit team and their 1940 world championship
are little remembered today.

Like the black baseballers before them, the **Globies'** ranks got watered down
after the integration of their sport's major pro league in 1950. Saperstein tried to
compete with the NBA with his own ABL (1961–63), which included Pittsburgh
Rens. The Steel City had contributed mightily to wartime production, and smoke-
control measures were part of a cleanup called the Pittsburgh Renaissance. So the
ABL **Rens** were named after both the civic overhaul and the old New York team.
New structures of the Renaissance, like the **Rens'** Civic Arena (the "Igloo"),
could be built only after the black neighborhood on the hill below the Crawford
Grill had been razed.

• • •

Just before the Civil War, white performers started fusing parts of the African American musical heritage into a new form of entertainment for white audiences. "Minstrel show" performers put greasepaint on their faces to appear extremely (perhaps *ridiculously*) black. Their characters always appeared happy, lest anyone reckon that enslaved people found plantation life disagreeable. Players aligned with their instruments by name. Mr. Tambo played the tambourine and Mr. Bones played wooden castanets ("bones"). Mr. Banjo and Mr. Fiddle helped popularize their stringed instruments, one derived from the African *banjar* and the other being a folk violin. Performances were advertised as showcases for "Ethiopian melodies."

A wildly popular fiddle tune from minstrelsy was "The Arkansas Traveler." Minor league baseball's Little Rock **Travelers** were playing by 1895 but they were the first pro team associated with an entire state when they became *Arkansas* **Travelers** ("A-Travs") in 1957, distinguishing between themselves and independent blackball's Little Rock **Black Travelers** of the 1940s and '50s. Barnstorming female basketballers behind Arkansas-born superstar Hazel Walker were also Arkansas **Travelers** (1949–65). (The Arkansas Traveler Certificate has been awarded to prestigious visitors since 1941.) The campus paper for the University of Arkansas **Razorbacks** (p. 79) became the *Arkansas Traveler* in 1920.

Minstrelsy relied on the presumption that persons of African descent were silly and incapable by nature. The same attitudes facilitated segregation ordinances in the post-Reconstruction South that kept blacks out of workplaces and voting booths. Those Jim Crow laws were named for the narrator in the most popular early minstrel song, "Jump Jim Crow." Some of the later minstrels were even black, presenting an "authentic" or "genuine" experience while sticking with the template set down by white predecessors, including the tradition of "blacking up" (adding another layer to the idea of whites pretending to be black).

Just as minstrelsy opened the backstage door for the large-scale entrance of African Americans into show business,[14] black athletes banned from the majors had to survive first if they were ever to be recognized as players inferior to none. They often added a little *clownin'*—flash and trickery—to their style of play, especially in warm-ups, but feigning an amicable witlessness might attract even more white patrons. That black teams toured as Miami **Ethiopian Clowns** (est. 1937) or Louisville **Zulu Cannibal Giants** (1934–37) might shock today's progressive thinkers. The **Zulus** even wore "grass skirts [...] red wigs and face paint, making it difficult to distinguish among the players. Consequently sometimes only the four best hitters would bat, with the opposition rarely noticing."[15]

The **Ethiopian Clowns** were Florida's Miami **Giants** before their clownin' days, and they muted their antics to enter the Negro American League as Cincinnati **Clowns** in 1943. (They're still considered the only clownin' team to have played in the black majors.) They were later the Cincinnati-Indianapolis **Clowns** (1944–45) and Indianapolis **Clowns** (1946–50).[16]

A popular and original baseball clown named Reese "Goose" Tatum broke in with the 1939 Louisville **Black Colonels** (p. 134) but played with other famous teams. Abe Saperstein saw Goose play first base and hired him to be the "Clown Prince" of the 1946 **Globetrotters**, accelerating their transition to an exhibition team. The Detroit **Stars** were an inaugural NNL team that barnstormed in later decades, becoming Detroit **Clowns** after hiring Goose (1958–60). But Tatum was all business when guarding George Mikan in exhibitions against the Minneapolis **Lakers**. Two such games in consecutive Februarys (1948 and '49) helped nudge the NBA toward integration in 1950.

In fact, by the time the Washington **Generals** were invented as their everyday "opponents" in 1953, the **Trotters** had already turned into a stage show. The last remnants of the clownin' tradition can still be seen in the hot doggery of the Harlem **Globetrotters'** warm-up routine, in which their Magic Circle—a term for the boundary from which spells are cast in voodoo (p. 66)—is accompanied by the 1949 version of "Sweet Georgia Brown" (in the upbeat minstrel style) by Brother Bones and the Shadows.[17]

• • •

Like other black athletes, the **Rens** and **Globetrotters** had to barnstorm to pay the bills before World War II, challenging professional and club teams in town after town. After a tough game (or two), they might drive for hours to find hotels that accepted black patrons or they just slept on the bus.

Black musicians were enduring similar hardships running from "apple to apple." New York's "Big Apple" nickname was the result, as were the New York **Apples** (1977–78) of World Team Tennis and Nassau County's junior hockey New York **Apple Core** (est. 1993).

Barnstorming is an old term for traveling theater groups or politicians who charmed impromptu audiences in rural sheds. It was later adopted by aviators who astounded those who might never have seen an airplane and who might pay up for the ride of a lifetime. Indoor football's Iowa **Barnstormers** (est. 1995) touched down at Des Moines, but—like the musicians before them—their flying ace mascot sought the bright lights of the biggest apple as New York **Dragons** (2001–08). Different Iowa **Barnstormers** returned to Des Moines in 2008. Here are some other perpetual "visitors":

- The New York **Wanderers** hadn't planned on wandering around, but after they won the first-ever AAU basketball championship as the **23ʳᵈ Street YMCA** in 1898, they were booted from the gym, playing for the next dozen years as pioneering barnstormers.[18]

- Some teams barnstormed within their own circuits. The Los Angeles (or "Pacific Coast") **Wildcats** were Californians by name only, never playing west of their Chicago base. Named for their star player-coach, former Washington **Husky** George "Wildcat" Wilson, the **Wildcats** were in the 1926-only AFL. The NFL felt curiously obligated to counter that with its own cartographical pipe dream, the Chicago-based "Los Angeles" **Buccaneers**.[19]

- Indoor football's Carolina **Sharks** (Charlotte, N.C.) folded before they ever even managed to take a snap. Their 2005 schedule was therefore exercised by the homeless (and winless) Greensboro **Ghostriders**. In Asheville for 2006 as *Carolina* **Ghostriders**, those beleaguered B-leaguers lost their first four games and were replaced by **Ghostchasers**, who gave up the rest.

Cardinals | Midshipmen | Black Knights | Browns

In 1893 football fans at Fordham University in the Bronx used this cheer: "One *damn*; two *damn*; three *damn*; For-*dham*!" Jesuit administrators encouraged a change to "One *ram*; two *ram*; three *ram*; For-*dham*." That allusion to a Christian symbol of sacrifice (p. 106) made athletes **Rams**. In the 1930s the prestige of the eastern colleges was often still manifest on the gridiron, and the **Rams** were known nationally for the Seven Blocks of Granite on their offensive line, including future pro Hall of Famers Alex Wojciechowicz and Vince Lombardi.

In 1936, Fordham's nick was copied by the AFL/NFL Cleveland **Rams**, which wasn't that unusual. College-educated men of that era who chose to don helmets and pads after graduation were suspected of lacking a certain adult dignity, so the attention-starved pros tried to legitimize themselves by creating subliminal associations with collegians. The **Rams** moved to Los Angeles in 1946 and then St. Louis in 1995.

Chicago's semi-pro Morgan [Street] Athletic Club first played football in 1898 and moved to the normal school field on Racine Avenue for 1901. (Chicago Normal is now Chicago State University, where **Cougars** do not reflect any deep history.) That same year those Racine **Normals** accepted some uniforms that were being discarded by the more-famous University of Chicago **Maroons**. The jerseys had faded from maroon to cardinal red, turning the **Normals** into Racine **Cardinals**. They were Chicago **Cardinals** by the time they entered the original 1920 APFA/NFL. Decades of competition started in 1921 with the arrival of the Chicago **Bears**, finally forcing the unprofitable **Cards** to St. Louis in 1960. Coincidentally, "St. Louis **Cardinals**" was already in place at Sportsman's Park through baseballers named after their own red threads. Without a stadium deal, the football side moved again to be Phoenix **Cardinals** in 1988 and Arizona **Cardinals** in 1994.[1]

New York lifted its ban on Sunday baseball in 1919. With football expected to follow suit, baseball's New York **Giants** assembled football's Brickley's **Giants** (named for its coach and former Harvard standout Charlie Brickley) to occupy the Polo Grounds on fall Sundays. But inconsistent blue laws still limited football, so the APFA/NFL New York **Giants** wouldn't play a down until regulations relaxed in 1921. They folded after that season, but the NFL finally cracked the country's largest market for good in 1925 with new New York **Giants**. To be distinct from local hardballers, they were (and are) New York *Football* **Giants**, Inc.

The last thing that pro football's battle for recognition needed was World War II. Facing travel restrictions and draft-drained rosters, some NFL squads didn't even have enough players to put on the field. The "Phil-Pitt" team of 1943 was an amalgamation of Pennsylvanians, including Pittsburgh **Steelers** and Philadelphia **Eagles**. Officially they wore Philadelphia's green and white as **Eagles** without any municipal allegiance, but just about everyone called them **Steagles**. (The **Steeler** and **Eagle** coaches disliked each other and split the responsibilities of offensive and defensive coordinators, the **Steagles**' remaining legacy.) The next season, Pittsburgh's new association with Chicago's **Cardinals** made them "**Card-Pitt**." The marriage dissolved after their 0-10 record gave the **Card-Pitts** the nickname of walkovers: "Carpets."

• • •

The typical college student during the war (or at any time) was a male of service age, so varsity ranks suffered alongside the pros. While some schools suspended athletics, recruits to the U.S. Military Academy at West Point, New York and the U.S. Naval Academy at Annapolis, Maryland dominated opponents in the late war years. (If nothing else, enlisting to play sports for one's county could insulate one from the draft and possibly combat duty.) Officers in training at "Army" and "Navy" are respective midshipmen and cadets. Therefore, **Midshipmen** and **Cadets**—and here you can add the U.S. Merchant Marine Academy **Mariners**— aren't so much athletic nicknames as objective designations.[2]

So well-matched were their footballers that Navy's only loss in 1945 came amidst Army's three consecutive undefeated seasons under coach Red Blaik. Those '45 **Cadets** were "Blaik's Black Knights of the Hudson," the first hint of Army's **Black Knights**. That moniker was undoubtedly advanced by the Military Gothic style of prominent USMA buildings like Cadet Chapel, although "**Cadets**" remains a viable alternate.

Collegiate enrollments were dwindling just when classrooms were needed to train officers, pilots, and mechanics. A partnership that would populate campuses with the fittest and brightest young men was struck. Athletic eligibility require- ments were relaxed for players at military institutions while "favored schools, such as Notre Dame, Northwestern, and Michigan, ended up with star student- athletes as transfers from other major teams."[3] In fact, Minnesotans attending a 1943 game "were outraged to find eight **Gophers** from the 1942 team in [the Northwestern] lineup."[4]

Service teams didn't necessarily represent their hosting institutions. As if the war years weren't tough enough, the University of Iowa's athletes had to share their Iowa City facilities with Navy Pre-Flight, a pilot school with monster teams. Disclaiming collegiate affiliations, their "Iowa **Seahawks**" name suited land- locked jocks only as long as they were naval aviators on Iowa **Hawkeye** turf.[5] The **Seahawks** dominated several sports and finished second in the nation in 1943 after losing only one football game to eventual number one Notre Dame.

In fact, ND's **Irish** remained undefeated until the Navy **Bluejackets** from North Chicago's Great Lakes Naval Training Station put them down 19-14 with only 33 seconds left in that season.[6] (The navy-blue Navy **Bluejackets** have the "bluejackets" nickname that's been historically applied all over the world to military sailors who seem to have all copied the navy blue of British sailors.) The '**Jackets** also had a wicked wartime nine that included major league baseballers like Hall of Famers Johnny Mize and Billy Herman.[7] Virginia's Norfolk Naval Training Station fielded unimaginatively named **Sailors** in wartime, including Cooperstown's Dom DiMaggio and Phil Rizzuto.

• • •

These colleges earned the attendance of pilots and ground crews:

- The Lewis Holy Name School of Aeronautics (Romeoville, Ill.) was overrun by Navy pilots in 1940, as suggested by Lewis University's current **Flyers**.[8]
- The University of Tennessee at Martin hosted Navy combat fliers and has therefore scrambled **Skyhawks** since 1995.[9]
- The federal Civilian Pilot Training Program was created in 1938. When World War II (unsurprisingly) started in Europe the next year, the CPTP was ready to develop combat aviators. That program relaunched Ohio's Embry-Riddle Flying School and moved it to Daytona Beach (in partnership with the University of Miami). Embry-Riddle Aeronautical University now hosts airborne **Eagles**.
- Mayor Fiorello LaGuardia encouraged his Great War buddy Casey Jones and famous fighter ace George A. Vaughn to move their aeronautics school from Newark to New York. In 1940 the cornerstone was laid next to the strip soon called LaGuardia Field. That was just in time to train 20,000 technicians for World War II duty, putting **Warriors** at the Vaughn College of Aeronautics and Technology. It's five miles from Long Island City and the flying **Red Hawks** of LaGuardia Community College.
- Boston brickmaker Charles Tufts donated the hilltop that would host his namesake Massachusetts university (p. 244) in 1852. His second cousin James Walker Tufts developed golf courses and resorts in Pinehurst, North Carolina. That required him to build an airstrip in 1929. It too was a military airfield during WW2, so Sandhills Community College—on Airport Road—scrambles **Flyers** squads.
- In 1943 the municipal airport in Nashua, New Hampshire was renamed for native son Paul Boire, a Navy pilot killed in a training flight. In 1965 the New England Aeronautical Institute was put next to Boire Field. Its main building, Daniel Webster Hall, opened the next year. The school was renamed Daniel Webster College in 1978 but sustains the flight of **Eagles**.
- Michigan's Jackson College has its Flight Center at the Jackson County Airport. That's mostly been a civilian field, but the Army Corps of Engineers did expand its runways during World War II. JC jocks are **Jets**.

• • •

The domination in sports by service squads wasn't all stateside. Among the CFL champs during wartime were Toronto's **RCAF Hurricanes** (1942) and Quebec's St. Hyacinthe-Donnacona **Navy** (1944). The '43 champs were the RCAF Hamilton **Flying Wildcats**, also called **Wildcats** during their tenure (1941–49). The Ottawa **RCAF Flyers** won hockey's 1942 Allan Cup. When stringent new definitions of amateurism gave Canada little hope for the 1948 Olympics, but the **Flyers** went anyway and won that country's most surprising gold.

The Patricia Bay [B.C.] RCAF **Gremlins** were Canada's 1943 basketball champs. The word *gremlin* was just coming to North America after Brits in the R.A.F. were heard blaming mechanical issues on gremlin saboteurs. (Gremlins were goblins in English legends.) A student poll in 1944 put **Gremlins** at Greenville [Ill.] College, but GC students soon scuttled their own folkloric identity, electing "**Panthers**" quite arbitrarily in late 1947.[10]

• • •

It was decided in 1944 that former pros shouldn't be playing college football. Teams like Iowa's **Seahawks** and Great Lakes Naval slipped a bit, but the new coach at Great Lakes earned an 8-2 record despite the reduced firepower. Legend-in-the-making Paul Brown had coached Ohio State to the national championship in 1942, the last year before service-team domination. After the war he went to the All-America Football Conference, a new league competing with the NFL. His team was in Cleveland, where the **Rams** had managed to lose money even as the 1945 NFL champs. In fact, the intrusion by Brown's AAFC squad sent the **Rams** to Los Angeles for the '46 kickoff, beginning west coast expansion of major sports in the post-war era. When Brown let fans vote on the new nickname, "**Panthers**" won but was discarded when the local owner of earlier team of independent **Panthers** demanded compensation. The enthusiasm that had welcomed Mr. Brown to the pros made "**Browns**" the next-best choice, it being an already familiar moniker for storied hardballers in St. Louis.

In 1996, Cleveland's **Browns** fluttered off to Baltimore. To implore the forgiveness of Clevelanders, the NFL forced owner Art Modell to leave behind the team records and nickname (which explains the different Cleveland **Browns** who were playing by 1999).[11] The ex-**Browns** became Baltimore **Ravens**, after Edgar Allen Poe's 1845 poem "The Raven." The Boston-born Poe spent more time in other eastern cities, but he's become associated with Baltimore, where he lived at his aunt's house after his 1831 expulsion from West Point, arriving just in time for the death of brother Henry from tuberculosis. It was also in the Charm City that Poe first charmed the 13-year-old first cousin he'd marry in Richmond. In 1847 she became the second Poe intimate tackled by TB—Poe's literary melancholy is irresistibly attributed to these deaths—and the increasingly depressed writer of macabre tales died somewhat mysteriously two years later while passing through Baltimore at age 39. He and Henry are in the family plot just blocks north of the **Ravens**' pitch. The team colors are from the "purple curtain" and "ebony bird" in the poem and their crow mascot is even named Poe. The Baltimore **Nighthawks** (est. 2008) of women's football are also black-and-purple birds.

• • •

Sports scribe Grantland Rice gave boxer Joe Louis his famous "brown bomber" nickname. In his autobiography, Paul Brown denied reports that said votes for "**Brown Bombers**" were counted toward "**Browns**" in his team-naming contest.[12] The fighter has had influence elsewhere though, being the stated inspiration when the CFL's **Winnipegs** (or '**Pegs**) became Winnipeg **Blue Bombers** in 1936 while Louis was on a meteoric rise to his first heavyweight title.

After his bout that June with Max Schmeling at Yankee Stadium, the Bomber was the most famous black American. The *New York World-Telegram* called the **Yankees** lineup "Bronx Bombers" for the first time a few weeks later.[13] Looking upstate, the 1937 Ithaca College yearbook called teams "**Bombers**" for reasons unknown, but any sporting application of "Bomber" at that moment inevitably called either Mr. Louis or the **Yanks** to mind.[14]

The aforementioned Winnipeg **Blue Bombers** close our service team loop. Their name was copied by pilots and flight crews on the Peg's RCAF **Bombers**, wartime CFLers who lost the 1943 Grey Cup final to the RCAF's new Hamilton **Flying Wildcats**, a side that remained intact after the war to compete for fans with the CFL Hamilton **Tigers** (est. 1869). Rather than drive each other to extinction, the **Tigers** and **Wildcats** merged as Hamilton **Tiger-Cats** in 1950.

• • •

The U.S. was abruptly brought into World War II on December 7, 1941 when planes from a Japanese carrier group bombed Pearl Harbor. One legendary aviator, Lt. Col. James H. Doolittle, was in Columbia, South Carolina two months later to assemble B-25 crews for a secret mission on Japan, as recalled by Columbia's Capital City **Bombers** (1993–2004, South Atlantic League).[15]

By March more intense training was under way at Eglin Field. Northwest Florida State College's original campus in Valparaiso and its current one in Niceville were surrounded by Eglin's airstrips. Sports started as soon as the school opened in 1964, and Jimmy Doolittle's fliers were instantly memorialized by NWFSC's **Raiders**, whose fox mascot is Jimmy Raider.

When the raid started on April 18, 1942, Doolittle himself commanded the first bomber to depart the carrier *Hornet*. According to the plan, crews had only enough fuel to make their bombing run before ditching in China (America's wartime ally). Damage to infrastructure was light, but the raid dramatically boosted American morale, and the newly fearful Japanese recalled planes and ships from Pacific patrols for homeland defenses.

Doolittle's 17th Bombardment Group is saluted even at air bases to which it has no connection. Two miles north of Doolittle Avenue on Tinker Air Force Base is Oklahoma City's Rose State College, where **Raiders** commemorate Doolittle's crews, but the base's eponym, Gen. Clarence L. Tinker, was every bit the daring air raider. The Oklahoma native bravely led bombing runs over Japanese positions during the 1942 Battle of Midway. All hands were lost when his B-24 went down on June 7.[16]

• • •

Although the specific attack on America's Pacific Fleet was a surprise, the war against the Axis powers (Japan, Germany, and Italy) was about as expected as such horrors can be. To work out the tactical and logistical issues associated with any future engagement of its mechanized force, the Army started running massive exercises in northern and western Louisiana and East Texas in the year leading up to Pearl Harbor. A major event in those Great Louisiana Maneuvers was the capture of Shreveport by Gen. George Patton's "Blue" army. Other generals on the scene included Omar Bradley and Dwight Eisenhower, all to be made famous by the coming war. The Maneuvers gave name to both the indoor football Bossier-Shreveport **Battle Wings** (2001–10) and the **Generals** at Louisiana State University at Alexandria.[17] A school in Seneca Falls, New York called Eisenhower College put **Generals** in the field during its years of operation (1968–83).

Texans | Rangers | White Mules | Roughriders

Rarely do state demonyms become athletic identifiers. While you're not likely to find Woonsocket **Rhode Islanders** or Eagle River **Alaskans,**[1] Texas is the exception, as the Texas timeline is teeming with **Texan** teams:

- Dallas **Texans** were in the NFL (1952) and the AFL (1960–62).
- The Houston **Texans** were a 1974 WFL team that moved to Louisiana amidst their only season to become the Shreveport **Steamer,** but NFL expansion in 2002 resulted in new Houston **Texans.**
- South Plains College in Levelland has **Texans** and **Lady Texans.**
- Tarleton State University has **Texans** (men) and **Texanns** (women).
- The San Antonio **Texans** (1995) were well south of most teams in the Canadian Football League.
- El Paso **Texans** played minor league ball most years from 1930 to 1957.

The self-image of Texans owes to a pride that theirs is the only state that was once its own country. Compared to the thirteen independent post-Revolution states, the subsequent Republic of Vermont, California's "Bear Flag" Republic, and the Republic of Hawaii, it's more accurate to say Texas was the only future state where white settlers experienced independence *and really meant it.*

• • •

Connecticut-born miner and banker Moses Austin was rewriting his rags-to-riches-to-rags story in New Spain's Missouri Territory when the 1803 Louisiana Purchase put him back under U.S. jurisdiction. In 1820, Moses asked Mexico City if he could bring Anglos to *la provincia de Tejas.* The governors knew such a deal would deter trespass onto the lightly occupied property by less amenable whites, but they'd agree only if the newcomers embraced Catholicism, learned Spanish, and accepted a ban on slavery.

Moses died suddenly of pneumonia, and the enterprise was run by his son Stephen, who led hundreds of Anglos to Texas over the next few years. Some of those first colonists—the Old Three Hundred—settled a site now called Wharton, where **Pioneers** have aptly represented Wharton County Junior College since its 1947 founding.

Mexico's 1824 constitution gave democratic rights to all, and *Texians* (white Texans) got along pretty well with the *Tejanos* (their neighbors of Mexican blood). El Paso Community College has the highest percentage of Hispanic students among U.S. colleges, as indicated by respective male and female **Tejanos** and **Tejanas.**[2]

Steven Austin recruited militias to roam Texas ranges and monitor Indians. Those "Rangers" had to think on their feet and on horseback. Texas formalized the Rangers in 1835 in response to the revocation of Mexico's constitution by President Antonio López de Santa Anna, who was centralizing dictatorial power at Mexico City. In 1880 the Texas and Pacific Railway ran past the Ranger camp that's now the town of Ranger, where Ranger College posts **Rangers.** Rangers kept the peace when the tiny town of Kilgore boomed into the "world's richest acre" after oil strikes in 1930, so Kilgore College has **Rangers** too. The junior hockey Fort Worth **Rangers** (1945–49) were followed by minor league baseball's Dallas-Fort Worth **Rangers** (1958–64) and the MLB's Texas **Rangers** (1972–, the former Washington **Senators**).

Texas Rangers evolved to serve many purposes. They were scouts in the Mexican-American War, Indian fighters, and then desperado nabbers. For post-pioneer times, the Rangers redirected attention to law enforcement, rounding up bank robbers and bootleggers. They are now the elite investigative force within the Texas Department of Public Safety. Outside Texas, *ranger* remains a romantic term for any Western rider, as evidenced by the **Rangers** at both Regis University in Denver and Northwestern Oklahoma State University in Alva.

• • •

Resenting the ban on slavery and suspicious of Santa Anna's power grab, Texians declared independence on March 2, 1836 and launched a Texas Revolution. They took the mission compound at San Antonio and its Alamo church, which had already been fortified against Comanche and Apache raids by the Spanish. Santa Anna surrounded the Alamo with 1,500 soldiers. A twelve-day siege was followed by an attack on March 6. After an hour, there were 600 Mexican casualties, but all 200 Anglo defenders were dead (ballpark estimates). Two weeks later, the 300 Texians who'd surrendered the Goliad mission were executed.

Using a new battle cry—"Remember the Alamo! … Remember Goliad!"—a Texas army under Sam Houston defeated the forces of Santa Anna at the April 21 Battle of San Jacinto, making Texas an independent republic. The Alamo is still the most famous historic site in Texas, one remembered by San Antonio **Missions** and **Missionaries** from a century of minor league baseball. Some of San Antone's sporting facilities include Alamo Stadium (built in 1940) and the Alamo Dome (1993).

In 1938, Texas commemorated the centennial of its independence by donating a sculpture to Texas Woman's University in Denton. Leo Friedlander's marble "Pioneer Woman" is a campus landmark, but "**Pioneers**" was adopted in 1979 to respect the pioneering spirit of the largest state-funded college for women in the country, one that established first-of-their-kind programs in medicine, library science, and graduate studies. (Despite its name, TWU went fully coed in 1994.)

In 2006 the MLS San Jose **Earthquakes** moved to Texas, where a fan poll gave them the name Houston **1836**. But Houston had a problem when Latinos protested that reference to Sam Houston's victory over Mexico, so the boys who finally took the field were the Houston **Dynamo**, indicating H-Town's dynamic energy industry and generating memories of the 1987 Houston **Dynamos** of the Lone Star Soccer Alliance and several famous *futbol* **Dynamos** in Europe.[3]

• • •

The Texans' trials didn't end with their Revolution. Indian raids along the Brazos River in the late 1830s killed several close kin to Scottish immigrant Neil McLennan, who later surveyed much of his namesake county. The county seat at Waco is where the McLennan Community College **Highlanders** remember the Scottish Highland birthplace of Mr. McLennan.

Guys like Neil McLennan would likely have had little sympathy when Sam Houston became an advocate in Washington for the rights of Western Cherokees (those who'd anticipated the removals of the 1830s and slipped into Mexican territory). Once a young runaway from Tennessee, Houston had been adopted by Cherokees who called him *Colonneh* (raven). Just months after the Revolution, the hero's surname was given to the biggest city in modern Texas, quickly followed by his election to the presidency of the new Republic of Texas. Another namesake was Huntsville's Sam Houston State Teachers College (now Sam Houston State University), where **Normals** became **Bearkats** or **Bearcats** or **Bear Cats** in 1923. It took a while to settle on the *k*-version, although none were historically significant. In the late 1940s, school president Harmon Lowman tried to trade "**Bearkats**" for the more justifiable "**Ravens**" (from Houston's Cherokee name), but alumni blocked the transition.

Ignoring Houston's measured efforts, the second Texas president, Mirabeau B. Lamar, wanted to rid East and West Texas entirely of their respective Cherokee and Comanche occupants. The Rangers became mounted rifles in Lamar's 1839 Cherokee War, which chased the eponymous people into Arkansas and Oklahoma. In the post-Revolution, post-Cherokee era, the lumber industry really took off in East Texas, and the "bonanza era" enjoyed by the large operations began when the railroads arrived in the early 1880s. That's why a Nacogdoches college that's named for the Father of Texas—Stephen F. Austin State University—runs teams of **Lumberjacks** and **Ladyjacks**.[4]

In fights with Comanches, small bands of Rangers held off several times their number with the world's first repeating firearm, the .36-caliber, five-shot Colt revolver. Improvements led to renowned six-shooters like Colt's single-action, .45-caliber Peacemaker revolver, carried by cavalrymen after 1873 and recalled as the "gun that won the west." The first MLB team in Texas was the 1962 Houston **Colt .45s**. Their emblem resembled that of Colt Firearms, so they were asked to change, becoming **Astros** after moving to the Astrodome in 1965.

• • •

Soon after independence, Texans wanted to gain statehood to firm up the border with Mexico and make Indians reluctant to attack U.S. ground. As a new slave state, however, it would upset an otherwise balanced U.S. Senate (p. 142). When presidential candidates at the Democrats' 1844 convention split on annexation issues, former president Andrew Jackson talked his protégé James K. Polk (ex-Tennessee governor) into joining the race. In the general election, Polk rode his platform for the annexation of Texas and that of the complementary "free state" of Oregon right over an old Jackson nemesis, the Whigs' Henry Clay.

President Polk was the first unlikely political contender to have been called a "dark horse" (a racehorse about whom gamblers knew uncomfortably little). Footballers at Colby College in Waterville, Maine had their own reputation for overachieving in 1924, and a student wrote in the campus news that the blue and grey shouldn't be considered dark horses if they continued defeating all comers. He successfully suggested an inversion: **White Mules**.[5]

Some buzzer-beating diplomacy by outgoing president John Tyler got Texas and Congress to agree on annexation terms a few days before Polk's inauguration in March 1845. Democratic columnist John L. O'Sullivan remained unsatisfied in July, writing that it was the states' "manifest destiny to overspread the continent" and free California from the "imbecile and distracted" Mexico. Polk failed to buy Alta California (and *Nuevo México*) from Mexico, and ill health prevented the Democrat from running again, but he gave a political boost to the Whig who would succeed him by sending Gen. Zachary Taylor onto the disputed ground between the Rio Grande and Nueces Rivers in March 1846. Mexico took the bait, and the Mexican-American War ran until September 1847. As expected, Mexico got pretty well smucked and the 1848 treaty gave most of the Southwest and California to the U.S. for a token cash settlement.

It was during that war that Americans became fascinated by the golden-blond Arabian palomino horse that Spanish-Mexican ranchers had bred for centuries. (*Palomino* is "white dove" *en español.*) There are **Palominos** at Laredo Community College in Laredo, an old Spanish ranching town on the Rio Grande. Southwest Minnesota State University opened at Marshall in 1967 and adopted colors of brown and gold, the next year fielding male **Golden Mustangs** (with a palomino mascot) and female **Pintos**. All have been **Mustangs** since 1988.

The U.S. military had a significant west-coast offense in waiting even before the start of the Mexican-American War. John C. Frémont's well-armed exploring party was near Sonoma while six ships of the Pacific Squadron were anchored off Monterey Bay. When news of war reached those commands in mid-1846, they took the area easily. Sonoma's Mexican flag was replaced by one for the new Republic of California, which was hastily scribbled onto available cloth. Its single star was probably from the recently annexed Republic of Texas, but more prominent was the profile of a golden bear (*Ursus arctos californicus*), which would be hunted to extinction by miners, settlers, and bounty hunters by the early 1920s.

The Bear Flag Republic lasted only three weeks before the U.S. annexed California. In 1854 the capital moved from Sonoma to Sacramento, but it wasn't until 1911 that the Sac-Town legislature adopted a modernized Bear Flag as the state flag. Its star and bear both appear on the badge of soccer's Sacramento **Republic** FC (2014–) of the USL's Pro division.

The bear banner made the California grizzly the state animal, as indicated by programs at two private institutions: the Golden State Baptist College **Bears** in Santa Clara and the Bethany University **Bruins** in Scotts Valley (closed in 2011). But ursine themes run amuck in the state system, the parent school of which, UC-Berkeley (or "Cal"), has **Golden Bears**.[6] Teams at UC's Southern Branch were **Cubs** and **Grizzlies** in the early 1900s. SBUC became the University of California at Los Angeles in 1927 and joined the PAC-10. Because Montana's **Grizzlies** were already in that conference, UCLA changed to **Bruins**.

Two public community colleges derive their sporting identities from their elders. Santa Rosa Junior College is a feeder for Cal, so its **Bear Cubs** can grow into **Golden Bears**. The Los Angeles City College's **Cubs** exhibit their subordinate position to the UCLA **Bruins** five miles east. Even when they aren't called **Golden Bears**, athletes in the UC system flash variations of their respective institution's blue and gold colors (also the official state colors). At UC-Merced, blue-and-gold **Golden Bobcats** are the result.

In a 1965 grass-roots election, students at UC-Irvine made athletes **Anteaters**, inspired by the anteater in the popular Johnny Hart comic strip, *B.C.* (The school cheer is "Zot! Zot! Zot!" … the sound made when said character sucks up ants.) Those **Anteaters** meant to explicitly avoid the bear-related nicknames of the larger UC campuses, but UCI fell into the bear trap anyway; the giant anteater (*Myrmecophaga tridactyla*) is colloquially the "ant bear."[7]

> The historical range of the Kodiak grizzly (*Ursus arctos middendorffi*) is north of the golden bear on southern Alaska's Kodiak Archipelago. Two two-year colleges on the Canadian mainland like that fearsome imagery enough to field **Kodiaks**, Lethbridge [Alta.] College and the College of New Caledonia (Prince George, B.C.). Elsewhere in Alberta are junior hockey's Camrose **Kodiaks**.

• • •

A War for Mexican Independence had freed Mexico from Spain in 1821, and American traders discovered a Mexico willing to stretch its mercantile legs. When modest packhorse trains left Missouri for Santa Fe in 1822, the exchange of American hardware and textiles for Mexican silver, fur, and mules proved so profitable that complete wagon trains were on the Santa Fe Trail within a year. After 1846 that road was getting American troops into the Mexican-American War. By then the Oregon Trail also departed Missouri, with other westward roads (like the Mormon and California Trails) passing nearby.

Military and immigrant caravans increased demand on draft animals in regions where the family mule had long been the sharecropper's best tool. Missouri mules famously took the top prizes at the 1904 St. Louis World's Fair, and **Normals** and **Teachers** at Warrensburg's teachers' college were **Mules** by 1921. It's now the University of Central Missouri, where women have been complementary **Jennies** since 1974. (Technically, a *jennet* or *jenny* is a female donkey, but those terms sometimes identify mare mules.) Athletes at an early-twentieth-century agricultural school rode miles on horse and mule to catch trains to road games, explaining the **Muleriders** (and female **Riderettes** until 2001) at Magnolia's Southern Arkansas University.

Mexican-American War units made good use of a federal arsenal that opened at St. Louis in 1827. A wheeled-cannon emblem represented independent football's St. Louis **Gunners**, established in 1931 as the **Battery A Gunners** (with National Guard sponsorship). The **Gunners** played the last three games on the 1934 NFL schedule of the bankrupt Cincinnati **Reds** (whose best players became **Gunners**). The **Gunners** were then minor leaguers and independents until dissolving in 1941, but the military theme returned with the BAA/NBA St. Louis **Bombers** (1946–50) and rugby's St. Louis **Bombers** (est. 1962).

After the war, a road straight west from Albuquerque was surveyed to tie California to the rest of the country. It went through today's Flagstaff (so named after passers-through from the east trimmed a ponderosa pine down to a flagpole for the 1876 national centennial). The Flagstaff normal school fielded **Normals**, but an ambitious logging industry had made them **Lumberjacks** by 1915. The school is now Northern Arizona University, still near the continent's largest ponderosa forests. The Stone Forest Sawmill was operating across the street when NAU opened in 1899 and didn't close until 1993.

• • •

In December 1845, four months after demanding annexation for Texas and California, John O'Sullivan used similar language to argue for the appropriation of "the whole of Oregon" (between Spanish California and Russian Alaska). This time when he said "manifest destiny," everyone seemed to hear. Back in 1818, the U.S.-Canadian border had been fixed at the 49th parallel from Minnesota to the Rockies, leaving the Oregon Country subject to "joint occupation" by British and American empires. That was just about as workable as it sounds, leaving open the "Oregon Question" that O'Sullivan was addressing.

Dr. Marcus Whitman had left New England in 1836 to become a Presbyterian minister to Indians. He joined a westward fur caravan with his new spouse and another missionary couple. Exiting southwestern Wyoming's South Pass in 1836, the wives were the first white women to cross the Rockies, convincing some that travel to Oregon suited families. The party's small wagon was the first on the Oregon Trail, but they ditched their ride at Fort Boise on the Snake River when HBC guides said it would become a drag in the Blue Mountains. They continued on horseback, so the end of the "Whitman Route" doesn't quite match the trail maps that would guide wagon trains within a few years.

The city of La Grande is on the eastern slope of the Blues. It's where Eastern Oregon University's **Mountaineers** and their trapper mascot recall the era before the wagon trains, but the Whitmans' trail guides had seen their future. When the craving for beaver hats and pelts died down, fur men became entrepreneuring pathfinders who exaggerated the ease of westward movement to stir up "Oregon Fever" and maintain an income. (Refer to indoor football's 2005-founded Tri-Cities **Fever**, Kennewick, Wash.) Mountaineers often blaze trails through dense forests (removing bark from successive trees to indicate the direction of travel), but that was quickly unnecessary on the Oregon, where wagon tracks across open prairies were evident after the first few caravans. Missouri's Metropolitan Community College–Blue River is in Independence, the Oregon Trail's traditional starting point, so teams are **Trail Blazers**. At the other end are the NBA Portland **Trail Blazers** (est. 1970), whose path was set by baseball's Salem **Trailblazers** (PCL, 1946–48).

The Cowlitz Trail ran south from Puget Sound to [Fort] Vancouver, Washington. HBC men discovered it as a centuries-old Indian footpath that didn't need much blazing, but Centralia College (midway on the Cowlitz at Centralia, Washington) keeps **Trailblazers**. By the late 1840s, the Cowlitz was the recognized northern branch of the Oregon Trail.

Establishing a mission west of the HBC's Fort Walla Walla, the Whitmans gave education and medicine to Cayuse Indians, but few Christian conversions occurred. In spring 1843 the trail's first great wagon train started the 2,000-mile trip from Missouri. Just then returning from a trip east, Dr. Whitman caught up with those pioneers near South Pass to guide them. White settlement was soon in earnest, and the Whitman house seemed better suited as a rest stop than as a base for evangelism.

Many newcomers settled the Willamette Valley from Portland to Eugene. The wet climate and soggy soil that were ideal for planting led to the locals' self-deprecating nickname, "webfooters," variations of which—Portland **Webfooters**, **Webfeet**, **Webfoots**—were used by turn-of-the-century minor leaguers. They were the **Beavers** by 1906 but sometimes **Buckaroos** (1918) or **Ducks** (1929). Reporters made **Webfoots** out of athletes at Eugene's University of Oregon in the 1930s, but they too were **Ducks** by the late 1970s.

Wolves (and bears and pumas) were soon making a picnic of Oregon's livestock, and joint occupation provided no bureaucratic solution. The informal Wolf Meetings of 1843 ostensibly addressed that problem, but it was really the inception of a provisional government to challenge HBC ("British") authority. There are still **Wolves** in the Willamette at Monmouth's Western Oregon University. Considering the Wolf Meetings, that's just about as historically informed as nicknames get, but those **Wolves** were tagged right after Mr. Larry Wolfe became football coach in 1928.

Once found throughout the region, wolves were pretty much eradicated from Washington in the 1930s, and Oregon made its last payout based on the 1843 wolf bounty in 1946. The federal government reintroduced wolves to native habitats in Idaho, Montana, and Wyoming in the 1990s. Those that have since snuck west found **Timberwolves** awaiting them at Blue Mountain Community College (Pendleton, Ore.) and **Wolves** at Washington's Walla Walla University. (The Washington Territory was cut out of the northwest Oregon Territory in 1853.)

Indians blamed the whites' medicine man—Dr. Whitman—for the endless stream of emigrants that got more endless when the 1846 Oregon Treaty stretched the international border along the 49th parallel to the Pacific. After measles wiped out half the Cayuse the next year, a small band killed the Whitmans and a dozen others. The ensuing Cayuse War was initially fought between Oregon militias and Indians, but a federal army helped effect the 1855 treaty that accelerated new settlement.

At the site of the Whitman mission, Rev. Cushing Eells opened Whitman Seminary as a memorial in 1863. It moved seven miles east to Walla Walla in 1866 and eventually became Whitman College, home of the (**Fighting**) **Missionaries**. With the Whitman killings resonating for generations, Cheney's Eastern Washington University fielded **Savages**, but they became **Eagles** in 1973.

Eells had arrived in Oregon two years after Whitman and spent a decade ministering to Spokane Indians alongside Elkanah and Mary Walker. *Spokane*—children of the sun—is what the area's Salish speakers call themselves, and there have been minor league Spokane **Indians** in Washington's second-largest city most years since 1903. (They've worked closely with the Spokane Nation to create respectful imagery since 2006.)

Reverend Walker was the first white man to record the Spokanes' legend of a large ape-like humanoid creature later called Sasquatch, still remembered by the Community Colleges of Spokane's **Sasquatch**. By the 1960s "Bigfoot" had become Sasquatch's English-friendly nickname, and CCS uses it as an alternate team ID. (Either is always singular.) *Sasquatch* isn't a Spokane form; it's from the Coast Salish word *sásq'ets*. In fact, the hairy mascot for the University of the

Fraser Valley **Cascades** is *Sásq'ets*. Other **Bigfoot** teams stomp through semi-pro and club soccer leagues in the Pacific Northwest.

Spokane is also where the influential Boston-born Presbyterian missionary and University of Washington president George F. Whitworth founded Whitworth University in 1890. Its teams became **Pirates** in 1926, mostly to avoid the collo-quialism of "**Preachers**," which had been assigned by reporters.[8]

Oregon missionaries were reined in from remote locations after the Whitman Massacre, so the Walkers got some land at Forest Grove (near Portland) and edu-cated their children at an academy run by fellow New England missionaries. In 1867 one Walker son, Joseph Elkanah Walker, did graduate from what by then was Pacific University. In 1898 he was amidst his fifty-year stint as the leading Christian missionary in China when a populist uprising broke out, one in which Chinese nationalists tried to abolish the foreign exploitation of domestic resources that had been going for decades. The most visible rebels, the Fists of Righteous Harmony—or "Boxers"—gave name to the Boxer Rebellion, in which mission-aries and their Chinese converts were listed among "foreign devils." When the armies of Western nations (and a Japan that was getting imperialist notions) crushed the rebellion in 1901, China found itself even more obliged to foreign intervention.

Late in that rebellion, Joseph Walker shipped home a statue of a Chinese dragon (or maybe a unicorn or a dog or a goat—it's a little weird). His mom promptly donated it to Pacific University. Current events gave the bronze the nickname "Boxer," so **Boxers** replaced **Badgers** in Pacific's 1967 student poll. Walker's bronze disappeared after the 1969 Boxer Toss (exactly the type of college prank it sounds0, so the school cast a replica in 1982.

• • •

Boundary disputes between the War of 1812 and the 1846 Oregon Treaty moti-vated the British to punch up their Canadian defenses. The modest hilltop fortifi-cations at Quebec and Halifax became impressive masonry citadels. AHLers of the past have been Halifax **Citadels** (1988–93) and *Citadelles de Québec* (1999–2002). Quebec's massive ramparts also inspired the junior hockey *Remparts de Québec* (1969–85, 1997–).

The Rideau Canal was completed in 1832 to move materiel and troops from Lake Ontario to Montreal if the U.S. invaded. Stonemason Thomas McKay ran the construction, and his Rideau Hall mansion in Ottawa became the residence for Canada's governors general in 1867. The sons of the sixth governor general, Frederick Arthur Stanley, flooded the yard in 1889 and skated as **Rideau Rebels** until the arrival of the next governor general in 1894. The violence at the **Rebels**' games compelled the family to create the Ontario Hockey Association in 1890. Three years later, the elder Stanley awarded the Dominion Hockey Challenge Cup to Canada's amateur English-speaking hockey champions, but Lord Stanley's Cup has been coveted by pros since 1907 and NHL champs since 1926.

In 1911, Queen Victoria gave the tenth governor generalship to her son, the Duke of Connaught. Canada's military secretary named a World War I battalion for the duke's daughter, so Princess Patricia's Canadian Light Infantry was in the midst of wartime heroics when the world's oldest continuous junior hockey team formed in 1917, Saskatchewan's Regina **Patricias** (officially "**Pats**" since 1923). The same duke gave a trophy to Canada's soccer champs in 1912.[9] The side that's claimed the most cups is today's [New] Westminster **Royals**, assembled from a detachment of Royal military engineers in 1862. Just three years earlier, Victoria had given their B.C. capital the name of the London district that includes Westminster Abbey and Parliament, so it's the Royal City, the longtime home of the Douglas College **Royals**, the many hockey incarnations of "New Westminster **Royals**," and senior lacrosse's Royal City **Capitals**. (By 1868 the queen's namesake city, Victoria, was B.C.'s capital.)

• • •

When self-government for the newly named Dominion of Canada was created by the British North America Act of 1867, the office of governor general was modified to protect Britain's continuing interests. To celebrate the centennial, Montreal hosted the 1967 International and Universal Exposition, or "Expo '67." The spirit of that world's fair was evident two years later when the first Canadian MLB team arrived, *les Expos de Montréal*. (The **Expos**' monogram was a heavily stylized *M* for *Montréal* with the initials E.L.B.: *Expos Le Basebol*.) Similarly, junior hockey's Ottawa **67's** are named for both the year of their own inception and the national centennial. Named in anticipation of the party were the Calgary **Centennials** (1966–77).

• • •

The first formal indoor hockey contest was on March 3, 1875 at Montreal's Victoria Rink, named for Her Majesty.[10] By 1881 it was a home to the Montreal **Victorias**, who won three Stanley Cups in the amateur era. The **Victorias** were not amused in 1896 when they were the first team to let the Cup leave Montreal, having lost to Manitoba's first organized team, the Winnipeg **Victorias**. The Montrealers reclaimed the Cup from their same-named opponents later that year because challenges in that era could be posted at any time.

In 1903 the Duke of Marlboro loaned his name to the Toronto Marlboro Athletic Club, which forthwith presented junior hockey Toronto **Marlboros** until 1989. A 2005-named AHL team revived "Toronto **Marlies**."[11]

• • •

In southern Africa's Second Boer War (1899–1902), the British Empire had a tough time countering raids on personnel, bridges, and telegraph lines by colonial Dutch *kommandos*. Canadian cowboys and Mounties were recruited as mounted rifles and scouts that were called "Queen's Cowboys" or "Rough Riders." After helping defeat the *Boers* ("farmers" in Dutch), both nicknames remained with the North West Mounted Police, first prefixed with "Royal" after the Boer Wars by an appreciative Edward VII.[12]

The Regina Rugby Club joined the Saskatchewan Rugby Football League in 1910, adopting the Mounties' red and black colors in 1912 and the corresponding "**Roughriders**" handle in 1924. At that same time, the Interprovincial Rugby Football Union had same-colored Ottawa **Rough Riders**.[13] They'd been named in 1898 for the Ottawa River basin's lumber industry, which boomed after some daring men took a long and rough ride on a huge raft that was disassembled so its composite logs could be sold at Quebec City in 1806 (the standard operating procedure for a century).[14] That history was obscured in 1995 when a new mascot appeared in the full dress of the Ceremonial Guard of the Canadian Forces, who have been trooping around in red and black since 1953 on Ottawa's Parliament Hill (copying the Queen's Guard at Buckingham Palace). Saskatchewan's Regina **Roughriders** moved to the new Western Interprovincial Football Union in 1936. They transitioned to a community-owned team with stockholders across the province in 1948, thus becoming *Saskatchewan* **Roughriders** and trading the Royal Canadian Mounties' red and black for green and white.

In 1958 the IRFU and WIFU became the respective East and West Conferences of the new Canadian Football League, so that circuit had **Roughriders** and **Rough Riders** until the Ottawans folded in 1996. The CFL returned to the capital for 2014 with Ottawa **RedBlacks** (*le Rouge et Noir d'Ottawa*). From the **Rough Riders** they took their colors and bold *R* logo, adding a sawmill blade for background. Red and black were already familiar locally through Ottawa's NHL **Senators**, junior hockey **67's**, NASL **Fury** F.C., and Carleton University **Ravens**.

The Boer War cavalries came to be called "Rough Riders" only after that term had been popularly associated with Theodore Roosevelt's 1st Volunteer Cavalry of 1898,[15] but that's no excuse for credible sources—including the CFL's own website—to suggest that the inspiration for monikers in either Saskatchewan or Ottawa owe to Canadian regiments that served with T.R. in the Spanish-American War.[16] Such a statement willfully ignores that Canadians stayed in line with the British Commonwealth's declared neutrality during that conflict.

But we're willing to exploit even that erroneous reference to the Spanish-American War to revive our discussion of Manifest Destiny. Propagandizing newspapers of the 1890s reignited expansionist fever in Americans by reminding them that they'd never quite gotten around to taking Cuba and other colonies from Spain. They blamed Spain for the (probably accidental) explosion of the battleship Maine at Havana in February 1898. That was the war's immediate cause, but its most celebrated event was a July charge up San Juan Heights by Col. Roosevelt, whose eclectic mix of volunteer frontiersmen, miners, and Indians (with ex–Ivy League athletes thrown in) had countenances and thrown-together uniforms that made them "Rough Riders." They actually ended up riding nothing in Cuba because there had been no room to ship the horses and mules.

Most of the Rough Riders—Roosevelt's "cowboy regiment"—were recruited from the dry unforgiving Southwest, thought to roughly approximate that of Cuba. That makes Las Vegas, New Mexico the right place for both a local museum's Rough Rider Memorial Collection and the Luna Community College **Rough Riders**. Other regional examples include the Yavapai College **Rough Riders** (Prescott, Ariz.) and Crowder College **Roughriders** and **Lady Riders** (Neosho, Mo.). The University of Oklahoma's squads were sometime **Rough Riders** until becoming **Sooners** (p. 156) in 1908.

When the war against the Spanish Empire ended in four months, the U.S. was suddenly a colonial power with control of Cuba, Puerto Rico, Guam, and the Philippines. Manifest Destiny had done its work and then some.

Stingers | Mountain City | Shamrocks | Fire | Sky

Utica College's **Pioneers** recall the early white families who settled at a shallow Mohawk River crossing. But life in upstate New York changed forever in 1820 when the first section of the Erie Canal from Rome to Salina opened. The 363-mile "ditch" linked the Hudson to Lake Erie by 1825, making Utica a mid-canal rest stop and a textile boom town. Midwestern goods had previously bypassed the great falls of the Niagara by going down the Mississippi, across the Gulf, and up the seaboard, but access to the Great Lakes launched New York ahead of Philadelphia, Baltimore, Boston, and New Orleans as the country's busiest port.

Mutually rising fortunes would make New York and Chicago the "Big Apple" and "Second City" respectively. Indoor football's Chicago **Rush** (est. 2001) make a not-so-passing reference to an offensive run,[1] but it's really a tribute to the hustlin' and bustlin' Second City. Similar thinking led to the WBL Chicago **Hustle** (1978–81). That was late in the disco era, the signature song of which was 1975's *The Hustle* by Van McCoy. *Hustler* is rarely a compliment, connoting all kinds of shady behavior and being especially indelicate for a WBL (women's) team because it can refer to a prostitute. Chicago's long history of business dealers, corrupt politicos, and crime bosses has yielded flimflammery of all kinds, and the Chicago of the 1930s was where hustlers pulled off a horse-betting scam for the ages in the 1973 film *The Sting*. They were followed shortly by soccer's Chicago **Sting** (1975–84) and later Chicago **Stingers** (1995–98).

Digging the Erie Canal was toughest where it cut across the northern Allegheny Plateau. The plateau had already blocked shipments from Pittsburgh to Philadelphia, so the Quaker State reacted to New York's canal by opening the Allegheny Portage Railroad in 1834, an ingenious series of inclined planes that pulled canal barges over mountains and up to North America's first railroad tunnels. The APRR National Historic Site in Cresson reports that draught animals towed the load along the flat tracks. That's why an Irish Draught horse represents **Mounties** at Cresson's Mount Aloysius College, although "Irish" therein alludes to the Sisters of Mercy, a Catholic order founded in Ireland in 1831 that sent nuns to Pennsylvania in 1846 for the sake of Irish-Catholic workers who were building the rail lines with hand tools. The Sisters that opened MAC in 1853 did so to educate those laborers' children.

The APRR's inclined planes were obsolete after the 1854 completion of the Pennsylvania Railroad's Horseshoe Curve in Altoona (near Cresson). It was an engineering marvel because a flat track bed had been blasted from the hillside at a consistent and steep grade, connecting Philadelphia's docks to the West. Minor league baseballers have included Altoona **Rail Kings** (1996–97) and the curve-ball-throwing Altoona **Curve** (est. 1998).[2] *Altoona* is from the Latin *altus* (high place), so rail workers called it "Mountain City," putting Altoona's **Mountain City** in the 1884 UA.

With the explosion of canals, Baltimore businessmen tried in 1827 to reclaim business for their port by chartering the Baltimore & Ohio Railroad to run from

Chesapeake Bay to the Ohio and beyond.[3] It was expanding into Pennsylvania two years before Altoona's Curve opened, and one of the B&O's own engineering feats is the 1835 Thomas Viaduct, which connects Howard and Baltimore Counties. Just west of the viaduct, rail history was recalled by Howard [County] Community College's **Iron Horse Express**. They became **Dragons** in 2001 because a dragon adorns the crest for England's Howard family, even though they have no relation to county eponym John E. Howard, a Maryland colonel in the Revolution and successful politician.

• • •

Blame for the Great Chicago Fire of 1871 long rested with the O'Leary family cow, which owes little to forensics and much to local prejudice against the many Irish who'd built the Erie Canal before moving on to the Illinois and Michigan Canal (connecting the Great Lakes to the Illinois River since 1848) and then into Chicago's growing factories. Later years saw an embrace of Irish-Catholic themes displayed by minor league hockey Chicago **Shamrocks** (1930–32), NLL Chicago **Shamrox** (2007–08), and W-League Chicago **Gaels** (2005–08). The soccer **Gaels** were especially at home in the "Windy City," being homophonically associated with *gale*-force winds.

An array of Chicago **Blaze**, **Flames**, and **Fire** sides remember the three-day fire, and Fire Prevention Week marks its anniversary.[4] In 1982 the University of Illinois at Chicago was created through the merger of UI's medical center and its Circle campus, bringing in **Flames** at the same time.[5] The Chicago Fire Academy is a training center for emergency personnel sited near the old O'Leary barn. The MLS Chicago **Fire** (est. 1998) runs its own "Chicago **Fire** Academy" to develop young soccer players.[6]

• • •

Despite the destruction, the trade center between the Great Lakes and the Mississippi watershed was too important to abandon, so leases on Chicago lots remained high. Civic fire codes required the reconstruction to be done with modern, fireproof materials, so Chicago became the proving ground for soaring buildings supported by steel skeletons (as opposed to outside walls) with relatively small architectural footprints. In the shadow of those "skyscrapers," the ABA Chicago **Skyliners** (2001/02) failed to gain much of a profile, but the WNBA Chicago **Sky** (est. 2006) has a skyline emblem. The city's literal rise from the smoldering ashes explains the phoenix symbol (p. 174) for the University of Chicago **Maroons**.

The four red stars on Chicago's city flag represent landmark local events. The earliest was the founding of Fort Dearborn there in 1803. The next was the Great Fire. The third was the World's Columbian Exposition of 1893, which commemorated the four-hundredth anniversary of Columbus's first New World voyage and flaunted Chicago's recovery from the fire for which it had become internationally famous. The last star is for another world's fair, the 1933–34 Century of Progress. Chicago **Red Stars** have played in top women's soccer leagues since 2009, the same time the abovementioned Chicago **Gaels** became the Chicago **Red Eleven** (the **Red Stars'** W-League affiliates), but they folded after 2010.

Clippers | Atlantics | Ducks | Windjammers

After Britain's Civil Wars (p. 69), Charles II regained the British throne for the Stuart family in 1660. He'd acquired a taste for tea during his wartime exile in the Netherlands, and his recent marriage to Catherine of Braganza brought Portugal's tea plantations in India into his empire. The Stuarts' New York namesakes are Kings and Queens Counties. The latter hosts Queens College's courtly **Knights**.

Kings County and Brooklyn have coterminous boundaries, so the major league **Dodgers** (p. 337) of the late 1800s were sometimes Brooklyn **Kings**, revealed in souvenir pennants by a bum wearing a crown. (After sports cartoonist Willard Mullin scribbled up a **Dodger**-bum in 1937, they were forever "Dem bums.") New York–Penn Leaguers were Queens **Kings** in 2000 only, moving to Coney Island as Brooklyn **Cyclones** (after a legendary rollercoaster). The Brooklyn College **Kingsmen** and **Kingswomen** became **Bridges** in 1994 (for the Brooklyn Bridge), but they've been **Bulldogs** since late 2009.

• • •

Tea will spoil over time, so it was too bad that Britain's East Indiamen were lumbering vessels. With a premium paid for quicker delivery, both commercial and romantic interests were served when the super-sleek American—or "Yankee"—clipper appeared in the mid-1840s. Still the fastest commercial sailers ever built, their massive sails and razor hulls *clipped* time off voyages. Most clippers took forty-niners from New York to Frisco before zipping over to Hong Kong for tea or Australia for wool and gold miners, so most **Clippers** play at Pacific ports:

- The San Francisco **Clippers** (1944–48) played in the west coast's top pre-war football leagues but infamously drew *seven* fans to one game.[1]
- The NBA Buffalo **Braves** (est. 1970) became San Diego **Clippers** with a 1978 move west, but they've been Los Angeles **Clippers** since 1984.
- Columbia Christian College (Portland, Ore.) had **Clippers**, but closed in 1993.
- Minor league Oakland **Clippers** started the 1936/37 season but quickly skated north as Spokane **Clippers** until 1939. Elsewhere in Washington are the **Clippers** of South Puget Sound Community College in Olympia.
- Crew members often hailed from the Northeastern ports that built Yankee clippers for Pacific seas, putting **Clippers** at the University of Maine at Machias.

• • •

Brilliant marine architect William Webb launched many clippers from New York. Predicting the end of wooden ships, he addressed the engineering demands of steel construction by opening Long Island's Webb Institute of Naval Architecture in 1894. Webb's **Webbies** are conveniently abbreviated "webfoots" (a nickname for sailors), but "**Clippers**" is a recognized alternate. Eastward on Long Island are Suffolk County Community College's **Clippers**. Across the sound are the Concordia College **Clippers** (Bronxville, N.Y.).

Despite its name, southern Saskatchewan's village of Caronport isn't a port; *Caronport* is a portmanteau for the WW2-era Caron Airport. It's also a thousand miles from the nearest ocean, but its Briercrest College is a base for **Clippers** because the winter storms that blow east from the Canadian Rockies are "Alberta clippers." Those dry low-pressure systems can cause large, coastal snowstorms when they collide with warm air over Atlantic waters.

• • •

Henry Eckford had been the master shipwright in the generation before William Webb. On eastern Lake Ontario he quickly built all of the U.S. Navy's Great Lake ships for the War of 1812 with the help of trusty apprentice Isaac Webb (William's father).[2] Eckford's Brooklyn shipyard was among that city's largest employers by the 1820s, and shipbuilders played baseball on Eckford Street as the **Eckford** Club (1857–72), an early NA power. The rival **Atlantic** Club (1855–75) was named for Brooklyn's Atlantic Avenue. The **Eckfords** and **Atlantics** are the working class crews oft-credited with turning their game away from domination by amateur gentlemen's clubs.

• • •

The millions of Long Island ducklings that have graced dinner plates for generations are subtle tokens of the Tea Trade. All were purportedly descended from just nine Pekin ducks brought back from China on an 1873 clipper run. By 1900 dozens of family farms produced ducks near Moriches Bay. Long Island **Ducks** have played minor league hockey (1959–72, Commack), hoop (1977/78, Commack), and hardball (est. 2000, Central Islip).

Across New York Harbor from Long Island is the Stevens Institute of Technology (Hoboken, N.J.). The Stute's **Ducks** are named for the waterfowl that mill about the Hudson River campus. Their cartoon webfoot is a Pekin, as are virtually all white ducks in North America. *Pekin* is from the French form of *Peking*, an alternate name for the Chinese capital Beijing. In fact, roasted Peking duck is China's national dish, so that country's top pro hoop league has Beijing **Ducks**.

• • •

The famous *Glory of the Seas* made record-breaking runs in the San Francisco-Liverpool-Melbourne trade. Like many clippers it spent its last years in the coal trade out of Nanaimo, B.C., explaining the name of junior hockey's Nanaimo **Clippers**. The *Glory* was the last clipper launched by famous shipbuilder Donald McKay in 1869, the same year the Suez Canal opened. From then on, steamships powered by coal could forgo the circumnavigation of Africa, ending the reign of the clippers like the coal-toting *Glory*.

Having been run hard, clippers had short lives, but wind-driven cargo ships had one last big play. The new "windjammers" could be twice as long as clippers with hulls of iron or steel (as foreseen by William Webb). Faster than steamers and more stable, windjammers didn't run out of coal in mid-ocean. Like **Clippers**, athletic **Windjammers** are on the coasts, as evinced by Portland's Maine **Windjammers** (1985/86), Nova Scotia's Halifax **Windjammers** (1991–94), and Florida's Tampa Bay **Windjammers** (1996–99). All played minor league basketball, where a monster *jam* finishes your path to the iron.

Bees | Tommies | Bonnies | Conquerors

Being tireless workers, bees came to represent a selfless Christian faith. It was even believed bees experienced virgin birth, mirroring New Testament events. When bees dropped honey down the throat of a well-born Roman infant, Mom and Dad realized the spiritual truths that mouth would later speak.

The pre-game hype was borne out in 374 CE when our boy Ambrose—then Rome's governor of northern Italy—talked a mob out of rioting in a Milan basilica. Those present had been split between candidates to succeed the recently deceased Bishop of Milan, and so eloquent was he that a reluctant Ambrose was drafted into service as bishop by the assembled.

A Catholic seminary founded at Davenport, Iowa in 1882 is now St. Ambrose University, where **Saints** became (male) **Fighting Bees** and (female) **Queen Bees** in 1937. Calgary's Ambrose University was named for the same saint in 2007 when Nazarene University College and Alliance University College merged. They'd united their **United** teams three years earlier, but the merger made them **Lions**, out of respect for the noble characteristics of *Panthera leo* and the lion imagery in Christian literature.[1]

Hawks at the Benedictines' Saint Anselm College refer to raptors on the quieter west side of Manchester, New Hampshire. The institutional namesake is Benedictine monk Anselm of Canterbury (1033–1109), the first person to seriously use reason (as opposed to faith alone) to explain Church teachings, a fused approach called *scholasticism*.

After Anselm's death, Latin translations of Aristotle's ancient Greek texts came to Christian Europe through scribes in Islamic Spain, but Aristotle's logic punched holes in the faith-based methods of Church Doctors (great doctrinal thinkers like Ambrose and Anselm). Soon a *doctor universalis*, Dominican friar Albertus Magnus, was filtering everything in his observable world through an Aristotelian prism. From his University of Paris chair, "Albert the Great" wrote diverse works that included a widely consulted *Treatise on Falconry* (c. 1258), but it's not remembered if that explains **Falcons** at the Dominicans' Albertus Magnus College (New Haven, Conn.).

Albert's Dominican protégé was St. Thomas Aquinas, known in his time as the "Wayne Gretzky of scholasticism" because his commentaries on Aristotle are among the Middle Ages' great intellectual achievements. Aquinas's namesake **Saints** represent the Dominicans' Aquinas College (Grand Rapids, Mich.).

The University of St. Thomas (St. Paul, Minn.) and St. Thomas University (Fredericton, N.B.) are both named for Mr. Aquinas and both host (male and female) **Tommies**. That irreverence isn't unprecedented; the study of Aquinian philosophy and theology is called "Thomism," and addressing saints with such familiarity is more of a trend at Catholic institutions than one might intuit. There are **Bonnies** at the Franciscans' St. Bonaventure University (Allegheny, N.Y.). In fact, Saints Thomas and Bonaventure of Bagnoregio both taught at the University of Paris in the 1250s. There was mutual respect, but some friction resulted from the rejection of Dominican-Thomist Aristotelianism by the Bonaventure-led Franciscans. SBU adopted "**Bonnies**" in 1979 after the Seneca people asked that **Brown Indians** and **Brown Squaws** be dumped. ("**Brown**" owed to the drab habit of Franciscans who worked among the western Iroquois.)

The Benedictines' Saint John's University (Collegeville, Minn.) backs all-male **Johnnies**. Its partner school is the all-female College of Saint Benedict, where volleyballers held a naming contest in 1976 expressly to avoid the tag historically applied to students: **Bennies**. All CSBers since then have been **Blazers**.[2] Red-and-white **Frannies** and **Franciscans** used to play for the country's oldest Franciscan college, Saint Francis University (Loretto, Pa.), but they're now the **Red Flash**.[3]

• • •

Dominican Sisters founded Siena Heights University (Adrian, Mich.) in 1919. It and its **Saints** remember the Dominican tertiary St. Catherine of Siena, who famously applied scholastic logic to her *Dialogue* of 1378. Catherine died in 1380, the year her city's other famed saint was born. The preacher Bernardine (or Bernardino or Bernard) was a great comfort to plague victims and the eponym for St. Bernardine of Siena College (Loudonville, N.Y.), founded by Franciscans in 1937. It's now Siena College, where **Indians** became **Saints** in 1988. A California city is also named for Bernard of Siena. It's where the CSU San Bernardino **St. Bernards** changed to wilder **Coyotes** when they moved up a division in the early 1990s.

Siena and CSUSB have both used St. Bernard mascots, as have many **Saints**, whether or not their home institution is affiliated with anyone named Bernard. The canine's popularity owes to the attending legend. In the tenth century, St. Bernard of Menthon (not he "of Siena") ran some hospices near Alpine passes. For centuries, the Augustinian monks at those shelters trained big dogs to sniff out avalanche victims. (The NHL's Colorado **Avalanche** have a St. Bernard mascot—*Bernie*—for that reason.) We don't know how many were lost during severe winters in the early 1800s, but it's probable that only a few that survived were crossbred with other dogs, making today's "pure breed" St. Bernard dramatically different from its ancestors. Those dogs represent the Carroll College **Fighting Saints** (Helena, Mont.) and the **Saints** at Ashford University (Clinton, Iowa), College of St. Scholastica (Duluth, Minn.), Presentation College (Aberdeen, S.D.), and Santa Fe College **Saints** (Gainesville, Fla.). The St. Bernard mascot for Aquinas College's **Saints** is Nelson, named for former college president Paul Nelson. The NFL New Orleans **Saints** had a pet St. Bernard at their inception because Orleans Parish abuts St. Bernard [of Clairvaux] Parish.

• • •

In mid-empire Rome, Christianity was an inconsequential sect, but those Christians who needled emperors with an adoration of their own "king of kings" could still get flung to the lions. Persecution was at its worst under Valerian (r. 253–260), who tried to massacre all Christian ministers. He beheaded Pope Sixtus II and ordered the cruel martyrdom (a literal grilling) of Lawrence of Rome, acts that stirred sympathy in non-Christians and nudged the empire toward acceptance of that faith.

The Feast of St. Lawrence is August 10, the day in 1535 on which Frenchmen named the St. Lawrence River. The St. Lawrence University **Saints** (Canton, N.Y.) are just a few miles south of their eponymous stream, a rare case of non-Catholic **Saints**. (SLU started as a Universalist seminary in 1856.) Restating the theme of casual address, St. Lawrence teams were **Larries** into the 1970s.

In about 304, Catherine of Alexandria told Emperor Maxentius that the on-going persecution of Christians by Rome was one messed up scene. Her argument actually won over the court's best counselors, so an enraged Max wheeled her out to her execution.[4] The athletic **Wildcats** at her namesake school—St. Catherine University (St. Paul, Minn.)—seem devoid of whimsy, but those 'Cats are derived from the **Katies** and **Kats** who'd represented "St. Kate's" in decades past.

• • •

Things would improve for would-be martyrs. Maxentius had to defend his emper-or's seat against the ambitious Constantine in 312. Before one battle the chal-lenger dreamed of a cross in the sky with a Latin instruction set: *In hoc signo vinces.* (In this sign, victory.) He awoke, told his soldiers to paint the cross of the merciful lord on their shields, and crushed his rival. As Constantine I, he quickly issued an edict of toleration for Christians across his empire.

The word is generally reserved for soldiers of later centuries, but Constantine is the earliest military leader we can call a literal *crusader*—one who does battle in the name of the holy cross. The College of the Holy Cross (Worcester, Mass.) is New England's oldest Catholic college. Its unsurprising Latin motto is *In hoc signo vinces*, and teams at "The Cross" are **Crusaders**. Their official purple is from the standard of Roman emperors, although a competing tale says it's a blend of Harvard crimson and Yale blue.

One might infer that the Division III **Lancers** at Worcester State University derived their name from the D-I Holy Cross **Crusaders** across town, but that ignores John W. Higgins, a local pressed steel manufacturer with a natural interest in European armor. The world's largest private stockpile of armor—including plenty of lances—opened in 1931 as the Higgins Armory Museum. (The collection was transferred to the Worcester Art Museum in 2014.)

A young Roman named Martin invoked the Christian soldier metaphor by putting down his sword before a 336 battle against Gauls to declare, "I am a soldier of Christ." He'd live to a ripe old age in post-Constantine Rome as the third Bishop of Tours and the first non-martyred saint. Saint Martin's University in Lacey, Washington is a proving ground for **Saints**.

• • •

The dawn of Imperial Christianity might have had as much to do with creating a uniform Roman presence across the empire as any devotion to Jesus. The mother of Constantine himself (St. Helena of Constantinople) was a Christian who built Jerusalem's Church of the Holy Sepulcher. It was destroyed in 1009 when the "mad" Caliph Hakim of Egypt and Palestine provoked Europe by cracking down on infidels (Christians and Jews) and closing the Holy Land to Christian pilgrims.

In 1071, Seljuk Turks took Jerusalem from the Egyptian Caliphs and handed the Christian Byzantines a defeat in the Battle of Manzikert. When Constantin-ople looked to Rome for help in 1095, Pope Urban II spotted a chance to reassert

Roman authority that some Byzantine states had lately been questioning. Urban's call for a volunteer army got a huge response from Central Europe's poor and disenfranchised, especially in his home country of France. In 1096, Crusaders warmed up for the war on distant infidels by slaughtering some they found closer to home. The killing of thousands of Rhineland Jews in the name of Jesus is among the earliest acts to have bloodied the Crusader-as-metaphor. The First Crusade ended when Christians took Jerusalem in 1099 and massacred Arabs, Jews, and some local Christians (!) who had the gall to not look very French. It is a narrative tradition to stop here to repeat the words of crusader-chronicler Raymond of Aguilers: "Wonderful things were to be seen [...] the corpses of men [...] horses waded in the blood up to their knees [...] a just and marvelous judgment of God."

Turks quickly snatched back a few of the new Crusader states, and French and German armies failed to retake them in a Second Crusade (1144–50). After the Crusaders lost Jerusalem in 1189 to Saladin Ayyub the Kurd, a Third Crusade (1189–92) brought England's King Richard to the Holy Land, but he won from Saladin little more than access to Jerusalem for pilgrims.

A Fourth Crusade would have put soldiers from Central Europe into Ayyubid-controlled Egypt and Palestine, but the money ran out in Italy. The merchants of Venice had suspended trade to build the invasion fleet, so would-be Crusaders discharged the debt in 1202 by conquering Venice's commercial competitors on the east Adriatic coast, a Christian (!) port with Byzantine sympathies (now Zadar, Croatia). That earned the Crusaders their excommunication and unemployment, so a Swabian prince paid them to invade Christian (!) Constantinople to knock off the Byzantine emperor in 1204. The victorious Latins then slaughtered, raped, and pillaged Eastern Christians (!) on a grand scale.

A Fifth Crusade (1217–21) attacked Ayyubid power along the Nile. Francis of Assisi—founder of the Franciscan order—arrived at camp in 1219 intending to end the fight between diseased and starving armies, although his plan to bring the enemy sultan to Jesus proved unrealistic. The two men did have a nice chat before the Crusader advance on Cairo was squashed. Citing their patron saint's mission of peace, the blue and gold at the Franciscans' Madonna University (Livonia, Mich.) have been **Crusaders** since intercollegiate sports began in 1987. Other Christian-backed **Crusaders** represent Christendom College (Front Royal, Va.), Evangel University (Springfield, Mo.), Tennessee Temple University (Chattanooga), and the University of Dallas (Irving, Texas).

• • •

Ever since those knight-combatants returned from the Crusades the character of knighthood has been inextricably Christian, so **Knights** represent these Christian schools: College of Saint Rose (Albany, N.Y.), Neumann University (Aston, Pa.), and Southwestern Adventist University (Keene, Texas).

After warfare subsided in the Middle Ages, knights were courtiers in an age of chivalry, fighting only each other in simulated military tests, such as jousting with lances. The **Knight** at Calvin College (run by the Christian Reformed Church) is named *Joust*, while team photos of **Knights** from Gannon University (Erie, Pa., Catholic) appear in its *Lance* yearbook. Among Christian **Lancers** are those at

Grace College (evangelical, Winona Lake, Ind.) and Mount Marty College (Catholic, Yankton, S.D.).

A knight-with-lance on a horse is a *charger*, so **Chargers** at Christian schools include Ancilla Domini College (Donaldson, Ind.), Briar Cliff University (Sioux City, Iowa), and Dominican College (Orangeburg, N.Y.). The symbol for the **Chargers** at Lancaster [Pa.] Bible College was once a knight with a Crusader's crossed shield, but it's now an advancing warhorse, also called a charger.

Crusade has evolved to describe any zealous advocacy. With colleges trying to win at all costs, athletic director Luther Grossman at Susquehanna University (Selinsgrove, Pa.) emphasized participation and true amateurism, a personal crusade that gave his Lutheran school **Little Crusaders** in the 1920s, long since shortened to **Crusaders**.[5]

• • •

In 2006, Northwest Nazarene University (Nampa, Idaho) set to "redefine [and] identify more contemporary uses" of *Crusader* for its own **Crusaders**, thereby invoking a metaphor while distancing itself from the very events that effected its metaphoricity. Considering team names in 1968, students at Alabama's University of Mobile eschewed Crusader atrocities by taking "**Knights**" and "**Crusaders**" off the table completely to make way for **Rams**.[6] Philadelphia Biblical University (Langhorne, Pa.) swapped **Crusaders** for **Crimson Eagles** in 1982 (and then **Highlanders** in 2012 when it became Cairn University.). As we'll show, evading "**Crusaders**" would be a more pronounced trend in the next century.

One Christian college, San Diego's Point Loma Nazarene University, cited the "changing international meaning of the term crusader" in a 2003 press release and dumped its **Crusaders**. No specifics were given, but that was when the U.S. was reacting to the terrorist attacks of September 11, 2001 by invading Afghanistan and Iraq, two predominantly Muslim countries. In fact, avowed Christian president George W. Bush characterized the impending U.S. response on September 16: "This Crusade, this war on terrorism, is gonna take a while." The new mascot for PLNU's renamed **Sea Lions** is a fantastical maned "sea-lion." That of the same city's WPSL San Diego WFC **SeaLions** (est. 1988) is an actual California sea lion (*Zalophus californianus*).

Bush would later apologize for his Crusader remark's lack of historical sensitivity. Some Christians, however, decided not to risk that some Middle Eastern web surfer would notice their self-comparison to bygone Crusaders. For example, administrator Matt Davis at Maranatha Baptist University (Watertown, Wis.), announced in early 2014 that his school would drop its **Crusaders**, saying, "Our world has changed since 9/11 and we've become a more global society with the Internet."[7] MBU teams had a ferocious new name that spring, **Sabercats**.

The **Crusaders** at Wheaton College (Wheaton, Ill.) switched to **Thunder** in 2000. The next year, **Crusaders** at Cardinal Stritch University became **Wolves**. One year further and their Milwaukee neighbors from Mount Mary College traded **Crusaders** for **Blue Angels**. Oregon's Northwest Christian College **Crusaders** in Eugene became **Beacons** in 2004. That same year, the Mascot Task Force at San Antonio's University of the Incarnate Word exhibited admirable humility by identifying the "**Crusaders**" nickname that dated to 1980 as "nothing to be proud of." The Catholic school then decided that its red and black would be **Cardinals**. Similarly, Eastern Nazarene College (Quincy, Mass.) threw its **Crusaders** out for **Lions** in 2009, conceding that Crusader imagery failed to evoke the standard of universal Christian love that is expected from students.[8]

• • •

Piedmont Baptist College (Winston-Salem, N.C.) and the Association Free Lutheran Bible School (Plymouth, Minn.) both sponsor **Conquerors**. Christians use *conqueror* as a sometime synonym for *crusader*, but PBC and AFLBS are spared the scrutiny directed at **Crusaders** thanks to a letter by the apostle Paul (Romans 8:37) that was written a thousand years before the Crusades. It says, "In all these things we are more than conquerors through Him that loved us." The AFLBS athletic badge is indeed a cross-endowed shield, but the school says it's meant to represent the "armor of God" from Ephesians 6:11 and not the kite-shaped shield of a Crusader.

Ravens | Monks | Centaurs | Hoyas

When Rome stopped its persecution of Christians (p. 205), a martyr's death was no longer a fast-track to heaven. This led to the rise of monasticism, a kind of living self-sacrifice. Western monasticism started when Benedict of Nursia gave up the advantages of a privileged Roman birth to live in solitude in about 500 CE. At his first Italian monastery (est. 529), "Benedictines" lived silently in self-contained communes where they studied scripture and demonstrated humility before God through manual labor. The "Rule of St. Benedict" implemented at the dozen monasteries he founded set the example for later monastics.[1]

Jealous priests who didn't like Benedict's rigorous Rule poisoned his bread. The intuitive raven who spirited away said loaf often accompanies the saint in Christian art. "Black monks"—black-robed Benedictines—founded Benedictine College (Atchison, Kan.) in 1859, home of black-and-red **Ravens**.

Benedict's raven recalls the prophet Elijah. After telling Israel's King Ahab that the Lord thought he (Ahab) was a punk, Elijah had to hide in a wilderness where he survived only because ravens brought him food. In light of that passage (1 Kings 17:2–6), black-and-orange **Tigers** at the Church of God's Anderson [Ind.] University became **Ravens** in 1937.[2]

The raven's association with hunger owes to its habitual scavenging. Noting that Coffeyville [Kan.] Community College's 1925 footballers were lean on wins, the *Coffeyville Journal* called them **Ravens** and later **Red Ravens**, saying the players were embarrassed—"red faced"—over their losses.[3]

• • •

A Spanish noblewoman dreamed of her unborn child as a dog enlightening the world with a torch. (Dogs had represented preachers for centuries.) At his 1170 baptism, the newborn took the name Dominic while a star of divine light warmed his forehead. That predicted the future saint's role as a spiritual beacon and gave **Stars** to the Dominican-founded Dominican University (River Forest, Ill.).

Dominic founded a radical new order of priests in 1216. Until then, monks had followed Benedict's strict rules, but Dominic thought his preachers should travel and spread the gospel in the tradition of the original twelve apostles of Jesus. Their activities beyond the monastery walls required reclassification because *monk*—along with *monastery*—is from the Greek *monos*: alone. Saint Dominic's "Dominicans" instead would be *friars*, from the Latin *frater*: brother. Female monastics are called nuns, which is ignored by the **Monks** and **Lady Monks** at Saint Joseph's College of Maine in Standish. In 1917, Rhode Island's Providence College opened with help from Dominican brothers, as appreciated by **Friars**. **Lady Friars**—"lady brothers"—would be as self-excluding as **Lady Monks** and no more politically correct, but that's what PC's women are called.

Dominic's mom's dream gave a nickname to friars, *Domini canis*, which is tortured Latin for "dog of God." That and the order's black-and-white habit make Dalmatians apt symbols for Dominicans and a mascot for their colleges (like Providence). The **Penguins** at San Rafael's Dominican University of California were named for faculty nuns who waddle around campus in black-and-white duds. The identity dates from the 1970s, so somebody probably would have noticed that DU's black, white, and gold colors matched those of the NHL's 1967-founded Pittsburgh **Penguins**.

• • •

After decades of fighting over their city with Latin Crusaders, the Byzantines were once again running Constantinople by the mid-1200s. The Muslim threat to the "Greek East" would prove too great, however, and Constantinopolitans were fleeing long before the city fell to the Turks in 1453. (It's now Istanbul, not Constantinople, having formally taken its traditional Turkish name only in 1930.) Influential Byzantine scholars were in Italy by 1400, bringing Greek texts that renewed appreciation for classical literature, architecture, art, and reason. The *Renaissance* (rebirth) soon overwhelmed Europe, but Florence is where lecturers from the East first had influence, so it's the world's Renaissance City.

In 1818 a surveyor gave the name of his Italian birthplace to a site on the Tennessee River. The Florences in Italy and Alabama are now sister cities. The latter hosts fall's Alabama Renaissance Faire and the tallest structure in town is the Renaissance Tower. More than a few associate that city's University of North Alabama **Lions** (named in the 1930s) with Marzocco, the heraldic lion of Italy's Florence, but no existing backstory confirms that suspicion.[4]

A popular Greek mythology course brought a micro-Renaissance to Purdue University North Central (Westville, Ind.) in the late 1960s, drawing students to a new athletic identity: North Central **Centaurs**. Mythological centaurs were half-human (upper body) and half-horse (back, legs, etc.). A few were healers and teachers, but most resembled the distant relatives who show up drunk and knock the cake into the bride. That made centaurs lousy role models for collegians, and PNC's **Centaurs** grudgingly accepted the inevitability of having their efforts called "half-assed" by opposing fans,[5] so PNC switched to alliterative **Panthers** in 2000. **Lady Centaurs** are also problematic; centaurs were born from a cloud—so, no mothers—which leaves female centaurs absent in mythology (although uninformed Roman artisans did immortalize female centaurs in mosaic and marble as Greek ideals pervaded the empire).

Alliteration like that within "[North] Central **Centaurs**" (above) was sought by literature professors at the University of Wisconsin Centers–Fond du Lac, who successfully advanced the "Centers **Centaurs**" nickname in the early '70s. When the school was renamed UW-Fond du Lac in 1997, major campus renovations were under way. Students decided to overhaul the team name too and scrambled the letters in "Fond du Lac" to get **Falcons** in 1999.[6]

The Center/**Centaur** pun was also played by Allentown College of St. Francis de Sales. It was renamed DeSales University in 2001 and decided its "wild [and] lawless" **Centaur** "no longer fits the school's image."[7] They became **Bulldogs** without moving from their home in Pennsylvania's *Center* Valley.

• • •

Nuns from a German orphanage traveled to Wisconsin in the 1870s to start the School Sisters of St. Francis. In 1887 they founded the Milwaukee school for

Catholic women that's now Alverno College, commemorating the 1224 appearance of Jesus before St. Francis of Assisi on Italy's Mt. Alverno. The "Alverno **Inferno**" has great assonance and even links to Italian literature through Dante Alighieri's *Divine Comedy*, an epic Renaissance poem about the author's spiritual journey through *Inferno* (hell), *Purgatorio* (purgatory), and *Paradisio* (heaven). Romance languages sometimes feminize *Alverno* as *Alvernia*, so don't confuse the Franciscans' Alverno College with their Alvernia University (Reading, Pa.). Like uncountable Christian colleges, Alvernia keeps **Crusaders**.

Many **Saints** are indebted to Mr. F. Assisi & Associates. Encounter **Fighting Saints** and **Lady Saints** at the University of St. Francis (Joliet, Ill.). The Sisters of St. Francis helped shape Mount St. Clare College in Clinton, Iowa. The Mount put forth **Mounties** until it became The Franciscan University in 2003, thereafter backing **Saints**. (It became Ashford University when its Catholic affiliation ceased in 2005 but kept its **Saints**.) California has long hosted AAU and minor league San Francisco **Saints** in the city named for him of Assisi.[8]

The traveling preachers in Assisi's order were compared to troubadours (a name for wandering minstrels). The saint himself is often "God's troubadour," which put **Troubadours** at Fort Wayne's University of Saint Francis when intercollegiate sports started in 1964. They became less cryptic **Cougars** for fall 1975,[9] but their cat mascot was later named Johnny Cougar, calling to mind rock troubadour and favorite Indiana son John Cougar Mellencamp.

• • •

John Carroll became America's first Catholic bishop in 1784. His seat was at Baltimore, in England's only former Catholic colony, Maryland. Carroll sponsored several colleges, including America's first Catholic one at D.C.'s Georgetown neighborhood in 1789. Like other Jesuit "Latin schools," it emphasized the study and use of the language of the Church and science. A nineteenth-century student supposedly corrupted Greek and Latin forms to come up with the cheer "Hoya saxa!" … roughly "What rocks!" Fans yelling "Hoyy-ahh!" gave **Hoyas** to Georgetown University in the 1920s.[10]

It was for that same Bishop Carroll that Jesuits renamed St. Ignatius College (Cleveland, Ohio) in 1923. John Carroll University's **Blue Streaks** were named for colors of blue and gold shortly thereafter.

In 1808, Carroll invited tireless educator Elizabeth Ann Bayley Seton to run a Maryland girls' school. There she set the template for parochial education in America. The next year, Carroll made her "Mother" Seton of the American chapter of the Sisters of Charity of St. Vincent de Paul, the order that opened Seton Hill College (Greensburg, Pa.) in 1918. Changing to Seton Hill University in 2002, **Spirits** became **Griffins**, either of which commonly represents Christian schools (p. 107).

Don't confuse Seton Hill University with New Jersey's Seton Hall University, although both recall the first American-born saint. Thirty-five years after Mother Seton's 1856 death, the latter was founded at Madison by her nephew, the first Bishop of Newark, James R. Bayley. (It moved to South Orange in 1860.) A Worcester reporter first called Seton Hall's **Blue and White** players "**Pirates**" in 1931 after a ninth-inning comeback stole victory from Holy Cross baseballers.

• • •

Tennessee's 1925 Butler Act prohibited the teaching of evolution at publicly funded institutions. When Governor Austin Peay signed Butler to mollify rural support, civil libertarians went ape. Businessmen in Dayton thought a "Monkey Trial" would put their town on the map, so science teacher John Scopes agreed to say he'd taught evolution from a state-approved textbook. The lead prosecutor was William Jennings Bryan, a famous Christian opponent of Darwinism (former Congressman, Secretary of State, and presidential candidate). Bryan won when the defense asked for a guilty verdict to jumpstart the appeals process, but the state's top court set aside that conviction on a technicality and bounced the test case from the courts. Butler would be law for another four decades.

At that time, "Fundamentalism" was a new term for old-time religiosity. Fundamentalists feared that their less secular worldview "would not be the dominant version of Protestantism in America. They responded [to the Scopes trial] by turning inward and building [churches and Bible colleges] that would enable them to maintain their faith within their own cultural system."[11] In fact, Bryan College opened in Dayton itself five years after the Monkey Trial, but it was a memorial. The "Great Commoner" had died just five days after the trial. Athletes were once **Commoners**,[12] but today's Bryan **Lions** are rhymin' … and they conform to the lion-as-Christian-symbol (p. 107).

> Governor Peay tirelessly campaigned for a teachers' college in Clarksville, and the Austin Peay Normal School opened there in 1929 (two years after the governor died in office). Austin Peay State University is now the seat of **Governors** and **Lady Govs**. (They'd been **Normalites** or **Warriors** until the late 1930s.)

Between the trial and his death, Bryan wrote a few upbeat letters. A sorry-you-were-not-there version went to the Fundamentalist who would continue the attack on Darwin.[13] Texas Baptist J. Frank Norris pioneered both broadcast evangelism and megachurchism. His vitriolic campaign against modernism within Baptist congregations and institutions (like the teaching of evolution at Baylor) got him booted from the Southern Baptist Convention in 1924. Such zeal often finds trouble, and Norris beat charges at different times for arson and murder, but he was a hero to many who embraced his conservative and anticommunist "Christian patriotism." **Patriots** represent the Arlington, Texas institute he founded in 1939, Arlington Baptist College. It's fifteen miles from Dallas Baptist University. DBU has no connection to Norris, but a student center—a replica of Independence Hall—hints that this place of "Christ-centered education" also keeps **Patriots**.

Norris would come to divide time between pastorates in Fort Worth and Detroit. His protégé G.B. Vick assumed some of the duties in Michigan, but when he dared question the administration of Arlington Baptist, Norris took enough (predictable) offense that a Vick-led faction split from Norris's World Baptist Fellowship in 1950 to form Baptist Bible Fellowship International, which immediately set up its own Baptist Bible College in its new home city, Springfield, Missouri. A cross is pinned to the tricorne hat of BBC's **Patriot** mascot to verify his own Christian patriotism.

Spiders | Giants | Mets | Athletics

In 1894 the **Colts** from Virginia's University of Richmond took the field around lanky pitcher Puss Ellyson like spiders in his web, as described by the *Richmond Times Dispatch*. They've been **Spiders** ever since,[1] but Cleveland's National Leaguers had already legitimized "**Spiders**" as a team name when the club's treasurer noted an inordinate number of lanky players at an 1889 practice.[2]

In 1897, Penobscot Indian Louis Sockalexis signed with the **Spiders**. Much was expected from the multi-sport Holy Cross star, but after a promising rookie year, big-league pressure mixed with alcohol and an off-field ankle injury to ensure that "Socks" saw only small parts of two more seasons.

In *Indian Summer: The Forgotten Story of Louis Sockalexis*, author Brian McDonald says "**Indians**" and "**Red Men**" were sometime identifiers when the Sockalexis-era **Spiders** played split-squad games,[3] but outside of those ad hoc circumstances, Sockalexis was never on any **Indians** team, and a so-named side from a different league that would claim to honor him was lying.

In 1901, two years after the **Spiders** folded, the AL put forth the Cleveland **Blues** (the same name as blue-suited NLers, 1879–84). Their lousy record made them **Bluebirds** in the press. That was intentionally short on bravado, so the players voted to be **Bronchos** for 1902.[4] The next year they were **Naps** in tribute to their second baseman and eventual player-manager Napoleon Lajoie, who'd been acquired under peculiar circumstances in June 1902. The AL's deep pockets had lured Lajoie from the NL's Philadelphia **Phillies** to the crosstown **Athletics** for 1901, and the **Phillies** sued to keep Lajoie. While his case went through the courts, the future Hall of Famer became the twentieth century's first Triple Crown winner as an **Athletic**.

Before the 1902 season, the state supreme court said Lajoie (and other local "jumpers") should have remained **Phillies** property. But instead of sending him back, the league shipped Lajoie off to Cleveland, beyond the jurisdiction of both the state courts and the NL. A fugitive in Pennsylvania, Lajoie expected to miss road games against the **Athletics** for the rest of his career, but that changed with a new National Agreement of 1903 in which "Major League Baseball" became a proper noun and the NL aligned with AL owners who suddenly appreciated their exclusive rights to players.

Lajoie even finished his career in Pennsylvania after being traded back to the **Athletics** for 1915, so the Nap-less **Naps** became Cleveland **Indians**. The **Indians** waited until their 1968 pressbook to say they'd been named for Sockalexis who'd died in 1913,[5] but that's possible only if history is "a set of lies agreed upon" (words attributed to the French general for whom Napoleon Lajoie was the namesake). In truth, the **Naps** were dead last in 1914, and it's likely that team owner Charles W. Somers wanted a Native American moniker to compare them to that season's last-to-first world champs, Boston's "Miracle" **Braves**.[6]

No one's ever suggested that Cleveland's **Indians** commemorate either the area's original Erie Confederacy or the Iroquois who displaced them in the 1650s, people whose descendents would likely be quick to forfeit any association with the buck-toothed, shifty-eyed Chief Wahoo mascot the team has had since 1947.

• • •

Louis Sockalexis fell so far so fast that he was actually cut from the NL's 1899 Cleveland **Spiders**, *the worst major league team of all time* ... which does little to champion Socks as the inspiration for "**Indians**."

But how'd the **Spiders** get to be so bad?

Mulling over Cleveland's poor gate receipts from 1898, team owners Stanley and Frank Robison decided to buy the St. Louis **Browns**. The brothers quickly traded most of the good **Spiders** (like Cy Young) for a bunch of pale **Browns**. The much-improved St. Louisans were recast as **Perfectos**, but they finished in a less than perfect fifth place in the 1899 NL. On the way to their 20-134 record,[7] the depleted **Spiders** stopped drawing fans, so the Robisons put them on the road for the last two months while the press derided them as "Exiles," "Wanderers," and "Misfits."

Buying multiple franchises to create one superteam was an old strategy called syndication. Two New York sides had joined the majors in 1883. The NL New York **Gothams** (or **Maroons** or **New Yorks**) and the AA New York **Metropolitan Club** were both run by tobacco merchant John B. Day and "**Mets**" manager Jim Mutrie. The 50-cent admission to NL games was twice that of the AA, so Day slid Mutrie and his best **Mets** to the '85 **Gothams**. When the **Gothams** rallied to win a big June game, Mutrie sprang from the dugout to congratulate "My giants!" They've been **Giants** ever since, even after their 1958 move to San Francisco.

But only in fantasy. In real life, the *New York World* had called Mutrie's boys "**Giants**" as early as mid-April for good reason. The 1885 **Gothams** bore an uncanny resemblance to Troy, New York's defunct 1882 NL team. In fact, Day's **Gotham-Metropolitan** syndicate had purchased the best Troy **Trojans** and thrown them on his 1883 Big Apple squads. The improved **Mets** gave the upstart AA some credibility, while the new NLers were instantly prestigious via membership in the senior circuit. But Day wanted a dream team and moved four Hall of Famers from his sack of Troy (Buck Ewing, Tim Keefe, Mickey Welch, Roger Connor) to the '85 **Gothams**, reuniting them with ex-**Trojans** and fellow HoFers Jim O'Rourke and John Montgomery Ward. Certainly, these were giants in baseball terms, but a few broke six feet, very tall for the era (especially Conner, the tallest NLer at 6'3"). That explains "**Giants**" sufficiently without summoning any suspect outbursts from Mutrie.[8]

• • •

The NL had added Day's **Gothams**/**Giants** and Philadelphia's **Quakers** in 1883.[9] The "**Quakers**" alternate was quickly lost, so if we accept "Philadelphia **Phillies**" as official as of '83, it's the longest-lived name for a continuously operated professional team in North America.[10] Some later owners, however, would try to screw that up. Sportswriter Horace Fogel bought the team and said "**Phillies**" was "too trite."[11] He called his 1910 squad **Live Wires**, but nobody else did. A later owner, Robert Carpenter, was the only person calling his **Phils** the **Blue Jays** for 1944 and '45. (He did cause a big hullabaloo a hundred miles away among fans of

the Johns Hopkins **Blue Jays**, who called the change a "reprehensible act.")
"**Blue Jays**" had no momentum when fans returned after World War II, and it's
gone from any official timeline. The problem these owners might have seen with
"**Phillies**" is its homophonic bond to *fillies*, a word for young female horses. The
corresponding masculine word is *colt*, a comparison made by two Philadelphia
Colts teams of the 1890s, minor league baseballers and international cricketers.

The multi-team syndicates imitated the consolidated empires of the era's
industrial robber barons. Baltimore owner Harry Von Der Horst and his Hall of
Fame manager Ned Hanlon invested in the AA Brooklyn **Bridegrooms** in 1899
and shipped most of the quality **Orioles** north. As with the revamped **Browns-
Perfectos**, the press gave Brooklyn's squad a splendiferous nickname: **Superbas**.
The transplanted Mr. Hanlon brought to mind the Hanlon Brothers' popular
vaudeville show *Superba*, and his regenerated Brooklyn nine won the next two
NL pennants. That irritated the often irritable **Giants** owner Andrew Freedman,
who thought Brooklyn shouldn't even have a team because the borough had been
annexed by New York in 1898. (League rules reserved each municipal market for
a single team.)[12] The club that finished second to the 1900 **Superbas** was the
similarly syndicated Pittsburgh **Pirates**, assembled from the **Pirates** and the Louisville **Colonels** organizations that were both owned by Barney Dreyfuss. If we
account for the less overt syndicates, the majority of NL teams were tied up in
such mini-trusts.[13]

The NL contracted after 1899 by folding up Washington's cellar-dwelling
Senators and three of the clubs on the losing side of syndication (Baltimore,
Cleveland, and Louisville). That would make markets and players available when
the American League challenge came in 1901.

· · ·

Sure-hitting **Oriole** third baseman John McGraw was his catcher Wilbert Robinson's neighbor and restaurant partner. When both men refused a trade to the
syndicate's Brooklyn team, McGraw became Baltimore's 1899 manager, where
his on-field aggression and volatile personality would make him "Little Napoleon." No amount of stubbornness would keep McGraw and Robinson in Baltimore after the diminished **Orioles** folded, so they demanded that the reserve
clause be struck from their contracts before their trade to the 1900 St. Louis
Cardinals. (The red uniforms of the year-old **Perfectos** had already effected a
new name.) That was prescient because the AL assumed major league status for
1901, and McGraw and Robinson jumped back to Baltimore without reservation
to join the AL's new **Orioles**.

AL president Ban Johnson needed a New York franchise and tried to put the
Orioles there. McGraw suspected that Johnson would fire him the second the
move was made, so he preemptively jumped to the helm of the NL's **Giants** in
the middle of 1902, leaving Robinson to run Baltimore. Quickly refocusing his
animosity, McGraw slid his ownership shares in the Baltimore team to **Giants**
owner Andrew Freedman. The resulting syndicate sent the best **Orioles** to the
Polo Grounds and relegated Maryland's remainders to last place. McGraw would
manage the **Giants** until his 1932 retirement, enjoying the services of his old
buddy Robinson as pitching coach from 1903 to 1913. Then "Uncle Robbie" left

the **Giants** to manage their Brooklyn rivals, soon dubbed "**Robins**" in his honor. That lasted until his 1931 retirement, at which time they became **Dodgers** for good (p. 337).

• • •

McGraw remained hostile toward his old league in 1902, referring to the AL's first-place **Athletics** as white elephants (a metaphor for a poor investment). With good humor, Philly manager Connie Mack adopted the **A's** now-famous pachyderm insignia and rode it to that season's AL championship.

By then, "Philadelphia **Athletics**" had been around a while. The Philadelphia Athletic Club (or "**Athletic** of Philadelphia") played in the NA (1860–75) before joining the new NL for 1876 only. A like-named AA team followed (1882–90), and Mack's **A's** were the former Western League Indianapolis **Indians** (1893–1900). (In fact, there've been major or minor league Indianapolis **Indians** every year since 1893 except for that 1901 season.) They've since been Kansas City **Athletics** (1955–68) and Oakland **Athletics**.

Little Quakers | Fords | Mighty Macs | Poets

English preacher George Fox believed that following one's internal spiritual light would create a closer relationship with God than would blind adherence to the instructions of churchmen, and he rejected even baptism and communion, the only biblical sacraments kept by Protestants. Fox's Society of Friends refused to pay taxes, show any deference to social betters, or march off to war. Charged with blasphemy in 1650, Fox advised the judge to "tremble at the word of the Lord." The curt reply from the bench pointed out that such an act would make "quakers" of Fox's flock.

In the 1660s, Charles II signed laws to bend Quaker allegiance toward his Church of England. His House of Stuart owed significant debts to Adm. William Penn. He was the father of an eternally pesky Quaker (also named William) who was jailed regularly for his beliefs. Penn the Younger nonetheless inherited the royal I.O.U. after his father died, and the king killed two birds with one keystone in 1681 by giving Penn a large colonial parcel, knowing he'd take a bunch of his Quaker-hippie Friends with him. Latinizing freely, the king named it Pennsylvania (Penn's woods) after the late admiral. The mid-Atlantic location was ideal for Quakers who'd been unwelcomed—if not banned or executed—in other colonies,[1] and Penn successfully established one of tolerance that was south of the Protestant English and Dutch (in New England and New York respectively) and north of the Catholics (Maryland) and Anglicans (Virginia).[2] Many thousands of Friends arrived at Penn's Delaware River port in the 1680s to become successful merchants and politicians.

In light of its Quaker City history, sportswriters have reflexively called almost any Philadelphia team **Quakers**.[3] Fans today are likely to recognize the **Quakers** at the University of Pennsylvania, which ironically isn't even a Quaker school. Although assisted by colonial Anglicans at its 1740 founding, Penn is the vision fulfilled of its secular proponent, Ben Franklin, who was determined to open an American college for purposes other than training ministers.

Quakers had started gaining traction in England back in 1652 when Thomas and Margaret Fell let Mr. Fox and Friends meet at their Cumbria home, Swarthmoor Hall. In 1864, Philadelphia Quakers founded the Westdale institute named after the "cradle of Quakerism," Swarthmore [*sic*] College. Its **Little Quakers** became the **Garnet** or **Garnet Tide** (either is always singular) in 1981 to reflect its garnet and gray colors. The Old Main building burned in 1881 and was quickly rebuilt, so the college paper was named *The Phoenix*. But it wasn't until 2006 that the **Garnet Tide** was represented by phoenix mascots (symbolism on p. 174).[4]

• • •

William Penn's first New World transplants were farming Welsh Quakers west of the Schuylkill River. Strong Quaker recruitment across Wales spilled over to the adjacent parts of England, including Chester County, so Penn renamed one Pennsylvania settlement Chester in 1681. In fact, Swedish settlers in the New Sweden colony (absorbed by Penn's charter) had been at that site for four decades. As the state's oldest settlement, Chester once kept **Pioneers** at Widener University, but they somewhat arbitrarily became the **Pride** in 2006.

The well-heeled of Wales had been more receptive to Quakerism than the English gentry, and those in the "Welsh Tract" west of Philadelphia "were better educated, and probably better off financially than the average English settler,"[5] so Welsh Friends unsurprisingly had the wherewithal to start the continent's first Quaker college in 1833 at Haverford. The former **Little Quakers** at Haverford College are now the suffixally derived **Fords**, but baseballers are the **Black Squirrels** because melanistic versions of the eastern gray squirrel (*Sciurus carolinensis*) patrol their diamond.[6]

Up the street from Haverford is the town of Bryn Mawr, named for the estate of influential local Quaker Rowland Ellis (born in Wales on Brynmawr Farm). Bryn Mawr College was conceived as a school for Quaker women but opened as a non-denominational school in 1885. Students are "Mawrters" (a near homonym for *martyrs*), so some believe it's the athletic moniker. But BMC athletes are **Owls** because its seal contains the Owls of Athena (p. 169).

The Welsh Tract was called the Main Line after the fat part of the Pennsylvania Railroad started running through in 1852, and commuter trains still run on those routes. A mile north of the Haverford stop is a station named for the Villanova University campus. As is common for colleges seeking national recognition for their athletes, that Catholic school's **Main Liners** or **Blue and White** changed to something less colloquial in 1926: **Wildcats**.

The Rosemont stop between Bryn Mawr and Villanova is where Irish-born whiskey magnate Joseph Sinnott built one of the Main Line's many pastoral estates in 1891. The house became the centerpiece of Rosemont College in 1921, where **Ramblers** were named for the wall-climbing rambling rose (*Rosa multiflora Thunb*).[7] That seemed too quaint when male students arrived in 2009, so teams were **Ravens** thereafter. (Renny Raven is their mascot, *Renny* being an Irish Gaelic name that means "small but mighty.")

Please stay seated after Villanova for respective lessons in alliteration, assonance, and consonance. The next stop is Radnor and the former Woodcrest Estate, now home to the blue-and-white **Cavaliers** of Cabrini College (Catholic). The St. Davids station is next and the closest stop to the **Eagles** of Eastern University (Baptist). The blue-and-white **Mighty Macs** of Immaculata University (Catholic) are nearer the end of the line in the Malvern borough, named by Welsh Quakers for the Malvern Hills on the Welsh-English border.

• • •

Revolutionary-era Patriots were uneasy with both the Quakers' pacifism and their English roots, so Quakers often joined Loyalists in heading for English-speaking or unsettled parts of Canada after the war. Those left behind often emulated their Scots-Irish neighbors by drifting down the eastern slopes of the Appalachians to the Carolina backcountry.

A love of freedom and tolerance didn't seem to stop the Quakers from owning slaves. When the irony dawned on them, most Quakers became vocal abolitionists who helped to outlaw slavery in Pennsylvania (1780) and New Jersey (1803). To protect its slave-based economy, North Carolina outlawed such emancipation in

1796. Carolina Quakers were suddenly facing peer pressure plus prison, so many crossed the Ohio River because the Northwest Ordinance of 1787 had made Ohio lands cheap while banning slavery there.

Without any formal creed to impart through higher education, the Quakers weren't obsessed with founding seminaries, and they watched from the stands while other denominations ambitiously started Bible colleges during the Second Great Awakening (p. 96). Quakers did open boarding schools to educate their children, and some evolved into respected colleges. A few have retained their novel **Quakers** while once-numerous **Methodist** and **Presbyterian** counterparts have long since been rebranded. An east-to-west discussion of **Quakers** nicely plots the migration from the Carolinas to Ohio and beyond by the Friends and their roamin' countrymen:

- **Quakers** represent Guilford College (Greensboro, N.C.), an 1837-founded Quaker boarding school.
- Quakers from North Carolina's same Guilford County founded Richmond, Indiana in 1806 and opened its boarding school in 1847. It was called Earlham College by 1859, after Earlham Hall, the English family home of famous Quaker minister Joseph John Gurney (1788–1847). Non-Quakers have attended Earlham since 1865, its **Hustlin' Quakers** notwithstanding.
- In 1870 more North Carolina Friends founded Wilmington College of Ohio, another **Quaker** base.
- A Bible college in Cleveland was founded by Quaker evangelicals J. Walter Malone and his wife Emma in 1892. It moved to Canton in 1957, where it's Malone University. **Pioneers** "honor those who exhibit courage and determination especially in regard to the Christian faith"[8] ... although we've not seen *pioneer* so defined.
- Quakers started William Penn University (Oskaloosa, Iowa) in 1873. It once fielded **Quakers**, but Mr. Penn's diplomacy is now remembered by **Statesmen** and **Lady Statesmen**, a rare example of **Statesmen** representing a privately funded institution.
- Some Quakers reopened a defunct Wichita, Kansas college as Friends University in 1898. FU's **Fighting Quakers** misrepresented the sect's pacifist teachings, so they're now **Falcons**.
- Down the road was Friends Bible College (Haviland, Kan.). It was renamed Barclay College in 1990 for early Quaker apologist Robert Barclay (1648–90). It now hosts alliterative Barclay **Bears**.
- Saskatchewan's farming Quakers help to explain the Saskatoon **Quakers** of minor league baseball and football in the first half of the twentieth century.
- By the 1880s there were Quaker settlements on the Pacific Coast. Friends from Chicago founded a town near L.A. and got New England's famous Quaker-poet-abolitionist John Greenleaf Whittier to loan his name to both the town and its Whittier College (est. 1887), home to purple-and-gold **Poets** since 1951.[9]
- Newberg, Oregon was the first Quaker town west of the Rockies. Its grade school adopted an orphaned *black* bear cub named Bruin ("brown") in 1887. The associated academy now called George Fox University opened in 1891.

Jocks were usually **Quakers** in the press, but sometimes **Bruins**. A fox mascot named Foxy George only confused things, so teams were officially **Bruins** as of 1970.[10]

Semi-pro **Quaker** baseballers once barnstormed the Midwest. Depending on which story you believe, they either stayed in Whitewater, Wisconsin (forever linking "**Quakers**" to the area) or they surrendered their uniforms to cover outstanding hotel and dinner bills. In the second scenario, the "**Quaker**" jerseys ended up on the Whitewater Normal School's (non-Quaker) athletes. Either way, "**Quakers**" was adopted because it was more colorful than the school's past **Purples**, but University of Wisconsin–Whitewater teams became **Warhawks** in 1958 just to duck the pacifism suggested by **Quakers**. (The **Warhawks'** Native American iconography had transitioned to a de facto hawk in 1979.)[11]

Mutuals | Yankees | Canucks | Knicks | Hawkeyes

William Penn's 1683 treaty with the Delaware (Lenape) sachem Tamanend was a celebrated model of cooperation between natives and newcomers. Painter Benjamin West famously memorialized the signing ceremony, but the treaty has otherwise proved hard to authenticate. The supposed good will of "Chief Tammany" would be central to many convenient legends created by white men.

Among the first to stretch the truth was Penn's son Thomas, a later and less revered proprietor of Pennsylvania. Relations between Indians and colonists were already getting iffy in 1737 when Thomas produced a document in which Tamanend had granted land to the elder Penn. With that suspicious deed (and Iroquois assistance), the whites drove from their ancestral lands the Lenape and Shawnee, some of whom set up on the far side of the Alleghenies. This was the midst of the colonial wars, and the removed Indians turned to the French. When those Indians backtracked over the hills to raid white settlements in the Juniata Valley, one target was Huntingdon, a former Indian village where you'll find Juniata College. To deemphasize that history of regional conflict, Juniata's **Indians** switched to **Eagles** in 1994.

• • •

In the pre-Revolutionary period, civic-minded Patriots named their organization the Sons of St. Tammany (after the famous *Tamanend*). After the Revolution, "Tammany Hall" members co-opted Indian titles to display uniquely American—that is, non-European—sensibilities. Rank-and-filers were braves, not brothers. Its councilors and deputies were sachems and sagamores. All convened at big-city wigwams.

Senator Aaron Burr steered New York's Tammany Society toward the Democratic Party in the 1790s, and it is with that city that Tammany politics are usually associated. Having suffered centuries of British rule (and fully grasping the language of the oppressor), Irish Catholics rose from New York's slums to become the natural champions of urban Democratic politics. Tammany Hall would soon include a number of Jews and Catholics from Central and Eastern Europe, but the Irish remained overrepresented in key Tammany positions.

Tammany-allied New York City alderman James Gaffney purchased Boston's NL **Red Stockings** after the 1911 season. Quickly renamed according to the wigwam's Indian protocol, they sported the machine's Delaware Indian chief emblem as Boston **Braves**. They went to Milwaukee in 1953 and they've been Atlanta **Braves** since '66.[1]

Many would-be politicos came up through NYC's volunteer firehouses, which by the 1820s bustled with political activity. Infamous Tammany boss William Tweed rose through the ranks of Americus Engine Company 6, so its "Big Six" tiger emblem was used by cartoonist Thomas Nast to mock corrupt "Tammany Tigers." In fact, Princeton's orange-and-black clad students of the 1870s initially resisted the adoption of **Tiger** symbols (p. 94) from fear of any vaguely assumed association with Tammany Hall.[2]

Evidence of Tweed's Ring was everywhere. From 1860 to 1871 he was even the president of the NA's **Mutual** club[3] from the city's Mutual Hook & Ladder fire brigade. Among the millions of dollars squandered during the Tweed years, the "amateur" **Mutuals** collected more than $30,000 annually to play ball while on the clock as city street sweepers, coroners, and clerks.[4] The **Mutes** were crooked on the field as well, becoming baseball's distinct bad boys in an era when almost all players had reputations for carousing and gambling.

Downtown Tammanites were perpetually irked by having to answer to upriver "hayseeds" in Albany's Republican-run statehouse, so it stung when the Ring's **Mutuals** lost to the Capital District's Troy **Unions** in 1867. In the language of the wigwam, frustrated **Mutes** called the **Unions** a bunch of upstate "haymakers" and the **Unions** immediately became **Haymakers**.[5]

In 1867 the mischievous **Mutual** club was reluctantly admitted to the National League, a new circuit that needed New York entrants and simply couldn't have the famous **Mutuals** lingering in the competing NA.[6] Still, NL president William Hulbert booted the **Mutes** and **Athletic** of Philadelphia after that season for refusing to finish their western schedules because they'd never catch the Chicago **White Stockings** (a Hulbert-owned team comprising the former core of the NA-dominating Boston **Red Stockings**). Hulbert aimed to preserve the NL's integrity even if it meant dismissing franchises in the country's two largest cities.[7]

Convicted on corruption charges, Tweed died in prison in 1878, but his spirit lived on. Through systematic patronage and outright bribery, Tammany Hall ran New York politics into the 1930s. But there were political machines like Tammany elsewhere. The MLL Chicago **Machine** (2006–10) recalled the last of the big-city machines, the Cook County Democratic Organization, which had its last hurrah during the administration of Irish-Catholic mayor Richard J. Daly (1955–76).[8]

• • •

In 1890 some key players on John B. Day's National League New York **Giants** jumped to new and different "New York **Giants**" in the rebel Players' League (p. 294). And they didn't jump far. Those PL **Giants** played at Coogan's Hollow in their new Brotherhood Park, a *few feet* from the older **Giants**' Polo Grounds II. There were often simultaneous games at the side-by-side parks because the senior circuit deliberately synchronized its schedule with the junior. Even so, the veteran NLers in the PL usually outdrew their old league in most cities with head-to-head competition.

The NL bluffed the PL into folding after its only season, and both **Giants** merged into a single NL team at Brotherhood Park (thereafter Polo Grounds III). But baseball's Brotherhood War (p. 294) had so strapped Day that team control shifted to the influential Republican owners of the PL **Giants**, a blow to Tammany Democrats that proved only temporary when city realtor Andrew Freedman bought the team in early 1895, finally placing the **Giants** in Tammany hands. (By 1902, Freedman was only a minority shareholder, having sold to John T. Brush.)[9]

AL president Ban Johnson and his Baltimore manager John McGraw weren't friends, but they worked together to jimmy the Baltimore **Orioles** (II) into New York to establish league credibility through a Big Apple franchise. Tammany Hall interfered with the move because Freedman didn't want his NL **Giants** to share the New York market. After his eleventy-zillionth falling out with Johnson, McGraw left the AL to coach the **Giants** in July 1902. He transferred his **Oriole** shares to his new owner, enabling Freedman to move the best **Orioles** to the **Giants**.[10] Johnson quickly collected some second-string ALers to restock an **Oriole** team he still hoped to bring north, but Tammany men were buying up or running trolley tracks through every potential city ballfield except for a difficult perch on the city's Washington Heights, way uptown. It could be built upon only by playing ball with Tammany contractors.

When New Yorkers elected Republican mayor Seth Low and his reform platform in 1901, Tammany Democrats resorted to finger pointing and factionalism. Freedman's influence declined after the retirement of his longtime patron, Tammany boss Richard Croker. Ban Johnson sucked it up and became bedfellows with Tammany investors who'd never liked Freedman. Their public face was coal shipper Joseph Gordon (a past investor in the **Giants-Mets** syndicate).[11] Johnson had assembled the migrated **Orioles** that opened the 1903 season in New York by raiding Pittsburgh's defending NL champion **Pirates** and by encouraging other AL clubs to send top talent to N.Y.C. for the good of the league. They played in the Heights' hastily built Hilltop Park as New York **Highlanders**.[12]

Had the **Giants** managed to keep the **Orioles/Highlanders** out of New York, they would have had nowhere to turn when a fire destroyed most of the Polo Grounds in spring 1911. Tammany still had fingers in both Gordon's **Highlanders** and Brush's **Giants** (through Freedman), so they shared Hilltop Park until the **Giants** moved back to Coogan's Hollow in June. The tables turned after the next season when the **Highlanders**' lease ended, putting them in the rebuilt Polo Grounds. Removed from Hilltop, the **Highlanders**' name didn't make any sense, so the 1913 team adopted what is now among the most recognized teams in sport: New York **Yankees** … which had been at least a casual alternative from the beginning. (Some historians say it was always as popular as "**Highlanders**.") "**Yankees**" might have referred to the **Orioles**' move to the most brazen of northern cities from their old home south of the Mason-Dixon Line, or it could have been an exaggeration of just how far uptown Tammany's men had forced them.

· · ·

So what's *Yankee* mean? In the 1600s the Flemish referred to the Dutch derogatorily as *Jan Kaas* (literally John Cheese), a name so common as to be compared to the Anglophones' *John Smith*. Copycat English colonists started referring to the Caribbean's Dutch pirates as *Jan Kaas* or *Jan Kees*. The Connecticut English and New York Dutch later called each other *Jan Kees*—"*yahn*-kees."[13]

After that, the context depended entirely on the accuser's perspective. British soldiers in the colonial wars looked down on their New England *Yankee* allies and mocked them with the song "Yankee Doodle." During America's Civil War, the Yankee city slicker was antithetical to the Southern gentleman-squire. British troops were calling G.I.s "Yanks" in World War I, but at least by then they had company; the Allies called Canadian soldiers "Canucks," after Johnny Canuck, the lumberjacking, hockey-playing manifestation of the Canadian subconscious.

He appeared in political cartoons as a youthful foil to *über*-Yankee Uncle Sam or Britain's John Bull. (Before heading for the timberlands, Mr. Canuck had been drawn in the traditional garb of New France's farming *habitants*.) Junior hockey had Moose Jaw [Sask.] **Canucks** (1935–84) and the minor league Vancouver **Canucks** (est. 1945) turned major when the NHL expanded in 1970. That same year, the Calgary **Canucks** formed to bring a "uniquely Canadian" hospitality and styled of play to rugby. Junior hockey Calgary **Canucks** started in '71.

• • •

Patriots of the Revolutionary era embraced a goddess of liberty named Columbia. She was a classicized, feminized namesake of Christopher Columbus. It was a bit curious that English-speaking Protestants had such regard for a Catholic Italian who sailed for Spain, never set foot on the mainland, and died thinking he'd found Asia, but Columbia popped up liberally in poems, paintings, and popular song. Ms. Columbia's namesakes included a new Potomac-side federal district, a New York college reopened as "Columbia" by Federalist benefactors, and a Pacific fur ship that gave its name to the great river of Oregon.

In 1791, New York's men of St. Tammany even changed their organization's name "to the more secular Tammany Society or Columbian Order and began making plans to celebrate the Columbian tercentenary."[14] Tammany Hall men all but invented Columbus Day the next year, and Tammany associate Washington Irving gave a boost to Columbianism by publishing his multi-volume *Life and Voyages of Christopher Columbus* in 1828.

It was Irving who popularized the falsehood that everyone in the Europe of 1492 except his hero thought the world was flat, a fear of The Edge alluded to by the Columbus **Horizon** (1989–94), minor league hoopsters in the captain's namesake Ohio capital. In fact, that "Discovery City" was founded and named by patriotic Ohioans exactly when the War of 1812 against Britain and its native allies was steering Americans away from Indian themes and toward Columbia. Undoubtedly Columbus's crewmen and their quest at least subliminally explain the MLS Columbus **Crew** (est. 1996) and ABL Columbus **Quest** (1997–98).

Following the Columbus theme, a patriotic Catholic fraternity called the Knights of Columbus was founded in Connecticut in 1881. The Knights' international headquarters are next to the former New Haven Coliseum, the rink for minor league New Haven **Knights** (2000–02) and the more subtle New Haven **Nighthawks** (1972–93). "K of C" members are often "Caseys," so the independent basketballers they sponsored in the 1920s and '30s were inevitably **Caseys**.

• • •

The Erie Canal opened in 1825, making many formerly remote places accessible. For the next half-century, artists of the Hudson River School painted wilderness scenes of an idealized New York and New England while writers in the Knickerbocker School set romantic tales in those regions. As patriotic fraternities like Tammany had done, these schools (of thought) embraced distinctly American aesthetics, often employing Native American tokens to distance the subject matter from the Old Country. The Knickerbockers were named for Diedrich Knickerbocker, the old Dutch narrator of *A History of New York*, first published in 1809.

Actually, Diedrich and the rest of the *History* were also inventions of Washington Irving. The surname alluded to the knicker pants that Dutch colonists wore in New Amsterdam (later New York). Protestant New Yorkers of Dutch and English lineage got to boasting on their old Knickerbocker blood to set themselves apart from the growing immigrant underclass represented by Tammany's Irish Catholics. The **Knickerbocker** Base Ball Club was created in 1845 when Alexander Cartwright and Doc Adams wrote the rules generally accepted as the basis for modern hardball. The first game between different teams was played on June 19, 1846, at which time the New York **Nine** knocked off the **Knickerbockers**, 23-1. ("**Nine**" revealed the number of players per lineup, which eventually became official.)[15] The NBA New York **Knickerbockers** (est. 1946) are only the latest of so-named teams playing various sports for nearly two centuries, but everyone uses their "**Knicks**" nick.

Irving had launched his writing career in 1807 with his *Salmagundi* magazine, wherein he first compared crazy Manhattan with the "renowned and ancient city of Gotham."[16] "Gotham City's" amateur **Gothams** and **Knickerbockers** later played every season in the National Association (1857–70). The NA divided into pro and gentlemen amateur leagues for 1871, with the **Gothams** and **Knickerbockers** trying to stay afloat in the latter, which folded in '74.

We could have mentioned earlier the part Irving played in the confused etymology of *Yankee* (p. 90). His *History of New York* blithely claims that coastal Indians gave white settlers "the name of *Yanokies*, which in the Mais-Tchusaeg (Massachusett) language signifies *silent men*." In fact, the next-most famous of the Knickerbocker writers was James Fenimore Cooper, who used an authentic looking footnote in his 1841 novel *The Deerslayer* to misreport that *Yengeese* is the Indians' failed attempt to say "English."

Shortly after James's 1789 birth in New Jersey, the Coopers settled in their namesake New York town on Ostego Lake. Today the Fenimore Art Museum is there, but its fine collection of Hudson River School paintings can't compete with Cooperstown's *other* museum. The National Baseball Hall of Fame celebrates the 1839 invention of baseball at Cooperstown by Civil War hero Abner Doubleday. Actually, there's no evidence Doubleday even liked baseball, much less created it, but his boyhood home is 100 miles west in Auburn, where the "Doubleday myth" survives through minor league Auburn **Doubledays** (or "**D-Days**").

Near the end of Cooper's *The Last of the Mohicans*, Chief Tammany (as *Tamenund*) shows up to provide thematic clarity for those who've been speed reading. The protagonist of both *Mohicans* (1826) and *The Deerslayer* (1841) is Natty "Hawk-eye" Bumppo. Born to white parents, Hawk-eye calls himself brother to several Indians and is among the best literary examples of an American *renegade*, a white man "turned injun." That means **Renegade** mascots can be picked from a variety of rebellious or nonconformist types: bandits, pirates, black knights, and—yes—Indians … although referring to "renegade Indians" can offensively suggest a traitorous disposition, but that doesn't stop the **Renegades** at Fremont's Ohlone College from getting behind Indian feather emblems. (The Ohlone people of central California's coast saw their numbers and influence decline after Spanish colonization.) Minor league baseball's Hudson Valley **Renegades** refuse to be iconographically tripped up, being vaguely represented by Rookie the Raccoon. They're in Fishkill, New York, which is generally accepted as the setting for J.F. Cooper's Revolutionary-era adventure novel, *The Spy*.

• • •

The end of the Black Hawk War (p. 136) opened Iowa for white settlement, starting with Burlington in 1833. Five years later, Iowa's oldest extant newspaper, the *Iowa Patriot*, was established. Publisher James Edwards renamed it the *Burlington Hawk-Eye and Iowa Patriot* to recall the protagonist in Cooper's crazy-popular *Mohicans*. It also remembered the recently defeated Sauk chief, Black Hawk, and Edwards was soon insisting that Iowans self-identify as "Hawkeyes."[17] For no better reason, Iowa is the Hawkeye State, with the most famous athletic **Hawkeyes** representing Iowa City's University of Iowa. The NBL/NBA Waterloo **Hawks** (1948–50) were abbreviated Iowa hawkeyes, and the same city keeps Waterloo **Black Hawks** (est. 1962) in junior hockey.

The Presbyterians' Coe College in Cedar Rapids fielded **Crimson and Gold** sides. In a 1922 naming poll, a language professor suggested taking the first syllable from *Hawkeye* and prefixing it with *ko*, supposedly an Indian word for "resembling." Thus, Coe's **Kohawks** would play like hawks.[18] The football **Kohawks** lost a 1924 intrastate game to Dubuque's Columbia College. The surging Columbians were headed for a showdown against the University of Detroit **Titans**, so a *Detroit Free Press* writer referred to them as "Dubuque Hawks" and "Duhawks." Columbia is now Loras College, but **Duhawks** remain.[19]

Speaking of U. Detroit and the *Free Press*, Stan Brink was the *DFP* reporter who thought UD's **Tigers** needed a nickname that was different from the city's pro baseballers, so he changed three letters in 1920 to make the college's tall basketballers **Titans**. So-named teams now represent the University of Detroit–Mercy, which was produced through the 1990 merger of two Catholic schools, UD and Mercy College of Detroit.[20]

Continuing to assign regional team names, the *Free Press* made **Dales** out of the **Blue and White** from Hillsdale [Mich.] College in 1924. That lasted until deliberately less pastoral **Chargers** were presented in 1968.

Pioneers | Tracers | Thundering Herd | Grays

Most **Pioneers** represent private colleges because the first academy on any given frontier was usually a private seminary. The nearby state-sponsored A&M or normal school generally came later. In fact, "As late as 1860, only 17 of America's 246 colleges and universities were state-funded. With a few exceptions, the others were paid for and closely administered by Protestant denominations to train ministers."[1]

We won't explain all **Pioneers** in all places. At some point, white settlers considered everything beyond Plymouth Rock or St. Augustine to be the wild frontier. But these few worthy **Pioneers** ignore geographical ambitions to be defined by some other trailblazing first:

- Wesleyan College (Macon, Ga.) has a variety of convincing backstories for its "First for Women" tagline and its corresponding **Pioneers**: [1] It was chartered in 1836 as the world's first college to grant degrees to women; [2] The first college sororities opened there in 1851; [3] Its alumnae association (est. 1860) is the country's oldest.
- Two Wisconsin schools celebrate firsts through **Pioneers**. Having received a territorial charter as the Pioneer College of Wisconsin in January 1846, Waukesha's Carroll University claims the oldest founding date of any Badger State college. In 1866 the state's first teachers' college was founded, today's University of Wisconsin–Platteville.
- **Pioneers** represent Pacific Union College (Angwin, Calif.), the first college to be established west of the Mississippi by the Adventist Church.
- The C.W. Post Campus of Long Island University (Brookville, N.Y.) is on the former estate of Marjorie Merriweather Post, heiress to a breakfast cereal fortune. CWP has **Pioneers** because it dared open as a new private college in the wake of World War II when so many extant institutions were struggling.[2]
- In the 1960s the term "community college" started to displace "junior college" at state-funded two-year schools. That pioneering idea gave extramural **Pioneers** to Western Piedmont Community College (Morganton, N.C.),[3] chartered in 1964.

Takoma Park, Maryland was the planned Victorian suburb of a planned federal city, putting it among the few places where **Pioneers** are ill-placed. Still, its Columbia Union College fielded such teams until it became Washington Adventist University in 2009. They're now the modern (but not more meaningful) **Shock**.

• • •

In 1787, Congress jumpstarted trans-Ohio expansion by selling much of the Northwest Territory to speculators in the Boston-based Ohio Company. Some profits went to found new colleges (the first federal fund for public education). The Company was run by Army officers—especially Rufus Putnam—who had spent years asking Congress to grant land to veterans of the Revolution.

The Ohio Territory's first college, Ohio University, opened in 1809 at classically named Athens. The campus was designed by two trustees, Ohio Company founders Manasseh Cutler and Gen. Putnam. OU's **Green and White** became **Bobcats** in 1925, but it took eight decades for history to catch up. Only in 2006 did students name their bobcat (*Lynx rufus*) mascot *Rufus*, for Rufus Putnam.[4]

The Ohio Company established Marietta on the far side of the confluence of the Muskingum and Ohio Rivers in April 1788. Marietta College was founded there in 1835. Athletes at the oldest permanent white settlement in the Old Northwest make a non-metaphorical claim to **Pioneers**. In early 2014 the "**Pios**" got a new gentleman mascot named Putnam, after Marietta's founder.

The images on Ohio's Great Seal suggest westward expansion: mountains, seventeen Indian arrows (Ohio became the seventeenth state in 1803), and a sun rising on a new day. The seal for the college that's now Kent State University faithfully reproduced the sun, but it's been modernized several times. Still, those rays explain KSU's **Golden Flashes**. (They were **Silver Foxes** until 1926 because Kent's first president owned the nearby Silver Fox Farm.)[5]

• • •

To appreciate the changing definition of "the West," we need look only at several generations of one family. Zanesburg, Virginia was established by Ebenezer Zane on the Ohio in 1769. Zane and his kin held the post through the Revolution, and the 1782 British-sponsored Indian raid there was the war's last battle. During the shooting, a young Zane sister scooted across sixty yards of open ground to fetch a powder keg for her brothers, actions recalled in the book *Betty Zane*.

To speed post-war settlement, Congress paid Ebenezer to build a 200-mile pass from Zanesburg to modern Maysville, Kentucky. As a veteran in good standing, Zane got some prime real estate at river crossings on the cheap, lots that had been drafted by the first U.S. Surveyor General (the ubiquitous Rufus Putnam). Midway along "Zane's Trace" the Zanes founded a mid-Muskingum town that's now Zanesville in 1797. The aforementioned Ohio University keeps **Tracers** at its Zanesville campus.

As for Zanesburg, it was renamed Wheeling in 1806 and would be part of the new state of West Virginia in 1863. (See p. 72). Congress funded a new National Road in 1811 with Zane's Trace as its core. By 1818, the Ohio River and the best route to the West intersected at Wheeling. After Zanesville, the road forked west to the Quaker town of Richmond (est. 1806). **Pioneers** at Richmond's Indiana University East remembered the road's early travelers, but they became **Red Wolves** in conjunction with expanded athletics in 2008. (IUE's *Canis lupus rufus* mascot is named Rufus.)

The National Road replaced the rocky Wilderness Road as the best way west. Daniel Boone had blazed the older trail through the Cumberland Gap in 1775 for the Transylvania Company. (Transylvania—"across the woods" in Latin—was the land beyond the Kentucky River.) Five years later, the seminary at Lexington was the first college west of the Alleghenies, giving **Pioneers** to Transylvania University.

• • •

By the time Ebenezer Zane's great-great-grandnephew was born in Zanesville in 1872, nobody thought Ohio was in the West. But Pearl Zane Gray was a pioneer of sorts, being among the first young men across the Ohio to throw a curveball. Pro scouts noticed the University of Pennsylvania star in 1892, but the mound was moved back to its modern distance the next year, and Pearl's hard-breaking deuce started running aground way short of the plate. (His big bat did keep him in Penn's outfield and the minors until about 1900.) Later disenchanted with his dental practice, Pearl dropped his first name, changed the spelling of his last, and turned family folklore into novels. His first privately published book was the aforementioned *Betty Zane*.

In 1912, *Riders of the Purple Sage* sold two-million copies and made Zane Grey a famous writer of the West. *The Thundering Herd* was his popular 1925 novel about Texas bison hunters. Within three years, the *Herald-Dispatch* newspaper in Huntington, West Virginia was calling the nearby **Indians** at Marshall College the **Thundering Herd**. (Huntington is just down the Ohio from the Zanes' Wheeling, but some factions felt the name was irrelevant for West Virginians and tried to advance "**Judges**" to honor institutional eponym and famous federalist jurist John Marshall.) The **Herd** got a live bison mascot named Marco (*Mar*-shall *co*-llege) in 1931, but an alternate nick that had been around since 1903—"**Big Green**"—would later dominate. In 1965, four years after the school became Marshall University, the administration wanted something conducive to costumed animal mascots, so the **Thundering Herd** was overwhelmingly reinstated by student vote.[6]

The Zanesville **Grays** (1933–37) were minor leaguers in Zane Grey's hometown, as were the *e*-version Zanesville **Greys** (1993–96). Ignoring the local boy made good, these crews tipped their steel-colored caps to the Louisville, Milwaukee, and Providence **Grays** ... National Leaguers of the 1870s and '80s who were named for their uniform color. The famous Homestead **Grays** were formed in a black Pittsburgh neighborhood after 1912.[7] Waiting around for clothes to dry in a launderette could screw up a team's road schedule, so travel kits have historically been gray instead of white to hide dirt.

• • •

As Zane Grey was becoming famous, Zanesville's independent **Mark Greys** played two games (0-1-1) in 1920, both against the NFL's Columbus **Panhandles**. The **Mark Greys** represented Clayton Mark's steel pipe plant of the booming Ohio Valley iron industry. Wheeling (the former Zanesburg) was itself an iron town renowned for cut iron nails, and "Wheeling **Nailers**" has been tacked to minor leaguers since the 1880s, as evinced by a 1981-founded hockey squad. The Wheeling/Ohio Valley **Ironmen** (1965–69) were in the Continental Football League.

The steel cities of Wheeling and Pittsburgh sold cigars a-plenty to Ohio River boatmen and the Cumberland Road's Conestoga teamsters. 'Stoga drivers gave the cheap smoke its name—"stogie"—and several Wheeling **Stogies** played minor league baseball between 1899 and 1934. Pittsburgh **Stogies** were in the 1884 Union Association (starting that season as Chicago **Unions**) and the 1914 Federal League. (The FLers were **Rebels** after Louisiana-born manager Ennis "Rebel" Oakes took over in mid-season.)

Steamrollers | Captains | Gamblers | Millers

Improvements in steam engines, power looms, and canals in eighteenth-century Britain drove an Industrial Revolution that coincided with the end of a thousand-year-long Agricultural Revolution, in which the tradition of hunting animals and gathering edibles gave way to efficiently produced crops.

New farming machines (Jethro Tull's 1701 horse-drawn seed drill is an oft-cited example) could keep pace with industry only if given room to roam, so politically disenfranchised peasants were run off their lots to redistribute historical "common land" to landlords. The fencing in of those large estates was facilitated by a century of Parliamentary Enclosure Acts after 1750.

Irishman Oliver Goldsmith's poem "The Deserted Village" waxes nostalgic for the fictional Auburn, a pastoral hamlet that enclosure had turned into an earl's estate. Most towns of *Auburn* are remembrances of that 1770 poem. Known for decades as East Alabama Male College or the A&M College of Alabama or Alabama Polytechnic Institute, the college at Auburn was always "Auburn" to locals, and it was indeed Auburn University by 1960. Its **Plainsmen** came from the opening line of Goldsmith's poem: "Sweet Auburn, loveliest village of the plain." (Auburn's baseballers still play at Plainsman Park.) A later stanza compared ruthless landlords to famous predators: "Where crouching tigers wait their hapless prey." That turned Auburn's 1891 **Plainsmen** into **Tigers** for good.

Stories persist that Clemson [S.C.] University players once wore long locks to engage in helmetless football and were thus hairy **Tigers**. Actually, engineering professor and football coach Walter Riggs was an Auburn alum who introduced both football and Auburn's "**Tigers**" name to Clemson in 1896. That later Clemson president also swapped his school's red and blue for orange and Northwestern purple to resemble Auburn's burnt orange and blue.

• • •

Samuel Slater was a mill superintendent who left home in 1789 disguised as a farmhand because Britain guarded domestic technologies enough to prohibit the emigration of engineers and machinists. In America, Slater learned that Moses Brown was building mills on Rhode Island's Blackstone River. With mechanical designs stored in his head, Slater helped Brown build America's first water-powered factory looms in 1793, kick-starting its own Industrial Revolution. The factory city that now surrounds Slater's Pawtucket Falls mill has long hosted minor league and amateur Pawtucket **Slaters**.[1]

Brown's nephew Nicholas was another of the area's successful industrial millers. After graduating from Providence's Rhode Island College in 1786, Nick became a reliable-enough benefactor that it was Brown University by 1804. Brown's **Bears** recognize the brown bear species.

In the late 1820s, America's mills followed England's by converting river water to vapor, which could be piped around factories as steam power. Rhode Islanders would come to hope their steam-powered teams would flatten the competition. The Providence **Steam Roller** (1925–31) was New England's first NFL team,[2] followed by hoop's BAA Providence **Steamrollers** (1946–49) and indoor football's New England **Steamrollers** (1988).

• • •

Before the age of steam, flatboats that carried cargo downstream were busted up for lumber at the last stop. Reversing direction would be a drag until boats were self-propelled. Robert Fulton didn't invent the steamboat that solved this problem, but a grasp of marine propulsion and connections to New York politico Robert Livingston allowed him to establish on the Hudson the first commercially viable service.

For travel in shallow western rivers, Henry M. Shreve reduced draft by lifting his steamboat's boilers to the main deck. Then he split them to drive independent port and starboard sidewheels, which—along with the older sternwheel—is a classic steamboat design. Shreve opened the West to river pilots by breaking the Fulton-Livingston steamboat monopoly at New Orleans and using a steam-powered snagboat to break the Red River's 160-mile Great Raft. That took most of the 1830s, with the thorniest part being near a bluff now called Shreveport. The Louisiana State University–Shreveport **Pilots** have a steamboat emblem, and there was a WFL Shreveport **Steamer** (1974–75). Captain Shreve's namesake city has hosted several baseball **Captains**, one of which became Shreveport **Swamp Dragons** (2001–02) to reference slow waters on the lower Red that had created the ancient raft. There have also been several hardballing Shreveport **Sports**, which lacks for both specificity and imagination unless we remember that Shreveport's colloquial abbreviation is "S'port."

• • •

Steam power came to dominate inland waterways too. Cotton, lumber, grain, and sugar moved steadily along, with passenger fares being a bit of a byproduct. Midwestern riverfront cities remain partial to romantic riverboat imagery. Indoor football's Quad City **Steamwheelers** (1999–2009) were Mississippi-side at Moline, Illinois.[3] The confluence of the Missouri and the Miss'sip was a major steamboat stop where St. Louis **Steamers** have floated through top soccer leagues since 1979.[4] In 2005 the largest city on the Illinois welcomed the AHL Peoria **Rivermen** and their steamboat captain mascot.

Showboats weren't steamboats. They were ornate multi-deck barges pushed along by tugs. (Boilers would have interfered with the stage and dance floor.) There were Memphis **Showboats** (1984–85) in the USFL.

After Bix Beiderbecke heard the sounds of New Orleans coming from the Mississippi showboats that passed his boyhood home in Davenport, Iowa, he became a great soloist and jazz's first major white contributor. Often confused with the trumpet, Bix's horn was the cornet, which has either everything or nothing to do with lady hoopsters that were called Iowa **Cornettes** (WPBL, 1978–80) and Iowa **Cornets** (NBBL, 1997–2007). Anyway, D-port's favorite son drank himself to death at age 28 in 1931, but his spirit was captured by the minor league **Swing** of the Quad Cities (2004–07) on Beiderbecke Drive.[5] The **Swing** had been Quad City **River Bandits** from 1992 to 2003, and they swung back to that name in 2008. That same year saw a **Swing** revival, as their stadium and old uniforms appeared in *Sugar*, an acclaimed true-to-life drama about Dominican players on the fictional Bridgetown **Swing**.

The Mississippi watershed has long hosted other minor league **Bandits**, along with **Aces** and **Gamblers** owing to a different part of steamboat history. It was easy for robber-bandits to monitor floating targets from riverbanks, and gamblers were only slightly more upright. (Card playing as a profession almost certainly required cheating.) By the 1840s, riverboat card sharks were cashing in on a per-petual supply of new acquaintances. If suspicions grew, they'd simply slip away at the next dock. Soccer's New Orleans **Riverboat Gamblers** anted up from 1993 to 1999. A rival suggested that University of Evansville basketball coach John Harmon was playing with "five aces up his sleeve" in 1926, after which UE's **Pioneers** were **Purple Aces**,[6] which is appropriate for an Indiana school on the Ohio's northern bank. (The Evansvillians can no longer be accused of hiding cards; after stalling for a half-century, the **Aces** cut the sleeves off of their T-shirts only in 2002.) The WTT St. Louis **Aces** (1994–2011) practiced the double enten-dre, being in riverboat gambling territory and taking a name from a tennis scoring term. (An ace is a winning serve of such filth that a receiving opponent can't even get a racquet on it.)

• • •

Massachusetts merchant Francis Cabot Lowell thought factories like those in Manchester, England could succeed near Boston. Even with the modest flow of the Charles River, his 1814 mill at Waltham successfully spun and wove a high volume of raw cotton into cloth in a single large building. After his death in 1817, Lowell's partners looked twenty miles north to the town of East Chelmsford— soon "Lowell"—where the dominant geographical feature is the Merrimack River, as indicated by the University of Massachusetts–Lowell **River Hawks**.[7]

By the 1820s improved canals around Lowell's falls were powering a "mile of mills." The sophistication of Lowell's looms "were planned for the employment of farmers' daughters,"[8] as opposed to being planned for strong and skilled (read: costly) English spinners. The demands of the equipment went back up after the Civil War, and Lowell put men back in the mills.[9] Baseball's Lowell **Spinners** (est. 1996) are named for those diligent spinners, but their Canaligator wasn't Lowell's only reptilian mascot; the Lowell **Lock Monsters** (AHL, 1998–2006) were named for the city's canal locks. Their dragon-lizard mascot clearly poked fun at Scotland's seldom seen but much discussed Loch ("lock") Ness Monster.[10] Referencing English industries, Lowell was soon the "Manchester of America."

A few older mills were thirty-five miles up the Merrimack at Brooklyn, New Hampshire. The men of the Waltham-Lowell system merged Brooklyn's opera-tions in 1831, and it was renamed Manchester in 1892 on its way to becoming the Granite State's "Queen City." The AHL's Manchester **Monarchs** (est. 2001) allude to that nickname and their Los Angeles **Kings** parent club.[11] Manchester **Millrats** (2007–11) were minor league basketballers.

• • •

New England's textilers relied heavily on Southern cotton in the antebellum period, and the North's victory in the Civil War put a huge ironic dent in its own economy. The Southern whites who'd been yeomen and tenant farmers in the old plantation system found themselves competing for farm jobs with four-million freed slaves. When northern industrialists noticed the cheap workforce and lax labor laws in the cotton states, Southern cities competed to be "Lowell of the South." (Rival footballers from schools in the Carolinas that developed ambitious textile programs—Clemson's **Tigers** and NC State's **Wolfpack**—have played the "Textile Bowl" since 1981.) The new Southern mills wanted to entertain their laborers and started recreational baseball circuits in the 1870s. Those "Textile leagues" gained stature as their players went to the majors. A South Carolina millhand since age 6, Joe Jackson was on some good textile teams. Playing for the 1908 Greenville **Spinners**, he removed the ill-fitting new shoes from his blistered feet and socked a homer, after which Scoop Latimer of the *Greenville News* called him "Shoeless Joe."

John W. Hanes and P.H. Hanes sold their tobacco business to R.J. Reynolds in 1900. The next year the brothers opened separate textile mills at Winston-Salem. They were merged into Hanes Corporation in 1965, but not before the **Hosiery Girls** of P.H. Hanes Knitting dominated AAU basketball through the late 1940s, especially when Hazel Walker was on the roster.

• • •

Navigation on the Mississippi was halted by its only major waterfall, the fifty-foot drop of St. Anthony Falls. The power those falls provided and the easy access to points south demanded that flour and sawmills be built, and the new grain shipping center considered calling itself "Lowell."[12] Instead it became Minneapolis in 1856, meaning "city of waters" when the Dakota word for a waterfall (*minnehaha*) meets the Greek suffix for "city" (*-polis*). Starting in 1884, the mill city had a string of hardball **Millers**. During World War II their park accommodated Minneapolis **Millerettes** of the All-American Girls Professional Baseball League. Later neighbors were the Minneapolis **Millers**, three different minor league hockey franchises between 1926 and 1963.[13]

Minnesota's future capital lost its original name (Pig's Eye Landing) after the Catholic French priest Lucien Galtier opened the modest St. Paul's Chapel in 1841. Loads of Protestant Scandinavians flocked to the mills that New Englanders established around Minneapolis, but nearby St. Paul maintained its Catholic character through the immigration of French-Canadian, Native Irish, and German-Catholic laborers. These distinctions have kept them "Twin Cities" rather than having them merge. The AL **Senators** moved from D.C. to the suburb of Bloomington in 1961 to become Minnesota **Twins**, alienating neither Twin City as the first major leaguers identified by state.[14]

• • •

Despite an exodus from Lowell, America's largest post–Civil War textile center remained in Massachusetts. The mills at Fall River, which—like Providence—were on the Narragansett Bay watershed, were backed by men from the dying whaling industry at nearby New Bedford. Entrepreneur Sam Mark bought the American Soccer League's Fall River **United** (est. 1921) and made them **Marksmen** (1922–30).[15] With home-grown talent in short supply, the ASL was the first

North American league to recruit heavily in Europe. New Bedford is Fall River's twin city, and the **Marksmen** and New Bedford **Whalers** (1924–31) both comprised a healthy number of British-born athletes.

• • •

The names for some of the dozen sides in the ASL at mid-life (the 1925/26 season) indicate corporate sponsorship:

- Bethlehem [Pa.] **Steel** F.C. represented a huge steel plant in the country's first soccer-specific stadium. (Today it's Moravian College's Steel Field.)
- Sponsored by the Wonder Works factory, Boston Soccer Club members were **Wonder Workers**.
- The New York Field Club (1921–24) was replaced by the corporate-backed **Indiana Flooring**. New York **Giants** owner Charles Stoneham bought up the **Flooring** team in 1927 and thought they might be **Giants** too, but a soccer team of that name (copied from Stoneham's baseballers) had been around since the 1890s, so the *National* League owner made them **Nationals**.
- James and Peter Coats were Rhode Island thread manufacturers who sponsored Pawtucket's **J&P Coats**.
- Kearny, New Jersey became the American base of Scotland's Clark Thread Co. in 1875. (Its merger with J&P Coats in 1952 created today's Coats & Clark.) British spinners flooded both the mills and the rosters of semi-pro sides of the 1880s, so ASL teams included Kearny **Scots** and Kearny **Irish** (or **Celtic**).

The ASL was pretty stable until its schedule clashed with tournaments run by the United States Football Association. That "Soccer War" forced individual clubs to choose sides. Breakaway ASL teams formed the Eastern Soccer League in 1928, but both circuits realigned as the ASL in late 1929 just in time to be wiped out by the Depression. Late-era ASLers and players in its immediate successor, a semi-pro ASL, were transparent about their ethnicities, as indicated by Philadelphia **German-Americans**, Brooklyn **Hispanos**, Philadelphia **Ukrainian Nationals**, and Boston **Celtics** that preceded a like-named NBA club by more than a decade.

The ASL's 1971 New York **Greeks** had evolved out of the **Greek-Americans** from the German-American Soccer League of the 1950s and '60s. As New York **Apollo** (from the Greek god of light, poetry, and healing), they were the league champions or co-champs in three of the next six seasons. They were the New York **United** for their last two seasons (1980 and '81). The **Greeks/Apollo/United** franchise had started in the metropolis the same year as another Greek-named team, the NASL's New York **Cosmos** (1971–85). That's abbreviated from *cosmopolitans*, a Greek form for citizens of the world.

Canada's own great immigrant city, Greater Toronto, is home to Canadian Soccer League sides that indicate immigration to Canada's largest city, including the Serbian **White Eagles** and Hamilton **Croatia**, but its Vaughan Italia **Shooters** and Portugal **FC** dropped their respective references to Italy and Portugal in 2009 and 2010 to be York Region **Shooters** and **SC** Toronto.

Commodores | Blue Devils | Hatters | Cuban Giants

"Vertical integration" is business-speak for controlling all of the services and supply chains relevant to a particular market. A few get rich when it works, and it's not unusual when folks in cities with ranching, drilling, mining, or manufacturing histories become fans of **Millionaires**, **Aristocrats**, or **Barons**.

• • •

Thomas Gibbons had a federal contract for steamboat service between New Jersey and New York, but Aaron Ogden had the same deal from New York State. Gibbons sued Ogden and won in the U.S. Supreme Court. Writing the unanimous 1824 decision, Chief Justice John Marshall said the regulation of interstate commerce was the exclusive purview of Congress. Within a year, the number of steamboats out of New York jumped from six to forty-three.[1]

> Aaron Ogden was the New Jersey governor during his court case, and he helped build one of the state's prominent families. Mr. Ogden's distant nephew was the banker Ogden Goelet, who built his Ochre Court summer estate at Newport, Rhode Island in 1892. Oggy's son left the house to Salve Regina University in 1942. As was true only for Newport's greatest "cottages," the lawn is separated from the Atlantic by a narrow cliff walk, so SRU's **Newporters** became the **Seahawks** in 1996.

After Gibbons died in 1826, his son William couldn't hang on to his ambitious business manager, Cornelius Vanderbilt. "Commodore" Vanderbilt bought out his competitor Daniel Drew in an 1834 price war and was a millionaire at age 50 before making his real money in railroads. Exhibiting the late-life generosity that was typical of industrial barons, Vanderbilt donated a million dollars in 1873 to start Nashville's Vanderbilt University. By the late 1890s, Tennessee newspapers had bolted Vanderbilt's own "**Commodore**" nameplate onto VU athletes.

Mr. Vanderbilt's steamers had shuffled miners to and from rail stations on both sides of the Central American isthmus so they could sail up to California's Gold Rush. That cut thousands of ocean miles, but Vanderbilt dreamed of a time-saving canal. In 1849 he partnered with Nicaragua's government to connect the world's two largest oceans, but engineering challenges, malaria, politics, and (after 1878) a competing French project in Panama killed his canal. By 1902 the U.S. had leased both canals and chose to finish Panama's, with the Pacific end (completed in 1914) at Panama City, Panama. To raise its profile, the port city of Harrison, Florida was renamed Panama City in 1906. The **Commodores** at its Gulf Coast State College are justified by their seaside location, but that's a little ironic because it was the Panama Canal that ultimately killed Commodore Vanderbilt's Nicaraguan project.

Vanderbilt's aforementioned adversary, Daniel Drew, became one of the most ruthless men of the age by mastering the short sell. It was a tricky way of profiting in a "bear" (down) market at the expense of others,[2] so Drew's Latin nickname was *Ursa Major* (Great Bear). In 1867 he purchased a New Jersey residence built by the aforementioned William Gibbons. Drew immediately turned the Madison estate—"The Forest"—into the Methodist seminary that's now Drew

University. Athletes at the "University of the Forest" are **Rangers** ... *forest* **Rangers** whose "Ranger Bear" mascot unwittingly alludes to their *Ursa Major* eponym.[3]

A younger Drew had driven cattle in upstate New York. Paid by the pound, he fed salt to his herd so they'd drink and gain weight as they neared Big Apple stockyards. Drew gives us the term "watered stock" to describe artificially overvalued commodities. During the post–Civil War rail boom, Drew—along with fellow barons Jim Fisk and Jay Gould—watered down Erie Railroad stock to sucker Vanderbilt out of millions. Then Fisk and Gould tried to corner the gold market through connections in the Grant administration, causing the Gold Panic of 1869. Undaunted, they pushed Erie stock upward the next year while former partner Drew was selling it short. The Great Bear's big losses were immediate and he was finished off by the Panic of 1873, losing the ability to fund his namesake university.

Jay Gould's close associate in Midwestern railways was Russell Sage, a politician and financier from New York's Rensselaer County. A decade after Mr. Sage's 1906 death, his progressive widow, Margaret Olivia Slocum Sage, endowed Troy's all-female Russell Sage College, now among three upstate institutions in The Sage Colleges, for which confederated teams wear white and green. It's a muted green—one definition of *sage*—and the adoption of "**Gators**" by jocks of the mid-1980s likely owes to that color.

In 1896, Gould's son, George Jay Gould, built a Georgian-style home at Lakewood, New Jersey, a winter hangout for industrial barons from both New York and Philadelphia. The women's academy that moved to "Georgian Court" in 1924 is Georgian Court University, where **Courtiers** ran the court in the Casino, the Goulds' ballroom and equestrian ring. The marble lions still guarding GCU's Casino and Sunken Garden changed **Courtiers** to **Lions** in the mid-1970s.[4]

• • •

Philadelphia banker Jay Cooke invested heavily in the Northern Pacific Railroad. A spring 1873 stock crash in Austria wiped out investment in the overextended railroads, and Cooke's bank—the largest in the U.S.—melted away by the fall. This caused a run on the banks and a five-year recession (the abovementioned Panic of 1873). The Texas and Pacific Railroad was forced to stop laying track at Dallas, thirty miles short of the Chisholm Trail's former booming "Cowtown," Fort Worth. Things there got so lifeless that the *Dallas Herald* satirically reported a panther sleeping downtown in 1875, effecting FW's "Panther City" nickname. Minor league baseball's Fort Worth **Panthers** (1888–1959) were alternately "Cats." New Fort Worth **Cats** started in 2001.

Fortunes were different on the side of Big D with tracks; the T&P's Mesquite stop quickly attracted farmers who shipped tons of cotton, hay, and sugar on the new rails, as recalled by Eastfield College's **Harvesters**.

• • •

Smoking was a rage in Europe after tobacco was discovered in the Americas. The New World's first African slaves were on Caribbean tobacco plantations by 1501, as Spain tried to monopolize the trade with a quality Cuban tobacco. In the Ten

Years' War (1868–78), Cuban patriots failed to gain autonomy from Spain, so cigar maker (and rebel backer) Vicente Martinez Ybor moved his Havana factory to Florida's Keys and then Tampa, where the cigar district is Ybor City. The Tampa **Smokers** appeared in various minor baseball leagues from 1919 to 1954.

In the early 1850s a Dr. Durham donated land for a North Carolina Railroad stop soon called Durham. Local tobacco man John Green labeled his "Spanish" tobacco with the bull's head from Colman's Mustard (which he thought was made in Durham, England),[5] bringing about both the Bull Durham cigarette brand and Durham's "Bull City" nickname. But Durham could have been the Bull City for entirely different reasons; *Durham* is an alternate name for some shorthorn cattle that Britons had brought to the colonies from northeast England. Males of that breed are therefore "Durham bulls." Starting in 1912 various minor league Durham **Bulls** played into the next century, gaining fame in the 1988 film *Bull Durham*.[6]

During the spring of 1865, soldiers waited around Durham for the Civil War to end. Both sides acquired a taste for Piedmont tobacco by raiding Green's storehouses, paying off as lifelong customers. After Green's 1869 death, his company was Blackwell Tobacco, run by W.T. Blackwell and later Julian Carr. Local competitors included the family of Washington Duke, whose ambitious son James Buchanan Duke exhibited pure robber baronism by aggregating various tobacco interests in 1890 to control 90 percent of the American market. His Duke of Durham cigarettes gave Carr's Bull Durhams a good fight,[7] but Carr and the Dukes agreed on one thing; all were Methodists who thought Durham should be a college town. They funded the relocation of Randolph County's Trinity College in 1892. (Six years later, Duke's tobacco trust bought out Blackwell and its Bull Durham label.)

Any sermon by Methodist founder John Wesley would likely touch on human responsibilities to transcend the "image of the devil, wherein we are born," so he wouldn't have anticipated Trinity trading its "**Methodists**" for "**Devils**" in 1918. Great War veterans returning to classes that year would likely have heard of France's *Chasseurs Alpins* (alpine rifles) of the mountain campaigns. The *Chasseurs* were valiant enough, but they also looked simply smashing in blue kits and matching berets that made them *les Diables Bleus*. Irving Berlin even wrote a popular 1918 song for the "Blue Devils of France." Just two weeks after busting up the Rockefellers' Standard Oil monopoly in May 1911, the Supreme Court did the same to the Dukes' tobacco trust. J.B. had by then amassed an additional fortune in hydroelectricity, and he started the Duke Endowment in 1924 to improve the quality of life for Carolinians. Trinity College—ever the family fascination—was a major donee. The appreciative school was renamed Duke University that year, but it maintains **Blue Devils** in "Duke blue" and white.

• • •

The former bottom of an equatorial salt sea, New York's Finger Lakes region has many salt mines. A "salty dog" is an experienced sailor, but the idiom stretched to cover the Salt City's Syracuse **Salty Dogs** (USL, 2003–04).

Sodium bicarbonate (baking soda) was among the salt products that shipped on the Erie Canal, and upstater Henry DeLand made enough money trafficking the white powder to buy a bunch of North Florida orchards. He founded DeLand, Florida in 1876 and its DeLand Academy in 1883. The Great Freeze of 1894/95 destroyed orange crops and Mr. Deland was broke. He passed the academy-funding hat to fellow Baptist and Sunshine State neighbor John B. Stetson.[8]

The delicate constitution that had brought Stetson to Florida in the 1880s had earlier led to his fortune. The young Philadelphia hat-maker's son had been diagnosed with tuberculosis as a boy, so he'd left for Colorado's dry mountain air and 1859 gold rush. For the extreme climate, Stetson sold prospectors headwear with exaggerated features. A super-wide brim offered sun and rain protection, a large crown kept warm air on the scalp, and treated beaver felt repelled water like it was still affixed to the beaver. The lining even made for a good three-quart bucket (despite its "ten gallon" designation).[9] Returning to Philly in 1865, novel marketing and business strategies soon turned Stetson's small shop into the world's largest hat factory. With Henry DeLand's blessing, the academy Stetson saved was renamed Stetson University in 1889. Athletes were **Hatters** right off the top, having fielded Florida's first football side in 1901. Heads-up hardballers in the Florida State League would be DeLand **Red Hats** (1939–54) and DeLand **Sun Caps** (1970).[10]

• • •

Flagler Hall, a Stetson University science building, was underwritten by another local mover and shaker, Henry Flagler. He was J.D. Rockefeller's founding partner in Standard Oil, the first big trust. His other grand American vision was modern Florida. A semi-retired Flagler built St. Augustine's Ponce de León Hotel, a Spanish Renaissance Revival wonder by McKim, Mead, and White. Its 1888 opening made the city a winter destination for industrial barons. By 1968, the Ponce was the main building at Flagler College. The city of St. Auggie and the Flagler College **Saints** are both namesakes of St. Augustine of Hippo, whose feast day in 1565 marked the first Spanish landfall at the site.

Flagler had purchased the lot for the Ponce from former mayor Dr. Andrew Anderson. The pair planned to put the city on the tourist map, and Anderson donated marble copies of Florence, Italy's Medici lions to flank the west end of a new city bridge in 1927. The Bridge of Lions was an instant landmark, and the city's Baptist college was fielding **Lions** within two years without explanation, but we are compelled to point out the coincidence. Relocated to Miami Gardens in 1968, Florida Memorial University retains **Fighting Lions**.

The ambition with which Flagler developed railroads and hotels on Florida's east coast made it hard to tell which business intended to jack up the other. Traveling from the Midwest to one's St. Augustine vacation got easier in 1892 when the popular Dixie Flyer train started going to Jacksonville via Nashville. It ran until 1966, overlapping with minor league hockey's Nashville **Dixie Flyers** (1962–71). The Nashville **Nighthawks** (1996/97) were **Ice Flyers** for their last season (1997/98). That Jacksonville had become Florida's major rail junction got noticed by the city's second WFL franchise in as many years, the 1975 Jacksonville **Express**.[11] Flagler's boss in the Cleveland-based Standard Oil, J.D. Rockefeller, spent winters in North Florida and died there in May 1937. Within months, the AHL Cleveland **Falcons** (1934–37) were renamed **Barons**, ironically moving to be Jacksonville **Barons** for the last half of the 1972/73 winter season before expiring.

• • •

Flagler's hotels served an underappreciated role in baseball history. Frank Thompson, the African American headwaiter at the Argyle Hotel in Babylon, New York, captained the 1885 Babylon **Athletics**,[12] which played good white teams to entertain guests at the Long Island resort. The **Athletics** were purchased by Trenton businessman Walter Cook after one season and turned into black baseball's first recognized pro side. That's about when New York's National Leaguers became **Giants**, and Cook called his nine **Cuban Giants**, thinking Latino players were more palatable to white vacationers than African Americans would be. Flagler decided "to provide his wealthy clientele with an extravagant array of first-class amusements that brought Frank Thompson and the Cuban **Giants** into [the] unlikely world of lavish, conspicuous leisure."[13] The **Cuban Giants**' success at the Ponce effected an immediate rise of black baseball in Florida. For instance, two of the many **Giants** named after the **Cuban Giants**—the Chicago **American Giants** and the Lincoln **Giants**—wintered at Palm Beach, representing Flagler's Royal Poinciana and Breakers hotels (respectively), where they "worked as bellhops and cooks [...] and played games whenever they could."[14]

In the 1920s, black players from the independent Jacksonville **Red Caps** supplemented incomes by redcapping (serving as porters) at the city train station.[15] Watching black baseball draw tourists to Florida, Atlantic City mayor Harry Bacharach invited Jacksonville's Duval [County] **Giants** to his city's resorts as Atlantic City **Bacharach Giants** (1916–29).[16]

Just two hours south of St. Auggie are the Johnson University–Florida **Suns** (Kissimmee). The best shot at winter warmth, however, is nearer the end of the peninsula, so Flagler extended his rails to a village called Miami. The Great Freeze that had damaged North Florida's reputation hadn't stretched so far south, a climate indicated by the NBA Miami **Heat** (est. 1998). With just a decade of development, Miami surpassed St. Augustine as Florida's prime resort.

• • •

In the 1890s, breakaway **Cuban Giants** formed the **Cuban X-Giants** (that is, *ex-Giants*) and barnstormed through Cuba, "marking the start of the symbiotic business relationship between black and [actual] Cuban teams."[17] Travel between Havana and Miami (perhaps on a Flagler-owned steamer) was steady. Threats of *revolución* sent Cuban exiles to south Florida, especially after a Communist takeover of Cuba in 1959. Cubans have richly mixed bloodlines, so Anglo-Cuban Miami quickly became an international city in which *fusion* is applied to culturally diverse fashions, foods, arts, and music. Miami **Fusion** F.C. (1998–2001) was an MLS soccer side in Fort Lauderdale.

Statesmen | Nuts | 66ers | Yellow Jackets

In January 1918, President Woodrow Wilson gave a speech to Congress that laid out Fourteen Points for post-war peace. Point 14 argued for a "general association of nations" that might avoid future wars. Indeed, the League of Nations assembled in January 1920 at Paris and found a permanent home in Geneva, Switzerland from that November until its 1946 dissolution. It failed to hold off World War II but was the necessary prototype for the United Nations (est. 1945).

For decades, Wilson was hailed as an exemplary President-statesman, and the **Statesmen** and **Lady Statesmen** at Chicago's Kennedy-King College are his namesakes. The eponyms for KKC are actually Robert F. Kennedy and Martin Luther King, Jr. (both assassinated in 1968), so **Statesmen** recall the school's name before 1969: Woodrow Wilson Junior College.

Geneva, New York isn't named after the Swiss burg. In fact it's believed that *S-E-N-E-C-A* was mistaken for *G-E-N-E-V-A* on an early map of Lake Seneca. Either way, Hobart College's footballers played to an opening day tie at Amherst in 1936, after which the *New York Times* called them the "statesmen from Geneva," a comparison to the League of Nations that has made all Hobart crews **Statesmen**.[1]

The same month as his Fourteen Points speech, Wilson put Bernard Baruch in charge of industrial wartime production. After his 1889 graduation from City College of New York, Baruch had been Wall Street's original whiz kid and an unofficial economic and diplomatic consultant to multiple presidents. He also popularized the term "Cold War" and discussed the great issues of the day from a D.C. park bench. In 1953, City College's business school was renamed for its early advocate, the "Park Bench Statesman," giving to Baruch College teams of **Statesmen** and **Stateswomen**. When a modern athletic facility opened in 2002, students moved for the alliteration of "Baruch **Bearcats**" but kept the name of the *Ticker* student news, a reference to a stock ticker.

• • •

Mr. Baruch famously liquidated his stocks before the October 1929 market crash. The ensuing Great Depression was especially hard on farmers on the lower Great Plains who overextended credit and over-farmed land to recoup war-time losses. The latter robbed soil of nutrients, and years of drought and dust storms followed. Many farmers from Missouri, Arkansas, Texas, and Oklahoma (all indiscriminately called "Okies") left the Dust Bowl for the long growing season for fruits and nuts in California's Central Valley. The Modesto **Nuts** (2005–) are only the latest local minor league hardballers to reference production and packing.[2] Fresno alone has hosted **Raisin Eaters** (1906), **Raisin Growers** (1909), and **Packers** (1913).[3] Fresno City College was California's first community college in 1910, intending to emphasize practical trades and agriculture, a legacy documented by **Rams**. Also in the valley are Stockton's San Joaquin Delta College **Mustangs** and the minor league Visalia **Rawhide**, who suggest both cowskin and the baseball coverings made therefrom.

Many migrant workers ended up in California simply because that's where the road went. Route 66 had opened in 1926 to serve rural communities between Chicago and Los Angeles. An hour east of the Pacific and just south of the Central Valley is another fertile valley, the Inland Empire. The California League's Inland Empire **Sixty-Sixers** (2003–) in San Bernardino are among the valley's many route 66 tokens.

Each spring since 1911, San Berdoo's National Orange Show has highlighted its citrus industry. That it always rains on the show is blamed on the fairgrounds being atop an old Indian cemetery. In 1927 that legend put **Indians** at San Bernardino Valley College. Since 2000 they've been **Wolverines**, which aren't native to the valley, indicating the degree to which SBVC went to ditch its Indian theme.

Icons of Americana that evolved along 66 include motor hotels ("motels"), neon signs, and drive-through restaurants. Phillips Petroleum contributed in 1927 with the first Phillips 66 "service station." In 1920 the Tulsa company had sponsored the Phillips **66ers** (or **Oilers**), which was an AAU hoop powerhouse into the 1960s. The NBA D-League's Tulsa **66ers** (est. 2005) followed. After sucking heaps of oil from the High Plains, company founder Frank Phillips funded public schools in the town of Pantex (renamed Phillips in 1938) and a junior college two miles away at Borger. The latter is home to the Frank Phillips College **Plainsmen** and **Lady Plainsmen**.

• • •

In 1899 footballers started representing Philadelphia's Frankford [Ave.] Athletic Association. As Frankford **Yellow Jackets**, they were strong contenders in the 1924 NFL. With few paying fans during the Depression and state laws that prevented play on the NFL's game day, the 1930 **Yellow Jackets** formed a visible two-team syndicate with the Minneapolis **Red Jackets**[4] (a dying powerhouse with a coincidentally similar name). The NFL looked the other way, hoping to save at least one of the tradition-rich franchises, but they finished ninth and tenth in an eleven-team circuit. By 1931 the absorption of the **Red Jackets** by the **Yellow Jackets** was complete, but the Depression crushed even the combined franchise halfway through that season. By then they'd moved to the **Phillies'** Baker Bowl, far enough from the old neighborhood that longtime fans who felt abandoned (and likely could no longer afford tickets anyway) started calling them *Philadelphia* **Yellow Jackets**.[5]

Franklin D. Roosevelt was elected president in 1932, having already implemented anti-Depression programs as New York's governor. He pushed more than a dozen industry, labor, agriculture, and social welfare measures through Congress as part of his New Deal program. The last bill passed during FDR's historic first 100 days was the National Industrial Recovery Act, for which the new National Recovery Administration would monitor industrial practices and union rights. Businesses displayed the NRA Eagle to verify their compliance and attract customers. Bert Bell, a former assistant for Penn's **Quakers**, did his part in 1933 when he bought Frankford's mothballed **Yellow Jackets**. Taking a walk after his purchase, Bell saw an NRA billboard and decided the art deco raptor was apt justification for "Philadelphia **Eagles**."[6]

Also noticing the NRA Eagle in 1933, the purple-and-gold **Purple Titans** at the Brethren Church's Ashland [Ohio] University became **Purple Eagles**, but they're now just **Eagles**.[7]

The NHL's famous Ottawa **Senators** had small-market problems during the Depression and left Canada for a larger U.S. city in October 1934. They were deliberately given an all-American name and symbol, the St. Louis **Eagles**. (Their sweater patch was suspiciously similar to the eagle emblem of the city's famous Anheuser-Busch brewery.) Travel expenses for the Heartland team were so large that it folded after that season.

Jumbos | Americans | Flyers | Wings

Cornelius Vanderbilt consolidated his New York train lines at Grand Central Station in 1871 and rented a vacated Madison Square rail lot to P.T. Barnum, who in 1874 opened the Monster Classical and Geological Hippodrome. The oval hosted sporting events, animal shows, and acts from Barnum's circus. It changed to Gilmore's Garden in 1875 after Vanderbilt leased it to Patrick Gilmore, who even John Phillip Sousa called the "father of the American band." Two years after Vanderbilt's 1879 death, his son William Henry Vanderbilt decided to keep the renamed Madison Square Garden in the family.

> W.H. Vanderbilt's son, William K. Vanderbilt, had an English country home called Idle Hour on Long Island. After W.K.V.'s death in 1920 the grounds were cut into neighborhoods. In 1963 the house itself became the center of what is now Dowling College's Oakdale campus. Sculpted Italian lions in its garden explain DC's blue-and-gold **Golden Lions**.

The Garden continued hosting dog and horse shows, boxing, and *Buffalo Bill's Wild West*. Barnum returned to the building in 1882 with his greatest prize, an African elephant purchased from the London Zoo named Jumbo. (The word *jumbo* immediately became an adjective for oversized things.) Jumbo made Barnum piles of cash quickly but was killed in Ontario by a train of the Grand Trunk Line (insert joke) in 1885. Ever the salesman, Barnum executed the "largest taxidermy job ever," allowing even a dead Jumbo to draw well. Eventually the big boy's stuffed hide became the centerpiece of the Barnum Museum of Natural History at Tufts University (Medford, Mass.), for which Barnum and his Universalist Brethren were longstanding benefactors. When Barnum Hall burned down in 1975, all that was left of Jumbo were the ashes that the athletic department stashed in a peanut butter jar. (Insert additional joke.) Before big games, the Tufts **Jumbos** rub that plastic urn for luck.[1]

• • •

The roofless Hippodrome wasn't conducive to New York's extreme seasons, so it was unloved in the otherwise happenin' Madison Square. In 1890 the Vanderbilts built a new Garden on the corner, a marvelous Moorish castle by Stanford White. Boxing was MSG 2.0's steadiest draw, but the building had never been consistently profitable. The Garden needed a gambler.

You'd come up with half the stuff in this book by following around George "Tex" Rickard. He'd been a Texas rancher, county marshal, cattle baron, and poker player before discovering gold in Alaska and running a dice joint in the Klondike. Rickard made fortunes off customer bets that he'd quickly lose on bad mineral claims. He set up boxing matches at temporary stadiums in mining towns then teamed with another product of the gold fields, Jack Dempsey, a saloon fighter turned heavyweight contender. Coming east in 1920, Rickard leveraged his relationship with Dempsey into control of the Garden's sporting events and the building was finally operating in the black. But past mismanagement had put

MSG in the hands of the mortgaging bank, New York Life, which flattened the building to put its own home office on the site.

The new Madison Square Garden of 1925 wasn't even in Madison Square. Tex Rickard's MSG Corporation hastily constructed Garden III some 25 blocks north at Pennsylvania Plaza.[2] It was a big box of a building built for boxing, but it handled a variety of carryover events from the old corner.

Arguments over playoff compensation at the end of the 1924/25 NHL season brought about a strike by Ontario's Hamilton **Tigers**, established in 1920 and named after the 1869-founded CFL **Tigers** (now the **Tiger-Cats**). Bootlegger Big Bill Dwyer bought the **Tigers'** contracts and made them New York **Americans**, conceding that the *Nation* in "National Hockey League" was Canada. (Big Bill's **Americans** and Pittsburgh's new **Pirates** were joining Boston's year-old **Bruins** as the only U.S.-based teams.) Dwyer's **Americans** brought hockey fans to the Garden, and Tex Rickard figured a house team could pack the seats when boxing and dog shows did not, and the team's rent would simply revolve from one MSG pocket to another. Rickard didn't mind the little personal chaffing when reporters called his skaters "Tex's **Rangers**" after the Lone Star State's lawmen (p. 190). The New York **Rangers** have been NHL stalwarts since that 1926/27 season.

The Chicago **Blackhawks** and Detroit **Cougars** joined that same season, so the NHL suddenly had more American teams than Canadian, which ironically put the Garden's **Americans** in a new Canadian Division to offset the American Division's **Rangers**.[3] In 1926, Dwyer's rum running got him locked up for a year. Then prohibition's 1933 repeal coincided with what was already the **Rangers'** second NHL crown. The financially and athletically weak **Americans** were taken over by the NHL in 1936. They collapsed early in World War II.[4]

• • •

Like its predecessors, Garden III is gone. Pennsylvania Station was razed in the 1960s to build MSG IV. The 1910 terminal had been a Beaux-Arts masterpiece by Stanford White's partner Charles McKim. But unlike White's Moorish Garden, Penn Station was defended by an outraged public. It still ended up in a Meadowlands landfill, but the protest heated up an architectural preservation movement. City ordinances later saved many buildings, including the Vanderbilts' magnificent Grand Central Station. MSG IV opened in 1968, overlapping slightly with the last events at Garden III.

From New York's Penn Station or Philadelphia's Broad Street Station, the Pennsylvania Railroad's more luxurious steam trains—or "flyers"—zipped passengers to remote destinations. Some think that's how "**Flyers**" got assigned to the 1967 NHL expansion franchise at Broad Street's Spectrum. In reality, the team's first general manager, Bud Poile, gave them that name after playing for and coaching senior hockey's Edmonton **Flyers**, a team that commemorated Alberta's rich aviation history. Remote Edmonton has been a base for bush pilots, airmail carriers, and combat pilots since the dawn of powered flight, but the Edmonton **Flyers** also fit nicely with their Detroit **Red Wings** parent club (p. 339), a convention repeated in 1987 when the Philadelphia **Flyers** owned lacrosse's NLL Philadelphia **Wings** (1986–2014). (Different Philadelphia **Wings** had been in an earlier NLL, 1974–75.)

Panhandles | Pistons | Pacers | Hoosiers

By 1900 miners, oilers, steelers, and chemists were working away along North America's interior lakes and waterways. Their company-sponsored teams laid the groundwork for enduring pro leagues, especially in football and basketball.

• • •

By the twentieth century, football was all the rage at the East Coast Ivies. Folks in the trans-Appalachian industrial cities, however, lacked universities of such international renown and therefore backed the working class crews of early pro ball.

In 1911, Irish factory laborers in Youngstown, Ohio opened St. Patrick's Church. It's because of St. Patrick that *patrician* describes any Irish Catholic, and the church's Youngstown **Patricians** (1914–19) were pro football's unofficial national champs of 1915.

The Massillon [Ohio] **Tigers** got named in 1903 when a retailer dumped cheap orange-and-black jerseys on them.[1] Largely to answer the Massillonians, nearby Canton fielded a team two years later. The Canton Athletic Company's players were soon **Bulldogs** for no outstanding reason. Each city "regarded the football team as the community's most important representative to the outside world and strongly supported the local boys."[2] A pair of Canton-Massillon games created a betting scandal in 1906, which (along with ballooning player salaries) shut down both franchises. New Cantonians in 1911 were called **Professionals** because the gambling controversy had rendered "**Bulldogs**" unpalatable, but they were **Bulldogs** again after Massillon's familiar **Tigers** regrouped in 1915.[3]

The **Bulldogs** and **Tigers** were in the Ohio League (1902–19), which was really an informal challenge circuit that improved with the absorption of college standouts who would otherwise have hung up the cleats.[4] The Ironton **Tanks** were great Ohio Leaguers. It made sense that a team formed in 1919 in an iron town would be named after the armor-plated vehicles first widely seen in World War I, and some **Tanks** were just back from the trenches themselves. Proving the power of Ohio's independents, the **Tanks** had three victories over NFL teams (the Chicago **Bears**, New York **Giants**, and Portsmouth **Spartans**) in their final season, 1930.[5]

The Ohio League was well-represented on a summer's day in 1920 when team reps met at Canton to create the American Professional Football Association. (It would be the National Football League by 1922.)[6] The **Bulldogs** joined, expecting the continuing Massillon rivalry to generate interest. But the financially strapped **Tigers** never showed up, so their famous name was pounced on by *two* inaugural APFA sides, the Cleveland **Tigers** and Chicago **Tigers**.

Other monikers conceded the distinction between the APFA and the popular college game. Not to be confused with amateurs, two teams in the inaugural APFA were overtly professional, the Akron [Ohio] **Pros** and Hammond [Ind.] **Pros**.[7] The same league's Buffalo **All-Americans** (1920–23) signed past collegiate All-Americans. The St. Louis **All-Stars** intended to recruit similarly, but the ambitious name didn't prevent poor play in their only NFL season, 1923. Behind a very college-sounding color, the APFA/NFL Evansville [Ind.] **Crimson Giants** (1921–22) were Midwestern ex-collegians who'd theretofore been the semi-pro Evansville **Ex-Collegians** (est. 1920).

• • •

The names of some early APFA/NFL squads revealed their histories as established neighborhood sides. Illinois's Rock Island **Independents** had a common (and obvious) name for many of that era's unaffiliated semi-pros, but they were decidedly less independent after committing to 1920 APFA charter. They jumped to the new AFL in 1926, a rival circuit that lasted for only that season, leaving the disassociated **Independents** with a pertinent moniker until they folded after 1927.

Western New York's Rochester **Jeffersons** made good as the easternmost APFA/NFL contestants from 1920 to 1925, despite humble amateur beginnings in the Jefferson Road neighborhood. Also named for a local avenue were Kentucky's Louisville **Brecks**. Starting on a Breckinridge Street lot in 1907, they were weak APFA/NFL entrants (1921–23). They weren't much better when the NFL reactivated them as the 1926 Louisville **Colonels** (p. 134), a "Kentucky" team that went 0-4 from their new home in Chicago.

Wisconsin reservists played semi-professionally after 1915 as the Racine **Regulars** (or **Battery C**). With sponsorship from a local American Legion hall and the Horlick brothers (Wisconsin's malted milk kings), they were the NFL's Horlick-Racine **Legion** from 1922 to '24.

Around 1915 the Staten Island **Stapletons** formed as independents from their borough's Stapleton neighborhood. They turned pro in 1926 after the AFL's Newark **Bears** beat them so badly the owner simply hired most of the New Jerseyans away (before adding some NYU standouts).[8] The **Stapes** were NFLers from 1929 to 1932.

Now part of Muncie, the Indiana town of Congerville had two pro teams, the Congerville **Athletic Club** and Congerville **Flyers**. They merged in 1916 and were later the APFA Muncie **Flyers** (1920–21), but "**Flyers**" has no historical relevance.

• • •

When a business sponsored NFLers, its name often ended up in the moniker:

• The Pennsylvania Railroad's Panhandle Division crossed West Virginia's panhandle to connect Pittsburgh and Ohio. Some boilermakers from PRR workshops in Ohio assembled as Columbus **Panhandles** in 1901. (Their six rough-and-tumble Nesser brothers get as much credit as Jim Thorpe for popularizing American football.)[9] The **Panhandles** played in the first three APFA/NFL seasons in Ohio but were a road team of Columbus **Tigers** from 1923 to '26.

• The first-ever game between two APFA/NFL contestants was on October 3, 1920 at Dayton's Triangle Park. The **Panhandles** lost to the Dayton **Triangles**, an Ohio powerhouse backed by three companies that composed that city's downtown "industrial triangle."

• Buffalo's Tonawanda suburb kept the All-Tonawanda **Lumbermen** at Lumberman Stadium. Their great 1920 record against APFA sides moved that league to bar challenges from independents, forcing the **Lumbermen** to join in 1921. As

Tonawanda **Kardex**, they lost badly at Rochester in their only league appearance. (A presumed relationship between team **Kardex** and the upstate filing cabinet maker American Kardex is tough to verify.)

- The Duluth **Kelleys** (1923–25) were NFLers in Minnesota that were sponsored by Kelley-Duluth Hardware. They were later the Duluth **Eskimos** (1926–27).[10]
- The A.E. Staley starch company of Decatur, Illinois sponsored semi-pros in 1919. Fixing to enter the APFA/NFL, they hired reigning Rose Bowl MVP George S. Halas to recruit and coach the Decatur **Staleys**.[11] Losing interest after the 1920 season, the company would pay to move Halas and his boys to a larger city if they kept the name for another year, so the *Chicago* **Staleys** replaced the Chicago **Tigers** and won the 1921 title. Clear of obligations to his former sponsor and sharing a park with baseball's **Cubs**, Halas decided his bigger players were **Bears**.[12]

• • •

After two decades in the NFL, Halas gambled on the National Basketball League. Like early pro football, the NBL (1937–49) was in the industrial heartland, having grown out of the modest Midwest Basketball Conference (1935–37). Following the bear track, Halas called his boys Chicago **Bruins** (1939–42). He even hired some football **Bears** as bench players,[13] but these were no sloths; at Chicago's 1940 World Professional Basketball Tournament, the **Bruins** lost the final in overtime to the Harlem **Globetrotters**.

The Cleveland **Allmen Transfers** (moving and storage), Cleveland **Chase Brassmen** (alloy rods), and Fort Wayne **General Electrics** (meters and motor drives) were corporate-sponsored NBL teams. An Indiana cylinder plant backed the NBL Fort Wayne **Zollner Pistons** (est. 1941), but that's pushing ahead in the story.

Wartime leagues suffered as workers went off to fight, but military contractors and civilian shops that converted to defense could insulate employees from the draft. The Grumman Corporation (Bethpage, N.Y.) built warplanes and sponsored basketball's Long Island **Grumman Flyers**. (They were often **Hellcats** after the Grumman F6F *Hellcat* became the most successful Navy fighter in the Pacific.) The **Flyers** were in the eastern Independent League, and they finished behind two NBL teams at Chicago's 1942 tournament.

A series of wartime ads for Studebaker hyped its Wright Cyclone engines for bombers while ignoring its auto division, so the company's NBLers were Chicago **Studebaker Flyers** (1942/43).[14] Unaccidentally, several of the **Globetrotters** worked at the Chicago aircraft plant, so the **Studebakers** (and their NBL rivals, Toledo's Jim White **Chevrolets**) are among the very first integrated teams in major pro sports, a progression necessitated by wartime manpower shortages.

The NBL brought top collegians to the Midwest, but its owners coveted the untapped fanbases and large (often empty) ice arenas of the seaboard. In 1946 east coast amphitheater owners with hockey tenants were moved by that same notion and started the Basketball Association of America in tiny hamlets called New York, Philadelphia, and Boston.

Millions of young men were returning from service as players and fans. The best prospects, however, kept going to the established NBL, so the BAA contracted from twelve to four teams after one season. It purchased some credibility for its third season (1948/49) by luring four NBL teams into the fold, largely owing to the efforts of NBL owner Fred Zollner. Reluctant to hawk for commercial shops, the BAA preceded all nicknames with the home city, and Zollner led by example, dropping "**Zollner**" from the Fort Wayne **Zollner Pistons** (the *Detroit* **Pistons** since 1957).[15] Likewise, grocer Frank Kautsky's NBL Indianapolis **Kautskys** became (meaningless) **Jets**. New York's Rochester **Royals** also jumped to the BAA, but the big catch was center George Mikan and his NBL champion Minneapolis **Lakers**. The six remaining NBL squads couldn't compete and were dissolved into the BAA before it was renamed the National Basketball Association for the 1949/50 season.

• • •

A handful of Michigan visionaries gave birth to an industrial tide that lifted all corporate boats on Great Lakes shores. The auto biz also drove the existing materials industries at Toledo (glass), Akron (rubber), and Pittsburgh (steel).

Goods bound for Detroit or Chicago often shipped through Toledo on the corner of Lake Erie, where the rail and freighting history explains the Owens Community College **Express** (whose speedy mascot is a jaguar). OCC eponym Michael J. Owens got a 1904 patent for mechanized bottle production that helped Toledo become the "Glass City," and the University of Toledo's stadium was officially renamed the Glass Bowl in 1945. Regional sand deposits are low in impurities and high in silica, both ideal for glass production.

Toledo produced vehicles too. Before World War I, its Willys-Overland plant bankrolled football's semi-pro Toledo **Overlands**. W-O produced more Jeeps than any other maker in World War II, after which Toledo **Jeeps** (1946–48) pounded the NBL glass. The (zero-plural) name of junior hockey's Toledo **Cherokee** (est. 1993) is north and west of any Cherokee homelands, so it's a subtle allusion to a popular Jeep model built locally since 1974.

East of Toledo is Akron, where Mr. B.F. Goodrich was making carriage and bike tires by 1870. Soon other rubber companies (Firestone, General Tire, Goodyear) would capitalize on Akron's canals and centrally located rail lines, making it the Rubber City. Many minor leaguers before 1920 were Akron **Rubbermen** or **Rubbernecks** and double-A baseballers became Akron **Rubber Ducks** before the 2014 season. The locally produced rubber that gets chewed up on asphalt tracks every year explains pro softball's Akron **Racers** (est. 2000).

Also justifying those **Racers** are the sloped lanes at Akron's Derby Downs, the site of the Soap Box Derby world championship since 1934. Those lanes are practically attached to the University of Akron stadium, officially named the Rubber Bowl. In a 1927 team nicknaming contest, one student suggested the model name of some rubber overshoes made locally by Goodrich, "Zippers." Eventually, UA's **Zippers** became **Zips**, with a swift kangaroo mascot.

The creation of the NBL in 1937 had been steered by Firestone and Goodyear, whose own Akron-based entrants were the **Firestone Non-Skids** and **Goodyear Wingfoots** (named respectively for Firestone's high-performance tire and Goodyear's flying foot, a symbol for the Greek god Hermes). A group of mostly deaf workers from Goodyear played semi-pro football quite successfully as Akron **Silents** (1919–23). Many **Silents** (sometimes "**Mutes**") were alumni of Washington D.C.'s Gallaudet University,[16] the world's oldest college for hearing-impaired persons. Communicating through American Sign Language, Gallaudet's **Bison** helped popularize football's closed huddle.[17]

Charles Goodyear worked in east coast labs, but his surname was appropriated by Goodyear Tire and Rubber (with which he was not affiliated). His 1844 patent for vulcanization outlined the manipulation of heat and pressure to produce practically applicable rubber. The Continental Football League's Akron **Vulcans** tried to stick in the Rubber City but melted away after one 1967 exhibition game.

• • •

Chuck Barnes was the son of an Ohio rubber baron. Merging interests in tires and sports, he became an agent for drivers like A.J. Foyt and Mario Andretti. A part-owner of Indianapolis's inaugural ABA team in 1967, Barnes said that "Indiana **Pacers**" would refer to both the Indianapolis 500's pace car and the pacing horses of the city's harness racing history. (The **Pacers** joined the NBA in 1976.) The Marywood University **Pacers** (Scranton, Pa.) are also near a harness racing track, Wilkes-Barre's Pocono Downs.[18]

> For many winters, well-bred New Yorkers retired to the mild climate of Aiken, South Carolina. They brought their penchant for polo and pacers with them and Aiken was a hotbed of equine activity. The annual Aiken Triple Crown included a thoroughbred race, a steeplechase, and a harness race. The latter race was sponsored by the University of South Carolina–Aiken, where **Pacers** replaced **Rebels** in 1970. (In 2004 the decades-old harness race became a polo match.)

Indianapolitans built a brick oval to test its machines at a time when Stutz, Duesenberg, Marmon, and other city factories rivaled those at Detroit. In 1911 a Marmon *Wasp* won the first Indianapolis 500, but the Depression closed the local assembly lines. Indianapolis **Racers** (WHA, 1974–78) were the **Pacers'** rhyming housemates. Then came minor league hockey's Indianapolis **Checkers** (1979–88), who referenced both the 500's checkered flag and an obstructing hockey move. Indy's female footballers were the Indiana **Speed** (2002–10). In 1924 the **Cardinal and Grey Warriors** at the University of Indianapolis became **Grey-hounds**, track dogs that dovetail nicely with the city's other racing sports.

• • •

Chuck Taylor was an Indiana high school basketball star who later joined Akron's Firestone **Non-Skids**, but that wasn't his only rubber interest. In his early 20s, Taylor moved to Chicago to join the **All-Stars**, sponsored by Converse rubber to promote the first real basketball shoe.[19] So famous was their star player and head clinician that "Chuck Taylor" was stamped on all Converse All Stars after 1932 as part of the first high-profile sports endorsement contract.

Athletes at Converse College (Spartanburg, S.C.) couldn't resist becoming Converse **All-Stars**, even though benefactor D.E. Converse (one of the many New England textilers who rushed to the Piedmont after the Civil War) was not connected to the shoe company. Because "**All-Stars**" implied an association between the sneaker brand and the school, Converse athletics had trouble getting other corporate sponsors, so they became the only **Valkyries** in collegiate sports in October 2007. The Valkyries of Old Norse mythology hovered over battles, selected combatants for heroic deaths, and ushered their souls to a heavenly banquet at *Valhalla* ("hall of the slain"), and—like Converse's jocks—the Valkyries of old were an all-female club. Their nickname comes with its own fight song, *Ride of the Valkyries*, from Richard Wagner's cycle of four operas based on Norse sagas. (The costumer for Wagner's Ring Cycle is often singled out for palpably and incorrectly putting horned helmets on Vikings.) It took a few years, but starting in 1861 a few Wagner fans in New York State got their town renamed Valhalla. That sense of Nordicism is deliberately maintained by its Westchester [County] Community College **Vikings**.

Chuck Taylor graduated from Indiana's Columbus North High School in 1919. That was great news for fellow future Hall of Famer Robert "Fuzzy" Vandivier, a sophomore whose Franklin Community High School (twenty-five miles north of Columbus) had struggled for years against Taylor. Now Franklin's **Wonder Five** would take three straight state championships. In 1922, **Wonder Five** coach Ernest "Griz" Wagner stayed in town to coach Fuzzy & Co. at Franklin College. An injury returned Vandivier to coach Franklin High in 1926, which was the year after Griz Wagner's collegian **Baptists** were renamed **Grizzlies**. (The high schoolers became **Grizzly Cubs** shortly thereafter.)

• • •

James Naismith invented basketball in Massachusetts in 1892, but after seeing another state's 1925 high school tournament, he conceded the sport "really had its origins in Indiana." If the anticipation of Friday- and Saturday-night high school games was as intense anywhere else, it would be called "basketball fever." (A charter WNBA team, the Indiana **Fever**, celebrate that ailment.) But in the Hoosier State it's "Hoosier Hysteria."[20]

So this is a good place to define *Hoosier*.

Indianans who crossed the Ohio River to Kentucky to build Louisville's Portland Canal worked for one Samuel Hoosier, and were thus "Hoosier men." Or … *hoosier* is a corruption of a frontier greeting: "Who's here?" Or … you can trust American Heritage co-founder Howard Peckham, who says immigrants from England's Cumberland County gave names to the Cumberland River and Cumberland Gap and applied the Old English word *hoozer* (which describes big things—especially hilly ones) to the backwoods people of the Cumberland Mountains. Whatever the reason, *hoosier* became a frontier fill-in for *hillbilly* and *cracker*,[21] and it has described a person or thing from Indiana for nearly 200 years.

Baseball's Western, National, American, and Federal Leagues all included Indianapolis **Hoosiers** between the 1880s and World War I. Ball State University jocks became **Cardinals** after the state bird in the 1920s, but they'd been the **Hoosieroons** (or **Normals**) before that. The **Hoosiers** familiar to most readers are those at Bloomington's Indiana University.

Golden Shield | Badgers | Rockies | Quakes

Many thoughtful persons have written books on geography, cosmology, and collisional foreland basins that would enthrall the average sports fan. We suggest you go read them because the sweeping generalizations we are set to employ will give any scientist the heebie-jeebies. Athletic **Miners** represent mining towns. **Mounties** have stadiums near mountains. Further detail may be for the super-curious only.

• • •

Unimaginable forces once packed every atom in our observable reality into something the size of a single proton. All that energy let loose 14-billion years ago when a Big Bang recast the space-time experience as a cloudy universe. Hydrogen nuclei then collided and fused into helium atoms that composed the cores of stars like our five-billion-year-old sun. Being too small to suck up everything in its zip code, the sun was orbited by a hydrogen-helium "protoplanetary disk." Gravitational coagulation within that cosmic goop produced spheres that might have grown large enough to produce light through nuclear fusion—the definition of a star—but instead those gas giants (Jupiter, Saturn, Uranus, and Neptune) simply reflect sunlight.

A rocky little ball o' fire like the infant Earth couldn't even aspire to such a grand failure. About four-billion years ago, its dense iron and nickel started to gravitate toward the core while lighter silicates floated outward, cooled, and hardened into a crust. Magma seepage and volcanic activity broke that crust into surface pieces—"plates"—that continue to slide over, crash into, and grind against each another.

A good place to find Earth's exposed metamorphic and igneous crust is at mid-plate, where time has afforded the most dramatic surface erosion. Geologists call such large expanses of rock a continental shield. The oldest Earth rocks ever found are along Hudson Bay's shore, which is part of the Precambrian Shield, a shield running from the Great Lakes and St. Lawrence River basins to the Arctic Ocean. Cambrian College in Sudbury, Ontario is a deliberate echo of "Precambrian Shield," as is its **Golden Shield** (always singular).

With so much exposed rock around, one might expect the soil on continental shields to be shallow and therefore relatively infertile, but those conditions are conducive to the wide-spreading root systems of slow-growing coniferous trees. Such boreal (northern) ecosystems support a variety of amphibians and reptiles. *Les Vipères* at *Collège Boréal* (also in Sudbury) refer to Ontario's only venomous viper, the eastern massasauga rattlesnake (*Sistrurus catenatus catenatus*).

One of Toronto's first sports fraternities was the Granite Curling Club (est. 1836), named after the many Ontario rock faces carved up during glacial retreat. (Also, the granite curling stone is a "rock.") The Granite Club's ice-**Granites** played in Toronto's first hockey match in 1889, then won gold for Canada at the 1924 Olympics. Lacrosse's Toronto **Rock** (est. 1999) play in the NLL.

• • •

Random plate movements occasionally bring Earth's landmasses into a single supercontinent, one subsequently separated by the rifting between plates. Today's dispersed continents indicate the middle of one such supercontinent cycle. The last supercontinent was Pangaea, which started smashing together 500 million years ago. Orogenic collisions 300 million years ago finished making central Pangaea's Appalachian chain. (*Orogeny*—"mountain building" in Greek—describes the folding and faulting of the Earth crust.) The northernmost Appalachians would once have rivaled today's Himalayas or Alps, but they were ripped into Atlantic Canada's rocky coast by glaciers. In fact, Newfoundland is called "The Rock," as is its St. John's **Atlantic Rock** of rugby. *Caput* is Latin for head, so the word *cape* describes a coastal headland. Cape Breton is the headland of its namesake Nova Scotia island (which is another detached piece of the northern Appalachians), so Sydney's Cape Breton University keeps **Capers**.

South America's super slo-mo slam into the future southern states came near the end of Pangaea's consolidation. That Ouachita Orogeny lifted the seafloor that's now the Gulf Coastal Plain and folded up both the Ouachita Mountains and the Ozark Plateau. The plateau's topography owes largely to subsequent erosion. You get clear views of the southern Ozarks in northeastern Oklahoma's Rogers County, especially at Claremore, where one erosionally resistant feature became "College Hill" after a preparatory school opened there in 1909. Owing to some fundraising by citizens called Hilltoppers, Rogers State University got **Hillcats**.[1] Wilburton's Eastern Oklahoma State College **Mountaineers** sit among the western Ouachitas. (EOSC is a former school of mines in coal country, which fielded **Miners** until 1927.)

Pangaea started busting up about 200 million years ago, when the Mid-Atlantic Ridge separated the Americas from Eurasia and Africa while a weaker split created the Mississippi valley. The latter is a "failed rift" because it wasn't dramatic enough to make a new ocean, but it did reveal the low-lying Mississippi Embayment, which cuts the Ouachitas off from the rest of the Appalachians. Where the eastern side of the embayment gets bumpy again, we find the Mississippi town of Blue Mountain, the hilltop home of the Blue Mountain College **Toppers**.

Another failed rift of about the same age is the Bay of Fundy between New Brunswick and Nova Scotia. Erosion of the Appalachians filled the wedge-shaped bay with sediments, making for extreme differences between high and low tides. Because the Petitcodiac River could never be deep enough to accommodate the high tide that funnels in from the bay, it experiences a twice daily tidal bore (a wave that charges upstream). At Crandall University (Moncton, N.B.), the river's killer crossover action made a **Blue Tide** of the Baptist school's blue and gold, but they've gone full bore ahead as **Chargers** since 2010.

• • •

The flow of groundwater brine and high heat are associated with plate tectonism. Evaporation in those hydrothermal conditions rearranges the atomic structures of gasses and water into solid crystals called minerals. A crustal region's particular mineralogical yield depends on the temperature, pressure, evaporation speed, and chemistry in the immediate environment.

Orogenic pressure often puts sags in continental crusts that are called foreland basins. They're usually parallel to new mountains, and the Ouachita Orogeny made one such basin in southeast Missouri. As French miners discovered after 1700, the area's ore yields goodly amounts of mineral lead. In fact, the lead-zinc deposits in the "Lead State" define what geologists call Mississippi Valley-type (MVT) ore deposits. In 1870 the University of Missouri School of Mines and Metallurgy opened at Rolla, a land-grant college now called the Missouri University of Science and Technology, where **Miners** dig in. Across the Mississippi from Missouri is Tennessee, where MVT minerals and building stones have long been jacked from the countryside, but the only diamonds there have bases on the corners; the Jackson **Generals** are the renamed West Tennessee **Diamond Jaxx** (1998–2010).

Way upriver from Missouri are the MVT deposits of the Upper Mississippi Valley Lead-Zinc District, where Wisconsin lead miners of the 1820s hunkered down for the winter in sod-covered hillside huts, or "badger holes." That comparison to the burrowing American badger (*Taxidea taxus jacksoni*) gave the "Badger State" a nickname and put **Badgers** at the University of Wisconsin–Madison. Following the parent school, UW-Green Bay fielded **Bay Badgers** until students voted in 1970 to be represented by the **Phoenix**, an arbitrary choice from mythology (p. 174). A two-year institution is UW-Sheboygan, whereat **Wombats** remember that members of the *Vombatidae* family are often "Australian badgers." For a spell, the NFL had its own Milwaukee **Badgers** (1922–26).

Iron isn't a mineral. It's a chemical element, which comprises only one kind of atom: iron. For our purpose, though, iron is mined like minerals or ores. About two-billion years ago, the not-yet-dug Great Lakes were under a shallow sea into which iron was injected by hydrothermal vents. The Marquette Iron Range is on Michigan's Upper Peninsula, where "Marquette **Iron Rangers**" recur in junior hockey. Northeastern Minnesota's Iron Range hosts the **Ironmen** and **Ironwomen** of Vermillion Community College in Ely. Even here, when regional geology so well informs the identity, there is a sports history. Vermillion's footballers won their conference in 1940 with a roster of only fourteen "men of iron," most having played all downs on both sides of the ball.[2]

• • •

Pangaea's pieces were well into their diaspora 70 million years ago when the Pacific Plate started sliding under North America. (Relatively light landmasses ride up on the denser oceanic plates if e'er the two should meet.) Events like this Laramide Orogeny usually create mountains near the fault zone, but geologists speculate that the Pacific Plate must have a shallow subduction angle to put the Rockies so much farther east than expected. Denver and Colorado Springs are in foothills called the Colorado Front Range, but the Rockies provide spectacular backdrops. Denver had Colorado **Rockies** (1976–82) in the NHL and got same-named hardballers in the 1993 MLB expansion.[3] Moving into the hills, you'll find Western State Colorado University in Gunnison, where **Mountaineers** remember the fur trappers of the 1800s.

The newer Rockies have yet to erode like the ancient Appalachians. In fact, they're still being pushed skyward by the Pacific Plate. Regional extremes of slope, altitude, and dryness make avalanches far more common here than in the east. Failing to regain their financial footing after the lockout-shortened 1994/95 season, the NHL's Quebec **Nordiques** slid west to become Denver's Colorado **Avalanche**.

• • •

Still skating over the Pacific Plate some 40 million years ago, North America raked up a heap of seafloor sediments and left them on the west coast. Two-million years ago, glaciers started carving that pile into the peaks of the Olympic Peninsula's Olympic Mountain Range. Water in the basalt ocean plate boiled as it slid down into the hot mantle, pressure that (over the last few million years) blew holes through the surface where the plates overlap (the subduction zone). The volcanoes from northern California to the Canadian border are called the High Cascades. That includes Mt. Hood, a stratovolcano easily seen from fifty miles away at Keizer, Oregon. The Salem-Keizer **Volcanoes** (est. 1997) play minor league ball there.

The Cascade Volcanic Arc is a piece of the Ring of Fire that runs around the rim of the Pacific Plate. The Ring goes due north from Mt. Hood to Mt. Rainier, the tallest volcano in the lower forty-eight states. The PCL's Seattle **Rainiers** (1938–64) were owned by Emil Sick's Rainier Brewing Company. It was British captain George Vancouver who named the volcano after Adm. Peter Rainier in 1792, but there's evidence the Coast Salish always called it (something like) *Tacoma*, so the PCL's 1995-named Tacoma **Rainiers** have a somewhat redundant name.

The area north of Rainer is a pivot foot for hundreds of millions of years of continental bumping and grinding. This mostly non-volcanic region—the North Cascades—is a heap of sediments, seafloor, crust, and mantle, but the occasional stratovolcano like Mt. Baker does pop up. Abbotsford, B.C. gets a great view of Baker's cone, putting **Cascades** at its University of the Fraser Valley.

The volcanic arc continues northwest through Vancouver. Outside town are the magma cores of long-eroded volcanoes that British settlers thought resembled the lion couchant from heraldry. "The Lions" gave name to both minor league hockey's Vancouver **Lions** (1928–41) and today's CFL BC **Lions** (est. 1954).

The Olympic and Cascade Ranges also explain the WTT Sea-Port (Seattle-Portland) **Cascades** (1977–78), the minor league hockey Seattle **Olympics** (1940/41), the Continental Football League's Seattle **Rangers** (1967–69), and the Tacoma-Seattle **Majestics** of women's football (est. 2002).

As all this science suggests, most volcanoes are near plate boundaries, but some are randomly distributed at mid-plate for reasons geologists argue about. That puts Hawaii's volcanoes far within the Pacific Ring of Fire. Only on its remote slopes do botanists find the *Argyroxiphium sandwicense*, or Hawaiian silversword fern. Mature silverswords can have six-foot stalks with hundreds of blossoms. (They weren't endangered until the introduction of hungry goats and sheep in the 1700s.) Honolulu's Chaminade University stands behind athletic **Silverswords**.

The Columbia River makes up much of the border between Washington and Oregon. Downstream from Portland, a hundred-mile gorge was carved when the river tried to stay at sea level while the rest of the greater Cascade region was lifted. Only a good ship's pilot should navigate there, which explains **Pilots** at the University of Portland. Washington's AL Seattle **Pilots** (1969) referred to tricky sailing in the glacier-carved Puget Sound. Their emblem was a ship's wheel, but the **Pilots** also fit with Seattle's Boeing aircraft company (p. 275).

The **Pilots** played in the **Rainiers**' Sick Stadium while a dome was being planned for them, but ground wasn't broken until 1972, two years after the **Pilots** were shipped out to Milwaukee as **Brewers** by Wisconsin car dealer Bud Selig. The tax dollars that had been dumped into the Kingdome anchored Seattle's lawsuit against the AL, which gained the city an expansion franchise in 1977. They're Seattle **Mariners** for the same seafaring reasons that had made their predecessors **Pilots**.[4]

From Seattle you can sail north to the former Malaspina College (Nanaimo, B.C.). The school, its *Navigator* newspaper, and **Mariner** teams were all named for an Italian sailing for Spain, Allessandro Malaspina, who docked at Vancouver Island in 1791 while looking for the western end of the Northwest Passage. Blue Thunder is the alligator-navigator mascot that still accompanies **Mariners** at the institution that was renamed Vancouver Island University in 2008.

• • •

The last geological events to reconfigure our landscapes were the retreats of great glaciers, the most recent of which was the Laurentide Ice Sheet. At its glacial maximum, it blanketed most of Canada and the northern U.S. with the last retreat beginning only 20,000 years ago. The area south of the Great Lakes was shaved down to open space to which French voyageurs applied their word for a grazing meadow, *les prairie*. In 1977 the Prairie State got **Prairie Stars** at its University of Illinois Springfield.

Continuing north, glaciers dug potholes that filled with meltwater, the biggest being the Great Lakes. Alpena, Michigan on Lake Huron (at the heart of a glacial outwash plain) hosts junior hockey's Alpena **IceDiggers** (est. 2001).[5]

Glaciers shaped some seriously hard rock into beautiful landforms like Puget Sound, an ocean inlet between the Olympic Peninsula and the Cascades. The NASL Seattle **Sounders** (1974–83) and USL Seattle **Sounders** (1994–2008) were followed by a new MLS franchise in 2009, one that got a familiar sound from a fan poll: Seattle **Sounders**.

A glacial dam blocked the north-flowing Monongahela River and filled a large basin that's now drained by several streams, the easternmost of which runs along western Maryland as the Youghiogheny River. Deep Creek Lake (like all Maryland lakes) is artificial, filled behind a hydroelectric dam built on the "Yawk" in 1925. The Garrett College **Lakers** (McHenry, Md.) are waterside.

The Wabash River watershed formed to drain the last glaciers. Dams on the Little Wabash filled in some valleys to create Illinois's Lake Paradise and Lake Mattoon, which are barely west of Lake Land College's **Lakers** (in Mattoon). The Little Blue River also drained glacial till. Damming it created metropolitan Kansas City's Longview Lake, next to the **Lakers** of Metropolitan Community College–Longview.

• • •

Long Island is part of an archipelago that includes Block Island, Martha's Vineyard, Nantucket, and Cape Cod ..."Outer Lands" that indicate the Laurentide Ice Sheet's terminal moraine (a bulldozed pile of sand that shows a glacier's farthest advance). The NHL's New York **Islanders** were put in Long Island's Nassau Coliseum in 1972 to crowd any potential WHA team out of the New York media market.[6] The invading New York **Raiders** did play the inaugural WHA season as tenants of the **Rangers** at Madison Square Garden, but an unsurprisingly high rent was among several financial problems and the team owners turned over the franchise to the league by midseason.

They didn't have better luck as New York **Golden Blades**, failing to skate all the way through the 1973/74 season in white boots with gold blades. By January they were Cherry Hill's New Jersey **Knights**. New Jerseyans might have found them suspiciously similar to the **Scarlet Knights** at Rutgers, but it may have simply been the case that a supplier was willing to cheaply dump jerseys that happened to say "**Knights**" on them.[7]

• • •

Like volcanoes, earthquakes remind us that the Earth is still evolving. The Pacific Plate is trying to snap northward along the San Andreas Fault, but it's being checked for now by the continental plate. Seismologists believe a major release is overdue by at least decades, and when the Big One hits California, the destruction will be like nothing the modern world has seen.

The NASL San Jose **Earthquakes** (1974–82) became the Western Soccer Alliance's Golden Bay **Earthquakes** (1983–84). After the 1999 season, the arbitrarily named MLS San Jose **Clash** (est. 1996) got new owners who revived "San Jose **Earthquakes**." In 2005 those '**Quakes** moved to Houston as the **Dynamo** (an energy reference) because the MLS had reserved both the old name and the attending franchise records for future San Jose **Earthquakes**, who did in fact take the field in 2008.

Los Angeles's sedimentary basin can amplify seismic waves that are miles off shore. Female semi-pro footballers in L.A. County are the California **Quake** (est. 2001), and players on the Long Beach **Aftershock** (est. 2003) came mostly from the **Quake**. The irony is that aftershocks usually follow earthquakes, but the **Quake** rumbles on while the '**Shock** faded in 2005. Since 1993 the California League's Rancho Cucamonga **Quakes** have played on a diamond east of L.A. called the Epicenter. They have a ready-to-rumble mascot called Tremor the Ralleysaurus. He wears number 4.8, the highest reading on the Richter scale before significant infrastructure damage is likely.

Oilers | Flames | Raptors | Mastodons

For millennia humans used unprocessed oil for such crude purposes as lighting torches and waterproofing boats. After refiners of the mid-1800s figured out how to extract an efficient lamp fuel—kerosene—the oil biz became highly profitable. The frontier method of soaking up oil from springs with blankets was inefficient, so Edwin Drake used a steam-powered drill to pioneer modern production in 1859 near Titusville, Pennsylvania. Drake's oil was pumped up to the surface with methods adapted from rock salt harvesting.

In the subsequent Quaker State oil rush, derricks popped up all over Pennsylvania, West Virginia, and Ohio. In an oil and gas boom at Findlay, Ohio in the late 1880s, the oil outlasted the gas, giving **Oilers** to the University of Findlay.[1] Ohio Valley oil fields would soon be surpassed by strikes farther west, owing to how hydrocarbon fuels form and where they are found.

• • •

Sediments—sand, silt, clay, and pebbles—are moved around by water, wind, and glaciers, usually settling on flood plains or at the bottoms of lakes and shallow seas. When those waters recede, sediment-covered plants bio-degrade, releasing hydrogen and oxygen to create carbon-rich goo called peat. Peat then experiences millions of years of oxygen deprivation, heat from the earth's interior, and the weight of surface sediments, all of which cook it into fossil fuels: petroleum (crude oil), coal, and natural gas. Coal seams of the "Pennsylvanian" geological period (320–286 million years ago) were once the bottoms of coastal swamps in states already mentioned.

The Great Plains region is a huge sedimentary basin. It's the former bottom of the shallow Western Interior Seaway, which started forming about 170 million years ago when the collision of the Pacific and North American Plates lifted the Rockies and depressed the continent's center, allowing the Arctic Ocean and Hudson's Bay to drain south and join the advancing Gulf of Mexico.

During the Laramide Orogeny (70–40 million years ago), the seaway was lifted and drained, with hot magma moving closer to the surface. Boiling water in the drying sediments created volcanic explosions still indicated by weathered cones all over Central Texas, especially near the 300-mile Balcones Fault Zone from Del Rio to Waco. It goes right through Austin, where one cone supports St. Edward's University and its **Hilltoppers**. Subsequent seismic activity (20 million years ago) along the BFZ jacked up former limestone seafloors to create the rest of Texas Hill Country. In the heart of those irregular hills are the Schreiner University **Mountaineers** in Kerrville.

Oil lies under the plains from coastal Texas to Canada's prairies. Accounting for minor leaguers, "**Oilers**" is among the most common team names. Its natural derivatives (**Drillers, Roughnecks, Boomers, Exporters, Millionaires**) are so common near oil fields that even a short list would bore the reader. We'll largely restrict discussion to the best-known such teams, which are unsurprisingly in oil towns on the former Western Interior Seaway.

In 1884 a crew searching for water to supply the growing Texas cotton town of Corsicana accidentally struck oil at what became the first commercially viable field west of the Mississippi. When Navarro College started there in 1946, an informal gathering of teachers and students almost made teams **Drillers**, but the less esoteric "**Bulldogs**" was chosen instead.[2]

An 1892 oil strike at the Norman No. 1 well in southeastern Kansas launched a rush on the Mid-Continent Field (Kansas, Oklahoma, and Texas). One well at Spindletop Field near Beaumont Texas became the world's first "gusher" in 1901, yielding 100,000 barrels a day when the average was 6,000.[3] That dropped oil prices down to almost nothing, but gave the U.S. an abundant resource to drive industrial and automotive production. Beaumont's minor league hockey players were Texas **Wildcatters** (2003–08) because "wildcatter" describes crews that drill randomly hoping to strike it rich.

John G. Hardin got rich leasing Texas fields to drillers in 1918. During the Depression, he and wife Mary funded several Baptist educational institutions in Texas. The Hardin Administration Building is at Abilene Christian University, a school the Hardins kept afloat.[4] ACC's **Wildcats** echo of the Texas wildcatters, but the nickname was an arbitrary choice in 1919.

West of Beaumont is Houston. Already a major cotton port, Houston was exporting loads of oil after Spindletop. Bud Adams, the son of the guy who succeeded Frank Phillips as the head of Phillips 66, bought into the inaugural 1960 AFL with his new Houston **Oilers**. (They're now the NFL Tennessee **Titans**, but they were Tennessee **Oilers** during two spillover seasons, 1997 and '98.)

The Mid-Continent Field in western Texas and southeastern New Mexico is called the Permian Basin, a former undersea shelf on Pangaea's coast. **Falcons** at Odessa's University of Texas of the Permian Basin were arbitrarily named, but Continental Football League players based at Odessa and Midland more accurately reflected the sedimentary basin's oil industry as the West Texas **Rufneks** (1965–69), followed by indoor football's Odessa/West Texas **Roughnecks** (est. 2003). The word "roughneck" usually describes oil drillers (although it can refer to any semi-skilled laborer). Another name for a rig worker is "gorilla," which supported the consonance of hockey's minor league Amarillo **Gorillas** (2002–10) of the Texas Panhandle. At the east end of the Mid-Continent Field is Pittsburg [Kan.] State University and the only **Gorillas** in college sports.[5]

Indoor football's Oklahoma **Crude** (2002–04) at Enid took their name from Columbia Pictures' *Oklahoma Crude* (1973), in which wildcatters stood up to the big drilling companies. Four Oklahoma minor league hockey teams since 1928 have been Tulsa **Oilers**, often "**Ice Oilers**." Minor league hardball's Tulsa **Oilers** (1905–76) were followed immediately by Tulsa **Drillers** (est. 1977). The derrick emblem for the AHL Oklahoma City **Barons** (est. 2010) concedes that they're oil barons in the Edmonton **Oilers** system.

• • •

Like many Canadian plains, northeastern Alberta's oil sands contain loads of untapped crude. Those prairies were exploited in a post–World War II boom, as evinced by junior Edmonton **Oil Kings** (1951–76). Bill Hunter, the **O.K.s'** GM, left to build a charter WHA franchise onto which he grafted "Alberta **Oilers**," identified by province because they had home ice in both Calgary and Edmonton.[6] By season two they were Edmonton **Oilers** and remained so after the 1979 merger of the WHA and NHL. (The NHL **Oilers** relaunched junior Edmonton **Oil Kings** in 2006.) An old HBC post among the northern oil sands hosts junior hockey's Fort McMurray **Oil Barons** (est. 1981).

Calgarians of the late 1970s wanted both a new arena and the 1988 Winter Olympics. They thought getting a major sports team might secure both. Indeed, the NHL's financially strapped Atlanta **Flames** relocated to Calgary's Stampede Corral in 1980, remaining **Flames** because petroleum is highly flammable. (Also, oil fields are dotted with flares that burn off casing head gasses.) In fact, "Calgary **Flames**" was a perfect lure for the Olympic torch, as the city was awarded the games in 1981. The Saddledome that opened in '83 was the **Flames**' home ice and the major indoor Olympic venue. Calgary's Olympic Oval houses 400-meter speed skating lanes, large enough to encircle the hockey rink that hosted a very successful senior women's team, the Calgary **Oval X-treme** (1995–2005).

Independent baseball's Edmonton **Cracker-Cats** (est. 2005) referred to a catalytic cracker, a reactor in which a catalyst induces a chemical reaction to convert heavy oils with high boiling points into efficiently burning fuels. (The Alberta capital's **C-Cats** became **Capitals** in 2009.) The list of teams named for Alberta's energy boom include the NASL Edmonton **Drillers** (1979–82), NASL Calgary **Boomers** (1981), NLL Calgary **Roughnecks** (est. 2001), and NLL Edmonton **Rush** (est. 2006).

• • •

Creatures that aspire toward an exhibition hall afterlife do well to get buried by floods or landslides immediately after death, protecting them from scavengers and decomposition. The hard bits (bones, teeth, claws, etc.) can be mineralized, the process of turning into fossils. Earth has hosted an enormous variety of creatures, but we're usually aware of only those that dropped dead in sedimentary basins. That means you'd look in the same places for animal fossils and fossil fuels.

Paleontologists have found many important fossils across Alberta, especially during the Great Canadian Dinosaur Rush (1910–17). The University of Calgary **Dinos** are abbreviated from the **Dinosaurs** it kept until 1998.[7] The Dinosaur Valley is eighty-five miles to the northeast. In its town of Drumheller is the Royal Tyrrell Museum of Paleontology and an eighty-six-foot T-rex observation deck, reptilian influences for junior hockey's Drumheller **Dragons** (est. 2003).

Utah was on the western shore of the Western Interior Seaway. It's where the huge dromaeosaurid (raptor) *Utahraptor ostrommaysorum* was pieced together in the early 1990s. A bunch of Utah's dinosaur-themed attractions are in Ogden, like the Pioneer League's Ogden **Raptors**. Raptor-mania was peaking just when those **Raptors** were named in '94; a groundbreaking 3D version of the Utahraptor's clever and vicious *Velociraptor* cousin had just had fame thrust upon her the 1993 blockbuster *Jurassic Park*.

A name-the-team contest would also soon put Toronto **Raptors** into the 1995 NBA. Unlike your stegosaurus, your T-rex, or your triceratops, the velociraptor had never previously been among the first-team dinosaurs, so it was undoubtedly momentum from *Jurassic Park* that advanced the syllabic bookending of the

TOR-onto rap-TOR. (In terms of regional relevance, the exposed bedrock of the Canadian Shield yields few ancient animal remains.)

The *Jurassic Park* of the megaplex followed Michael Crichton's same-named 1990 novel in suggesting that dinosaurs and birds have linked evolutionary histories, ideas advanced in the 1960s by paleontologist John Ostrom (the afore-mentioned *U. ostrommaysorum's* eponym). In fact, talons on carnivorous birds are so similar to those of dromaeosaurids that winged hunters were raptors first; clawed dinosaurs were called raptors only later. The Latin *rapere* means to seize and carry away, exactly describing the technique of birds of prey (exemplified by American University's **Eagle**, "Clawed"). Bard College's **Raptors** (Annandale, N.Y.) and Rutgers-Camden's **Scarlet Raptors** use hunting bird emblems. The three campuses of Montgomery [County] College in Maryland combined their **Falcons** (MC-Takoma Park), **Gryphons** (MC-Germantown), and **Knights** (MC-Rockville) as more general **Raptors** in 2012.

Hawk is from the Old English word *hafoc*, which—like *rapere*—means seize or grab. (Refer to Lehigh's **Mountain Hawk** "Clutch.") Hunting hawks, there-fore, include the Hunter **Hawks** from New York City's Hunter College. When switching from **Raiders** for **Redhawks** in mid-2012, Roberts Wesleyan College (Chili, N.Y.) noted that the concept of grasping was "a profoundly meaningful concept for an education institution."[8]

• • •

The Colorado Plateau was lifted over the last tens of millions of years by plate activity and pressure from interior magma, but it too was once the Seaway's bot-tom. The Colorado River starts in its namesake state's Rockies and flows south-west on the plateau. The riverbed is not eroded consistently along its course, and when water tumbles over rocks it picks up speed creating turbulence we call rapids. Indeed, the MLS Colorado **Rapids** (est. 1996) are at Denver (even though the Colorado's really big "holes" are hundreds of miles downstream in Arizona's Grand Canyon).

Columbian mammoths once ranged from Alaska to Mexico. Many left their remains on the Colorado Plateau, giving an impressive fossil collection to Den-ver's Museum of Nature and Science. One of the museum's *Mammuthus columbi* skulls was the backdrop for the press conference that announced the relocation of the Washington **Power** (p. 296) to Denver as the Colorado **Mammoth** (singular) in 2003.

M. columbi's slightly smaller cousin was the American mastodon (*Mammut americanum*). Recognized by a sloping forehead, its name refers to cone-shaped teeth (*mastodon* in Greek) that could chew a variety of plant life. There've been hundreds of mastodon finds in the American heartland, and many Midwestern museums display fossil skeletons. The one encased at Indiana University–Purdue University Fort Wayne was excavated from a nearby farm by students in 1968. Two years later, IPFW teams became **Mastodons**, usually "**Dons**." The mascot for the Wheaton [Ill.] College **Thunder** is a thundering mastodon because its science center's specimen was excavated by the geology department in 1963.

Paleontologists don't fully understand the mass extinction of North American mammoths, mastodons, and other large mammals at the end of the last ice age.

Maybe they were killed by human hunters arriving from Eurasia. Human disease or climate change could have thinned their numbers. Or other species might have arrived with the humans and competed for food. That latter theory may explain the extinction of the stag-moose (*Cervalces scotti*) just after its slightly smaller cousin the true moose (*Alces alces*) showed up. In fact, the name of the ambitious herbivore and largest member of the deer family (which Europeans call elk) is from the Algonquian forms *moz*, *muz*, or *moos* … meaning anything from "twig eater" to "bark stripper." Today, *A. alces* has healthy numbers in northern New England and eastern Canada and from Colorado's Rockies to Alaska. The University of Maine at Augusta keeps **Moose**, and Winnipeg's minor league Manitoba **Moose** (1996–2011) had already been St. Paul's Minnesota **Moose** (1994–96).

• • •

Tectonic twisting and stretching in southern California over millions of years created the Los Angeles Basin, an undersea bowl that collected sediments and microorganisms before being raised out of the Pacific by seismic activity some five-million years ago. Local wells were gushing by the late 1880s, and the 1892 discovery of the city oil field (around today's Dodger Stadium) made it the world's leading oil port after World War I. That overlooked history was drilled home by West Los Angeles College's **Hustling Oilers**, but in 2008 they became **Wildcats**.

Mexico's government approved an 1828 land grant for a ranch near some of the L.A. Basin's larger oil seeps. Sites like that *Rancho la Brea* (ranch of the tar) are predator traps. When animals get bogged down, their imminent demise attracts an array of predators. Those scavengers get stuck, attracting even larger hunters. So the La Brea Tar Pit is a goldmine of fossils, including many examples of *Smilodon fatalis*, the saber-toothed cat. California's official state fossil was the mascot for Arena Football's San Jose **SaberCats** (1995–2008).

Tennessee's Nashville Basin has yielded exactly one instance of *S. fatalis*, but at 10,000 years old, it's younger than any of La Brea's 2,000 fanged cats. In 1971 its cave was discovered during construction in Nashville, a half-mile north of today's NHL Nashville **Predators** (est. 1998). (*Gnash* is Nashville's saber-tooth–grinding mascot.) The basin's modest oil history allowed Nashville's Tennessee **Titans** to remain **Oilers** for two NFL seasons after leaving Houston. The high ground around the Nashville Basin is the Highland Rim. Its northern rim loops into Kentucky as the Pennyroyal Plateau. Bowling Green is atop one rolling hill ("The Hill"), so its Western Kentucky University rolls with **Hilltoppers** and **Lady Toppers**.[9]

Barons | Bankers | Steelers | Vulcans

Fifteen-year-old John D. Rockefeller dropped out of his Cleveland high school in 1855, but not for lack of ambition. He was soon enrolled in a ten-week bookkeeping course at a local commercial college later absorbed by Chancellor University. Other attendees would include rubber king Harvey Firestone and accountant Theodore Ernst (of Ernst & Young). Those three "titans of commerce" were recalled by **Titans** until CU closed in 2013.[1] (Until 2008 the school had been Myers University, with alliterative **Mustangs**.)

In the post-1859 Pennsylvania oil rush, Rockefeller let wildcatters chase the oil while he bought up and consolidated refineries and secured exclusive contracts with railroads in Pittsburgh and Cleveland. When incorporated at Cleveland in 1870, Rockefeller's Standard Oil Company controlled one tenth of America's supply. In the 1872 "Cleveland Massacre," Standard men pressured twenty-two more Ohio competitors into selling out over just a few weeks, and Rockefeller was refining 90 percent of the country's oil within that decade. Those moves put J.D.R. at the top any list of "robber barons," the notorious industrialists who mercilessly sought competitive advantage in the late nineteenth century. He inspired the Cleveland **Barons** in the NHL (1976–78) and AHL (1936–72, 2001–06).

Standard Oil acquired Charles Pratt's successful Brooklyn kerosene refinery in 1874. Before running that operation, Pratt had been in the whale oil biz. (It took a few greedy oil barons to inadvertently save the whales from certain extinction.) Pratt financed a Brooklyn school to address America's booming tech sector in 1887. In 1899 his Pratt Institute was the recipient of a relic of Spanish colonial times, a cannon captured at Havana's Morro Castle a year earlier in the Spanish-American War. It's the insignia for P.I.'s **Cannoneers**.

Rockefeller funded the new University of Chicago, which would combine the qualities of a liberal arts college with those of the great German graduate research institutes. J.D.R. unsurprisingly ran that "best investment I ever made" with his distinctive winner-take-all attitude, by controlling the sector's major assets. The opening-day faculty in 1892 had been built through what Frederick Rudolph called "the greatest mass raid on American college faculties in history."[2] One acquisition was Amos Alonzo Stagg, a former Yale end from Walter Camp's first-ever All-American football team (1889) and the first football coach at the YMCA training school in Massachusetts (now Springfield College). Not long after Yale connections got him to Chicago, Stagg thought its goldenrod colors got dirty too fast, and he didn't want anyone saying his players were yellow. (It was bad enough the occasional nickname was "**Rockerfellerites**.")[3] He secured some reddish-brown uniforms for 1894, quickly making them **Maroons**.[4]

Just five months after U. Chicago opened, an Act of Congress established American University in the nation's capital. It too was intended to meld the best of the German research universities with that of the liberal arts colleges, but the American **Eagles** favor America's bald eagle.

• • •

Removing impurities and excess carbon from iron gets you a material with greatly improved strength, steel. A quick recipe for steel calls for coal, iron ore, crushed limestone, and a blast furnace: [1] Cook the mineral impurities out of the coal to get coke, an efficiently burning fuel. [2] In a preheated blast furnace, mix the coke with limestone and iron ore. [3] Introduce air to the chamber so oxidation can mix the limestone and impurities into unwanted "slag." [4] After releasing the river of molten steel, skim the slag off and discard it. [5] Pour the steel into molds to make girders, train rails, or really hard muffins.[5]

Steel plants are near abundant supplies of raw materials, often at places where good shipping infrastructures exist. Wedged among the Ohio Valley's coal mines, mineral deposits, and rivers, western Pennsylvania is an ideal spot for production. It was to there that William Carnegie moved his family in 1848 after Scotland's giant new factory machines put his four handlooms out of business. In Pittsburgh, son Andrew quickly worked his way from bookkeeper and telegraph operator to become a successful investor in oil and railroads. On an 1872 trip to England, he saw that the mass production of steel was possible with Henry Bessemer's blast furnaces, making skilled workmen redundant. Realizing the new metal would soon replace wrought iron as the material of choice for locomotives, bridges, and tracks for the soon-to-boom railroad industry, Carnegie redirected all investment toward steel.

Andrew became the world's richest man after Federal Steel's John Pierpont Morgan bought Carnegie Steel in 1901. From a banking family already, things had taken off for J.P. when he became a partner in Drexel Morgan & Co. in 1871. It was renamed J.P. Morgan & Co. in 1895, two years after the death of associate Anthony J. Drexel. He'd endowed Philadelphia's Drexel Institute of Art, Science and Industry (renamed Drexel University in 1970). In 1928 its **Engineers**, **Blue & Gold**, and **Drexelites** were replaced by Drexel **Dragons**.[6]

Immediately after the big purchase, J.P. Morgan's right-hand man Elbert Gary merged Federal Steel and Carnegie Steel into the great steel trust, U.S. Steel. By 1908, Gary was the first president of the American Iron and Steel Institute, the industry's PR and strategy-development organization. In 1962 the AISI talked the Pittsburgh **Steelers** into slapping the organization's emblem onto their helmets (on just one side, the only such case in the NFL). The three hypocycloids in the Steelmark are yellow for coal, orange for iron ore, and blue for steel. The **Steelers** are the athletes that are best identified with their iron-working city, but they'd been the **Pirates** from 1933 to '39 while renting Forbes Field from like-named hardballers.[7]

A couple of years after forming U.S. Steel, Elbert Gary opened a Lake Michigan ore-shipping center. Gary, Indiana's baseball park is U.S. Steel Yard, home of the 2001-founded Northern League's SouthShore **RailCats** (a half-mile walk from the steel rails of the city's huge lakeside railyard). Blast furnaces in Gary gave a **Blast** to its Indiana University Northwest. IUN upgraded its athletic facilities in 1999 and decided then to avoid taunts that the **Blast** would forever "b-last." Learning that red-tailed hawks were predators at the nearby Indiana Dunes National Lakeshore, the crimson-and-cream **Blast** became **Redhawks**.[8]

Minor league basketball's Gary **Steelheads** (2000–08) don't recall steel history, but we'd bet they're happy for the coincidence. Their emblem and their tag line—*Get hooked!*—associate them with the steelhead rainbow trout (*Oncorhynchus mykiss*). You'll find steelhead fish and **Steelhead** teams from the Great Lakes to the Pacific.[9]

• • •

After decades of typical robber baronism, Andrew Carnegie threw money at thousands of charities and public buildings bearing his name (often libraries). The year before he sold out to Morgan, he founded a vocational school. Carnegie Institute of Technology footballers coached by Walter Steffen became **Tartans** in the early 1930s, named for Clan Carnegie's Highland roots.[10]

In 1924, Carnegie Tech had traveled north to trounce Thiel College's **Huskies** (Greenville, Pa.), 22-0. Steffen nonetheless complimented Thomas Holleran's boys for fighting like wildcats. A newspaper made that "Tom's cats," which evolved into "**Tomcats**" to complement Thiel's initials.[11]

The heirs of Pittsburgh banker and Gulf Oil founder William L. Mellon were later patrons of the Carnegie Institute of Technology, establishing a separate Mellon Institute on campus. A merger effected Carnegie Mellon University in 1967, but the Mellon family's own Scots-Irish roots justified keeping **Tartans**.

Ottawan Arthur Sixsmith was the personal secretary of banker (and future U.S. Treasury Secretary) Andrew W. Mellon, who was W.L. Mellon's mentoring uncle. Sixsmith played amateur hockey in the Banker's League, from which the Pittsburgh **Bankers** were assembled. The **Bankers** later were successful in their sport's first openly semi-pro circuit, the Western Pennsylvania Hockey League (1901–04), with "**Bankers**" representing a willingness to pay players. Almost all WPHL players were from Canada, where hockey was too cherished to transcend its amateurism. But the WPHL (and its successor, the all-pro IPHL,[12] 1904–07) forced the creation of Canada's first pro leagues, many teams in which were called simply **Pros** or **Professionals**.[13]

• • •

In 1900, Carnegie alone had produced more steel than all of Britain's Bessemers. Still, Pittsburgh was the "Birmingham of America," a reference to England's "workshop of the world." Near Alabama's iron and coal deposits, an actual Birmingham was founded as a post–Civil War industrial center and railroad hub. "Birmingham: The Birmingham of America" lacked shrewdness, so it is instead called the "Pittsburgh of the South."

Birmingham's rich industrialists gave a name to several baseball **Barons**, including **Coal Barons** (1880s), **Black Barons** (1920–60), and **Barons** (1981–). Basketball's Birmingham **Steelers** (1947–49), baseball's Birmingham **Ironmakers** (1887), and indoor football's Birmingham **Steeldogs** (2000–07) were minor leaguers. The Birmingham **Steel Magnolias** played women's football (2002/03), reminding us that "steel magnolias" are the feminine but strong Southern women revered as the backbones of family and social institutions.

Birmingham's rapid industrial rise made it the "Magic City," and some locals magically went poof after one season. For example, the 1982 Alabama **Magic** were Birminghamians in the short-lived American Football Association. In the

2005/06 hoop season, the city had both D-League Magic City **Court Kings** and ABA Birmingham **Magicians**.

B-ham hosts football's annual Magic City Classic, half way between intrastate participants from Normal (Alabama A&M University's **Bulldogs**) and Montgomery (Alabama State's **Hornets**). The first Classic was in 1924, but since 1892 Birmingham's mineral-rich reddish-brown hills had already been the neutral backdrop for the Iron Bowl, an annual gridiron test between the University of Alabama–Tuscaloosa and Auburn. 'Bama's early football teams were the **Crimson White** or the **Thin Red Line**. In the 1907 Iron Bowl they played Auburn's heavily favored **Tigers** to a 6-6 tie in a driving rain. Writing for the *Birmingham Age-Herald*, Hugh Roberts covered every game in town and he called Alabama the **Crimson Tide** for being awash in rust-colored mud that day.[14]

• • •

Auburn and Alabama argued over expenses from that 1907 Iron Bowl and didn't play each other for forty-one years. (The schools now alternately host the IB at home.) Birmingham didn't go without championship football for all that time, though; it hosted New Year's Day's Vulcan Bowl (1940–49, 1952), the HBCU title game.

So who's Vulcan? The Roman god of forge, fire, and volcanoes had his smith shop under Sicily's volcanic Mt. Etna. **Vulcans** appear regularly near volcanoes, as is the case at the University of Hawaii at Hilo, but the nickname lives longer and prospers in steel towns, where it takes little imagination to compare volcanism to erupting Bessemers and rivers of molten product.

California—a town south of Pittsburgh—hosts the California University of Pennsylvania **Vulcans**. Back in the Pittsburgh of the South, Vulcan is Birmingham's civic mascot, guarding the city as the world's largest cast-metal statue atop Red Mountain. The Birmingham **Vulcans** had the best record until their WFL went dormant half way through the 1975 season. (They'd replaced the WFL's only crowned champions, the 1974-only Birmingham **Americans**, whose name differentiated them from the Birmingham in England.)

The emblem for the XFL's Birmingham **Thunderbolts** (2001) flashed the thunderbolt weapons that Vulcan forged for the god Jupiter. Those 'bolts turned up again to represent amateur women on basketball's Birmingham **Power** (2001–05). You'd think the University of Alabama at Birmingham's **Blazers** fit that motif, but they were actually named when intercollegiate competition began in 1978 to *blaze* a new trail in the *Sun* Belt Conference. Some speculate that UAB adopted "**Blazers**" because Portland's **Trailblazers** had just grabbed the '77 NBA crown. What's more easily verified is that teams at North Lake College (Irving, Texas) are **Blazers** because Hall of Famer Neil Johnston was their coach between his time as a Portland assistant (1972–74) and his death in 1978.

A *maul* or *mall* can be any heavy mallet, perhaps one used to pound the anvil in a steel forge, so the Pittsburgh **Maulers** (1984) were the USFL's first expansion team. Their owner Edward DeBartolo was the world's leading developer of (*ugh!*) shopping *malls*.[15] Back in Alabama, Birmingham's female footballers were the 2001/02 Alabama **Slammers** (although the Alabama slammer is also a cocktail). In fact, Alabama **Slammers** (2003/04) in minor league hockey were represented by a steeler who pounded a maul much like Vulcan's. Alabama also had indoor footballers called Montgomery **Maulers** (2005–06).

• • •

The entire WLAF moved to Europe in 1995, with its Birmingham **Fire** (1991–92) becoming the *Rhein Fire* of Düsseldorf, Germany. *Rhein in Flammen* (Rhine in Flames) is a summer fireworks festival at Rhineside cities. Medieval lords hit up cargo ships for toll after toll on that great river of European commerce back when German lands were still hundreds of tiny political states. The tax regulator was supposed to have been some faraway Holy Roman Emperor, so it was hard for a captain to know which toll takers were on the up-and-up and which were history's original *Raubritter*—"robber barons."

Stanford University dropped its "**Indians**" identity in 1970. Alumni drove a new vote in 1975 to revive the **Indians**, but students elected "**Robber Barons**" instead. Administrators wouldn't abide that slander against their founder Leland Stanford,[16] a railroad magnate, California governor, and U.S. senator, so the "**Cardinal**" was maintained. (See p. 287.) The emblem for the Palo Alto school is a tree because Spanish explorers used *palo alto* (tall tree) to describe California's redwoods. (The university is called "The Farm" because it was cut out of Mr. Stanford's breeding ground for harness horses.)

During America's Progressive Era from the 1890s to the 1920s, social reformers fought for improved working conditions and women's voting rights. Progressive lawyer Louis D. Brandeis famously opposed the robber barons' concentrated economic power and waged a decade-long legal battle to keep J.P. Morgan from monopolizing New England's railroads. The stand that Brandeis took against "bigness" (the trust mentality) interested President Woodrow Wilson, who consulted him on economic reforms. When Wilson nominated him for the Supreme Court in 1916, Brandeis's forward-looking politics (and his Jewish heritage) effected bitter confirmation hearings, but he served on that bench until 1939. He died in 1941, seven years before Jewish persons at Waltham, Massachusetts founded Brandeis University, "a name that stressed its commitment to 'American' rather than 'Jewish' standards of greatness."[17] Court opponents have to face the conviction of the Brandeis **Judges**.

49ers | Claim Jumpers | Argonauts | Swastikas

Samuel F.B. Morse was a successful Hudson River School painter who was also politically active in New York, but real fame followed his 1837 patent for the telegraph, which transmitted coded electrical pulses on copper wire.

Morse enlisted plow salesman Ezra Cornell to bury the first long-distance telegraph line between Washington and Baltimore in 1844. The underground wire failed, so Cornell improved its insulation and ran cables from pole-to-pole, forever changing the American landscape. In 1865 he endowed Cornell University in Ithaca, New York with the profits from his decade-old telegram delivery service, Western Union. Cornell's **Big Red** wear carnelian and white. Either *Carnelian* or *cornelian* can describe flesh-red gemstones, and it's less than coincidental that both resemble Ezra's surname.

Mr. Cornell's Western Union Company had no connection to Western Union College in Le Mars, Iowa, but students there made athletes **Golden Eagles** in 1930 just to get reporters to stop calling them "Western Union **Telegraphers**."[1] (The renamed Westmar University closed in 1997.) Other Iowans attend a Cornell College on "The Hilltop" in Mount Vernon, sometimes mistaken for the (newer) Cornell University on "The Hill" in Ithaca. In fact, Ezra's distant cousin, iron magnate W.W. Cornell, had endowed the Iowa seminary in 1857. Its **Purples** or **Hilltoppers** became **Rams** after a 1949 vote in the *Royal Purple*.[2]

Junior hockey's Brantford **Alexanders** (1978–84) remembered that Alexander Graham Bell's family left Scotland for Ontario in 1870. His work there and in Boston led to the 1876 invention of the telephone. Copper was already required for telegraphing, and its conductivity facilitated an explosion of phone networks and the global spread of electricity. Previously ignored in gold- and silver-rich areas, copper was suddenly being dug up all over the Southwest. But copper is useless unless it can be extracted from the ore or fused with other metals through the high-heat smelting process. El Paso was a small town until the railroad arrived in 1881, followed by a huge smelting works in 1887. The Texas State School of Mines and Metallurgy was established in 1913, but it's now the University of Texas at El Paso, where former **Orediggers** or **Muckers** (both nicknames for prospectors) have been **Miners** for all of living memory.[3]

• • •

A diamond is a lump of coal that's had heat and pressure applied for a heck of a long time. Because it's a valuable commodity, coal's "black diamond" nickname straddles the literal and the metaphorical. William Lethbridge was the president of Alberta's North Western Coal and Navigation Company, so baseball's minor league Lethbridge **Black Diamonds** (1996–98) were appropriately named,[4] especially when their affiliation with Arizona's **Diamondbacks** is considered.

• • •

Swiss immigrant John Sutter built a small empire near the juncture of Alta California's Sacramento and American Rivers in the 1840s, even buying out Russia's California posts in 1841. (Sac's earliest baseball teams included the Sacramento

Altas [1879–94, from *Alta California*] and its latest are Sacramento **River Cats** [est. 2000].) After Mexico lost California in the U.S.-Mexican War, Sutter's Fort was a regular stopover for westward immigrants.

In January 1848 (the month before California's formal cession), a Sutter crew found some gold nuggets. Despite the boss's order for secrecy, the California Gold Rush was on by summer. The largest influx of would-be miners came during 1849, when uncountable "Forty-Niners" poured in to San Francisco and boarded steamboats for the inland boom towns of Marysville and Yuba City. Within a few years, hydraulic mining methods were blasting away hillsides on the Sacramento watershed, causing mud flows that exacerbated seasonal flooding. That drowned the twin cities' plan to compete with San Fran as a business center, but there's one local claim the latter city can't jump; Marysville's Yuba College **49ers** are decades older than the NFL team that became their neighbors in 1946, the San Francisco **49ers**.[5]

In 1848, John Sutter, Jr. helped found the city of Sacramento two miles west of his father's fort. That mining center hosted many gold-themed teams, including the minor league **Gilt Edge** club (1897–1900, backed by Gilt Edge beer), minor league football's Sacramento **Nuggets** (1946–47), and the ASL Sacramento **Gold** (1977–80). The gold *rush* yielded the WFL Sacramento **Surge** (1991–92), who became Sacramento **Gold Miners** (1993–94), the CFL's first U.S.-based team. The Bay Area's WPS FC **Gold Pride** (2009–10) were in Santa Clara.

Often overlooked are the significant gold deposits in the state's southern mountains, as indicated by the CSU Long Beach **49ers**, although they're also partly named for CSULB's founding in 1949 and the *rush* for education in the post–World War II era.[6] (Its baseballers have been **Dirtbags** since first practicing on an all-dirt diamond in 1989.)

California's "Golden State" nickname owes to its yellow poppy fields and its Gold Rush days. In fact, the entrance to San Francisco Bay was the Golden Gate Strait long before anyone thought of bridging it. The NBA's San Francisco **Warriors** (1962–71) became Golden State **Warriors** after crossing the Bay to Oakland, but they've lately considered returning to San Fran in the near future.

Claim Jumpers stake out ground at Sonora's Columbia College. Although claim jumping was the entirely legit practice of taking over abandoned mines, it's popularly associated with those unscrupulous miners who overran excavations in progress. When such incidents did occur, improvised courts substituted for genuine legal authorities. How such assemblies came to be "kangaroo courts" isn't clear, although itinerate judges often *hopped* among frontier settlements. Or maybe it was claim *jumping* that brought kangaroo-ness to mind.

With the verdict invariably being one of guilt, modern kangaroo courts are usually show trials in totalitarian states (although the modest fines still handed down by kangaroo courts in pro clubhouses address such infractions as dropping a pop-up or wearing an ugly tie to a team dinner). Upperclassmen at Austin College in Sherman, Texas intimidated defenseless freshmen in Kangaroo Kourts until such sessions ended in 1915, but **Kangaroos** still sit on AC's bench.

Steamshiploads of Chinese immigrants found work in the gold rushes and railroad projects of the 1850s and '60s. They were resented by white workers, even while doing more dangerous jobs at lower pay. San Fran has the oldest and largest Chinatown in North America. It's likely the MLL San Francisco **Dragons** (2006–08) were named for this history because Westerners generally recognize dragons as quintessentially Chinese. However, the dragon segreant on the club's shield imitated European heraldry, plausibly denying any association that might be unwelcome in an era when team names tied to regional ethnic histories are scrutinized.[7]

• • •

Sailing the *Argo* with his band of Argonauts, the Greek hero Jason had to retake his father's kingdom from a cunning uncle by going on a lengthy voyage to find a lost family heirloom, the Golden Fleece. Miners bound for California—especially those going aboard ship—compared their own wild-goose chase to that of Jason by calling themselves "Argonauts." That justifies Frisco Bay's current gold-and-blue **Argonauts** at Belmont's Notre Dame de Namur University.

Florida's westernmost port is Pensacola, home of the University of West Florida **Argonauts**. The 1967 basketball schedule for Montana's University of Great Falls was a daunting Jason-like challenge, so well-read administrators successfully floated "**Argonauts**" as a team name.[8] Jason's shipwright Argus had given his *Argo* fifty long oars, so it was no great reach when club rowers in Toronto became **Argonauts** in 1872. The next year they formed the rugby-football **Argonauts** to keep fit in winter. They've evolved into the CFL side that fans call "Boatmen."[9]

The women of tackle football's Sacramento **Sirens** (est. 2001) fit into the Jason theme. In both the story of Jason and that of Odysseus, female sirens used their beautiful singing voices to lure ship pilots into the rocks just to see the look on their faces.

• • •

Several eastern shippers consolidated under the American Express brand in 1850. Two years later, AMEX founders Henry Wells and William Fargo formed Wells, Fargo, and Company. They set their sights expressly on California's miner forty-niners and quickly became the West's preferred shipping, banking, and postal enterprise.

In 1868, Mr. Wells started a female seminary on his estate in Aurora, New York, but Wells College has been coed since 2005. Alumni of its **Express** teams can join the Wells Friends and Recent Graduates Organization—*Wells FARGO*.

After buying out coach king Ben Holladay in 1866, Wells Fargo was forever associated with stagecoaches. Holladay put his own profits in railroads and mines and was ruined by the Panic of 1873 (p. 237). He lost his chateau in Purchase, New York, which was eventually bought by publisher and politico Whitelaw Reid. After it burned down in 1888, architects McKim, Mead, and White replaced it with an ambitious castle. Manhattanville College still bears the name of its original New York City borough, but it moved to the Reid estate in 1952. The castle—now Reid Hall—is the campus's architectural heart, inspiring MC's courtly **Valiants** and their knight mascot.

• • •

In 1858 gold prospectors at Cherry Creek named their new settlement for the territorial governor of Kansas, James W. Denver. California Fever was then subsiding, and forty-niners returning to homes in the east made one last gamble on the Rockies' eastern slopes, where they met optimistic wagoners from the other direction still hoarse from yelling "Pike's Peak or Bust."

So many "fifty-niners" went to western Kansas that the Colorado Territory was cut from it in 1861. The next year a capital was established at the mining supply center called Golden (after miner Thomas Golden). The Colorado School of Mines opened there in 1873. Colorado's gold-certified athletes include CSM'S **Orediggers**, the ABA/NBA Denver **Nuggets** (est. 1974),[10] the Denver **Gold** (USFL, 1983–85),[11] and Colorado Springs **Millionaires** (in several minor league baseball clubs).

The Pike's Peak Rush was over by the early 1860s, but an 1891 gold strike at Cripple Creek launched another Colorado rush. By then, dynamite was being used to either blast away mountain passes or unlock buried ore, explaining Denver's ABL Colorado **Xplosion** (1996–98) and Arena Football's Denver **Dynamite** (1987–91). The new explosive was subtly referenced by the NASL's Denver **Dynamos** (1974–75), although "**Dynamo**" is long familiar to fans of so-named European soccer sides. Junior hockey's Kimberley **Dynamiters** (est. 1972) represent a lead- and zinc-mining town in B.C. that was named in 1891 after a huge diamond mine in Kimberley, South Africa. (Two senior teams, 1932–42 and 1946–81, won Allan Cups with that name.)

• • •

Western Canada experienced the Fraser River Gold Rush in 1858. The 30,000 miners suddenly on hand required an improved administrative infrastructure, so the Colony of British Columbia was created. A second stampede to B.C. occurred during the 1862 Cariboo Gold Rush. The PCHA's Vancouver **Millionaires** and Victoria **Aristocrats** won Stanley Cups in 1915 and 1925 respectively,[12] although either could have been named for the men who made lumber fortunes after the Canadian Pacific Railroad was completed in 1885.[13] There were once lady **Gold Rush** and gentlemen **Chiefs** at Cariboo College (Kamloops B.C.), but all became **Sun Demons** in 1991, owing to the Cariboo region's ample sunshine. In 2005 they were the **WolfPack** of the renamed Thompson Rivers University.

• • •

History's greatest mineral strike was at a silver vein east of Lake Tahoe in 1859. The Comstock Lode lured so many miners to Carson City and Virginia City that the Nevada Territory had earned statehood by 1864. It also put "The Silver State" on license plates and **Silver**- teams in various stadiums. Las Vegas **Silver Streaks** (1988–90) went to the hole in the World Basketball League, and the Las Vegas **Quicksilvers** were a 1977 NASL team. Longtime minor league baseballers were Reno **Silver Sox** (1947–92, 2006–08).

• • •

When Montana's gold rush started in 1862, miners set to dig up a large butte. That quickly settled town of Butte would remain a collection of gold, silver, and copper mining camps for years, but by 1900 it was the largest city between the

Mississippi and the Pacific. To see a home game for Butte's Montana Tech **Orediggers**, one would pass the bronze statue of Marcus Daly at the campus entrance. (The 1907 work is the last by the great Augustus Saint-Gaudens.) Mr. Daly, W.A. Clark, and F.A. Heinze were the "Copper Kings" at Butte who ruthlessly fought to control turn-of-the-century mineral wealth. Hockey's minor league Butte **Copper Kings** (1975/76) were followed by same-named Pioneer Leaguers (1978–2000) in baseball.

• • •

The westward flow of emigrants slowed to a trickle during the Civil War. Plains Indians decided to ramp up resistance to white settlement and federal armies that were distracted and depleted by events elsewhere. Cheyenne and Sioux warriors overran the cavalry of Lt. Casper Collins in 1865 at the spot where westward trails crossed the North Platte (soon Fort Casper). Today, Casper, Wyoming hosts indoor football's Wyoming **Cavalry** (est. 2000).

 The military campaign of the Oglala Sioux's Red Cloud was the most successful war against Federals by Native Americans, so the 1868 Treaty of Fort Laramie gave the Sioux "absolute and undisturbed use and occupation" of their sacred Black Hills. Oglala warriors likely heard their women sing "brave heart" songs as they set for battle, so teams of **Bravehearts** at Oglala Lakota College on South Dakota's Pine Ridge Reservation face high expectations.

 The Fort Laramie treaty kicked miners and soldiers off the Bozeman Trail, an Indian route from the fort to Montana's gold fields. French trappers had long spoken of gold just lying around the Dakota Territory's Black Hills, but fear of the Lakota-Sioux prevented confirmation. When the 7th Cavalry of Gen. George Custer verified the stories in 1874, men came from all over on the new rails. After the Indians refused to sell their land in 1875, the cavalry was more forgiving of the miners' trespass.

 As always, the first arrivals were independent placer miners who pan, sift, and sluice through stream sediments to find gold nuggets that were eroded from the lode trapped by solid rock. For a lone prospector and his pickaxe, it was a tough go. More efficient were the corporations that showed up later at any gold rush to work teams around the clock and tunnel right up to the mother lode, a method called hard rock mining. Intuition would suggest that South Dakota's Rapid City (founded in 1876) was named for its boom-town character, but it's actually on Rapid Creek. (Similarly, minor league baseball's 2008-founded Rapid City **Rush** are named for being only twenty miles from Mt. Rushmore.) A better indication of Rapid City's growth is its South Dakota School of Mines and Technology; it was founded in 1885, just ten years after the initial gold rush. "South Dakota Tech" has run **Hardrockers** crews since the 1920s.

 Violent Indian reactions to white incursions gave President Grant an excuse to round up the Black Hills' natives. The ensuing Great Sioux War (1876–77) pitted the Lakota-Sioux (of Sitting Bull and Crazy Horse) and their Cheyenne allies against the Army and the Lakota's traditional Crow enemies. Custer miscalculated enemy strength near eastern Montana's Little Big Horn River in June 1876 and set his 225 men on a camp holding thousands of braves. The glorified Last Stand was more likely a quick slaughter of Custer's entire force, and absent from the many retellings are the handful of slain Arikara companions, who were often the cavalry's scouts. Some of them rest at the Old Scouts Cemetery (New Town, N.D.), where Fort Berthold Community College's **Scouts** represent the Three Affiliated Tribes (Mandan, Hidatsa, and Arikara).

After Little Big Horn,[14] Americans spared little humor for Indians. In December 1890 a reconstructed 7th Cavalry brutally massacred hundreds of Lakota Sioux at South Dakota's Wounded Knee Creek to end the Indian Wars.

• • •

We might have added hockey's Colorado [Springs] **Gold Kings** (1998–2002) to Colorado's previously discussed **Gold-** teams, but they'd already been Alaska **Gold Kings** (1995–97) before relocating from Fairbanks. The last great North American gold rush was north to Alaska when prospectors from the Yukon/Klondike Gold Rush (1897–1900) pushed west from Canada.

Skaters from the Yukon Territory's mining camps got together as Dawson City **Nuggets**. The traveled by dog sled and train to Ottawa in 1905 to challenge the **Senators/Silver Seven** for the Stanley Cup. Exhausted from the three-week trip (and rudely awakened to the quality of play in the east) the black-and-gold **Nuggets** lost the two-game, total-goal series, 31-4.

• • •

A swastika is a cross with its arms bent at right angles. *Svastika* is a Sanskrit word for good luck, and the oldest swastikas are indeed in India. Variations on the design, however, appear independently in the native cultures of every populated continent, almost always associated with good luck, the sun, wealth, or all three. That included some Iron Age Germanic kingdoms, so the *Hakenkreuz* (crooked cross) was adopted in 1933 by the *Nationalsozialistische Deutsche Arbeiterpartei* (National Socialist German Workers' Party). "Nazi" Germany would systematically murder six-million Jews and millions more Romani (Gypsies), Soviet war prisoners, disabled persons, political reformers, and homosexuals during the World War II era.

The shadow cast in the last century by the once-revered swastika requires us to make an emotional adjustment before recognizing those **Swastikas** of sport. We found so-named teams exclusively in mining communities, where luck-seekers often put a swastika above the tunnel entrance:

• Nova Scotia's Windsor **Swastikas** (1905–16) were popular amateurs skating near the world's richest gypsum deposits (an area also loaded with coal).
• The 1916 Edmonton **Swastikas** were hockey-playing women from Alberta's coal capital.
• B.C.'s Fernie **Swastikas** were female hockey players of the mid-1920s from a mining town named for coal magnate William Fernie.
• The Canon City **Swastikas** of baseball's 1912 Rocky Mountain League played in a Colorado supply depot that had sprung up in the Pikes Peak Rush.

Early-twentieth-century athletes that put the ancient emblem on their uniforms included the intercollegiate basketball **Indians** from Oklahoma's Chilocco Indian Agricultural School (Ponca City). From 1884 to 1980 it served Indians of the Southwest, who embraced swastika (or *fylfot*) designs until World War II.

Sycamores | Buckeyes | Banana Slugs | Lumberjacks

Indiana State University's **Fighting Sycamores** are named for the continent's largest hardwood (*Platanus occidentalis*). Persistent stories say that pranksters suggested "Sycamores" in 1922 just to dump "**Fighting Teachers**," the name with which the Terre Haute normal school's athletes seemed stuck.

Indians of the Ohio Valley long thought the glossy chestnut of a common tree resembled a deer buck's eye. The Ohio buckeye (*Aesculus glabra*) is now the state tree, and Columbus is home to The Ohio State University **Buckeyes**.[1]

The **Sycs** and **Bucks** are tokens of the once-vibrant timber industry of the Upper Midwest, where great forests reclaimed tundra after the last glacial retreat. Dakota College at Bottineau keeps **Ladyjacks** and **Lumberjacks**, and that's OK because it was originally North Dakota's state school of forestry. There were **Lumberjacks** and **Lumberjills** at Northland College (Ashland, Wis.), but the '**Jills** tumbled out of favor and were **Lady Lumberjacks** by 1985. Don't confuse Northland's **Jacks** with the Northland International University **Pioneers** in Dunbar, although both are in Wisconsin's Northland ("Up North") region, where the first white pioneers were foresters.

In *Democracy in America*, Frenchman Alexis de Tocqueville harshly evaluated America's political and social systems of the early 1830s. In a less somber moment, he called Cleveland the "Forest City," giving name to the NA's 1870-founded **Forest City** club, which played the first-ever major league game the next year. The NA had another **Forest City** in Rockford, Illinois (a town better known for wooden furniture than raw lumber).[2] The **Lumberjacks** at Alpena [Mich.] Community College indicate the Thunder Bay River's timber industry. Tons of logs from the Upper Midwest floated down the Mississippi to sawmills at Clinton, Iowa, home of the lumber-swinging Clinton **LumberKings** since 1994.

Lutherans opened Milwaukee's Concordia Teachers College in 1855, but it was in the Chicago suburb of River Forest by 1913. The maroon and gold were usually **Foresters**, but sometimes **Pedagogues**, **Teachers**, or **Maroons**. It's now Concordia University Chicago, where a 1933 student poll made athletes **Cougars**. Thirty miles north of River Forest is the city of Lake Forest, settled upon the founding of Lake Forest College in 1857. After Chicago's 1871 Fire, the city's elite built beautiful mansions on what became Lake Michigan's "Gold Coast." Locals have actively preserved their green spaces, a respect for nature mirrored by LFC's red-and-black **Foresters**, who replaced **Gold Coasters** and **Red Devils** after World War II.

• • •

Hardwood trees in the *Quercus* (oak) genus are used in framing and flooring, and **Mighty Oaks** and **Lady Oaks** are at Indiana's Oakland City University. Those "Oakland City **Oaks**" aren't even redundant compared to the oaky California aftertaste of "Oakland **Oaks**" (PCL, 1903–55; ABA, 1967–69). Menlo College's **Oaks** are down the bay from Oakland in Atherton, and the Sacramento Valley had single-A Visalia **Oaks** (1977–2008). The **Giants** at Visalia's College of the

Sequoias refer to the giant sequoia, the largest tree species by weight and volume. Loggers couldn't exploit the brittle *Sequoiadendron giganteum*, but its cousin the California redwood (*Sequoia sempervirens*) is taller and more conducive to lumbering. Old-growth redwoods are the pride of Humboldt County, where the Redwood Bowl at Humboldt State University holds those who root, root, root (*ha-ha!*) for **Lumberjacks**. (They were "Humboldt **Thunderbolts**" until 1936.)

It's easy to find a slithering banana slug (*Ariolimax dolichophallus*) on the redwood forest floor at UC Santa Cruz. The banana slug is curvy, yellow, and long (up to eight inches). UCSC started intercollegiate sports in 1981, but blue-and-gold club-level **Banana Slugs** were ignored by its chancellor and athletes who favored "**Sea Lions**." Five years of mascot ambiguity followed, but a 1986 student vote overwhelmingly restored the **Slugs**.

The Robin Hood Oak at SUNY College of Environmental Science and Forestry supposedly sprang from an acorn from the Major Oak in England's Sherwood Forest. It was the inspiration when SUNY-ESF's **Mighty Oaks** took the hardwood in 2009. The Syracuse school's first varsity teams had been the 1912 **Woodsmen**, an identity maintained by coed lumberjack athletes.

By definition, deciduous trees (like buckeyes and most oaks) lose their leaves in the fall and stay bear until spring, which conveniently approximates the academic year. Marlboro [Vt.] College adopted a naked maple as its emblem shortly after its 1946 founding. The "dead tree" (as the dormant mascot is affectionately known) led to extramural **Dead Trees** in the 1990s.[3]

• • •

Great Lakes timber supplies collapsed around 1900, but abundant trees gave name to the "Evergreen State," so Michigan lumber heir Wilhelm Böing started a logging company at Aberdeen, Washington (putting some profits toward his aviation hobby, eventually creating Seattle's huge Boeing firm). Aberdeen's Grays Harbor College has **Chokers** because a choke-setter is the lumberman assigned the dangerous task of wrapping hauling cables—*chokers*—around felled trees. We assume GHC intends some irony; "choking" describes the snatching of athletic defeat from the jaws of certain victory.

Aberdeen and abutting Hoquiam have long hosted minor league **Loggers** and **Lumbermen**. Also, Tacoma's first white settlers were lumberman of the 1850s, so its University of Puget Sound backs **Loggers**. (Their "Griz the Logger" bear recalls the **Grizzlies** that UPS presented until 1910.) The NLL's Portland **Lumberjax** (est. 2006) are Oregon's LAX side. Teams in different soccer leagues have been falling for "Portland **Timbers**" since 1975. The country's tallest team won the first NCAA Division I basketball tournament in 1939. They were the **Ducks** of Eugene's University of Oregon, famously labeled "Tall Firs" by Portland's *Oregonian*. In fact, Eugene is the "Emerald City," owing to its green flora, indicated by minor league baseball's Eugene **Emeralds** (est. 1995).

The sawmills at Klamath Falls, Oregon slowed down after 1980, mostly over environmentalists' complaints that the old-growth habitat of the northern spotted owl (*Strix occidentalis caurina*) was disappearing. The Oregon Institute of Technology at K-Falls hosts **Hustlin' Owls**.

Cyclones | Hurricanes | Lightning | Rainbow Warriors

In January 1933 the basketball team from Ohio's Youngstown State University had to repeatedly get out to push their cars through a blizzard in West Virginia's mountains to play the West Liberty University **Hilltoppers** (p. 72). At game time, the Youngstowners were still shivering and flapping their *wings* to keep warm, being called **Penguins** thereafter.

Most talk about weather-related team names is less anecdotal. Just try getting to the game under the following conditions.

• • •

Tornadoes—or "twisters"—are relatively small rotating wind systems that form over land. The larger rotating systems that form over tropical oceans are called hurricanes (in the Atlantic) or typhoons (Pacific). Tornadoes, twisters, hurricanes, typhoons, and water spouts are cyclonic systems, so all are called *cyclones*.

Like the thunderstorms that they accompany, tornadoes are born of unstable air masses. They touch down in flat, dry areas, so the Iowa prairie is a hotbed of cyclonic activity. When Iowa State University's football **Cardinals** wiped out heavily favored Northwestern in 1895, the *Chicago Tribune* made report of the "Iowa Cyclone." By the time they got home to Ames, the **Cardinals** had already been upgraded to **Cyclones**. ("Cy" has been the **Cyclones'** redbird mascot since 1954, an artifact of the displaced "**Cardinals**" identity.)

The Great Tornado of 1882 was a not-at-all metaphorical Iowa cyclone that struck the town of Grinnell and destroyed Grinnell College. Minister J.B. Grinnell claimed in 1891 that it was he to whom *New York Tribune* editor Horace Greeley had famously advised "Go west, young man!" It's therefore natural that athletes at the school Grinnell co-founded in 1856 would be **Pioneers**, but their yearbook is *The Cyclone*.

Iowa is in the eastern Tornado Alley, a loosely defined area somewhat conterminous to the Great Plains. Texas is at the southern end of the alley, where **Tornadoes** represent Austin's Concordia University Texas. (They were **Stags** until gaining university status in 1995.) The Employers Casualty Insurance of Texas sponsored the Dallas **Golden Cyclones**, female basketballers who reminded fans to bulk up on weather-related coverage while dominating AAU tourneys in the 1930s behind multi-sport legend Babe Didrikson. At Waco, a three-day tornado event in May 1953 killed 114 people and caused $400 million in damage. Waco's Texas State Technical College first presented **Tornadoes** in the 1980s.

There are often twisters in another zone called Dixie Alley (the upper Tennessee and lower Mississippi Valleys) that kill more people than those in Tornado Alley simply because more people live there, so we respect the power of the Talladega College **Tornadoes** (Talladega, Ala.).

Spring and summer thunderstorms bring tornadoes to the Carolinas. The Brevard [N.C.] College **Tornados** use the variant plural form (no -*e*). We touch down on the other side of the Great Smoky Mountains to find King University (Bristol, Tenn.), which avoids this issue by sticking to the singular "**Tornado**."

The University of Tulsa switched its orange and black for yellow and black in the early 1920s. Football coach Howard Acher wanted to blow through competition as a **Golden Tornado**, but he learned Georgia Tech claimed that nickname (from its G.T. initials). A second-wind effort effected the **Golden Hurricane**.[1] The first choice had been more meteorologically apt; it's unlikely a hurricane of any significant smack could move as far inland as Oklahoma because they fizzle when robbed of their ability to draw power from cold ocean water.

Tornadoes zip groundward through a condensation channel in a storm cloud. A tiny cyclone that forms from the ground up is found in deceptively mild and sunny conditions when the air near a relatively warm surface gets heated. The resulting vortex that can suck sand and dirt upward is called a dust devil, which explains **Dustdevils** at Laredo's Texas A&M International University.

• • •

European explorers made fast Atlantic crossings by plying the northeast-to-southwest trade winds, and tropical storms follow the same groove. Such storms don't form near the equator because the Coriolis force (which creates the counterclockwise spin of cyclones) is weakest at 0 degrees latitude. Even if a hurricane made a run for the southern hemisphere, it would break up when ol' Coriolis tried to reverse the spin. Instead, tropical storms get a long rebound off the equator and move slightly north and west. (Reverse all of these directions in you're in the southern hemisphere.) This puts the coastal Southeast and the Gulf Coast in harm's way, giving those places the heaviest concentration of fans that chase **Hurricanes**.

The gods put a low-lying peninsula called Florida right across the likely path of hurricanes. On September 18, 1926 the Great Miami Hurricane slammed ashore and killed 300, wreaking devastation on the economy and delaying the ribbon cutting for the new University of Miami in Coral Gables until October 15. Its football game the next week was played by newly named **Hurricanes**.[2]

Tracking north from Florida, we find the Georgia Southwestern State University **Hurricanes** (Americus) and NHL Carolina **Hurricanes** (Raleigh, N.C.). The emblem for the latter is a highly stylized version of the red-and-black U.S. storm flag. Two such flags are hoisted to indicate hurricane-force winds, those that exceed 73 miles per hour.

Thirty miles from Raleigh is Louisbourg, where the Louisburg College **Hurricanes** predate the like-named NHLers by decades. Still in North Carolina, Lexington's Davidson County Community College introduced the **Storm** in 2007, replacing the vowel (*o*) in their logo with the storm symbol. In 1988, Charlotte's new NBA team came with a Hugo the **Hornet** mascot. A hurricane named Hugo would leave a path of destruction from the eastern Caribbean to the Carolinas just twelve months later, but the mascot stayed on the job, even returning with the second hoop version of Charlotte **Hornets** in 2013.

Hurricanes usually lose steam as they move north to cooler waters, but the warm north-flowing Gulf Stream can sometimes deliver an ocean cyclone to the Canadian Maritimes, placing **Hurricanes** at Prince Edward Island's Holland College in Charlottetown.

In winter, cold deep-ocean currents that move south along the mid-Atlantic coast in the company of cold Canadian air masses can run into the Gulf Stream. In such cases, the warm air rises and leaves the cold against the warm ocean, a convergence that can turn ocean moisture into driving snow. As the system crawls north, the coast experiences the western half of the counterclockwise rotation as winds from the northeast. New Englanders call such unpredictable and extreme winter storms "nor'easters," which is either an old salt's description of northeast winds or an affectation of same. In coastal Maine, where the New England accent is most extreme, **Nor'easters** serve Biddeford's University of New England. In French a northeasterly wind is a *nordet*, giving le ***Nordet*** *du sport à l'Université du Québec à Rimouski* (in *northeastern* Quebec).

> Because the northern hemisphere's trade winds go east to west, Pacific typhoons make landfall in Asia. That makes for few North American **Typhoons**, but there are California **Cyclones** at Mills College in Oakland. The former women's seminary is named after Cyrus and Susan L. Mills (its missionary benefactors), so Mr. Mills— perhaps "Cy"—is the best guess to justify its **Cyclones**.

• • •

Florida's panhandle acts like a frying pan that heats air near the ground during long days in the sun. When that air rises into the cooler ocean air that surrounds it, the instability is released in late-afternoon thunderstorms with electrical discharges so pronounced that central Florida from Tampa Bay to Titusville is called Lightning Alley. The word *Tanpa*—from southwest Florida's Calusa people— means "stick of fire," illuminated literally by pro softball's Tampa Bay **FireStix** (1997–2000). Tampa proper is also home for indoor football's Tampa Bay **Storm** (est. 1991) and the NHL Tampa Bay **Lightning** (est. 1992). Spring basketball's Tampa Bay **Flash** (1986/87) and the ABA Tampa Bay **Thunder Dawgs** (2000) were shorter-lived teams. Travel northeast from the bay on I-4 to the domain of indoor football's Lakeland **Thunderbolts** (est. 2005) and continue to the former home of the WLAF Orlando **Thunder** (1991–92).

Atmospheric instability can also occur when cold air moves over the surface of relatively warm water in cooler months, creating ocean-, bay-, or lake-effect storms. Fair-weather fans won't escape **Storms** by heading for a port. Minor league soccer's Seattle **Storm** (1986–90) are echoed by the WNBA Seattle **Storm** (est. 2000). Oregon's Portland **Storm** (1974) was replaced in the WFL by the Portland **Thunder** (1975). Painesville, Ohio is home to the Lake Erie College **Storm**.[3] Southwestern Ontario is socked in by three Great Lakes and Georgian Bay, as are its junior hockey Guelph **Storm**. Goldey-Beacom College (Wilmington, Del.) has colors of blue and yellow, the latter leading to GBC's **Lightning** and reminding us to take cover when thunderstorms roll in from Delaware Bay.

In summer, Great Lakes waters are cooler than the surrounding land masses, putting **Thunder-** teams all around the Ontario side of Lake Superior's Thunder Bay. Refer to Lakehead University's **Thunderwolves** and Confederation College's **Thunderhawks**,[4] both in Thunder Bay proper. Clear across Lake Superior are the **Thunderbirds** at Algoma University (Sault Ste. Marie, Mich.). There's more **Thunder** on the eastern end of the lakes at Ottawa's Algonquin College.

New York's Finger Lakes and the Great Lakes release relatively cool air in the summer and relatively warm air in the winter, limiting spring and fall frosts and extending the growing season to accommodate wine, juice, and jam producers. On Chautauqua Lake is the grape mascot of the Jamestown **Jammers** (est. 1994) of the New York–Penn League. The NYPL's St. Catharines **Stompers** (1996–99) referred to laborious grape squashing on southwestern Lake Ontario, as do the Frontier League's lakeside Lake Erie **Crushers** (est. 2009, Avon, Ohio).

Being surrounded by the Canadian Rockies, Okanagan Lake moderates the temperature of the Okanagan Valley, which is drier and sunnier than the rest of British Columbia. The city at the southern end of the lake first hosted amateur hockey's Penticton **Vees** in 1951. "**Vees**" indicates three varieties of local peach: Vedette, Valiant, and Veteran. Halfway up the lake is Kelowna, where **Lakers** represented Okanagan University College. In 2005 it split into two institutions: Okanagan College (still with **Lakers**) and the University of British Columbia Okanagan (which sustains **Heat**).

• • •

The parallel belts of color in the sky that we call rainbows appear when white light from a low-angle source is divided into different wavelengths by atmospheric moisture acting as a prism. Remote tropical islands with significant rainfall and broad ocean horizons are great places for viewing, and a rainbow auspiciously appeared after the **Fighting Deans** of the University of Hawaii at Mānoa unexpectedly beat their Oregon State guests to end the 1923 football season. UHM teams were **Rainbows** thereafter and then **Rainbow Warriors**.

By 2000 a spectrum of names were in use. Most men remained **Rainbow Warriors**, but baseballers were just **Rainbows** and footballers just **Warriors**.[5] Women were the **Rainbow Wahine** (a Polynesian word for a woman that became hipster talk for a surfer girl), except for the **Rainbow Wahine Harriers** of cross-country. In mid-2013, UHM simplified those coalitions by breaking them into distinct bands of **Rainbow Warrior** men and **Rainbow Wahine** women.

Huskies | Nordiques | Eskimos | Penguins

The Chukchi people of northeast Asia bred Siberian sled dogs for strength and endurance. In North America they were called *huskies*, which was a severe corruption of either *Chukchi* or *Ehuskemay* (an Inuit variant of *Eskimo*). The first huskies to cross the Bering Strait did so in 1909 to pull a sled in the All Alaska Sweepstakes race.

The last three Sweeps (1915–17) were swept by the huskies of Norwegian-born Leonhard Seppala. That team was more famous after pulling the longest leg of a 1925 relay in which twenty mushers drove 625 miles over six days from Nenana to the iced-in port at Nome, delivering antitoxin to prevent a diphtheria epidemic among the native children.[1] Former Nome hotelier Tex Rickard arranged for Seppala's subsequent coast-to-coast publicity tour to finish up at his **Rangers'** Madison Square Garden rink in October 1926.

Seppala stayed east to run some New England races and won his first test in January 1927 at southern Maine's Poland Spring Derby. Being convinced to open a local kennel, "Seppala's participation in subsequent races led to a surge in the popularity of the sport in New England as well as to an increased interest in Siberian Huskies."[2] Northeastern University's **Red and Black** were just then looking for a live mascot, and on March 4 Seppala personally delivered a lovable husky to Boston's North Station. Students met the train and paraded the pup to the Back Bay campus that's backed **Huskies** since.

Due south of Seppala's Maine kennel was Gorham's Townhouse Hill and the state normal school's **Teachers** and **Hilltoppers**. They became **Huskies** in 1967 and kept that name when Gorham State College merged into the University of Southern Maine in 1970. That's just one example of many **Huskies** across the northern states and Canada:

- The **Huskies** at Bloomsburg University of Pennsylvania were named in the 1930s for a teacher's pet (literally) that had supposedly been in the company of Admiral Richard E. Byrd on his recent Antarctic expeditions.[3]
- Houghton's Michigan Technological University keeps **Huskies** on the Upper Peninsula.
- Saint Mary's University (Halifax, N.S.) has been represented by (Siberian) **Huskies** since 1960.
- St. Cloud State University was a Minnesota teachers' college. Its **Normals**, **Teachers**, and **Peds** became **Huskies** in about 1940.
- Howler is the mascot of Saskatoon's University of Saskatchewan **Huskies**.[4] In that province, dog sledding used to be among the more reliable ways of getting around.
- The *Northern Star* is the campus paper of the Northern Illinois University **Huskies** (DeKalb). Its pages refer to any given player as a **Huskie**, the variant singular form.[5]

- In 1946 the Toronto **Huskies** lost to the **Knicks** in the first-ever BAA/NBA game then folded after that inaugural season. George Brown College reclaimed **Huskies** for Toronto after its 1967 founding.
- Junior hockey's Rouyn-Noranda **Huskies** (est. 1996) are in Quebec.

School administrators and civic leaders thought the University of Washington's **Sun Dodgers** didn't put Seattle in the best light, so they became **Huskies** in 1922 to align with the metro region's "Gateway to Alaska" slogan.[6] UW has Alaskan malamute mascots, which is only possible through a broad definition of *husky* that includes Siberians and similar Arctic sled dogs. Unlike *true*—that is, Siberian— huskies, the malamute is most closely associated with northwestern Alaska's Inuits. Those that are casually labeled "Alaskan huskies" are usually working dogs that have been crossbred from various Arctic breeds.

In 1965, Houston Baptist University wanted to trade its **Spartans** for something conducive to live mascots. From an assembly of hopeful critters, "**Huskies**" was chosen. That ignored the school's Texas location and the on-hand candidate, which was actually a Samoyed (a north-Eurasian breed that meets only the more liberal definition of *husky*), but HBU's pets of recent years have more often been true Siberians.[7]

When Connecticut Agricultural College became Connecticut State College in 1933, students traded **Aggies** for **Statesmen**. The next year they were **Huskies** quite arbitrarily. The school at Storrs wouldn't be the University of Connecticut for four more years, so any speculation that "**Huskies**" owes to the homophony between *UConn* and *Yukon* doesn't pull its chronological weight. Besides, Siberian huskies had no part in the Yukon Gold Rush (1896–98) simply because the breed wouldn't be seen in North America for another decade. To compound the confusion, the Yukon-Klondike prospectors did have plenty of malamute companions, which—explained above—are "huskies" only retroactively.

• • •

North, *Norway*, *Norse*, and a bunch of other *N*- words are from old European forms for "north." *Nordique* is French for "of the north," often referring to Scandinavian (or *Nordic*) persons. For the *Québécois* in Canada, that word referred to the northernmost team in the new-for-1972 WHA, the Quebec **Nordiques**. Their fleur-de-lis emblem and French-language press reports appealed to Francophones in the way Montreal's **Canadiens** once had. (There are still **Nordiques** in Sainte-Thérèse, Quebec at the *Collège Lionel-Groulx*.) In 1995 the '**Diques** (by then in the NHL) moved south and west to Denver, but it was little comfort to *Canadiens* that the Colorado **Avalanche** sported a French-derived name, one describing the gravitational tendency of high-altitude snow resting on a slope greater than its natural angle of repose. There'd already been some MISLers called the Denver **Avalanche** from 1980 to '82.

For reasons hard to compass, schools in septentrional—*north-y*—locales lean toward team names that are etymologically or zoologically in step with their geographical prefix to a degree that *South-*, *East-*, and *West-* institutions do not. Even ignoring the aforementioned **Huskies** at Northeastern, Northern Illinois, and Rouyn-Noranda (*Noranda* means "North-Canada"), this idea of *North-* yields the

Northern Kentucky University **Norse** (Campbell County) and Northeastern Okla-homa A&M College **Golden Norse** and **Lady Norse** (in Miami). (Many in Oklahoma do enjoy a rich Nordic heritage.) The mascot for the NHL's Minnesota **Wild** is Nordy, a sort of lion-wolf-bear-badger from northern Minnesota. Every season at Ohio Northern University (in Ada) sees **Polar Bears**.

Male athletes at Montana State University–Northern (in Havre) are **Lights**, so the MSU-Northern **Lights** remind one of the *aurora borealis*. That's "dawn of the north" in Latin, but we usually refer to the "northern lights," a spectacular glow in the sky that can happen when charged particles from the sun stimulate the Earth's magnetic field. (MSUN's female **Skylights** are allusions to Montana's "Big Sky Country" nickname from *The Big Sky*, A.B. Guthrie's 1947 novel about frontiers-men in the Montana Territory of 1830.) Canadian University (Lacombe, Alta.) has **Aurora** athletes. Auroras usually occur in polar latitudes beyond 60 degrees, so they're rarely sighted from either MSUN (48.5 degrees) or CUC (52.5 degrees). Sitting at 61 degrees north, Alaska's largest city is on the bubble for good aurora viewing, as illuminated by minor league basketball's Anchorage **Northern Knights** (1977–82).

The gray wolf (*Canis lupus*), or *northern* timber wolf, has only recently been reintroduced to Michigan, justifying Northwood University's **Timberwolves** in Midland. Hiding among "University of Northern British Columbia **Timber-wolves**" is "northern timberwolves." The school at Prince George recalls the pro-vince's native timber wolf subspecies (*C. l. columbianus*), which was hunted to extinction by 1941.

• • •

Molecular anthropologists are using DNA to figure out when the Asian ancestors of the Arctic people of Alaska, northern Canada, and Greenland came to North America. It was probably significantly later than the First Nations and Native American peoples to their south from whom they are ethnically distinct.

Eskimo is the Algonquian-derived term often applied to Inuit and Yupik people in the Eskimo-Aleut language family. It's historically been understood to mean "eaters of raw meat," but linguists today are leaning toward "snowshoe netters." The Frenchmen in Canada were the first whites to hear the word, and their spelling was used by rugby's Edmonton **Esquimaux** (est. 1892). Angliciza-tion effected "Edmonton **Eskimos**" in 1910, still used by the CFL team into which they evolved.

The plural form *inuit* means "people." A single person is *inuk*, so those sports fans who are grammar nerds—there aren't that many—root against the **Inuks** from the University of Quebec at Chicoutimi. Tracking such nuances within the Aleut-Eskimo and Inuit language group is the Alaska Native Languages Center at the University of Alaska Fairbanks. UAF's **Nanooks** Anglicize the Inuit word *nanuq* (polar bear). In fact, the UAF teams were **Polar Bears** until 1962. *Nanuk* is also name of the white ursine mascot at the sports-less College of the North Atlantic (Stephenville, N.L.).

Kelsey's Saskatchewan Institute of Applied Science and Technology fields **Amaruks**, an Inuit word for Arctic wolves (*C. l. arctos*), a gray wolf subspecies. Also in the Arctic you'll see the snowy owl (*Bubo scandiacus*), but only if you can pick out white feathers against an icy tundra. Its Inuktitut name is *ookpik*, which is the root word if you root for **Ooks** at the Northern Alberta Institute of Technology in Edmonton.

The women of hockey's Edmonton **Chimos** (1973–2011) played in western Canada's top league. *Chimo* is an Inuit inquiry as to whether one is friendly.

• • •

Donald B. MacMillan took some thirty trips to the Arctic before his last in 1957 at age 82. Having graduated Bowdoin College in 1898, MacMillan was among many Arctic researchers associated with the Brunswick, Maine school. In fact, his first trip was with the 1908/09 expedition of Adm. Robert Peary (Bowdoin class of 1877), which claimed to have put men on the geographic North Pole for the first time. Both men are on the marquee at Bowdoin's Peary-MacMillan Arctic Museum. The alumni association successfully pushed Bowdoin toward its **"Polar Bears"** identity in early 1913. MacMillan was thrilled, and agreed to bring a hide back from his upcoming voyage. A lot of that expedition went painfully wrong, but the polar bear guarding a gym lobby is MacMillan's 1918 gift.

The Racquette River flows out of the Adirondacks, through Potsdam, New York, and then a few winding miles to the St. Lawrence and the Canadian border. Teams at SUNY Potsdam were **Racqueteers** in the campus news (the *Racquette*) until becoming **Polar Bears** in 1964. It took about a decade for the transition to **Bears**, with **"Polar"** hanging around a little longer for hockey teams.

• • •

An Inuit family likely lived in a tent made of caribou or seal hide called a *tupiq*, which was covered with snow for winter insulation. But the public's imagination seized on the Inuits' domed *igluvigak*, in which explorers sometimes took shelter. The structural sphericality of Pittsburgh's Civic Arena made it the "Igloo" when it opened in 1961. The Inuit ice houses are literal polar opposites to the flightless marine birds of the southern hemisphere, a fact ignored when naming the Igloo's NHL tenants in 1967, the Pittsburgh **Penguins**. Otherwise, **"Penguins"** adheres naturally to ice-bound athletes, especially when **"Pens"** alliterates so well with "Pennsylvania."

No one's sure if the great auk (*Pinguinus impennis*) of Maritime Canada or the Magellanic Penguin (*Spheniscus magellanicus*) of South America's southern coasts was the first animal called *penguin*. Both are flightless, black-backed, white-bellied birds with white facial marks that could have evoked the Welsh description *pen gwyn* (white head).[8] The Lindsay/Frost campus of Ontario's Fleming College is way inland from the great auks of Atlantic Canada (including those on their namesake Penguin Islands), but it fields extramural **Auks**.

Sox | Purple Storm | Crimson Eagles | Golden Bears

Hall of Famers Harry and George Wright were the sons of accomplished cricket player Sam Wright. Sam moved from his native England to Staten Island in 1837 to become a groundskeeper and club pro at St. George's Cricket Club, where he played in the world's first international cricket match (USA v. Canada) in 1844. Cricketers and hardballers often shared fields, so it really wasn't surprising that the Wright brothers gravitated toward the American game.

Harry played for baseball's Cincinnati's **Red Stockings**, whose only 1867 loss was to the **National Baseball Club** of Washington D.C. and their star shortstop George. Showing off their advertised hosiery, the **Stockings** of 1868 were the first players to adopt short knicker pants. As the **Stockings'** manager in 1869, Harry hired George to play for the first openly salaried team.[1] Sponsored by Cincinnati businessmen and carried by George's defense and bat, they amassed a season record of 65-0 on the first-ever coast-to-coast tour (made possible by the new transcontinental railroad). They won twenty-seven games to start 1870, but lost the next one to **Atlantic** of Brooklyn owing to the first known use of extra innings. That started the **Stockings** toward a 68-6 season record ... a winning percentage of .921 that was so unacceptable that Cincy's city fathers decided to stop bankrolling a team that was always on the road.

The quick growth of salaried teams made necessary a centrally administered circuit. Some of the better amateurs joined the 1871 National Association of Professional Base Ball Players, which many historians consider the first major league. (Major League Baseball chauvinistically counts only its own AL and NL as major.) Sponsorless in Cincy, the Wrights and some teammates went east to play the inaugural NA season as *Boston* **Red Stockings**. But the NA had its problems. Fans had few recreational dollars once the Panic of 1873 hit (p. 237), and they had trouble embracing players who were sure to follow ever-higher paychecks from one team to another, a nomadism called "revolving." The hot revolvers always seemed to end up on Boston's **Stockings**, who won every NA championship from 1872 to '75.

Chicago **White Stockings** owner William Hulbert thought more organization would yield more profit, so in early 1876 he molded eight select NA teams into the National League of Baseball Clubs, the very name shifting emphasis from a pastime for "Base Ball Players" to a money-maker for "Baseball Clubs." Having watched their former players' success in Boston, Cincinnatians eagerly joined the new National League. Local pork packer Josiah Keck owned a franchise called the **Porkopolitans** and then **Red Stockings**. By 1878 they were **Reds** to be distinguished from those **Red Stockings** lately of Boston.

The NL expelled the **Reds** after 1880 for selling beer and playing on Sunday. Cincinnati's many Germans observed a Continental Sabbath, which meant the Lord's Day could be one of recreation after morning services. So Sunday baseball didn't seem at all odd to them, even though Ivy Leaguers at the eastern Calvinist colleges would never dream of taking to the gridiron on the Sabbath day. (Baseballers in greater New York had even been arrested for Sunday play.) Cincinnati Germans owned and patronized a large numbers of breweries, so only a beer-friendly league would bring back pro ball. Cincinnati investors put together an entirely new major league for 1882, the American Association. It would play games on Sundays, and four of its six teams had brewers in the ownership group,[2] but the AA collapsed after 1891, a victim of the 1890 Brotherhood War (p. 294).

• • •

With the Cincinnati **Red Stockings** setting the precedent, socks became an easy way to make uniforms distinct. The inaugural National League had both St. Louis **Brown Stockings** and Chicago **White Stockings**. By 1882 that league was dictating that each team display a unique color in the most prominent field of their nearly all-white uniforms, their socks.[3]

When Constantine Anson became the innovative player-manager of Chicago's 1879 **White Stockings**, he got his famous nickname, "Cap." Cap's larger-than-life presence and subsequent absence led to a series of unofficial team names. As a pioneer crossover celebrity, he starred in the 1895 vaudeville play *Runaway Colt*, turning his young **Stockings** into **Colts**. When Anson left to manage the 1898 New York **Giants**, the orphaned **Colts** became **Orphans**.[4]

After one season in New York, Cap retired from field duty to run a revived American Association, a second major league for 1899 and 1900. He tempted teams from Ban Johnson's well-run Western League, but they were obligated to serve as the NL's minor league by virtue of Johnson's signature on an early National Agreement. It was on those terms that the NL's West Side **Orphans** blocked Chicagoan Charles Comiskey from moving his Western League St. Paul **Saints** to his hometown. But the looming AA made it hard for the NL to alienate the WL owners, so the **Saints** enjoyed a conditional relocation from Minnesota: they would have to [1] stay on the South Side, [2] annually forfeit two prospects to the **Orphans**, and [3] avoid identifying the club with "Chicago." By the time Comiskey's team took the field for 1900, the WL had become the *American* League. Respecting his pledge to eschew any "Chicago" association, the Old Roman slyly grabbed the "**White Stockings**" name that the **Orphans** had recently abandoned. When the National Agreement expired after that season, Ban Johnson declared that his 1901 American League was a major one in competition with the NL.[5] Within a few seasons, headline writers at Chicago's papers would chop "**White Stockings**" down to "**White Sox**."

Jealous of the NL's quarter-century head start, the AL was playing catch-up baseball. To attract fans, AL teams shopped for recognizable crosstown talent, and seven veterans of the 1899 and 1900 **Orphans** ended up on the 1902 AL **White Sox**. Those remaining were called the "Chicago **Cubs**," which—like "**Orphans**"—suggested a lack of maturity, but the name has aged pretty well.[6]

• • •

After the AL **White Stockings/Sox** claimed the lost laundry of their NL neighbors, the scenario was repeated in St. Louis and Boston.

The 1875 NA had **Brown Stockings** and **Red Stockings** in St. Louis. The next season, the **Brown Stockings** joined the new NL and the **Red Stockings** got lost in the wash. The **Brownies** themselves folded in 1878, but a same-named team was in the new-for-'82 AA. They were simply **Browns** by season two, and they moved to the NL after the AA folded in late 1891. As the 1899 St. Louis **Perfectos**, they adopted cardinal red uniforms, leaving little chance that sports-writers would reattach "**Browns**." Just to be sure, they started 1900 as the now-familiar St. Louis **Cardinals**. Then the AL Milwaukee **Brewers** moved to the Gateway City in 1902 and immediately adopted the "St. Louis **Browns**" name that the **Perfectos/Cardinals** had dropped. Those **Browns** became today's Baltimore **Orioles** in 1954.

In the absence of any official monikers, it's probably safest to refer to the early Boston National League Baseball Club as "**Nationals**," even though those red-hosed remnants of Cincinnati's former team are often "**Red Stockings**." The **Nationals** had new neighbors in 1901 with the arrival of the Boston American League Baseball Club … "**Americans**" if you will. For 1907 new owner John Dovey replaced the **Nationals**' red trim with blue. **Americans** owner John I. Taylor saw that as a forfeiture of "**Red Stockings**" and switched his colors from blue to red. His 1908 players became today's **Red Sox**, following the spelling of Chicago's **White Sox**.[7]

• • •

In ancient times, dyed clothing was rare, and purple dye—an extract from Medi-terranean sea snails—was rarer still. Snails secrete worthwhile amounts of said fluid only before the spring egg-laying season, and folks quickly learned it took a thousand crushed gastropods to color a single pair of skimpy volleyball shorts.

Owing to that scarcity, Tyrian purple (from the Phoenician city of Tyre) was reserved by law for Roman emperors. It was consequently "royal purple" across Europe. In Los Angeles a 1967 NHL expansion team became "**Kings**" because owners just thought that sounded good, although they're inevitably compared to the 1944–50 Los Angeles **Monarchs** of the Pacific Coast Hockey League. To their credit, the arbitrarily named **Monarchs** and **Kings** often injected purple into the wardrobe, as do many **Regents** and **Royals**.

Christians associate royal purple with Jesus, but Roman guards in the New Testament were first to make the comparison. Mocking the "King of the Jews," they made him wear a crown of thorns and a purple robe on the way to his crucifixion, so purple is a common color at Christian colleges:

- Royal purple **Regents** represent the former Rockford, Illinois seminary that evolved into Rockford University.
- Purple-and-gold **Golden Eagles** in Minnesota represent the old Northwestern Bible and Missionary Training School, today's University of Northwestern–St. Paul.
- Niagara University's **Purple Eagles** (Lewiston, N.Y.) are perched on the Niagara Gorge's Monteagle Ridge.
- Like Niagara, Saint Michael's College (Colchester, Vt.) is a Catholic school. Its **Purple Knights** were **Michaelmen** until 1947.
- **Purple Raiders** represent a non-denominational school that's historically been Methodist-backed, the University of Mount Union (Alliance, Ohio).

- Royally named is Crown College in St. Bonifacius, Minnesota, where a **Purple Storm** represents the former St. Paul Bible Institute.
- Nyack [N.Y.] College is the successor to New York City's Missionary Training Institute (est. 1882), the country's first Bible college. Its purple-and-white **Fighting Parsons** switched to **Purple Pride** in 1996 but have been **Warriors** since the school took crimson as the dominant color in 2004.[8]

Purple is a mix of blue and red, and Tyrian purple skewed more toward the crimson than we might expect. In fact, after the fall of Constantinople in 1453 the trade routes to Tyre shut down just as the mollusk supply declined, so the Vatican approved a "Cardinal's Purple" in 1464. That cheaper and more bluish tone for clergy robes better jibes with our modern notions of purpleness. Also, Christian theology associates crimson with the sacrificial blood of Jesus, and is therefore oft-worn at Christian institutions (making Nyack's purple-for-crimson swap not very surprising). Refer to the Southern Nazarene University **Crimson Storm**, Calumet College of St. Joseph **Crimson Wave** (Whiting, Ind., Catholic), and crimson-and-cream **Crusaders** at Belmont [N.C.] Abbey College (Catholic).

• • •

Many teams take names from their shirt colors. Refer to McDaniel College's green-and-gold **Green Terror** (Westminster, Md.), Lawrence Technological University's blue-and-white **Blue Devils** (Southfield, Mich.), and tons of **Bluejays** and **Yellow Jackets**. Eureka [Ill.] College's maroon-and-gold colors explain both its **Golden Tornadoes** and the **Red Devils** that replaced them in the 1920s. Henderson State University (Arkadelphia, Ark.) presents red-and-gray **Reddies** (former **Red Jackets**, **Reds**, **Red Men**, and **Indians**). Wellesley [Mass.] College never gave teams an official name, but *everyone* calls them the **Blue** after the color "Wellesley blue." The Capilano University **Blues** (North Vancouver, B.C.) likewise exhibit "Capilano Blue." The **Blue Devils** at Brooklyn's Long Island University became **Blackbirds** in 1935 when their uniform colors changed accordingly. In New Orleans, Tulane University's green-shirted footballers were the **Olive and Blue** until "The Rolling Green Wave" became the cheer song in 1920, after which everybody was riding the **Green Wave** (always singular). Cardinal has always been Stanford University's color. White was added in the 1940s when conference rules said home and away uniforms had to be distinct, but devotion to the original hue gives us the Stanford **Cardinal** (always singular). (Stanford was famously ahead of the curve when it dropped "**Indians**" in 1972.) Quebec City's *Université Laval* **Rouge et Or** (red and gold) and the *Université de Sherbrooke* [Que.] *Vert & Or* (green and gold) players communicate their colors in French. Of course, Quebec is *la Cité de l'Or* (the city of gold) owing to gold and copper rushes in the 1920s.[9] The University of Ottawa initially fielded *Grenat et Gris* or **Garnet and Gray** based on the bilingual school's colors, but they're now **Gee-Gees**.[10]

They had been good independent players, but Milwaukee's **Cream Citys** (est. 1865) finished last in their only NL season, 1878. "Cream City" owes to 'Waukee's yellow-white brick buildings, made from the light clay from Lake Michigan's western shore. (Several later teams were **Cream Citys** or **Creams**.)

Don Striegel owned an independent Pottsville football team (est. 1920), and he wasn't particular when he ordered their kits: "The color isn't important." After reddish-brown jerseys landed on his doorstep his players were the Pottsville **Maroons**.[11] They wore that name in the NFL from 1925 to '28 (but were Boston **Bulldogs** for their last NFL season, 1929). The maroon-and-white football powerhouse at Lafayette College in the 1920s had already associated "**Maroons**" with football in eastern Pennsylvania. Some say Pottsville's **Eleven** were never even **Maroons** until signing Lafayette standout Charlie Berry for 1925 … about the time that Lafayette's **Maroons** changed spots to be **Leopards**.

> The word *varsity* can refer to the principal teams at a secondary school or college, but it's really just old British shorthand for *university*. With a long history as part of the British Empire, Canada has two conspicuous 'versity teams. The red and black at the University of New Brunswick–Fredericton were **Red Shirts** (soccer), **Red Bombers** (football), **Red Bloomers** (women's football), and **Red Devils** (hockey) until all became **Varsity Reds** in the mid-1990s. The University of Toronto supports **Varsity Blues**, although attendees of U of T's famous dental school won hockey's 1917 Allan Cup as Toronto **Dentals**.

• • •

After the brown-and-gold footballers from Baldwin-Wallace University in Berea, Ohio swarmed opponents in 1930, they were **Yellow Jackets**. In fact, contrasting stripes of any color can yield **Hornets** or **Wasps**, but gold helps:

- The Harris-Stowe State University **Hornets** (St. Louis) are brown and gold.
- Black and gold wrap the Alabama State University **Hornets** (Montgomery), Emporia State **Hornets**, Savannah [Ga.] College of Art and Design **Bees**, West Virginia State University **Yellow Jackets** (in Institute), and the University of Wisconsin–Superior **Yellowjackets**. The American International College's **Internats** (Springfield, Mass.) are now **Yellow Jackets** (with white as a third color), and the Randolph-Macon College **Yellow Jackets** (Ashland, Va.) trade their gold for "lemon."
- Blue and gold are modeled by the Morris College's **Hornets** (Sumter, S.C.) and those **Yellow Jackets** at Allen University (Columbia, S.C.), Howard Payne University (Brownwood, Texas), Montana State University–Billings, New York City Technical College, and Cedarville [Ohio] University. The same tones are worn by the **YellowJackets** (one word) and **LadyJackets** at LeTourneau University (Longview, Texas).
- Green-and-gold are used by the **Yellow Jackets** at Black Hills State University (Spearfish, S.D.) and **Hornets** at both CSU Sacramento and Lyndon [Vt.] State College.
- Defiantly flashing colors that are unique in this class are the purple-and-gold **Yellow Jackets** and **Lady Jackets** from the Restorationist-founded Defiance College in Defiance, Ohio.

• • •

"**Tigers**" is often assigned to athletes wearing either orange or gold. Those at Savannah State are orange and blue. Blue-and-gold **Tigers** represent Grace Bible College (Grand Rapids). Gold and purple cover Olivet Nazarene University's

Tigers (Bourbonnais, Ill.). For alternating stripes of gold and maroon, see the Hiwassee College **Tigers** (Madisonville, Tenn.).

Of course, the most anthropomorphically correct **Tigers** are orange and black, like those at Reedley [Calif.] College or any school that copies Princeton's colors by design. Thomas Doane was a New England Congregationalist pastor whose railroad superintendent job brought him to Nebraska. He envisioned a "Harvard of the prairies," but installed a graduate of Yale and Princeton—Rev. David B. Perry—as the first president of Doane College in 1872. The college says an orange-and-black pennant was stitched together for an 1887 meeting by the daughters of Thomas Doane, colors that led to **Tigers** by 1907. (The **Tiger** mascot was later named Thomas.)[12] This endearing anecdote always fails to report that Mr. Doane's adorable daughters by then ranged in age from 27 to 34, the eldest of whom was likely able to exercise some influence over administrative decisions through her husband, school president D.B. Perry.

• • •

Unlike **Blue Bears** or **Purple Eagles**, golden bears and golden eagles are actual critters. California's golden bear (*Ursus arctos californicus*) is an extinct grizzly subspecies and the golden eagle (*Aquila chrysaetos*) inhabits much of the northern hemisphere. When other explanations are absent, you can probably attribute "**Golden**" jocks to gold-and-*something* uniforms.

For many **Golden Eagles**, that *something* is blue, as seen at Clarion University of Pennsylvania (Clarion), La Sierra University (Riverside, Calif.), Northeastern Illinois University (Chicago), Northland Pioneer College (Holbrook, Ariz.), Rock Valley College (Rockford, Ill.), Spalding University (Ky.), and Utah State University–College of Eastern Utah (Price). There are maroon-and-gold **Golden Eagles** at the University of Minnesota–Crookston and West Virginia's University of Charleston. Green-and-gold **Golden Eagles** represent Feather River College (Quincy, Calif.) and SUNY Brockport. Black-and-gold **Golden Eagles** are at CSU-Los Angeles.

Mostly making a habitat in high hills, the golden eagle is called the "mountain eagle," as subliminally referenced by **Eagles** at Green Mountain College (Poultney, Vt.), Colorado Mountain College (Steamboat Springs), and Sierra Nevada College (Incline Village, Nev.), which is on the slope of the Sierra Nevadas. Find collegiate **Eagles** in California's Coastal Range at the College of the Siskiyous [Mountains] in Weed and Mendocino College in Ukiah.

With no native grizzlies, eastern states can explain their athletic **Golden Bears** only through their choice of gold. Refer to those in blue and gold at the West Virginia University Institute of Technology (in Montgomery). Gold-and-black **Golden Grizzlies** are from Michigan's Oakland [County] University.

• • •

Cardinals usually wear cardinal red uniforms. That color isn't named after the red bird. It's the other way 'round. When white pioneers noticed the dramatic colors in the male of a particular North American finch, they called it the "northern cardinal" because the feathers and crown looked like the red robes and crested hats of Catholic Church Cardinals (the very representatives of Papal authority from whom many European Protestants had fled). Almost all **Cardinals** are casually "Redbirds." In 1969, Saginaw Valley State University (University Center, Mich.) called its red-and-blue the **Redbirds**, but they were **Cardinals** within a year. Illinois State teams have managed to remain **Redbirds**, although they're clearly identified with cardinal imagery.

Seven states claim *Cardinalis cardinalis* as the state bird: North Carolina, Virginia, West Virginia, Kentucky, Ohio, Indiana, and Illinois. The following colleges of **Cardinals** are in those contiguous red states: Ball State University (Muncie, Ind.), North Central College (Naperville, Ill.), Otterbein University (Westerville, Ohio), the University of Louisville [Ky.], Stratford University (Falls Church, Va.), and Wheeling [W.Va.] Jesuit University.

Of course, WJU could have gone the **Cardinal** direction through its Catholic roots; the College of Cardinals comprises the super-bishops whose authority is surpassed by none but the Pope. In 1888, American bishops opened the only North American college that answers to the Vatican's cardinals, the Catholic University of America in Washington, D.C., which keeps **Cardinals**. Another Catholic school, Winona's Saint Mary's University of Minnesota, replaced **Cardinals** with **Red Men** in 1932. To distance itself from the Indian mascots that followed, SMU re-hatched **Cardinals** for 1992.

• • •

Many colleges have changed academic colors to match their highly visible teams, but a few maintain two separate sets. CUA's red-and-black **Cardinals** (above) ignore the gold and white academic colors still worn at graduation. Andrews University (Berrien Springs, Mich.) has colors of blue and gold, and no one can recall how it came to sponsor red-clad **Cardinals**. The academic colors at Skagit Valley College (Mount Vernon, Wash.) are blue, green, and black, but teams are red-and-white **Cardinals**. In 1907 baseballers at Roanoke College (Salem, Va.) couldn't find uniforms in the (still-official) blue and yellow, so they bought gray-and-maroon duds. Basketballers followed suit in 1911, and as **Maroon and Grays** they solidified team colors that were independent of school colors. They'd be **Maroons** within a few years.[13]

Kicks | Ice Dogs | GreenJackets | Lynx

When you watch The Beautiful Game, don't be surprised by sides that have self-referencing names; the word *soccer* itself is a distortion of *assoc.*, which is British shorthand for association football (a name to distinguish it from rugby football). That gives Europe plenty of teams like Sunderland **AFC** (Association Football Club) or **FCB** (Futbol Club Barcelona). Most *futbol* teams do have nicknames—Sunderlanders are the **Black Cats**—but the game's long history of regional rivalries makes identification by municipality the norm.

The MLS Dallas **Burn** got named in 1996 for the Texas heat, but they were **FC** Dallas by 2005, two years before Toronto **FC** arrived in the league. (Toronto players are informally the "**Reds**.") American soccer teams of the 1920s, like New York **FC** and Philadelphia **FC**, were Field Clubs, not Football Clubs, although the English Premier League's Manchester City **F.C.** have joined New York's baseball **Yankees** in backing an MLS expansion team, New York City **FC** (Football Club), to start in 2105 at Yankee Stadium.

A bunch of S.C. ("sporting club" ... or *clube sporting* or *sportclub* or *club sportif*) sides are in the top national leagues of Portugal (**Sporting** Braga, **Sporting** Lisbon), Spain (**Real Sporting** Gijón), Belgium (**Sporting** Lokeren, **Sporting** Charleroi), Panama (**Sporting** San Miguelito), Peru (**Sporting** Cristal), and Brazil (Ceará **Sporting**). Such names were absent from the U.S. until Missouri's MLS team was renamed **Sporting** Kansas City in 2011.[1]

San Diego has twice had indoor-soccer **Sockers** (1978–96, 2001–04), while Chicago hosted soccer **Shoccers** (NPSL, 1985–87). Texas's Dallas **Sidekicks** (1984–2004) were doubly clever because a sidekick is either a lateral foot-pass or the friendly ever-present foil of movie cowboys. The USL Austin **Sockadillos** (1987–89) punned upon "armadillo," the official small mammal of Texas. *Striker* is British *futbol*-speak for a high-scoring forward, and the NASL Fort Lauderdale **Strikers** (1977–83) moved from Florida to Minneapolis as the 1984 Minnesota **Strikers** (in the MISL from 1985 to '88). In 1995 the Fort Lauderdale **Kicks** became Fort Lauderdale **Strikers** and finished as *Florida* **Strikers** (1996–97), but the NASL relaunched some Fort Lauderdale **Strikers** in 2006. Other **Kicks** (and **Kix** and **Kickers**) kick their aptronyms around all over semi-pro and club circuits.

Two new MLS franchises expanded the league's international flavor in 2005 by taking Spanish-language names. **Real** Salt Lake copied the name of Spain's spectacularly popular *Real Madrid CF* (**Royal** Madrid *Club de Fútbol*).[2] **CD Chivas USA** (Carson, Calif.) repeated the name of its *Primera División* parent club in Mexico, *Chivas Rayadas de Guadalajara* (striped goats of Guadalajara). A reporter had given those original *Chivas* their *nombre* in 1948 when he said they resembled hopping goats.[3] (Before the 2014 season the MLS took over the **Chivas**. It's expected they'll be renamed by new owners for 2015.)

• • •

Kentucky is famous for the Louisville Slugger baseball bats made by Hillerich & Bradsby. The mascot for the minor league Louisville **Bats** is a winged, nocturnal mammal in the *Chiroptera* order and not a lathed wooden club, but they do swing away at Louisville Slugger Field.

. . .

While you'll probably not encounter a lot of football **GrassWildcats** or basketball **Hardwood Bears**, many minor league hockey teams slip "**Ice-**" in front of a standard moniker, which can be a necessary reminder in those places where ice hockey would seem about as likely as hell freezing over:

- Swampy Lafayette hosts the Louisiana **IceGators** (1995–2005, 2009–).
- The Austin **Ice Bats** (est. 1996) referred to the one-million Mexican free-tailed bats (*Tadarida brasiliensis*) that live in the Texas capital, taking off in a black ribbon at sunset from March to November from under the Congress Avenue Bridge to hunt insect prey. The **Ice Bats** folded in 2008, but Austin Community College adopted a "River Bat" mascot two years later, not yet having athletic teams.
- Elsewhere in the Texas heat, the Corpus Christi **Ice Rays** (est. 1998) became **Rayz** in 2002 and **IceRays** in 2008.
- California's Long Beach **Ice Dogs** (1996–2007) were formerly Los Angeles **Ice Dogs** (1995/96).
- The Winston-Salem [N.C.] **IceHawks** (1997–99) had been the Adirondack **IceHawks** (Glens Falls, N.Y.) until 2004 and the similarly chilly Adirondack **Frostbite** until 2006.
- An ice pilot is a captain who specializes in navigating frozen waters, but sunny Florida's Pensacola **Ice Pilots** (1996–2008) changed shifts on the fly while tipping their wings to aviators at the Pensacola Naval Air Station.
- The town of Upper Maryland had Chesapeake **Icebreakers** with a polar bear mascot from 1997 to 1999.
- The bear that represents Tennessee's Knoxville **Ice Bears** (est. 2002) is a black bear, which isn't a real "ice bear," as *Ursus maritimus*—the polar bear—is sometimes called.
- Our favorite sunglass-wearing polar bear (*Shades*) represented Florida's IHL Orlando **Solar Bears**, 1996–2001.

You'd think a team simply called **Ice** is either not very imaginative or desperately short on ink, but different Indianapolis **Ice** teams since 1988 (and the 2007-named AHL Rockford **IceHogs**) recall the ice harvesters upon whom Midwestern meatpackers relied in the pre-refrigeration age. Cranbrook, B.C. hosts the College of the Rockies **Avalanche** and junior hockey's Kootenay [Region] **Ice**. Cranbrook is at the heart of the Canadian Rockies near the glaciers of the Jasper, Banff, and Kootenay National Parks, but the **Ice** had already been Alberta's Edmonton **Ice** (1996–98).

As with the *Ice-* prefix, minor league hockey has a corresponding weakness for the *-Blades* suffix. North Little Rock on the Arkansas River was home to the Arkansas **RiverBlades** (1999–2003). (They'd wanted to be **RazorBlades**, but the Arkansas **Razorbacks** [p. 79] campaigned against the potentially confusing name.) Lexington's Kentucky **Thoroughblades** (AHL, 1996–2001) were in the Thoroughbred City. Estero's Florida **Everblades** (est. 1998) are next to the swampy Everglades. Maryland's WHA-ers were Baltimore **Blades** (1973–75). The Western Hockey League had Los Angeles **Blades** (1961–67). The Boston **Bruins'** bear mascot is "Blades."

• • •

Two team identities link to a famous annual sporting event in Georgia. The Augusta National Golf Club's members first donned green sportcoats to identify themselves as officials in the 1937 Masters Tournament. Sam Sneed was the first winner to get a Green Jacket with his trophy package in 1949. Augusta's minor league baseballers are **GreenJackets** (1994–). That otherwise transparent reference to the Masters is obscured by Sting, their clearwing dragonfly (*Erythemis simplicicollis*) mascot.

Golf was invented on Scotland's seaside about 500 years ago. In fact, the artificial sand and water traps with which you're probably too familiar are artifacts of those coastal origins. A golfing ground cannot be a called "links course" unless it's on natural, seaside terrain, but that doesn't keep any ol' duffer from saying "I'm off to the links" whenever he grabs his clubs. Even Augusta isn't on the very short list of true American links courses, but its minor league hockey Augusta **Lynx** (1998–2008) unaccidentally resembled *links*. The **Lynx** mascot and name defied local fauna because the feline commonly called *lynx* lives in Canada and along its southern border. The *Lynx* genus of the southern U.S. is actually the bobcat, so **Bobcats** at East Georgia College (Swainsboro), Georgia Northwestern Technical College (Rome), and Georgia College (Milledgeville) better represent the state's wildlife.

• • •

Sticking with the lynx's scientific name—*Lynx canadensis*—there are lots of **Lynx** crews in Canada proper. International League baseball included Ontario's Ottawa **Lynx** (1993–2007). Soccer's USL Toronto **Lynx SC** (est. 1997) has had **Lady Lynx** W-League counterparts since 2004. There are *les Lynx du Collège Édouard-Montpetit* (Longueuil, Que.). The WNBA Minnesota **Lynx** (est. 1999) at Minneapolis are in a border state. **Lynx** in Illinois bobcat country are at Lincoln College in Lincoln and Lindenwood University–Belleville, both helped by alliteration, as are the Lesley University **Lynx** in Cambridge, Massachusetts.[4]

The aforementioned southern—or *Florida*—bobcat (*Lynx rufus floridianus*) explains **Bobcats** at Miami's St. Thomas University, but bobcats are all over the continent, as indicated by uncountable **Bobcats** and **Wildcats**. In strict taxonomical terms, *wildcat* refers only to *Felis silvestris* of Africa and Eurasia (which looks like a wild housecat). That which North Americans call *wildcat* is a lynx or bobcat, although the *wild cats* (two words) that serve as mascots for **Wildcats** (one word) are mountain lions, jaguars, or any fierce non-domestic cats.

Yes. It's confusing.

Outlaw Reds | Alleghenies | Federals | Innocents

St. Louis millionaire Henry Lucas watched baseball's AA and NL join in the first National Agreement in 1883 and saw room for a third major league. He and other team owners of the era (like the Robison brothers of Cleveland's **Spiders**) owned streetcars that made money on the same fannies twice on otherwise slow weekends. The best pros in the 1884 Union Association always seemed to end up on Lucas's own St. Louis **Maroons**, who provided color contrast to the city's AA **Brown Stockings**.

The "outlaw" UA had a team of Cincinnati **Outlaw Reds** and several simply called **Unions** (or "Onions" to detractors.) Stacking the **Maroon** deck backfired when Lucas's redshirts won the championship by such a margin that fans had lost all interest. The circuit collapsed after one season and the champion **Maroons** were the only UA-ers good enough for the '85 NL. (The NA's best team finished last and sixth in their two NL campaigns, so many historians won't call the UA a major league.) Indy clothier John T. Brush bought the **Maroons** and moved them to the NL cellar as Indianapolis **Hoosiers** (1887–89).

• • •

For the most part, only players with expiring contracts had joined the UA out of fear of the NL's reserve clause, which let players re-sign only with their former teams, although they could be traded, sold, or cut at the club's discretion. A larger threat to hardballers was a looming salary cap, so in 1885 they created the first labor organization in sports, the Brotherhood of Professional Base Ball Players. The guild's president was John Montgomery Ward, a Columbia-trained lawyer and the New York **Giants'** star shortstop.

In 1889 the **Hoosiers'** Mr. Brush proposed capping NL salaries by putting players in performance-based categories, so Monte Ward's union took the best NLers (and some from the AA) into a new cooperative circuit, the 1890 Players' League. Ward himself managed Brooklyn's Ward's **Wonders**. PL squads surgically targeted established teams during the "Brotherhood War." The PL's Chicago **Pirates** revealed by name that they'd raked the 1889 rosters of the NL Chicago **White Stockings** and AA St. Louis **Browns**. Half of the PL Pittsburgh **Burghers** had played for the 1889 **Allegheny** club.[1] The remaining helpless **Alleghenies** played the 1890 NL schedule as Pittsburgh **Innocents**.

To rub it in, PL squads co-opted the nicknames of established neighbors. The PL New York **Giants** often played right next to NL New York **Giants** on the same afternoon. The NL's **Quakers** became today's **Phillies** in 1890 to avoid confusion with Philly's upstart PL **Quakers**. The NL Buffalo **Bisons** (est. 1879) had dropped to the International League in 1885 but went bust after 1890 as fans followed the familiar faces on the PL's last-place Buffalo **Bisons**. The same-name trend was bucked in Cleveland, where PLers were named for the youngest of rookies and not for the veterans of the 1889 Cleveland **Spiders** that filled its ranks. The presence of 16-year-old pitcher Willie "Kid" McGill was notable enough to make teammates Cleveland **Infants**. (He's still the youngest major leaguer with a complete-game victory.) The PL champs were Boston's **Reds**, neighbors of the NL **Red Stockings**.

The PL generally outdrew the NL in shared markets. The NL even folded Brush's **Hoosiers** to allow him (and **White Stockings** owner Albert Spalding) to buy into the **Giants** and thus avoid having the PL bust its big-city team. Not suspecting they had the senior circuit on the ropes, top PL backers were talked into selling out the Brotherhood after a single season to merge their squads with local NLers. The Spalding-brokered deal consolidated New York's two **Giants** as well as rival pairs in Brooklyn, Pittsburgh, and Chicago.

The NL and AA agreed the reserve clause would return PLers to their former teams, but the AA Philadelphia **Athletics** blew the paperwork on the **Wonders'** star second baseman Lou Bierbauer and he was snapped up by the NL **Innocents**. That bit of plunder made Pittsburgh owner J. Palmer O'Neill "J. Pirate O'Neill" in the press and made his **Innocents** today's Pittsburgh **Pirates**, a name used later by NHLers (1925–30) and NFLers (1933–39, now **Steelers**).

> As seen in Chicago and Pittsburgh, players often become **Pirates** after some misbehaving. In 1928, Elmhurst College's ambitious president wanted to soften the school's evangelical reputation and give it quality teams. He got both when news broke that the new football coach had recruited **Blue and White** players based on their athletic skills (*gasp!*) while he'd collected a bigger salary than the prez himself (*double-gasp!*). With rivals calling them **Pirates**, the conference concluded that Elmhurst had placed "a higher value on athletics and physical education than on academic accomplishments."[2] (*Triple-dog-gasp!*) Things really unraveled when there seemed to be merit behind suggestions that some players weren't even students while others had gotten paid. Elmhurstians got tired of being reminded of their piratical past, so the blue-and-white **Pirates** became **Bluejays** in a 1940 name-the-team contest.

• • •

Baseball's next forgotten league started in good economic times in 1912 as the minor Columbia League, but it was the Federal League the next year. In 1914 and '15 it was an eight-team major league that usually added -*feds* to the city name. There were Buffalo **BufFeds** (or **Blues**), Chicago **Federals** (or **Whales**), Indianapolis **Hoosiers** (or **Hoosierfeds**), and St. Louis **SlouFeds** (or **Terriers**). Brooklyn's **Tip-Tops/BrookFeds** were owned by Robert B. Ward of Tip-Top bakeries. Baltimore's "**Terrapins**" was lifted from the University of Maryland teams, and Kansas City's **Packers** were named after local beef shippers.

The FL had an antitrust suit against Organized Baseball (the AL and NL) that ended up before Judge Kenesaw Mountain Landis. The sport's future first commissioner dragged his feet until the FL collapsed. Some FL owners reinvested in major league teams (as with the PL buyout), but Baltimore alone continued to the U.S. Supreme Court. The unanimous decision came in 1922 (a little late to help the **Terrapins**). In it, Justice Oliver Wendell Holmes said the baseball biz wasn't interstate commerce because the travel of players across state lines was incidental and "not the essential thing." The antitrust exemption thereby granted to Organized Baseball is a luxury still enjoyed by no other sport.

Senators | Capitals | United | Golden Gophers

The Latin word *senex* refers to an old man, so ancient Rome's ruling *Senatus* was composed only of elders from elite families. That exclusivity runs counter to all egalitarian instincts, but a modern democracy very often calls its senior legislative body the *Senate*.

If you didn't know the U.S. or Canadian capital, you'd figure it out from their **Senators**, **Nationals**, **Statesmen**, **Capitals**, and **Capitols**. Readers who are satisfied with that explanation can skip a bit.

• • •

The Roman gladiator emblems associated with the NHL's Ottawa **Senators** (est. 1992) acknowledge the original Latin root of *senate*, although their lion mascot Spartacat is named for the ex-gladiator Spartacus, whose slave revolt truly threatened the Senate's armies until being put down in 71 BCE.

The current **Senators** aren't the first of that name in O-Town. Amateur players for Ottawa **H.C.** ("Hockey Club," est. 1883) were **Senators** from 1902 to '08, but they're often the "**Silver Seven**" on lists of Stanley Cup champs. *Seven* indicated the players per side before it was trimmed to six in 1911. By then, "**Senators**" was dominant, and they were so known as charter NHL members (1917–34).

The CFL's **Rough Riders** (1876–1976) were "Ottawa **Senators**" only in 1925 and '26, a name reused by a senior hockey side (1945–55).

• • •

Basketball in the U.S. capital has seen BAA/NBA Washington **Capitols** (1946–51) and abbreviated Washington **Caps** (ABA, 1969/70). Minor league hockey's Washington **Presidents** served a four-year term (1957–60). The Baltimore **Bullets** moved to Landover, Maryland for the 1973/74 season as Capital **Bullets**. The next year they were Washington **Bullets**, having ceded "Capital" to new housemates, the NHL Washington **Capitals**. A couple of soccer sides have been Washington **Diplomats** (NASL: 1974–81; ASL: 1988–90).

Despite their lightning bolt emblem, the NLL Washington **Power** (2001–02, Landover, Md.) alluded to political influence, not electrical capacity, although the subliminal suggestion of "D.C. power" (as opposed to A.C.) is appreciated. The MLS D.C. **United** represent the capital of the *United* States, but they're willing to capitalize on the familiarity of English sides like Newcastle **United** and the exceptionally famous Manchester **United**.[1]

The W-League's D.C. **United Women** entered the 2013 NWSL as the Washington **Spirit** … a "spirit of freedom" that reminded soccer fans of the WUSA Washington **Freedom** (est. 2001). Their league was in hiatus after 2003, but **Freedom** endured in exhibition and W-League games until joining the new WPS in 2009. In 2011 they relocated to Boca Raton and took the name of their Florida-based tech company sponsors, **magicJack**. Their owner ruffled feathers that season, so the WPS ejected the franchise. When the '**Jacks** sued, it pushed the already-struggling league into oblivion.

Minor league hockey's Washington **Eagles** (1939–42) and the American University **Eagles** are D.C. residents named for the national symbol, but the bald eagle is more often a mascot. Screech the Eagle represents the MLB Washington **Nationals**. There are W-shaped eagle's wings for the NHL's **Capitals**. An eagle with wings outstretched is D.C. **United's** emblem.

In 1972 the Secret Service contracted Virginia's Kastle Systems to develop strategies for presidential security. In 2008 the owners of Kastle established the WTT Washington **Kastles**, incorporating the crenellated walls from the company trademark into that of the tennis team.

• • •

We'll combine the names of the Federal City's baseball teams in a single discussion because their chronologies are otherwise confused. (It's confusing anyway.) Many NA clubs were called Washington **Nationals** or **National** of Washington. The first (1859–75) toured nationally in 1867. Most had been recruited as Treasury Department clerks, unchallenging positions that didn't require perfect attendance. More Washington **Nationals** were in the 1884 UA. The NL **Senators** of 1886 to '89 were alternately "**Statesmen**." The AA's 1891 Washington **Statesmen** were different players that transitioned into new NL **Senators** (1892–99). Then an AL team (1901–60) tried to separate themselves from past **Senators** of the rival NL by stitching *N-A-T-I-O-N-A-L-S* on their shirts in 1905 (the first time a team name had so appeared).[2] The fans called them **Senators** anyway, and *S-E-N-A-T-O-R-S* finally turned up on the 1959 apparel, just before a 1961 move made them today's Minnesota **Twins**. (In 1921 those **Senators** had shared the capital with like-named APFA/NFL Washington **Senators**.) In a case of isomorphism (structural identicality), there were still AL Washington **Senators** in D.C. the next season, a 1961 expansion franchise that would become Texas **Rangers** in 1972.

More than three decades passed before another MLB franchise switched cities, and Washington was involved again. The unprofitable Montreal **Expos** moved to D.C. for 2005, and "**Senators**" was the presumed nickname nominee, but the **Rangers** claimed that name as part of their franchise history. Irony was also at work; D.C.'s civic leaders didn't like "**Senators**" because its residents had no voting representation in Congress, even while paying federal taxes. (Such taxation without representation had once led to rebellion.) In light of that, players became Washington **Nationals**, a self-evident alternative with its own local history.

• • •

State and provincial capitals also seat **Capitals** and **Senators**. The AHL Indianapolis **Capitals** (1939–52) played in Indiana's capital and there were Indianapolis **Capitols** (1968–69) in the Continental Football League. That makes this a good time to explain that a *capital* city is the seat of a centralized government while a *capitol* is the building in that city in which legislators meet. **Capitals** often confuse the issue by employing capitol dome emblems.

The WTT's Sacramento **Capitals** (est. 1988) represent California's capital. The PCL Sacramento **Senators** did the same (intermittently) from 1891 to 1935. They were then **Solons** (1936–60, 1974–76) because the statesman and reformer who laid much of the groundwork for Athenian democracy was named Solon (c. 639–559 BCE).

The state capitol is in Charleston, but the West Virginia town of Elkins fields **Senators** at Davis & Elkins College. They remember two U.S. senators instrumental to the school's 1904 founding, Henry G. Davis and his son-in-law Stephen B. Elkins.[3]

Nashville is Tennessee's capital, but there are red-white-and-blue **Senators** at Morristown's Walters State Community College, named for U.S. Sen. Herbert S. Walters (in office 1963–64).

Lander University (Greenwood, S.C.) was the only four-year liberal arts college in the U.S. run by a county. It was a state school by 1992, but "**Senators**" had been chosen for the inaugural 1968/69 basketball season simply because no other regional team was so called.[4] LU's switch to **Bearcats** in 2003 was just as arbitrary.

• • •

Entrepreneurs in St. Paul in the late 1850s wanted their city to become a hub for westward railroads. A political cartoon grafted the faces of politicians and industrialists onto striped gophers that were happily speeding across the prairie by rail and munching through millions of dollars in railroad appropriations as gophers do through crops. The newly nicknamed Gopher State soon had **Gophers** at the University of Minnesota. After footballers donned gold jerseys in 1934, they were the **Golden Gophers** (with a mascot named Goldy). St. Paul's **Colored Gophers** were black baseball's top team of 1909 (although it was hard to declare national champs before the organization of the first Negro league in 1920).

• • •

New Hampshirites are proud that theirs is the first state to cast votes in each presidential primary season. Baseball owners, therefore, thought that the same crowd would love Manchester's new-for-2004 minor league **Primaries**, but fans who hated that reference to the democratic process (and who were apparently unfamiliar with irony) campaigned for a vote on the moniker. The newly named New Hampshire **Fisher Cats** refer to the seldom-seen fisher (*Martes pennanti*), a nocturnal member of the weasel family that lives among North America's boreal forests. The -*cat* appendage is a New Englandism.

Bloomers | Belles | Trojanettes | Athenas

In the 1850s social reformer and newspaper editor Amelia Bloomer was championing loose ladies' trousers that were derived from Turkish fashions. The skirts worn over them were shorter than ever without revealing additional flesh. The obvious name for Ms. Bloomer's blooming knickers was "bloomers," a word sometimes directed at those who wore them. In fact, the fashion never fully blossomed because many prudent ladies sacrificed the comfort of bloomers to avoid the association with progressive politics.

Late-century female athletes dropped their restrictive skirts and bloomers got a second life as uniforms. In fact, male spectators were sometimes barred from watching women's basketball, lest they witness players running around in what many still considered underwear. Sportswriters reflexively identified more than a few barnstorming teams as **Bloomers** or **Bloomer Girls**, and female baseballers might have been described as "bloomer girls" regardless of their official team name or legwear.[1]

A century removed from the bloomer era, many team names remain bent on indicating the otherness of female athletes. The University of Central Arkansas **Bears** are joined by female **Sugar Bears** (former **Bearettes**). The female **Bears** at Baltimore's Morgan State University were **Honey Bears** in press reports into the twenty-first century, and Mercer University's basketball **Bears** were matched with **Teddy Bears** through the 1970s. The gold and white colors at Xavier University of Louisiana (New Orleans) make for a male **Gold Rush** and female **Gold Nuggets**, the former suggesting ambition and speed and the latter a nearly serendipitous discovery of modest mineral pieces. In past decades, Seton Hall's female **Pirates**—especially those shooting buckets—were often **Bucettes**.

You'd certainly notice if your local grocer had one check-out line for "Customers" and another for "Lady Customers." For greatest parallelism, shouldn't the first sign say "Gentlemen Customers"? Otherwise, can we assume that people who buy groceries are male by default and female only by unforeseen exception? Readers will establish for themselves the degree to which they are bothered by **Lady Tigers**, **Lady Pirates**, and **Lady Hawks** that are so qualified at many colleges. What is undeniably more irksome is the habit of substituting *Lady* for some more ambitious modifier. **Fighting Tigers** or **Blue Jackets** correspond to **Lady Tigers** or **Lady Jackets**, subliminal propositions that female athletes lack either the fight or color of the boys. For example, Montana State University in Bozeman once hosted **Fighting Bobcats** and **Lady Cats**, but all are now **Bobcats**. (The few bobcats in Yellowstone National Park are usually in its northern half, closest to Bozeman.) Oregon Tech keeps **Hustlin' Owls** alongside **Lady Owls**. Missouri's Crowder College hosts **Roughriders** and **Lady 'Riders**. Merced [Calif.] College keeps **Blue Devils** and **Lady Devils** (occasionally "**She-Devils**").

• • •

A huge number of colleges were all-male institutions through the 1960s. Congress ended sex discrimination at federally assisted institutions only in 1972,[2] opening up athletic opportunities for young women long after male **Lions, Barons**, and **Mounties** had been established. Some say the **Lady Lions, Lady Barons**, and **Lady Mounties** appearing thereafter were named to effect both agreement and distinction and are not in any way indicative of a masculine-by-preference model. (One defense might cite black baseball's New York ***Black* Yankees**, Brooklyn ***Brown* Dodgers**, or Washington ***Black* Senators**, who chose to divorce their product from recognized local entities even while capitalizing on the familiarity of same.)

There's a different problem for **Lady Peacocks** or **Lady Stags**, who expect *lady* to create distinguishment from that which can refer only to the male of those species. The **Rams**—male sheep—at Shepherd [W.Va.] University are shepherded together with **Lady Rams**. That avoids *ewes*, a perfectly good English word for an adult female of the *Ovis aries* (sheep) species.

• • •

Exhibiting one's school spirit with a letter sweater or sportjacket (blazer) used to be a staple of collegiate life. Senior "big sisters" at the all-female Elms College (Chicopee, Mass.) used to present underclasswomen with such garments after the annual Soph Show. Likewise, Hood College for women (Frederick, Md.) recognized a student with good grades and appropriate spirit with its white blazer award starting in 1928. (It was a sweater before that.)[3] Elms and Hood are now coed, but both retain **Blazers** to commemorate those traditions.

Connecticut College was a women's institution with a weekly tea social. The New London school went coed in 1969 with men's sports starting the next year. The "One lump or two?" inquiry as to how much sugar was taken at tea may explain CC's **Camels**, but that's among several wildly different creation stories recalled by alums. Another says male students were still so scarce in 1970 that all of them—talent notwithstanding—were required to fill out the basketball roster. Those athletes (such as they were) considered themselves to be about as nimble as lumbering desert camels.[4]

Each incoming class at the all-female Winthrop College (Rock Hill, S.C.) used to elect its own mascot, a tradition deemed unworkable when the athletic profile was raised after men arrived in 1974. **"Eagles"** was thereafter applied uniformly to athletes at what's been called Winthrop University since 1992, the "Campus of Champions."[5]

The yearbook at Harrisburg, Virginia's State Normal School for Women was named the *Schoolma'am* in 1910. Dr. Samuel Page Duke (a former coach) started his thirty-year tenure as president in 1919 and strongly supported **Schoolma'am** teams.[6] When Mr. Duke welcomed World War II vets by making the college coed in 1946, male basketballers were immediately **Dukes**. The **Schoolma'ams** would later be complementary **Duchesses**, but all were **Dukes** in 1982 at what was by then James Madison University.

JMU's post-war embrace of men wasn't entirely altruistic. Women's colleges had a huge incentive to go coed as veterans' tuition payments were guaranteed after 1944 by the G.I. Bill. The number of women receiving such aid was negligible, and no one knew if they would drop their newfound educational ambitions to resume domestic duties. Adelphi University (Garden City, N.Y.) didn't have an official pre-war nickname, but immediately after going coed in 1946 it chose a big-time label for newly assembled teams: **Panthers**. In fact, readers may note the large number of colleges among these pages that traded esoteric nicknames for some that were more recognizable in the late 1940s, just when veteran-students were starting to contribute to high-profile athletic programs as both players and fans.

• • •

As JMU's **Duchesses**-to-**Dukes** transition illustrates, masculine sports imagery is dominant. As prolific writer of the sociology of sport D. Stanley Eitzen says:

> Since the traditional masculine gender role matches most athletic qualities better than the traditional feminine gender role, the images and symbols are male. [Women] are 'others,' even when they do participate. Their team names and logos tend to perpetuate and strengthen the image of female inferiority by making them secondary, invisible, trivial, or unathletic.[7]

For example, U.S. Naval Academy's **Midshipmen** have a goat mascot because sailors traditionally kept goats on board to dispose of garbage in return for milk and butter, but the Navy billy goat (he-goat) is "Billy," whereas only a nanny (she-goat) is a capable dairy producer. "**Midshipmen**" also indicates an imperfect language that applies *freshman* and *second baseman* to members of either sex, which is why the Navy nearly always calls its female jocks "**Mids**." In rare cases, though, men inadvertently adopt a moniker with subliminal femininity:

- The Philadelphia **Phillies** owe some of their familiarity to the plural of the homophone *filly*, a young female horse.
- Marlin fishermen most want to catch "granders," those exceeding a thousand pounds. Male marlins are half as heavy, so only those big enough to give birth are the trophy-mascots for **Marlin** jocks.
- Canadians think nothing of assuming the names of revered British queens or princesses, so it has hosted multiple all-male **Victorias** and **Patricias**.
- There are certainly teams of male **Pumas** or **Aztecas** around, even though the final vowel (-*a*) indicates a feminine noun in Romance languages.
- Wanting to avoid cockfights, farmers maintain a rooster-to-hen ratio of any-where from six or twenty to one. It's therefore understandable that the flock would be called "hens," meaning that athletic **Sagehens**, **Blue Hens**, and **Mudhens** aren't always women.

• • •

Belle (beautiful) is a French feminine form that Southerners have long used to describe women of external beauty and internal strength. Historically the ideal belle was the white mistress of the antebellum plantation, but today any woman can aim for belle-ness, including those who toil on the playing field:

- Saint Mary's College (Notre Dame, Ind.) is a women's academy founded by the Sisters of the Holy Cross, an order from Le Mans, France. Saint Mary's blue-and-white French-form **Belles** echo of "The Bells of St. Mary's," a 1917 song revived by Bing Crosby in a 1946 movie of the same name. That same association gave **Belles** to Saint Mary's University (Halifax, N.S.), but they and the male **Saints** became **Huskies** in 1979.[8]

- In 1873 freed slaves were the first students at a coed institution opened by the Methodists' Freedman's Society in a Greensboro, North Carolina church basement. Northern industrialist Lyman Bennett financed improvements at what's now Bennett College. The "Vassar of the South" has been an all-female academy since 1926, one that requires students to conduct themselves as exemplary ladies, as indicated by **Belles**. The school bell on the college shield further supports the name; Mr. Bennett died of pneumonia on a campaign to raise money for said ringer.

- Like many institutions, Seminole [Okla.] State College hosts **Trojans**, but female basketballers have been **Belles** since the early days when they were outfitted by the local Blue Bell plant (makers of Wrangler jeans).

- There are **Tigers** and **Lady Tigers** at Nashville's Tennessee State University, but the women of track remain **Tigerbelles**, a name made famous by multiple TSU stars who won Olympic gold at Rome in 1960.

- Two single-sex schools in Louisville, Kentucky merged to create the coed Bellarmine University in 1968. The women were Bellarmine **Belles**, as if they required a little chivalric protection from BC's gentlemanly **Knights**. All are now **Knights** (never "**Lady Knights**").

• • •

Long before there were male **Knights** (and the unnecessarily sexualized female **Knighties** of the 1950s), basketballers at Michigan's Calvin College informally rivaled other Grand Rapids teams as **Rivals** (1920–21). They were respected a little more than the corresponding female **Rivalettes**, who played to empty stands to negate fallout from the occasionally exposed ankle.[9] But the **Rivalettes** bring us to a new French subject, one in which *-et* and *-ette* are respective masculine and feminine suffixes that mean "little" in an endearing way. For example, a *brunette* would be dark-haired or dark-complected little girl. *Brunette* lost its diminutive angle after jumping to English, where it can describe a dark-haired woman of any complexion or age.[10] Otherwise, *-ette* in English refers to quaint-sized objects; a cigarette is a little cigar and a kitchenette is a scaled-down cookery. When London's *Daily Mail* called female suffragists "suffragettes" in 1906, *-ette* reclaimed its feminizing suffixation, although male *Mail* readers certainly understood that the word aimed to diminish the credibility of voting rights advocates who happened to be female. (It hardly helped that *-ette* is sometimes employed to suggest a cheap imitation, as in *leatherette*.)

Colleges were once quick to use *-ette* to create feminine counterparts for established team names (just as Nicolette or Antoinette might be named after an uncle named Nick or Tony). Few examples of the once-plentiful **Crusaderettes**, **Trojanettes**, or **Yellow Jackettes** survive,[11] although the convention still occurs among high schoolers or cheerleading **Pantherettes**, **Rebelettes**, or **Bullettes**. Female **Golden Eaglettes** played for Tennessee Technological University into the twentieth century. They were the teamette most etymologically in line with the original French form. Even in English, *eaglet* is a young eagle of either sex, but TTU's men were **Golden Eagles** when "**Eaglets**" would have effected the best parallelism. All TTU teams are now purple-and-yellow **Golden Eagles**, recognizing actual eagles near the Cookeville campus.

When Mississippi Valley State University opened its doors at Itta Bena in 1950, administrators wanted a team name. Because it was hot as hell on the Delta, "**Delta Devils**" carried the day, now joined by female **Devilettes**. On the other side of the Mississippi Valley is Northwestern State University in Natchitoches, Louisiana. It's hot there too, but the creation story for NSU's **Demons** and **Lady Demons** (named in 1923) is lost.

• • •

As discussed elsewhere, teams with monikers from the animal kingdom, like **Wildcats** and **Mustangs**, err on the side of power and aggression. Some cute and fluffy fauna, however, seem to give the impression that there is no male of their respective species. For example, about half of Australia's cuddly koalas (*Phascolarctos cinereus*) are male, but the only **Fighting Koalas** are at the all-female Columbia [S.C.] College.

The small, gray, fuzzy, and fighting theme continues at Mary Baldwin College (Staunton, Va.), a women's school with **Fighting Squirrels**. Different **Fighting Squirrels** represented Bradford College (Haverhill, Mass.), an 1803-founded women's institution that went coed in 1970 and closed in 2000.

Edmonton's University of Alberta fielded male **Golden Bears** in the mid-1930s and (presumably adorable) female **Pandas** shortly thereafter. Biologists long argued over whether the giant panda (*Ailuropoda melanoleuca*) of south-central China's bamboo forests was a bear or a big raccoon, but recent genetic testing has put it squarely in the *Ursidae* (bear) family. That conveniently realigns Alberta's **Golden Bears** and **Pandas**, but a respective ferocity and gentleness continues to distinguish them.[12]

Sweet Briar, Virginia in the Blue Ridge foothills is barely bigger than the women's school it contains. Prey eludes Virginia fox hunters by sticking to a briar patch, so Sweet Briar College teams are **Vixens**, the female form of the Old English word for a fox, *vix*. Other foxes are the Minnesota **Vixen** (est. 1999), the world's oldest continuously operated pro football team for women. Some of the pastoral innocence is lost when we consider that a secondary definition of *vixen* describes a badly tempered woman, or that *fox* is slang for a sexually appealing person.

• • •

Angels are spiritual beings that can adopt a human shape to act as divine intermediaries. The angels mentioned by name in canonical Christian literature are all male (Michael, Gabriel, and Raphael), which is curious because athletic **Angels** are almost exclusively the opposite.

If you have an angel on your tail, it's one of two kinds. A guardian angel is there when your well-being is part of some vast, eternal plan, but an avenging angel gets your case if you've messed up. To put some edge on their game, **Angels** at the Baptists' all-female Meredith College (Raleigh, N.C.) became **Avenging Angels** in 2007 (overlapping with indoor football's Los Angeles **Avengers** [2000–08] from the City of Angels). Some say "**Angels**" meant to compare

Meredith's athletes to the **Demon Deacons** at the formerly all-male Wake Forest University (p. 98) a hundred miles west.

The WBL Houston **Angels** (1978–80) of women's basketball were a celestial presence in a city with loads of space-themed teams. Two Catholic women's schools, Mount Mary College (Milwaukee) and the College of New Rochelle [N.Y.], keep blue-and-white **Blue Angels**. Men's teams at New Brunswick's *Université de Moncton* are *Aigles Bleus* (blue eagles), but the women swap a couple of French letters as *Anges Bleus* (blue angels). Kaskaskia College (Centralia, Ill.) has blue-and-white **Blue Devils** and **Blue Angels**, and we trust the reader's intuition to reveal which be men and which be women.

The above-listed teams show that **Angels** bend disproportionately toward the blue. That's because the Christian angelic hierarchy includes seven colored rays of light. The first (and most often cited) is the "blue sword" of the Archangel Michael, whose guardian angels travel on the beam and are illuminated by it.

• • •

The first person to organize women's *basket ball* was Senda Berenson. She was the athletic director at Smith College in Northampton, Massachusetts, just up the Connecticut River from the Springfield YMCA at which basketball had been invented in 1891. In fact, Berenson corresponded with James Naismith about how a women's version might be played. Victorians would have been scandalized by sweating ladies, so Berenson's game emphasized passing by assigning players to one of three zones (offense, defense, centre). The first collegiate women's game was in 1893 when Smith's class of '95 beat up on the class of '96 by a score of 5-4. This sporting first, the institution's advancement of women's athletics (spearheaded by Berenson), and Northampton's place at the heart of the Pioneer Valley serve to explain Smith's **Pioneers**.[13]

Down at Sophie Newcomb College in New Orleans (now part of Tulane), Clara Baer was trying to understand Dr. Naismith's game without ever having seen it live. (Following aforementioned spelling conventions, Baer's rulebook called her game *basquette*.) When her students started running plays in 1895 there were as many zones of confinement per side as there were players. Eventually, the games of Berenson and Baer evolved into the six-on-six affair played at some high schools into the 1990s. With only the ball crossing half court, it was like two three-on-three games played alternately back to back.

Among those who'd raise expectations were the women at black colleges—notably Bennett's abovementioned **Belles**—who ran all ninety-four feet.[14] The Philadelphia **Tribunes** (occasionally the "**Hustle**") were sponsored by the black-owned *Philadelphia Tribune*.[15] Those barnstorming African American women played full-court.

The most successful team of traveling women came out of Casserville, Missouri in 1936. Mr. C.M. Olson was already famous for attaching his Scandinavian surname to barnstorming men, Olson's **Terrible Swedes**. Now his hairdressing wife Doyle colored her friends' locks and took on the men at their own game for fifty years as All American **Red Heads**.[16]

With many men off to fight in World War II, the All-American Girls Professional Baseball League (1943–54) filled in, especially in Midwestern cities that were crucial to wartime production. To the modern reader, most of that circuit's monikers seem unnecessarily quaint: Chicago **Colleens**, Fort Wayne **Daisies**, Milwaukee/Grand Rapids **Chicks**, Muskegon/Kalamazoo **Lassies**, Racine/Battle Creek/Muskegon **Belles**, Rockford **Peaches**, and Springfield **Sallies**.[17] Don't expect much better from those teams in the first women's pro basketball circuit, the Women's Basketball League (1978–81), which included Dayton **Rockettes**, Houston **Angels**, Milwaukee **Does**, Minnesota **Fillies**, Philadelphia **Fox**, California **Dreams**, and New England **Gulls**.

$$\bullet\ \bullet\ \bullet$$

Fans of orthographic ingenuity can appreciate the silent *W* carried through the late 1970s by the University of Rhode Island's female **WRams**. Otherwise, sticking a *W* in front of *NBA* doesn't seem all that different from prefacing "**Lions**" with "**Lady**." Or as Casey Miller puts it in *The Handbook of Nonsexist Writing*, there's a "putdown implicit in such non parallel titles as the Professional Golfers' Association and the *Ladies* Professional Golfers' Association" [emphasis added].[18]

The 1997-founded WNBA would finally avoid such gender-specific identities. Putting its teams under local NBA owners might have yielded **Hornettes** or **Lady Lakers**. And few people would have blinked if the NBA's **Kings** had been joined by WNBA **Queens**, but the Sacramento **Monarchs** would be co-regents, not consorts (until folding in 2009). The WNBA Charlotte **Sting** joined the Charlotte **Hornets**.[19] The Houston **Rockets** burned less brightly than the Houston **Comets**, who won the first four WNBA crowns (then burned out financially and folded after 2008). The NBA Phoenix **Suns** and WNBA Phoenix **Mercury** are named for our solar system's star and its closest patron planet. The NBA Utah **Jazz** paired with the similarly spelled WNBA Utah **Starzz**, a name from bygone ABA men, the Utah **Stars** (1970–75).[20]

Later WNBA teams fit the same pattern. With expansion in 1998, the Detroit **Pistons** ran the WNBA **Shock** (as in absorber thereof). For 2010 the **Shock** moved to Oklahoma where it actually took a fan poll to rename them "Tulsa **Shock**." Their lightning-bolt symbol begs comparison to the existing NBA Oklahoma City **Thunder**, as thunder is in fact a sonic shock wave. The Washington **Mystics** magically appeared alongside the NBA **Wizards** in 1998, while the Orlando **Magic** were joined by the Orlando **Miracle** (1999–2002). The coupling of Minneapolis's Minnesota **Timberwolves** and Minnesota **Lynx** in 1999 was mildly sexist at worst, as the former are wild canines and the latter are wild felines.[21] In 2000 the Miami **Heat** watched the rise of the WNBA Miami **Sol** (Spanish for *sun*), and the WNBA Portland **Fire** took their identity from the second half of "**Trail Blazers**." (Both the **Sol** and **Fire** were extinguished after the 2002 season.)

Utah's **Starzz** were sold to NBA owners in the Lone Star State for 2003. As San Antonio **Silver Stars**, they matched the NBA **Spurs**. By then, the required NBA-WNBA partnerships had proved economically untenable. Orlando's team was the first to exit the arrangement when the Mohegan Tribe bought the **Miracle** and moved it for 2003. The renamed Connecticut **Sun** entertain gamblers taking a break from the slots at Uncasville's Mohegan Sun Casino. To respect their sponsors (and avoid confusion with Phoenix's NBA **Suns**), *Sun* is always singular.[22]

The WNBA's **Fever, Fire, Liberty, Lynx, Mercury, Miracle, Shock, Sky, Sol, Sting, Storm**, and **Sun** indicate a modern trend having nothing to do with gender. Until the last years of the twentieth century, you could count the number of major league teams with singular monikers on one hand.

So much for pluralism.

• • •

In some cases, attempting to get around these gender issues has had interesting and varied results:

- In the Cotton State, the University of Arkansas–Monticello fields male **Boll Weevils**, named for the insects that devoured immeasurable cotton plants in the twentieth century. UAM's women are **Cotton Blossoms**, the delicate targets of boll weevil intentions. At Alabama's Enterprise State Community College, male **Boll Weevils** correspond to **Weevil Women**.

- A tough 'tude made **"Ironsides"** out of footballers representing Shreveport's Centenary College of Louisiana. The players even got into a big fight during a 1921 game, after which the school president told them they would thereafter act as gentlemen. They did just that as **Gents**, joined in the 1960s by complementary **Ladies**.[23]

- Carthage, Texas hosts the Panola College **Ponies**. A pony can be male or female, but by choosing to chase its origin to the French root *poulain* (colt), the school's women are complementary **Fillies**.

- The University of Puerto Rico at Mayagüez (or the *Recinto Universitario de Mayagüez*) runs with ***Tarzanes*** and ***Juanas*** (Tarzans and Janes), but there's no other connection to *Tarzan of the Apes*.[24]

Like most Indo-European languages, Spanish solves this issue with grammatical gender, wherein end-vowels indicate masculine or feminine words. **Zorros** and **Zorritas** are respective male and female foxes at *el Centro de Enseñanza Técnica y Superior Mexicali* ("CETYS Universidad") in the Mexican state of Baja California, and we've elsewhere discussed colleges with both **Vaqueros** (cowboys) and **Vaqueras** (cowgirls). A WPS soccer team in Missouri started in 2009 and folded half way through 2010 as the St. Louis **Athletica** … a Romanized female athlete.

The same language group has a neuter grammatical gender, nouns that are neither masculine nor feminine, which applies to ***Delfines*** at the Catholic *Universidad del Sagrado Corazón* (University of the Sacred Heart) in San Juan, Puerto Rico. That's "dolphins" to those who recognize the Christian symbolism of fishes (p. 107). Even then, the definite article in *las **Delfines*** identifies sides composed only of women, while the masculine-by-preference model uses *los **Delfines*** to refer to either the men's sides or all ***Delfines*** collectively.

• • •

The big sagebrush plant (*Artemisia tridentate*) is all over the West, but only Nevada is the Sagebrush State. Early white settlers were "Sagebrushers" and turn-of-the-century teams at the University of Nevada–Reno were **Sagebrushers** and **Sage Hens**. (The campus paper is still the *Sagebrush*.) Looking for fierceness, they were **Wolves** by the early 1920s and a **Wolf Pack** later in that decade.

UNR's former **Sage Hens** seem to contradict English's masculine-by-preference track, but *sage-hen* is the gender-neutral name commonly assigned to the western plains' greater sage grouse (*Centrocercus urophasianus*), although it's acceptable to call the male a sage-cock.

The Pomona-Pitzer College **Sagehens** are composed of male and female athletes from Pomona and Pitzer Colleges (Claremont, Calif.), hundreds of miles south of native sage grouse habitat.[25] Pomona and Pitzer are part of The Claremont Colleges, a consortium of resource-sharing schools east of Los Angeles. Its other undergraduate institutions—Claremont McKenna College, Harvey Mudd College, and Scripps College—have combined teams of CMS (Claremont-Mudd-Scripps) **Stags** and **Athenas**. The former is a male red deer (*Cervus elaphus*) and the latter is ancient Greece's goddess of learning.

From CMS, go across L.A. to the foothills of the Santa Monica Mountains to find Mount St. Mary's College. That women's school hosted purple-and-gold intercollegiate **Athenians** from the mid-1980s until about 1993. Students and alums still identify as "Athenians."

Mighty Ducks | Admirals | Harvest Queens | Gators

White hunters and settlers noticed many black bears on the Ozark Plateau, which makes Arkansas the "Bear State." The **Tutors** and **Normals** at Conway's state normal school became **Bears** in 1920, since joined by female **Sugar Bears** at the renamed University of Central Arkansas.[1] Follow the plateau into Missouri to the pair of bears on the state seal and the athletic **Bears** at both Washington University in St. Louis and Missouri State University in Springfield, the latter having some bearing on the **Grizzlies** at MSU's West Plains campus.

Vocal fans of those abovementioned sides love their "Bahrs" … which is the way *bears* sounded after backcountry settlers developed a unique accent drawn from Scots-Irish and English West Country roots. The name of independent pro hockey's Hershey **B'ars** (est. 1932) was a self-deprecating linguistic joke and an unsubtle promotion of the Pennsylvania city's chocolate bars. In 1905 the town of Derry Church had been renamed for chocolate king Milton Hershey, who constructed numerous facilities during the Depression. When he opened a new ice arena in 1936, the **B'ars** addressed concerns about their commercialized name by becoming more orthodox **Bears**. Like Hershey's famous bar, the **Bears** in today's AHL are all wrapped up in chocolate-brown.

No such objections were made in 1993 when the Walt Disney Company expanded the NHL into the California home of its Disneyland theme park. The **Mighty Ducks** of Anaheim were named after Disney's supremely mediocre 1992 movie *The Mighty Ducks*, in which pee-wee hockey players in Minneapolis learn to play the coolest game on earth while sorting out their coach's emotional baggage. Their arena's owners bought the team in 2005, and by the '06/07 season both "**Mighty**" and Disney's duck-shaped goalie mask were history; they're now Anaheim **Ducks**.[2]

Walt Disney's original famous duck, Donald, appeared in 1938, and the animator allowed the University of Oregon **Ducks** to call their white-feathered mascot "Donald" for decades (as did his studio after his 1966 death). In 1968 a Disney artist drew up "Denver Boone" for the University of Denver (replacing "Pioneer Pete"). D.B. was dropped in 1998 when administrators decided his white maleness didn't represent its diverse **Pioneers**.

Walt Disney had spent his late boyhood in Kansas City, where he opened his first animation studio in 1922. The KC Zoo purchased two baby kangaroos in 1936 and the already famous creator of Mickey Mouse was persuaded the next year to draw the cover for the *Kangaroo* humor magazine at the University of Missouri–Kansas City. (*Kansas City* and *kangaroo* have the same initial syllable.) The debate team embraced Kasey (*K.C.*) the Kangaroo as mascot, and athletes were soon **Kangaroos**.[3]

The Disney Company also made a movie about a real sports franchise. In 1994 the studio remade *Angels in the Outfield*, a 1951 baseball film in which a coach's emotional baggage is sorted out through the suddenly divine performance of his Pittsburgh **Pirates**. When MGM made the original, there wasn't the luxury of real **Angels**, but Disney's version featured the California **Angels**, whom the studio would purchase from Gene Autry two years later. As part of a stadium deal with the host city, Disney made them *Anaheim* **Angels** for 1997, associating them with both Disneyland and Disney's **Ducks**. Preparing to defend their 2002 World Series title, the **Angels** were bought by advertising exec Arte Moreno, who instinctively wanted to identify with the huge L.A. media market. However, the long-term lease with the city said the team name would include "Anaheim." Spying the inverted syntax of "**Mighty Ducks** of Anaheim," Moreno renamed his 2005 team "Los Angeles **Angels** of Anaheim." Civic leaders and the Disney folks who'd spent decades promoting Anaheim as a travel destination in its own right felt very much bamboozled.

Anaheim is to Disney as Orlando is to … well … *Disney.* Traffic in Central Florida got worse in 1971 when Walt Disney World's Magic Kingdom opened. O-Town's tourism slogan is "Come to the Magic!" … but the NBA Orlando **Magic** came to it in 1989.

• • •

In 1970, Wisconsin appliance dealer Erwin Merar founded an independent amateur hockey team he called Milwaukee **Admirals** after a brand of TVs and refrigerators he sold.[4] A similar story in New York explains minor league basketball's Rochester **Zeniths** (1978–83), owned by a Zenith TV retailer. If you worry that such advertising might eventually affect amateur collegians, you're a little late:

- When women's hoop began at Wayland Baptist University (Plainview, Texas) in the 1940s, uniforms were supplied by a local granary, the Harvest Queen Mill, so jocks were **Harvest Queens**. By 1950, WBU grad and oilman and airline owner Claude Hutcherson was flying them to away games in private planes as **Flying Queens**,[5] but Wayland athletes in other sports are **Pioneers**. Their hare mascot recalls WBU's former **Jackrabbits**, from the black-tailed jackrabbit (*Lepus californicus*) of western states.

- The lower-case *d* logo of the Dawson College **Blues** is transposed to an eighth note, but those Montrealers aren't musical. Dawson flashed the corporate blue of Eastern Airlines only after that carrier sponsored its 1970 hockey team.[6]

- When Labatt's Brewing introduced a blue-labeled Pilsner in 1951, fans of the CFL Winnipeg **Blue Bombers** called it "Labatt's Blue." Labatt's owned many shares in Toronto's 1977 AL expansion team, and was able to inject some color into "Toronto **Blue Jays**."[7] Another large Canadian brewer, Moosehead, funded the establishment of Nova Scotia's Halifax **Mooseheads** in 1994, spurring the expansion of major junior hockey in the Maritimes.

- Being hip persons of the 1980s, **Roadrunners** at the Notre Dame of Maryland University wore crocodile-emblazoned Izod Lacoste polo shirts.[8] As NDMU's moniker was falling out of favor, people noticed that field hockey and lacrosse squads (often the marquee teams at women's schools) wore those alligator polos on fields next to a Baltimore marsh. The environs and the embroidery conspired to make athletes **Gators**.[9] Pine Manor College (Chestnut Hill, Mass.) remained a women's college from its founding in 1911 until fall 2014. Its library staff tells us that Izod sportswear most likely brought about that school's own **Gators**.[10]

Whirlwinds | Jets | Supersonics | Astros

For three decades, Milton Wright was a bishop in the Church of the United Brethren in Christ. Most UBC congregations entered a liberal new constitution in 1889, so Wright led conservatives into the (new) Old Constitution branch, based in Huntington, Indiana. In a wooded area outside that town, Wright laid the cornerstone for Huntington University in 1896. HU has its own arboretum, herbarium, and teams first called **Foresters** in 1931, although that identity may owe a little to their green apparel, which reminded one sportswriter of Robin Hood's Merry Men of Sherwood Forest.[1]

Some of the new branch's early pamphlets were published by Bishop Wright's mechanically inclined sons. Orville and Wilbur worked on printing presses and bicycles but became fascinated with powered flight. Among the dunes of North Carolina's Outer Banks the Wrights found the seclusion, steady winds, and soft landing areas needed to test their contraptions. Setting up shop at Kitty Hawk in 1900, they used gliders to improve stability and control. When they finally strapped on an engine in late 1903, the toss of a coin made Orville the first person to experience a successful powered flight.

The Wrights spent their autumns and early winters at Kitty Hawk. The rest of the year was at Dayton, Ohio, where Wright Flyers were improved at the field that's now the enormous Wright-Patterson Air Force Base. The WBL Dayton **Rockettes** (1978/79) aimed to indicate Wright-Patt's Propulsion Directorate.

The 1903 Wright Flyer is the emblem of Dayton's Wright State University. Its past mascots its **Raider** have been pirates, Vikings, and wolves, but never air raiders. (Nor do **Rams** at Chicago's Wilbur Wright College seem particularly germane to the elder brother.) There are **Flyers** at the University of Dayton, named for the Wright Flyer in 1920.[2]

Mercy College (Dobbs Ferry, N.Y.) was just going coed and starting intercollegiate athletics in 1969 when a transfer student from Dayton was heard referencing his old **Flyers**. Mercy's athletic director decided his teams would be so known. In 2007 the athletic department wanted to brand the **Flyers** with inspired symbols but failed to find appropriate imagery precisely because the identity had been lifted from elsewhere. Horse sense suggested a complete change, so teams became Mercy **Mavericks** with a wild mustang trademark.[3]

• • •

Three years after Wilbur's 1912 death from typhoid fever, Orville sold to investors who produced engines in the already crowded aeronautics field. The Navy asked Wright Aeronautical to work with the Lawrance Aero Engine Company to produce the Wright J-5 Whirlwind at a Paterson, New Jersey plant in 1925. In fact, a J-5 powered Charles Lindbergh's "Spirit of St. Louis" when he was famously first to fly nonstop across the Atlantic alone in 1927, publicity that propelled the Paterson **Whirlwinds** through the 1928/29 ABL season.[4] Lindy's backers were St. Louis businessmen, so his monoplane was the *Spirit of St. Louis*, as commemorated by ABA **Spirits** of St. Louis (1974–76) and AHL St. Louis **Flyers** (1944–53).

Lindbergh's first ride was a Curtiss JN-4 (the "Jenny"), a surplus Great War training biplane he bought in 1923 from Souther Field in Americus, Georgia. Pilots of two world wars trained there, and it's now Jimmy Carter Regional Airport, which can land modest business jets. Some of the airfield's former apron is a parking lot for students at South Georgia Technical College, including **Jets** jocks.

• • •

In 1916 aircraft builder Clyde Cessna moved to Wichita, Kansas. Matty Laird arrived there in 1920 and designed the Laird *Swallow*. That first commercial aircraft addressed the inefficiencies of the Curtiss Jennys that had been retrofitted for use in a new national airmail service. By the mid-1920s, Cessna and Laird were working alongside guys named Beech and Stearman on the Wichita scene. Congress privatized airmail operations in 1925 to create the commercial aviation industry, and Wichita successfully lobbied to become a major stop on the transcontinental route. Seattle's Boeing Company (p. 275) purchased Stearman in 1929 and called it Boeing Wichita.

Every time you look up there are teams paying homage to the "Air Capital of the World": Wichita's Newman University maintains **Jets**; minor league baseballers have been Wichita **Aviators, Aeros**, and **Pilots**; Wichita **Wings** were longtime soccerists (1979–2001) and independent baseball's Wichita **Wingnuts** took off in 2008; indoor football's Wichita **Stealth** (2001–04) used as an emblem the B-2 *Spirit* bomber, a Stealth (radar-invisible) aircraft.

Pilots become "air hogs" when fellow military aviators note their habit of taking flight at every possible opportunity. The Grand Prairie **AirHogs** (est. 2008) play independent ball in a Dallas suburb that hosts the world headquarters for both American Eurocopter and Triumph Aerostructures–Vought Aircraft Division.

• • •

Minor league baseball's Lancaster **JetHawks** (1996–) are between Air Force installations in Edwards and Palmdale, California. Lockheed's Skunk Works developed supersecret military aircraft at both sites and later at the remote dried bed of Groom Lake. That Nevada lake's less romantic name on a military grid is "Area 51." It's there that conspiracy theorists say the Feds are hiding a crashed alien spacecraft to keep the rest of us from getting freaked out. Nevada's route 375 is the "Extraterrestrial Highway," and minor league ball's Las Vegas **Stars** (named in 1983) became Las Vegas **51s** in 2001.

• • •

Frederick Lothrop Ames, Jr. was heir to a shovel fortune and the president of a small commercial airline. At age 29 he died in a 1932 monoplane crash just north of the private landing strip on his Stonehill estate in North Easton, Massachusetts. That's now the grounds of Stonehill College, which replaced its Indian-themed **Chieftains** with **Skyhawks** in 2005.

• • •

Seattle ended 1966 with a boom. It got an NBA expansion team on December 20, and on New Year's Eve the U.S. government gave the Boeing firm the huge contract to develop the supersonic transport (SST), an intercontinental passenger jet to compete with the *Concorde* SST, a French-British project nearing production. The Seattle **Supersonics** took the floor in October 1967.[5]

The European *Concorde's* first commercial flight was in 1976. Montrealers lobbied for regular service, but—except for token promotional stops—all they got were the CFL Montreal **Concordes** (1982–86). The **'Cordes** struck a chord with folks who knew the city's Latin motto, *Concordia salus*, "sanctuary through harmony." Congress dropped the extraordinarily expensive SST in 1971. A terrifying Paris crash grounded Europe's SST in 2000.

An arena dispute sent Seattle's NBA-ers to Oklahoma for the 2008/09 season, leaving "**Supersonics**" and the green and gold colors behind to become the Oklahoma City **Thunder**. The team could have made at least a modest effort to tie "**Thunder**" to "**Supersonics**": a supersonic aircraft does produce a *thundering* audio shock wave when it exceeds the speed of sound. And thunder is an actual *sonic* boom, a phenomenon produced naturally when lightning causes heated air to expand at a speed that exceeds that of sound.

• • •

In San Diego's Miramar neighborhood is the Marine Corps Air Station Miramar. It's been the pilot-training base for the TOPGUN program since its inception in 1969 and was a shooting location for the 1986 film *Top Gun*. Many active duty personnel take classes at San Diego Miramar College, where **Jets** play on fields that cover a former Navy runway.

The Palomar Observatory is also in San Diego County. It's on Mount Wilson, a remote site removed from the light and dirt of urban campuses. (It's administered by Caltech.) Palomar's 200-inch Hale reflector made it the world's largest telescope for nearly three decades after its 1948 completion. The Palomar College **Comets** are in the nearby city of San Marcos.

In 1949 nameless minor leaguers in New York State accepted a suggestion to become Clinton **Comets**. No one recorded why that name was so applicable to Mohawk Valley players, although one notices that both hockeyists and comets shoot and pass and they have icy surfaces in common. (Also, Palomar's huge mirror had been produced at Corning, New York. Its 1947 roadtrip to California was closely followed nationally.) In any case, upstate **Comets** had come to stay. In Utica, the ACHL Mohawk Valley **Stars** (1981–85) became **Comets** (1985–87). They were followed by semi-pro Mohawk **Comets** (2003, Whitestown) and the AHL Utica **Comets** (named in 2013).

The Smithsonian Institute launched Operation Moonwatch in 1956, a Cold War call to track artificial satellites. Citizens had nothing to look at until October 1957 when the Soviet Union launched Sputnik 1, an unmanned satellite that went "beep." But that was one more beeping orbiter than America had and the Space Race was on. NASA's answer to Sputnik was the Pioneer program, a twenty-year series of probes to other planets and the sun. California State University–East Bay adopted a Pioneer Pete astronaut mascot after its 1961 opening, followed by **Pioneers**. (Pete was a frontiersman in the 1970s and a gold miner thereafter.)

Speaking at Rice University in 1961, President Kennedy reiterated a challenge to put America on the Moon in that decade. Rice had donated land for NASA's

Mission Control, and Houston—"the Space City"—was using a build-it-and-they-will-come strategy by constructing the first domed stadium with hopes of luring a major league ballclub. Indeed, the new-for-'62 Houston **Colt .45s** played in a temporary park while the Harris County Domed Stadium went up next door.[6] When NASA coined *astronaut* (star sailor) from Greek parts, locals started to prefix everything with *Astro-*, including the "Astrodome." Even the **Colt .45s** were **Astros** after going indoors in 1965. Some dome-based NASLers circumvented translation as Houston **Stars** (1968).

The connection between NASA and the NBA Houston **Rockets** may not be the one that launches quickly to mind. The U.S. Army's first intercontinental ballistic missile was the Atlas. Its ability to put payloads and warheads into orbit made it the liftoff booster for NASA's manned Mercury missions (1958–63). The high-profile Atlas was built at San Diego's General Dynamics plant, so NBA expansion in 1967 gave the "City in Motion" San Diego **Rockets**. Four years later they went to Houston, where the Space Age name was kept.

The ABA started competing with the NBA in 1967 with its own **Rockets**, Denverites who had been named after their owner's Rocket Trucking company. Anticipating both the decline of their ABA and a hopeful merger with the NBA, Denver's **Rockets** avoided potential confusion by becoming **Nuggets** in 1974. As hoped, the Denver **Nuggets** were amalgamated into the NBA in 1976.

Like the NBA **Rockets**, the WHA Houston **Aeros** (1972–78) had their name before skating to the Space City. Unable to secure an arena as *Dayton* **Aeros**, they never played in Ohio, but in Houston the **Aeros** formed a near-perfect seal between two different minor league Houston **Apollos** (1965–69, 1979–81). NASA's Apollo program had started in 1960 and put men on the Moon in 1969 in accordance with the late president's schedule. Houston's current AHL **Aeros** started in the 1994 IHL.

Business and academic leaders in Texas wanted to attract bright young minds to its emerging technology sector. They started a research center in the Dallas suburb of Richardson in 1960. By 1969 it was the University of Texas at Dallas, where ongoing partnerships with aerospace firms made athletes **Comets**. (UTD's fire-haired mascot is Temoc, *comet* backwards.)

Similarly, Florida Technological University opened in 1963 to fill aerospace and engineering jobs at Cape Canaveral, the Apollo launch site. On its fifth anniversary, FTU revealed its "Reach for the stars" motto and a new shield that featured Pegasus, the winged horse of Greek mythology with a famous namesake star constellation. By 1970 the Orlando school's black-and-gold were **Knights of Pegasus**, having dodged momentum already gained by a *Citronaut* mascot. (Yes; an orange wearing a space helmet.) Teams at the renamed University of Central Florida became **Golden Knights** in 1993 and **Knights** in 2007. Somewhat north of Cape Canaveral's "Space Coast" are Jacksonville's Florida State College **Stars**. From 1964 to 1972 minor league hockey had Jacksonville (or "Florida") **Rockets**.

Scorpions | Lopes | Wolverines | Horned Frogs

In 1974, Oakland **Athletic** Reggie Jackson described the feeling of the bat in his hands to *Sports Illustrated:* "I'm out of my cage. I'm free to move, to run, to go. I'm like an animal running through the woods."[1] Judging by all the **Wildcats**, **Bears**, **Tigers**, and **Wolves** in the sports pages, the feeling is not unique to Mr. October.

After hanging on like bulldogs, attacking like hawks, or clawing back like bears in newspaper reports, athletes often sally forth as respective **Bulldogs, Red Hawks,** and **Bears**. "Tearing through the defense" can make teams **Tigers**. "Picking apart their prey" effects **Raptors**. A defensive trap might draw opponents into a "lion's den" or a "hornet's nest" of soon-to-be **Lions** or **Wasps**.

In other words, zoomorphism—the description of human feats in terms of comparable animal behavior—is alive and well in our sporting world. But don't expect a peaceable kingdom, as the adopted mindset is inevitably that of the hunter, not the hunted. For example, Georgia's 1966-founded NFLers are Atlanta **Falcons**, not **Field Mice**. The NBA team in St. Paul since 2000 is the Minnesota **Wild**, not the **Mild**. **Hawks** would most surely devour **Doves**. Teams march in as **Lions** hoping to go out like lions.

We're going to go on like this for a bit.

• • •

Scorpions are common in the Desert Southwest, although members of the *Scorpiones* order on other continents live in forests and tropical grasslands. We intuitively fear scorpions, but American species don't usually inject enough venom to kill an adult. Still, Texas Southmost College's **Scorpions**, the Central Hockey League's New Mexico **Scorpions** (1996–2009, Rio Rancho), and the NASL San Antonio **Scorpions** (est. 2012) let fearsome reputations preceded them.

• • •

No member of the family *Bovidae* (Asian and African antelopes) is native to the Americas. What we call the pronghorn "antelope" is the only animal that annually sheds the outside of its forked horns and is therefore the sole member of the family *Antilocapridae*. **Pronghorns** at Gillette [Wyo.] College and Alberta's University of Lethbridge properly identify the continent's fastest land animal. (Until 1971, ULeth fielded **Chinooks**, after the Chinook salmon, *Oncorhynchus tshawytscha*.)

Also in Alberta, Medicine Hat College once had **Antelope** men. That shows that North American colleges aren't shy about using the pronghorn's inexact colloquial name, but MHC further strained geographical credibility with **Kudus**, female athletes that referred to certain members of *Tragelaphus*, an antelope-like genus from Africa's bush. In 1985 all MHC teams became **Rattlers** after the province's only venomous snake, the prairie rattler (*Crotalus viridis*).

The **Lopers** at the University of Nebraska at Kearney are derived from the numerous pronghorns in the Antelope State. Arizona's pronghorns are most often found on its northern plains (near the Antelope Valley), but down in Phoenix are the **Antelopes** of Grand Canyon University, very often "**Lopes.**"

• • •

Unlike most terrestrial mammals, the coyote (*Canis latrans*) has expanded its range in the face of human settlement. The flattening of forests has made the "prairie wolf" more at home while eradicating its upstream food chain competition, the gray wolf. Still, the coyote is most often associated with its original prairie and desert homelands, where most athletic **Coyotes** play. Good examples are found at Kansas Wesleyan University (Salina), the University of South Dakota, and Weatherford [Texas] College.

In 1996 the emblem of the NHL's new Phoenix **Coyotes** featured the bold lines and block colors of traditional Navajo artwork because desert coyotes are gods and tricksters in Navajo tales. They switched to more zoologically realistic graphics in 2003. A deal between the Glendale arena and their new Canadian owners made them *Arizona* **Coyotes** going into the 2014/15 season. In 2000 the **Plainsmen** and **Lady Plainsmen** at Lincoln's Nebraska Wesleyan University became **Prairie Wolves**, a step toward gender neutrality that recalls the **Coyotes** that NWU fielded from 1907 to 1933.

Prairie dogs (*Cynomys ludovicianus*) aren't canines at all. They're rodents, but they do share grassland habitats with prairie wolves. Athletes at New Mexico's College of Santa Fe held heads high as **Prairie Dogs** when intercollegiate sports began in fall of 2008, but programs were canceled at the end of the same semester. When the school was renamed Santa Fe University of Art and Design the next year, a program to relocate the campus's significant number of real prairie dogs to non-urban spaces was under way.

• • •

The aforementioned gray wolf is on the rebound in Michigan's Upper Peninsula. That wolves once inhabited all corners of the state could explain **Wolves** at the University of Michigan–Dearborn and the short-lived Detroit **Wolves** of the Depression-era (black) East-West League. There are reasons to suspect that these were really abridged *wolverines* … although we're about to learn that wolverines may in fact be named after wolves.

In the 1940s, Coach Fielding Yost couldn't find a live wolverine mascot for his University of Michigan footballers, who'd been **Wolverines** since about 1900. The frustrated coach asserted that there had never been any wolverines in the Wolverine State, an off-the-cuff remark that was reported as fact for decades. In 2004 came evidence that a scant few wolverines do still roam northernmost Michigan,[2] but the largest member of the weasel family prefers Canada's arctic tundra, where its powerful jaws chop through frozen hides and bones. In fact, the carnivore's Latin name is *Gulo gulo*, the "glutton," but its wolf-like appetite probably explains why those beasts were called wolverines in the first place.

If sightings in Michigan are so rare, why is it the Wolverine State? There are two theories: [1] *Gulo* pelts from the north and west were among the beaver and moose hides that French traders funneled through Sault St. Marie, forever associating the area and the animal; [2] Indians saw white settlers devour both food and raw materials and made the wolverine comparison.[3] Elsewhere in Wolverine State history, Detroit **Wolverines** were in the NL (1881–88). The NFL Canton **Bulldogs** moved to Michigan for 1928 as Detroit **Wolverines**, being led by quarterback Benny Friedman, a future pro Hall of Famer and two-time All American for Yost's **Wolverines**.[4] The occasional wolverine can be sighted in Utah's Rocky Mountains, as suggested by the Utah Valley University **Wolverines** in Orem.

• • •

The nine-banded armadillo (*Dasypus novemcinctus*) of Texas and the Southeast is the northernmost 'dillo, all other species being found in Central and South America. Independent baseball in Texas had Amarillo **Dillas** (abbreviated armadillos) from 1994 to 2010.

• • •

Arizona's state reptile is the ridgenose rattlesnake (*Crotalus willardi*), but when major leaguers arrived at an Arizona diamond in 1998, "Arizona **Diamondbacks**" was deemed more appropriate. In fact the Western diamondback rattlesnake (*Crotalus atrox*) slithers across the Southwest and Mexico, and the **Diamondbacks** share Phoenix with indoor football's Arizona **Rattlers** (est. 1992).

Tucson **Sidewinders** (1998–2008) played southeast of Phoenix as a **D-Backs** farm team. They were named after another regional terror, the sidewinder pit viper (*Crotalus cerastes*). Texas diamondbacks gave the name *Rattler* to the campus paper at San Antonio's St. Mary's University, with **Rattlers** jocks following in 1926. Appleton's species-specific Wisconsin **Timber Rattlers** (1995–) play minor league ball. The timber rattler (*Crotalus horridus*) haunts dense woodlands of the eastern U.S. and Canada. Northern Florida is the extreme southeastern range of the timber rattler, but it and several other rattler species put **Rattlers** at Tallahassee's Florida A&M University.

The diamondback terrapin turtle (*Malaclemys terrapin*) is Maryland's state reptile. Found in brackish waters from southern New England to the Gulf of Mexico, terrapins were plentiful in the Delaware and Chesapeake Bays until being harvested to near-extinction in the 1920s. Originally an Indian meal, they were plucked from marshes and dropped into terrapin soup in colonial times. That became a dietary staple for Maryland's slaves and then a restaurant delicacy. Teams for the University of Maryland in College Park became **Terrapins** in 1935 after the name was suggested in the campus *Diamondback* paper.[5]

Spaniards called Florida's swamp thing *el lagarto* (the lizard). Anglicized as the American *alligator* (*Alligator mississippiensis*), it leads to the University of Florida **Gators**.[6] The north campus of San Jacinto College (Pasadena, Texas) was constructed in the early 1960s after alligators were removed from the site, an event commemorated by **Gators**.[7]

Eastern Arizona College's **Gila Monsters** are on the Gila ("*hee*-lah") River in Thatcher. The river's namesake is the Gila monster (*Heloderma suspectum*), the two-foot long venomous lizard of the desert Southwest.

Geckos are small, chirping lizards of the *Gekkonidae* family found globally in warm places. Arizona has one native species, the western banded gecko (*Coleo-*

nyx variegatus), and one introduced one, the Mediterranean gecko (*Hemidactylus turcicus*). **Geckos** represent GateWay Community College in Phoenix.

The Texas horned lizard (*Phrynosoma cornutum*) is a wide-bodied desert dweller that looks like a creepy member of the frog and toad order (*Anura*), so it's the "horned frog." It became the state reptile in 1992, but **Horned Frogs** have represented Texas Christian University since 1897. The horned frog is in trouble because its main food source, the harvester ant, has been getting wiped out by human pest controls and the invasive red imported fire ant.

• • •

The abovementioned fire ant (*Solenopsis invicta*) was unwittingly imported to the U.S. when ships from Brazil discharged cargoes at Gulf Coast ports in the early 1930s. With no natural predators, fire ants waged decades of war on the agriculture of the Southeast. Their sting burns something wicked and makes for mean mascots, as appreciated by the University of South Carolina–Sumter **Fire Ants**, indoor football's Tupelo [Miss.] **FireAnts** (2001–05), and minor league hockey's Cape Fear/Fayetteville [N.C.] **FireAntz** (est. 2002).

Brazil brewed up new trouble in the late 1950s when African honey bees (*Apis mellifera scutellata*) were crossbred with European species to create a strain more conducive to tropical areas. Twenty-six African queens escaped and have since been expanding their domain with the cooperation of domestic drones. Those Africanized—or "killer"—bees aren't so distinct from their European cousins, except that numerous predators in Africa have made them far more likely to swarm and sting. Killer bees are now across the American South, first noticed stateside at Hidalgo, Texas in 1990. Two years later the town unveiled a twenty-foot killer bee statue, joined in 2003 by the junior hockey Rio Grande Valley **Killer Bees**.

Uniform colors can easily lead to insect sides called **Greenjackets**, **Bluejackets**, or **Yellowjackets**. You can also get jacketed as such by swarming all over opponents, but the threat is sometimes literal. The main building at Lamoni, Iowa's Graceland University was overrun by wasps in 1926, as recalled by its **Yellowjackets**.[8] A similar (and possibly apocryphal) story says that Shenandoah University athletes at the Dayton, Virginia campus lived in a wasp-infested dorm, giving rise to **Hornets**.[9] (SU moved to Winchester in 1960.)

• • •

A touch of gray is a sign of distinction. Grizzly bears often have gray hair along the spine and are thus "silvertips," giving a name to minor league hockey's Everett [Wash.] **Silvertips**. Also owing to light-colored back hairs, mature males in the *Gorilla* genus are "silverbacks." Minor league soccer's Atlanta **Silverbacks** adopted gorilla mascots when they were named in 1998, two years before the death of the beloved Willie B., a mountain gorilla who lived thirty-nine years at Zoo Atlanta. Coho salmon (*Oncorhynchus kisutch*) are also "silverbacks." A variety of salmon species (coho, sockeye, chinook, pink) are caught near Salmon Arm, B.C., and junior hockey's Salmon Arm **Silverbacks** are likely named after shiny cohos, but their gorilla emblems strike more fear into opponents.

Mudcats | Sharks | Rays | Dolphins | Marlins

The flathead catfish (*Pylodictis olivaris*) is a fisherman's prize in the Ohio, Mississippi, and Missouri watersheds. It can be four feet long and weigh a hundred pounds. Feeding at night and resting on muddy bottoms during the day, the flathead is commonly the "mud cat." Minor league baseball had Columbus [Ga.] **Mudcats** (1989–90), but they've since been Carolina **Mudcats** (at Zebulon, N.C.). The most widely distributed North American catfish is the large channel cat (*Ictalurus punctatus*) of lakes and rivers east of the Rockies. Alabama's Huntsville **Channel Cats** (1995–2003) skated in various minor leagues.

The Franco-Ojibwa word *Muskellunge* sort of means "ugly long-faced pike." Up to five feet in length, the muskellunge (*Esox masquinongy*) is the largest pike, so "muskies" are caught across the Upper Midwest. Bloomington's Minnesota **Muskies** were in the 1967/68 ABA. It's the state fish of Wisconsin, so Sheboygan's Lakeland College **Maroons** were renamed **Muskies** in the 1930s by athletic director Elmer Ott, an avid fisherman and longtime administrator of a lakeside YMCA camp upstate.

Alongside western New York's Chautauqua Lake, Jamestown Community College had **Muskys** until a student poll made them JCC **Jayhawks** in the mid-1950s.[1] Ohio's Muskingum River gives a name to Muskingum County and its Muskingum University. The origin of the Delaware-Algonquian word *muskingum* isn't clear; it might mean "river town" or "elk eye." That it doesn't seem to refer to the muskellunge is contradicted by the fish mascots for the **Muskies** at Muskingum U.

The greenback cutthroat trout (*Oncorhynchus clarki stomias*) was thought to be extinct until being rediscovered in the Rockies. It became Colorado's state fish in 1994, confirmed by minor league hockey's Denver **Cutthroats** (est. 2012).

• • •

The Pacific Ocean's Red Triangle—defined by San Francisco Bay, Point Reyes, and the Farallon Islands—is a feeding ground for the great white shark (*Carcharodon carcharias*). When the southern Bay's NHL's San Jose **Sharks** were introduced in 1991, all the buzz was about their emblem, a toothy shark on a triangle background. Farther south, the WHA Los Angeles **Sharks** (1972–74) were followed by the NASL San Diego **Jaws**, a 1976-only team that surfaced the year after Steven Spielberg defined the summer blockbuster with his same-named shark flick. The MLL Los Angeles **Riptide** (2006–08) warned of dangerous coastal undertows, but their great white emblem was even scarier.

Great whites hunt for California elephant seals and sea lions. They can mistake a paddling surfer for either, but because they spit out bony humans after the initial chomp California sharks kill only about one person per year. Tourists run down to see pinnipeds all over San Francisco's docks, and the NHL's Oakland **Seals** (est. 1967) became California **Golden Seals** (1970–76) after new owner Charlie Finley renamed them for cross-bay appeal (and gave to them the green and goldenrod colors of his Oakland **A's**). San Francisco **Sea Lions** of the 1940s were barnstorming black baseballers named like the PCL's San Francisco **Seals** (1903–57), a legendary team remembered by the Luigi Seal ("Lou Seal") mascot of San Fran's **Giants**.

The shallow bays around the Sea Islands of Georgia and South Carolina are haunted by sand tiger sharks (*Carcharias taurus*). The University of South Carolina–Beaufort first floated **Sand Sharks** in 2007. Florida's Miami Dade College keeps **Sharks** at its Kendall Campus, not too far south of where Fort Lauderdale's Nova Southeastern University **Knights** became **Sharks** in 2005. Other Florida sharks below the major league level include the MISL Orlando **Sharks** (2007–09) and baseball's Clearwater **Threshers** (named in 2004 for the thresher shark of temperate coasts, *Alopias vulpinus*). The Jacksonville **Sharks** struggled through only part of the 1974 WFL season. The Jupiter **Hammerheads** (named for the T-shaped heads of *Sphyrnidae* family sharks) have pounded basepaths since 1998.

Sharing the *Elasmobranchii* subclass of cartilaginous fishes (*Chondrichthyes*) with sharks are the "flat sharks," or skates and rays. The largest, the manta ray (*Manta birostris*), is also called the "devil ray" because forward-projecting fins can resemble satanic horns. They're found in tropical and subtropical continental shelf waters like those from the Gulf Coast to the Carolinas, giving **Sea Devils** (with manta ray mascots) to Cape Fear Community College (Wilmington, N.C.). St. Petersburg's MLB Tampa Bay **Devil Rays** (est. 1998) became **Rays** for 2008, a ray being a drop of golden sun in the Sunshine State, but they maintain manta ray mascots.

The bottlenose dolphin (*Tursiops truncatus*) lives in temperate and tropical waters across the globe, including northern Florida's St. Johns River. It winds past Jacksonville University, where students voted on December 12, 1947 to create **Green Dolphin** teams (now simply **Dolphins**).[2] That conformed to their green-and-white colors, but we've noticed that this was a mere five weeks after the release of the MGM film *Green Dolphin Street*, a big-budget tale of clipper ship days. (It had everyone talking about an earthquake that would win the Oscar for special effects.) Florida's AFL/NFL Miami **Dolphins** (est. 1966) followed JU's **Dolphins** by two decades.

Shoreline [Wash.] Community College opened its original Pagoda Union Building in 1965. Its low lines and faux thatched roof were influenced by Japanese architecture. That same year, athletes became the **Samurai**. Different people saw the Japanese warrior mascot as too cartoonish, too geographically irrelevant, or too straight-up racist, so SCC teams resurfaced in 1992 as **Dolphins**. Their bottlenose mascot remains out of place because the only *Delphinidae* family member that is native to cold Puget Sound is the killer whale—*Orcinum orca*—indicated by the **Orcas** at Whatcom Community College in Bellingham, Washington.

The geoduck ("*goo*-ee-duck," *Panopea abrupta*) is a huge salt-water clam along the coasts of Washington and British Columbia. They're abundant in south Puget Sound near Evergreen State College in Olympia. ESC's Latin motto is *Omnia Extares*, "Let it all hang out," which refers to the three-foot neck of the **Geoducks**' bivalve mascot.

• • •

National League expansion in 1993 created the Florida **Marlins**. There had already been minor league Miami **Marlins** from 1955 to 1982, and the major leaguers flopped back to that identity in 2012 as part of their city- and county-financed stadium deal. Up the coast, "**Marlins**" was in place at Norfolk's Virginia Wesleyan College before the first students arrived in 1966. Like most **Marlins**, those at VWC and Miami salute the east coast's largest sport fish, the Atlantic blue marlin (*Makaira nigricans*).

The Atlantic sailfish (*I. albicans*) is named for a sail-like dorsal fin. It's in the *Istiophoridae* family of marlins and sailfish. Palm Beach Atlantic University's **Sailfish** (West Palm Beach) are just north of their Miami **Marlin** cousins.

The University of Corpus Christi was founded in 1947 on Ward Island. Early teams were **Tarpons** after the Atlantic tarpon (*Megalops atlanticus*), which gives salt-water anglers a good fight. After a long absence, athletics at "The Island University" returned with **Islanders** in 1996, but the tarpon was retained as a mascot for the renamed Texas A&M University–Corpus Christi. Local fisheries are still commemorated by minor league baseball's 2005-named Corpus Christi **Hooks**.

Retrievers | Pointers | Terriers | Thoroughbreds

Gray wolves hunt in packs with a multi-step gameplan: find, stalk, chase, kill. They have few qualms about picking on prey that's either dangerous, much larger than themselves, subject to irregular plurals, or some combination thereof (like moose or bison), so there are many athletic **Wolves**. Basketballers at Northern State University (Aberdeen S.D.) were so named in 1923.

Some of the wolves that picked through the garbage of early humans were noticeably more sociable than others. The loud barkers among them might have been adopted to keep a night's watch against other critters, unfriendly humans, or anyone trying to deliver a package. Over thousands of years, wolves of such bearing were bred to bring out desirable instincts like hunting or herding. Every domesticated dog is therefore some deliberately engineered descendent, making your family pup (*Canis lupus familiaris*) a recognized subspecies of the gray wolf (*Canis lupus*).

• • •

Dogs are appreciated for their ferocity, vigor, loyalty, and dedication to the task at hand. Some breeds are identified with a particular region or activity. Some are beloved everywhere. Many are team mascots:

- Brown-coated Chesapeake Bay Retrievers were bred by Maryland hunters to retrieve downed waterfowl in marshes. In 1878 the Chessie became the first American breed recognized by the American Kennel Club, and the CBR has been the state dog since 1964. When the University of Maryland, Baltimore County opened two years later at Cantonsville, athletes found "**Retrievers**" irresistibly fetching. The state had already hosted CBR-inspired **Retrievers** at St. Mary's College of Maryland (in St. Mary's City) since 1959, but they became **Saints** in 1968 and **Seahawks** in 1983, taking up osprey mascots.

- The state dog of Wisconsin is another purpose-bred retriever, the American Water Spaniel. One in-state school, however, is represented by a different field pup, the German Pointer. Of course, the reason the University of Wisconsin–Stevens Point is partial to "**Pointers**" is a phonetic one, a point taken by the **Pointers** at the University of Connecticut at Avery Point.

- The MLL Charlotte **Hounds** (est. 2012) identify the Plott Hound as the only North Carolina breed and the state dog. It was developed by the Plott family to hunt wild boars in the western part of the state.

- A few pups in 1860s Boston were mixes of English bulldogs and (now-extinct) English white terriers. The mild manners of their "Boston terrier" ancestors make it the "American Gentleman." In 1893, Bostons were recognized by the AKC. Boston University athletes became **Terriers** in 1922.[1] Wofford College athletes (Spartanburg, S.C.) adopted Boston mascots in the early twentieth century, resulting in their own **Terriers** teams.[2] Brooklyn's St. Francis College fielded **Terriers** in 1933 because the scrappy determination of terriers resembles teams that often compete against larger and better-funded programs,[3] which is consistent with SFC's slogan, "Small College of Big Dreams."

- The University of Ontario Institute of Technology fielded its first **Ridgebacks** in 2006. The Rhodesian Ridgeback is a cross of European and short-haired African guard dogs bred to assist southern Africa's hunters. UOIT assumed that the canine known also as the "Rhodesian lion dog" could handle the **Lions** (and **Mustangs** and **Badgers**) that were its conference opponents.

• • •

The domestication of the horse thousands of years ago can't be traced to a single place, but there are now almost 300 horse breeds cultivated toward various purposes (riding, pulling, racing). Equine athletic monikers don't tend to be as breed-specific as those in the canine class.

Thousands of years ago, Bedouins of the Arabian deserts had domesticated the camel. That beast had limited speed and agility, so strong and swift horses were bred for raiding and warfare in a harsh environment. European knights of the medieval Crusades noticed the enemy's superior mounts, but only when English nobles hooked up Arabian stallions with quality domestic mares did they produce comparably athletic foals. All true thoroughbreds trace their bloodlines to that trio of Arabians imported between 1689 and 1730, and entitled persons lined up with their stud fees to make racing the "sport of kings."

The rolling fields near Lexington are tinted blue by nutrients in phosphate-rich soil. The durability and traction of "Kentucky bluegrass" (*Poa pratensis*) makes for an extremely popular cool-weather athletic turf. (There is much argument as to whether bluegrass is native to North America or imported from cooler spots in Eurasia.) With an additional ability to thrive under continuous grazing, it's perfect for producing race horses, so it's somewhat ironic that that football's Lexington **Horsemen** (2003–09) played indoors on artificial turf.

Kentucky State University in Frankfort sits between Lexington's horse farms and Louisville's Churchill Downs, which is home to the country's oldest continuous sporting event, the Kentucky Derby. The thoroughbred standard is maintained by the non-standard spellings of KSU's **Thorobreds** (men) and **Thorobrettes** (women). The Louisville **Nightmare** (2009–10) fit that horse history only after some word parsing: "night-mare." As their ghost-horse emblem suggested, those female footballers played home games at night. In earlier days, the Kentucky school of agriculture at Murray hosted **Aggies**, but Murray State University teams are now **Racers**, although baseballing **Thorobreds** concede that those **Racers** are equines.

The natural mineral spas that gave a name to Saratoga Springs, New York attracted nineteenth-century barons and bankers who introduced horse racing. North of the main drag's many mansions is Skidmore College, where students voted to field **Wombats** in 1973, the only four-year athletes named for Australia's *Vombatidae* marsupial family. (In fact, that uniquity seems to be the best explanation for the name.) With the racing world in the Northeast captivated by events at the Saratoga Race Course in late summer, Skid kids steered toward the horsepower in 1981, changing to **Thoroughbreds**.

Jaguars | Bengals | Pumas | Cougars | Cheetahs

Big cats roar. Small cats can only purr, which owes to their restrictive throat structure. That's the distinction taxonomists use when splitting the *Felidae* (cat) family between big cats of the genus *Panthera* and small cats of the genus *Felis*.

The only big cat of the Americas is the jaguar, *Panthera onca*. It's similar to leopards of Africa and Asia, but with a different spot pattern. Jaguars remain in the rainforests of South and Central America (best represented by *los Jaguares de Chiapas* of first-division Mexican soccer), but they once seeped across today's U.S.-Mexican border. Texas **Jaguars** are at South Texas College (McAllen), Jacksonville College (Jacksonville), and the University of Houston–Victoria. The University of North Texas at Dallas has a jaguar mascot, but no intercollegiate teams.

Southern University has **Jaguars** at Baton Rouge and **Port City Jaguars** at its Shreveport campus, indicating that Louisiana is (at best) the eastern limit of historical jaguar country. Continue east to Mobile's University of South Alabama, where the **Jaguars**' spotted mascot is Southpaw. **Jaguars** at Georgia's Spelman College (Atlanta) and Georgia Perimeter College (Alpharetta) are in places never seen by real instances of *P. onca*, but a third Georgia college has a unique claim to **Jaguars**; somebody saw the *J-A-G-S* in sequence within "Junior College of Augusta" at what has become Georgia Regents University.[1]

We run into real jaguars again in Florida, albeit captive ones. A rare all-black jag named Zorro was a city symbol from his 1967 arrival at the Jacksonville Zoo until his 1986 death. His legacy is the Range of the Jaguar exhibit that opened in 2004, partly funded by his namesake NFL Jacksonville **Jaguars** (est. 1996). (The alliteration of "Jax **Jags**" had already been appreciated for decades at the aforementioned Jacksonville College.)

Some **Jaguars** represent schools at which regional wildlife wasn't the major consideration when it came to team names. **Jaguars** at Indiana University–Purdue University Indianapolis suggest the "fast pace" of their urban campus. (In fact, they were **Metros** until 1998.) The jaguar's reputation as the cat family's best swimming hunter helped because IUPUI's world-famous Natatorium has hosted many national pool events and Olympic trials since 1982.[2]

Spaniards recorded the Mexicas' Uto-Aztecan *Náhuatl* language with Latin characters. The *Náhuatl* word for jaguar, *ōcēlōtl*, was misapplied to its smaller spotted cousin, the nocturnal ocelot, *Leopardus pardalis*. A school in Livonia, Michigan is too far north, but students voted to follow **Ocelots** in 1966, probably realizing that *O-C-E-L-O-T-S* is scattered throughout "Schoolcraft College," or that such a name would give Schoolcraft the continent's only so-named teams. In 2012, however, athletic **Ocelots** appeared at the University of Texas–Brownsville, much closer to that cat's historical range.

• • •

Big cats outside the Americas include leopards (*Panthera pardus*), lions (*Panthera leo*), and tigers (*Panthera tigris*). Most teams go "big cat" with *leo* or *tigris* instead of their smaller cousin *pardus*, which is why there are more **Lions** and **Tigers** jocks than **Leopards**. When *P. pardus* does show up, it's often for alliterative value, as is true for the **Leopards** at four-year institutions like Lafayette College (Easton, Pa.) and the University of La Verne [Calif.].

The coasts of Asia's Bay of Bengal (accent the second syllable) are stomping grounds of a short-haired subspecies, the Bengal tiger (*P. tigris tigris*). In 1934 the Cincinnati Zoo opened its big-cat grottos and a captive breeding program for Bengals. Black baseball's Cincinnati **Tigers** (1934–37) followed quickly, and pro football's Cincinnati **Bengals** (with the accent moved forward: *BEN-gals*) played in several leagues (usually the AFL) from 1937 to 1941. New Cincinnati **Bengals** led by Ohio native Paul Brown joined a later AFL in 1968, but they have been NFLers since 1970.

> Cincy's **Bengals** and J'Ville's **Jaguars** bring us to another zoo-kept mascot. Charles Towne Landing is the park where the English first made landfall in South Carolina. It recreates a colonial plantation of 1670, including the exhibition of many aboriginal species. Its mountain lion inspired the maroon-and-white **Maroons** at the nearby College of Charleston to become **Cougars** after the park opened in 1970.

• • •

Extinct North American cave lions (*P. l. atrox*) were the big-cat cousins to the largest feline ever, the Eurasian cave lion (*P. l. spelaea*). Those members of *atrox* that didn't sink in L.A.'s La Brea tar pits (and there were plenty) died out at the end of the last ice age along with their megafauna prey.

The lion of the Americas looked enough like the mane-less females of sub-Saharan Africa's recognizable lion subspecies (*P. leo*) to confuse Europeans, but it isn't actually a *Panthera* because it can't roar. The "mountain lion" is the mammal with the broadest historical distribution in the western hemisphere. Formerly *Felis concolor*, this apex predator never fit comfortably into the same league as your housecat Fluffy (*Felis catus*), so it got its own genus in the late twentieth century: *Puma*. "*Puma concolor*" indicates the collision of cultures when Spain conquered Peru's Inca Empire to loot gold and silver reserves in 1533; *puma* is the Quechuan (Incan) word for "magical animal" and *concolor* is Latin for "one-colored."

Livestock near Saint Joseph's College (Rensselaer, Ind.) was getting slaughtered by a carnivorous beast in the 1930s, so a local headline read "County Goes to Guns in Puma Hunt." A farmer's dog turned out to match the culprit's prints, but the puma rumor was hottest just when St. Joe's was looking to rebrand its **Cardinals** ... thereafter **Pumas**.[3] Otherwise, "**Pumas**" isn't as popular a team name among English speakers as it is in Mexico, where the ***Pumas*** *de la Universidad Nacional Autónoma de México* (the National Autonomous University of Mexico) play soccer. Those first-division pros began as UNAM squads and they continue to occupy the university stadium.

Writing in 1898 of the pioneer period in Dryden, New York, George Goodrich (editor) says, "The only animal which seriously endangered human life [...] was the cougar, or puma, or American lion as it was sometimes called, and often referred to by old people as the painter or panther, but improperly so, the true panther being a denizen of Africa."[4] Little wonder there are **Panthers** at Dryden's

Tompkins Cortland Community College, but we're more immediately intrigued by the many names for the beast described; North America's various **Catamounts**, **Cougars**, **Lions**, **Panthers**, and **Pumas** are usually named after regional subspecies of the same *Puma concolor*. Those finding this explanation satisfactory may skip ahead. Gluttons for punishment who read on should be aware that names for *Puma concolor* vary by region, in accordance with local languages, and for no good reason. Accounting for colloquialisms like "mountain screamer," "deer tiger," "sneak cat," and "purple feather," there are dozens of ways to identify *P. concolor*.

The Amazon's Tupi-Guarani speakers call the puma *yaguar* or *suasuarana*, roughly "false deer." Portuguese colonizers heard that as *çuçuarana*, from which Louisiana's French derived *cuguacuarana*. Anglicized contortions are *jaguar* and *cougar*, names now applied to different species. If you're not confused yet, *Puma concolor* has more than twenty subspecies:

- The home of *P. c. californica* is the west coast's varied terrain, so there are California **Cougars** at Azusa Pacific University (Azusa) and CSU San Marcos.[5] San Diego's Alliant International University keeps **Mountain Lions**.
- *P. c. hippolestes* is called the "Colorado cougar," but it creeps into Wyoming and South Dakota too. Refer to the Colorado Christian University **Cougars** (Lakewood), the University of Colorado–Colorado Springs **Mountain Lions**, and the University of Sioux Falls [S.D.] **Cougars**.
- Presumed extinct in the north-central U.S. since the 1920s is the Wisconsin cougar (*P. c. schorgeri*), but live and kicking **Cougars** represent the University of Wisconsin–Waukesha and University of Minnesota–Morris.
- By the time you get to Phoenix, you're in the eastern domain of *P. c. browni*, or the "Yuma puma" of western Arizona and southern California. That city's Paradise Valley Community College hosts **Pumas**.
- The eastern cougar (*P. c. cougar*) is endangered throughout its historical range from eastern Canada to the Carolinas. One old Pennsylvania hangout is Oakland, where famous bronze panthers by Giuseppe Moretti have guarded Panther Hollow Bridge since 1897. After the University of Pittsburgh moved near the hollow in 1909, teams were cast as **Panthers**. At Pitt's Johnstown campus, **Mountain Cats** and **Lady Cats** are foils to the parent **Panthers**.
- The mountain lion is also the *catamount* (from the archaic "cat o' the mountain"). **Catamounts** at the University of Vermont show that the word is more common in the Northeast, but there are **Catamounts** as far south as Potomac State College (Keyser, W.Va.) and Western Carolina University (Cullowhee, N.C.), which backed **Teachers** until 1933.
- West Virginia is the Mountain State, with **Mountain Lions** at Concord University in Athens and **Cougars** at Mountain State University in Beckley.

• • •

A genetic variation can create seemingly all-black (melanistic) cats, but African or Asian leopards and South or Central American jaguars with black coats actually retain their spots (a black-on-black pattern seen when the light is right). *Panther* is a variation on *painter* that describes all-black leopards or jaguars.

Melanism is unrecorded in the New World's *P. concolor* species, but that doesn't keep North America **Panthers** from running out all-black mascots. For instance, the 1995-founded NFL Carolina **Panthers** (Charlotte, N.C.) are in the southern range of the Eastern cougar,[6] but they're represented by black cats that are indicative of the Old World jaguar. High Point University has had dark (**Purple**) **Panthers** in High Point, North Carolina since the 1920s.

As those Carolinians suggest, *panther* is a common name for the monochromatic pumas of the Southeast. When nicknameless footballers from Alabama's Birmingham College traveled to Mobile to defeat Spring Hill College (p. 424) in 1916, they were compared to a "pack of panthers" in the next *Birmingham College Reporter*.[7] Teams remained **Panthers** two years later when BC merged with Southern University to create Birmingham-Southern College.

The once-abundant Florida panther (*P. c. coryi*) is cornered by the eastern cougar and the Texas cougar. The fewer than 100 such cats in the Everglades may be the only remaining wild lions east of the Mississippi. Florida's Clearwater Christian College fields **Cougars**, but for decades there have been way more **Panther** teams in Florida than actual Florida panthers:

- Orlando **Panthers** (1966–69) were in the Continental Football League.
- Gold-and-blue **Sunblazers** at Miami's Florida International University became **Golden Panthers** in 1988 and just **Panthers** in 2010.
- The **Engineers** at Florida Institute of Technology (Melbourne) became **Panthers** in 1986.
- Lake Worth's Palm Beach State College traded **Pacers** for **Panthers** in a 1990 student vote and adopted a live Florida panther at the Palm Beach Zoo to publicize its endangered status.[8]
- Sunrise is home to the NHL Florida **Panthers** (est. 1993).
- Florida panthers and eastern cougars overlap in Georgia, which is the home state for **Panthers** at Georgia State University, **Cougars** at Columbus State University, and **Mountain Lions** at Young Harris College in Towns County's Blue Ridge Mountains.

• • •

The cheetah (*Acinonyx jubatus*) is sub-Saharan African's spotted *Felidae* hunter and the fastest land animal. In a world overrun by **Tigers**, **Lions**, and **Jaguars**, there are surprisingly few **Cheetahs**. Maybe the near-homonymity of *cheetah* to *cheater* makes it ill adapted for fair play. Montreal's Vanier College is alone in hosting **Cheetahs**, and how they got that name is unrecorded.

Pelicans | Orioles | Roadrunners | Gamecocks

In an ancient allegory adapted for medieval Christian bestiaries, a mother pelican tore her own breast to feed blood to nestlings during a famine. That makes her representative of both the blood atonement of Jesus and a more general Christian charity. One Catholic school, Spalding University (Louisville, Ky.), had **Pelicans** for those reasons, but they've been blue-and-gold **Golden Eagles** since 2006.

A strong Catholic history and coastal brown pelicans (*Pelecanus occidentalis*) make Louisiana the "Pelican State," so the bird appears on the college seals of LSU, Loyola NOLA, and Tulane. (Riptide is the pelican mascot for Tulane's **Green Wave**.) Minor league baseball's New Orleans **Pelicans** played most years from 1887 to 1959, joined later by **Black Pelicans** (c. 1920–53). The city's NBA **Hornets** were made **Pelicans** in 2013.

Georgia's state bird, the brown thrasher (*Toxostoma rufum*), explains the Atlanta **Thrashers** (1999–2010). (Conveniently, a Mr. John Thrasher established "Thrasherville" in 1939 as the terminus of the Western & Atlantic Railroad. It's now downtown Atlanta.) Thrashers migrate to the American South for the colder months, having left summer perches from southern Alberta to New England. That trek was reversed by the **Thrashers'** relocation to Manitoba, which revived "Winnipeg **Jets**" for the 2011/12 season.[1]

The black-orange-and-white Baltimore oriole (*Icterus galbula*) lives east of the Mississippi. Hardball's first Baltimore **Orioles** were in the 1882 AA and moved to the 1892 NL.[2] Hall of Famers John McGraw, Wilbert Robinson, Hugh Jennings, and Wee Willie Keeler anchored those "Old **Orioles**" under manager Ned Hanlon. They ground out runs through the sacrifice, the steal, the hit-and-run, and the firm hack toward the packed dirt that created a high bounce still called the "Baltimore chop." The franchise folded after 1899, having traded most stars to their Brooklyn syndicate partner. The next AL **Orioles** (1901–02) became the 1903 New York **Highlanders** (then **Yankees**). In 1954 the AL St. Louis **Browns** became **Orioles** III. Successful minor league Baltimore **Orioles** (1903–53) filled the half-century gap between **Orioles** II and III, during which the Baltimore oriole became the state bird (1947).[3]

Rhode Island's state bird is the Rhode Island Red, a maroon chicken first bred in Newport County from Asian fowl. Hockey's minor league Providence **Reds** (1926–76) were Rhode Island **Reds** in their last season (1976/77).

• • •

Florida Atlantic University hosts **Fighting Owls** because the Audubon Society designated its Boca Raton campus a sanctuary for the burrowing owl (*Speotyto cunicularia*) in 1971. The coastal Jacksonville campus of the University of North Florida is also a wildlife sanctuary, partly to accommodate the *Pandion haliaetus* population that has inspired its **Ospreys** since 1979. As the osprey's alternate name suggests, "fish hawks" live near open water and have a fish-heavy diet. (UNF is between the Atlantic Ocean and the brackish St. John's River.) Another good place to see fish hawks is among New Jersey's barrier islands, near the **Ospreys** at Stockton College in Pamona.

Pennsylvania's Lock Haven University is near Bald Eagle Mountain, so called because of exposed rock on its scalp. But the occasional real bald eagle (*Haliaetus leucocephalus*) dines in the nearby Susquehanna River, or you can spot **Bald Eagles** and **Lady Eagles** on LHU playing fields.

The northern goshawk (*Accipiter gentilis*) is among the many hawk species that frequent the Mohonk Preserve. It's near SUNY New Paltz, where a goshawk was in the care of the biology department in 1951, just when students wanted a live mascot for teams consequently called **Hawks**. In fact, the Hudson Valley is a major migratory path for hunting birds, putting **Hawks** at Hunter College (New York City), **Raptors** at Bard College (Annandale-on-Hudson), **Fighting Hawks** at SUNY Rockland Community College (Ramapo, N.Y.), and **Red Hawks** at RPI (p. 54). East of New Paltz, the Mid-Hudson Bridge crosses over the Hudson to Poughkeepsie. One bridge tower has an artificial nesting box for peregrine falcons (*Falco peregrinus*), and Po-Town is home for those **Falcons** at Dutchess [County] Community College.

The **Peregrines** at Purdue University–Calumet (Hammond, Ind.) are refreshingly species-specific. There are nearly forty species in the *Falco* genus, but *F. peregrinus* is a common **Falcon** mascot because its clean aerodynamics make it the fastest animal of any kind, achieving 200-plus miles per hour in dives from rocky ledges. It turns out that the stone facing of big-city office towers looks an awful lot like cliffs, so indoor football's New York **CityHawks** (1997–98) were named for the peregrines that nest among Big Apple high-rises. Ohio conservators fixed artificial nests to skyscrapers in the 1980s, and the mating pair at the Terminal Tower became Cleveland's beloved new residents. In 1991—when interest in the blue-gray peregrines was hottest—the blue and gold athletes at Notre Dame College in the South Euclid neighborhood became **Blue Falcons**.[4]

The continent's largest raptor, the California condor (*Gymnogyps californianus*), once ranged from the Baja Desert to southwestern Canada but was nearly wiped out by ranchers who thought they hunted livestock. In reality, those scavengers rarely chase large prey, but they were susceptible to lead poisoning from bullets and pesticides in carcasses. In the 1980s, the two-dozen remaining condors were brought into a captive breeding program. Reintroduction to the wild started in 1992 at Los Padres National Forest between Oxnard and Bakersfield, respective hosts of Oxnard College's **Condors** and minor league hockey's Bakersfield **Condors** (est. 1995).[5]

The American coot (*Fulica americana*) rhythmically nods its head in strolls along its marshy turf, so it's the "mud hen." The Maumee River entrance to Lake Erie at Toledo, Ohio is home to coots a-plenty, so minor league baseballers have been Toledo **Mud Hens** on and off for over a century.

In a spring mating dance, the male Greater Prairie Chicken (*Tympanuchus cupido pinnatus*) inflates his neck sacks to amplify his cooing. Illinois is on the eastern edge of the "boomer's" much-reduced historical range, but it's where you'll find the Frontier League's Schaumburg **Boomers** (est. 2012).

The chukar partridge (*Alectoris chukar*) is from southern Eurasia's dry mountain slopes. Introduced in many states as a game bird in the 1930s, the "rock partridge" thrived only in the arid Mountain West. The Treasure Valley Community College **Chukars** (Ontario, Ore.) are (way) down the Snake River from Idaho's Idaho Falls **Chukars** (2004–) of minor league baseball.

• • •

Geococcyx genus birds of the American Southwest and Central America are often called roadrunners or chaparral cocks. Arizona's first professional sports team was hockey's minor league Phoenix **Roadrunners** (est. 1967). They were so known in the major WHA from 1974 to '77, and two later skating teams used that name (1989–97, 2005–09). In Mexico, **Correcaminos** (road runners) are players of American football at *Universidad Autónoma de Tamaulipas*.

Metropolitan State University of Denver opened in the mid-1960s. Students hustling to class across downtown intersections were "roadrunners," and athletic **Mustangs** were also **Roadrunners** by 1974 (an identity maintained at the current, less urban Auraria campus). The **Chaparrals** at the College of DuPage (Glen Ellyn, Ill.) were named when it opened in 1967 for students shooting across city blocks to get from one temporary classroom to another.[6]

Community leaders and ABA execs discussed a 1967 team for Dallas at the Chaparral Club. One attendee suggested that the club's chaparral cock emblem suited the enterprise.[7] Indeed, they were Dallas **Chaparrals**, occasionally *Texas* **Chaparrals** to broaden the fanbase through home games at Lubbock and Fort Worth. (The former had already hosted the Lubbock Christian University **Chaparrals** and **Lady Chaps** since 1963.) Before the 1973/74 season, the **Chaps** moved to San Antonio. They were slated to be **Gunslingers**, but by the time they took the floor they were San Antonio **Spurs**, a name they rode into the NBA the next season. ("**Gunslingers**" was therefore available for San Antonio's 1984–85 USFL team.) The University of Texas at San Antonio elected to have **Roadrunners** in 1977. Midland College and Vernon College keep **Chaparrals** in their eponymous Texas cities.

The Latin name of the Greater Roadrunner—*Geococcyx californianus*—is roughly "California ground cuckoo," so **Roadrunners** at Golden State schools include CSU Bakersfield, the College of the Desert (Palm Desert), Rio Hondo Community College (Whittier), and Butte College (Oroville).

The *Geococcyx* fast tracked to fame when Warner Brothers unveiled its *Road Runner* cartoon in 1948. The president of State Fair Community College (Sedalia, Mo.) was thinking about a potential athletics mascot in 1975 when his daughter reminded him of his favorite animated character. The school then decided to run with **Roadrunners**.[8]

It's no coincidence that SFCC, Midland, Vernon, COD, RHCC, and Butte are community colleges. Even outside *Geococcyx* habitat, roadrunner imagery is often employed by scholar-athlete-commuters. Coach Melvyn Ottinger called basketballers at Dalton [Ga.] State College "**Roadrunners**" in 1968 specifically because it was a "fitting nickname for a commuting college."[9] Other community colleges with **Roadrunners** are Angelina College (Lufkin, Texas), Rowan

College at Gloucester County (Sewell, N.J.), Linn-Benton Community College (Albany, N.Y.), and the University of Wisconsin–Richland.

Ramapo College of New Jersey sits near the Ramapo Mountains in Mahwah. It's a top-rated "regional university," which—by definition—emphasizes undergraduate studies. That puts a disproportionate number of commuter-students on RCNJ's **Roadrunners**.

• • •

Cockfighting is a gambling sport in which two roosters have at it in a small pit. In the end, one bird is killed or crippled by either the opponent's beak or the sharp weapons attached to the legs. The Moors brought cockfighting from northern Africa to the southern parts of Spain they occupied from 711 to 1491. It was also a rage in medieval England (having come from Persia via the Romans), so Spaniards and Englishmen independently introduced cockfighting to their colonies.

Alabama's Jacksonville State keeps **Gamecocks** in a city named for cockfighting fan Andrew Jackson. The University of South Carolina has **Gamecocks** in Columbia. USC's Union campus is smaller, as are its **Bantams**. (The bantam is a small breed of fowl sometimes used for cockfighting.) Similarly, the USC system's two-year branch in Conway—Coastal Carolina College—wanted to trade **Trojans** for something to complement "**Gamecocks**" and so became **Chanticleers** (often "**Chants**") in 1963. (The rooster Chanticleer in Chaucer's *Canterbury Tales* gets by on his wits because he lacks physical strength.) The popular moniker was kept when Coastal Carolina University became independent of USC in 1993.[10] (In fact, the *Chanticleer* is the student news on the campus of JSU's abovementioned **Gamecocks**.)

As a graduate and trustee of Trinity College (Hartford, Conn.), federal judge Joseph Buffington boasted to Princeton alumni at an 1899 dinner that the "Trinity bantam" was fit company for the "mighty chanticleers of the collegiate barnyard," i.e., Harvard, Yale, and Princeton. Coincidentally (or not—no one seems to know), the *Detroit Free Press* evaluated Trinity's 1905 football schedule against those same powerhouses and called the school the "game-bantam of the intercollegiate poultry," a remark that hatched Trinity's **Bantams**.[11]

With breaks in the action during the Revolution, Delaware Valley soldiers entertained themselves by pitting Kent County blue hen chickens against one another. When the regiment's fighting fierceness matched that of their fowl, other soldiers called them "blue hens." Newark's University of Delaware teams have been **Fightin' Blue Hens** since 1911.[12]

A few animal rights advocates find cockfighting so objectionable that even **Gamecock** teams cause offense, but some Hispanic-Americans insist this testing of the bloodlines links to a proud cultural heritage. Only in 2008 were cockfights banned in all states. The tradition continues legally in Puerto Rico in small, attractive arenas. In fact, *la Universidad de Puerto Rico* at Río Piedras hosts male **Gallitos** and female **Jerezanas**. A *gallito* is a scrappy bantam, and *jerezana* is a feminization of *jerezano*, the prized breed from Jerez de la Frontera (a city in Andalusia, Spain) that had been crossed with English fowl to yield stunning colors.

Gorlocks | Bearcats | Werewolves | Devils

When regional critters fail to fulfill the role of mascot, athletes might just take the liberty to make something up.

• • •

At the heart of the Webster Groves neighborhood in St. Louis is the jogged junction of avenues named Gore and Lockwood. That inspirits the **Gorloks** at Webster University one mile east. The fakeloric Gorlok is endowed with the face of a St. Bernard, the horns of a bison, and the paws of a cheetah.

• • •

Do jackalopes really have jackrabbit bodies and antelope horns? *Yup.* Were any of them ever alive? *Nope.* Any jackalopes you encounter owe to a crypto-taxidermic trick wherein the antlers of a small deer have been fused to the noggin of a prairie rabbit. It looks pretty darned real, and the whole idea is too never—*ever*—admit to anyone from the coasts that the jackalope is just so much flim-flam. For our lack of discretion, we don't want to be spotted in Texas by Slap Jack, the face of the slapshooting Odessa **Jackalopes**. That name was slapped on minor leaguers (1997–2011) then junior hockeyists.

• • •

The Greek prefix *cyber* (to steer or govern) lately refers to computer-driven machines and applications. Everyone became cyber-savvy to some extent after companies in California's Santa Clara Valley led the software and Internet service boom of the 1990s. The capital of "Silicon Valley" is San Jose, the home of the WUSA Bay Area/San Jose **CyberRays** (2000–03). An organic ray with a technical name and the ability to deliver an actual electric shock does live off the coast, and that Pacific electric ray (*Torpedo californica*) inspired California's ABL Long Beach **Stingrays** (1997/98).[1]

• • •

Speculators who swindled pioneer squatters out of land before selling it at inflated prices were called land sharks. In a more literal incarnation, comedian Chevy Chase donned a foamy fish costume for a recurring land shark skit during the debut 1975 season of NBC's *Saturday Night Live*. When Landmark College (Putney, Vt.) opened in 1985, the similarity between *Landmark* and SNL's *landshark* baited teams into becoming Landmark **Sharks**.[2]

• • •

With his team down to Kentucky's **Wildcats** in a 1914 football game, one University of Cincinnati cheerleader decided to exploit the name of fullback Leonard Baehr, telling fans that the **Wildcats** would be defeated by *Baehr*-cats. The **Red & Black's** miraculous second-half comeback cemented their "**Bearcats**" nick. (The -*cat* theme is repeated by **Cougars** at UC Clermont College, a regional campus opened at Batavia in 1972.)

While Cincy's basketballing **Bearcats** were making five consecutive Final Four appearances (1959–63), an intramural team 200 miles down the Ohio River at Brescia University (Owensboro, Ky.) casually copied their nickname. Joining intercollegiate competition in the mid-1980s, Brescia retained **Bearcats**.[3]

We're not surprised that we can't find any sporting **Bearcats** before 1912, the year the Stutz *Bearcat* appeared in the emerging sports car category. But suddenly **Bearcat** athletes were popping up all over the place for no better reasons than the scrappiness implied and the instant familiarity owing to Stutz.

A tribal word for Malaysia's "bear cat" is *binturong*, a raccoon cousin that lives in Southeast Asia's rainforests. With a diet of mostly fruit, the nocturnal binturong eats nothing bigger than field mice, so actual bearcats don't conjure up ferocity. The mascots for athletic **Bearcats** are therefore almost always fantastical hybrids of ursine and feline features, as is the case at Columbia Bible College (Abbotsford, B.C.), Lander University (Greenwood, S.C.), Lon Morris College (Jacksonville, Tenn.), Saint Vincent College (Latrobe, Pa.), Southwest Baptist University (Bolivar, Mo.), Willamette University (Salem, Ore.), and Rust College (Holly Springs, Miss.).

Before one intra-Missouri basketball game in 1916, Coach Dan Nee of Springfield's Drury University was the first to call the **Normals** from the Maryville normal school "bearcats." The latter is today's Northwest Missouri State University, which kept its **Bearcats** and corresponding female **Bearkittens** for decades until they too were **Bearcats** by 1993.[4] Nee had actually thrown an unintended cheap shot. His own Drury **Panthers** were named in 1896 after the campus paper explicitly shunned bears (too clumsy) and most other cats, citing the tiger's willingness to be subdued and the lion's habit of quickly tiring in a hunt.[5]

• • •

Many European immigrants brought fables and fairy tales to North America. Reynard the fox, who had all-too-human emotions and motivations, was prominent in a cycle of medieval folk tales that were popular in Europe, especially France. In 1905 the Marist Brothers (a French-founded order) started Marist College at Poughkeepsie, New York. The ever-crafty Reynard stole his way onto the Marist arms and was adopted by basketballers in 1961, thereafter the **Red Foxes**. French trappers called one set of Meskwaki people around the Great Lakes the *Renard* clan, forever identifying them as "Fox" Indians. That provides the (otherwise obvious) Fox Valley Technical College **Foxes** in Appleton, Wisconsin with a little history.

Bruin is from Germanic forms for *brown*. A brown bear named *Bruin* or *Bruyn* (like the one in the Reynard epic) is a little like a red fox named Red or a polar bear named Snowflake, but *bruin* became a charming reference to bears of any color. Charles F. Adams was already a successful businessman when he bought an NHL franchise. He owned a chain of grocery stores that were brown with yellow trim. When he started his Boston club in 1924, Adams was indifferent toward the identifier, wanting only a fearsome something that was brown with yellow trim. He accepted the "Boston **Bruins**" alliteration suggested by an associate.[6]

Lycanthropic folk tales have been around forever, but two pop culture events firmly associated werewolves with the English capital: Warren Zevon's 1978 hit "Werewolves of London" and the 1981 movie *An American Werewolf in London*.

In historically Loyalist Ontario, you'll find a second London, one that hosted the Frontier League's London **Werewolves** (1999–2001). The next FL team to take their rips in town were the London **Rippers**, whose Jack-the-Ripper mascot came forth from Victorian London's spooky fog, but they were ripped from the league half way through their only summer, 2012.

Mountain-dwelling trolls from Scandinavian lore are either gigantic or pocket-sized. The **Trolls** at Trinity Christian College (Palos Heights, Ill.) are the result of deliberate alliteration; influential persons at the college simply wanted to repeat Trinity's *Tr-* in the team name.

• • •

The closest thing the U.S. has to a creepy fairy tale monster haunting misty woods is the devil of New Jersey's Pine Barrens. The story begins in 1735 when one Mrs. Leeds was delivering her thirteenth kid. In the pain of childbirth, she hollered, "The Devil can take this one!" … or "Gosh, this one's a devil!" … or "Yikes!!" The exact words are unknown because the lady's existence can't even be verified. Anyway, not having been at all careful for what she'd wished, Mrs. Leeds gave birth to the Jersey Devil, a monster with human, equine, and reptilian attributes that even a mother couldn't love. Strange things happen anywhere, but when they happen in the Pine Barrens the blame goes to Leed's Devil. Its athletic namesakes include Cherry Hill's minor league Jersey **Devils** (1964–73) and the NHL New Jersey **Devils** of East Rutherford (1982–2007) then Newark (2007–).

We'd advocate for the **Devils** at Farleigh Dickinson University's Madison, New Jersey campus being linked to the Jersey Devil, but there is no confirming backstory. (Also unexplained are the **Knights** at FDU's College at Florham.)

Cobras | D-Men | Nets | Racqueteers

We admit it. Every team name doesn't have a rich or ironic anecdotal backstory. Luckily, language lends phraseological frameworks for producing plenty of parallel pairings that articulate particular points. Instead of hitting the history books to find an identity, some new teams look to phonetics.

The most inspiring such agent is one of alliteration, the repetition of (usually) consonant sounds at the beginning of words or stressed syllables.[1] Beloit College tried hard to go alliterative with its new nick in 1949, choosing to replace **Blue Devils** with either **Braves**, **Bulldogs**, **Bobcats**, or **Buccaneers**.[2] Wisconsin is well removed from any ocean, but students went for "Beloit **Buccaneers**" anyway. Similarly, Tennessee's Crichton College put forth **Crusaders** until 1989, **Cougars** until 1996, **Cardinals** until 2005, and then **Comets**, but alliteration was lost when the Memphis school became the for-profit Victory University in 2010, quickly making teams Victory **Eagles**. (The Victory Eagle symbolized American pride and resolve during the world wars.) VU closed in mid-2014. **Comet** teams elsewhere tend to remain particularly alliterative, as is true at Cottey College (Nevada, Mo.) and Contra Costa College (San Pablo, Calif.). The student news at Concordia University (St. Paul) was the alliterative *Concordia Comet*, a name transferred to blue-and-gold **Comets** in 1926.[3] They became **Golden Bears** when moving up a division in 1999, but their bear mascot is still named Comet.

Coker College (Hartsville, S.C.) students thought their unofficial Coker **Nuts** (coconuts) and Coker **Cocos** were a bit timid, so they adopted "Coker **Cobras**" in the mid-1970s[4] (even though hooded snakes of the venomous *Elapidae* family don't live in North America). Florida's Kissimmee **Cobras** (1995–2000) were also alliterative. They had been the Osceola [County] **Astros** (1985–94), but became **Cobras** to avoid the phonetic difficulties invariably associated with "Kissimmee **Astros**."[5]

Iowa baseball had Des Moines **Demons** (1925–37, 1959–61). The unis at Chicago's DePaul University used to have a big *D* on the chest, but the **D-Men** were already gender-neutral **Blue Demons** by the time women's teams arrived. (The DePaul mascot is Dibs, "demon in a blue suit.") Similarly, the junior varsity **(Red) Demons** at Dean Academy (Franklin, Mass.) became **Bulldogs** when the institute upgraded to Dean College in 1994.[6]

Two North Carolina schools had an identity clash in 2003 when Raleigh's Peace College joined a conference in which Greensboro College already had **Pride**. Peace swallowed its **Pride** and fielded equally alliterative **Pacers**. In fall 2012 it went coed and changed its name to William Peace University, so Peace's **Pacers** are but a few letters removed from New York City's pace-setting Pace University **Setters**, who use Irish setter mascots.

A year-old California community college in San Luis Obispo was nameless until it became Cuesta College in October 1965. Just a week earlier a student poll had made CC's teams **Cougars**, the hard-*c* of which is actually believed to have effected the alliterative institutional name.[7] The same sound put **Cougars** at Kean

University (Union, N.J.), Kuyper College (Grand Rapids, Mich.), and Indiana University Kokomo. There are some hard-*k* **Kougars** at Kishwaukee College in Malta, Illinois.

Santa Barbara's Westmont College had **Wildcats** for two years before a 1947 student poll made them Westmont **Warriors**.[8] We needn't sermonize on the origins of the Mount Allison University **Mounties** (Sackville, N.B.), Mt. San Antonio College **Mounties** (Walnut, Calif.), or Mount St. Mary's University **Mountaineers** (Emmitsburg, Md.).

• • •

Assonance is the repetition of vowel sounds within words. For team naming, it's not nearly as popular as alliteration. The Sault College **Cougars** (Sault Ste. Marie, Ont.) are "Soo **Cougars**," as are the University of *Sioux* Falls **Cougars**. Olivet [Mich.] College keeps "Olivet **Comets**." The Frostburg [Md.] State University mascot is Frosty the **Bobcat**. Vowel sounds shared by "Vincent" and "mystic" put **Mystics** at Mount Saint Vincent University (Halifax, N.S.). Assonance pans out for the Canadore College **Panthers** (North Bay, Ont.). Storer College (Harpers Ferry, W.Va.) shut down in 1955, as was its Storer (**Golden**) **Tornado**. Kansas City's Avila University practiced assonance through its Avila (*ah*-ve-lah) **Avalanche** until a student poll made them Avila **Eagles** in 1990.

A parallel construction called *consonance* repeats consonant sounds, as exemplified by **Lancers** at the University of South Carolina–Lancaster. (Of course, "Lancaster **Lancers**" is also alliterative.) The purple-and-gold **Purples** at a women's tech in Montevallo, Alabama became arbitrarily named **Falcons** just a couple of years after the first men were admitted in 1956. The soft assonance and consonance of "Montevallo **Falcons**" was more explicit when Alabama College was renamed the University of Montevallo in 1969. Look also for shared vowel and consonant sounds in the NFL's city-nickname tandem, "Atlanta **Falcons**."

Assonance and consonance are *general* rhymes, in that some phonetic similarity exists. Of course, enough combined assonance or consonance between words with the same number of syllables can yield *perfect* rhymes. Refer to minor league baseball's Hannibal [Mo.] **Cannibals** (1908–12) or Connecticut's minor league New Haven **Ravens** (1992–2004).

No place rhymes like the Big Apple. When the **Dodgers** and **Giants** left NYC after the 1957 season, lawyer William Shea's Metropolitan Baseball Club of New York, Inc. proposed a new stadium for Flushing Meadows. Failing to either lure an existing NL club or get the league to expand, Shea and company created the Continental League, a new circuit that barely existed outside their imaginations. With its antitrust exemption then being examined by Congress, Organized Baseball was compelled to expand. In 1962 two new NL teams were added in the "Continental League cities" of Houston (the **Colts**/**Astros**) and New York. The latter's **Mets** abbreviated the name of Shea's Metropolitan Club and recalled the AA **Metropolitans** of the 1880s.

Before facing the wrecking ball in April 1964, the Polo Grounds had been the home of the **Mets** and the 1960-founded AFL New York **Titans** (whose name begged comparison to the NFL's **Giants**). That year the **Mets** and **Titans** moved to the world's first all-purpose sports facility, Shea Stadium. It was a mile from

LaGuardia Airport, so new **Titans** owner Sonny Werblin made them **Jets** to rhyme with the **Mets**.[9] (The buzz around early jet travel is now hard to appreciate, but the first jet-propelled transatlantic flight didn't happen until 1958.)

Werblin's friend Ben Hatskin was a Manitoba sportsman and entrepreneur. He called his 1967 team the Winnipeg **Jets** just so they'd match Werblin's footballers. Those junior **Jets** became minor league WHA-ers in 1972 and NHLers in 1979. A 1996 move to Arizona made them Phoenix **Coyotes**, but the relocation of Atlanta's **Thrashers** to Manitoba after the 2010/11 season created a successful demand from fans to take "Winnipeg **Jets**" out of mothballs.[10]

In 1967 it seemed that at least one team in the new *American* Basketball Association would be **Americans**. That fate fell to New Jerseyans who really wanted to be New Yorkers, but they could only get as close as a Teaneck armory. In 1969 those New Jersey **Americans** dribbled their red-white-and-blue ball over to the Long Island Arena in Commack. It wasn't Manhattan, but it was close enough to hook up the desired prefix, and as New York **Nets** they completed the **Mets-Jets-Nets** rhymed triplet. The NBA absorbed the ABA in mid-1976, forcing the crew back to the Garden State as New Jersey **Nets** for the 1977/78 season. In the fall of 2012 they were back on Long Island as Brooklyn **Nets**.

• • •

The New York **Sets** (later the **Apples**) arrived in the Big Apple in 1974. **Sets** didn't just rhyme with **Mets-Jets-Nets**; it was typical of the self-referencing monikers that World Team Tennis clubs served up, such as the Chicago **Aces**, Cleveland **Nets**, Detroit/Indiana **Loves**, and Los Angeles **Strings**.

The WTT has been a stop-and-go operation for decades, and later incarnations included Idaho **Sneakers**, Milwaukee **Racqueteers**, St. Louis **Aces**, Phoenix **Smash**, and the (unassociated) Delaware **Smash**. Some WTT names got more clever the longer you looked at them. Capital Off Track Betting once sponsored a prestigious tourney in Schenectady. OTB later owned that city's WTT New York **OTBzz** ("O.T.B.s"), then moved them to Albany as the New York **Buzz**. Just as Colorado's ABA Denver **Nuggets** were becoming Denver **Rockets**, along came the phonetically similar WTT Denver **Racquets**. California's Newport Beach **Breakers** (est. 2000) make sense for a coastal WTT team because a game won on an opponent's serve is called a service break.

Dodgers | Red Wings | Whalers | Colts

Favoring historical contexts, we've pretty much avoided tracking nicknames on a team-by-team basis. For your favored side, you can easily find such timelines elsewhere (especially on the Internet). In some cases, though, the history behind the moniker turns out to be the history of the team itself.

• • •

At what point does a recognized and revered team name become more important to a franchise than the local history that informs it? Ask the **Dodgers**.

Above-ground trolley tracks in the late 1800s were formidable obstacles. The tangled maze on the east side of the Brooklyn Bridge made pedestrians "trolley dodgers." Indeed, "**Trolley Dodgers**" was one name for the AA's Brooklyn Base Ball Club. They'd been **Atlantics** or **Grays** from the beginning (1883), but reporters offered many unofficial options.

Four Brooklyn players got married in 1888 and were **Grooms** or **Bridegrooms** by the time they joined the 1890 NL. They'd be so named until 1899, but management changes had sportswriters batting around these alternates:

- John Montgomery Ward's 1891 and '92 NLers were often called the Brooklyn **Wonders** because Ward had managed the Brooklyn **Ward's Wonders** in the 1890 Players' League, three of whom joined the 1891 **Bridegrooms**. Ward retired after the next season, leaving Dave Foutz to run **Foutz's Fillies** through 1896.

- Manager Ned Hanlon came to Brooklyn from Baltimore in 1899. He happened to share a surname with vaudeville's Hanlon Brothers, pantomimists and acrobats famous for their *Superba* show. The **Bridegrooms** were therefore **Superbas** from 1899 to 1910, even after Hanlon left to run Cincinnati's **Reds** in 1906. (This was no obscure reference. The *Superba* show debuted at the Brooklyn Academy of Music in 1890 and toured nationally until 1911.)

- At baseball's winter meetings in December 1909, Brooklyn owner Charlie Ebbets famously remarked that "baseball is in its infancy," so his nine were often **Infants** between 1911 and 1913.

- Starting in 1914, manager Wilbert Robinson's own sobriquet led to "**Robins**." Uncle Robbie retired after '31, and "**Dodgers**"—doggedly associated with the franchise from the beginning—could no longer be dodged.

- L.A. had the world's largest electric trolley system through the 1920s, but by the time the Los Angeles **Dodgers** moved there in 1958, the complete transition to an automobile-based system was nearly complete.[1]

• • •

One ABA franchise is a case study on evolving team identities. Named for Gulf Coast pirates, the New Orleans **Buccaneers** (1967–70) played some games in Memphis. In fact, they were soon the Memphis **Pros** (1970–72) simply because *P-R-O-S* covered up *B-U-C-S* on the uniforms. (True.) The league turned the club's finances over to Charlie Finley, whose name-the-team contest gave him **Tams**. That acronymically targeted fans in *T*ennessee, *A*rkansas, and *M*ississippi, but the emblem was a braided Scottish bonnet called a tam o'shanter. (Team colors were Celtic too, matching the kelly green and gold of Finley's Oakland **A's**.) By the 1974/75 season, the **Tams** were back in league hands. Local musicians tried to buy them, and they were Memphis **Sounds** until financing fell through. They would have been Baltimore **Hustlers** for 1975/76, but the ABA found that too risqué, instead naming them **Claws** after the Chesapeake Bay's famous blue crab (*Callinectes sapidus*). That didn't matter because the **Claws** never took hold, folding after a few exhibition games.[2]

• • •

Upstate New York's independent Rochester **Seagrams** lost a decade-old whiskey company sponsorship in 1943 and were simply **Pros**. They joined the top hoop league for the 1945/46 season as Rochester **Royals**, hoping to "seize the NBL crown."[3] (They were, in fact, champs that season.) They slid to the NBA in 1949 and moved to the Queen City in 1957, staying regal as Cincinnati **Royals**.[4] A 1972 shift to K.C. found baseballers already called **Royals**, so they were Kansas City-Omaha **Kings**, representing the biggest respective cities in Missouri and Nebraska. "Omaha" was dropped in 1975, and they've been Sacramento **Kings** since moving to California in 1985.

• • •

The ABL/BAA/NBA Baltimore **Bullets** (1944–54) were named for a city ammo factory, the Phoenix Shot Tower.[5] In 1964 the NBA Chicago **Zephyrs** moved to Maryland as new **Bullets**. In 1973 owner Abe Pollin (a construction magnate) moved them to Landover, Maryland, five miles from D.C. The new building—Capital Centre—effected the new team name: Capital **Bullets**. That lasted one season until "Washington **Bullets**" was called upon to avoid confusion with Pollin's new NHL Washington **Capitals**. The District was the nation's murder capital throughout the 1980s and '90s, making Pollin increasingly uncomfortable with "**Bullets**" (especially after a gunman assassinated his friend, Israeli Prime Minister Yitzhak Rabin, in 1995). Again coordinating a change in venue with a new name, Pollin made his NBA-ers alliterative Washington **Wizards** when moving them to D.C. proper in 1997.

• • •

Bret "Hitman" Hart is from a famous Canadian pro wrestling family. He originally had a large financial stake in junior hockey's Calgary **Hitmen** (est. 1995). Because a good, clean hit is part of the game, "**Hitmen**" is an apt name for other hockey teams, like junior hockey's New Jersey **Hitmen** (est. 2004). Different New York/New Jersey **Hitmen** had been in the 2001 XFL, a football league started by Hart's old wrestling federation after his 2000 retirement. (Both **Hitmen** sides capitalized on the popularity of the acclaimed HBO series the *Sopranos*, which followed Garden State mobsters from 1999 to 2007.)

The XFL Chicago **Enforcers** highlighted their own city's gangster past. (Arena Football had already fielded Chicago **Bruisers**, 1987–89.) Other XFLers that aimed to intimidate were the Memphis **Maniax**, Orlando **Rage**, and San Francisco **Demons**.

• • •

"Casey at the Bat" is Ernest Lawrence Thayer's mock epic poem in which the Mudville **Nine**'s slugger represents the winning run with two out in the ninth. (We won't give away the ending.) It originally appeared in an 1888 edition of the *San Francisco Examiner*. You can sail from Frisco Bay to the inland port of Stockton, and Stocktonians claim Mr. Thayer did just that, writing "Casey" after seeing the town's semi-pro nine. Locals so strongly believe that their city is Mudville that Stockton's California League **Ports** were the Mudville **Nine** for two seasons (2000–01). New owners in 2002 reverted to "Stockton **Ports**."

• • •

British Columbia's Victoria **Aristocrats** formed in 1918. In 1922 they became **Cougars**, after Vancouver Island's *Puma concolor vancouverensis* subspecies. They were the last non-NHL Stanley Cup winners in 1925 and the last to challenge for it in 1926. Lester and Frank Patrick realized that their Western Canada Hockey League couldn't compete with the NHL's salaries and expansion ambitions, so they folded it up and sold the **Cougars** into the NHL. Waiting for Olympia Stadium to be built, those *Detroit* **Cougars** played the 1926/27 season on the Ontario side of the Detroit River. They became Detroit **Falcons** in 1930 to divorce themselves from an unimpressive recent history. In 1832, Chicago grain broker James Norris bought the **Falcons** and made them **Red Wings** to acknowledge a team for which he'd played in his Canadian youth, the **Winged Wheelers** of the Montreal Amateur Athletic Association (in some chronicles the "MAAA").[6] Originally a cycling club, the **Wheelers**' mark was a winged wheel, which fit the Motor City.

In little more than a decade, the Norris family would be invested in the Olympia (and the **Wings**), Madison Square Garden (and therefore the **Rangers**), and Chicago Stadium (and the **Black Hawks**), giving them control of half of the NHL's six teams.[7] Norris consequently supported the 1946 BAA, a major hoop league designed to for large eastern arenas, and he ran two BAA franchises, the Stadium's Chicago **Stags** (1946–50) and the Olympia's Detroit **Falcons** (1946/47), the latter having adopted the "**Falcons**" name previously discarded by Norris's **Red Wings**.[8]

• • •

Various Fort Wayne **Komets** have played minor league hockey in Indiana since 1952. The first such side was deliberately misspelled to correspond with the name of original owner Ernie Berg's wife Kathryn, or "Kay."

• • •

Over the San Gabriel Mountains from L.A. is California's High Desert, where the **Marauders** at Lancaster's Antelope Valley College have used scimitar-wielding mascots since 1939 to suggest Bedouin marauders of Arabian deserts.

• • •

Having lunch in 2006, two Garden State men were planning a soccer league for girls and women. One arbitrarily scribbled "Sky Blue" on the back of a napkin, and Sky Blue Soccer soon had offices in Somerset. They ran the W-League's Jersey **Sky Blue** (2007–08) and then **Sky Blue FC** (WPS: 2009–11, NWSL: 2013–).[9] Somerset was in the several northern New Jersey counties already called the Skylands Region by the state tourism board. (The eponymous Skylands estate home is in the New Jersey Botanical Garden.) That makes **Skylanders** and **Lady Skylanders** at home at Sussex County Community College.

• • •

Skaters on Boston's 1972 WHA team displayed their league allegiance as New England **Whalers** (*WHA-lers*). Boston had been a whaling base, but not much competition for southern New England's ports. (Connecticut's New Bedford **Whalers** of 1920s soccer had a stronger historical claim to the identity.) The "New England" prefix proved prophetic; unable to compete with the NHL's established **Bruins**, the **Whalers** moved to Hartford in 1974 after being sold to a congregation of Connecticut businessmen. They skated up the frozen Connecticut River to Springfield, Massachusetts after their roof collapsed in a 1978 snowstorm. (No wonder female basketballers who split home games between Hartford and Springfield would be the ABL's New England **Blizzard**, 1996–99.) As one of four squads absorbed by the NHL when the WHA went belly up, they started the 1979/80 season as *Hartford* **Whalers**, even as they remained in Springfield for the first half. "New England" had been dropped as a league-imposed fishing limit to keep the **Whalers**' hooks out of the **Bruins**' territory. The **Whalers** became the Carolina **Hurricanes** in 1997.

• • •

In 1970 the editors of the first staff-and-student directory at Hampshire College (Amherst, Mass.) arbitrarily put a photo of a frog on the cover, probably without the foggiest idea they'd endowed HC with a frog mascot and **Frog** athletes.[10]

• • •

Seventh Day Adventists founded Salem International University (Salem, W.Va.) in the Tenmile District along Tenmile Creek, so athletes were **Seven Days** and **Tenmilers**,[11] but "**Fighting Tigers**" came to dominate in the 1960s.

• • •

Baltimore's Pimlico Race Course hosts the Preakness Stakes, an annual race for 3-year-old colts and fillies (the Triple Crown's middle stage). The thoroughbred is Maryland's state horse and Baltimore County is "Horse Country," owing to its equine breeders and hunt clubs, facts not lost on the Stevenson University **Mustangs** or several Baltimore **Colts** teams. You'd do well to accept that recap. The uncut version—*read on if you must*—is a bit of a tangle.

Good numbers of ospreys, hawks, and falcons in southern coastal Florida explain the AAFC Miami **Seahawks** of 1946. They moved after that season to be Baltimore **Colts**. (**Seahawks** returned to southern Florida in 1959 to represent Fort Lauderdale's Broward [County] College). A regional rivalry with Washington's **Redskins** was expected when the NFL absorbed the **Colts** and two other AAFC teams in 1950, but the **Colts** folded after both sides finished at the bottom of their respective divisions.

The bloodline for the next **Colts** is more involved. Setting sights on the 1944 NFL, singer Kate Smith and her manager Ted Collins already owned one of basketball's most storied teams, Kate Smith's **Original Celtics**, but Collins wanted an NFL franchise for Yankee Stadium. He was blocked when the **Giants**' owner, Tim Mara, exercised his territorial rights. Making a base farther north, Collins's New York state of mind was revealed by Fenway Park's Boston **Yanks**. It had taken real gumption to start a new franchise during those war years in which existing teams were struggling. In fact, Boston's **Yanks** were already absorbing the NFL Brooklyn **Dodgers/Tigers** in 1945, which gave them use of Yankee Stadium for a single *home* game by "Boston-Brooklyn" **Yanks**. The next year, the **Dodgers/Tigers** were in the rival AAFC, which already had Brooklyn **Dodgers**, so Collins's former NFL partners stuck it to him, not only becoming the AAFC's own New York **Yankees**, but by settling into the House that Ruth Built. The NFL was anticipating the demise of the AAFC and Collins was finally allowed to move his 1949 **Yanks** from Boston to the Polo Grounds (technically as a new franchise). His baseball **Giant** landlords didn't want to advertise for the city's American Leaguers, so Collins's **Yanks** became New York **Bulldogs**. The AAFC's **Yankees** and Brooklyn **Dodgers** merged for 1949 to remain afloat but were too late. The NFL absorbed the AAFC in 1950 and Collins bought the rights to the good **Yankees** and put them on his **Bulldogs**. (Lesser **Yankees** went to Mara's **Giants**.) The team played in Yankee Stadium as New York **Yanks**. His Big Apple dream was finally fulfilled, but Collins quickly tired of the exercise and sold the franchise back to the NFL after 1951. In '52, the **Yanks** turned up as Dallas **Texans**. Again they struggled and again the NFL was running the franchise by midseason.[12] For 1953 a Baltimore group purchased the **Texans'** players and draft rights and moved them east (again as a *new* franchise) under the name of the former AAFC/NFL team: Baltimore **Colts**.

Don't confuse the 1952 NFL Dallas **Texans** with the AFL Dallas **Texans**. The latter team was started in 1960 by oil scion and AFL founder Lamar Hunt. Hunt's 1962 champion **Texans** followed the old cowboy trails north to Kansas City after being lured there by Mayor H. Roe "Chief" Bartle. (The NFL's plan to compete directly with Hunt's AFL **Texans** by creating the 1960 Dallas **Cowboys** had apparently paid off.) Hunt called his relocated side Kansas City **Chiefs** in the mayor's honor, a team in the NFL since the 1970 merger.

Air conditioning magnate Robert Irsay bought the Los Angeles **Rams** in 1972 and immediately traded *the entire franchise* for Baltimore's **Colts**. On a March day in 1984, Irsay took the **Colts** to Indiana in a bit of unsportsmanlike conduct that Marylanders still recall as "The Move." In Indianapolis, "**Colts**" could be kept because the NBA **Pacers** already saluted the city's harness racing history.

After years of trying to revive football, Maryland's big burg landed a 1994 Canadian Football League team. They thought they'd be called Baltimore **Colts** (or the Baltimore **CFL Colts**), but a federal court upheld the Indianapolis **Colts'** trademark. They enjoyed anonymity as the Baltimore **Football Club** (or in Euro-soccer style, **B.F.C.**), but many preferred "a horse with no name." By 1995 they were Baltimore **Stallions**, another masculine equine moniker. After becoming the first U.S.-based team to claim the CFL's Grey Cup, they learned they'd be the only CFL team in an NFL market after the announcement that another bitter civic divorce would make Cleveland's **Browns** the 1996 Baltimore **Ravens**. Plucked immediately northward, the **Stallions** became the third installment of Montreal **Alouettes** in CFL history.

AA: American Association (1882–91), a major baseball league. Same-named later circuits were prestigious minor leagues (1902–62, 1969–97). In 2006 the American Association of Independent Professional Baseball started.

AAFC: All-America Football Conference (1946–49), absorbed by the NFL in 1950.

AAU: Amateur Athletic Union, developing community teams and athletes since 1888.

ABA: American Basketball Association (est. 1967), absorbed by the NBA in 1976. A second ABA—sometimes "ABA 2000"—started in 2000 and has since struggled.

ABL: American Basketball League (1925–31), among the very first national hoop circuits (although all teams were east of the Mississippi without black players). The Depression killed it. Another ABL (1961–62) was formed by Abe Saperstein from top AAU and independent clubs but folded during its second season. A women's ABL (1996–99) was crushed by the NBA's 1997-founded WNBA.

AFL: American Football League (1926 only), started by former college star Red Grange and his manager. A same-named circuit (1936–37) couldn't compete with the NFL. The downfall of a *third* American Football League (1940–41) was hastened by the outbreak of World War II. The most successful AFL (est. 1960) would merge with the NFL. The two circuits played a single championship game starting in January 1967 (retroactively "Super Bowl I") and waited for their respective TV contracts to expire before fully consolidating in 1970.

AHL: American Hockey League (1940–), the NHL's premier minor league.

AL: American League (of Professional Baseball Clubs), started as Ban Johnson's (minor) Western League. It became the AL for 1900 and assumed *major* status in 1901.

APFA: American Professional Football Association, founded in 1920. It became the NFL in 1922.

ASL: American Soccer League (1921–33), North America's first pro soccer league. When its schedule clashed with another organization's Open Cup championship, renegade ASLers formed a new league in 1928. Both circuits realigned in 1930, just in time to disintegrate in the Depression. We've listed squads in the ASL before or after that 1928/1929 "soccer war" as ASL teams. Readers seeking greater exactitude are enthusiastically directed toward Colin Jose, *The American Soccer League, 1921–1931: The Golden Years of American Soccer* (Lanham, Md. and London, 1998), American Sports History Series, no. 9. See also Dave Litterer, ed., "The American Soccer History Archives," http://homepages. sover.net/~spectrum (accessed 16 September 2013). A semi-pro ASL (1933–83) revived some team names from the old ASL. It was later a second-division NASL circuit from which teams formed the USL in 1984. A third ASL lasted from 1988 to '89.

BAA: Basketball Association of America (1946–49), absorbed the NBL to form the NBA for the 1949/50 season.

CFL: Canadian Football League, started as the Canadian Rugby Football Union in 1884, which is about when Canada's "rugby football" started looking more to the open formation of U.S. colleges (as opposed to rugby's traditional scrum). *Rugby*, however, managed to remain in the name of one league division or another until 1958.

FL: Federal League (1914–15), considered major owing to its recruitment of MLB players. It had been the (minor) Columbia League (1912) and (minor) FL (1913).

HBCU: Historically Black Colleges and Universities. Colleges established primarily to educate African American students between the Civil War and 1964 were reclassified as HBCUs as part of the Higher Education Act of 1965.

IHL: International Hockey League, three main incarnations: 1929–36, 1945–2001, 2007–2010.

MBL: Metropolitan Basketball League (1921–33), with teams around New York City.

MISL: Major Indoor Soccer League (1978–89). A different league of that name (2001–08) comprised remainders of the NPSL.

MLB: Major League Baseball, the result of a 1903 alliance between former competitors, the AL and NL. After ninety-eight years of cooperation, those leagues dissolved as separate legal entities and re-formed as a new MLB only in 2000.

MLL: Major League Lacrosse, started outdoor play in 2001.

MLS: Major League Soccer (1996–), North America's top professional league.

NA: National Association (of Base Ball Players), started in 1858 with clubs around New York City. Within a decade there were hundreds of teams. The NA standardized the "Knickerbocker rules," sentencing Philadelphia's "town ball" and New England's "Massachusetts game" to footnote eternity. The circuit disappeared a few seasons after the coming of the National Association (of Professional Base Ball Players) in 1871, which added only *Professional* to the name. (A National Association of *Amateur* Base Ball Players tried to compete with the new NA but was gone by 1875.) Considered the first major league, the NAPBBP folded when its select teams formed the NL in 1876.

NASL: North American Soccer League (1968–84), the continent's top professional league of its day. A second-division league established in 2011 has the same name.

NBA: National Basketball Association, created by merging the BAA and NBL before the 1949/50 season.

NBA D-League: The Basketball Development League (NBDL, est. 2001) was renamed the NBA Development League ("D-League") in 2005 when it became the NBA's official minor league.

NBL: National Basketball League (1937–49), with teams sponsored by Midwestern factories. It merged with the BAA to form the NBA for the 1949/50 season.

NFL: National Football League, the former APFA (1920–21).

NFL Europe: This NFL-sponsored league (the progeny of the 1991–94 WLAF) played in European cities (mostly Germany) from 1995 to 2005. It was "NFL Europa" by 2006 but folded after the 2007 season.

NHA: National Hockey Association (1909–17), the forerunner of the NHL.

NHL: National Hockey League (est. 1917), comprising most teams in the soon-to-collapse NHA.

NL: National League (of Professional Baseball Clubs), founded in 1876 to succeed the professional National Association (of Base Ball Players).

NLL: National Lacrosse League (1974–75), a box lacrosse circuit. Teams usually owned by hockey arenas played indoors on hard floors. A 1987-founded indoor NLL uses artificial turf.

NNL: Negro National League (1920–31), baseball's first successful black league. A different NNL (1933–48) was also the top black league of its day.

NPSL: National Professional Soccer League, two leagues: 1967 only and 1990–2001.

NPSL: National Premier Soccer League (est. 2003), an amateur league with regional circuits.

NWSL: National Women's Soccer League (est. 2013), America's top women's league comprising four former WPS sides.

PCHA: Pacific Coast Hockey Association, a major senior league founded by Lester and Frank Patrick with their father's lumber money in 1911.

PCL: Pacific Coast League (est. 1903), an almost-major baseball league on the west coast. The legendary PCL lost prestige with the advent of televised MLB games and the 1958 arrival of the **Giants** and **Dodgers** in the biggest PCL markets.

PL: Players' League (or Players' National League of Professional Base Ball Clubs), an 1890 major league composed of most of the NL's players and about a fifth of the AL's.

UA: Union Association (1884), tried to compete with the major baseball leagues of its day. Poorly managed, it lasted one year and is not generally considered a *major* league.

USFL: United States Football League (1983–85), a spring league that followed the 1982 NFL player strike. The upstart league won its antitrust suit against the senior circuit, but because USFL administrators were found largely liable for their own demise, the NFL paid a settlement of $3.76 (plus $6 million in legal fees).

USL: United Soccer League (1984–85), a remnant of the collapsed ASL.

USL: United Soccer Leagues, a confederation of more than 100 minor league teams.

WBL: Women's Basketball League (1978–81), the first major pro league for women.

WFL: World Football League (1974–75), a bust in terms of fan interest. It folded during its second season with no teams welcomed into the NFL.

WHA: World Hockey Association, a big league established to compete with the NHL in 1972. After it folded, four of its teams entered the 1979/80 NHL.

WL: Western League (1894–99), a minor baseball league that became the 1900 AL, which turned major in 1901. Before 1894 it was a circuit of Great Lakes region teams.

WLAF: World League of American Football (est. 1991), the NFL's ten-team spring minor league. Its three European sides laid the groundwork for NFL Europe.

W-League: Established in 1995, this was North America's most prestigious women's league between the 2003 suspension of the WUSA and its resurrection as the 2009 WPS.

WNBA: Women's National Basketball Association (est. 1997), run by the NBA.

WPS: Women's Professional Soccer (2009–11), the reorganized WUSA. Financial and legal pressures wiped out the 2012 season, with some WPS teams joining the new 2013 NWSL.

WPSL: Women's Premier Soccer League (est. 1997), a pro-am development circuit. It added a WPSL *Elite* component when it absorbed some WPS teams in 2012.

WTT: World Team Tennis, a circuit that's struggled for definition since 1974. It matches pro and amateur players in long- and short-season exhibition series.

WUSA: Women's United Soccer Association (2001–03), the world's first all-salaried soccer league for women. (The later WPS was largely the restructured WUSA.)

XFL: X Football League (2001), the *X* standing for "X." The XFL was backed by World Wrestling Entertainment, who quickly learned that "Xtreme Football League" had belonged to Alabama sports promoter Art Clarkson since 1999. Clarkson's XFL never played a down, but he protected the name because he was sure the WWE would come to raid his semi-pro ranks. It was therefore said that *XFL* "stood for nothing," which it proved by folding after three months of uninspired play. The league did maintain an *x*-tra edge through its Los Angeles **Xtreme**. That name may have subliminally intended to bring to mind the famous abbreviation for the L.A. International Airport—L.A.X.—in which *X* (again) stands for nothing. It was added arbitrarily when the growing number of airports (and their associated National Weather Service stations) exploded in the 1930s, forcing the conversion from two-letter codes to three.

Notes

Chapter 1 Notes

[1] *New York Times*, "On the Baseball Field," 4 Oct. 1899, http://query.nytimes.com/mem/archive-free/pdf?res=FA0A1EFD385913738DDDAD0894D8415B8985F0D3 (accessed 11 April 2011).

[2] Fred Pettijohn, "In the Pressbox," *Tallahassee Daily Democrat* (9 Nov. 1947), www.nolefan.org/summary/seminoles.html (accessed 23 July 2012).

[3] WNBA Enterprises, LLC, "Atlanta's WNBA Team Named Atlanta Dream," www.wnba.com/dream/dream_080123.html (accessed 25 April 2014). A retrofitted story says "**Dream**" came from the 1963 "I Have a Dream Speech" by Atlanta native Martin Luther King, Jr.

Another women's hoop **Dream**—L.A.'s WBL California **Dreams** (1979/80) inevitably called to mind the Mamas & the Papas' 1965 hit "California Dreamin'."

[4] The **Niners** will retain "San Francisco" when they move south to Santa Clara in 2014.

[5] For example, a California normal school became Fresno State College in 1921 and started intercollegiate football. Athletes were **Bulldogs** because one such canine often waited for his owner outside the main building. (FSC became CSU Fresno in 1972.)

An English bulldog owned by basketball coach Ellis Verink at McPherson [Kan.] College made its teams **Bulldogs** in 1917. A bulldog owned by athletic director Walter Hellwege at Seward's Concordia University Nebraska put **Bulldogs** there in the 1920s.

[6] Denton's University of North Texas planned to turn its extension school at Dallas into an autonomous institution by 2009. That was delayed until 2010, even though blue and gold colors and a jaguar mascot had been waiting on deck since a January 2007 "branding event." Students at the University of Minnesota–Rochester elected a raptor mascot in September 2010. The University of Houston–Clear Lake has a hawk mascot. Eastern New Mexico University–Roswell has a cougar mascot. The University of Alaska–Southeast (Juneau) adopted a humpback whale mascot in 1980. None of those field corresponding intercollegiate teams.

[7] Taylor University, "Donating Materials," http://library.taylor.edu/archives/donating.shtml (accessed 22 July 2013). When Hannibal College and LaGrange College merged into today's Hannibal-LaGrange University (Hannibal, Mo.) in 1929, a member of the new football team suggested "the fanciful name **Trojans**" for reasons known only to him. (J. Hurley and Roberta Hagood, *Hannibal-LaGrange College: History* [Hannibal, Mo.: Hannibal-LaGrange College, 1995]: 49–51.) (LaGrange's pre-merger teams had been **Owls**, motive also unknown.)

[8] Kaye Lundgren (UALR archives), email to the author, 26 May 2010.

Chapter 2 Notes

[1] Joseph B. Oxendine, *American Indian Sports Heritage* (Lincoln: U. Nebraska Press, 1995): 306.

[2] Fergus M. Bordewich, *Killing the White Man's Indian* (New York: Doubleday, 1996): 17.

[3] The Tomahawk Chop—which mimics football's first-down signal—started with fans of Florida State's **Seminoles**. FSU football and baseball star Deion Sanders played for Atlanta's **Braves** from 1991 to '94, and it's believed the chop followed him there from Tallahassee.

[4] The 2005 NCAA report encouraged members to follow the Universities of Iowa and Wisconsin by rejecting non-conference contests against teams with the offending imagery.

[5] Their stories are throughout, but here are the eighteen colleges that were asked to reexamine their potentially "hostile or abusive" names and symbols by the NCAA in August 2005: Alcorn State, Arkansas State, Bradley, Catawba, Carthage, Central Michigan, Chowan, Florida State, Illinois, Indiana U.-Pennsylvania, McMurry, Midwestern State, Mississippi Coll., Louisiana-Monroe, Newberry, North Dakota, Southeastern Oklahoma State, and Utah. Absent is William

and Mary, having already agreed to self-reflection. Another thirteen schools had already agreed to wash their identities of any trace of Indian characteristics: CSU Stanislaus, East Stroudsburg, Eastern Connecticut State, Hawaii-Mānoa, Husson, Lycoming, Merrimack, San Diego State, Southeast Missouri State, West Georgia, Stonehill, Winona State, and Wisconsin Lutheran.

[6] *Phoenician* is a Greek form of "red men" that Rome applied to Tyrian purveyors of royal purple dye. In 814 BCE the Phoenicians/red men founded North Africa's city-state of Carthage, closing the historical distance between *Carthage* College and its **Red Men**. The closest the school comes to acknowledging that is its recently adopted flaming torch and shield of classical design, best dated to the Roman conquest of Carthage in 146 BCE.

[7] Scott Bigelow, "Statue of Hawk Mascot Unveiled," *UNCP University Newswire* (1999), www.uncp.edu/news/1999/tommy_statue.htm (accessed 23 July 2012).

[8] Mutual distrust of the Snohomish allied Sealth with the white pioneers who named their settlement after him in 1853, thirteen years before his death. A good orator in Salish, Sealth's famous 1854 speech didn't appear in English until 1887, and even that was reconstructed from incomplete notes. The version popularly quoted was further amended for an environmentalist film in 1972. Refer to Bordewich, *Killing the White Man's Indian*: 131–133, 161.

[9] Charles Canon (Roberts Wesleyan Coll. archivist), email to the author, 23 April 2014.

[10] Ken Leiviska, "Ripon Redmen, History of the Name, Mascot Changes," *College Days* (12 April 2006): 1, 11.

[11] Arbitrarily named **Eagles** not listed elsewhere include those at Alice Lloyd Coll. (Pippa Passes, Ky.), Chadron [Neb.] State Coll., U. Toronto–Mississauga, and Trinity Lutheran Coll. (Everett, Wash.). **Running Eagles** represent Life U. (Marietta, Ga.).

[12] Frenchmen supposedly thought the Indians' shaft-and-basket equipment resembled a bishop's staff and cross, so they called the sport *la crosse*. A more believable story has the French putting up a cross, naming the place *Prairie La Crosse*, and calling the local game *la crosse*.

UW-La Crosse is a former normal school where maroon-and-grey **Peds** became **Maroons** (which may have led to the "**Red Raiders**" alternate to "**Indians**"). "**Maroons**" led to the "**Roonies**" sobriquet that was used by female athletes until 1990. In the past, UW-L fielded **Hurricanes** (unexplained) and **Racqueteers**, likely a reference to lacrosse sticks.

[13] As a collegiate football powerhouse, Colgate often had its identity appropriated by other schools. **Blue Raiders** appeared at Middle Tennessee State in 1934, and **Red Raiders** were presented by Iowa's Northwestern College (Orange City) in 1945. Both admit to having respectfully derived those names from Colgate's **Red Raiders**. (Matt Bos [Northwestern sports info. dir.], email to the author, 6 Jan. 2006.)

[14] "Newspaper Redesigned as *The Shield*," *North Star* (vol. 42, no. 2, spring 2001): 4.

[15] Robert L. Santos, "California State University, Stanislaus: A History," http://wwwlibrary. csustan.edu/bsantos/chap2.html (access 12 Nov. 2013).

[16] WLC was formerly St. John's Lutheran College, with **Saints** and **Johnnies**. **Johnnies** represented the Lutherans' other St. John's College (Winfield, Kan.), which closed in 1986. Maryland's (non-Lutheran) St. John's College in Annapolis has club-level **Johnnies**.

[17] *Merrimack* is *merruh* (strong) plus *auke* (place), the middle *m* "thrown in for the sake of the sound," according to Chandler E. Potter, *The History of Manchester* (Manchester, N.H.: C.E. Potter, 1856): 7. The Merrimack River (near Merrimack College) isn't etymologically related to the Meramec River associated with St. Louis Community College in the text. *Meramac* also has Algonquian roots, but it means "ugly [cat-] fish."

A mile from North Andover's Merrimack College **Warriors** is Andover's Balmoral Park, where a premiere soccer field of the 1920s is now a modest running track. That park abuts a tributary of the Merrimack called the Shawsheen River ("great spring" in Algonquian). Its Shawsheen **Indians** were soccerists sponsored by Lawrence's nearby mills. The **Indians** were national champs in 1925 and joined the top pros in the ASL immediately thereafter.

[18] Greg Knowlden, ed., "ESU Athletic Traditions," *ESU Football Media Guide* (2007): 18.

Chapter 3 Notes

[1] The **Arrows** were **Braves** from 1974 to '79. Indian themes thrive in Ontario's box lacrosse leagues, as shown by Ontario's Whitby Brooklin **Redmen** (1966–), Whitby **Warriors** (1984–), Burlington **Chiefs** (1992–), Kitchener-Waterloo **Braves** (1967–), and Elora **Mohawks** (1967–). The province's 1973-founded Mississauga team has been **Arrowheads**, **Chiefs**, and **Toma-hawks**. (Southern Ontario's Mississaugas were the Ojibwas' cousins.) The St. Regis **Indians** (2006–09) represented New York's St. Regis Mohawk Reservation.

[2] The 1830/31 Winter of the Deep Snow forced central Illinoisans south for food, a trip compared to one made by the sons of Jacob, who went from Canaan to Egypt to buy grain during a famine (Genesis 42). This reinforces southern Illinois's "Little Egypt" nickname.

[3] Seeking an institutional identity that was distinct from that of the sister campus in Carbondale, students at SIU Edwardsville elected to have **Cougars** in 1967.

[4] Eleven ancient Egyptian pharaohs were named Ramesses, the most famous and powerful being Ramesses II (r. 1279 to 1213 BCE). Rams named *Ramses* (or *Ramesses* or *Rameses*) have represented **Rams** at Fordham, U. Mobile, and U. Rhode Island.

[5] We know little of the Muskogean-language Chatot people of northwest Florida's upper Chipola River. They are often confused with—possibly related to—the Choctaws. The Chatots revolted in the 1670s against zealous Spanish missionaries near modern Marianna, home of the Chipola College **Indians**.

[6] Southeastern State Teachers College fielded its first **Fighting Teachers** in 1910. after 1920 they were **Indians**, then **Savages**. In fall 2013, SOSU's **Savage Storm** added a buffalo mascot named *Storm*.

[7] Warfare and disease nearly wiped out the Catawba by the late 1800s. Half of the survivors were recruited to the Southwest by Latter Day Saints, whose Book of Mormon says Native Americans descended from persons who left Israel around 600 BCE.

[8] Betsy Brinson, *Kentucky Civil Rights Oral History Project: Interview with Anne Butler* (Frankfort: Kentucky Hist. Soc., 2007): 29. Interviewee Butler was one of the first African American students at EKU. Her account says "**Maroons**" was dropped when administrators became aware of the connection to fugitive slaves: "of course, the university wanted to disassociate with that image." See also William E. Ellis, *A History of Eastern Kentucky University* (Lexington: U. Press of Kentucky, 2005): 122–123.

[9] In 1946 the Tallahassee Branch of the University of Florida opened to educate war veterans on the campus of the Florida State College for Women. TBUF and FSCW merged as the coed FSU in '47 with teams of **Seminoles**, which copied UF's yearbook (called the *Seminole* since 1910). After a ten-year break, the *Seminole* returned in 1983 as the *Tower* (after UF's Century Tower) to avoid confusion with FSU's rival '**Noles**. Similarly, Michigan State's *Wolverine* yearbook appeared in 1900, just when Michigan jocks became **Wolverines**. MSU's annual wasn't renamed the *Red Cedar Log* until 1976.

[10] Osceola was lured to negotiate with the Army in October 1837. He was imprisoned and soon died of malaria. Since 1978 the mascots for FSU's **Seminoles** have been Chief Osceola and his horse Renegade. (Refer to Florida's 1985 USFL Orlando **Renegades**.) An alternate FSU mascot is a horse named Cimaron, from the *cimarrón* root of *Seminole*.

The roles of Red Seminoles (usually Lower Creeks) and Black Seminoles (having the blood of freed or escaped slaves) varied. Some Black Seminoles were full tribal members and some resembled slaves. Those sent to Oklahoma experienced the same segregation as other children of Africa, making it hard to establish exactly who's a Seminole when issues of tribal recognition arise. Some Seminoles in Florida take pride in FSU's '**Noles**, but (speaking in broad terms) those in Oklahoma are often more sensitive to the co-option of that identity by their evictors.

FSU trustee Richard McFarlain made few friends out West while defending "**Seminoles**" in 2005: "They got run out of here by—who was it?—Andrew Jackson or somebody? […] the 'Veil of Tears'? The real Seminoles stayed here." That astonishing misread of history (the *Trail of Tears* is almost always associated with Cherokees) was dismissive enough of their identity that some previously apathetic Oklahoma Seminoles joined the debate. McFarlain's subsequent apology was so politically necessary that its sincerity was impossible to gauge, but he did maintain his eloquence: "I just should have shut up." See Steve Bousquet, "FSU Trustee Apologizes to Tribe," *St. Petersburg Times Online*, 16 Aug. 2005, http://www.sptimes.com/2005/08/16/Tampabay/FSU_trustee_apologize.shtml (accessed 1 March 2012).

[11] UTC's **Moccasins**-to-**Mocs** transition coincided with its retirement of Chief Moccanooga, whose name combined *moccasin* and *Chattanooga*. (Compare that to the Milwaukee/Atlanta **Braves'** longtime mascot, Chief Noc-a-Homa: "knock a homer.") UTC's mascot is now Scrappy the Mockingbird, whose striped hat and overalls of traditional engineers recall 'Nooga's history as a large rail hub. Glenn Miller's 1941 version of "Chattanooga Choo-Choo" was the first gold record, so Negro Leaguers were Chattanooga **Choo Choos** later in that decade. The Chattanooga **Locomotion** (est. 2005) of women's football were on the same track.

The mockingbird is Florida's state bird too, but the Florida Southern College **Mocs** are named after the Southeast's venomous water moccasin (*Agkistrodon piscivorus*). The Florida cottonmouth (*A.p. conanti*) lurks in the state's waterways, including those around FSC's Lakeland campus. Several cottonmouth subspecies overlap in Georgia, indicated by minor league hockey's Columbus **Cottonmouths** (1996–), or the "Snakes" to fans.

[12] The NCAA listed Central Michigan among the institutions with potentially hostile or abusive nicknames in 2005 but agreed to accept "**Chippewas**" (named in 1941) so long as CMU maintained approval from the Saginaw Chippewa Tribe. Former CMU-ers were **Normalites** or **Pedagogs**, **Dragons** (1925–27, after the homecoming bonfire), then **Bearcats** until 1941.

[13] William E. Unrau, "The Ottawa Indian University: C.C. Hutchinson, the Baptists, and Land Fraud in Kansas," *Arizona and the West* (autumn 1983): 229. See also Cary Michael Carney, "Ottawa University," *Native American Higher Education in the United States* (New Brunswick, N.J.: Transaction, 1999): 76–79.

[14] UI professor Carol Spindel examines the chief's case in her book about Indian mascots, *Dancing at Halftime* (New York: New York U. Press, 2000).

There were similar problems for Arkansas State's **Indians** (now **Red Wolves**), whose Chief Big Track (named for an Osage leader) donned a "war shirt […] of an authentic Cherokee design" (Arkansas State Red Wolves, "ASU Glossary," *2007 Arkansas State Football Media Guide*: 171), even though the Osage and Cherokees fought bloody wars over hunting grounds after the latter arrived from the east in the early 1800s.

[15] A bobcat represented the **Braves** from 1993 to 2000 but never caught on. A gargoyle became the mascot in fall 2013. The limestone gargoyles on the Collegiate Gothic tower of Bradley Hall were repeated when an alumni center wing was added in 2011 (part of a construction program within the "Bradley Renaissance" campaign).

[16] Trading **Redskins** for **Redhawks** brought Miami of Ohio into formation with the **Harriers** (marsh hawks of the *Circus* genus) at its regional campus in Hamilton. (UM-Middletown's **Warriors** became **ThunderHawks** at around the same time.) Miami's **Big Red** became **Redskins** in around 1930 to gain distinction from Denison U.'s **Big Red** (a hundred miles away in Granville). See "Miami Nickname History," *This is Miami Basketball* (2010–11): 19. (Denison's **Big Red** briefly used Indian imagery in the 1950s.) The Maumee (Miami) people who remained in the Old Northwest (mostly Indiana) after 1867 forfeited their tribal status. They did not influence the naming of Florida's Miami, near the Seminoles' Everglade haunts. The origin of that *Miami* isn't clear, but it's probably from a regional native language.

Chapter 4 Notes

[1] *Fútbol americano* is a big deal at universities around Mexico's capital, although football nicknames don't always match those of other sports. For instance, *Politécnico's* other athletes are **Burros Blancos** (white donkeys).

[2] Minor league basketball's Mexico City **Aztecas** played the 1994/95 season, and the Mexico **Aztecas Dorados** (Monterrey N.L.) were in the 1969 Continental Football League.

[3] Oklahoma Baptist U. Public Relations Office, "OBU Traditions," www.okbu.edu/alumni/traditions.html (accessed 13 Nov. 2013).

[4] New Sioux City **Soos** were scheduled for 1993, but some Winnebagos and Santees asked to be distanced from the unflattering history and mascots of earlier **Soos**. The newcomers were instead **Explorers**. See Coleman McCarthy, "Sioux City's Lesson Of Enlightenment" (Washington Post Writers Group, 22 Feb. 1993), reproduced by the *Seattle Times*, http://community.seattletimes.nwsource.com/archive/?date=19930222&slug=1686828 (accessed 27 Feb. 2012).

[5] "Flickertail State" refers to Richardson's ground squirrel (*Spermophilus richardsonii*) of short-grass prairies in the northern U.S. and southern Canada. Its tail trembles—*flickers*—nervously at all times. UND's **Flickertails** were occasionally **Nodaks** (*NO*-rth *DAK*-otans).

[6] NDSU's bison is Thundar [*sic*] because "Thundering Herd" is applied to the **Bison** and their fans. Conversely, Rumble the bison accompanies Oklahoma City's **Thunder**.
    The first Buffalo Nickel was minted in 1913. (It's called the Indian Head Nickel if "heads" wins the coin toss.) In its last year of issue—1938—the **Sioux-Bison** game was played for the Nickel Trophy, an oversized copy. It would be cool if the Nichols College **Bison** (Dudley, Mass.) were also named for the famous five-cent piece. Get it? ... *Nichols Bison ... buffalo nickels*? Unfortunately, no one knows the intent of the reporter who first called the Nichols **Bulls** the "Bison" in the 1930s, effectively changing the moniker. (Dick Scheffler and Michael Serijan of the Nichols athletic department, separate emails to the author, 29 Aug. 2007.)

[7] Many UND fans fought hard to keep "**Fighting Sioux**" for decades. A fall 2007 deal with the NCAA gave them three years to get permission to maintain that identity from the region's Standing Rock and Spirit Lake Sioux tribes. The State Board of Higher Education decided to pursue thirty-year agreements with those Indians to avoid fighting the same battle every few years. By fall 2009, however, the lack of a resolution was interfering with UND's bid to join Division I football, and the board voted to drop "**Fighting Sioux**." Resistance then came from a surprising direction. Folks from the Spirit Lake tribe argued in court *for* the nickname, believing it kept Siouan people in the public mind. Because the 2007 NCAA-UND settlement said the Sioux had "important contributions in determining [...] the athletic traditions at UND," Spirit Lakers claimed third-party beneficiary status. But there was no such urgency at Standing Rock, where a referendum wasn't even scheduled. (Mandates from its tribal council could be overturned by future councils, so UND's thirty-year requirement was impossible to satisfy). On April 8, 2010, the state's highest court said Spirit Lakers had no standing in the case. This coincided with the monthly meeting of the state board, which by the afternoon had voted to stick with "**Fighting Sioux**" only through the 2010/11 school year. Then—coming *way* late to the party in March 2011—North Dakota's legislature passed House Bill 1263, making it unlawful for UND to drop "**Fighting Sioux**" and the associated Indian emblem. The NCAA agreed to meet with the state's governor and legislative leaders at its Indianapolis headquarters, but after listening politely to the pro-**Sioux** argument, they flatly reiterated their commitment to the 2007 agreement. Within minutes, the **Sioux** faction dropped opposition to the repeal of HB 1263. In November the governor signed a new senate bill (SB 2370), which said UND could drop the nickname and choose a new in 2015. (This short version leaves out protests from alumni, a state-wide referendum vote, efforts to amend the state constitution, arguments about the cost of removing Sioux logos from campus arenas, and a slate of other legal filings.)

[8] The University of. Manitoba's **Bison** and Winnipeg's senior rugby Manitoba **Buffalo** both display Manitoba's provincial symbol. Brandon University was once a UM affiliate, but its alliterative **Bobcats** were independent of the **Bison**, as indicated by this report of a women's game: "Manitoba **Bisonettes** survived last half pressure by Brandon University **Bobbies** to win." (See Frank Luba, "Winston on Target in Bisonette Win," *Winnipeg Free Press* [4 Dec. 1976]: 77.) According to Morris Mott (email to the author, 31 Aug. 2007), history professor at Brandon U. and former NHL winger, the school's pre-**Bobcat** teams were (male) **Caps** and (female) **Capettes**, possibly referring to the Winnipeg *Capital* Region in which UM sits.

[9] Linguist Steven Pinker says **Maple Leaf** players are neither maples nor leaves, and "a noun that does not get its nounhood from one of its components cannot get an irregular plural from that component either; hence it defaults to the regular form *Maple Leafs*." See Pinker, *The Language Instinct* (New York: Harper Perennial, 1995): 145.

[10] Confusion could have been avoided if American frontiersmen had remembered Europe's heftiest land animal, the wide-ranging European bison, *Bison bonasus*. Some scientists say *B. bonasus* and America's *B. bison* are a single species.

Chapter 5 Notes

[1] Two-year **Thunderbirds** in the West are at Casper [Wyo.] Coll., Mesa [Ariz.] Comm. Coll., and New Mexico Junior Coll. (in Hobbs). Johnny Thunderbird is the mascot for the St. John's University **Red Storm**. **Thunder**- has become a viable-enough prefix; the Richland Coll. **Thunderducks** (Dallas), CSU-Pueblo **Thunderwolves**, Terra Comm. Coll. **ThunderCats** (Fremont, Ohio), and indoor football Houston **Thunderbears** (1998–2001) are not representative of historical or mythical animals. They just sound cool.

Chapter 6 Notes

[1] Joseph B. Oxendine, *American Indian Sports Heritage* (Champaign, Ill.: Human Kinetics, 1988): 184.

[2] Oxendine, *American Indian Sports Heritage*: 192.

[3] Jack Newcombe, *The Best of the Athletic Boys: The White Man's Impact on Jim Thorpe* (New York: Doubleday, 1975): 222. Refer also to *Canton Repository*, 4 Nov. 1915, quoted in Keith McClellan, *The Sunday Game* (Akron, Ohio: U. Akron Press, 1998): 64. Also see Bob Curran, *Pro Football's Rag Days* (Englewood Cliffs, N.J.: Prentice-Hall, 1969): 13.

Thorpe was a bench player for baseball's **Giants** (1913–15, 1918–19), Cincinnati **Reds** (1917), and Boston **Braves** (1919). (In 1916 he played exclusively for Canton's football **Bulldogs**.) His .252 career batting average *exactly* matches the NL average over those years.

[4] Here's *too much information* for the tangled **Bulldogs** and **Indians** of the 1920s. A 1923 team recycled the name of the 1921-only APFA/NFL Cleveland **Indians**. After that season their owner Sam Deutsch bought Canton's strapped **Bulldogs** and made its best players **Indians**. Canton's team and moniker therefore skipped the 1924 season, so Deutsch recast his Cleveland **Indians** as **Bulldogs** and immediately won that city's first NFL title. The original **Bulldogs** were sold back to Canton men, yielding Cleveland *and* Canton **Bulldogs** for 1925.

[5] Bill Crawford, *All American: The Rise and Fall of Jim Thorpe* (Hoboken, N.J.: John Wiley & Sons, 2005): 11.

[6] The **Indians** played the only home game of their tenure in nearby Marion, spending the rest of the time practicing at LaRue and traveling to advertise Lingo's pups.

[7] Dietz's term included victory in the first *annual* Rose Bowl (1916). A 1902 Rose Bowl had seen Michigan defeat Stanford, but the game wasn't played every year until 1916.

[8] Sportswriter Dave Zirin suggests that team success would likely leave "casual fans asking how this name could still exist." See Zirin, "Dump the 'Redskins' Slur," *The Nation* (30 Oct. 2013), http://www.thenation.com/article/176900/dump-redskins-slur (accessed 17 July 2013).

[9] Washington State let Coach Dietz go before the 1918 season after Spokane's draft board said his claim to be a noncitizen Indian wasn't strong enough for a draft exemption. If Dietz's birth mother was an unnamed Oglala Sioux, it's only because his German-immigrant father and white (and therefore adoptive) mother said so. In any case, Lone Star Dietz publicly self-identified as Sioux only after making friends with an Indian named One Star while working at the 1904 St. Louis World's Fair when he was 19 according to Tom Benjey, *Keep A-Goin': The Life of Lone Star Dietz* (Carlisle, Pa.: Tuxedo Press, 2006): 20. For doubts about Dietz's ethnicity in his own day, see "Famed Gridiron Star Indicted as *Slacker*," *Idaho Statesman* (1 Feb. 1919), reproduced by Washington State U. Libraries at http://content.wsulibs.wsu.edu/cdm/singleitem/collection/clipping_II/id/45589/rec/12 (accessed 25 Feb. 2014). If Dietz's Indian identity was one that he only assumed, it gives leverage to those who would deny that the Boston-Washington **Redskins** were named out of any kind of reverence for his heritage.

Chapter 7 Notes

[1] Ontario's junior hockey St. Catharines **Teepees** (1947–62) were way east of the Plains' conical tents but, they were owned by Thompson Products auto parts, or "TP."

[2] There are no bison as far east as Buffalo, but the continent's largest land animal did roam from the Rockies to the Appalachians when Europeans arrived. Milligan College's **Buffaloes** (Johnson City, Tenn.) and the abutting Buffalo Creek are both named for the historical bison presence, but no wild bison were east of the Mississippi by 1830.

[3] Buffalo's **Bisons** were **Rangers** for 1926. They were renamed for mounted Texas Rangers after **Bison** Jim Kendrick recruited collegians from Texas (and Oklahoma). When Kendrick joined New York's **Giants** for 1927, the Buffalonians reverted to **Bisons**. See Jeffrey Miller, "Jim Kendrick: The Man with the Plan," *Coffin Corner*, Vol. XXV, No. 6 (2003): 3, 5.

[4] Many theories behind the naming of Buffalo are in Nancy Blumenstalk Mingus, *Buffalo: Good Neighbors, Great Architecture* (Mount Pleasant, S.C.: Arcadia, 2003): 9–11.

[5] Collis Huntington bought most of an Ohioside West Virginia town and renamed it Huntington in 1871. It became the C&O's gateway to the Midwest, as recalled by Huntington's River Cities **Locomotives** (2001, indoor football). Another regional railroad was the Norfolk and Western, which ran from Chesapeake Bay to West Virginia and the Carolinas. The N&W built such fine steam locomotives at its Roanoke, Virginia headquarters that it was the last major line to convert to diesel, as indicated by indoor football's Roanoke **Steam** (2000–02).

[6] The WFL Chicago **Winds** (1975) folded after five games. Their city isn't particularly windy. It's often reported that politicians expended so much hot air to land the 1898 World's Columbia Exposition that the "Windy City" nickname followed, but the reference is older than that. Chicago hosted a ton of presidential nominating conventions in the decades before the fair, so all that political wind was probably more to the point.

The major league Colorado **Rockies** came to Denver in 1993, sending the minor league Denver **Zephyrs** to New Orleans. The name was kept because a legendary wooden Pontchartrain Beach rollercoaster (1938–83) was coincidentally called *Zephyr*. The Coney Island *Cyclone*—opened in 1927—is perhaps the world's most famous wooden coaster. It's now just a long fly ball from the Brooklyn **Cyclones**. Soccer's USL Hershey **Wildcats** (1997–2001) were owned by the Pennsylvania chocolatier and named after a Hersheypark coaster (1923–45).

Chapter 8 Notes

[1] Caesar used Gaul to cushion his empire against Germanic invaders across the Rhine. In 50 BCE, Rome left two legions at the Rhine outpost that's now Cologne, Germany. The city's consequent Roman character explains NFL Europe's Cologne **Centurions** (2004–07). (A centurion commands up to 100 Roman infantrymen.)

[2] When St. Leo's Prep reimagined itself as a college in 1959, teams became **Monarchs**. (Like "**Lions**," it indicated the *king* of beasts, p. 107.) In 1999 came university status, a new pair of

panthera leo sentries, and reclaimed **Lions**. (See Francis Crociata, "Theodore 'Fred' Rust, '54," *Spirit: The Magazine of Saint Leo University* [fall 2005]: 41.) Fancy entrances have influence elsewhere. The Ashner Gateway at Tennessee's Rhodes College was erected when the Clarksville school moved to Memphis in 1925. Its lynx-topped stone pillars made all athlete-scholars at Rhodes **Lynxes**.

³ Jerry Anhorn, Sr. (Walla Walla Comm. Coll. workforce ed.) and Jim Rice (Walla Walla Comm. Coll. ref. lib.), separate emails to the author, 19 Oct. 2011.

⁴ Martha Chambers, ed., *Dragons, Dragons, Dragons* (Oneonta, N.Y.: The Alden Room at the Milne Library, SUNY Oneonta, 1983). Multiple assisting correspondences in May and June 2008 from Heather Heyduk, the Milne's acquisitions and special collections librarian. (The Cortland Normal **Normals** played in the pre-**Dragons** era.)

⁵ After the war, McCormack maintained rights to "**Celtics**," so the players added "**Original**." See Alex Sachare, ed., *The Official NBA Basketball Encyclopedia* (New York: Random House, 1994): 4, and Robert W. Peterson, *Cages to Jump Shots* (New York: Oxford U. Press, 1990): 70. With an Irish theme, the early **Original Celtics** often relied on great Jewish players from NYC, like Hall of Famers Nat Holman and Barney Sedran. Purchased by a famous singer and her manager, they were **Kate Smith's Celtics** during their final years in the early 1940s.

When Celts got to Ireland (c. 300 BCE) they marveled at the carvings of earlier inhabitants they called *Tuatha Dé Danann*, "people of the [Celtic] goddess Danu." Most of the info about those Stone Age people comes from myths that the Celts invented. *Leprechauns*, a Gaelic-Latin construction meaning "little bodies," were diminutive shoemakers who guarded pots of gold. The leprechauns you encounter today are likely the mascots for **Celtic** and **Irish** sides.

While looking to explain the Holy Trinity to Ireland's fifth-century Celtic priests, St. Patrick showed that the three leaves of the shamrock represented distinct parts of a unified whole. That's why merchandise and memorabilia for Irish-themed **Celtics**, **Gaels**, **Irish**, and **Shamrocks** are often covered with clovers.

How are *Celt* and *Celtic* pronounced? The hard-*c* version ("*kelt*-ic") from the Greek *Keltoi* may have disappeared until a few hundred years ago. It's now often used adjectively, as in Celtic music or Celtic languages. As a noun, a soft *c* is articulated ("*selt*-ic"), as in "Grampy is a good old Celtic" or "The **Celtics** played well." The four-letter form—*Celt*—almost always uses a hard-*c*, but you're really on your own because these rules are unreliable and subject to regional variation. Working to avoid such phonetical ambiguities are Indiana's NBL Kokomo [Ind.] **Kelts** (1932/33) and rugby's Nova Scotia **Keltics** (Halifax) and Cincinnati **Kelts**. (The latter followed the Ohio League's *k*-sounding Cincinnati **Celts**, founded in 1910 and in the APFA [NFL] for four games in 1921.)

⁶ A 1984 student body vote at the University of St. Thomas (Houston, Texas) decided that teams would be **Fightin' Celts** and **Lady Celts**, so no single person is on the hook for placing British-Celtic themes at a school started by the French-founded Congregation of St. Basil in 1947. It may just be true that the psychohistorical connection between *Irish* and *Catholic* already mentioned justifies **Celts** at any Catholic college. UST's pre-**Celts** were **Saints** and **Warriors**. The **Celts** dropped "**Fightin'**" and "**Lady**" in 2005, and the red lion on the Scottish coat of arms became the team emblem two years later. See Sandra Soliz, ed., "UST Chooses New Logo for Mascots," *Shining Star* (U. of St. Thomas, summer 2000): 7.

Chapter 9 Notes

¹ Jeff Sauve (St. Olaf Coll. archives), email to the author, 14 Jan. 2004.

² Diarmaid MacCulloch, *The Reformation* (New York: Penguin, 2004): 113. The same page says Frederick founded U. Wittenberg to "offer an up-to-date humanist education, in contrast to the prevailing scholasticism" of the Holy Roman Empire, which was then ingrained at rival universities on the Rhine.

³ Wartburg's earlier teams were **Teutons**. The change from **Teutons** to **Knights** probably saw

a transitional period of **Teutonic Knights**, named for a medieval German order that protected Christian pilgrims in Palestine. (The college's Lutheran founder was a Bavarian-born academic.) See a communication (15 Nov. 1935) from Wartburg president O.L. Proehl in George Earlie Shankle, *American Nicknames: Their Origin and Significance* (New York: H.W. Wilson, 1955): 489.

[4] MacCulloch, *The Reformation*: 345.

[5] Canada's 1872 Dominion Lands Act intended to settle Europeans (and willing Americans) in the Prairie Provinces. Among the first takers were Icelanders. To the usual Scandinavian troubles—harsh weather, famine, limited inheritance—Icelanders added a fear that was commensurate with a heavily volcanic homeland. Many settled the west shore of Lake Winnipeg in the 1870s and '80s. The first Canada-born generation formed hockey's Winnipeg **Falcons**. (The largest falcon species, the gyrfalcon [*Falco rusticolus*], lives along colder northern coasts and is Iceland's national bird.) Most of the **Falcons** served in World War I, later winning the right to represent Canada in the 1920 Olympics by seizing amateur hockey's Allan Cup. They defeated their Nordic cousins from Sweden in hockey's first-ever Olympic gold medal game.

[6] The **Viking** at South Dakota's Augustana College was named Ole in 1939, the year Norway's Prince Olav visited campus. But we're pretty sure "Ole" aims more toward Professor Ole Edvart Rolvaag, who wrote much of *Giants in the Earth* while at Augustana. Published in the 1920s, *Giants* follows a Norwegian family transplanted to the Dakota Territory in the 1870s. (Don't confuse Augustana's Ole with St. Olaf College's **Oles**, and Augustana's former Augie Doggie bears no relation to the Augsburg College **Auggies**.)

[7] Kim-Eric Williams, "Upsala College: 1893–1995" (Torrington, Conn.: New England Lutheran Hist. Soc., n.d.), http://www.upsala.org/histouc.html (accessed 18 July 2012).

[8] The **Gusties** are former **Shrouds** and **Galloping Swedes**. The latter easily associates with Sweden's master cavalry tactician, but the origin of "Shrouds" is—*forgive us*—shrouded. We do know King Gustavus opened Stockholm's Royal Armory in 1628 to exhibit his blood-stained battle clothes, but the shirt in which he was slain and his embalming sheets would soon be main attractions, objects revered by Swedes as are the death shrouds of saints elsewhere.

[9] Besides towing canal boats, mules were the early engines of Pennsylvania's farming and mining industries. Penn State's beloved mule Old Coaly (1855–93) hauled the limestone that built the Old Main. For three more decades he helped agriculture students in the fields, and his bones are displayed on campus. Penn State calls Coaly a "former mascot" (one that predates the **Nittany Lion** [p. 91]), but nothing suggests jocks were ever **Mules**.

[10] The "Lion of Finland" is actually Swedish. The Finns were within a confederation of Viking factions after 1150. Gustav I freed Sweden from that alliance in 1521, and Swedes ruled the Finns for 300 years, mapping onto it their language, culture, Lutheranism, and lion heraldry of Gustav's family.

[11] "**Warriors**" is associated with the Winnebagos in a communication (13 Nov. 1935) from Waldorf's own president, J.L. Rendahl, cited in George Earlie Shankle, *American Nicknames: Their Origin and Significance* (New York: H.W. Wilson, 1937): 558.

[12] Minor league hockey included Rochester **Cardinals** (1935/36). SJFC's **Cardinals** are a mile down Rochester's East Ave. from their rivals, the purple-and-gold **Golden Flyers** of Catholic-founded Nazareth College, named in 1977 for an eagle on the (old) school emblem. (See Nazareth Coll. Office of Undergraduate Admissions, *Magazette* [winter 2010]: 1.) Another Nazareth College (also Catholic) in Kalamazoo, Michigan closed in 1992. Its blue-and-white **Moles** owed to students who ran to class via the campus's system of tunnels. (See Associated Press, "College Bids Adieu by Holding Auction," *Beaver County Times* [21 Sep. 1992]: D6.)

[13] Thomas More College's first blue-and-white teams were **Blue Rebels**. Being in the historically Unionist Kenton County, it ducked possible associations with Confederate rebels by going with **Saints** in 1994.

Chapter 10 Notes

[1] Abby Cress, president (Columbia College Chicago Student Athletics Assn.), email to the author, 20 Jan. 2013. The CFL Ottawa **Renegades** (2002–05) had a masked rider to indicate their rebelliousness, perhaps alluding to the CFL Ottawa **Rough Riders**, who'd folded in 1996.

[2] Rebecca Miller, "Extreme Makeover: Longtime Chipmunk Replaced with More Realistic Wolverine Mascot," *GeDUNK: Grove City College Alumni Magazine* (fall 2006): 53.

[3] Emerson Coll., "History of Emerson College Athletics," www.emerson.edu/athletics/history/timeline.cfm (accessed 14 May 2010).

[4] Joe Scanlon, *The History of Football at Carleton* (Ottawa: Old Crow Society, 1966): 12. (Lloyd Keane [Carleton U. archives technician], assisting email to the author, 6 June 2007.)

Don't be confused by the chicken/egg conundrum; a tiger got on the shield at Georgetown [Ky.] College only in 1997, long after teams were arbitrarily named **Tigers**.

[5] JWU's oral history, as reported by John Parente (JWU athletics), emails to the author, 15 and 16 Aug. 2013.

[6] Jeannette Browning, "Evolution of Griffons a Continuing Story," *Griffon News* (25 April 2000): 4. More French-language **Griffons** represent *Cégep de l'Outaouais* (Gatineau, Que.).

[7] Mary Levine (SLC athletic dir.), email to the author, 21 Jan. 2005.

[8] Communication (18 Nov. 1935) from D.B. Wekoff (Wentworth Mil. Acad. treasurer) in George Earlie Shankle, *American Nicknames: Their Origin and Significance* (New York: H.W. Wilson, 1937): 573.

[9] Sara Mata (SGU sports info. dir.), email to the author, 14 Jan. 2005. Junior hockey's Longueuil [Que.] **Chevaliers** (1982–87) were also French **Cavaliers**. Ohio's Walsh University (Canton) was founded and is run by Brothers of Christian Instruction, Catholic educators organized in France in 1819, likely leading to Walsh's own **"Cavaliers"** *nom de guerre*.

Chapter 11 Notes

[1] Inconveniently, members of the *Delphinidae* family aren't fishes; they're mammals in the toothed whale suborder, *Odontoceti*. Dolphins on Roman frescos, coins, and jewels are adapted from Greece, where they represented the god Apollo.

[2] Le Moyne Coll. Office of Admission, "Dolphin Determination," *Le Moyne: Educating the Whole Person, For Life* (2006): 21. **Dolphins** at the (Catholic) College of Mount Saint Vincent in the Bronx salute that creature's admirable intelligence and social nature, not its symbolism.

[3] "Gonzaga Mascots," *Gonzaga Soccer 2006*: 5.

[4] Nicholas Varga, *Baltimore's Loyola, Loyola's Baltimore* (Baltimore: Maryland Hist. Soc., 1990): 239–240.

[5] Michael Leo Donovan, *The Name Game: Football, Baseball, Hockey & Basketball: How Your Favorite Sports Teams Were Named* (Whitby, Ont.: McGraw-Hill Ryerson, 1997): 175–176. Drawing a nickname from a letter is a capital idea. The University of Baltimore's past intercollegiate teams were "UB's **Super Bees**."

[6] Paul Lynch O'Connor, *Xavier University* (New York: Newcomen Soc., 1956): 10.

Chapter 12 Notes

[1] Rollins Coll. Office of Public Relations, "Welcome Back, Rollins: What is a Tar?" *Winter Park Observer* (fall 2004 insert).

[2] The **Tar Heels'** ram mascot first showed up in 1924 when UNC cheerleaders wanted to call attention to star fullback Jack "Battering Ram" Merrit. That same year, UNC's undefeated white-suited basketballers were called **White Phantoms** by Atlanta sportswriters who thought the speedy **Heels** looked like "shadows and ghosts." The transition back to **"Tar Heels"** wasn't absolute until 1950. See Ken Rappopo, *Tales from the Tar Heel Locker Room* (Champaign, Ill.:

Sports Publishing L.L.C., 2005): 9. One "tar heel" creation myth dates to a Civil War battle in which the "tar boiler" insult was redirected when North Carolinians caught up with deserters from Virginia and then threatened to "tar their heels" so they'd better stick to future positions.

UNC's freshman basketballers were once **Tar Babies**, a term from a cycle of African American folk tales in which Brother Rabbit and a doll made of tar become hopelessly entangled. The **Tar Babies'** occasional foes were freshman **Blue Imps** from nearby Duke. Since ancient Greece, folkloric imps have been small demons with limited abilities to mess with you, making **Imps** appropriate foils to Duke's more senior **Blue Devils**. See Alwyn Featherston, *Tobacco Road: Duke, North Carolina, NC State, Wake Forest* (Guilford, Conn.: Lyons Press, 2006): 35.

[3] Another Kansas Mennonite school is Hesston College in Hesston. Its **Larks** exalt the state bird of Kansas, the western meadowlark, *Sturnella neglecta*.

[4] With a bat-like schedule, the common nighthawk (*Chordeiles minor*) feeds on insects at dusk. It's colloquially the "bull bat," appreciated on the Plains for eliminating crop-eating grasshoppers, so Nebraska's early nickname was "Bugeater State" and Nebraska's pre-**Cornhusker** sides were **Bugeaters**. (See Frederick Ware and Gregg McBride, *Fifty Years of Football: A Condensed History of the Game at the University of Nebraska* [Omaha: Omaha World-Herald, 1940]: 14. Carmella Orosco [UN-Lincoln archives], assisting email to the author, 30 Jan. 2007.) When Ewald Stiehm coached Nebraska footballers (1911–15), they were **Stiehm Rollers**. As for "Planter State," it refers to Nebraska's ambitions to get the Timber Culture Act of 1873 passed. It encouraged tree planting to create orchards, prevent wind erosion, and produce wood fuel. In fact, the first Arbor Day was a Nebraska celebration in 1872, and Nebraska's Lincoln **Tree Planters** (1886–88, 1907) were in baseball's Western League.

[5] Patrick J. Nicholson, *In Time: An Anecdotal History of the First Fifty Years of the University of Houston* (Houston: Gulf Publishing, 1977): 35–36. (Dick Dickerson [UH archives], assisting email to the author, 9 Jan. 2006.) Bender's nickname—"Chief"—forever confused him with Charles Albert "Chief" Bender, the Hall of Fame inventor of the slider who'd attended Carlisle. The mix-up wouldn't matter if it didn't suggest to so many that Johnny Bender was of Indian extraction, especially when one learns that he coached Haskell Indian Nations University's **Indians** (1908–09) or that his coaching tenure at Washington State falls amidst those of four Native America head coaches who were Carlisle alums. Bender's German-Russian ancestry is verified by Jerry Johnson (Sutton [Neb.] Hist. Soc.), emails to the author, 31 Oct. and 3 Nov. 2010.

[6] Dani Tifft, "College Mascots: What's in the Name? The Stories Behind Worcester's Menagerie of Mascots," *The Pulse* (Mar. 2005), 36.

[7] A flame depicts the spirit of God in the Holy Trinity, and John's gospel (8:12) borrows from Matthew, with Jesus saying, "I am the light of the world; he that followeth me shall not walk in darkness, but shall have the light of life." So the **Flames** at Welch Coll. (Nashville) and Liberty U. (Lynchburg, Va.) and the **Firestorm** at Arizona Christian U. indicate Christian backing, as does ACU's phoenix mascot (Christian symbolism on p. 174), just north of downtown Phoenix. Some Christians were called Pentecostals around 1900 after being overcome by God's spirit in the same way Christ's apostles were moved when the Holy Ghost appeared as a flame during the first Pentecost celebrations. Playing with fire on behalf of their Pentecostal benefactors are the Lee U. **Flames** (Cleveland, Tenn.) and Southeastern U. **Fire** (Lakeland, Fla., former **Crusaders**). In 1998 the **Flames** at the Pentecostals' North Central U. (Minneapolis, Minn.) became **Rams** (Christian symbolism on p. 106). New Hope Christian Coll. (Eugene, Ore.) presents the Pentecostals' flame emblem and **Deacons**. Similarly, the Pentecostal-backed Messenger Coll. (Joplin, Mo.) has a Bible-flame-globe emblem and **Eagles** teams.

[8] Bustling Buffalo was the "Queen City of the Lakes," suggested by Queen City **F.C.** (NPSL, 2006–08) and the 1974 Buffalo-Toronto **Royals** of World Team Tennis. But "Toronto **Royals**"

long described second-tier sides in loyalist Ontario (including a current junior hockey side). Quebec's Francophones call Toronto *La Ville-Reine*—the Queen City—to indicate the Anglican character of Ontario's capital. Also legitimizing "Toronto **Royals**" is the annual Royal Agricultural Winter Fair—"The Royal"—the world's largest indoor agricultural and equestrian festival since 1922 (explaining Toronto's Centennial College **Colts**). The WHA's phonetically inspired Toronto **Toros** (Spanish "bulls," 1973–76) moved to Alabama, where there happened to be a historically important ranching industry, so they kept their bovine theme as Birmingham **Bulls** until 1979.

[9] The Buffalo YMCA recalls the many gyms in German-American neighborhoods that owe to a particularly German tradition. In 1811, German advocates of regimented exercise started turner associations: *Turnvereins*. Turners—tumblers or gymnasts—rubbed elbows with labor activists, free thinkers, and nationalists during the War of Liberation against Napoleon. The Congress of Vienna reinstated Europe's conservative regimes after the wars and Prussian authorities closed the turner halls, fearing they would remain incubators of leftism. But turners returned in the more liberal 1840s, just in time to become avowed radicals in the Revolutions of 1848. Losing that battle, many sought refuge in North America where they promoted exercise at gyms and social clubs, inspiring many colleges to create their first athletic programs.

[10] "World's Champions Come to Give Varsity a Tussle," *Wittenberg Torch* (17 Feb. 1916): 1. (Suzanne Smailes [WU tech. services lib.], assisting email to the author, 28 Oct. 2005.) See also Donald Sayenga, "The 1904 Basketball Championship" *Citius, Altius, Fortius* (Autumn 1996): 7–8. Before being **Orioles**, they were **German Ramblers** for a short time, enjoying sponsorship from Buffalo's Rambler Bicycle Club, according to Robert W. Peterson, *Cages to Jump Shots* (New York: Oxford U. Press, 1990): 60–61.

Chapter 13 Notes

[1] Jon Entine, *Taboo: Why Black Athletes Dominate Sports and Why We Are Afraid to Talk About It* (New York: PublicAffairs, 2000): 200. See also Steven A. Riess, ed., *Sports and the American Jew* (Syracuse: Syracuse U. Press, 1998): 27.

[2] Entine, *Taboo*: 200.

[3] Entine, *Taboo*: 201. The store was Passon's, owned by **SPHA** Harry Passon. He later revived black baseball's Atlantic City **Bacharach Giants** as a Philly-based team (1931–42).

[4] Riess, *Sports and the American Jew*: 27. See also Robert W. Peterson, *Cages to Jump Shots* (New York: Oxford U. Press, 1990): 121.

[5] The Philadelphia **Warriors** had goofy Indian mascots in the mid-1940s. As San Francisco **Warriors** (1962–71), they displayed an Indian headdress but changed for their last year in the city with only "The City" on home jerseys. (That Bay Area folks defer to Frisco as "The City" is verified by minor league baseball's Oakland **Commuters**, 1901–15.) The **Warriors** crossed the Bay to Oakland in 1971, becoming Golden State **Warriors**.

[6] Entine, *Taboo*: 203. See also Peterson, *Cages to Jump Shots*: 123.

[7] Charles Rosen, *The Scandals of '51: How the Gamblers Almost Killed College Basketball* (New York: Seven Stories Press, 1978, 1999): 27, 28.

[8] Colin Jose, *The American Soccer League, 1921–1931* (Lanham, Md. and London, 1998): 11.

[9] Gerald R. Gems says American Jews sponsored the Vienna **Hakoah** tour to counter "a resurgent anti-Semitism." See his essay "The Rise of Sport at a Jewish Settlement House" in Riess, *Sports and the American Jew*, 157. Jewish minor leaguers and semi-pros (especially in New York and Philadelphia) have been called *Hakoah* for decades, as have European teams that were created when Jews tried to resume normalcy after World War II. *SC Hakoah Wien* was reassembled for the immediate post-war period. In 2000, Vienna's Jews created a new team for the **Hakoah's** old field, *SC Maccabi Wien*, named from the Maccabees story in the main text.

[10] David B. Biesel, *Can You Name That Team?* (Lanham, Md.: Scarecrow, 2002): 60.

[11] *Israel* refers to the Jewish people (see Genesis 32:28), and since 1948 it's been the name of a mostly Jewish country in the Middle East. At the 1972 Munich Olympics, armed Palestinian Arabs entered the Olympic Village and took members of the Israeli team hostage, demanding the release of prisoners from Israel's jails and a flight out of Germany. Eleven Israeli athletes would be killed in the kidnapping and the botched rescue attempt at Munich's airport. Later that year, businessman Bernard Levin donated the first eleven ducks to the campus of the College of the Mainland (Texas City, Texas) as a memorial to those athletes. Their descendents led to COM's **Fighting Ducks** in 2006, according to Rebecca Sauer (COM's communications coordinator), email to the author, 7 Feb. 2013.

[12] "Joseph Krauskopf," (Delaware Valley Coll., 2009), http://www.delval.edu/cms/index.php/library/archives/joseph_krauskopf (accessed 2 May 2012).

Chapter 14 Notes

[1] The word *Dauphin* has a complicated history. A dolphin represented some twelfth-century French nobles, possibly because a lost family name resembled *dauphin*/dolphin. (Heralds call such puns *canting*.) The last *Dauphin du Viennois* was a crusader-turned-priest who forfeited his domain to the king in 1349. It went to the eldest royal son, and French crown princes have since been *Dauphins de France*. (Junior hockeyists in Manitoba since 1967 anticipate their own ascension as Dauphin **Kings**.) The eponym for Verrazano's *Dauphine* was probably the French prince, not the ocean mammal. Astute readers notice that *La Dauphine* is feminine and therefore fit for neither prince nor king, but using that gender to reference French vessels is consistent with the Anglophonic application of *she* and *her* to watercraft.

[2] The **Original Celtics** are *Brooklyn* **Celtics** in some ABL standings because they replaced Brooklyn's **Arcadians** for the 1926/27 season. Until then, the ABL had blocked its teams from accepting **Celtic** challenges, forcing them to sign on. (See Charles Rosen, *The Scandals of '51: How the Gamblers Almost Killed College Basketball* [New York: Seven Stories Press, 1999]: 16.) Others say the **Celtics** joined the ABL owing to pressure from their own Madison Square Garden court. (See Kareem Abdul-Jabbar with Raymond Obstfeld, *On the Shoulders of Giants: My Journey Through the Harlem Renaissance* [New York: Simon & Schuster, 2007]: 156.) Marshall's own ABL Washington **Palace Five** of the late 1920s got named for his family's Palace Laundry chain. (He later owned the NFL's Boston **Braves**/Washington **Redskins** franchise.)

[3] Brooklyn's spires made it the City of Churches, so an early nickname for the **Dodgers** was "Church City **Nine**." When the Washington **Palace Five** quit the ABL in the middle of the 1927/28 season, they were replaced by Brooklyn **Visitations** (1921–39), sometimes "**Visitation Triangles**" because their Visitation Church court anchored a three-sided park. See David B. Biesel, *Can You Name That Team?* (Lanham, Md.: Scarecrow, 2002): 11.

[4] Manhattan's first thirty "Dutch" families were actually Walloons and Flemings (both from modern Belgium) and Huguenots (French Protestants). Like their Calvinist counterparts who would soon sail from England to Plymouth, these outcasts had hung out in Holland's Protestant city of Leiden to plan their next move. Britain wouldn't settle them in Virginia, so they became the first colonists of New Netherland, where their familiarity with Germanic languages got them by. In fact, New York City's official colors of orange, blue, and white are from the Prince's Flag, the House of Orange tricolor. It's where "**Dodger** blue" and "**Giant** orange" come from (both adopted by the New York **Mets** in 1962). Orange and/or blue and/or white still wrap most Big Apple pros, including blue-and-white **Yankees** and blue-orange-white **Islanders** and **Knicks**. The flag's orange often faded to red, a reality the Netherlands conceded by officially swapping orange for red by the 1640s. With the same substitution, we can account for the red-and-blue of NYC's hockey **Rangers** and football **Giants**.

Adopted in 1778, New York's state flag contains a single word, *Excelsior* (Latin for "superior"). The National Association's **Excelsior** of Brooklyn (1855–67) popularized baseball in upstate towns and Atlantic ports during an 1860 tour. Excelsior College—in the capital city of Albany—has no intercollegiate teams.

[5] RPI's baseball, basketball, golf, lacrosse, soccer, softball, and aquatics teams are **Red Hawks**. Its **Engineers** (with red hawk mascots) play football, hockey, tennis, and track. When referring to the cherry-and-white collectively, RPI usually uses "the **Red**." (The **Engineers** were sometimes **Bachelors** in the 1950s, when the male-to-female ratio of students at the college that had been coed since 1942 was still about 10-to-1.)

[6] Robert P. Swierenga, *Faith and Family: Dutch Immigration and the Settlement in the United States, 1820–1920* (New York: Holmes & Meier, 2000): 175.

[7] "Flying Dutchman" comes from an old legend. With his ship sinking, one Dutch captain of the 1600s swore he'd clear the Cape of Good Hope if he had to keep sailing to Judgment Day. (Nice going.) Until then, the Flying Dutchman will haunt the tip of Africa.

[8] Robert P. Swierenga, *The Dutch in America: Immigration, Settlement, and Cultural Change* (New Brunswick, N.J.: Rutgers U. Press, 1985): 183.

[9] Elton J. Bruins et al., *Albertus and Christina: The Van Raalte Family, Home and Roots* (Grand Rapids: Eerdmans, 2003): 25.

Chapter 15 Notes

[1] Laurentian's partner is the nearby Huntington University. Its athletes play for LU's **Voyageurs**, but eponym Silas Huntington was certainly well traveled by canoe; that legendary itinerant Methodist missionary paddled, rode, and hiked all over Ontario in the 1880s and '90s to found many congregations. Other **Voyageurs** include the AHL Montreal **Voyageurs** (est. 1969, a **Canadiens** farm team), later Halifax's Nova Scotia **Voyageurs** (1971–84).

[2] The first Montreal **Alouettes** (1946–81) were replaced by Montreal **Concordes** (1982–85), but even they were **Alouettes** in their last season (1986). The next **Alouettes** (ex-Baltimore **Stallions**) appeared in 1996, but the CFL combines the records for all **Alouettes**.

[3] Muskrat Portage was an Ojibwa path from I-Falls to Canada. It was simply 'Rat Portage by the time an HBC post opened in 1836. In the 1880s the Canadian Pacific started bringing many immigrants, including the usual high volume of Scots. Hockey's Rat Portage **Thistles** of the 1890s were boys named for Scotland's national emblem, the cotton thistle (*Onopordum acanthium*). The **Thistles** evolved into a senior team with four future Hall of Famers (Tommy Phillips, Tom Hooper, Billy McGimsie, and Silas Griffis) and challenged unsuccessfully for the Stanley Cup in 1903 and 1905. Rat Portage became Kenora in '05, and HoFers Joe Hall and Art Ross (son of an HBC agent) were added to the 1907 Kenora **Thistles**, immediately making theirs the smallest Cup-winning city ever. In the 1263 Battle of Largs, an invading Viking yelped after stepping on cotton thistle thorns, alerting defenses and creating the Scottish symbol. (Scottish footballers still play for Largs **Thistle** F.C., est. 1889.) James II restored the ancient Knights of the Thistle in 1687. Members are the "Knights of St. Andrew," a good-enough reason for **Knights** at St. Andrews University (Laurinburg, N.C.) in Scotland County.

Scotland's G. MacKay whiskey company popularized the phrase "the real Mackay" in ads of the 1850s, and a slip-up may have changed *Mackay* to *McCoy* in common parlance. An Elijah McCoy was born in 1844 to fugitive slaves in Ontario. His steam engine lubricator was oft copied, but customers wanted "the real McCoy." Elijah wasn't identified as the McCoy in the "real McCoy" until a 1966 bourbon ad in *Ebony* magazine, but its repetition thereafter is enough for an Ontario town to justify its senior hockey Dundas **Real McCoys** (1985–).

[4] Canadian Anglophiles would certainly have been familiar with English football's famous Bolton **Wanderers** F.C. They started in 1874 as Christ Church **F.C.**, but broke their partnership with the vicar in 1877 to be **Wanderers**.

[5] The UFO film was shot by Nick Mariana, coach of the American Legion's Great Falls **Electrics**. (G-Falls is the "Electric City" owing to hydroelectric dams on the Missouri.) Local minor

league **Electrics** date back to 1911.

[6] Walter Spokesfield, *A History of Wells County, North Dakota and Its Pioneers* (Valley City, N.D.: n.p., 1929): 26–27. (Jim A. Davis [ref. services at State Hist. Soc. of North Dakota, Bismarck], assisting email to the author, 16 Feb. 2006.) The Jacques or James is officially the Dakota, but even Lewis and Clark's journals (1804–06) note their camps along the "River au Jacque" or "R. Jacque." The transition to "James River" was reinforced when former Confederate officer Thomas Lafayette Rosser came to the area in 1872 with the railroads and named a riverside city Jamestown after his Virginia birthplace.

[7] The CCNY lavender-and-black from St. Nicholas Terrace were either the **Lavender** or the **Saint Nicks** from 1907 until a student suggestion made them **Beavers** in 1934. See Jo Ann Winson, "A Mascot's Tale," *The Campus* (7 April 1978).

[8] T.A. Larson, *Wyoming: A Bicentennial History* (New York: W.W. Norton, 1977): 11.

[9] Russia and the Scandinavian countries were major purveyors of fur. Sweden's King Gustavus Adolphus (Gustavus Adolphus **Golden Gusties**, p. 38) revolutionized warfare by integrating cavalry, artillery, and infantry attacks in the Thirty Years' War, but his cavaliers were all the more famous after their beaver hats launched the fur craze.

Chapter 16 Notes

[1] If you think "Canadian Hockey Club" lacks color, the precedent had been set by Montreal **H.C.**, four-time Stanley Cup champs in the amateur era (including an 1894 victory over Ottawa **H.C.**, later the first Ottawa **Senators**).

[2] The top NHL scorer gets the Richard Trophy, named for Montreal-born **Canadien** legend Maurice "Rocket" Richard (played 1942–60). His namesake junior hockeyists were Montreal **Rockets** (est. 1999), later Charlottetown's P.E.I. **Rocket** (2003–13, now P.E.I. **Islanders**).

Players in the 1968-only National Lacrosse Association were Montreal **Canadians** to distinguish them from hockey's **Canadiens**. The *-ian* version is right at home in B.C., where French is a foreign language, as evinced by baseball's Vancouver **Canadians** (various minor leagues) and hockey's Vernon **Canadians** (1956 Allan Cup winners). Alberta's junior hockey Calgary **Canadians** won two Memorial Cups in the 1920s.

Today's French speakers in Quebec are *les Québecois*, and *le mouvement Québecois* is a celebration of French-Canadienism often linked to calls for Quebec's nationhood. Lacrosse's Montreal **Quebecois** played in the NLL's only two seasons (1974, 1975) just before the separatist *Parti Québécois* made major gains in the 1976 provincial elections.

A grossly Anglicized version of *Québécois* is presented by minor league basketball's Quebec City/Laval **Kebekwa** (2006–12). The **Kebs**' amphibian mascot is a remnant of the original name, "**Jumping Frogs**," but French-speakers forced the shedding of that slang term for French people. (The pejorative use of *frog* probably owes to a French delicacy, frog legs.)

[3] *Ahuntsic* corrupts *Auhaitsique*, the reported name of a Huron who converted to Christianity in New France (the likely inspiration for *Collège Ahuntsic's Indiens*). But acclaimed Canadian historian Bruce Graham Trigger says *Auhaitsique* was actually the nickname that Hurons gave a young Frenchman among the Recollet friars. He and pioneer French missionary Nicolas Viel drowned in the rapids near Montreal's modern Ahuntsic neighborhood in 1625. See Trigger, *The Children of Aataentsic: A History of the Huron People to 1660* (Montreal: McGill-Queen's University Press, 1987): 396.

[4] Before incorporating French-Canadians, the **Shamrocks** had improved with the 1895 absorption of the Montreal **Crystals** (amateurs at the Crystal Palace rink). Different Montreal **Shamrocks** are now associated with the Montreal Gaelic Athletic Association, a Gaelic football and hurling club founded by Irish immigrants in 1884. Exclusively French-blooded sports teams appeared in Montreal with the establishment of the *Association Athletique d'Amateurs Nationale* in 1894 and the *Association d'Amateurs Le Montagnard* (a snowshoe club) in 1898.

Their hockey sides would be respective **Nationals** and **Montagnards** (mountain men), rival hearts for local Francophones. Both climbed into prestigious leagues, but the **Montagnards** reverted to amateur status in 1908 and the **Nationals** folded after their best players ended up on the new "Flying Frenchmen," the 1910 **Canadiens**. For the evolution of Francophone hockey in Montreal, see "French-Canadian Tradition" by Michel Vigneault, part of *Backcheck: A Hockey Retrospective* at the web site of Library and Archives Canada, www.collectionscanada. gc.ca/hockey/024002-2101-e.html (accessed 4 June 2013). Also refer to Michael McKinley, *Hockey: A People's History* (Toronto: McClelland & Stewart, 2006): 19, 24, 25, 40.

[5]   The train from Ottawa to see O'Brien's **Millionaires** was the Timberwolf Special, remembered by junior hockey's Renfrew **Timberwolves** (est. 1987). Another O'Brien-owned team in the inaugural NHA was the 1910 Haileybury [Ont.] **Comets** (successful semi-pros back to 1906). Haileybury is named for an English prep school, but "**Comets**" references Halley's Comet, which appears about every seventy-five years, including 1910.

[6]   The 1917/18 NHL had four teams: the Ottawa **Senators**, Toronto **Arenas** (later **Maple Leafs**), and Montreal's **Canadiens** and **Wanderers**. But "Original Six" is often applied to teams that were the exclusive NHL contestants between 1942 and the 1967 expansion that doubled that number to twelve. Those six were the carryover **Leafs** and **Canadiens** plus the Boston **Bruins**, New York **Rangers**, Chicago **Blackhawks**, and Detroit **Red Wings**, but no amount of fuzzy math can make those the *original* half-dozen NHL teams.

[7]   Significant numbers of Canada's Irish Catholics had fought with the (Catholic) French against the British in the colonial wars. Afterwards, many Scots and "native" (Catholic) Irish came from the British Isles. Some Irish Catholics in the new (predominantly Protestant) U.S. went to Ontario alongside Loyalists after the Revolution. England brought boatloads of native Irish to Ontario to button down the border in the wake of the War of 1812. Subsequent building booms for canals, railways, and fortifications brought many more wage laborers from the Emerald Isle (including large numbers of Protestant Anglo-Irish and Scots-Irish).

Peter Robinson was a war hero in Upper Canada's legislature who fostered the relocation of many Catholics from Ireland's County Cork to Canada. His Ontario namesake is Peterborough, northeast of Toronto, where junior icemen are the 1966-named Peterborough **Petes**. Ontario's other Irish communities were logical destinations when the big exodus from Ireland occurred during its potato famine (1845–50), suggested by the NHA's Toronto **Shamrocks** (1915) and Montreal **Shamrocks** (1886–96, from the powerhouse Shamrock Lacrosse Club).

[8]   Athletes at Arkansas State (an A&M until 1933) were **Aggies** or **Farmers** in 1911, **Gorillas** in 1925, **Warriors** in 1930, and **Indians** in 1931. Switching again in 2008, ASU folks probably thought they had the only **Red Wolves** among four-year schools, but Richmond's Indiana University East was just then replacing **Pioneers** with **Red Wolves**.

[9]   Marquette's first teams on University Hill were **Hilltoppers**. After 1924 its blue-and-gold footballers were the **Golden Avalanche**, presumably rumbling down from that hill for road games. All were **Warriors** in 1954 and **Golden Eagles** in 1994. Marquette trustees made them the **Gold** in 2005, but a campus uproar brought the **Golden Eagles** back within weeks.

[10]   "New Newsfeature Makes Initial Bow," *The Griffin* (29 Sep. 1933): 1. Also on p. 1, see Rudolph J. Eichhorn, "The President Greets the Griffin Graciously."

[11]   In 1685, J.B. de la Salle founded the *École Normale* in Reims, France, the "normal school" model for many teachers' colleges. The LaSallian Christian Brothers started several North American colleges, being obviously eponymous for Tennessee's Christian Brothers University on Memphis's East Parkway. CBU's Treasure Chest Players staged four plays between 1949 and 1951 that incorporated a pirate ship prop, and a few students got hold of a black flag to menace the quad as "Parkway Pirates." Surrendering to the spirit in early '51, the campus news became the *Buccaneer* and athletes **Bucs**. (Joy Christie Di Cresce, "*Buccaneer* Born in Theater," *The Cannon* [6 Nov. 1990]: 1. Assisting email to the author from Deborah Babb [CBU electronic services lib.], 6 Aug. 2013.) **Lady Bucs** came with coeducation in 1970.

Another Christian Brothers academy, Manhattan College, was founded in downtown NYC in 1853 but moved to the Bronx in 1922. Manhattan's **Jaspers** remember LaSallian Brother Jasper Brennan, who introduced baseball to campus. Manhattan insists the good Brother Jasper invented the seventh-inning stretch to settle a crowd at an 1882 game, but the super-shortstop of the professional Cincinnati **Red Stockings**, Harry Wright, had noted the practice back in 1869: "The spectators all arise between halves of the seventh inning, extend their legs and arms and sometimes walk about." The extent to which Manhattan students might have popularized the stretch during exhibition games against major leaguers is unknown. A different story says fans followed suit when President William Howard Taft stood up to stretch in the middle of the seventh of an opening-day **Senators** game in 1909, a sight easily seen throughout Griffith Stadium. (Taft was huge.) Despite this fiction, Taft certainly was the first Chief Executive to throw the ceremonial first pitch before the first **Senators** game in 1910, starting an entirely different tradition. For the stretch's history, see Bruce Anderson, "Perspective: A Pause That Refreshes," *Sports Illustrated* (16 April 1990).

[12] Later Omaha **Knights** skated from 1945 to '51 and 1959 to '75. Omaha's last Ak-Sar-Ben **Knights** (2005–07) were AHLers. Compare "Ak-Sar-Ben" to the Coquitlam [B.C.] **Adanacs** (senior lacrosse, est. 1965), the plural of *Canada* backwards.

Chapter 17 Notes

[1] Centenary football coach Bo McMillin probably first called Georgia Tech a **Golden Tornado** in around 1920. He went to Geneva in 1925, possibly with that nick in tow. Tales that a tornado ripped the gold roof off Geneva's Old Main to yield the nickname are apocryphal. See Van Zanic, ed., *Geneva College Golden Tornadoes Football* (2011): 14.

[2] Julie Haas (JCCC assoc. v.p. of marketing/communications), email to the author, 25 July 2014. See also Johnson County Community College, "Meet Jean Claude," *Annual Report to the Community* (2012–13): 15.

[3] Victor Fleming, dir., *Gone With the Wind* (Metro-Goldwyn-Mayer, 1939).

[4] UVA has the only campus that's a UNESCO World Heritage Site, sharing that honor with Monticello, home of UVA founder and architect Thomas Jefferson. In fact, Patrick B. Miller reports that UVA's first baseballers were **Monticellos** in "The Manly, the Moral, and the Proficient: College Sport in the New South" in the volume he edited, *The Sporting World of the Modern South* (Chicago: U. Illinois Press, 2002): 31. The same page says pre-**Generals** baseballers at Washington College (later Washington and Lee) were **Shoo Flies**. (Miller cites Ollinger Crenshaw, *General Lee's College* [New York: Random House, 1969]: 215.) That probably refers to shoofly pie, a sticky molasses desert Southerners famously defend against flying insects.

The **Cavaliers** have alternately been **Wahoos** or **'Hoos** ever since Washington and Lee fans called rambunctious UVA baseballers a "bunch of wahoos" in the 1890s. *Wahoo* can be a cry of exuberance (or the person who releases same), but the wahoo (*Acanthocybium solandri*) is a tropical mackerel, giving fish mascots to Florida's 2012-named AA Pensacola **Blue Wahoos** and fastpitch softball's Florida **Wahoos** (Plant City, 1997–98).

[5] The South has more **Cavaliers** at Darton College (Albany, Ga.) and Bossier Parish [La.] Community College. Southern Virginia University (Buena Vista) and Southern University at New Orleans both host *Southern* **Knights**. Minor league Charlotte **Knights** (est. 1989) represent North Carolina's Queen City. Our favorite Southern **Knights** were in Duluth, the ABA **Reigning Knights** "of Georgia." They played a single season (2004/05) while referencing Brook Benton's last big single, 1970's "Rainy Night in Georgia." Two-year colleges in the Southeast are **Knight**-heavy. Refer to those Southern **Knights** at Surry Community College (Dobson, N.C.). There are **Golden Knights** at West Central Technical College (Carrollton, Ga.) and **Fighting Knights** at Lynn University (Boca Raton, Fla.).

A *squire* is an apprentice knight, but it later described an English country gentlemen.

Virginia planters imagined themselves within such a "squirearchy." In fact, George Washington is affectionately the Squire of Mount Vernon, and ABA Virginia **Squires** (1970–76) played in several cities. The general's roots run deep in Virginia's gentry class, and he bought his widowed mother a Fredericksburg house in 1772. In 1908 the University of Mary Washington opened a half mile away. Its **Eagles** were named in 1986 from respect for the national symbol.

[6] Ben Hay Hammet, *The Spirit of PC: A Centennial History of Presbyterian College* (Clinton, S.C.: Jacobs Press, 1982): 44.

[7] Carolina was a single province from 1663 to 1712. The teams prefixed only with "Carolina" include Carolina **Cougars**, **Ghostriders**, **Hurricanes**, **Mudcats**, **Panthers**, **Phoenix**, **Sharks**, **Queens**, and **Thunder**, all with homes in the more northern state (as do East Carolina U. and Western Carolina U.). This *North*-as-the-default-*Carolina* model seems broken only by Coastal Carolina U. (Conway, S.C.), even though the capital of the Carolina province had actually been in modern South Carolina at Charleston. A June 2013 baseball matchup between the UNC **Tar Heels** and USC **Gamecocks** saw both home and away jerseys with only "Carolina" across the front, as noted by Phil Hecken at Uni Watch, http://www.uni-watch.com/2013/06/09/louisville-unveils-the-worst-baseball-uni-of-all-time (accessed 12 June 2013).

[8] Junior hockey's Windsor [Ont.] **Spitfires** (1946–53, 1975–) salute the Royal Canadian Air Force pilots who flew Supermarine *Spitfires* to victory in history's greatest air battle, the 1940 Battle of Britain. New Westminster [B.C.] **Spitfires** were a senior service team during the 1941/42 season. The slowly produced *Spitfire* was actually outperformed during the Battle of Britain by the less elegant Hawker *Hurricane* fighter, inspiration for Toronto's wartime rugby football **RCAF Hurricanes** (1942–43). North American Aviation in California designed the P-51 *Mustang* fighter for Britain's Royal Air Force, but by the time it was unleashed in 1942, it was beloved by U.S. and Canadian flyers. The P-51s in Calgary's No. 401 squadron gave name to senior hockey's Calgary RCAF **Mustangs** (1942–45). Junior hockey Calgary **Mustangs** were named in 2010. (C-Town's historic rodeo further justifies these **Mustangs** sides.)

[9] Exceeding our geographical charter, Celtic League rugby players in Galashiels, Scotland were **Border Reivers** (1999–2007). (In fact, the world's first rugby union league was the Border League along the Scottish Borders in 1901.)

[10] "What's a Reiver?" *Iowa Western's Men's Basketball 2013–2104 Media Guide*: 28.

[11] Started as a Methodist seminary in 1853, Beaver College kept its name when it moved cross-state from Beaver to northern Philadelphia in 1925. In fact, the **Knights'** old mascot was Sir Castor, after the North America beaver, *Castor canadensis*. Administrators would never admit it, but in the twenty-first century a former all-female academy called "Beaver U." sounded way too much like a B-movie title, so the change to Arcadia U. was made.

[12] See Theodore Roosevelt, *The Winning of the West, Volume One* (New York: G.P. Putnam's Sons, 1889): 102, 103, 105.

[13] Competing sentiments on the Virginia-West Virginia line were indicated by Bluefield **Blue-Grays** (1937–55) in the former Virginia town of Graham, renamed Bluefield in 1924 to associate itself with the prosperous town of that name just over the state border. Their Bowen Field diamond was a thousand feet from West Virginia. Both Bluefields are named after the area's abundant violet-colored flower of the chicory plant (*Cichorium intybus*). West Virginia's Bluefield State College keeps **Big Blues** and **Lady Blues** two miles from Virginia's similarly named Bluefield College, which has **Ramblin' Rams**, as do other Christian schools (p. 106).

[14] Chester Bailey, "Mansfield Classical Seminary," in Joyce M. Tice, ed., *Tri-Counties Genealogy & History*, www.joycetice.com/articles/cbsemina.htm (accessed 11 Aug. 2010).

[15] One possible origin is from the Middle English *cracker*, meaning boaster. England's second Lord Dartmouth—eponym of Dartmouth College—famously called the Scots-Irish boasters in the Southeast "Crackers" in 1766, and it would continue to be derogatorily applied to poor, rural white folks by better-off urban white folks. Families in Georgia and Florida now proudly

use *Cracker* to distinguish themselves from more recent arrivals.

[16] The **Crackers** and **Black Crackers** may actually represent abbreviations from the Southern League's 1892 Atlanta **Firecrackers**. Or "**Firecrackers**" might have already been an enhancement of "Crackers."

Settlers in shacks on Georgia's great Okefenokee Swamp were "swamp crackers" or "swampers." The closest city is Waycross, where the Waycross College **Swamp Foxes** were combined with the South Georgia College **Tigers** (in Douglas) in summer 2013 to create **Hawks** for the two campuses of the new South Georgia State College.

[17] The winning Pittsburghers **Pipers** became Minneapolis's 1968/69 Minnesota **Pipers**, but they returned to the Golden Triangle the next season. A fan poll said the 1970/71 team would be Pittsburgh **Pioneers**, but that brought protests from the city's super-alliterative Point Park University **Pioneers**. The ABA solved the problem by arbitrarily assigning "**Condors**" to the team that folded after the '71/72 season. See Terry Pluto, *Loose Balls: The Short, Wild Life of the American Basketball Association* (New York: Simon and Schuster, 1990): 125.

[18] Also feeling a need for speed were Arena Football's Richmond **Speed** (2000–03), who shared Virginia's capital with one of racing's premier short tracks, Richmond International Raceway. The University of Northwestern Ohio in Lima has motorsports teams and its own race track. UNOH's racers are in fact **Racers**, as are its other athletes.

[19] Hugh Howard, ed., "Origin of the Fighting Scot," *College of Wooster Football Media Guide* (2004): 4. As for the Philadelphians, their longtime in-state affiliates, the Reading **Phillies**, became **Fightin Phils** for 2013. (Their Crazy Hot Dog Vendor wears an ostrich costume and chucks franks to fans for reasons neither historical nor comprehensible.)

[20] Brooks Blevins, *Lyon College, 1872–2002* (Fayetteville: U. Arkansas Press, 2003): 338, 341. Blevins discusses other Arkansas College team names (**Lambs**, **Panthers**, **Highlanders**, and **Scots**), pp. 64, 101, and 183.

[21] R. Douglas Brackenridge, *Trinity University* (San Antonio: Trinity U. Press, 2004): 103. Baseball's formal pre-season workouts were three decades old at this point and were standard by 1900, but the idea of spring training as a local festival was just taking off when Detroit's **Tigers** came to Waxahachie. Neither Trinity University in Texas nor its **Tigers** are affiliated with the Trinity Washington [D.C.] University **Tigers** or the Trinity College of Florida **Tigers** (in Trinity). The coincidence probably owes to a fondness for alliteration, which presumably applies to **Trojans** at Trinity International University (Deerfield, Ill.).

[22] Francis Collinson, *The Bagpipe* (London: Routledge & Kegan Paul, 1975): 171.

[23] The "Hillbillies" taunt is from a letter (17 June 1935) from C.U. Money (Hanover athletic dir.) in George Earlie Shankle, *American Nicknames: Their Origin and Significance* (New York: H.W. Wilson, 1937): 228.

[24] Walter B. Hendrickson, *Forward in the Second Century of MacMurray College* (Jacksonville, Ill.: MacMurray Coll., 1972): 49. (Assisting email to the author from Bob Tobin [MacMurray Coll. P.R. dir.], 18 Oct. 2005.)

[25] Dr. Phil Sturm (OVU history dept.) and Marty E. Davis (OVU marketing dir.), emails to the author, both dated 16 Jan. 2005.

[26] The evolution of Rockhurst's athletic identity is from a letter (21 Nov. 1935) that was written by a witness to the events, athletic director Patrick W. Mason, as cited in Shankle, *American Nicknames* (1937): 449.

[27] A timeline of ND team names is in chapter 12 in Murray Sperber *Shake Down the Thunder: The Creation of Notre Dame Football* (New York: Henry Holt, 1993). Coach Knute Rockne had one great backfield on his **Irish** squads between 1922 and '24. Sportswriter Grantland Rice compared quarterback Harry Stuhldreher and backs Jim Crowley, Elmer Layden, and Don Miller to the Book of Revelation's Four Horsemen of the Apocalypse. Stuhldreher and Layden

joined a 1926 AFL team consequently called Brooklyn **Horsemen**. The NFL set up rival Brooklyn **Lions**, which by November had absorbed the **Horsemen** (sometime "**Horse-Lions**"). Both franchises were absorbed by the AFL New York **Yankees**, who moved to the NFL for 1927 and '28.

[28] Sperber, *Shake Down the Thunder*: 80. Many roaming collegians had such early nicknames. Founded in 1966, classrooms for York College of The City University of New York bounced all over Queens. Without a home gym, teams scattered among local high schools as **Nomads**. Those white-red-and-black players became **Cardinals** some time after settling on a permanent campus in 1986.

Basketballers from the University of West Alabama were called **Ramblin' Tigers** in 1940 but are now simply **Tigers**. See "There's Something About this Place: Significant Moments at UWA," http://175.uwa.edu/timeline.htm (accessed 12 Sep. 2012).

[29] Jack Jumper (SJU athletic communications assoc. dir.), email to the author, 10 Nov. 2008.

[30] The forward pass explanation for "**Rockets**" is from a communication (28 June 1935) by David Connelly (Toledo athletic dir.) in George Earlie Shankle, *American Nicknames: Their Origin and Significance* (New York: H.W. Wilson, 1955): 474. Other sources say Toledo's speed in recovering fumbles in that same Carnegie game explains "**Skyrockets**," quickly shortened to "**Rockets**." We trust Connelly's proximity to events, especially considering that "**Skyrockets**" makes infinitely more sense as a *passing* reference.

Chapter 18 Notes

[1] "Hungry, Hungry Homer" aired on March 4, 2001. (A 1999 episode exposed a plot to move the **Isotopes** to Moose Jaw, a Saskatchewan town that's long hosted minor leaguers.) Springfield's **Ice-O-Topes** adhere to standard minor league hockey conventions, as do the junior **Iso-Tots**. Footballers named for the powerplant include Springfield **Atoms** and the (proposed) Springfield **Meltdowns**. Women of wartime baseball were Springfield **Floozies** (barely less respectful than the real team names). Rivals in Shelbyville are **Shelbyvillians** and **Visitors**.

[2] WSMR's old Goddard [baseball] Field was named after Robert Goddard, who ushered in rocketry's modern age in 1926 by test flying liquid-fuel vehicles in Massachusetts. He experimented secretly throughout the 1930s at Roswell, New Mexico (just east of White Sands). It hosted minor league baseball's Roswell **Rockets** (1949–56), but their space alien mascot recalled the 1947 Roswell Incident, in which the Army says it reclaimed a weather balloon while conspiracists say they're hiding a crashed alien spacecraft.

[3] "Padre brown" is linked to Franciscans who established many New Spain missions. Quincy [Ill.] University was founded by German Franciscans in 1860. Its Padre-brown and white must have reminded QU students of brown-feathered hunters because in the early 1930s the school paper was named *The Falcon* while athletes became **Hawks**. (Patricia A. Tomczak [Quincy U. lib. and info. resources dean], email to the author, 14 Aug. 2007.)

[4] Most collegiate **Dons** have **Lady Don** counterparts. The grammatically appropriate feminine complement to *Don* is *Doña*, which even in Spanish is rare because Europe's power structure of dukes and counts was male-dominated. "*Donnas*" at first seems a suitably Anglicized alternative, but that's an Italian honorific for a noble lady who doesn't need to be tramping around a wilderness. It is therefore inconsistent with California's Spanish colonial heritage.

Chapter 19 Notes

[1] Hockey's **Indians** often dominated the Springfield-based AHL. The last **Indians** were later Worcester [Mass.] **IceCats** (1994–2005) and Peoria [Ill.] **Rivermen**.

[2] Tupper the bulldog mascot salutes Earl Tupper, the inventor of Tupperware who donated land to move today's Bryant U. from Providence to nearby Smithfield in 1967.

[3] The Chatham **Cougar** is "Carson," after Rachel Carson. She got her biology degree from CU's institutional predecessor in 1929 and all but launched the modern environmental movement through her 1962 anti-pesticide book *Silent Spring*.

[4] In the heart of Ottawa territory is Pontiac, Michigan, where General Motors started stamping Pontiacs with Indian-head emblems in 1925. In 1952 an Alberta GM dealer sponsored a senior hockey team, thereafter called Bonnyville **Pontiacs**. (That survives as the name of juniors.) Gear heads inevitably see that as a deliberate inversion of "Pontiac *Bonneville*," but that revolutionary performance model wouldn't be introduced until 1957. It was named after Utah's Bonneville Salt Flats, where drivers have set land speed records since 1914. The Flats were named for a U.S. Army captain made famous after notes from his Western expedition (1832–36) were worked into *The Adventures of Captain Bonneville*, an 1837 book by Washington Irving. There is no relationship between the Bonneville Flats and Bonnyville, Alberta. The latter memorializes Father Francis Bonny, a French-Catholic minister in the West after 1907.

Team sponsorship by a local dealership can be mutually beneficial. Hockey's Edmonton **Mercurys** were backed by Alberta's Waterloo Motors, the "Forgotten Team" that won the 1950 World Championship and 1952 Olympic Gold. Four years later, Waterloo was outselling all North American dealerships. See Ron Kuban, *Edmonton's Urban Villages* (Edmonton: U. Alberta Press, 2005): 74.

[5] Jim Hogan, *Plymouth: Where My Viewpoints Crossed* (Plymouth, N.H.: Clifford Nicol, 1985): 54. (Susan Jarosz [PSU archives], assisting email to the author, 5 Jan. 2010.)

[6] The mascot for the UL Lafayette **Cajuns** is Cayenne, a costumed cayenne pepper. While that pepper is often used in Cajun food, there's no etymological relationship between *Cajun* and *cayenne*. The latter is from Cayenne, the capital of South America's French Guiana.

[7] Pierre Nobert (U. Sainte-Anne athletic dir.), email to the author, 6 Sep. 2007. Like *Sainte-Anne's* **Dragons**, teams in French Canada often try to have it both linguistic ways. There's little explanation else for basketball's Montreal **Dragons** (1993) and the WLAF Montreal **Machine** (1991–92), the respective *Dragons de Montréal* and *Machine de Montréal*. The same goes for minor league soccer's Montreal **Impact** (*Impact de Montréal*, est. 1992), who brought their deliberately bilingual name to the MLS in 2012.

[8] Roger Grindle, "The University of Maine at Fort Kent: A Century of Progress," reproduced at www.umfk.edu/library/cataloged/Century (accessed 2 Jan. 2014). Other assistance from Kathryn Donahue (UMFK archives), email to the author, 2 Jan. 2014.

[9] Bishop's U., "Historical Timeline 1908–1950: The "Gaiters" Story," http://www.ubishops.ca/library/old-library/historical-timeline/1908-1950.html (accessed 5 Aug. 2014).

Chapter 20 Notes

[1] England's Emmanuel College was founded in 1584 to give Protestant ministers educations on par with those historically received by Catholic friars in other Cambridge halls. A Catholic school in Boston took the Emmanuel College name in 1919 because *Emmanuel* is Hebrew for "God with us." EC's **Saints** refer to several Saints Emmanuel canonized by the Catholic Church. *Cambridge* itself refers to an ancient bridge over England's River Cam. *Cantabrigiensis* is the city's Latinized name, so you'll see "Cantabs" casually applied to athletes or students at Cambridges on either side of the Atlantic.

[2] Ironically, the man who first wrapped Harvard's **Crimson** in crimson would threaten to ban football at his university after a spate of serious injuries and a few game-related deaths. Mr. Eliot's ideas conflicted with those of Yale's anti-reform coach Walter Camp, who'd almost single-handedly developed football's rules. In 1905 a successful Harvard grad (and father of one **Crimson** player) summoned athletic representatives from football's Big Three (Harvard, Yale, and Princeton) to his Oval Office. Teddy Roosevelt wanted football to continue and encouraged the founding of a rules committee, the Intercollegiate Athletic Association of the

United States, which was the National Collegiate Athletic Association (NCAA) after 1910.

[3] The passage from William and Mary's charter echoed the First Charter of Virginia (1606): "[…] propagating of Christian Religion [to] Infidels and Savages, living in those parts, to human Civility." The Brafferton School for Indians—which W&M was running by 1697—is cited as a legitimizing factor whenever "**Tribe**" is scrutinized. In fact, it was on that basis that the NCAA approved its continued use in 2006, although W&M did forfeit its Indian feather emblems. The school charter also said it should be called "forever, The College of William and Mary, in Virginia," so the name of "The College" didn't change with university status in 1967.

After 2001 the **Tribe** mascot was Colonel Ebirt (*tribe* backwards). He was replaced in 2010 by a griffin, a convergence of the American bald eagle and Britain's heraldic lion.

Williamsburg had the country's first public psychiatric hospital. W&M teams found out they were called "**Loonies**" by attendees at U. Richmond, accelerating the move to "**Indians**." See Office of University Relations, "Glimpse of Tribe Baseball History," *W&M News* (5 May 2006), reproduced at http://web.wm.edu/news/archive/?id=5814 (accessed 1 Jan. 2014).

[4] The red deer was the ultimate English hunting prize and a symbol of nobility. That's reinforced by **Kings** and **Queens** at Alberta's Red Deer College.

[5] Cotton Mather was a well-regarded theologian whose writings on witchcraft fueled the legal persecution of witches at Boston and Salem (although the Mathers eventually spoke against the proceedings). "**Witches**" has been a popular name for high school and semi-pro athletes in eastern Massachusetts since the late 1800s.

[6] With Yale setting the precedent, "**Bulldogs**" is among the most common team names. Find such sides throughout this book and at U. Montana–Western, UNC-Asheville, Selma [Ala.] U., Southwestern Oklahoma State U. (Wetherford), and Union U. (Jackson, TN). There are **Runnin' Bulldogs** at Gardner-Webb U. (Boiling Springs, N.C.).

[7] Margaret Smagorinsky and Wink Einthoven, *The Tigers of Princeton University* (Princeton, N.J.: Princeton U. Office of Communications, 1992): 3. See also Raymond Rhinehart, *Princeton University* (New York: Princeton Architectural Press, 2000): 22.

[8] Jackie Esposito and Steven Herb, *The Nittany Lion* (University Park, Pa.: Pennsylvania State U. Press, 2000): 3. The same book (p. 15) says Penn State's 1887 footballers were the **Pink and Black** before they were the **Blue and White** and then **Nittany Lions**. *Nittany* may be an Algonquian description of a solitary mountain, like nearby Mt. Nittany.

PSU has nearly twenty "commonwealth campuses" with their own **Lions** or **Nittany Lions**. The exception is Penn State Fayette [County], which has **Roaring Lions**. This is a good place to say that "Roary" is a **Sea Lion** at Point Loma Nazarene, a **Panther** at Florida International, a **Lion** at Missouri Southern State University (Joplin), and a **Tiger** at East Central University (Okla.). The **Lion** is Roar-ee at Columbia University.

[9] Christopher Jencks and David Riesman, *The Academic Revolution* (New York: Doubleday, 1968): 315.

[10] Penn opened America's first medical school in 1765. That followed the model of European universities that have graduate schools in various disciplines, so Penn claims to be North America's oldest university.

[11] Horace Mather Lippincott, *The University of Pennsylvania: Franklin's College* (Philadelphia & London: J.B. Lippincott, 1919): 113. Lippincott gives further evidence that William Penn might have been turned off by the Anglican school in his Quaker City, reporting that the university's first provost (Anglican bishop William Smith) had historically been "a vigourous [*sic*] opponent of the Quakers." He also says Penn's red and blue were selected ahead of an 1876 rowing match against Harvard and Yale to "beat them with their own colours" (p. 115).

[12] Benjamin Spener, "Story Behind Lion Sheds Light on University, Athletics," *Columbia Daily Spectator* (28 Sept. 2011), www.columbiaspectator.com/2011/09/28/story-behind-lion-

sheds-light-university-athletics (accessed 3 April 2014). Also see Paul Hond, "Year of the Lion," *Columbia Magazine* (winter 2009-10): 64.

[13] "School Colors," *Undergraduate Studies in Liberal Arts and Engineering* (Baltimore: Johns Hopkins Office of Undergraduate Admissions, 2008): 12.

[14] Gordon M. Morton, *Brown University Athletics* (Portsmouth, N.H.: Arcadia, 2003): 21, 79.

[15] UMaine's first cub made students go bananas at a 1914 pep rally, so he's named Bananas.

[16] Queen's College and New Brunswick were respectively named for George III's consort (Charlotte of Mecklenburg) and the king's German dukedom of Brunswick. It opened with strong support from New Jersey's last royal governor, William Franklin. He'd be a Loyalist during the Revolution despite being the illegitimate son of super-patriot Ben Franklin.

[17] "Why Scarlet? Why Knights?" *Rutgers Soccer Media Guide* (2008): 107. Other Rutgers campuses field **Scarlet Raiders** (Rutgers-Newark) and **Scarlet Raptors** (Rutgers-Camden).

[18] James Axtell, *The European and the Indian* (New York and Oxford: Oxford U. Press, 1981): 88. Dartmouth's early history is in the chapter "Dr. Wheelock's Little Red School."

There's no known relationship between Dartmouth's Congregationalist educator Eleazar Wheelock and Lucy Wheelock, the educator and daughter of a Congregationalist minister in Vermont. In 1888 she founded a Boston school to train kindergarten teachers. Wheelock College teams are alliterative Wheelock **Wildcats**.

[19] See Kenneth Raymond, *The History of Johnson State College: 1828–1984* (Johnson, Vt.: Johnson State Coll., 1985): 132. Some of the timeline was assembled through multiple emails to the author (Oct. 2011) from Linda Kramer (JSC public services lib.), Michael Osborne (JSC sports info. dir.), and Peter Albright (the JSC athletic dir. when "**Badgers**" was adopted).

[20] Dennis M. Burke, *A Report by the Rev. D.M. Burke on the Green Knight* (De Pere, Wis.: St. Norbert Coll., c. 1977): 1, 2. (Olivia Dart [SNC archives], assisting email to the author, 24 Sep. 2008.) Norbert founded the Norbertine priests in 1120, so **Green Knights** fit that age of chivalry. The navy-and-gold Green Bay **Packers** started using the **Knights'** field for training camp in 1958. Rookie coach Vince Lombardi gave his team their now famous green-and-gold uniforms the next season, which isn't necessarily seen as a coincidence at SNC, where the same hues have been used since 1931.

[21] Jason Erickson, ed., *2005–06 Idaho State Women's Basketball Media Guide* (2005): 1.

[22] Communication (19 Nov. 1935) from A.G. Paul (Riverside Jun. Coll. president) in Shankle, *American Nicknames* (1937): 447.

Chapter 21 Notes

[1] Threatening hellfire and damnation, New Light evangelicals provided exemplary religious zeal. Connecticut preachers seem to have been remembered by minor league baseball's Bridgeport **Orators** (1899–1912). (A current vintage team uses that name.) In fact, they were a tribute to Bridgeport native and Yale-trained lawyer Jim "Orator" O'Rourke (1850–1919), a Hall of Fame **Giant** nicknamed for his persistent and erudite outfield chatter.

[2] *Yeomen* came to describe naval petty officers, military guards, or independent farmers. When established in 1833, Oberlin was named for Rev. J.F. Oberlin (d. 1826) who advanced education and agriculture for France's poor farmers, so the definition of *yeoman* that's the most pastoral (and the oldest) perhaps best applies to Oberlin's **Yeomen**. Or it might simply be that a student in 1926 suggested the name from a cheer: "Ye-*O*-Men" ... *O* as in "Oberlin." (See "So They Called 'Em," *The Day* [25 Jan. 1935]: 16.)

Toronto was called York during the English colonial period. **Yeomen** and **Yeowomen** at its York University probably referred to the Yeomen of the Guard (attendants of English monarchs for five centuries). YU moved to gender-neutral **Lions** in 2003.

[3] Fitch's stories in the *Saturday Evening Post* made "Old Siwash" a term of endearment for all

alma maters. Refer to Christopher Jencks and David Riesman in *The Academic Revolution* (New York: Doubleday, 1968): 315: "[W]hat's good for Old Siwash is good for the country. And what seems good for Old Siwash is determined not by the transient adolescents who constitute the student body […] but by the tenured [faculty]."

⁴ Anne Devereaux Jordan and J.M. Stifle, *The Baptists* (New York: Hippocrene, 1990): 87.

⁵ Spright Dowell, *A History of Mercer University, 1833–1953* (Mercer, Ga.: Mercer U. Press, 1958): 164.

⁶ Communication (12 June 1935) from Mercer coach Lake Russell in George Earlie Shankle, *American Nicknames: Their Origin and Significance* (New York: H.W. Wilson, 1937): 343.

⁷ Dowell, *A History of Mercer University*: 164. Besides being contradicted in Shankle (*loc. cit.*), this story has problems. "Whence cometh that bear?" is suspiciously reminiscent of a line from "Elene," a ninth-century Anglo-Saxon poem by Cynewulf: "Whence cometh it that ye bear in mind so many things […]?" Also, Mercer's athletes would likely have been bushy haired and mustached, but probably no more so than other Victorian-era footballers. The moppy "chrysanthemum" cut that players felt protected their heads was mocked in newspaper cartoons and probably gave us a few **Tiger** and **Lion** teams whose backstories are long lost. Ivy League rowers started sporting "crew cuts" to keep their hair out of their faces in the 1890s, just about when the first helmets were making the long-hair approach obsolete.

⁸ "Band, Spirit & Tradition," *Wake Forest Football* (2008): 30.

⁹ Campbell U., "Spirit & Tradition," www.campbell.edu/about/spirit-tradition (accessed 21 Aug. 2012).

¹⁰ "Bulldog Adopted as Name for Team," *Howard Crimson* (14 Dec. 1916): 1.

¹¹ Communication (25 Nov. 1935) from W.I. Walton (OBU athletic dir.) in Shankle, *American Nicknames* (1937): 401.

¹² In 1896, Baptists founded Wingate [N.C.] University, named for Wake Forest's late president, Rev. W.M. Wingate. Wingate's **Bulldogs** lack a dramatic backstory but give us excuse to address their mascot, Victor E.—*victory*—Bulldog, perhaps the most common mascot name, indicated by Victor E. Bulldog (CSU Fresno), Victor E. Bull (U. Buffalo), Victor E. Hawk (Viterbo U.), Victor E. Huskie (Northern Illinois), Victor E. Bear (Central Arkansas), Victor E.Tiger (Fort Hays State), Victor E. Ram (Bluefield College), and Victor E. Lancer (Mount Marty). Victor E. Viking has represented **Vikings** at Western Washington, Portland State, and Dana College, as well as Northern Kentucky's **Norse**. Victor Viking represents arbitrarily named silver-and-blue **Vikings** from Berry [Ga.] College (**Blue Jackets** until 1962). Viktor-with-a-*k* is a **Viking** at Grand View University and in Minnesota's NFL clubhouse.

UW-Milwaukee's Victor E. Panther was replaced by a cat named Pounce in 2007. Other **Panther**-backing Pounces are at Davenport U. (Grand Rapids, Mich.), Ellsworth Comm. Coll. (Iowa Falls, Iowa), Georgia State, Purdue–North Central, and Tompkins-Cortland. Pounce is a **Cougar** at U. Wisconsin–Morris and a **Lion** at Lambton. The U. Memphis **Tiger** is Pouncer.

Minor league hockey Louisville [Ky.] **IceHawks** (1991–94) and baseball Greenville [S.C.] **Braves** (1984–2004) had mascots named Tommy Hawk, as do the NHL Chicago **Blackhawks** and UNC-Pembroke **Braves**. "Tommy Hawk" is a play on *tomahawk*, so that name is starting to fade along with other Indian themes.

¹³ Wesleyan doesn't tell us if that **Cardinals** jacket replicated those of the 1931 world champion St. Louis **Cardinals**. We do know that one freshman at Coeur d'Alene's North Idaho College—the fantastically named Glen Noglenn—was a huge fan of the major league **Cards** and successfully suggested his school adopt "**Cardinals**" in 1939. See North Idaho Coll., "History & Tradition," www.nic.edu/history (accessed 30 July 2014).

¹⁴ Nathan Graybeal (EHC sports info. dir.), email to the author, 2 Dec. 2003. (EHC's co-eponym is Patrick Henry.)

[15] Consider that Methodism's founder John Wesley often sermonized on being carried to heaven on eagle's wings. Refer to "Upon Our Lord's Sermon on the Mount" (Discourse 1, II.1), "Earnest Appeal to Men of Reason and Religion" (34, 54), "A Farther Appeal to Men of Reason and Religion" (Part 1, III.11), and "On the Resurrection of the Dead" (II.3).

Missouri's Central Methodist University was founded at Fayette in 1854 by circuit rider Nathan Scarritt and Methodist minister D.R. McAnally. Methodists started Reinhardt University (Waleska, Ga.) in 1883 with cooperation from Confederate officers A.M. Reinhardt and John J.A. Sharp. A Methodist seminary at Jackson, Tennessee was renamed Lambuth University in 1921 after the recently deceased W.R. Lambuth, a ridiculously well-traveled missionary. Like many Christian schools, CMU, RU, and LU host **Eagles**, and there are blue-and-gold **Golden Eagles** at John Brown University (Siloam Springs, Ark.), named for evangelical Methodist John E. Brown (1879–1957). (Lambuth closed in mid-2011 and the site immediately became the "Lambuth Campus" of U. Memphis.)

[16] Hamline's 1895 team hosted the first-ever intercollegiate basketball game, a 9-3 loss to the State School of Agriculture. Some sources call that HU team "**Porkers**"—a syllabic derivative of *Ham*-line—but the school adamantly denies using any such moniker.

[17] Baker U. Office of Alumni Relations, "History of the Wildcat," *Baker World*, www.bakeru.edu/bakerworld/?p=4785 (accessed 17 July 2014).

[18] Larry LaTourette, *Northwestern Wildcat Football* (Chicago: Arcadia, 2005): 10.

[19] Northwestern's switch to **Wildcats** ironically came only one year after a live wildcat mascot had been removed from its sidelines after getting blamed for a disastrous 1923 season.

The speed with which Northwestern's "**Wildcats**" caught on was evident at California State University–Chico, where Northwestern fans successfully campaigned to apply "**Wildcats**" to their own teams, also in 1924. See "Our History and Traditions," *2003–2005 University Catalog* (Chico, Calif.: CSU Chico, 2005): 14.

[20] James D. McLaird, *The Dakota Wesleyan University Memory Book: 1885–2010* (Mitchell, S.D.: Dakota Wesleyan U., 2010): 98.

[21] It's often said that SMU's small but powerful football **Mustangs** traveled to Ann Arbor for a 1963 game and so impressed **Wolverine** fan and Ford president Lee Iacocca that he called his small but powerful sports car the *Mustang*, but most sources say the real inspiration for the car was a legendary fighter plane, the P-51 *Mustang*.

[22] A.G. Bedford, *The University of Winnipeg* (Toronto: U. Toronto Press, 1976): 182–183. A later merger of Methodist-minded and Baptist Canadians (1966) switched control of Bethany Bible College (Sussex, N.B.) from Reformed Baptists to the Wesleyan Church. BBC jocks are **Blazers**, inspired by God's light.

[23] Bedford, *The University of Winnipeg*: 209.

[24] As ever, some Methodist or Wesleyan schools arrived at common sporting identities without much of a story. **Tigers** represent Central Christian Coll. of Kansas (McPherson), Dakota Wesleyan U. (Mitchell, S.D.), and Iowa Wesleyan Coll. (Mount Pleasant). Methodist **Bulldogs** are at Adrian [Mich.] Coll., Tennessee Wesleyan Coll. (Athens), and Union Coll. (Barbourville, Ky.). There are **Wildcats** at Indiana Wesleyan U. (Marion). Methodist-backed **Panthers** frequent Ferrum [Va.] Coll. and Kentucky Wesleyan Coll. (Owensboro). There are Methodist **Mustangs** (Morningside Coll., Sioux City, Iowa) and **Pioneers** (Spartanburg [S.C.] Methodist Coll.). The blue-and-gold-and-Methodist **Blue Jays** at Spring Arbor [Mich.] University became **Cougars** with the addition of varsity soccer in 1967.

[25] Mark A. Noll, *A History of Christianity in the United States and Canada* (Grand Rapids: Eerdmans, 1992): 169.

[26] Starting slowly in a 1924 game at Atlantic Christian (now Barton College), the nicknameless baseballers from Lenoir-Rhyne University (Hickory, N.C.) sprang "out of the dugout like

mountain bears," so said the *Raleigh News and Observer*, giving LRC **Bears**. See Tim Peeler and Brian McLawhorn, *Baseball in Catawba County* (Charleston, S.C.: Arcadia, 2004): 67.

[27] Douglas A. Foster et al., *The Encyclopedia of the Stone-Campbell Movement* (Grand Rapids: Eerdmans, 2005): 104.

[28] Jim McGrath, ed., "Why Bulldogs?" *2010–11 Butler Basketball Guide* (2010): 6.

[29] Casey L. Gradischnig, ed., "John Griffith, First Bulldog," *Drake Blue* (fall 2005): 18. The same page says Drake teams were sometimes **Tigers** in the pre-**Bulldog** era.

[30] We shouldn't call out the Campbellites' Tougaloo and Jarvis Christian for favoring "**Bull-dogs**"; it's a ridiculously popular name at HBCUs. For instance Alabama A&M, Bowie [Md.] State U., Fisk, North Carolina A&T, South Carolina State, Wilberforce, and Knoxville [Tenn.] College all have such teams.

[31] Jeff Hoedt, ed., "About the Terriers," *Hiram College Women's Soccer Guide* (2006): 14.

With a roster of regional farm boys, Hiram College's football team started 1928 as **Farmers**, but three quick victories in downpours made them **Mudhens**. The year-end banquet that same season was the setting for the comment that led to their being **Terriers**.

The 1914 football team at Truman State University (Kirksville, Mo.) wasn't great, but—like Hiram—"hung on like bulldogs." Hoopsters at Ferris State University (Big Rapids, Mich.) were "hanging on like bulldogs" in 1930. Losing a 1917 football test 20-0 to the University of Redlands [Calif.], Whittier College's coach said the Redlanders "might well be called the Bull-dogs of the conference." (University of Redlands, "About Redlands: Mascot," www.redlands. edu/about-redlands/294.aspx [accessed 26 July 2013].) TSU, FSU, and RU keep **Bulldogs** as a result. The first football coach at Texas Lutheran University (Sequin) wanted players "strong and tenacious, so he named them **Bulldogs** in 1926." (TLU, "History & Traditions," www.tlu. edu/student-life/traditions (accessed 5 Aug. 2014).

[32] Communication (30 June 1935) from Joe Malcor (California Christian Coll. [now Chap-man U.] athletic dir.) in Shankle, *American Nicknames* (1937): 90.

[33] E.B. Andrews, ed., "Higher Education," *A History of Education in the State of Ohio* (Colum-bus: Ohio General Assembly, 1876): 247.

[34] **Flames** and **Blazers** appear at Christian schools outside the Restoration Movement because the flame is the symbol for the spirit of God in the Holy Trinity. But Trinitarianism is one doc-trine that Restorationists reject as part of their core non-denominationalism.

[35] Sides with regal names (like the Kansas City **Royals** or Los Angeles and Sacramento **Kings**) claim lion emblems through the beast's sovereign nature, a trend more apparent at Christian colleges. The King's College **Monarchs** (Wilkes-Barre, Pa.) have a lion mascot, and these other Christian colleges train **Lions**: Bryn Athyn [Pa.] Coll., Emmanuel Coll. (Franklin Springs, Ga.), Lindenwood U. (St. Charles, Mo.), Mars Hill [N.C.] U., Molloy Coll. (Rockville Centre, N.Y.), and Piedmont Coll. (Demorest, Ga.). The North Dakota State Normal and Indus-trial School had **Dusties** (in-*dust*-rials) until a 1970 fire closed it, but Trinity Bible College re-located to Ellendale two years later, eventually fielding **Lions**. Regis College (Weston, Mass.) is a Catholic school with **Pride** because *pride* describes a lion group and *regis* is Latin for a ruler. (Sister Mary Regis Casserly founded the school.) Multnomah Bible College's **Ambas-sadors** (Portland, Ore.) were **Lions** after its upgrade to Multnomah University in 2008.

We found just one college that liked its team name enough to make it the name of the insti-tution itself. Costa Mesa's Southern California College considered itself the most ambitious college within the Assemblies of God denomination and therefore "on the vanguard" of Chris-tian education. Its **Vanguards** replaced **Deacons/Deaconettes** in 1958. (Refer to Lewis Wilson, "Vanguard's Football Team," *Vanguard* [fall 2005]: 47. Wilson also says the first teams were the 1930s' **Sky Pilot** basketballers, "sky pilot" being a folky term for an emphatic preacher.) The school became Vanguard University of Southern California in 1999 and avoided "Van-guard **Vanguards**" by making teams **Lions**. There had been varsity **Lions** within the same denomination since 1963 at Southwestern Assemblies of God University (Waxahachie, Texas). SAGU's mascot is Judah because a lion represented the Israelites' ancient Tribe of Judah. The Lion of Judah was also noted when athletes at Lincoln [Ill.] Christian University became **Red Lions** in fall 2009, although LCU also claims inspiration from lions in Psalms (104:21), Job (38:39), Revelation (5:5), and even Aslan, the Jesus-lion in C.S. Lewis's *Chronicles of Narnia*. (See Brian Mills, "Student Life," *Lincoln Christian University Restorer* [fall 2009]: 15.)

[36] There are **Eagles** at Morehead [Ky.] State University, a state school that's only coincidentally on the site of the Restorationists' former Morehead Academy. The following Christian-but-not-Restorationist schools presumably adopted "**Eagles**" for the described reasons: Benedictine U. (Lisle, Ill.), Biola U. (La Mirada, Calif.), Bridgewater [Va.] Coll., Coll. of Saint Elizabeth (Morristown, N.J.), Edgewood Coll. (Madison, Wis.), Emmaus Bible Coll. (Dubuque, Iowa), Northwest U. (Kirkland, Wash.), Oklahoma Wesleyan U., Southwestern Christian U. (Bethany, Okla.), and U. of the Ozarks (Clarksville, Ark.). Blue-and-gold **Golden Eagles** represent the Seventh-day Adventists' La Sierra University.

When Boston College's nameless maroon-and-gold athletes won a 1920 track meet, a news cartoon showed the team from University Heights on Chestnut Hill as a stray cat lapping up the competition like so much milk. An editorial by Rev. Edward McLaughlin in the Catholic school's own *Heights* reacted quickly, proposing "the Eagle, symbolic of majesty, power, and freedom. […] Surely the Heights is made to order for such a suggestion." A subsequent drawing of an eagle in that June's *Heights* made future athletes **Eagles**. See Nathaniel J. Hasenfus, *Athletics at Boston College* (Worcester, Mass.: Heffernan Press, 1943), cited in Reid Oslin, *Tales from the Boston College Sideline* (Champaign, Ill.: Sports Publishing L.L.C., 2004): 43. BC's bald eagle is "Baldwin," emphasis on -*win*.

[37] After teaching a semester at Mount Holyoke in 1850, Williams College professor Edward Lasell was inspired to start the country's first all-female junior college. Lasell died from typhoid fever the next year, immediately after the seminary now called Lasell College (Newton, Mass.) opened. For a century-plus, seniors have passed literal flames of knowledge to juniors in spring's Torchlight Parade, and the yearbook is the *Lamp* … themes of light with which Lasell's alliterative **Lasers** fit.

A maned lion represents Wheaton's **Lyons**, even though *Lyon* and *lion* have a strictly homophonic relationship. The school was financed by Judge and Mrs. Laban Wheaton as a memorial to their deceased daughter and should not be confused with Illinois's Wheaton College.

Saint Mary-of-the-Woods College (Saint Mary-of-the-Woods, Ind.) is another women's college with teams named for a longtime administrator. SMWC's **Pomeroys** remember 1921 grad and subsequent professor Mary Joseph Pomeroy SP.

[38] Having gone coed in 1988, Wheaton is out of the running for World's Oldest Women's College. Mount Holyoke is still the oldest among the Northeastern women's colleges called the Seven Sisters (from the myth in which seven daughters of Atlas were placed in the heavens by Zeus as the constellation *Pleiades*). The Sisters—which include Vassar, Wellesley, Smith, Radcliffe, Bryn Mawr, and Barnard—got together in 1927 to promote elite education for women at a time when most Ivy League colleges admitted only men.

[39] Barnard athletes compete as Columbia **Lions**. A similar relationship in Cambridge had athletes from the all-female Radcliffe College playing for Harvard's **Crimson**, but Radcliffe was fully absorbed by Harvard in 1999.

[40] Gwendolyn Evans Jensen, *Wilson College* (New York: Newcomen Soc., 1995): 22.

Chapter 22 Notes

[1] Good black baseballers in Kansas—the **Black Wonders**—became Wichita **Monrovians** for the same reasons. They dominated the 1922-only Colored Western League and hosted black and white teams for years. They famously beat Wichita's [Ku Klux] **Klan Number 6** in 1925, indicating some curious measure of coexistence. See Jason Pendleton, "Jim Crow Strikes Out:

Interracial Baseball in Wichita, Kansas, 1920–1935" in John E. Dreifort, ed., *Baseball History From Outside the Lines* (Lincoln: U. Nebraska Press, 2001): 147, 151.

[2] Shifting regional demographics and court-ordered diversity measures have given to some HBCUs—like Bluefield State and West Virginia State—student bodies that are mostly white. Black attendees at Missouri's Lincoln U. are no longer a vast majority.

[3] Britons crossed bulldog strength and terrier tenacity in fighting dogs, but much aggression has since been bred out of "pit bull terriers." Pitt [County] Community College (Greenville, N.C.) keeps "Pitt **Bulldogs**." That presumably puns on "pit bull," as did Pittsburgh's ABA Pennsylvania **Pit Bulls** (2004/05) and indoor lacrosse's Pittsburgh **Bulls** (1990–93).

[4] *Student Handbook 2012–2013* (Wilberforce, Ohio: Central State U., 2012): 21.

[5] See Kenneth J. Kinkor, "Black Men Under the Black Flag," in C.R. Pennell, ed., *Bandits at Sea* (New York: New York U. Press, 2001): 195.

[6] LMU had **Braves** until 1924 and **Airedales** until '31. The Aire River valley (*Airedale*) and England's own town of Harrogate are in Yorkshire, birthplace of many Cumberland Gap pioneers. America's first Airedale terriers may have been on Tennessee farms.

[7] Here are notes on institutional histories. Bethune-Cookman resulted from the merger of academies named for Mary M. Bethune (a civil rights leader born to slaves) and influential Methodist abolitionist Alfred Cookman. Coppin State's eponym was Fanny Jackson Coppin, born to slavery to become the longtime president of Cheyney. Hampton was founded after the Civil War by Presbyterian and Congregationalist missionaries. Maryland-Eastern Shore was a land-grant established because UMD College Park barred black attendees. Morgan State is named for prominent Methodist minister L.F. Morgan. North Carolina Central opened as the only black liberal arts college in the country funded by state taxes. Winston-Salem State was a black teachers' college. Delaware State, FAMU, and South Carolina State are land-grants.

[8] Alabama State's **Hornets** got named after playing like "underdogs that attack larger prey," according to a letter (18 Nov. 1935) from H. Councill Threnholm (president of State Teachers Coll., Montgomery) in George Earlie Shankle, *American Nicknames: Their Origin and Significance* (New York: H.W. Wilson, 1937): 498.

[9] AAMU and UAPB opened as black teachers' colleges. Alabama State and Alcorn State were land-grant colleges. Charles P. Adams graduated from Tuskegee and applied the principles of Booker T. Washington as Grambling State's first president. Jackson State was a Baptist school for freedmen. PVAMU was the state's black land-grant complement to Texas A&M. MVSU opened in 1950 to give white Mississippians something to indicate equal education for blacks in the face of federal pressure. One founder of Southern University (a Louisiana land-grant) was former Union captain P.B.S. Pinchback, who became the first state governor of African descent during Reconstruction. His namesake New Orleans **Pinchbacks** of the late 1880s were among black baseball's first great teams.

[10] See Miller's essay "Sport at Historically Black Colleges" in the volume he edited, *The Sporting World of the Modern South* (Chicago: U. Illinois Press, 2002): 134–135.

Morristown [Tenn.] College closed in 1994 after presenting a rare case of a team name designed to indicate an African American student body. "**Red Knights**" at first seems to indicate only red-and-black uniforms, but it did "pertain to the racial color and the fact the 'knight' is black." Don't blame us; we found that in a communication (21 Nov. 1935) from Morristown's own president, E.C. Paustian, who says "**Red Knights**" was chosen for those reasons by coach A.P. Graves in the early 1930s. Refer to Shankle, *American Nicknames* (1937): 362.

[11] Representing only 4 percent of colleges that play at the NCAA Division I level in at least one sport, "**Eagles**" is nonetheless the most popular team name. **Tigers** appear at the HBCUs at a rate two-and-a-half times that.

[12] Fast historical facts: Benedict's first teams were (Baptist) **Deacons**, but a student vote made

them **Tigers** in 1938; Jackson State was a Baptist Seminary at Natchez that moved to Jackson in 1882; Saint Paul's was founded by Episcopalians; Mr. Edward Waters was the third bishop in the African Methodist Episcopal Church; William Paul Quinn was the fourth; Stillman is a Presbyterian institute founded by Rev. C.A. Stillman. (In 1990, Paul Quinn College moved from Austin to the Dallas campus of a former HBCU, Bishop College, which was founded in 1881 and hosted **Bears** until closing in 1988.)

[13] Real tigers live in the jungles of India and Southeast Asia, but not everyone knew that, so African American athletes needed be only as confused as anybody else to have an affinity for "**Tigers**." Edgar Rice Burroughs put tigers in Africa in the 1912 serial version of *Tarzan of the Apes* but corrected that by the 1914 book publication. Cartoonists showed Teddy Roosevelt bagging tigers on a post-presidency African safari, and Melville listed tigers among interior Africa's dangers in *Moby Dick*. Nelson Mandela repeatedly debated fellow political prisoners in Africa as to whether tigers ever roamed their continent. See Mandela, *Long Walk to Freedom* (Boston: Little Brown, 1994, 1995): 430, 434.

[14] After the Civil War, Gen. O.O. Howard of the Freedmen's Bureau (and Howard U. fame) visited Atlanta schoolhouses. The inspiration he drew from the youngest of the newly freed was dramatized in the 1869 poem "Howard at Atlanta" by John Greenleaf Whittier. (See the Whittier College **Poets**, p. 221.) When Whittier's Howard asks what message he should bring north, one student exclaims, "Tell 'em we're rising." Having attended a makeshift school in Atlanta, Savannah State's founding president Richard R. Wright has been popularly identified as Whittier's vocal "black boy of Atlanta," although he's unnamed in the poem. See Andrew Billingsley, *Mighty Like a River* (New York: Oxford U. Press, 1999): 42–43.

[15] Evelyn Brooks Higginbotham, *Righteous Discontent: The Women's Movement in the Black Baptist Church, 1880–1920* (Cambridge, Mass.: Harvard U. Press, 1993): 25.

[16] Ron Chernow, *Titan: The Life of John D. Rockefeller, Sr.* (New York: Random House, 2007): 241.

[17] Morris Brown College was another HBCU component of the AUC Center until losing accreditation in 2002. That ending the run of its arbitrarily named **Wolverines**.

[18] Shortly after Union forces seized the Confederate capital of Richmond, Baptists founded two schools that have since unionized as Virginia Union University. Funds for Claflin's campus were donated by industrialist William Claflin, a progressive Methodist and a Massachusetts governor. Denmark Tech is a 1947-founded trade school. Philander Smith's widow financed missions in Asia before helping educate freed slaves. Prairie View A&M is a Texas land-grant. Programs at Simmons were established by ex-slave Dr. William Simmons, who'd run the normal school at Howard University.

[19] *Historical Barber-Scotia College: Student Handbook, 2008–2010* (Concord, N.C.: Barber-Scotia Coll., 2008): ii.

[20] Monika Rhue (JCSU lib. services dir.), email to the author, 13 Jan. 2005. "**Golden Bulls**" harkened back to the **Bull Pen** footballers that JCSU (then Biddle U.) presented in its inaugural 1890 season. (They won the first inter-HBCU gridiron game at Livingstone in 1892.)

[21] Miller, "Sport at Historically Black Colleges": 135. "**Sons of Milo**" probably seems unnecessarily paternalistic. We offer as only the mildest defense the great wrestler Milo of Croton, who famously triumphed in several sixth-century-BCE Olympiads, so scholarly athletes might have found some small bit of the comparison to appreciate.

Similarly, [Ichabod] Washburn University's **Ichabods** (p. 143) were originally **Sons of Ichabod**. The men at Michigan's Gogebic [County] Community College were "Sam's Sons" during the coaching tenure of Sam Dubow (1946–52), leading to **Samsons** and **Lady Samsons**. We're indebted to the institutional memory of Jeanne Graham (GCC dean of students) as relayed through an email to the author (6 Feb. 2013) from Dennis Mackey (GCC athletic dir.).

Chapter 23 Notes

[1] Beehives have suggested order, industry, and perseverance since Roman times. Bees represent the duality of God's pure love (honey) and his wrath (stinger). The Freemasons, a fraternity to which some early influential Mormons belonged, used beehive symbols liberally.

[2] "Elements of the Brand Identity System," *Communications Guide* (Torrington, Wyo.: Eastern Wyoming Coll., n.d.): 6.

[3] The Ute Tribal Council endorses UU's "**Utes**," insulating it from scrutiny. (The U's gymnasts are **Red Rocks**, for the red Navajo sandstone formations all over the Colorado Plateau.)

The **Utes**' mascot is a red-tailed hawk named Swoop. Other Swoops represent **RedHawks** at Miami of Ohio, **Cardinals** at Gadsden [Ala.] State Comm. Coll., and **Hawks** at both Hartwick and Roger Williams. The **Patriot** Eagle at the University of Texas at Tyler is named Swoop, as are **Eagle** mascots for Eastern Michigan, Eastern Washington, Emory, Houston Comm. Coll., Post University (Waterbury Conn.), and the NFL's Philadelphians.

You don't have to be an ethnogeographer to know there were never Uto-Aztecan people in upstate New York. Minor league baseball's Utica **Utes** (1910–17) were phonetically inspired, but based on the unavoidable psycholinguistic connection, Utica's basketball **Utes** (1913/14) were alternately "**Indians**."

[4] D. Louise Brown, "The Fire in the Bookstore and What Came of It," devotional address at the LDS Business College (Salt Lake City), 22 June 2010.

[5] By 1882 the Salt Lake-to-Butte line ran to the Yellowstone Valley, where the stop was named for recently retired Northern Pacific president Frederick Billings. Billings grew like magic and is now Montana's Magic City, explaining minor league hockey's Montana **Magic** (1983/84). Cattlemen, homesteaders, and mineral and coal miners continued arriving for decades. The last justify minor league basketball's Billings **RimRockers** (1998–2001).

[6] A leader of the St. George Stake was Erastus Snow, a Mormon elder and pioneer eponym of Snow College. (Snowflake, Arizona is named after Mr. Snow and fellow Mormon W.J. Flake.) Seeking wider recognition as part of the state university system, "**Rebels**" had to go when the former Dixie State systematically removed any references to southern themes except those that recognize the history of the Cotton Mission, although calling it U-of-U's "Dixie campus" isn't objectionable. (Owing to the Mormons' pioneer tradition, local independent baseballers were the Zion/St. George **Pioneerzz** from 1999 to 2001.)

Chapter 24 Notes

[1] Not all "German Quakers" were Quakers. Some weren't even German. That adjective applied to anyone from German-speaking principalities or neighboring parts of Switzerland, Poland, Bohemia, or France. The Amish and Mennonites did have Quaker-like beliefs, revering an inner light and embracing pacifism. One third of Pennsylvanians adhered to Peace Churches, so resentment from neighbors trudging off to various wars was common.

[2] *Deutsche* is really an Old High German autonym meaning "we non-Romanized locals."

[3] Baron Von Richthofen shot down more aircraft than any other Great War flier. The many German immigrants in eastern Pennsylvania could explain minor leaguers named for that "Red Baron," but despite their WWI fighter emblem, baseball's Scranton/Wilkes-Barre **Red Barons** (1998–2006) were named for two older clubs, the Scranton **Red Sox** (1939–51) and the Wilkes-Barre **Barons** (1888–1955).

[4] Baseball's UA Philadelphia **Keystones** played at Keystone Park in 1884. The next year Philly's black **Keystone Athletics** were formed (only to be absorbed by the famous **Cuban Giants** within months). Pittsburgh **Keystones** were in both the 1887 National Colored Base Ball League (the first black league, lasting only two weeks) and the 1922 NNL. Minor league hockey had Pittsburgh **Keystones** (1901–04). Baseball's Reading **Keystones** (1923–32) were International League contenders followed by minor league basketball's Reading **Keys** (1940s–

'50s). Allentown's NPSL Pennsylvania **Stoners** (est. 2007) copied the name of that city's ASL **Stoners** (1979–83). "**Stoners**" is at least a double entendre, being both a sobriquet for "Keystoners" and a reference to local limestone quarries. A 1977 WTT team of stars from the USSR was to play at both ends of the state in Philadelphia and Pittsburgh, and so would be Pennsylvania **Keystones**, but when the tennis season started they were the **Soviet** National Team.

[5] "A New Nickname," *University Hatchet* (27 Oct. 1926): 2. (Courtesy of GWU's Special Collections Research Center at the Gelman Library.) The yearbook at the University of [George] Washington in St. Louis is also the *Hatchet*.

[6] Stony Brook acknowledges seawolves as good luck totems of the Tlingit people on Alaska's southeastern coast, but **Seawolves** return the school to the aquatic theme of its first teams of **Soundsmen**. In early 1959 that became the sporting identity after being suggested by a member of the school's oldest team, crew, which practices on the inlets of Long Island Sound. The front page of the campus paper made a gleeful report: "We are glad that we now have a name like other colleges for our teams […] that will last throughout the years." That lasted one year, until teams were recast as **Warriors**. "**Patriots**" followed in 1966. See J. Rodger Morphett, ed., "Soundsmen, New Nickname," *Sucolian* (18 Feb. 1959): 1.

[7] There's no such critter as a sea wolf, so Stony Brook's mascot is an oceangoing wolf. Ditto for the **Seawolves** at Southern Maine Community College (South Portland), the University of New Brunswick-Saint John, and minor league baseball's Erie [Pa.] **SeaWolves** (1995–). Erie's pup wears an eyepatch because "sea wolf" is a sometime synonym for "pirate," and the **SeaWolves** were in fact Pittsburgh **Pirate** affiliates at their 1998 founding. Similarly, "sea dog" describes a veteran sailor or privateer, and the only **Sea Dogs** we can find are in two of those same towns: minor league baseball's Portland **Sea Dogs** (est. 1994) and junior hockey's Saint John **Sea Dogs** (est. 2005). (Both have seal mascots, which are also colloquial "sea dogs.")

[8] "**Ephmen**" and "**Ephwomen**" are casual alternates to "**Ephs**." British soldiers of the Revolution added a verse to *Yankee Doodle* in which a cowardly "Brother Ephraim sold his cow, and bought him a Commission," indicating the lack of respect Continental officers received from the British, their brothers-in-arms in past wars. The **Eephs**' purple cow mascot comes from a campus humor magazine called *The Purple Cow*, having printed the whimsical single-verse poem "The Purple Cow" by humorist Gelett Burgess on the first cover in 1907. Did the choice of Burgess's cow have anything to do with the *Doodle* ditty? We'd like to think so, but only because that's the most historically apt of many proposed backstories. We do know that purple became the school color when female fans came to see Williams players off to a Harvard match in 1865. Realizing there was no counter to Harvard's **Crimson** they hurriedly slapped purple ribbons on the players. See Leverett Wilson Spring, *A History of Williams College* (Boston and New York: Houghton Mifflin, 1917): 297–298.

Animosity between the teams from their eponymous college would likely have surprised Col. Williams and fellow British officer Jeffery Amherst. The rivalry between the **Ephs** and **Lord Jeffs** dates to a time when some of Williams's own trustees thought they were too far west in Massachusetts. They moved east to found Amherst College in 1821. First played in 1884, the season-ending D-III football game between the **Ephs** and those they can only call the "Defectors" is The Biggest Little Game in America. The same rivalry led to history's first intercollegiate "base ball" game at Pittsfield on July 1, 1859. Amherst edged out Williams 73-32 using the rules of the Massachusetts Game, which called for overhand pitching and catching the ball in the air to record an out (as opposed to one hop), ideas absorbed by the New York Knickerbocker rules that would become the blueprint for modern baseball in the Civil War era.

[9] *Vert Mont* is not an artifact of French exploration; it was the pseudo-archaic placename that English speakers invented by translating "green mountain" to French. See Joseph-Andre Senecal, "Samuel de Champlain and the Naming of Vermont," *Vermont History* (Barre, Vt.: Vermont Hist. Soc., summer/fall 2009): 119.

[10] The state's two-letter abbreviation is "Vt.," but U. Vermont's call letters are UVM because its Latin name is *Universitas Viridis Montis*: "university of the green mountains." Its 1791 founding was driven by Ira Allen, the politician most responsible for turning Burlington into an important Lake Champlain town.

Similarly, Middlebury's shield abbreviates the Latin phrase *Collegium Medioburiense Viridis Montis*: "Middlebury College of the Green Mountains." (Middlebury had **Black** **Panthers** in the early 1920s, but the adjective was later dropped.)

[11] Lauren Davidson, "What's in a Name?" *Dickinson Magazine* (1 Oct. 2009): 13. Davidson also reports on administration efforts to make teams **Colonials** in 1936. That was rejected by students, which makes sense because DU was established in 1783, which actually made it the first U.S. college to open *after* independence was secured through revolution.

[12] The **Tea Men** were backed by the Lipton tea company. They kept their name and clipper ship emblem when they set off for the port of Jacksonville, Florida for 1984 and 1985. Philip J. Deloria uses Boston's Tea Party to examine metaphorical Indianness and the history of co-opted Indian mascots in *Playing Indian* (New Haven, Conn.: Yale U. Press, 1998).

[13] WC's **Shoremen** participate in the annual "War on the Shore" lacrosse game against Salisbury U.'s **Sea Gulls** (whose women were **She Gulls** from 1966 to '83). Salisbury's Delmarva **Shorebirds** are affiliates of the Baltimore **Orioles**. *Delmarva* is a peninsula east of Chesapeake Bay that includes parts of Delaware, Maryland, and Virginia. Having strayed this far, we might mention that the University of Maryland Eastern Shore (in Princess Anne) fields **Hawks**, represented by flying raptors, which—like **Seagulls** and **Shorebirds**—live in Delmarva's wetlands and forests. Other bay neighbors included the MLL Baltimore **Bayhawks** (est. 2001). They moved to the nation's capital as the Washington **Bayhawks** in 2007 but returned to bayside Maryland (Annapolis) in 2010 as Chesapeake **Bayhawks**.

Chapter 25 Notes

[1] Henry's words weren't in print until 1816, after Washington insider William Wirt had used interviews and recollections to reconstruct the ideal oration for his Henry biography.

[2] UMass's **Minutemen** were maroon-colored **Aggies** (until 1948) and **Redmen** (until 1972). An NASL side anticipated the 1976 Bicentennial as Boston **Minutemen** (1974–76). Women play tackle football in the Somerville suburb as the Boston **Militia** (est. 2007).

Bostonians called Redcoats "lobsters" (although members of the olive green *Homarus americanus* species of New England and Canadian Maritime coasts turn red only when boiled). In the 1970s, the World Team Tennis Boston **Lobsters** weighed in, and Portland's Maine **Red Claws** (est. 2009) play D-League basketball.

[3] The **76ers** are the former Syracuse **Nationals**, revealing origins in the *National* Basketball League. When they moved, "Philadelphia **Nationals**" would have been patriotic enough in the birthplace of America. In fact, Philadelphia **Nationals** did play pro football as early as 1902, backed by baseball's *National* League **Phillies**. (See Harold "Spike" Claassen, *The History of Professional Football* [Englewood Cliffs, N. J., Prentice-Hall, 1963]: 13.) But in 1963 the Syracusans filled the void left by the recently departed Philadelphia **Warriors** as "76ers." Owing to the team's origins in 1939, the **Sixers** claim to be the NBA's oldest franchise.

In 2013 the **76ers** acquired Orem's D-League Utah **Flash** (2007–11) and moved them to Newark as Delaware **87ers**, commemorating the first state to ratify the Constitution on December 7, 1787.

Viterbo University (La Crosse, Wis.) started intercollegiate sports in 1972 with male basketballers anticipating the Bicentennial as **Seventy-Sixers**. When a new athletics center opened in 1986, the name with no esoteric appeal was abandoned for "**V-Hawks**."

[4] Stan Gorski (PhilaU archives), email to the author, 11 June 2010.

[5] Twain was born Samuel Clemens in 1835 and experienced boyhood in Hannibal, Missouri. His 1868 short story "Cannibalism in the Cars" was suggested by minor league baseball's Hannibal **Cannibals** (1908–12).

[6] In 1975, Elton John had a huge hit with a tribute song for Ms. King, "Philadelphia Freedom." His 1973 smash "Bennie and the Jets" gave the name *Benny* to the furry mascot of the Winnipeg **Jets** … then owned by *Ben* Hatskin.

[7] When the **Eclipse** faced Toledo's **Blue Stockings** on May 1, 1884, the **Stockings'** star catcher Moses Fleetwood Walker became the first African American major leaguer.

[8] Being named after British ground troops makes IUS's **Grenadiers** similar to the Frontier League's Ohio Valley **Redcoats**. The '**Coats** had trouble finding a ballpark, playing much of their interrupted history (1993–2005) in various Ohio and Indiana cities.

[9] Poor health kept Stark from attending an 1809 reunion of Bennington veterans. From his native New Hampshire he wrote in: "Live Free Or Die; Death Is Not The Worst of Evils." The first part is now the state motto, inspiring the New Hampshire/Manchester **Freedom** (est. 2001) of women's football.

[10] Basketball's MBL Kingston **Colonials** of the 1920s recalled Kingston's early history. Same-named ABLers (1935–39) may have been sponsored by the Colonial Cities gas stations. See David B. Biesel, *Can You Name That Team?* (Lanham, Md.: Scarecrow, 2002): 36.

[11] Two Mecklenburg County basketball crews, the Davidson College **Wildcats** and UNC Charlotte **49ers**, play annually for the Hornet's Nest Trophy.

[12] On August 25, 2005, Katrina crashed upon the Gulf Coast as a category 3 hurricane. It was the third-strongest hurricane ever to make landfall in the U.S., but most of the death and destruction owed to subsequent levee failures. That sent the **Hornets** north as "New Orleans-Oklahoma City **Hornets**." They had some success, but the NBA didn't want the PR nightmare of abandoning a historic city that was reeling from catastrophe, so the **Hornets** returned for the 2007/08 season. With the OKC market having proved viable, the league allowed Seattle's **Supersonics** to become the **Thunder** in 2008.

[13] Stories persist that Franklin and Marshall footballers were called **Diplomats** after a 1935 loss to Fordham's favored **Rams**. Leading at halftime, the **Big Blue** or **Nevonians** (named for an F&M president of the previous century, John W. Nevin) supposedly wasted enough time in the locker room to earn a delay of game penalty, spurring Fordham to victory. Sportswriters are said to have compared that careful but ineffective deliberation to the snail's pace of diplomacy. Jill Schoeniger, however, has uncovered evidence to disprove all; "**Diplomats**" clearly predates the Fordham game by at least a season, reinforcing notions that the diplomacy of the institutional eponyms yielded the team name. See Schoeniger, "Deciphering Our Diplomatic Heritage," *Franklin and Marshall Magazine* (spring 2005): 28–31.

[14] Kentucky's Fayette County was named for the Marquis de Lafayette in 1780, and the village of Hopewell became *Paris* in appreciation. (Many cities named after the marquis—Lafayette, Fayetteville, Fayette—often host minor league **Generals**.) Fayette County split in 1785, and Paris went into Bourbon County, named for the family that would rule France until 1830. More than thirty new counties were later cut from it, but distillers remained identified with "Old Bourbon." That's how Kentucky whiskey—*bourbon*—became a moniker for regional teams, including Paris **Bourbonites** (1909–12) and Paris **Bourbons** (1922–24), both in baseball's Blue Grass League. Kentucky **Bourbons** of men's pro softball are more recent (1977–82).

[15] The NPSL New York **Generals** (1967–68) had a four-star insignia but were named for owners at RKO General, created by the 1955 merger of RKO Pictures and General Tire.

[16] Correspondence from Coach Ira Wilson (eponym of SUNY-G's ice arena) in George Earlie Shankle, *American Nicknames: Their Origin and Significance* (New York: H.W. Wilson, 1937): 498. SUNY-G's aquatic athletes are a **Blue Wave**.

[17] Stacy Johnson (CCC athletics coordinator), email to the author, 28 May 2009. Also turning to the funny papers, students at Bismarck [N.C.] State College made basketballers **Mystics** in 1940 after somebody saw a cartoon of "a wizard or magician or something." See Irene Voth, "Mystic Mascot Derived From 1940 Cartoon," *BSC Mystician* (28 March 1988).

[18] Thanks anyway to multiple emails to the author (Feb.–Mar. 2012) from OSU Lima reference librarians Rene Hunter and Tina Schneider and athletic director Rob Livchak.

Chapter 26 Notes

[1] See George and Darril Fosty, *Black Ice: The Lost History of The Colored Hockey League of the Maritimes* (New York: Stryker-Indigo, 2007): 57.

[2] Fosty and Fosty, *Black Ice*: 57.

[3] The **Dutchmen's** Olympic coach was Bobby Bauer, from Boston's high-scoring line of the 1930s and '40s (alongside **Bruins** Woody Dumart and Milt Schmidt). Owing to their German surnames, the Hall of Fame trio was the Kraut Line. But even references to German cuisine were distasteful during World War II—sauerkraut was "liberty cabbage" for the duration—so the boys were usually "Kitchener Kids." They were together in the military on Ottawa's Royal Canadian Air Force **Flyers**, wartime semi-pros that won the 1942 Allan Cup. For the '43 cup, the Canadian Army's Ottawa **Commandos** used star New York **Rangers** to beat Victoria **Army**. (For the dispersal of NHL talent to Canada's amateur leagues during World War II, see Don MacEachern, "Where the Stars Were: Service Hockey in Western Canada in 1942–43," *Hockey Research Journal* [fall 2004]: 39 *ff.*) Canadians began resenting amateur leagues stocked with NHL talent while sons and neighbors fought the war, so **Flyers** and **Commandos** found themselves flying and commando-ing all over Europe, and all three Kitchener Kids spent the last two years of the war on combat duty. The **Bruins'** Kraut Line reassembled for 1945, playing two seasons until Bauer retired to help sell the family's Bauer skates. As juniors, all three had been Kitchener **Greenshirts**. (We've been unable to confirm that the first team of that name—as early as 1917—commemorated the green jackets worn by loyalist British corps, including the Queen's Rangers, whose namesake **Rangers** are mentioned in the main text.)

[4] The University of Waterloo's women became the **Athenas** in 1968 just to slip away from "**Bananas**," a nickname from their yellow one-piece court uniforms, but they joined the men as **Warriors** in 1997. These identities are of a tangled history. Waterloo College Associate Facilities started as part of Waterloo College, itself subordinate to London's University of Western Ontario. UWO teams were **Mustangs**, so **Mules** and **Mulettes** at WCAF/WC indicated their smaller stature … a precedent already established by Western's junior varsity **Colts**. By 1960 these were three independent universities, so WCAF presented independent **Warriors**. At the same time, Waterloo College became Waterloo Lutheran University and switched colors to purple and gold and changed **Mules** to **Golden Hawks**. (Waterloo Lutheran has been Wilfrid Laurier University since 1973.) U. Waterloo's team names are chronicled in its athletics alumni newsletter: "A Fruitful Beginning," *Gold and Black* (July 2006): 1–2.

One might wonder why the University of Western Ontario isn't in westernmost Ontario. When it was still British Upper Canada, land beyond the Ottawa River was settled in an east-to-west direction across the top of Lakes Ontario and Erie, where populations remain the most dense. Ontarians still give directions in those terms.

[5] The "**Little Corporals**" nickname is verified by a communication (25 Nov. 1935) from Leonard L. Thomas (Bethel's president) in George Earlie Shankle, *American Nicknames: Their Origin and Significance* (New York: H.W. Wilson, 1937): 42.

Chapter 27 Notes

[1] The 1871 **Kekiongas** (or simply "**Kekionga**") comprised players from the disbanded Maryland Base Ball Club. When they folded half-way through the NA season, club **Kekionga** was replaced by Brooklyn's **Eckford** Club.

[2] A fort named for Gen. Wayne was in Michigan's Wayne County, where—like Indiana Tech—Detroit's Wayne State University hosts **Warriors**. That's not Indian-related; it has ties to former **Tartars** teams. The Tartars are a Turkic-Mongolian people across Eastern Europe, but they have a long history of armed conflict with neighbors in east-central Asia.

Wayne State's early squads were **Griffins** and **Munies**, respective names from the mythical bird and the university's midtown (*municipal*) location. "**Tartars**" was adopted in 1927, and "**Warriors**" in 1999. California's El Camino College Compton Center posts the other collegiate **Tartars**, named presumably for their warrior spirit. Wayne College is a branch of U. Akron in Ohio's Wayne County (which is also named from Mad Anthony), but we've been unable to find a backstory for its own mascotless **Warriors**.

[3] Earlier LCSC teams were **Pioneers** (1923–39) and **Loggers** (1938–51). The school closed in 1952 and reopened three years later with **Warriors**.

[4] Alternate explanations for **Penguins** in Clark's huddle involve toy or mechanical penguins left lying around its original building (possibly other promotional items from *Kool*.) See Tom Koenninger, ed., "Let's Give Clark College a Mascot with a Little Bit of Historical Bite," *The Columbian*, 14 March 1999: b.11. (Assisting emails to the author, 7 and 10 April 2006 respectively, from Joey Merritt-Dennis [ref. lib.] and Lukas Bardue [assoc. P.R. dir.], Clark Coll.) The world's northernmost penguins are equatorial straddlers off Ecuador's coast called Galapagos penguins (*Spheniscus mendiculus*), so Clark's yearbook is the *Galapagon*.

[5] North Bridgewater, Massachusetts was renamed Brockton in 1874 after a local traveler suggested that the name of Brockville, Ontario (another Isaac B. namesake) was pleasant-sounding enough to be modified. Heavyweight champ and favorite son Rocco "Rocky" Marciano (1923-1969) was the "Brockton Rock," commemorated by minor league baseball's Brockton **Rox** (est. 2002) … spelled like the **Red Sox** just to the north.

[6] Blockade-running Baltimore clipper's inspired minor league basketball's Baltimore **Bayrunners** (1999/2000). To rub in the privateering innuendo, their blue crab wore an eyepatch. Maryland's state crustacean, the blue crab (*Callinectes sapidus*), is economically important to the Chesapeake region. A crab suspiciously similar to that of the **Bayrunners** represented Baltimore County's minor league basketball Maryland **Bayraiders** (2008).

[7] The land of the **Vols** is "Big Orange Country." The UT color was supposedly adopted in 1889 from the orange-and-white daisies growing on "The Hill" on the east campus … although there are no orange daisies in North America.

[8] Minor league baseballers in Iowa have historically poked fun at the numerous sporting **Colonels** while good naturedly drawing attention to their own reputations as corn-fed hicks. Contemporary examples are the single-A Cedar Rapids **Kernels**, so named in 1993. Minnesota's Concordia College **Cobbers** have a corn-cob mascot named Kernel, and the *Kentucky Kernel* has been the campus newspaper of the UK **Wildcats** since 1915.

[9] Ken Golner (Curry sports info. dir.), email to the author, 4 Jan. 2005. The School of Elocution had actually started in 1879 as the vision of Anna Baright, who became Mrs. Curry three years later. Together they nurtured the institution renamed for them in 1943.

[10] Baltimoreans tried replacing the **Colts** with an NFL franchise of Baltimore **Bombers**. That bubble burst when expansion teams went to Jacksonville and Charlotte in '95, but it was all good the next year when Cleveland's **Browns** became Baltimore **Ravens**.

[11] Illinois's Fort Dixon went up on the Rock River during Black Hawk's War. Today, the city of Dixon's Sauk Valley Community College explains **Skyhawks** through vague references to a "mythical bird." The University of Wisconsin–Baraboo/Sauk County doesn't really explain its **Fighting Spirits** or cartoon ghost mascot either. **Hawks** and **Spirits** elsewhere sometimes owe to Indian traditions, but if these *Sauk* schools co-opt such themes, they do so without saying.

[12] An earlier PCHA team had already been Portland **Rosebuds** (1914–18), as had a team in Abe Saperstein's 1946 West Coast Negro Baseball League. Portland's climate is ideal for rose

growing, and rosebush-lined avenues made it a "City of Roses" even before its first annual Rose Festival in 1907. The main arena is the Rose Quarter's Rosegarden. The alternate "Rose City" jersey of the Portland **Timbers** has a rose-and-thorn motif, so their women partners in the NWSL are Portland **Thorns** F.C. (est. 2013).

[13] Eric Duhatschek et al., *Hockey Chronicles: An Insider History of National Hockey League Teams* (New York: Checkmark, 2001): 63. The **Black Hawks** moved their farm team (the Edmonton **Oil Kings**) back to the **Rosebuds'** old turf in 1976 and dumped used pro uniforms on them. The chief-on-the-chest made them Portland **Winter Hawks**, but they too have been one-word **Winterhawks** since 2009.

Chapter 28 Notes

[1] The Arawaks also roasted the American manatee (*Trichechus manatus latirostris*), which lives in brackish and warm coastal waters of the Caribbean and Southeast. They're loaded with meat, but hunting the state marine animal is now illegal. The Brevard County **Manatees** (est. 1994) are Florida State Leaguers in Melbourne. The Gulf Coast's Sarasota and Manatee Counties were served by Manatee Community College, renamed the State College of Florida in summer 2009 when **Lancers** became **Manatees**.

[2] Lafitte's Galveston refuge was called *Campeachy*, after a Spanish port on Mexico's Yucatan Peninsula, *San Francisco de Campeche*. Its massive fortifications defended against Maya warriors and English privateers, the latter inspiring triple-A ball's *Piratas de Campeche*.

[3] ECU's black-bearded mascot is PeeDee the Pirate. (The Pee Dee River's banks were buccaneer hideouts.) A century later a different Blackbeard appeared, a British pirate. He was lying low at Baltimore when the War of 1812 broke out. Blackbeard II thought the U.S. was wise to his Spanish silver, so his crew made for Canada on the Susquehanna watershed. Fearing the American forces near the Niagara Frontier, Blackbeard buried his booty in a yet-undiscovered location in Pennsylvania's McKean County. His cruise past Millersville is the best explanation for the black-bearded pirates associated with the alliterative Millersville University **Marauders** (although the school provides no backstory).

As with Millersville, the relatively few collegiate **Marauders** usually represent some *M*-school. They're at the University of Mary (Bismarck, N.D.) and the University of Wisconsin–Marshfield/Wood County, both a thousand miles from any ocean but with pirate-marauder mascots. For raptor raiders, see the **Marauders** at McMaster U. (Hamilton, Ont.) and **Marauding Eagles** at Marycrest International U. (Davenport, Iowa) (which closed in 2002). The only four-year school with non-*M* **Marauders** is Ohio's Central State U. (McMaster's jocks had been **Maroons** [1930s–45] and **Rams** [1945–48], according to Ian Speers, "A History of Football at McMaster," *McMaster Marauder Football: 2006 Media Guide*: 9.)

[4] Cal Maritime's teams were **Seawolves** until 1974. Their bearded captain mascot was named Golden Beard in 2014 to refer to their state grizzly symbol, their training vessel (the *Golden Bear*), and other **Golden Bears** in California (p. 194).

[5] Five years after Oakland's NFL **Raiders** appeared, Michigan's Oakland [County] Community College opened, now fielding its own *Oakland* **Raiders**. Founded in Cook County, Illinois in 1969, Oakton Community College has recognizable *Oakton* **Raiders**. When the NFL **Raiders** moved to Los Angeles in 1982, their abandoned territory was seized upon by USFL Oakland **Invaders** (1983–85).

[6] Herbert G. Florcken, *The History of Modesto Junior College* (1956), cited by Shawn M. Cramton, "Analyze This: Shiver Me Timbers!" *Innovations* (Yosemite Comm. Coll. Dist., vol. 5, Jan./Feb. 2006): 4.

[7] Saint Patrick introduced Roman masonry and clay construction techniques to Ireland, so March 17 (the Feast of St. Patrick) sees special events at several tech colleges.

[8] Brian Gibboney (MSOE sports info. dir.), email to the author, 3 April 2008.

[9] Randy Kennedy, "Joseph Driscoll, 70; Educator Opposed Antiwar Protesters," *New York Times Biographical Service*, vol. 24 (New York: New York Times, Arno Press, 1977): 1481.

[10] In 1774 the Continental Congress first convened in Philadelphia but sat later at many virtual national capitals. During its stay at York, Pennsylvania, the Articles of Confederation were drafted, patriotism commemorated by baseball's minor league York **Revolution** (est. 2007).

[11] Lindsay Anderberg (NYU-Poly archives), email to the author, 8 Nov. 2011.

[12] Todd Rudat (Millikin archives), email to the author, 17 Jan. 2006. There were often Decatur **Commodores** in minor league baseball between 1900 and 1974.

[13] WIU's bulldog is Colonel Rock (after Rock Hanson). The Marines' association with bulldogs dates to World War I, when German soldiers (at least according to American reporters) called them *teufelshunde*—"devil dogs"—after a bad-ass canine in Bavarian myths.

Chapter 29 Notes

[1] U. Missouri's mascot is Truman the Tiger, after the Missouri-born and -bred president who is also the eponym for K.C.'s Harry S Truman Sports Complex (which includes stadiums for the **Chiefs** and **Royals**).

[2] In his later years Mr. Lawrence founded Lawrence University (Appleton, Wis.). LU's **Vikings** are typical of the Scandinavian-settled Midwest. (They replaced **Blues** in 1926.)

Any head-to-head test between the Kansas **Jayhawks** and Missouri **Tigers** is part of the Border Showdown, a unique cross-sport rivalry. (Even in meets that neither KU nor "Mizzou" wins, their relative standings are compared.) Until 2004 it was a Border *War*, but that metaphor was ditched out of respect for Americans on combat duty in Iraq and Afghanistan. Also, the original Kansas Jayhawkers and Missouri tigers both had Union sympathies and were therefore never opposed in armed conflict.

The abbreviations for the Universities of Kansas and Missouri are KU and MU because teams that are inland from older colleges often reverse their initials to avoid confusion. Observe that convention at CU (University of Colorado), DU (University of Denver), NU (University of Nebraska), OU (University of Oklahoma), and TU (University of Tulsa).

[3] Scrappy blue jays often stand up to larger hawks and owls. Elizabethtown College athletic director Ira R. Herr noted this attitude when he switched blue-and-gray **Gray Ghosts** (or **Phantoms**) to **Blue Jays** in the late 1930s. See "Traditions and Special Events" (Elizabethtown, Pa.: College Life Office of Elizabethtown Coll., 2007): 2.

[4] Communication (22 Nov. 1935) from Robert H. Ruff, president of Central Coll., in George Earlie Shankle, *American Nicknames: Their Origin and Significance* (New York: H.W. Wilson, 1955): 99. Assisting email to the author from Nicholas Petrone (CMU sports info. dir.), 15 May 2013.

[5] See James L. Forsythe, *Lighthouse on the Plains: Fort Hays State University* (Hays, Kan.: Fort Hays State U., 2002): 272, and Pat Jordan, "Tiger Mascot Reaches His Prime," *University Leader*, 14 Oct. 1982): 13. (Patty Nicholas [FHSU archives], assisting email to the author, 18 Dec. 2009.)

[6] Tiger Sports, "Tiger Hall of Fame: Dan Stark," http://www.cowleytigers.com/halloffame/hofstark.html (accessed 6 Jan. 2012).

Chapter 30 Notes

[1] LMU's teams were **Braves** until 1926, **Airedales** until 1930, and then **Railsplitters**.

[2] Alderson-Broaddus resulted from a 1932 merger of two Baptist institutions, so pre-**Battlers** on Battle Hill were sometimes **Battling Bishops** according to a communication (19 Nov. 1935) from Jeannette Samuals (A-B's phys-ed dir.) in George Earlie Shankle, *American Nicknames: Their Origin and Significance* (New York: H.W. Wilson, 1937): 14.

[3] The **Blue Jackets'** stars-and-bars imagery always tied them to the Ohio state flag and Union

sentiments, but only at the 2011 All-Star Game was the **Blue Jacket** explicitly identified as a Union soldier. (The NHL had hired legendary superhero creator Stan Lee to produce thirty franchise-specific "guardians.") Until then, the **Jackets** claimed no particular backstory. Some suggested the honoree was Chief Blue Jacket of the Shawnee, who handed the young U.S. some disheartening military defeats in the Ohio Country. Nationwide Insurance built a downtown arena to lure an NHL team, effecting rumors that blue-suited insurance agents were the original *jackets*. But when the **Blue Jackets** were activated in 2000 (along with the Minnesota **Wild**), all expansion in the preceding decade had occurred in California, Canada, and the American South, so it's been offered that "**Blue Jackets**" was a Yankee-friendly counterbalance. Another Columbus team was the 1992-only WLAF Ohio **Glory**, also wrapped in the flag's colors. One of the more popular Civil War movies, *Glory*, had been released just three years earlier (although it was about a Massachusetts regiment). Minor league hockey's star-spangled Columbus **Stars** collapsed halfway through their only season in 2004.

[4] Some think Auburn University's "War Eagle" is either the mascot or the nickname, but it's neither. "War Eagle!" is a game-day battle cry from the post–Civil War period.

[5] Brittany Columbia (LWC public services lib.), email to the author, 2 June 2010. Ms. Columbia says that LWC formerly fielded **Blue and White**, **Blue Tornadoes**, and **Hillers**. (Today's Blue Raider Bob mascot is a musketeer with no Civil War connection.) **Eagles** at Lock Haven University of Pennsylvania were once "Morgan's **Raiders**," but only during the coaching tenure of Raymond Morgan (1929–30). Lock Havenites were also **Wolverines** when Sol Wolf coached them (1923, 1934). See Shankle, *American Nicknames* (1937): 501.

[6] Another Sheridan College is in an Oakville, Ontario neighborhood named for Irish playwright and politician R.B. Sheridan (1751–1816). Its **Bruins** were named arbitrarily in 1967.

[7] Kimberly Stokes Pak, "Dr. Lindsey Mock Interview," CSU Oral History Project, http://archives.columbusstate.edu/oral_history/Mock_Lindsey.pdf (accessed 15 Aug. 2013).

[8] Richard Bak, *A Place for Summer: A Narrative History of Tiger Stadium* (Detroit: Wayne State U. Press, 1998): 40. See also Mike Lessiter, *The Names of the Games* (Chicago: Contemporary Books, 1988): 13.

[9] Bak, *A Place for Summer*: 46–48.

[10] Being east of the Mississippi floodplain, Ole Miss had the **Flood** until 1935. Its red and blue are from Harvard crimson and Yale blue, according to "The Bondurant Years," http://classics.olemiss.edu/history/the-bondurant-years (accessed 16 March 2011).

Chapter 31 Notes

[1] "Old West" can refer to anything beyond the Mississippi, so let's include those **Mustangs** at Central Baptist Coll. (Conway, Ark.), Marygrove Coll. (Detroit), Los Medanos College (Pittsburg, Calif.), and two Iowa schools, Morningside Coll. (Sioux City) and Mount Mercy U. (Cedar Rapids). As the last few schools suggest, **Mustangs** are often alliterative, explaining eastern **Mustangs** at Monroe Coll. (New Rochelle, N.Y.), Morrisville [N.Y.] State Coll., and Mount Ida Coll. (Newton, Mass.)

[2] The only source floating this backstory is UAH's concrete canoeing club, www.uah.edu/student_life/organizations/ASCE/Articles/YoungHistory/Youngarticletext.htm (accessed 5 Sep. 2013). "Concrete canoeing" itself adequately describes a design and racing competition among engineering schools.

Accomplished equestrians are among the **Chargers** at Colby-Sawyer College (New London, N.H.), where the rural campus consumes some of the former Colby family farm.

[3] UTPA is scheduled to merge with UT-Brownsville in 2015 to create UT-Rio Grande Valley. At press time, there's no word on a nickname or mascot for the new institution.

A.J. Rider became the first president of Trenton [N.J.] Business College in 1865. It was Rider Business College by 1897 and Rider University in 1994. The eastern college inevitably got saddled with Rider **Broncs**.

[4] The Kansas City **Chiefs'** pinto mascot is *Warpaint*. A Virginia college had a pinto mascot for its **Indians** from the 1930s to the 1960s. He was Wampo: *William And Mary pony*.

[5] Another Texas Tech token of Spanish history is its mounted Masked Rider, who gallops in ahead of the **Red Raider** footballers. Except for his crimson Spanish cape, the rider is all black, while a mask and bolero hide his identity. This inevitably effects comparisons to Zorro, the caped vigilante of Spanish-era Los Angeles who appeared in a 1919 Johnston McCulley novel and nearly every media format since. Northwest of L.A., Moorpark's Moorpark College **Raiders** ditched their pirate in 2008 for an explicitly Zorro-like mascot.

[6] *Sahuaro* is Spanish for the Sonoran Desert's tall saguaro cactus (*Carnegiea gigantea*), but the ranch was set up and named by Anglo settlers from Illinois in 1886. Several teams of **Sahuaros** have played minor league soccer and baseball around Phoenix since the early 1990s.

[7] Klein was at home throwing around potential names for his team, including **Matadors** and **Toreadors** (both being bullfighters). His son joked that those were "a bunch of bull," thus "Chicago **Bulls**." (Alex Sachare, *The Chicago Bulls Encyclopedia* [Chicago: Contemporary, 1999]: 7.) Klein's obituary differs but has the same son wandering in to the living room with Munro Leaf's popular 1936 children's book about a peaceful bull, *Ferdinand*. (Walt Disney's cartoon adaptation, *Ferdinand the Bull,* won a 1938 Oscar.) See Michael Hirsley, "Dick Klein, Bulls' Founder And 1st Ceo, Dies At 80," *Chicago Tribune*, 12 Oct. 2000.

[8] The timeline is from a letter (19 Nov. 1935) from John J. Schourmer (Armour Inst. athletic dir.) in George Earlie Shankle, *American Nicknames: Their Origin and Significance* (New York: H.W. Wilson, 1937): 20.

[9] The NBL/NBA Anderson [Ind.] **Packers** (1945–51) were also Midwesterners. They were alternately "Anderson Duffy" **Packers** for meat processor Ike Duffy (the NBL president who helped create the NBA in 1949). The city of Anderson is named for Delaware chief William Anderson (*Kikthawenund*), so the early **Packers** were sometime **Chiefs**. The Kansas City **Packers** were in baseball's Federal League, and the 2003-named minor league Kansas City **T-Bones** (with a bullish mascot *Sizzler*) represent one cut of meat. The Western League had two sets of baseball **Packers** (Sioux City: 1900s–20s; Omaha: 1930s). Omaha was once a stopover for hooves headed to Chicago and later a pork- and beef-packing center in its own right, as indicated by the WL Omaha **Omahogs** (1888–1901) and indoor football's Omaha **Beef** (est. 2000). The Iowa **Chops** (2008/09 AHL, Des Moines) referred to the Iowa chop (a lean center-cut of loin or rib meat). We're reminded of Iowa's packing industry (which is now the country's largest) by the bronze hog trophy that goes to winners of the football match between the Universities of Iowa and Minnesota, but that story ain't cute. **Hawkeye** Ozzie Simmons took an inordinate number of rough hits in a 1934 game against the **Golden Gophers**. That raised suspicions because Simmons was black, effecting memories of Jack Trice, an African American from Iowa State who'd died from injuries inflicted by **Gophers** in 1923. (ISU's Jack Trice Stadium is his memorial.) To ease tensions before the '35 game, governors of both states bet a prize hog. In defeat, an Iowa pig from Rosedale was shipped to the St. Paul offices of Gov. Floyd Olson, forever remembered by the Floyd of Rosedale prize.

[10] Colorado Mesa's **Mavericks** are explained in a communication (15 Nov. 1935) from the unnamed athletic director at what was then Grand Junction Community College. It's referenced in Shankle, *American Nicknames* (1937): 211.

[11] The origin for NOC's **Mavericks** is from a letter (19 Nov. 1935) from Horace Threlkeld (Tonkawa prep school dean) in Shankle, *American Nicknames* (1937): 544. An hour from Tonkawa is NOC-Enid, where **Jets** owe to that city's Vance Air Force Base.

[12] Jim Patterson, "How a Grubbworm Became a Maverick," *UTA Magazine* (fall 2003): 33.

[13] At Des Moines in 1912, white ex-pitcher J.L. Wilkinson put together the **All Nations** team of white, black, and Latino players (with individual Hawaiians, Japanese, and Native Americans). They were in K.C. from 1915 until World War I. Its black players reassembled in 1920 as Kan-

sas City **Monarchs**. (A new **All Nations** squad barnstormed for several more years.) In remembrance, K.C.'s Metropolitan Community College–Maple Woods traded **Centaurs** for **Monarchs** in 2007. See Metropolitan Comm. Coll., "Monarchs Baseball: History" (2012), http://athletics.mcckc.edu/mwbball/history.asp (accessed 18 April 2012).

[14] WTU's women were **Dusters** through 2004, the first year of indoor football's Amarillo **Dusters** (2004–09). Both referred to the dust kicked up by trail riders.

[15] Fort Worth's Tarrant County College adopted a bull mascot (Toro) in fall 2011 and the "Trailblazers" *identity*, apparently making no plans for **Trailblazer** teams.

[16] For example, the evangelical Columbia [S.C.] International University launched varsity **Rams** in fall 2012 explicitly to suggest "strength […] and its biblical significance" (symbolism on p. 106). See "CIU Announces Mascot" (24 March 2011), www.ciu.edu/newsstory/ciu-announces-mascot-prepares-intercollegiate-athletics (accessed 1 Sept. 2011).

[17] Texas State Hist. Assn., "Goodnight College," *Handbook of Texas Online*, www.tshaonline.org/handbook/online/articles/GG/kbg14.html (accessed 20 Aug. 2010).

[18] "University Traditions," www.wtamu.edu/traditions.aspx (accessed 20 Aug. 2010).

[19] An enterprising doctor who had helped create the rail hub at Chicago, John Evans was already appreciated in the name of Evanston, the Chicago suburb where he and fellow Methodists opened Northwestern University in 1855.

[20] The University of Idaho newspaper is the *Argonaut*, from the Idaho panhandle's gold rush history. (After California, any miner in the West might be called an Argonaut.) It was the *Argonaut* that suggested officializing "**Vandals**" for UI teams in 1921.

[21] Here are the excruciating details and interlocking histories of Cincinnati's **Red Stockings** and **Reds**. Independent **Red Stockings** took that name to Boston when the NA started in 1871. Keck's 1876 NL **Porkopolitans/Red Stockings** were next, but they lost money and were being run by the league by mid-1877. Those **Stockings** were expelled after 1880 after new owner Justus Thorner sold beer and used his park for Sunday games. Thorner and Cincy sportswriter O.P. Caylor drove the creation of the AA in 1882, a circuit with more **Red Stockings**. In 1884 the new UA included Cincinnati's **Outlaw Reds**, owned by Thorner, who had been chased from the AA **Stockings**' ownership in 1882 for violating a league order to not play the NL champion Chicago **White Stockings (Cubs)**, in what would have been considered the first World Series if schedules had allowed the completion of more than two games. In 1890 the Players' League was pushing the AA toward disintegration while the NL expanded to counter that threat. The AA **Red Stockings** moved to the 1890 NL as today's Cincinnati **Reds**.

In their final season (1891) Cincinnati's AA **Reds** were alternately **Porkers** and **Kelly's Killers**, after Hall of Fame outfielder Mike "King" Kelly. Today's NL **Reds** have *more or less* kept their name since 1890. After World War II, the U.S. believed Joseph Stalin would blanket Eastern Europe with the red flag of his Soviet Union, and Russians feared the U.S. would start throwing its nuclear weight around. During this Cold War, Congress conducted witch-hunts for Soviet-friendly Communists allegedly within the government. To grasp the measures taken to avoid suspicion during the "Red Scare," consider that the long-established **Reds** were officially "Cincinnati **Redlegs**" from 1953 to '58 (although it never really caught on with the press).

Chapter 32 Notes

[1] The Pentathlon (discus, javelin, long jump, running, and wrestling) was added to the Olympics in 708 BCE to satisfy Spartan demands for a test of war skills. It appeared at the modern Games only in 1912, 1920, and 1924. A modern pentathlon also first appeared in 1912. Its crosscountry running, fencing, equestrian jumping, swimming, and pistol-shooting events are elements of a fanciful escape from behind enemy lines to challenge a late-nineteenth-century European warrior.

[2] Alvin J. Straatmeyer (Joel Samuels, ed.), *Child of the Church: University of Dubuque 1852–2008* (Cedar Rapids, Iowa: WDG Publishing, 2008): 120.

[3] A bit of D'Youville's "oral history" from DYC's late archivist Sister Alice McCollester, as told to D. John Bray (DYC public relations dir.), email to the author, 13 Aug. 2013.

[4] Kaylee Moore, "A Look Into the Past," *The Minaret* (27 April 2012): 11. It's also suggested that **"Spartans"** contrasted nicely with **"Trojans"** nearby at St. Petersburg College (who switched to **"Titans"** in 2001).

[5] Lynn Wilkinson, *Oral History Project: Interview of Leland Asa* (29 Jan. 1983): 11, at http://archivessearch.twu.ca/uploads/r/twu/9/8/98534/aud218-transcript.pdf (accessed 15 Aug. 2013).

[6] **Spartans** at these four-years are likely named for such reasons: Aurora [Ill.] U., Castleton [Vt.] State Coll., Manchester U. (North Manchester, Ind.), and Missouri Baptist U. (St. Louis).

[7] Speaking on the Senate floor on April 20, 1858, Morrill said the land-grants "would prove (if they should not literally, like the schools of ancient Sparta, hold the children of the State) the perennial nurseries of patriotism, thrift and liberal information." But there's an even more obscure justification for MSU's **Spartans**. Much of the Upper Midwest—including Greater Lansing—is covered with glacial drift called "Sparta loamy" soil. (Homer had noted the loose Peloponnesian loam in his description of the 425 BCE battle between Sparta and Athens at "sandy Pylos.") Some smarty-pants connected to the aggie college may have known this and nominated **"Spartans."** Also, the town of Sparta, Michigan (and its loam planting fields) is only eighty miles from Lansing.

MSU lore says **Aggie** catcher Perry Fremont either suggested **"Spartans"** or had it placed in his game reports by Alderton (but no motivation is given). Michigan State's football **Spartans** usually finish their season against Penn State's **Nittany Lions** in the battle for the Land Grant Trophy. They're the two oldest land-grants, both chartered by their home states in 1855.

When colleges are identified only by state name, it means "university thereof." In other words, "Michigan" refers to the University of Michigan … a distinction well understood at Michigan State, where **Spartan** uniforms often simply read "STATE."

[8] "Traditions and Legends," *Traditions Handbook* (Stephenville, Texas: Tarleton State U., 1 Oct. 1999): 20. Texas A&M University–Central Texas opened as the Killeen satellite campus of Tarleton State U. in 1999, but it became an independent branch on the Texas A&M tree in 2009. Its classical "Warrior" mascot was unveiled to much fanfare in January 2010, but the development of corresponding teams is for the future.

[9] Pamela Grundy and Susan Shackelford, *Shattering the Glass: The Dazzling History of Women's Basketball* (New York: New Press, 2005): 189. In 1899, Louisiana Tech students brought a stray bulldog home. When the house caught fire that night, the pup went room to room to wake everyone up. All escaped except the dog, who's buried on campus in a blue-and-red jacket. The school soon had a football team, and both the **"Bulldogs"** name and red-and-blue scheme were adapted from that hero's tale.

[10] *2005–2006 Student Handbook* (Arkansas Tech U., 2005): 5.

[11] VPI's Hokie Bird is a guy in a turkey suit. Tech's former **Gobblers** described the ambition with which athletes ate in the dining hall. You might hear that a hokie is a castrated turkey, but not at VPI. The story was invented at other Atlantic Coast Conference schools, and online dictionaries that are "enhanced" by anonymous contributors have recently been duped by some tech-savvy rivals of Tech, making the slander increasingly hard to discredit.

[12] This point is better made by Christopher Jencks and David Riesman in *The Academic Revolution* (New York: Doubleday, 1968, p. 224): "The liberal arts colleges [made] clear that applied science was a very inferior subject, suitable for inferior students. […] The animosity, moreover, was mutual. The scientists mostly regarded the traditional liberal arts curriculum as uninteresting, impractical, undemanding, and effete." Because the cylindrical boiler was a steam engine's prominent feature, "boilermakers" referred to the men who built and repaired

locomotives, so Purdue's Boilermaker Special emblem is a choo-choo.

[13] Kevin Thorie (UW-Stout archives), email to the author, 9 Nov. 2010.

[14] *MSPO Handbook* (Atlanta: Georgia Inst. of Tech., 2005): 28.

[15] Shane O'Donnell (Tiffin sports info. dir.), email to the author, 10 Oct. 2003.

[16] Rick Marsi, "The Evolution of a College," *Significance* (fall 2007): 14.

[17] Michael S. Neiberg, *Making Citizen-Soldiers: ROTC and the Ideology of American Military Service* (Cambridge: Harvard University Press, 2000): 33.

[18] West Point—and subsequent "techs"—followed the example of Paris's *École Polytechnique* (Polytechnic School). After the French Revolution, Napoleon implemented its decidedly military program to train engineers for his *Grande Armée*.

[19] Catherine S. Manegold, *In Glory's Shadow: Shannon Faulkner, the Citadel and a Changing America* (New York: Knopf, 1999): 51. When VMI's **Keydets** play football against the Citadel's **Bulldogs**, somebody goes home with the Silver Shako, a gleaming version of a ceremonial military hat. The **Keydets** have a kangaroo mascot only because cheerleaders in 1947 wanted to get behind a rarely seen animal.

Many Southern schools that started with Morrill funds after the Civil War resembled military schools. Until the anti-war movement of the late Vietnam era, land-grants all over the country required that first- and second-year male students be ROTC enrollees.

[20] "Football," *The Kentuckian* (U. Kentucky yearbook, 1911): 131–137. Cited in Gregory Kent Stanley, *Before Big Blue: Sports at the University of Kentucky, 1880–1940* (Lexington: University Press of Kentucky, 1996): 48–49. (When women's teams first joined UK's male **Wildcats**, it was as **Lady Kats**.)

[21] NGCSU's women **Saints** were once **Gold Diggers**. That seemed to question the ambitions of female collegians, but it's somewhat justified through Dahlonega's history as the site of America's first gold rush. Gainesville State had been the "Home of the Fighting Geese" with a goose mascot named Laker but hadn't fielded varsity teams since its **Lakers** of the 1980s.

Chapter 33 Notes

[1] Alicia Hutzler, ed., "Redbird Traditions," *Illinois State Women's Tennis 2013-2014*: 15.

[2] Hilda R. Carter and John R. Jenswold, *The University of Wisconsin–Eau Claire* (UW-Eau Claire Foundation, Inc., 1976): 9, as quoted by Lark Keating-Hadlock, "The Origin of the Blugold," *Off the Shelf* (Mar. 2009): 4.

[3] Georgia Southern was previously an A&M (called Culture Hill) and a normal school that fielded the **Culture**, **Aggies**, or **Teachers**. (They were a **Blue Tide** [1924–41] after changing from green and gold to navy and white.) See F. Erik Brooks, *Pursuing a Promise: A History of African Americans at Georgia Southern University* (Macon, Ga.: Mercer U. Press, 2006): 12.

[4] V.A. Lowry, *Forty Years at General Beadle: 1922–1962* (Madison, S.D.: Dakota State College, 1984): 36.

[5] Rebecca Tavernini, ed., "Inside the Suit: Life as Wildcat Willy," *Northern Horizons* (winter 2007): 28.

[6] A college and pro Hall of Famer played tackle for UNT from 1966 to '68. "**Mean Green**" followed "Mean" Joe Greene to the Pittsburgh **Steelers'** "Steel Curtain" defense of the 1970s.

[7] Charles H. Ambler, *A History of Education in West Virginia* (Huntington, W.Va.: Standard Printing & Publishing Co., 1951): 794, cited in Charles H. McCormick, *This Nest of Vipers* (Champaign, Ill.: U. Illinois Press, 1989): 25.

[8] Communication (11 June 1935) from Peter Dwyer (Clarkson athletic dir.) in George Earlie Shankle, *American Nicknames: Their Origin and Significance* (New York: H.W. Wilson, 1937): 112.

[9] Jason Gum (GSC archives), emails to the author, 9 and 12 April 2010. See also an excerpt from the *Glenville Mercury* (13 July 1948) in the *Glenville State Alumni News* (fall 2007): 13.

[10] Donald Weast, ed., "Yaps, Yellow Jackets, and Hornets," *Emporia State University Hornets Soccer Media Guide* (2011): 23. This story also reports that black uniforms of the '36 football **Yellow Jackets/Hornets** gave them the alternate name "**Mud Daubers**," referring to the *Sphedidae* and *Crabronidae* wasp families, which nest in mud.

[11] An unofficial alternate at Delta State is the deliberately silly **Fighting Okras**. The pod of the okra plant (*Abelmoschus esculentus*) is a main vegetable in regional gumbo recipes. In fact, *gumbo* may be derived from *ki ngombo*, a word for okra in the West African Bantu language. Another popular gumbo staple is crayfish, a fresh-water crustacean. It's also called *crawdad* or *mudbug*, verified by minor league Hickory [N.C.] **Crawdads** (baseball, 1993–) and Bossier-Shreveport [La.] **Mudbugs** (1997–2011, hockey).

Students at Scottsdale [Ariz.] Community College weren't obsessed with their teams (often the case at two-year colleges). Administrators promoted the sports program anyway, asking students to elect a nickname in 1972. A protest vote effected the most meaningless epithet possible: **Artichokes** (another green African veggie) … which ironically draws more perpetual attention to SCC athletics than does the moniker at any other community college.

The UNC School of the Arts (Winston-Salem) makes every list of weird mascots without even fielding teams. UNCSA's Fighting Pickle owes to the pickle plant that once sponsored a touch football game against frat boys from Wake Forest. (A different story says one student was simply obsessed with the local absence of quality pickles.) See Lauren Whitaker, "The Evolution of the Pickle," *NCSA High School Life Handbook* (2006/07): 8.

[12] UW-Milwaukee Student Activities Office, "UWM History and Traditions," *Student Activity Guide* (fall 2008): 4.

[13] Dave Newhouse, "Spartan Romp," *Washington Square* (spring 2007): 11. Newhouse says San Jose State's first teams were **Daniels** for reasons unknown.

[14] Troy Katen, ed., "The Bobcats," *Peru State: Bobcat Basketball, 2008–2009*: 6.

[15] Ken Weigend, "Falcon Mascot Rich in History," *Student Voice* (27 March 2009): 8.

[16] Waheedah Bilal (WC archives), email to the author, 1 Feb. 2006. WWU's owl was pulled down in 1940 to save money on paint remover, according to Myldred Fox Fairchild, *Thru the Woods: William Woods* (Fulton, Mo.: Ovid Bell Press, 1998): 136–137. (Tena Edwards [WWU ref. lib.], assisting email to the author, 17 Jan. 2006.)

[17] **Knights**—unlike **Nighthawks** and **Owls**—aren't inordinately popular at night schools. In fact, **Knights** represent community and junior colleges with a dramatically lower frequency than they do schools founded as four-years. Identities that did often appear at two-years were **Jucos** and **Jaycees**, both abbreviations for "junior college."

[18] Thomas A. Scott, "History of Kennesaw State University" (Kennesaw, Ga.: Kennesaw State U., 1998): 1.

[19] "Identity and Sports," *Monmouth University Magazine* (winter 2008): 7.

Chapter 34 Notes

[1] Carl M. Becker, *Home and Away: The Rise and Fall of Professional Football on the Banks of the Ohio* (Athens: Ohio U. Press, 1998): 162.

[2] When the **Lions** arrived in '34, the cat theme set by baseball's **Tigers** was well worn. The 1926/27 ABL Detroit **Lions** had been the 1925/26 Pulaski Post **Five**, named for their five starters and not the post (no. 270) of their American Legion sponsors. The city's first NFLers were Detroit **Panthers** (1925–26). There have since been NASL Detroit **Cougars** (1968), and USFL Michigan **Panthers** (1983–84, Pontiac).

[3] "University Colors and Nickname," *Board Policies and Procedures Manual* (Norfolk State

U. Board of Visitors, 2008): 4. Virginia State's **Hilltoppers** became **Trojans** in 1936. VSU's first president was John Mercer Langston (1829–97), the former dean of the country's first black law school (at Howard) and the first African American Congressman from Virginia. His namesakes include his great-nephew, the poet John Mercer Langston Hughes, and Langston, Oklahoma (est. 1890), where Langston University (est. 1897) hosts alliterative **Lions**.

[4] In February 1962, the University of New Haven *News* first called teams **Chargers** for reasons unknown (but it was just weeks after the Los Angeles/San Diego **Chargers** appeared in their second consecutive title game of the new AFL). Separate columns in a June '61 issue of the *News* introduced Don Omrod as the first athletic director and asked for mascot suggestions. Through the fall the *News* referred to **Blue and Gold** hoopsters as "Omrod's charges" or "cagers." Putting a couple of vowels into either *charges* or *cagers* could have yielded **Chargers** by February, or maybe they wanted to be the only **Chargers** in their south New England conference. (Marion Sachdeva [UNH tech. services lib.], multiple assisting emails to the author [Aug.–Sep. 2008].) "Cagers" is a description unique to basketballers. In refers to the game's early days when spectators would grab the ball or punch players, so a wire cube surrounded the court of the first pro team, the 1896 Trenton **Trentons**. (Backboards had already been invented in 1893 to prevent goaltending from balcony fans.) Soon most courts in the Northeast had chain-link enclosures, and safer rope corrals were used in the late cage era of the 1920s.

[5] Barbara Braden Guffey and Debora Swatsworth Foster, *Westminster College* (Charleston, S.C.: Arcadia, 2007): 114.

[6] The Houston **Oilers** (1960–96) changed to Tennessee **Oilers** (1997–98) then Tennessee **Titans** (1999–).

[7] Alison Stankrauff (IU-South Bend archives), email to the author, 11 March 2009.

[8] In a spring 1928 edition of Illinois Wesleyan's campus paper, baseballers were both **Titans** and **Hillmen** (after Coach Hill). Tennis players on the same page were **Green and White**, so we assume the transition to **Titans** was complete shortly thereafter. See "Bradley Defeats Wesleyan 5-2 in Great Old Game," *The Argus* (19 May 1928). (Meg Miner [IWU archives and special collections], assisting email to the author, 18 Aug. 2008.)

[9] For example, we know the junior Springfield [Mass.] **Pics** are shortened **Olympics** because they use the Olympia Ice Center.) Boston Garden owner Walter Brown managed American hockey players in international competition in the 1930s. They took bronze at the '36 Olympics and were minor league Boston **Olympics** until 1952.

[10] That John Dryden was the source is supported by the town of Dryden, south of Syracuse next to Virgil, named after the Roman poet for whom Dryden was a famed translator. Dryden's translation of Virgil's *Aeneid* (c.25 BCE) includes the line, "The more with fury burns the blazing fire." The proximity of *burns* to *fire* therein was enough to justify an intra-MLS rivalry between the Dallas **Burn** and Chicago **Fire**. For that reason alone (*yup!*), those teams play a season-long total-points series for the Brimstone Cup, engraved with the Virgil-Dryden quote. The rivalry continued after the **Burn** became "FC Dallas" in 2005.

The *Aeneid* adapts the story of Rome's founder, Romulus, to make him the descendent of the Trojan hero Aeneas. Abandoned as infants, Romulus and twin brother Remus were suckled by a generous she-wolf, putting **Wolves** and **She-Wolves** at the American University of Rome.

[11] For a history of SU's nicknames and mascots see Dick Case, "Mascot Memories," *Syracuse University Magazine* (spring 1997): 38 *ff.*

Another Salt City team that dumped Indian themes was minor league baseball's Syracuse **Chiefs** (est. 1937), who became **Skychiefs** in 1997. By 2007 they were again **Chiefs**, this time employing locomotive emblems to recall a railroad's *chief* engineer, drawing attention to the freight trains that rumble past the outfield wall just about every inning.

[12] As a normal school, Buff State had **Normals** and **Teachers**. Their "**Frontiersmen**" alternate was from a post-colonial designation for the land between Lakes Erie and Ontario, the Niagara

Frontier. (Daniel DiLandro [BSC archives], assisting email to the author, 4 Oct. 2006.) Niagara County Community College (Sanborn, N.Y.) had **Frontiersmen** until about 1981 but switched to another pioneering handle, **Trail Blazers**. Since 2010 they've been **Thunderwolves**.

[13] Harpur College's 1950 relocation was technically to the southwestern Binghamton suburb of Vestal. The classical goddess Vesta and her Vestal Virgins were the keepers of the home fire and family. Vestal town is on the far side of Binghamton from Harpursville, named for Robert Harpur himself, noted also as an architect of New York's late-colonial and post-Revolutionary constitutional framework.

Greater Binghamton's Triple Cities (Binghamton, Endicott, and Johnson) followed baseball's minor league Binghamton **Triplets** (1923–67). Broome County had minor league hockey's Binghamton **(Broome) Dusters** (1973–80). Endicott-born Johnny Hart based the **Dusters'** caveman mascot on the protagonist in his famous comic strip *B.C.* Other ice-bound locals who used Hart's art in the Broome County arena were minor league B.C. **Icemen** (1997–2002).

[14] Carol Lee and Jerry Wadian, ed., "History of the Peacock Mascot," *The Bridge* (summer 2003): 4.

[15] Michiel Pauw was a well-connected director of the Dutch West India Company. His Pauw surname means "peacock" in Dutch, and Mr. Pauw's patroonship between the Hudson and Hackensack Rivers—now New Jersey's Hudson County—during the Dutch colonial era was *Pavonia*, from the Latin word for peacock (*pavo*). Jersey City is the county seat, so as of late some have irresistibly linked the Saint Peter's **Peacocks** to that history.

[16] Durward T. Stokes, *Elon College* (Elon, N.C.: Elon Coll. Alumni Assn., 1982): 190. (Connie Keller [Elon archives], assisting email to the author, 8 Feb. 2005.)

[17] In Greek, *Kosmos* refers to the ordered universe or the star-filled heavens. "**Cosmos**" would have fit the team-owning Ertegun brothers, who ran Atlantic Records. Those sons of a Turkish ambassador were born in Istanbul, which under its former name—Constantinople—had been the jewel of the Greek world. Also, the **Cosmos** would have been aware of the 1923-founded Cosmopolitan Soccer League, where teams still display the colorful ethnic history of greater NYC as Brooklyn **Italians**, Astoria **Gaels**, FC **Bulgaria**, FC **Japan**, Manhattan **Celtic**, NY **Ukrainian** S.C., **Shamrock** S.C., NY **Croatia**, and NY **Greek-American/Atlas**.

Chapter 35 Notes

[1] Cuba sponsored a baseball series against visiting African Americans in 1925. The hosts and their guests were distinguished as *Criollos* (or **All Cubans**) and **[All] Yankees**. Puerto Rico's top pro basketball league once included *Criollos de Caguas* (1976–2004).

[2] Fans of a dozen British soccer teams sing "When the Saints Go Marching In" at matches and victory parties. About half of those aren't even **Saints**, substituting "**Reds**," "**Blues**," "**Blades**," or "**Spurs**" when the chorus comes 'round.

Accounting for regional musical traditions, it seems appropriate that the Mississippi University for Women in Columbus has the **Blues**, but they were named after their Columbia-blue uniforms of the 1920s. (MUW's gym was destroyed by a 2002 tornado, and intercollegiate sports were canceled to fund more inclusive intramurals.) A better musical example could be found straight across the state, where minor league baseball's Greenville **Bluesmen** (1996–2001) played in the city that's hosted the Mississippi Delta Blues and Heritage Festival since 1977. In Florida, the Jacksonville **Dixie Blues** (est. 2001) are football women of note.

[3] The Pla-Mor Ballroom opened in 1927 outside K.C.'s black neighborhood, but black bands led by George E. Lee, Count Basie, and Andy Kirk entertained its white audiences. It also hosted minor league hockey's Kansas City **Pla-Mors** (1927–33, or "**Greyhounds**" when owned by the bus company, 1933–40). There were also Junior **Pla-Mors** (1945–49).

Professor Curtis Smith finds strong suggestions that **Blue Birds** at his Kansas City Kansas Community College became **Blue Devils** in 1928 to capitalize on the familiar resonance of

Oklahoma City's Blue Devils, barnstorming jazzers featuring pianist Count Basie. See Smith, "Legend: The Blue Devils," *KCKCC e-Journal* (Kansas City Kansas Comm. Coll., 2007), http://www.kckcc.edu/ejournal/archives/march2008/article/legendTheBlueDevils.aspx (accessed 29 Sept. 2012).

[4] New industries and a new Air Force base near Macon during World War II attracted black workers. The city was the "Song & Soul of the South" after the Douglass Theater and radio station WIBB launched the careers of Little Richard, Otis Redding, and James Brown. Minor league baseball's Macon **Music** (2007) were among the local teams that are full of puns. The Macon **Whoopees** struggled through half of the 1973/74 Southern Hockey League season while remembering Gus Kahn's popular 1928 song "Makin' Whoopee." A later Macon **Whoopee** (1996–2002) made tracks to Kentucky as Lexington **Men O' War** (2002/03) and were replaced by Macon **Trax** (2002–05), named after the city's rail history. Indoor football's Macon **Knights** (2000–06) were phonetically identical to *Maconites*, the demonym for locals. Brooklynites include Long Island's USL development team, the Brooklyn **Knights** (est. 1999), and the Brooklyn **Nets'** knight mascot.

[5] Other Berklee cats play for Emerson College's **Lions** as part of a consortium of arts schools that includes Boston Architectural Coll., Boston Conservatory, the School of the Museum of Fine Arts, and Massachusetts Coll. of Art and Design.

Chapter 36 Notes

[1] Paul Debono, *The Indianapolis ABCs* (Jefferson, N.C.: McFarland, 1997): 15–16.

[2] Debono, 116. Leading black baseball historian James A. Riley has a different take, saying the 1938 **ABCs** became the '39 St. Louis **Stars**, with Atlanta's '38 **Black Crackers** simply going to Indy as the new **ABCs**. See Riley, *The Biographical Encyclopedia of the Negro Baseball Leagues* (New York: Carroll & Graf, 1994): 406.

[3] G. Edward White, *Creating the National Pastime* (Princeton, N.J.: Princeton U. Press, 1996): 139. See also Donn Rogosin, *Invisible Men: Life in Baseball's Negro Leagues* (New York: Atheneum, 1983): 103–113. Newark's **Eagles** formed in 1936 when numbers runner Abe Manly merged his Brooklyn **Eagles** with his newly acquired black Newark **Dodgers**. (The 1841-founded *Brooklyn Eagle* was then one of America's most popular daily papers.) The **Eagles'** hands-on manager was Abe's wife Effa Manley, the first female Hall of Famer.

[4] Dominant in 1935 and '36, the **Crawfords** of 1937 weren't so good because Satchel Paige had taken several of them (including Gibson and Bell) to the Dominican Republic to play for *los **Dragones** de Ciudad Trujillo* (Trujillo City **Dragons**). Brutal dictator Rafael Trujillo had just renamed the capital after himself. (It would be "Santo Domingo" again after his 1961 assassination.) Returning home with their uniforms, the **Dragons** toured the Midwest as Trujillo **All-Stars**. (See William Brashler, *The Story of Negro League Baseball* [New York: Ticknor & Fields, 1994]: 72.)

The **Crawfords'** financially troubled owner, Gus Greenlee, witnessed the collapse of the NNL after the 1938 season and the demolition of Pittsburgh's Greenlee Field. Investors from Ohio rebranded the team for '39 as Toledo **Crawfords** in the newer Negro American League. They were gone for good after spending 1940 as Indianapolis **Crawfords**.

[5] Lawrence D. Hogan, *Shades of Glory: The Negro Leagues and the Story of African American Baseball* (Washington, D.C.: National Geographic, 2006): 36. After a stint in Philadelphia, the 1891 **Gorhams** absorbed some rival **Cuban Giants** and were **Big Gorhams**.

[6] Leland and Peters split in 1908, effecting separate Peters **Union Giants** and **Leland Giants**. In 1917 player Robert Gilkerson bought the Peters **Union Giants** and barnstormed them across the upper Midwest for two decades as Gilkerson **Union Giants**.

[7] The **Renaissance** had been Harlem's **Spartan Braves**, great amateurs assembled by Spartan Field Club manager Bob Douglas. After losing to Pittsburgh's professional Loendi **Big Five** (from the Hill District's black Loendi Social and Literary Club), Douglas realized black New

York needed an elite team, setting the **Braves'** transition to the **Renaissance**. Some **Braves** joined the competing Commonwealth **Big Five**, assembled in 1922 at the Commonwealth Casino by the McMahon brothers, white promoters who'd given black fighters fair shots in Madison Square Garden bouts. The **Rens'** age of dominance began after the Commonwealth and Loendi sides folded in 1923, leaving good players available. They even became the "home team for blacks in two cities" after hosting some games in Philadelphia after 1928. (See Kareem Abdul-Jabbar with Raymond Obstfeld, *On the Shoulders of Giants: My Journey Through the Harlem Renaissance* [New York: Simon & Schuster, 2007]: 145–157.)

The brothers McMahon already had experience with black baseballers. In 1911 they took some of Philadelphia's **Giants** and built New York's Lincoln **Giants**, a name copied from the Nebraska capital's good semi-pro black team. Giving up control of the Lincoln **Giants** in 1914, Jess McMahon took some of their key players and formed the rival Lincoln **Stars**, which lasted for three seasons. (In the 1940s, Jess would turn a carnival sideshow into an arena event, forever linking the clan McMahon to pro wrestling.)

[8] Robert W. Peterson, *Cages to Jump Shots* (New York: Oxford U. Press, 1990): 100.

[9] "**Vagabond Kings**" referred to the Michigan team's former barnstorming ways and their owner's name, C. King Boring. In terms of name recognition, *The Vagabond King* is Rudolf Friml's oft-revived 1925 operetta.

[10] Ron Thomas, *They Cleared the Lane: The NBA's Black Pioneers* (Lincoln: U. Nebraska Press, 2002): 15–16.

[11] Female housemates of the **Big Five/Globetrotters** were Savoy **Colts**, even though *colt* describes a young male horse. "**Globe Trotters**" was already associated with white barn-stormers from Minneapolis and Herkimer, New York. See Ben Green, *Spinning the Globe: The Rise, Fall, and Return to Greatness of the Harlem Globetrotters* (New York: HarperCollins, 2005): 37, 43, 46, 49. Frank Basloe's successful Herkimer **31st Separate Company** (or Oswego **Indians** or **Globe Trotters**) stopped the Buffalo **Germans'** 111-game win streak in February 1911. (See Peterson, *Cages to Jump Shots*: 64–65.) The Minneapolis **Globe Trotters** were **Fat Emmas** for 1928, backed by a local candy factory with a so-named chocolate bar.

[12] Saperstein may have created a second **Globe Trotters** team (possibly remainders of the Savoy **Big Five**) to tour simultaneously with Brookins's originals. Brookins quit in protest (and in part to become a singer). Refer again to Green (*Spinning the Globe*), who sorts through the **Globetrotters'** early days and the origin of their team name in chapter 3.

[13] Green, *Spinning the Globe*: 51. See also Nelson George, *Elevating the Game: The History and Aesthetics of Black Men in Basketball* (New York: Fireside, 1993): 42–44.

[14] Robert C. Toll, *Blacking Up: The Minstrel Show in Nineteenth-Century America* (New York: Oxford U. Press, 1974): 195.

[15] Riley, 894. One may wonder why the minstrel shows' "Ethiopian melodies" and baseball's **Ethiopian Clowns** were identified with East Africa when most slave ancestors had been from West Africa. Ethiopia is the sub-Saharan (black) African land most mentioned in the Hebrew Bible, and it's simply the case that Ethiopia was in the news. After the Suez Canal opened in 1869, countries wanted to monitor Red Sea traffic. Italy tried to get a foothold during the Euro-peans' land grab called the Scramble for Africa. Ethiopia's 1895–96 war to remain independent was successful, but a second one (1935–36) brought about the state of Italian East Africa, which lasted until World War II. As for the **Zulu Giants**, the Zulus are the largest native tribe of southeasternmost Africa who fought fiercely against British colonization in the 1879 Anglo-Zulu War. To less informed persons, half-naked, spear-wielding Zulus would represent stereo-typical Africans for generations.

[16] After the NAL's collapse, Indy's **Clowns** cranked the horseplay back up, distinguishing their independent product from the newly integrated majors until 1962. ("Indianapolis **Clowns**" was revived by touring teams of the 1970s and '80s.)

[17] A 1953 contract dispute with Saperstein led Marcus Haynes out of the magic circle to form the (Fabulous) Harlem **Magicians** with fellow future Hall of Famer Goose Tatum. Ex-**Trotter** Bill "Showboat" Dumpson toured with **Court Jesters** in the 1960s. Promoter Howie Davis started the Harlem **Wizards** in '62. He'd earlier run baseball and basketball Kokomo [Ind.] **Clowns**, making them play in actual clown costumes.

[18] Peterson, *Cages to Jump Shots*: 38.

[19] To their credit, the **Wildcats** and **Bucs** did recruit heavily from west coast colleges. Like Los Angeles's 1926-only **Buccaneers**, the NFL Louisville **Colonels** also made Chicago home during just that season while parading as Kentuckians.

Chapter 37 Notes

[1] St. Lou's baseball and football **Cardinals** were the only major league teams with the same nickname in the same city when neither was named for the other. The NFL **Cardinals** still have red mascots, even though two species overlap in Arizona, the red *Cardinalis cardinalis* and the less colorful *Cardinalis sinuatus*, the gray or desert cardinal.

[2] The Army pack animal puts mule mascots at West Point. The first showed up at an 1899 football game to counter the **Midshipmen's** goat (which dates to 1893). *Midshipman* itself refers to an officer candidate who walks the center of the ship along the keel (amidship).

The Army Air Forces broke off from the Army right after World War II but didn't open the U.S. Air Force Academy (Colorado Springs) until 1955. The first class of flyers adopted a falcon mascot, which led directly to **Falcons** teams.

[3] James P. Quirk, *The Ultimate Guide to College Football* (Chicago: U. Illinois Press, 2004): 15–16.

[4] Murray Sperber, *Onward to Victory: The Crises That Shaped College Sports* (New York: Henry Holt, 1998): 111.

[5] The University of North Carolina at Wilmington made jocks **Seahawks** in 1947, but school chronicles split over whether that references Iowa Pre-Flight's teams or UNCW's oceanside location. (At least one alum recalls the name coming from the 1940 Warner film *The Sea Hawk*, with Errol Flynn as one of Queen Elizabeth's privateers, which was re-released to much fanfare in spring '47.) See LuAnn Mims and Adina Riggins, "Transcript of Oral History of Medlin, Jim" [UNCW's William Madison Randall Library, 22 June 2005], http://library.uncw. edu/web/collections/oralhistories/transcripts/526.xml [accessed 28 July 2013].)

Other coastal **Seahawks** are at Lamar State Coll. (Port Arthur, Texas), Los Angeles Harbor Coll. (Wilmington, Calif.), Northwood U.-Florida (West Palm Beach), and Wagner Coll. (Staten Island, N.Y.).

[6] The 8-2 **Bluejackets'** had a final-game victory over the **Irish**, but the AP poll gave ND the national championship anyway for compiling great stats during a 9-1 season against tough teams. Great Lakes Naval had been a power in World War I too, winning the 1919 Rose Bowl over that game's defending champs, the Mare Island Naval Shipyard **Marines** (Vallejo, Calif.).

[7] Mickey Cochrane and Bob Feller managed the **Jackets**. Segregation still ruled the service, so fellow Hall of Famer Larry Doby played for all-black **Bluejackets** and served in the Pacific before joining Cleveland's **Indians** as the AL's first African American. Playing an exhibition schedule, hardball service teams rarely faced collegians.

More service teams: [1] UNC Chapel Hill hosted the Navy's V-5 (pre-flight) **Cloudbusters** of baseball and football, led by Hall of Famers Ted Williams and Otto Graham; [2] Among the greatest U.S. hockey sides ever was the Coast Guard **Cutters** (1942–44, Curtis Bay, Md.).

[8] Mickey Smith (LU sports info. dir.), email to the author, 23 June 2005.

[9] UT Martin evolved from the Baptist's Hall-Moody Bible Institute. HMBI's **Sky Pilots** teams further justify the current **Skyhawks**. ("Sky pilot" is an archaic term for a preacher.) When UTM became a state junior college in 1927, teams were **Junior Vols**, relative to the **Volun-**

teers at Knoxville's flagship school. When UT Martin was the new name in 1967, **Pacers** were picked to reflect the fast pace of the campus until 1995. (UTM's paper is still *The Pacer.*) See Matthew Maxey, ed., "Skyhawk Traditions," *UT Martin Women's Basketball Media Guide* (2008): 80.

Point University (East Point, Ga.) had (unofficial) **Sky Pilots** in the '40s because "sky pilot" also refers to military chaplains, which mentioned when **Chargers** replaced **Skyhawks** in 2011. See Sarah G. Huxford, ed., "New Mascot Announced," *Point Magazine* (fall 2011): 11.

[10] Marilyn Starr (GC archives), email to the author, 7 Jan. 2009. Starr uncovered poll results for "**Gremlins**" and "**Panthers**" in the 16 Feb. and 25 Oct. 1944 issues of *Papyrus*. (The Massachusetts College of Liberal Arts also fielded **Gremlins** in the late 1940s.)

[11] The players and administrators that Modell moved to Baltimore were technically an expansion franchise and not a relocated one, but they didn't participate in an expansion draft. The opposite is true in Cleveland, where two distinct sets of **Browns** are considered a single franchise, even though the newer club did pick in the 1999 expansion draft.

[12] Paul Brown with Jack Clary, *PB: The Paul Brown Story* (New York: Atheneum, 1979): 123.

[13] See Barry Popik, "Bronx Bombers," in Paul Dickson, ed., *New Dickson Baseball Dictionary* (New York: Harcourt Brace, 1999): 85.

In 1920, future college and pro Hall of Famer Fritz Pollard was one of two African American players in the new APFA/NFL. The offensive back was also the league's first black co-coach, leading Akron's **Pros** to the first NFL title. During the NFL's (unwritten) ban on blacks from 1934 to '45, Pollard had a Harlem barnstorming team, the New York **Brown Bombers** (1935–37), who many say were named for Joe Louis. But Pollard had already coached Chicago's (black) **Brown Bombers** (1927–33), named when Louis was 13, and it's likely his own standout seasons at *Brown* University made Pollard partial to "**Brown Bombers**." Pollard simultaneously ran an independent all-black all-star team of Chicago **Black Hawks**, named in 1927 after Chi-Town's year-old NHL **Black Hawks**. The football **Hawks** helped proved that barnstorming black and white sides could face off without incident.

[14] Previously fielding the **Blues**, **Blue and Gold**, and **Collegians**, Ithacans chose in 1937 to make athletes **Cayugas**, after its *Cayugan* yearbook. The vote was to have been binding, but the *Cayugan* itself was soon calling teams at the end of Lake Cayuga "**Bombers**." Rumors say a local paper simply repeated "**Bombers**" until it stuck, but too-cute-for-true stories say basketballers played in a theater tiny enough to effect half-court *bombs*. See "Students Pick *Cayugas* As Name For Teams," *The Ithacan* (22 Jan. 1937): 1.

[15] Moving from the Cap City to South Carolina for 2005 they were Greenville **Bombers**, but they were hitting line drives as the Greenville **Drive** the next year to recognize G'ville's transition from a textile city to a hub of automotive research and technology.

[16] During World War II, Japan's government solidified patriotic reverence for the emperor by arresting liberal and religious persons for thought crimes. Tsunesaburō Makiguchi founded the Sōka Gakkai (value creation society) movement in 1930 to steer national education toward humanistic sensibilities. He died in prison in 1944, but his principles are applied to two colleges, Tokyo's Soka University and the associated Soka University of America (Aliso Viejo, Calif.). SUA's **Lions** are named after Shishi, the snarling stone lion from ancient China that migrated to Japan's Buddhist temples after 600 CE.

[17] LSU-Alexandria, "Points of Interest," http://www.lsua.edu/About/History/PointsOfInterest (accessed 24 Jan. 2013).

Chapter 38 Notes

[1] The ABA's Miami **Floridians** (1968–72), or simply **Floridians** for their final two seasons had home games at Miami Beach, Tampa, Jacksonville, and West Palm Beach. The name of the WFL Honolulu **Hawaiians** (1974–75) was also only a geographic distinction. There've been

baseballing Richmond **Virginians** in the minors (1954–64) and the major AA (1884).

2 Gambling in Mexico dates to the Aztecs, and casinos opened across Mexico during France's attempted colonization in the early 1860s (about which few Americans are aware, owing to their simultaneous Civil War). Gambling was legal in Mexico long after bordering U.S. states banned it. The USFL Houston **Gamblers** (1984–85) referred to both gambling in old Mexico and the many gaming saloons on Western frontiers. ABC's Roone Arledge said Houston's **Gamblers** would force his network to flaunt an association between sports and wagering, but the team said it only intended only to suggest the high-risk play they would exhibit, and Kenny Rogers—famous singer of "The Gambler"—was associated with the ownership group. See Jan Reid, "Gambling on the Gamblers," *Texas Monthly* (Jan. 1984): 115. See also Jim Byrne, *The $1 League: The Rise and Fall of the USFL* (New York: Prentice Hall, 1986): 81.

3 In the 1830s, Europeans invented the dynamo, the first industrial electrical generator. Houston's **Dynamo** would be recognized by Eastern European soccer fans, as would Colorado's NASL Denver **Dynamos** (1974–75). *Dinamo* and *Dynamo* clubs across the Communist Bloc were tied to police agencies and loaded with top talent. Europeans in various sports still use "**Dynamo**" to plug in to the power of those clubs, not the politics. More explicitly indicating local energy plants are the Houston **Energy** (est. 2001) of women's football.

4 The Caddo people were natives of the Piney Woods (eastern Texas, southern Arkansas, western Louisiana, and southeastern Oklahoma). In fact, the Spanish form of the Caddo word for *friend* is *Tejas*, from which *Texas* is derived. Old World diseases nearly wiped out the Caddos, and their influence diminished further after Osages and Apaches picked up European weapons. The Caddo towns of Nacogdoches (Texas) and Natchitoches (La.) are the oldest settlements in their respective states. Today those cities host athletic rivals, SFAU's **Lumberjacks** and Northwestern State University's **Demons** (origin unknown), who compete for college football's largest (physical) prize, the Chief Caddo Trophy.

5 Colby Coll., "History: Mascot," www.colby.edu/athletics/glance (accessed 15 May 2009).

6 Cal's **Golden Bear** mascot is named *Oski*, from a meaningless turn-of-the-twentieth century cheer: "Oski Wow-Wow! … Whiskey Wee-Wee! … " etc.

7 Irvine Valley College is a feeder for UC-Irvine, so "**Ants**" (as compared to **Anteaters**) was considered to replace **Wolverines** in 1990. Cooler heads decided **Lasers** would refer to IVC's technical studies. See Steve Kresal, "Stanley Building Irvine Valley Program from Ground Up," *Los Angeles Times*, 24 Oct. 1990, http://articles.latimes.com/1990-10-24/sports/sp-2854_1_irvine-valley (accessed 14 May 2012).

8 Communication (21 Nov. 1935) from Estella Baldwin (Whitworth alumni secretary) in George Earlie Shankle, *American Nicknames: Their Origin and Significance* (New York: H.W. Wilson, 1937): 580.

9 The Connaught Cup has been the Canadian National Challenge Cup since 1926. Lord Stanley and Duke Connaught aren't the only esteemed persons of the realm with eponymous shiny cups. The ninth governor general, Lord Albert Grey, gave a trophy to U. Toronto for winning Canada's Senior Amateur Football Championship in 1909. It's now the CFL Grey Cup. After the 1925 NHL playoffs, the wife of Lord Byng of Vimy (the twelfth governor general) gave a silver cup to a player she admired, Ottawa **Senator** Frank Nighbor. The Lady Byng Trophy has been the NHL's sportsmanship award since.

10 The organizer of Victoria Rink's first nine-on-nine test was James Creighton, who'd seen similar games growing up in Nova Scotia. McGill students played in that game, and the university formed the world's first stable team to compete against a side from the Victoria Rink on January 31, 1877. That was just a month before the city's Metropolitan Club published Creighton's "Montreal Rules," guidelines that incorporated key features of his "Halifax Rules" (especially the pass forward) to become the template for modern hockey.

11 There've been plenty of **Marlboros** (or derived **Marlies** and **Dukes**) in local hockey history,

including Toronto **Marlboros** (1927–89, an NHL **Leafs'** farm team). The first (Protestant) Marlboro Club's rivals were the St. Michael's **Majors**, formed in 1906 at St. Michael's College School, an Irish-Catholic high school. They were junior Mississauga St. Michael's **Majors** after moving to a T.O. suburb in 2007 but became Mississauga **Steelheads** in 2012.

[12] *Hottentot* was a derogatory Dutch description of Khoisan speakers from southwest Africa's bush who had a long history of conflict with Dutch and British colonizers even before the Boer Wars. A string of white minor league baseball teams in Indiana were alliterative Terre Haute **Hottentots** after 1891 (just "**Tots**" from 1921 to '27). Basketball's Chicago's **Hottentots** of the mid-1930s included some (black) Harlem **Globetrotters**.

[13] Probably noticing the new **Roughriders** out in Regina, the Ottawans became **Senators** in 1925 but were **Rough Riders** again by '31.

[14] Up the Ottawa are Pembroke's junior hockey **Lumber Kings**, who explicitly reference Ontario's timber industry. A lumber town in Quebec hosted the *Trois-Rivières* **Draveurs** (1973–92), a French word for lumbering raftman.

[15] "Rough Riders" was familiar through William Cody too. His show "Buffalo Bill's Wild West and Congress of Rough Riders of the World" toured nationally since 1893.

[16] Canadian Football League, "History of the Ottawa Renegades," http://www.cfl.ca/page/his_ teams_ott (accessed 25 March 2013) and "History of the Saskatchewan Roughriders," www. cfl.ca/page/his_teams_sask (accessed 6 Feb. 2012).

Chapter 39 Notes

[1] The same can be said for the USFL Chicago **Blitz** (1983–84). *Blitzkrieg* is German for "light-ning war," referring to the quick bombardment and immediate ground attack that Germany used early in World War II. In football's blitz, defenders sacrifice pass coverage to send more rushers than the offensive line can handle.

[2] Before the 2006 season, the **Curve** formed an association with a newly named Pennsylvania single-A team, the State College **Spikes**, whose moniker is a three-pointer of sorts. In addition to being the L-shaped nail that secures train tracks, *spike* refers to either cleated sneaks or a young male deer whose antlers have yet to branch.

[3] The Baltimore **Orioles'** Camden Yards was purposefully positioned on a former rail lot to show off the old brick B&O Warehouse (c. 1900) behind right field.

[4] The Chicago blaze wasn't even close to being the largest or deadliest fire on Lake Michi-gan's western shore *on October 8*. The same drought that made Chicago a disaster waiting to happen created the biggest fire in North American history when cleared brush and timber lit up near the lumber town of Peshtigo, Wisconsin. Whereas 300 died in Chicago's vaporized down-town, Peshtigo's flames scorched 600 times as much earth and extinguished 1,500 lives. Peshtigo's only telegraph line burned while eyewitness accounts on the line out of Chicago turned its inferno into the first real-time international media event.

[5] UIC is the former Chicago Undergraduate Division, a two-year with teams of **Chi-Illini**, derived from the famous **Illini** at the flagship campus in Urbana-Champaign. In 1966 the Chi-Town school first awarded four-year degrees and was renamed UIC-Circle. ("Circle" euphe-mistically describes a massive traffic interchange.) Circle athletes were soon **Chicas**, a cutesy abbreviation for Chicagoans. Some say it was a sobriquet for the Chickasaw people of the mid-Mississippi Valley, but *chica* is also Spanish for a little girl, so the name quickly became "Chikas" and remained so until the '82 merger that ignited the **Flames**.

[6] Dalmatian mascots represent the MLS Chicago **Fire** and many other **Blaze** and **Fury** teams. The English had used the sleek spotted canine to run alongside carriages to dissuade highway robbers and more vicious dogs, so Dalmatians and horses formed a bond. It was a smooth tran-sition for them to pave the way for city fire pumpers. After the 2004 season, the minor league Peoria **Chiefs** moved away from Indian imagery to a Dalmatian wearing a fire helmet, as in

"fire chief." ("**Chiefs**" originally owed to the Peoria tribe of the Illini Confederation.)

In the semi-arid climate of California's southern San Joaquin Valley, a Dalmatian represents the minor league Bakersfield **Blaze** (so named in 1995). In the early 1980s their sprinkler system automatically went off during a long night game and the coach (of the then Seattle-affiliated Bakersfield **Mariners**) suggested burning off the puddles by igniting gasoline. The game went on, but the field remained scorched for the rest of the year.

Chapter 40 Notes

[1] Harold Claassen, *The History of Professional Football* (Englewood Cliffs, N.J., Prentice-Hall, 1963): 13.

[2] There are still warships on Lake Erie at the Buffalo and Erie County Naval & Military Park, a retirement home for Navy vessels opened in 1979. From the deck of the destroyer *USS The Sullivans* (DD-537), you can see the arena in which Buffalo **Destroyers** played indoor football (1999–2003). They were later Ohio's Columbus **Destroyers** (2004–08).

Chapter 41 Notes

[1] Ryan Willison, "Message from the Athletic Director," *Ambrose Lions Athletics* (2007/08): 1.

[2] CSB's strong nursing program may explain why **Blazer** boosters of the mid-1970s were the "Burn Unit." This fast fact—along with the **Johnnies/Blazers** timeline—is courtesy of Peggy Roske (CSB/SJU archives), emails to the author, 15 and 16 Sept. 2008.

[3] Joanne Sloan and Cheryl Watts, *College Nicknames: And Other Interesting Sports Traditions* (Northport, Ala.: Vision Press, 1993): 253.

[4] No one's sure which emperor signed Catherine's death warrant in *about* 305. In fact, doubt about the saint's existence resulted in the erasure of her feast day from the liturgical calendar from 1969 to 2002.

[5] Donald D. Housley, *Susquehanna University: A Goodly Heritage, 1858–2000* (Danvers, Mass.: Rosemont, 2007): 178.

[6] Kathy Dean, "A Ram I Am," *University of Mobile Magazine* (spring 2011): 33.

[7] Joshua Rhett Miller, "Christian College Drops 'Crusaders' Nickname in Bow to 'Global Society,'" *Fox News* (31 Jan. 2014), http://www.foxnews.com/us/2014/01/31/christian-college-in-wisconsin-drops-crusaders-nickname (accessed 31 Jan. 2014).

[8] Founded as a state community college, Spoon River College (Canton, Ill.) really had no strong love for "**Crusaders**" and reacted to the political climate in 2007 by becoming **Mudcats** (after the big catfish from the eponymous river). Two years of legal squabbling with the minor league Carolina **Mudcats** enticed SRC to change again in 2010, their frustration being manifest in the new name, **Rage**, ostensibly as in "raging river." In spring 2013 SRC used a tournament-style bracket to arrive at a new name, **Snappers**.

Chapter 42 Notes

[1] Tradition says that Benedict's twin sister was St. Scholastica (c. 480–543). She inspired Catherine Kerst to become Sister Scholastica upon taking the veil of the Benedictine Sisters in Minnesota in 1862. (Rita Rosenberger [St. Scholastica Monastery, Duluth], email to the author, 17 Jan. 2005.) As Mother Scholastica, she helped found a college in Duluth in 1912. It's now the College of St. Scholastica, where athletes are **Saints**.

[2] Justin Bates (Anderson sports info. dir.), email to the author, 26 Nov. 2003. Bates cites Ced White's 1937 article in the *Anderson Herald* (Anderson, Ind.). (AU had been founded in 1917 by the Church of God, also headquartered at Anderson.)

[3] *Coffeyville Red Ravens: The Tradition Continues* (Coffeyville Comm. Coll., 2008): 47. This media guide says this "true or not" backstory is from 1948 and '56 editions of the *College Dial*.

[4] The famous manifestations of Florence's lion include Donatello's sandstone sculpture and

the oft-copied Medici lions at the Loggia dei Lanzi. Florences elsewhere are drawn to **Lion**-like team names. Florence, South Carolina's minor league hockey players were the Pee Dee **Pride** (1998–2005), as in a pride of lions. Other than that, there's no connection to Italy's Renaissance city; a railroad manager named the South Carolina stop after his daughter Florence.

[5] L. Edward Bednar (PNC vice chancellor for academic affairs), emails to the author, 6 and 7 April 2005.

[6] "UW-FDL Unveils New Mascot," *Fond du Lac Reporter* (30 May 1999). (Lee Watson [UW-FDL athletic dir.], assisting email to the author, 14 April 2006.)

[7] Associated Press, "College Drops Centaur Mascot," *Sun Journal* (20 Oct. 2000): A4. Also in Allentown was the vaguest of classical team names; the Cedar Crest College **Classics** became **Falcons** in the early 1990s.

[8] Be on the lookout for redundancy at cities or institutions named for canonized persons. The St. Paul **Apostles** (referring to the apostle Paul) bounced around several baseball leagues before joining a resurrected AA in 1902. They were the St. Paul **Saints** from 1915 to 1960. The WHA Minnesota **Fighting Saints** battled through the 1976/77 season in St. Paul.

[9] Bill Scott (USF sports info. dir.), email to the author, 5 Oct. 2011. Scott cites the cover story in the campus *Jongleur* (27 March 1975). Like *troubadour*, *jongleur* is a French-derived description of a wandering minstrel.

[10] Another theory suggests that both *hoya saxa* (what rocks) and "**Stonewalls**" (a name for early GU baseballers) refer to the old campus's walled quadrangles. Either way, "**Hilltoppers**" was the most official name until newspapers used "**Hoyas**" consistently in the late 1920s. (Georgetown's bulldog mascots predate its use of "**Hoyas**" by a decade.)

Leading into Civil War, there were debates and brawls at Georgetown, with the majority of student-soldiers leaving the U.S. capital to become Confederates. Blue and gray colors were first worn by the 1876 crew team to suggest post-war unity between North and South.

[11] Julie Ingersoll and J. Gordon Melton, *Baptist and Methodist Faiths in America* (New York: Infobase, 2003): 77.

[12] "**Commoners**" (and lady "**Lassies**") are reported by D.W. Ryther (dean at Bryan College) in a letter (26 Nov. 1935) in George Earlie Shankle, *American Nicknames: Their Origin and Significance* (New York: H.W. Wilson, 1955): 509.

[13] Bryan's letter is referenced in Gerald Priest, "William Jennings Bryan and the Scopes Trial: A Fundamentalist Perspective," *Detroit Baptist Seminary Journal* (fall 1999): 71–72.

Chapter 43 Notes

[1] Reuben E. Alley, *History of the University of Richmond* (Charlottesville: University Press of Virginia, 1977): 75. UR's web slinging mascot is named WebstUR.

[2] Brian McDonald, *Indian Summer: The Forgotten Story of Louis Sockalexis* (Emmaus, Pa.: Rodale, Inc., 2003): 31.

[3] McDonald, *Indian Summer*: 57, 174. McDonald further states (p. 57) that spectators had a tough time disassociating "**Indians**" from the real Amerindian in right field, a man newspapers called "the Indian." An 1897 nickname from the manager, "Patsy Tebeau's Indians," appears in Terry Pluto, *Our Tribe* (New York: Simon & Schuster, 1999): 42.

[4] Pluto, *Our Tribe*: 45. Pluto devotes a chapter to various names for Cleveland's ALers. Also see Daniel P. Barr, "Looking Backward: The Life and Legend of Louis Francis Sockalexis" in C. Richard King, ed., *Native Athletes in Sport & Society* (Lincoln: U. Nebraska Press, 2005): 34–35. Mr. King (along with Charles Fruehling Springwood) also edited *Team Spirits: The Native American Mascot Controversy* (Lincoln: U. Nebraska Press, 2001), which includes Ellen J. Staurowsky's oft-cited essay "Sockalexis and the Making of the Myth at the Core of Cleveland's 'Indian' Image."

[5] Bruce E. Johansen, *The Native Peoples of North America: A History, Vol. 2* (Westport, Conn.: Praeger, 2005): 430.

[6] Pluto, *Our Tribe*: 50–51. Pluto also says (p. 49) that Somers was in debt and dumped Lajoie to get rid of his hefty contract. Besides admiring the miracle of the 1914 **Braves**, Somers already had Beantown sympathies. His coal fortune funded the early AL, and he brought a 1901 team to Boston (today's **Red Sox**) that was sometimes **Somersets** in his honor. A variant of *somersault*, *somerset* hints at athleticism. Also, the Somerset social club on Somerset Street has been a prestigious Boston address since the 1850s.

[7] Rob Neyer and Eddie Epstein, *Baseball Dynasties: The Greatest Teams of All Time* (New York: W.W. Norton, 2000): 155. Despite the title, some terrible squads are discussed. If we count the 1884 Union Association as a major league (some historians don't), the .111 winning percentage (2-16) of the Wilmington [Del.] **Quicksteps** made the **Spiders** look good at .130.

[8] Peter Mancuso's Mutrie bio tracks the **Gothams/Maroons/Giants** names through press accounts as part of *The Baseball Biography Project*, an online presentation of the Society for American Baseball Research, http://sabr.org/bioproj/person/430838fd (accessed 21 Sep. 2011). Mancuso says Mutrie's celebration of "My Giants!" in 1885 is probably a twentieth-century fabrication by Mutrie and others. In fact, headlines from the *New York World* show the casual evolution from "**Maroons**" to "**Gotham Giants**" to "**Giants**" over the summer of 1885. See them for yourself at *The Big Apple*, www.barrypopik.com/index.php/new_york_city/entry/giants_national_league_baseball_team_now_in_san_francisco (accessed 14 Aug. 2014), a web site that contains the backstories for hundreds of New Yorkisms compiled by Barry Popik, to whom we are grateful for assistance via email (29 Dec. 2007).

The 1883 NL **Giants** were a new franchise built from the old Troy **Trojans**, but the **Mets** were an existing AA team. Since the 1870s, Day had owned an independent Brooklyn team for which he desired a Manhattan fanbase, so they were **Metropolitans**. (The city of Brooklyn would be independent of New York for another two decades.) That name didn't persuade enough Manhattanites to ferry over to Brooklyn's Capitoline Grounds, and there would be no famous bridge across the East River until 1883. So in 1880, Day moved his **Mets** to a recreation field historically called the "polo grounds" immediately north of today's Central Park. The creation of the **Gothams/Giants** allowed Day to accept invitations to bring (what was presumed to have been) the **Mets** into both leagues after 1882. The **Giants** had their own grandstand and diamond at the polo grounds, but both clubs moved to Polo Grounds II for '89.

[9] The New York **Mutuals** and Philadelphia **Athletics** were expelled after the 1876 season for not making road trips to the westernmost NL parks, so the league embarrassingly didn't have teams in the country's two largest cities for six seasons. The circuit returned to both burgs in 1883 to counter the threat of the year-old AA, and the new **Gothams** absorbed and replaced the Troy [N.Y.] **Trojans** while the **Quakers/Phillies** replaced the Worcester [Mass.] **Worcesters**. Troy and Worcester were compensated with the "National League City" status they maintain, although neither has hosted MLB entrants since.

[10] For a team name with the most hang time, consider the 1873-founded CFL Toronto **Argonauts**, who suspended a few seasons only so that players could fight in two world wars.

[11] Rich Westcott, *Tales from the Phillies Dugout* (Champaign, Ill.: Sports Publishing L.L.C., 2006): 17. On p. 43, Westcott says manager Hans Lobert tried and failed to officially shorten "**Phillies**" to "**Phils**" in 1942.

[12] The City of Greater New York was the consolidation of five administrative areas in 1898. Those boroughs are The Bronx, Brooklyn, Manhattan, Staten Island, and Queens. The latter's Queensborough Community College once had **Burros**. Uninspired by the Spanish word for donkey, jocks switched to **Tigers** in 1989. (Pete Marchitello [QCC athletic dir.], email to the author, 18 April 2008.)

[13] "Moreover, half a dozen NL owners had a financial interest in the New York [**Giants**],

dating back to some rescue work that had been done during the PL war of 1890." So say James Quirk and Rodney D. Fort in *Pay Dirt: The Business of Professional Team Sports* (Princeton, N.J.: Princeton U. Press, 1992): 310. In 1901, Andrew Freedman almost talked the other NL teams into a single super-syndicate in which the team in the largest city—Freedman's own **Giants**—would own the most stock.

Chapter 44 Notes

[1] Several "Boston Martyrs" were executed in 1659 for their Quakerism by John Endicott, the Massachusetts Bay Colony governor. Endicott came to lead the colony after taking control of Salem's fledgling settlement in 1628. The town of Beverly was cut from Salem in 1668. It's where the Endicott College **Power Gulls** refer to the oceanfront campus.

[2] See Sydney G. Fisher, *The Quaker Colonies* (New Haven: Yale U. Press, 1919): 5.

[3] The NA's **Quaker** of Philadelphia (1867–68) was followed by NL Philadelphia **Quakers** (1883–89). Only when new **Quakers** appeared in the 1890 Players' League did the latter permanently switch to their "**Phillies**" alternate. In semi-pro and pro football, Philadelphia **Quakers** go back at least to 1921, with one such team winning the AFL's only title (1926). The NHL's Pittsburgh **Pirates** were named after local baseballers in 1925 but the skated cross-state as Philadelphia **Quakers** for their final season (1930/31). Fifteen miles east of Pittsburgh were independent football's powerful Pitcairn **Quakers** (est. 1904), who chose not to join the APFA/NFL in 1920 and fizzled out thereafter.

[4] The birthplace of the first internationally famous American painter, Quaker son Benjamin West (1738–1820), is now Swarthmore's visitor center. The part of Springfield Township that William Penn gave to Quakers in 1681 was later Westdale (after the artist) and then Swarthmore upon the college's founding. Club teams in intercollegiate disc football are **Earthworms** (men) and **Warmothers** (women), both anagrams of *Swarthmore*.

[5] Diane M. Laurent, ed., "History," Old Haverford Friends Meeting, http://www.oldhaverford.org/history (accessed 14 August 2014). In fact, "in Wales [Quakerism] appealed to the gentry far more frequently than to the educated classes in England" if you ask Edward Digby Baltzell, *Puritan Boston and Quaker Philadelphia* (New York: Free Press, 1979): 116.

[6] Some Haverford sources say that their **Hornets** or **Scarlet and Black** were never called **Little Quakers** (see Joanne V. Creighton, "View from Founders," *Haverford* [winter 2012]: 3), but we found plenty such references in newspaper archives from the interwar period.

Union College (Lincoln, Neb.) is also nearly overrun with red and black versions of the eastern fox squirrel (*Sciurus niger*). Union students embrace unofficial squirrel mascots, but basketballers were arbitrarily called **Warriors** in 1986, giving name to subsequent UC teams.

Only Haverford has **Black Squirrel** jocks, but such campus critters have given less official black squirrel mascots to Kent State, Sarah Lawrence, and Albion. *Albion* is from the Latin for white (*albus*), so it's too bad AC isn't home to the even rarer white squirrel, which is the opposite of the black squirrel in that it has *too little* melanin. White squirrels are campus symbols at Brevard College, Oberlin College, Western Kentucky, Louisville, and UT–Austin.

[7] Sinnott's mansion was *Rathalla*, Gaelic for "chieftain of the highest hill," possibly a good-natured jab at the Welsh *bryn mawr* (high hill). Haverford, Villanova, Bryn Mawr, and Rosemont are "Main Line communities," not incorporated towns. And we don't know how officially "**Main Liners**" applied to Villanovans; Lehigh's *Brown and White* repeatedly called teams from Villanova, Haverford, or Swarthmore **Main Liners** (or **Mainliners**) through the 1930s, and Haverford's side is called "main liners" in "No Match for Lehigh," *New York Times* (20 Oct. 1912), reproduced at http://query.nytimes.com/mem/archive-free/pdf?res=9502E2D6113 AE633A25753C2A9669D946396D6CF (accessed 15 Aug. 2014).

[8] Malone U., "Mission Statement, School Colors, Mascot & Motto," www.malone.edu/student-life/handbook/mission-statement.php (accessed 4 June 2013).

[9] John W. Oliver et al., ed., *Founded by Friends: The Quaker Heritage of 15 American Colleges and Universities* (Lanham, Md.: Scarecrow Press, 2007): 189.

[10] Tamara Cissna, ed., "Mascot à la Carte," *George Fox University Life* (summer 2004): 8. The same page says Bruin grew to unmanageable size and was converted to bear steaks in 1892. This wasn't the only black bear cub to have astounded collegian handlers by getting bigger. Arizona's Phoenix College **Bears** are named for a cub purchased from a circus in 1920, but he was passed to a zoo when he began to exhibit the very ferocity that inspires athletic **Bears**. Refer to Joe Gacioch, "Mascot Bumstead Once Roamed Campus," *Bear Tracks* (6 May 1966), reproduced on the Phoenix College website at www.pc.maricopa.edu/information/bear/mascot.html (accessed 21 Sep. 2011).

[11] Karen Weston (UWW archives), email to the author, 28 Jan. 2005.

Chapter 45 Notes

[1] The **Braves** tried to duck recent mediocre seasons by becoming Boston **Bees** ("**Bs**") in 1936, but they were **Braves** again by 1941. Lou Perini owned the **Braves** and Milwaukee's minor league **Brewers**, so he used his territorial rights to nix the relocation of the St. Louis **Browns** to Wisconsin. Enraged Milwaukeeans threatened to revoke the **Brewers**' lease, forcing Perini to make his Bostonians the Milwaukee **Braves** for 1953. (They hadn't drawn well against the AL **Red Sox** anyway.) That was the first city-switch for major leaguers since the 1902 **Orioles** had become the '03 **Highlanders/Yankees**.

In Atlanta, the **Braves** owned soccer's 1967 NPSL/NASL Atlanta **Chiefs**. They were sold to the Atlanta **Hawks** for their final season (1973) and became Atlanta **Apollos**, probably just because *Atlanta* and *Apollo* are both derived from Greek gods (Atlas and Apollo, respectively). A later **Braves** owner (Ted Turner) ran different NASL Atlanta **Chiefs** (1979–81).

[2] Margaret Smagorinsky and Wink Einthoven, *The Tigers of Princeton University* (Princeton, N.J.: Princeton U. Office of Communications, 1992): 6.

[3] Harvey Frommer, *Primitive Baseball* (New York: Atheneum, 1988): 9. The independent **Mutuals** (sometimes Mutual **Green Stockings**) joined the NA in 1871 and the NL in '76. The 1858 *New York* **Mutuals** of Hoboken, New Jersey moved to Brooklyn in 1868 with the same name, although Brooklyn wasn't part of New York for another thirty years.

[4] Frommer, *Primitive Baseball*: 9. See Steven A. Riess, "The Baseball Magnates and Urban Politics in the Progressive Era: 1895–1920," in *The American Sporting Experience: A Historical Anthology of Sport in America* (Champaign, Ill.: Leisure Press, 1984): 280. See also Robert F. Burk, *Never Just a Game: Players, Owners, & American Baseball to 1920* (Chapel Hill: U. North Carolina Press, 1994): 11, 31.

[5] Before the Civil War the **Unions** were created by the *union* of greater Albany teams, the Lansingburgh **National Club** and Troy **Priams**. (Priam was Troy's king during the Trojan War.) After they became **Haymakers**, the name stuck in Troy with basketball's ABL Troy **Haymakers** (1938–40), and "**Haymakers**" was an alternate for the NA Troy **Trojans** (1880–81). As for "**Haymakers**" itself, read accounts of Tammany attitudes toward Albany Republicans in either "New York City Is Pie for the Hayseeds" or "Brooklynites Natural-Born Hayseeds" in William L. Riordan, *Plunkitt of Tammany Hall* (1905; reprint, New York: E.P. Dutton, 1963), a compilation of speeches by Tammany ward boss George Washington Plunkitt.

[6] Neil W. Macdonald, *The League That Lasted* (Jefferson, N.C.: McFarland, 2004): 30–31.

[7] After the **Mutes** left the NL, the slack was picked up by the blue-socked Hartford [Conn.] **Dark Blues**, started in 1874 as an NA road stop between New York and Boston. As Brooklyn **Hartfords**, they played at the **Mutes**' Union Grounds in 1877 but folded at season's end.

[8] The Chicago **Machine** re-geared as Columbus's Ohio **Machine** in 2012. Despite the political pun, the Chicago **Machine's** gear emblem alluded to both the city's industrial power and famous basketballers of the past. Maurice White's American Gear and Manufacturing Com-

pany sponsored the Chicago **American Gears** (est. 1944). After winning the '47 NBL crown with rookie center George Mikan, White got greedy and formed the Professional Basketball League of America, in which he controlled all teams. Unable to compete with the BAA and NBL, it crashed in a month. The **Gears** were stripped and seeded back to the NBL. Mikan went to the Minneapolis **Lakers** and promptly won the '48 NBL crown.

[9] Let this monster note illustrate Tammany control of New York sports. Brush's heirs sold the **Giants** to the machine's Wall Street man, Charles Stoneham, whose shady trading was through mobster Arnold Rothstein, who owned a pool hall with **Giant** manager John McGraw. Rothstein had brokered the 1919 sale of the **Giants** to Stoneham and (probably) fixed that year's **White Sox-Reds** World Series. Tim Mara was Tammany's [then-legal] bookmaker who started the NFL's 1925 New York *Football* **Giants**, named after Stoneham's baseballers.

That Rothstein and Andrew Freedman were Jews indicates the Irish-Democratic machine's sway with other ethnic groups: "In some Tammany-controlled lower Manhattan wards, Jewish immigrants came to hold the balance of power" (says Moses Rischin, *The Promised City* [Cambridge, Mass.: Harvard U. Press, 1962]: 228). In 1915, Joseph Gordon's Tammany faction sold the AL **Yankees** to "the Colonels." Former Tammany-backed U.S. Senator Jacob Ruppert (D-New York) had served briefly in the National Guard and thereafter maintained his honorary captaincy. Tillinghast Huston was a Spanish-American War captain and an actual Great War colonel. Ruppert wanted the team to be **Knickerbockers** after his famous brewery, but sportswriters urged him to leave the famous name of Alexander Cartwright's pioneering team alone. (See Richard J. Tofel, *A Legend in the Making: The New York Yankees in 1939* [Chicago: Ivan R. Dee, 2002]: 8.) With its guys running Stoneham's **Giants** and Ruppert's **Yankees**, Tammany politicians overturned New York's blue laws in 1919 so that working-class constituents could catch a game on their day off. The 1920 **Giants**—who'd been getting outdrawn by the **Yanks**' newly acquired baby-faced slugger—evicted the ALers to capitalize on new Sunday dates on which they'd often host teams from remaining blue law cities (Boston, Philadelphia, Pittsburgh). That pushed the 1923 **Yankees** across the Harlem River into a new House that Ruth Built. But owing to MLB's territorial rules, the **Giants** still couldn't compete with the **Yankees**' Sunday games. For the **Yanks**' eviction from the Polo Grounds see the "Fall of the Giants" chapter in Henry D. Fetter, *Taking on the Yankees* (New York: Norton, 2003). For the connections between big city politicos like Tammany and their baseball teams, refer again to Riess, *The American Sporting Experience* ("The Baseball Magnates and Urban Politics in the Progressive Era: 1895–1920"). Also see the first chapter in Glenn Stout and Richard A. Johnson, *Yankees Century* (New York and Boston: Houghton Mifflin, 2002).

August Belmont was an agent of Europe's Rothschild family whose Democratic politics somewhat allied him with Tammanites. He financed the building of the Bronx's Jerome Park in 1866 and sponsored its first Belmont Stakes race the next year. As a reform advocate, he fell from Tammany favor in 1872, but his son (August, Jr.) bankrolled New York's subway system and was on the steering committee with Andrew Freedman (who'd sold baseball's **Giants** in 1902 to concentrate on that effort). Junior built Belmont Park in 1905, which has since hosted his father's race (the last jewel in the Triple Crown). At age 65 he volunteered for service in France during World War I. In his absence, his wife named a new foal Man O' War for him. Not knowing the yearling would become history's most revered thoroughbred, the Belmonts sold him in 1918. Starting with a Belmont Park win the next year, "Big Red" lost only one of twenty-one races (to a challenger name Upset). Man O' War retired to a Kentucky farm in 1920, as remembered by minor league hockey's Lexington **Men O' War** (2002/03).

[10] Jules Tygiel, *Past Times: Baseball as History* (New York: Oxford U. Press, 2000): 53. Two Hall of Famers went from the **Orioles** to the **Giants** in the swap. They were "Ironman" Joe McGinnity and Roger Bresnahan.

[11] The buyers that Gordon represented were bookie Frank J. Farrell and crooked police captain William Devery. Farrell and "Big Bill" had been left vulnerable in the reform tide and were

diverting gambling investments into the legit baseball biz.

[12] To repeat, nicknames of the era were rarely official, and Hilltop's **Highlanders** had plenty, including "**Hilltoppers**" and "**Americans**," the latter distinguishing them from the *National* League **Giants** south of Washington Heights and indicating Hilltop's actual name, American League Park. It's probable that club president Joseph Gordon's surname had advanced "**Highlanders**" as well; the 92nd Gordon Highlanders were Scottish regimentals who'd served famously throughout the British Empire in the previous century.

[13] Several possible etymologies for *Yankee* are famously listed in H.L. Mencken, *The American Language: Supplement One* (New York: Knopf, 1962): 192–197.

[14] Philip J. Deloria, *Playing Indian* (New Haven: Yale U. Press 1998): 49–53. Deloria fully examines Tammany's "Indianness" and its later embrace of Columbus and Columbia.

[15] The Knickerbocker Rules didn't address the number of players, and to some this June 19 contest seems no more profoundly regulated by those guidelines than were games in the previous season. (See Joel Zoss and John Bowman, *Diamonds in the Rough: The Untold History of Baseball* [New York: Macmillan, 1989]: 57.) The **Nine** are sometimes listed as "**New Yorks**," and many suggest they were a collection of **Knickerbocker** stars.

The **Knickerbockers** introduced matching team uniforms, although they ironically left one permanent innovation—the knicker pants from which their name was derived—to a later team, the 1868 Cincinnati **Red Stockings**.

[16] Long before Irving, English folktales associated "Gotham" with mad city dwellers. "Wise fools of Gotham" first appeared in a story in which courtiers looked into building a royal road through a Nottinghamshire town. Such projects had a way of exhausting local taxes with little to show for it (like the modern Olympics), so Gothamites conspired to seem so sufficiently cuckoo that the ambassadors were unable to make a favorable report to the king.

[17] Edwards wanted Iowans to be "Hawkeyes" to avoid "a more opprobrious title, something similar to that by which the people of Missouri are frequently designated." (Refer to a letter to the editor of the *Burlington Hawk-eye* [21 Nov. 1878] in Edward H. Stiles, "David Rorer," *Annals of Iowa* [April 1907]: 122.) The unnamed opprobrium was "Puke State." So many lead seekers had rushed to Missouri that it appeared the earth had thrown them up through mine shafts near the "badger dens" (sod houses) that gave name to Wisconsin's **Badgers**.

[18] "Hot Off the Press: History of the Kohawks," *Coe College Class News* (fall 2009): 3.

[19] *Loras College 2005–2006 Student Handbook* (Dubuque: Loras Coll., 2005): 5. The Cooperstown **Hawkeyes** of collegiate summer baseball (at Doubleday Field) reclaimed "hawkeye" for J.F. Coopers' hometown in 2010.

[20] Mark Engel (UDM sports info. office), emails to the author, 4 and 9 March 2009. Some U. Detroit footballers got together as semi-pro Detroit **Heralds** in 1905 and later played against Ohio League and APFA sides. They officially played (half of) the 1921 APFA (NFL) schedule under UD's former moniker, Detroit **Tigers**.

Chapter 46 Notes

[1] Joseph Conlin, *The American Past* (Boston: Wadsworth, 2009): 274.

[2] L.I.U., "Traditions," www.liu.edu/cwpost/about/history/traditions (accessed 14 May 2012).

[3] Mavis Burnette, "Pioneers Never Had it So Good," *The Pioneer Press* (Western Piedmont Comm. Coll.: May 1979): 6.

[4] The scientific name for the bobcat/wildcat had been punned upon before. The University of Arizona's **Varsity Blue and Red** traveled to California to lose to Occidental's football **Tigers** in 1914, after which *L.A. Times* scribe Bill Henry said the Arizonans had fought "like wildcats." They've been **Wildcats** since. The next year their mascot was a real live desert bobcat (*Lynx rufus baileyi*) named Rufus, after newly arrived UA president Rufus B. von KleinSmid.

The NBA's 2004 expansion team zoomorphized the first name of owner Bob Johnson to get

Charlotte **Bobcats**. Their *Lynx rufus* mascot is Rufus Lynx. (Johnson's proprietorship was noteworthy because he was the first African American to own a major sports franchise, having successfully run the Black Entertainment Television network.) Of course, the NBA might have noticed other North Carolina **Bobcats** at Lees-McRae College in Banner Elk, a hundred miles northwest of Charlotte. The first collegiate **Bobcats** were so named in 1920 at Texas State University–San Marcos after the biology department cited bobcats as four-tool players with "claws, teeth, speed, and brains." See Diana Finlay, ed., "Spirit and Tradition," *Celebrate San Marcos 150!* (1 March 2001): 10C.

[5] Ramona Stamm (KSU communications/marketing office), email to the author, 13 April 2006.

[6] See "Why the Thundering Herd?" *Marshall Football 2007* (Huntington, W.Va.: Marshall U., 2007): 123–127, 200. On November 14, 1970 nearly everyone associated with Marshall's football program died when their chartered plane crashed on return from a game against East Carolina's **Pirates**. The 1971 team of underclassmen was the **Young Thundering Herd**.

In the Days of the Thundering Herd was a 1914 movie with cowboy star Tom Mix. The 1920 powerhouse team at Washington, D.C.'s Howard University—now the **Bison**—was also a **Thundering Herd**, according to Michael Hurd, *Black College Football: 1892–1992* (Virginia Beach: Donning Co., 1993): 156. Both events predate Zane Gray's 1925 novel.

[7] Pittsburgh's African American population grew after Southern black coal miners were brought to the steel mills during an 1892 strike. From 1937 to 1948, Pittsburgh's popular **Grays** played some Sunday "home" games at D.C.'s Griffith Stadium, often outdrawing their **Senator** landlords. (They're sometimes "Washington-Homestead **Grays**" for those years.) Before 1910 the **Grays** had been the Germantown **Blue Ribbons** and Murdock **Grays**.

Chapter 47 Notes

[1] Pawtucket **Slaters** have played class B baseball (1946–49) and one ABL season (1952/53). Pawtucket **Slaterettes** (est. 1973) are in the country's oldest all-female baseball league.

[2] More anecdotally, the independent club's owner heard a fan say the Providence **Pros** were "getting steam rolled" in their first-ever game in 1916. He thereafter attached "**Steam Roller**" to his future NFLers. See Robert W. Peterson, *Pigskin: The Early Years of Pro Football* (New York: Oxford U. Press, 1997): 64 and David B. Biesel, *Can You Name That Team?* (Lanham, Md.: Scarecrow, 2002): 59.

[3] Other locals included hockey's minor league Quad City **Mallards** (1995–2007). They were immediately replaced by Quad City **Flames** (a Calgary farm team). Minor league hoop had the Quad City **Thunder** (1987–2001). Despite the multi-city nickname, these clubs—and the **Steamwheelers**—all played in the same Moline arena.

[4] Indoor soccer had two sets of St. Louis **Steamers** (1979–88, 2000–06). The 1999-named River City **Rascals** play minor league ball in the St. Louis suburb of O'Fallon, tucked between the Missouri and the Mississippi. The **Rascals'** Jack Russell terrier mascot copies the dog from *The Little Rascals* (1922–44), a popular film series about kids in an American Anytown.

[5] Since 1975, D-port's weekend warriors have run the Bix 7 and Quick Bix, seven- and two-mile road races that coincide with the Bix Beiderbecke Jazz Festival.

[6] *Student-Athlete Handbook* (Evansville, Ind.: U. Evansville, 2004): 1.

[7] Transitioning from the University of Lowell to UMass Lowell in the early 1990s, the **Chiefs** became **River Hawks**. (The earliest teams were **Indians** and Lowell Tech **Terriers**.)

[8] Elizabeth Faulkner Baker, *Technology and Woman's Work* (New York: Columbia U. Press, 1964): 10.

[9] Baker, *Technology and Woman's Work*: 16.

[10] The AHL **Lock Monsters** were sold to the New Jersey **Devils** in 2006 and became Lowell

Devils. (They've been Albany [N.Y.] **Devils** since 2010.) The lake monster "Champy" was first spotted in Lake Champlain by Samuel de Champlain himself in 1609 and by hundreds of folks since, so lakeside Burlington's single-A guys are the Vermont **Lake Monsters**. (They were the Vermont **Expos** from 1993 until the year after their Montreal parent club became the 2005 Washington **Nationals**, but Champy was the franchise mascot even in those days.) Cleveland's 2007-named AHL Lake Erie **Monsters** salute the Nessie-like "Bessie," a large, strange serpent spotted multiple times since 1793. (She's named for southwestern Lake Erie's Davis-Besse Nuclear Power Station.) "Loch" is the creature from the campus lakes at Clayton State University (Morrow, Ga.). He's the mascot for **Lakers**.

[11] The **Kings'** and **Monarchs'** regally named ECHL feeder teams are the 2001-named Reading [Pa.] **Royals** and 2008-named Ontario [Calif.] **Reign**.

[12] Isaac Atwater, ed., *History of the City of Minneapolis, Minnesota* (New York: Munsell, 1893): vol. I, p. 39.

[13] Peoria, Illinois on the Illinois River had clear water and Midwestern cereal grasses to feed its whiskey mills, and the "whiskey capital of the world" hosted minor league Peoria **Distillers** (1902–17). After 1880, the sale and consumption of alcohol was outlawed on a state-by-state basis. The Midwestern temperance movement was tied to a resentment of recent immigrants, especially Germans who tended to run the beer biz. Iowa passed a prohibition measure in 1882. Enforcement was delayed for decades by technicalities, despite the minor league Des Moines **Prohibitionists** (1888–1904). Suspicions of German people during World War I gave the pro-Prohibition movement some gas and the U.S. Constitution was so amended in 1917.

[14] *T* and *C* are superimposed on the Twin City team's caps. The **Twins'** mascot, T.C. Bear, remembers the Hamm's Beer bear, a token of the team's former brewery sponsorship.

Baseball's Fargo-Moorhead **Twins** (1933–66) united those Northern League fans from North Dakota and Minnesota who were otherwise divided by the Red River. Two minor league ball-clubs in North Carolina were bursting with multiple-birth pride in the 1930s and '40s as Winston-Salem **Twins** and Leaksville-Spary-Draper **Triplets**. There's a 2009-named hardball side called the Winston-Salem **Dash** (as in the punctuation), and minor league hockey had semi-identical Winston-Salem **Polar Twins** (1973–77, 2004/05).

Thunder Bay was created by merging the twin Ontario cities of Fort William and Port Arthur in 1970, so junior hockey's Fort William **Beavers** and Port Arthur **Bearcats** combined as Thunder Bay **Twins**. The Port Huron [Mich.] **BorderCats** (1996–2001) played minor league hockey. The Texarkana **Twins** were of a couple of short-lived minor league baseball teams in Texarkana, Texas, where the main street—State Line Ave.—straddles the Arkansas border. (Twenty miles away is Louisiana, which accounts for Texarkana's *-ana* suffix.) Collegians on this theme are rare, but Columbia-Greene Community College's **Twins** (Hudson, N.Y.) are named for counties separated by the Hudson. Some minor leaguers dashed past the obvious as **Hyphens**. Refer to baseball's Saginaw-Bay City [Mich.] **Hyphens** (1890), Sheldon-Primghar [Iowa] **Hyphens** (1903), and Amsterdam-Gloversville-Johnstown [N.Y.] **Hyphens** (1903–04). The *Twin* States League's Springfield-Charlestown (respective Vermont and New Hampshire towns) **Hyphens** drew fans on both sides of the Connecticut in 1911.

[15] Fall River's **Marksmen** actually played over the border in North Tiverton, Rhode Island to avoid Puritanical Massachusetts blue laws that forbid Sunday games.

Chapter 48 Notes

[1] Isabel Simon Levinson, *Gibbons v. Ogden* (Springfield, N.J.: Enslow, 1999): 78.

[2] To sell short you'd borrow 500 shares of MascotCorp stock from a broker at $10 per share. Then you'd sell them at their total market value, $5,000. It looks like you've broken even, but you do have to pay back the 500 shares (not the five grand). If you drove MascotCorp down to $8 by dumping shares onto the market that you'd purchased earlier on the cheap, paying up would cost you only $4,000 (that is, 500 x $8), yielding a $1,000 gain.

[3] The strong forestry program in the early days of Olympic College (Bremerton, Wash.) justi-
fied its **Rangers**. Like the *forest* **Rangers** of Drew U. and Olympic, there are *park* **Rangers** at
U. Wisconsin–Parkside. (UWP was created through the 1968 merger of UW-Racine and UW-
Kenosha. Naming the school for the nearby Petrifying Springs Park was a compromise.) West
London's top-tier soccer fans will recognize the *park* **Rangers** trick in the Queen's Park
Rangers. More **Rangers** represented Portsmouth's Shawnee State University, smack between
two large Ohio state forests. They became **Bears** 1988.

[4] Sister Barbara A. Williams (GCU archives), email to the author, 11 June 2008.

[5] Green was mistaken; Colman's Mustard was from Norwich, England. Yellow dominates the
uniforms of Norwich City F.C., a soccer side often sponsored by Colman's and named **Mus-
tardmen** accordingly. (They're also **Canaries**.) Flemish Protestants of the late 1500s sought
refuge from Spanish Catholic lords by moving to Norwich, bringing their Canary Island birds
with them to start a famous line of "Norwich canaries." Durham, New Hampshire is named for
the English city. Before arbitrarily becoming **Wildcats** in 1926, its University of New Hampshire teams were often Durham **Bulls** in press reports.

[6] Much of *Bull Durham* was shot at the **Bulls**' park. The Raleigh-Durham **Triangles** were
locals from 1971 to '72, but the **Bulls** returned in 1980. As for "**Triangles**," Raleigh, Durham,
and Chapel Hill are the respective homes of NC State, Duke, and UNC, all of which partnered
with government and business in 1959 to create the world's largest research park, the Research
Triangle. Durham's first baseballers were the **Tobacconists** (1902), and an hour east are the
Wilson [N.C.] **Tobs** (a nick dating back to 1908) … "tobacconists" of collegiate summer ball.

   Bull Durham's lead character chased the minor league home-run record. Cut from the **Bulls**,
he ended up hitting his record dinger with the Asheville **Tourists**, another real North Carolina
team (first named in 1915). Asheville is the gateway to the Great Smoky Mountains, and
"**Tourists**" refers to summer vacationers who flock to the area's cool air. "Altitude affects attitude" is the Asheville adage that inspired development basketball's Asheville **Altitude** (2001–
05). From Asheville, hop over the Smokies to Line Drive in Kodak to see baseball's Tennessee
Smokies. (They're former Knoxville **Smokies** from just ten miles west, so named in 1925.)

[7] Carr promoted the Bull Durham brand on a national scale with painted billboards on downtown bricks and outfield walls. The latter is often cited as the reason the pitchers' warm-up area
is the bullpen, although those enclosures already looked enough like corrals.

[8] The DeLand Academy timeline owes to multiple emails to the author from Gail Grieb
(Stetson U. archives), Feb.–Mar. 2005. Mr. DeLand's downfall came when he honored a
gentlemen's agreement to buy back frozen orchards from some of the growers he'd lured to
Florida. (Bill Dreggors, West Volusia Hist. Soc. [DeLand, Fla.], email to the author, 16 Feb.
2005.)

[9] Stetson may have copied his ten-gallon hat from England's Christy's firm (to whom he lost a
famous patent case). *Vaqueros* wove braids called *galóns* into their sombrero brims as badges
of ranching merit, so the first ten-*galón* hats probably commented on the attired, not the attire.

[10] Local rivers and easy access to New York's port attracted enough cap factories to make
Danbury, Connecticut "Hat City" by 1900. In fact, the Stetson Company bought a hat factory
there in 1950. Danbury **Hatters** (1912–17) played pro hoops in greater New York leagues.
Minor league Danbury **Mad Hatters** (2008/09) tried for hockey hat-tricks. They and a same-
named rugby squad (est. 1978) recall the Mad Hatter from Lewis Carroll's 1865 book *Alice's
Adventures in Wonderland*. Summertime's Danbury **Westerners** (est. 1995) play collegiate
baseball under a cowboy hat emblem.

[11] Jacksonville's first WFLers—the 1974 Jacksonville **Sharks**—failed three ways: [1] They
had a 4 for 14 record; [2] They lost a boxcar of money; [3] Civic leaders thought the name hurt
coastal businesses, although indoor footballers resurrected "Jacksonville **Sharks**" in 2010.

[12] Most **Athletics** (or Babylon **Black Panthers**) had played for Washington's **Manhattans**,

Philadelphia's **Orions**, and Thompson's own **Keystone Athletics** of Philadelphia.

[13] Jerry Malloy, "The Birth of the Cuban Giants," in William Kirwin, ed., *Out of the Shadows: African American Baseball from the Cuban Giants to Jackie Robinson* (Lincoln: U. Nebraska Press, 2005): 6. See also Michael E. Lomax, *Black Baseball Entrepreneurs* (Syracuse: Syracuse U. Press, 2003): 95. The **Cuban Giants'** arrival in Florida prompted the creation of the Jacksonville-based Southern League of Colored Base Ballists, ten clubs in the first organized black league. (It lasted only for 1886.) The **Cuban Giants** were probably the first "Jints" in New York papers, a phonetic facsimile still applied to football's **Giants**.

[14] Donn Rogosin, *Invisible Men: Life in Baseball's Negro Leagues* (New York: Atheneum, 1983): 28. See also William F. McNeil, *Baseball's Other All-Stars* (Jefferson, N.C.: McFarland, 2000): 16, 44.

[15] The independent "JAX **Red Caps**" (as uniforms would have it) were Negro American Leaguers in 1938 and '41 (spending '39 and '40 as Cleveland **Bears**). "Red Cap" indicated racial pride because smartly dressed railroad porters were often the first persons of their own complexion that Southern blacks had seen in a professional capacity.

[16] By 1900, Atlantic City had recruited thousands of Southern blacks to service jobs. After the Bacharach **Giants**, white politicians in A.C. continued attaching their own names to African American baseballers to attract black votes. Finishing his pro career with the **B-Giants**, Hall of Fame shortstop Pop Lloyd stayed as player-coach for the Johnson **Stars**, named for the Republican emperor of the boardwalk, Nucky Johnson. Pop Lloyd Stadium opened in 1949 with help from longtime state senator Frank "Hap" Farley, changing Johnson's **Stars** to Farley **Stars**.

[17] Lomax, xxiii. The **X-Giants** motivated the original **Cuban Giants** to bill themselves as *Genuine* **Cuban Giants**.

Chapter 49 Notes

[1] "Origins of the Hobart Statesmen," *H Book* (Alumni Assn. of Hobart Coll., 2006): 16. See also Eric Reuscher, ed., "The Statesmen Nickname," *A Celebration of Hobart Athletics* (April 2003): 7. *The H Book* further states that the **Orange and Purple** became **Deacons** around 1930 to honor athletic director *Deak* Welch. (Hobart's founding bishop John Henry Hobart did have Episcopal deacons as direct reports.) Hobart is a men's college that is a coordinate institution with Geneva's all-female William Smith College, collectively the "Hobart and William Smith Colleges." WSC's **Herons** reference the well-shanked birds of the *Ardeidae* family that wade in the pond next to the field hockey pitch.

[2] Refer to the Merced **Fig Growers** (1910), Stockton **Producers** (1913), San Bernardino **Valencias** (1948), and Salinas **Packers** (1954–58, 1973–75).

[3] In other California sports, the Bakersfield **Aggies** (1977) played pro women's softball and the San Jose/Bakersfield **Jammers** (1990–92) were minor league basketballers. Bakersfield has had another **Jam** team since 2006, but this one in the NBA D-League had already been the Long Beach **Jam** (2003–05), named for a rim bending move, not a fruit preserve.

[4] David S. Neft et al., ed., *The Football Encyclopedia* (New York: St. Martin's Press, 1991): 83. The **Red Jackets** (1929–30) were the rebuilt Minneapolis **Marines** (independent: 1905–21; AFFA/NFL: 1921–24), for whom no naming story is known.

[5] Robert Lyons, *On Any Given Sunday: A Life of Bert Bell* (Philadelphia: Temple U. Press, 2009): 46.

[6] Lyons, *On Any Given Sunday*: 47. North Carolina baseballers sponsored by Asheboro's Acme-McCrary hosiery mill were named after the NRA symbol as McCrary **Eagles** (1933–57), sewing the government's unmistakable eagle onto their jerseys.

[7] John L. Nethers, "Ashland University: Patterns of Expansion," in John William Oliver et al, ed., *Cradles of Conscience: Ohio's Independent Colleges and Universities* (Kent, Ohio: Kent State U. Press, 2003): 34. Ashland's multi-sport coach and athletic director, Fred C. Schmuck,

had a different story, saying jocks became **Eagles** in 1933 because eagles "fly by night and the members of the teams often travel by night." See his correspondence (19 Nov. 1935) in Shankle, *American Nicknames* (1937): 22.

Chapter 50 Notes

[1] Barnum's circus wintered in Bridgeport, Connecticut. His estate is now the University of Bridgeport campus. The Canada geese (*Branta canadensis*) who hang out there led to the goose as the first UB mascot in 1935, but **"Geese"** was never the athletic moniker. (See Janet Greenwood, *The University of Bridgeport* [New York: Newcomen Soc., 1988]: 13.) It's not known why or when UB teams became **Purple Knights**.

[2] The misplaced Madison Square Garden would have reminded New Yorkers of the Polo Grounds, which hadn't occupied a former polo field since baseball's **Giants** moved uptown four decades earlier. If you think a Madison Square Garden that isn't in Madison Square is a bit of a stretch, Rickard's MSG Corporation opened the *Boston* Madison Square Garden in 1928. "Madison Square" was quickly dropped from what was home for **Bruins** and **Celtics** until 1998. In the age of naming rights, the replacement arena sometimes incorporates "Garden" into the name and sometimes does not.

[3] A later team of Rochester [N.Y.] **Americans** (est. 1956) was named by their Montreal **Canadien** parents for international distinction. (They're now Buffalo **Sabre** affiliates.)

The Garden's senior New York **Rovers** (est. 1935) fed the NHL **Rangers** and their AHL **Ramblers**. Being synonymous with ranging and rambling, *rover* was also a position from the early days of hockey for a seventh skater who lacked a fixed position.

[4] British Commonwealth subjects got sucked into WW2 earlier than their U.S. counterparts, so the Canadian-heavy NHL rosters were drained ahead of the other major leagues. So many Canadians from New York's **Americans** were serving by 1941 that an attempt was made to distract fans with a new name, *Brooklyn* **Americans** (who practiced in Brooklyn and played at the Garden). America was heavily into war after Pearl Harbor was bombed in the middle of the 1941/42 season, and the last-place **Americans** folded in the spring.

Chapter 51 Notes

[1] Keith McClellan, *The Sunday Game* (Akron: U. Akron Press, 1998): 4. Some sources say Massillon's orange-and-black jerseys copied those of Princeton's **Tigers**.

[2] Steven A. Riess, *City Games* (Chicago: U. Illinois Press, 1989): 155.

[3] Jack Newcombe, *The Best of the Athletic Boys: The White Man's Impact on Jim Thorpe* (New York: Doubleday, 1975): 221.

[4] Pros in the 1903-founded Ohio League were (mostly) in Ohio cities. The league gave quality football to Midwesterners who were distanced from the east coast Ivy League colleges until the 1920 establishmend of the APFA (NFL) in Canton.

[5] Carl M. Becker, "The 'Famous' Ironton Tanks," *Coffin Corner*, Vol. XIX, No. 3 (1997): 15–19, and Bob Carroll (Professional Football Researchers Assn. exec. dir.), emails to the author, 27 and 28 July 2007.

[6] The founding of the APFA/NFL in Canton gives that city the Pro Football Hall of Fame, where legends are enshrined. It was also the home city for the American Indoor Football League and its Canton **Legends** (2005–08).

[7] Akron's **Burkhardts** (est. 1916) were named for a local brewing family, but footballers took jobs "oddly enough, not in the Burkhardt brewery, but in one of the city's many rubber factories." (Source: *Cleveland Plain Dealer*, 29 Oct. 1916, cited in Marc S. Maltby, *The Origins and Early Development of Pro Football* [New York and London: Garland, 1997]: 137.) Those independents became APFA/NFL **Professionals** (1920–25) and **Indians** (1926). As for Hammond's **Pros**, most home games were at Wrigley Field, thirty miles north of their Indiana base.

[8] Despite an early history as independents, the 1929 **Stapletons** technically operated under the same franchise charter as the 1927 Brooklyn **Lions** and 1928 New York **Yankees**.

[9] The Panhandle **White Sox** (est. 1901) were popular baseballers named for Chicago's new ALers. The Columbus native and sports reporter who ran the football and baseball **Panhandles** was future NFL president Joe Carr.

[10] Duluth's **Eskimos** were alternately the "Ernie Nevers **Eskimos**" (for their former Stanford All-American). They played all 1927 games on the road and were dormant for '28 before reappearing as Newark [N.J.] **Tornadoes** (1929–30). Boston's **Braves** (now Washington's **Redskins**) were assembled in '31 partly from the **Tornadoes'** wreckage, but it's not officially one continuous franchise.

[11] Halas improved the **Staleys** by draining the Hammond **Pros** of talent. (Having been a young New York **Yankees** bench player in 1919, Halas also starred on Staley's baseball squad.) In 2003 the NFL Chicago **Bears** created a uniformed mascot named Staley Da Bear.

[12] Halas wasn't the first to indicate the **Cubs'** relative smallness. In 1914 restaurateur Charles Weeghman built a brick Federal League park on Chicago's North Side. Wanting the **Chi-Feds** to dwarf the park's **Cubs** and **White Sox**, his players were **Whales**. The deal with Organized Baseball that sent the FL and its champion **Whales** belly up after 1915 allowed Weeghman into **Cubs** ownership, so the 1916 **Cubs** absorbed some good **Whales** and moved to Weeghman Park. Minority owner William Wrigley, Jr., bought out his partners in 1920 and renamed the stadium Cubs Park, but it's been Wrigley Field since 1926.

[13] Robin Deutsch and Douglas Stark, "The Roots: Early Professional Leagues," in Jan Hubbard, ed., *The Official NBA Encyclopedia* (New York: Doubleday, 2000): 46.

[14] Wagons made by the Studebaker Brothers in South Bend set out for California's gold fields. From the 1920s to the 1960s, a huge local plant stamped out Studebaker's *Hawk* line: *Golden Hawk, Power Hawk, Silver Hawk*, etc. Near that factory are minor league baseball's 1994-named South Bend **Silver Hawks**.

[15] Michigan's Detroit **Pistons** have been in nearby Auburn Hills since 1988. There's a virtual parts bin of motoring Michigan monikers: IHL Saginaw **Gears** (1972–83), indoor football's Detroit **Drive** (1988–93), MISL Detroit **Ignition** (2006–09), NLL Detroit **Turbos** (1989–94), WFL Detroit **Wheels** (1974), minor league basketball Flint **Fuze** (2001), and minor league hockey Motor City **Mechanics** (2004–06). Lansing **Lugnuts** (est. 1996) play single-A ball ninety miles west of Detroit at Oldsmobile Park in the hometown of auto pioneer Ransom Olds. Early-twentieth-century Michigan makers moved to Ontario's industrial cities, forming General Motors of Canada at Oshawa in 1915. Players from its senior hockey Oshawa **Generals** (1934–53) became the Dunlop Rubber-sponsored Whitby **Dunlops** (1954–60). Junior **Dunlops** and junior Oshawa **Generals** both appeared in 1962.

[16] Marc S. Maltby, *The Origins and Early Development of Pro Football* (New York and London: Garland, 1997): 137–138. See also Carl M. Becker, *Home and Away: The Rise and Fall of Professional Football on the Banks of the Ohio* (Athens: Ohio U. Press, 1998): 85.

[17] Former Postmaster general and Washington insider Amos Kendall was gave some D.C. land to a school for deaf and blind children. He asked Edward Gallaudet to run the academy in 1857, and Gallaudet teams were **Kendalls** for decades. Their colors of buff and blue made them **Blues**, but *buff* (as in *buffalo*) led to **Blue Bisons** in 1941 and then **Bison** in 1958, according to Tom Harrington, ed., "FAQ: Gallaudet Bison–Origin," (2006: Gallaudet U. Library) http://libguides.gallaudet.edu/content.php?pid=351760 (accessed 22 July 2013).

Three miles away, George Washington U. also uses buff and blue, which both schools say copy Continental Army uniforms (and not each other). Reportedly unknown to Gallaudet, Howard University—only *two* miles away—had **Bison** teams before 1941.

[18] The fastest gait, the gallop, is a bumpy ride, so harness horses learn two smoother strides, the trot or the pace. Trotters move diagonally opposed legs together. The unnatural (slightly faster)

pacing gait has both right legs moving forward while both left legs go back and vice-versa. Harness racing at Indianapolis's Indiana State Fairgrounds predates the Indy 500 by decades.

[19] Abraham Aamidor, *Chuck Taylor: Converse All Star* (Bloomington: Indiana U. Press, 2006): 51. Aamidor disproves reports that Taylor played for the Buffalo **Germans** and New York **Original Celtics** (pp. 8, 49, 50, 60). Taylor is a Hall of Famer as a contributor because his sales trips made him a leading ambassador for his young sport.

[20] Indiana has seventy-plus Hoosier Temples, as high school field houses that can accommodate more than 4,000 fans are called. Indiana's rural communities couldn't field enough students for football in the early twentieth century, and cold winters were conducive to indoor sports. The ABA Indiana **Legends** (2000–02) were named after the many native Hoosiers who've made the transition from high school hardwood to national superstardom (Chuck Taylor, Larry Bird, Oscar Robertson, John Wooden, Bobby Knight, etc.).

What boys' hoop is to Indiana, girls' basketball is to Iowa. In fact, Iowans were crazy for their championship tourney based on the girls' six-on-six format until 1993. The AAU's national six-on-six tournaments of the 1930s and '40s were dominated by home-grown squads from two Iowa business colleges, the American Institute of Business **AIBs** in Des Moines and the American Institute of Commerce **Stenos** (stenographers) in Davenport (now Kaplan U.). The last six-on-six state tourney was in Oklahoma in 1995, where different **Stenos** from Tulsa Business College won three AAU crowns from 1934 to '36. The AAU moved to five-on-five play in 1969 to prepare women for international and college competition. (Des Moines's AIB College of Business now has golf, basketball, and volleyball **Eagles**.)

[21] Howard H. Peckham, *Indiana: A Bicentennial History* (New York: W.W. Norton, 1978): 11, 12.

Chapter 52 Notes

[1] Rogers State's earliest squads were **Spartans**, a military theme that may owe to its occupation of the former campus of Oklahoma Military Academy (1919–71). (OMA fielded **Flying Cadets**.) Other pre-**Hillcats** were **Thunderbirds**.

For mascot purposes, the Rogers **Hillcat** is an Ozark bobcat. Elsewhere on the Ozark Plateau, **Bobcats** at Missouri's College of the Ozarks indicate *Lynx rufus*, but we're not sure if that's the westernmost Florida bobcat (*L. r. floridianus*) or the Maine bobcat (*L. r. gigas*). That's because St. Louis sportsmen purchased the Maine Building from the city's 1904 World's Fair and moved it to the White River in southwest Missouri as a Point Lookout hunting lodge. It became the home of C-of-O in 1915. While celebrating a win in 1924, basketballers took the "**Bobcats**" name from the feline mounted on the wall. We'll never know that bobcat's subspecies because the building burned down in 1930. As for New England's "Maine bobcat," it's the emblem for **Wildcats** at Westbrook College (Portland, Maine), Bates College (Lewiston, Maine), and the University of New Hampshire.

[2] In 1933, Oregon State's **Beavers** stopped the USC **Trojans**' twenty-five game win streak with a 0-0 tie using only eleven "Ironmen." A depleted bench forced the University of Iowa to put its 1939 football season on the backs of just a few quality double-duty **Hawkeyes** who are remembered fondly as **Ironmen**. Hampton U. had **Ironmen** for a few years after they "played through the [1925/26 football] season sans substitution." (See Bill Gibson, "Hear Me Talkin' To Ya," *The Afro-American* [6 May 1933]: 17.) Playing the same boys all day was common until World War II, after which available bodies gave way to the game's two-platoon system.

[3] Colorado's fifty-four "fourteeners" (peaks exceeding 14,000 feet) justified D-League hoop's Colorado **14ers** (2006–09, Metro Denver). It gets frosty up that high, and the Colorado **Chill** (2003–06, Loveland) were quality amateurs who failed to get funding to join the WNBA.

[4] Bellevue College's **Bulldogs** (across Lake Washington from Seattle) were **Helmsmen** until 2004. The yearbook at Indiana's Bethel College is the *Helm* and teams are **Pilots** based on the navigable St. Joseph River that runs through Mishawaka. Like many **Pilots**, the Bethel symbol

is a captain's wheel, but as an evangelical college it also claims inspiration from Jesus through the motto "Forward, With Christ at the Helm."

New Jersey's minor league Newark **Co-Pilots** (1968–79) got their name from their parent Seattle **Pilots**, but they were the **Brewers'** property after 1969. After the **Mariners** bought the Everett **Giants** (est. 1984) from San Francisco's MLB **Giants** in 1994, they adopted Seattle's "northwest green" color and were **AquaSox**.

5 Here are more **Lakers** near glacial lakes in the Great Lakes Basin and the Midwest: [1] Nipissing U. (North Bay, Ont.) is on Lake Nipissing. [2] Silver Lake Coll. (Manitowoc, Wis.) is on Silver Lake, four miles west of Lake Michigan. [3] New York's Finger Lakes are ancient river valleys that have been exaggerated by glaciation, putting Finger Lakes Comm. Coll. on Canandaigua Lake. [4] Iowa Lakes Comm. Coll. (Estherville) is surrounded by the Iowa Great Lakes, a scattering of glacial potholes.

6 Trying to keep the WHA off of Long Island was William Shea, who sat on the board of the NHL's Los Angeles **Kings**. See James Quirk and Rodney D. Fort, *Pay Dirt: The Business of Professional Team Sports* (Princeton, N.J.: Princeton U. Press, 1992): 207. Shea—soon of Shea Stadium fame—had created an amorphous 1959 Continental League franchise to force the NL's return to New York, so irony was abundant when he helped crush the WHA and its **Raiders** by creating the **Islanders** just a few years later, a suspiciously timed inception that would be cited in the WHA's antitrust suits against the NHL.

7 Scott Surgent, *The Complete Historical and Statistical Reference to the World Hockey Association* (Tempe, Ariz.: Xaler Press, 2004): 127. (The New Jersey **Knights** were the seaside San Diego **Mariners** from 1974 to '77.) With no respect for the NHL's reserve clause, the WHA was responsible for ballooning salaries, and not since soccer's ASL of the 1920s had a premier league recruited so heavily from Europe. By one vote, the NHL refused to absorb some of the struggling WHA teams in early 1979, so fans of the WHA **Oilers**, **Nordiques**, and **Jets** boycotted Molson beer, who owned the **Canadiens**. Within days Montreal's vote changed and those three teams (plus Hartford's **Whalers**) were in the NHL.

Chapter 53 Notes

1 Junior hockey's Wooster **Oilers** (est. 2006) are between Titusville and Findlay. Other regional teams had oil-rich nicknames. A coal and oil town in West Virginia hosted the NBL Clarksburg **Oilers** (1939/40). Baseball's Interstate League had these Pennsylvania entrants in 1907: Bradford **Drillers**, Oil City **Oilers**, and Franklin **Millionaires**. An Allegheny River processing town barely over the border in New York hosted that same league's Olean **Refiners**. In fact, the only fully professional turn-of-the-twentieth-century footballers were in industrial western Pennsylvania towns, and Oil City and Franklin outbid each other to assemble rival powerhouses, often luring players from the Pittsburgh **Stars** and Philadelphia **Athletics**, so oil money was ultimately behind the all-stars on the Franklin **All-Stars** who won the second annual (and last) World Series of Football at Madison Square Garden in 1903. (See Robert W. Peterson, *Pigskin: The Early Years of Pro Football* [New York: Oxford U. Press, 1997]: 36–37, 42.) Pennsylvania actually had a three-team league called the National Football League in 1902 (only). It included (Homestead) Pittsburgh **Stars**, Philadelphia **Athletics**, and Philadelphia **Phillies**, the latter two operated by same-named baseball neighbors.

2 Tommy Stringer, *Dreams and Visions: The History of Navarro College* (Waco, Texas: Davis Brothers, 1996): 19–20.

3 Spencer W. Robinson, ed., *Spindletop* (Beaumont, Texas: Spindletop 50th Anniversary Commission, 1951): 7.

4 Other Texas schools benefited from the Hardins: [1] Hardin-Simmons U. hosts **Cowboys** and **Cowgirls**; [2] Mrs. Hardin is the eponym at the University of Mary Hardin-Baylor in Belton, a Baptist academy associated with Baylor U. that first fielded **Crusaders** in 1975; [3] In Wichita Falls is the Spanish-colonial Hardin Hall at Midwestern State University (p. 6), which was

called Hardin College until 1950.

[5] A gorilla mascot of the 1920s was called Gus, so PSU's women became **Gussies**. But being "gussied up" puts appearance before performance, so they too were **Gorillas** after 1989.

[6] "**Oilers**" works in Calgary and Edmonton. With oil discoveries in southern Alberta in the early twentieth century, corporate offices were at Calgary. Huge reserves near Edmonton put large refineries there after World War II, but Calgary remained the business center. Both cities shared the WHA Alberta **Oilers**, which was a truce in the long-running Battle of Alberta, which dates to both cities fighting to become the territorial capital in the 1880s. Those battle lines are redrawn whenever the **Oilers** play the **Flames** or the **Eskimos** face the **Stampeders**.

E-Town says it's Canada's City of Champions, starting with the Edmonton **Grads** from Commercial High School. The **Grads** dominated women's hoop from 1915 to 1940 with a record of 502-20 (the best winning percentage of any known team), going undefeated at four Olympiads (1924–36) in the demo sport of women's basketball.

[7] *Dino* is pronounced "*dee*-no." Calgary's women were **Dinnies** from 1964 to '98.

[8] "Redhawks Roundup," *Roberts Today* (summer 2012): 20.

[9] WKU teams were **Teachers** or **Pedagogues** in the press until 1925, based on its normal school past. From the 1920s to the 1960s basketball coach E.A. Diddle riled up fans with his swinging red towel, which brought about the fluffy Big Red mascot in 1979.

Chapter 54 Notes

[1] Chancellor University Communiqué (Cleveland: Chancellor U., 15 Dec. 2008): 2.

[2] Frederick Rudolph, *The American College and University* (New York: Knopf, 1962): 350.

[3] Robin Lester, *Stagg's University: The Rise, Decline, and Fall of Big-Time Football at Chicago* (Chicago: U. Illinois Press, 1995): 35.

[4] Lester, *Stagg's University*: 22. After four decades at Chicago, Stagg coached the football **Tigers** (named in 1908 for orange and black colors) at the University of the Pacific (Stockton, Calif.) for fourteen years, then he spent five as an assistant to some guy named Amos Alonzo Stagg, Jr. of Susquehanna U.'s **Crusaders** (Selinsgrove, Pa.). He returned to the Sunrise Seaport to coach **Mustang** kickers at Stockton Junior College (now San Joaquin Delta College) from 1953 to 1960 before retiring. (He was 98.) Stagg's namesakes include the Division III championship game, the Big Ten football trophy, a prestigious coaching award, and campus football fields at Chicago, Pacific, and Susquehanna. Stagg is credited with inventing tackling dummies, cleats, uniform numbers, and a bunch of now-standard trick plays, and he's in the College Football Hall of Fame. His track team at Chicago earned him a coaching spot on the 1900 Olympic team. The New York **Giants** tried and failed to sign him as a pitcher out of Yale. And—*oh yeah*—Stagg is also a *basketball* Hall of Famer. In earlier days at Springfield, Stagg saw James Naismith's indoor sport that would keep occupied his "group of bored and often rowdy future YMCA […] instructors and administrators." (Peter C. Bjarkman, *The Biographical History of Basketball* [Chicago: NTC/Contemporary, 2000]: 5.) It was Stagg who trimmed Naismith's nine-on-nine game to five-man sides and brought high school's national tournament to Chicago. There's no acknowledged link between Stagg and the BAA/NBA Chicago **Stags** (1946–50). As far as is admitted, they referred to adult male deer, but one couldn't ignore Mr. Stagg's impact on Chicago's sports scene in the first half of the century.

[5] You can also get molten steel by melting scrap in an electric arc furnace. Niles, Ohio—in the Steel Valley—hosts the Mahoning Valley **Scrappers** (est. 1999). Barely south is Youngstown, where the Carnegie Steel Ohio Works sponsored minor league baseball's successful Youngstown **Ohio Works** (1901–06), followed in that sport by Youngstown **Steelmen** (1910–15) and in minor league hockey by Youngstown **Steelhounds** (2005–08).

[6] Stephen Janick, "The Origins of the Drexel Dragon" (Drexel U. Libraries), http://archives.library.drexel.edu/dragon-origins (accessed 15 Oct. 2013).

[7] Like the **Pirates** and **Penguins**, the **Steelers** wear Pittsburgh's official black and gold colors. Pennsylvania's other men of steel included BAA Pittsburgh **Ironmen** (1946/47) and the Johnstown **Steal** (1995–97) of baseball's Frontier League.

Charles M. Schwab brokered Carnegie's sale to Morgan before leaving U.S. Steel to run Bethlehem Steel in 1903. Bringing European workers to his plants, Schwab created an independent football team in 1914, Bethlehem **Steel** F.C. (Dominating the ASL of the 1920s, the **Steel** was alternately "Philadelphia **Field Club**," although another good side had the same name.) Bethlehem's was the largest factory in the Bethlehem-Allentown area, as indicated by A-Town's minor league baseball Lehigh Valley **IronPigs** (named in 2008). (Pig iron is an "intermediate material," having been through the Bessemer, but not yet processed into finished product.) The devil mascot of lacrosse's Pittsburgh **Crossfire** (2000, NLL) was clearly inspired by heat from the steel plants, but you wouldn't want to have been in the crossfire of the "monster cannons" cast at Fort Pitt Foundry late in the Civil War (some of the largest ever produced in North America), which also explains the ASL Pittsburgh **Cannons** (1972).

[8] Scott Fulk (IUN athletics coordinator) and Stephen G. McShane (IUN archivist), emails to the author, 25 Aug. and 5 Sep. 2008 (respectively).

[9] After success with basketball's Harlem **Globetrotters**, Abe Saperstein started the (1946-only) West Coast Negro Baseball League. His own Seattle **Steelheads** (named for Washington's state fish) were mostly **Globetrotters** trying to keep fit during the off-season.

[10] Past Carnegie Techsters were **Plaids**, **Scots**, or **Skibos**. (Mr. Carnegie had bought Scotland's Skibo Castle.) See a correspondence (7 June 1935) from Max Hannum (Tech's P.R. dir. and hoop coach) in George Earlie Shankle, *American Nicknames: Their Origin and Significance* (New York: H.W. Wilson, 1937): 95. Other **Tartans** are at Sinclair Community College (Dayton, Ohio), founded as a YMCA training school by Scottish-born David A. Sinclair.

[11] Thiel College Sports Info. Office, "Why Tomcats?" *Tomcat Gameday* (1 Sep. 2012): 25. T.C.'s **Tomcats** can be compared to the Anna Maria College **AMCats** (Paxton, Mass.).

[12] The International Pro Hockey League (1904–07) had three teams in Michigan's Upper Peninsula and one in Pittsburgh. Ontario's club in Sault Ste. Marie made it *International*.

[13] See Daniel S. Mason, "The International Hockey League and the Professionalization of Ice Hockey, 1904–1907." *Journal of Sport History*, volume 25 (1): 1–17.

[14] Several points 'Bama: [1] In Rudyard Kipling's famous 1892 poem "Tommy," the phrase "Thin Red Line of 'eroes" was a salute to unsung front-line infantrymen, a natural comparison to the linemen who gave Alabama its old "**Thin Red Line**" nickname. [2] The **Crimson Tide's** "Roll tide!" cheer is from the shanty "Roll, Alabama, Roll," celebrating the exploits of the Confederate commerce raider *CSS Alabama*. [3] A reporter called Alabama's undefeated footballers red elephants after they stomped opponents in 1930, so teams from Tuscaloosa are often represented by a tusked mascot, Big Al. (An alternate story says a Birmingham *trunk* company gave the **Tide** elephant-emblemed luggage that same season.) [4] Birmingham's rust colored soil owes to its hematite ore, making for a **Crimson**-not-*Brown* **Tide**.

[15] DeBartolo owned Pittsburgh's NHL **Penguins** from 1978 to '91 and the MISL **Spirit** (1978–86). During the USFL years, his son owned the San Francisco **49ers** in the competing NFL.

[16] Associated Press, "Stanford Vote Favors *Robber Barons* Tag," *Spokane Daily Chronicle* (5 Dec. 1975): 17.

[17] Christopher Jencks and David Riesman, *The Academic Revolution* (New York: Doubleday, 1968): 319.

Chapter 55 Notes

[1] Correspondence (19 June 1935) from D.O. Kemie (Western Union Coll.) in George Earlie Shankle, *American Nicknames: Their Origin and Significance* (New York: H.W. Wilson, 1937): 575.

[2] "Rams," *Cornell Football* (Mount Vernon, Iowa: Cornell Coll. Athletics, 2009): 7.

[3] The **Miners** won the 1966 NCAA championship, the first time an all-black starting five had done so. They're in the Hall of Fame under UTEP's old name, Texas Western University.

British Columbia has a long mining history. The town of Trail (on the Dewdney Trail to B.C.'s gold fields) became a processing center for zinc and lead in 1896. The smelting process produces clouds of sulfur and arsenic that aren't good for you, but it was all part of the job for the workers whose self-deprecating handle was adopted by the Trail **Smoke Eaters** (or "**Smokies**"), amateur hockey locals since the 1920s.

[4] The Lehigh Valley **Black Diamonds** were baseballers in the Atlantic League's inaugural 1998 season. They lost their field (Quakertown, Pa.) in the owner's 2000 bankruptcy, and they played through 2004 as a road team of Pennsylvania **Road Warriors**.

[5] Rod Beilby (Yuba Coll. athletic dir.), email to the author, 17 Jan. 2006.

[6] Barbara Kingsley-Wilson, "Forty-Niners nickname reflects early boom years of college," *Long Beach Press Telegram* (29 July 2014), http://www.presstelegram.com/opinion/2014 0729/forty-niners-nickname-reflects-early-boom-years-of-college-guest-commentary (accessed 4 Aug. 2014).

[7] In China dragons were associated with specific imperial houses and are not emblematic of any unified Chinese consciousness. The AFL Iowa **Barnstormers** (1995–2000) were bought by New York **Islanders** owner Charles B. Wang and moved to Long Island's Nassau Coliseum in 2001 as New York **Dragons**. As a boy, Wang's family moved from Shanghai to Flushing, Queens, which claims to have the largest Chinatown in the U.S. outside San Francisco. Unlike Frisco's MLL **Dragons**, the symbol for the software zillionaire's indoor footballers was a Chinese dragon. (New York's **Dragons** and the AFL folded in 2008, but the Wang-owned New York **Islanders** retain the Sparky the Dragon mascot.)

We don't know what a *sound tiger* is, but Wang's AHLers on Long Island Sound are the Bridgeport **Sound Tigers**—not the Bridgeport Sound **Tigers**—a tiger being Asia's apex predator. Likewise, the **Lions** at Estrella Mountain Community College (Avondale, Ariz.) are near the Sierra Estrella range, but they're Estrella Mountain **Lions** instead of **Mountain Lions**.

[8] Heather Lawton and Peggy Roske (UGF archivists), emails to the author, 18 Jan. 2005 and 15 Sep. 2008 (respectively). Montana's western valleys do have gold and silver mines to support UGF's claim to **Argonauts** (often "**Argos**"). Miners went there after the Bozeman Trail hooked up with the Oregon Trail in east-central Wyoming in 1862.

[9] Quality teams in other sports were often sponsored Greater Toronto scullers. The **Parkdale Canoe Club** lost to U. Toronto in rugby football's first Grey Cup final in 1909. The Toronto **Rowing Association** lost the 1915 cup to the Hamilton **Tigers** (which had absorbed **Parkdale** in 1914). Team **Balmy Beach** represented T.O.'s Balmy Beach Canoe Club (Grey Cup champs in 1927 and 1930). Hockey's Toronto Canoe Club **Paddlers** won the 1920 Memorial Cup, and the Winnipeg **Rowing Club** challenged for the 1904 Stanley Cup.

[10] The ABA Denver **Rockets** became **Nuggets** in 1974 and joined the NBA in '76. Different Denver **Nuggets** had won three national AAU titles (1937, '39, and '42), and more **Nuggets** played the 1948/49 NBL season and then the first BAA/NBA season. Typical of the AAU, the oldest **Nuggets** had alternately represented their sponsors as **Safeway-Piggly Wigglys/Pigs** (1935–38), **American Legion** (1941–44), and **Ambrose Jelly Makers** (1945/46).

[11] Denver boomed as the fifty-niners' business center, but "no significant gold finds have been uncovered in the immediate Denver vicinity," according to Howard N. Stone and Lucille Stone, *A Pictorial History of American Mining* (New York: Crown, 1970): 158.

[12] Perhaps Vancouver's **Millionaires** were named after the NHA's popular Renfrew **Millionaires**. See Michael Mckinley, *Hockey: A People's History* (Toronto: McClelland & Stewart, 2006): 65. (The **Millionaires** were maroon-and-white **Maroons** from 1922 to '26.)

[13] For millennia, agrarian people worked from sunup to sundown and didn't really care what time it was. Station-to-station shipping on the new railroads created a fascination with the correct time. The visionary behind twenty-four zones of "Standard Time" was Sanford Fleming, the Scottish-born chief engineer and surveyor for the Canadian Pacific. He also designed the three-penny beaver (Canada's first postage stamp and the rodent's introduction as a national symbol), was chancellor at Queen's University, and—most importantly—fiddled around with early inline skates. He was knighted for his various achievements in 1897, making Sir Sanford the eponym of both Fleming College and its **Knights** (Peterborough, Ont.).

[14] The Bighorn and Little Bighorn Rivers of Wyoming and Montana are named for the bighorn sheep subspecies (*Ovis canadensis auduboni*) of the Rocky Mountain foothills. Little Big Horn College in Crow Agency, Montana (capital of the Crow Nation) has unsheepish **Rams** and **Lady Rams** on the Little Big Horn's bank. Basketball has had several minor league Reno **Bighorns** (1978/79, 1982/83, 2008–). Camosun College (Victoria, B.C.) has **Chargers**, but their mascot is a charging thinhorn sheep (*Ovus dalli*), the bighorn's Vancouver Island cousin.

Chapter 56 Notes

[1] OSU officialized "**Buckeyes**" in 1950, but it had been in use for decades. Long-lost baseballers in Columbus were the NA's **Buckeyes** (1883–84). Cincinnati **Buckeyes** were the Queen City's first organized amateurs (1859–70), and the black majors saw **Buckeyes** in Columbus (1921), Cincinnati (1942), and Cleveland (1943–49).

[2] Neither **Forest City** was prefixed by a municipality. "Cleveland **Forest Cities**" and "Rockford **Forest Cities**" are inventions of later indexers. Rockford pitcher Albert Spalding handed Washington's **Nationals** their lone defeat of their 1867 Midwest tour, but his side folded after the NA's inaugural 1871 season. Cleveland's **Forest City** lasted through '72, but the sylvan theme reappeared with the IHL Cleveland **Lumberjacks** (1992–2001). Early-twentieth-century newspapers invented tales about Great Lakes lumberjack Paul Bunyan, so Michigan's **Wolverines** and Michigan State's **Spartans** play for football's Paul Bunyan Trophy while Wisconsin's **Badgers** battle Minnesota's **Golden Gophers** for Paul Bunyan's Axe.

[3] Marlboro Coll. oral history from Bill Horridge (class of '51), recorded by Emily Alling (lib. dir.) and communicated to the author, 10 Sept. 2013. Marlburians argue about which campus tree is on the institutional mark, but we're assured there was no specific model.

Chapter 57 Notes

[1] Eric Proctor, "Captain Cane: Another Mascot Memory?" *University of Tulsa Collegian* (11 Feb. 2003): 3. Formerly the Presbyterian School for Indian Girls, U. Tulsa may have taken its orange and black from Princeton's **Tigers**. It became Henry Kendall College in 1894, after the first general secretary of the Presbyterians' Home Missions Board. So pre–**Golden Hurricane** teams were **Presbyterians**, **Kendallites**, or **Orange and Black**.

[2] From the very beginning, the '**Canes**' wading bird mascot has been an American white ibis (*Eudocimus albus*), the last creature to seek shelter before a hurricane and the first to reappear after. His name, Sebastian, is from the U's former San Sebastian dorm.

[3] Before going coed in 1986, Lake Erie College's female athletes were **Unicorns** because of their famous equestrian center. (Fanciful unicorns have long been depicted as white horses with long horns that could be subdued only by a virgin woman.)

Taking a short trot to Lake Erie's southern shore, you can see clear across to Canada on those occasions when atmospheric refraction creates a lake-effect mirage. Enough people have done so to explain the Erie [Pa.] **Illusion**, pro female footballers since 2003.

[4] Until 1988, the Confederation College **Thunderhawks** were the **67s**, commemorating the college's 1967 founding and the centennial of the British North America Act (which created a Canada that was politically independent from England). A similarly evolved team was senior hockey's Durham **72's**, who started on the hundredth anniversary of Durham's founding in

1972, but became **Thundercats** in 1988. Team names from calendar years seem particularly Canadian. Former USL soccer players were Vancouver [B.C.] **86ers/Eighty Sixers** (1986–2000), remembering the team's founding in 1986 and their city's in 1886. In 2001 the **86ers** assumed the name of the NASL Vancouver **Whitecaps** (1974–84) because their city is between the Pacific's breaking waves and the white-capped peaks of the North Shore Mountains.

[5] UHM's athletic director told Honolulu TV station KGMB in 2000 that "**Rainbow**" had been dropped from some teams after athletes voiced discomfort with that symbol of gay and lesbian groups (who equate coexistent colors with tolerance). Institutional spokespersons quickly spun that to say the only concern had been one of potential brand confusion.

Chapter 58 Notes

[1] The All Alaska Sweepstakes was revived in 1983, but by then it was overshadowed. Another race that had first been run over a 1,000-mile course in 1973 had begun as a twenty-seven-mile sprint in February 1967 to celebrate the centennial of the Alaska Purchase. That inaugural event was called the Iditarod Trail Seppala Memorial Race because the famous driver had died just the month before at age 90. Through Seppala's association with that race, many folks think the Iditarod commemorates the Nenana-to-Nome serum run, but most of the Great Race of Mercy in 1925 had been run way north of the Iditarod's Seward-to-Nome route.

[2] Gay Salisbury and Laney Salisbury, *The Cruelest Miles: The Heroic Story of Dogs and Men in a Race Against an Epidemic* (New York: W.W. Norton, 2003): 252.

[3] Tom McGuire, ed., *Bloomsburg Football* (2011): 3. The Byrd story is the one repeated at Bloomsburg, but it's contradicted (at least ignored) by former athletic director E.H. Nelson, whose correspondence (20 Nov. 1935) says "**Huskies**" owes simply to a teacher who owned sled dogs and loaned one as mascot. See George Earlie Shankle, *American Nicknames: Their Origin and Significance* (New York: H.W. Wilson, 1937): 501. (Bloomsburg's husky is named Roongo, for colors of maroon and gold.)

[4] USask leads research in radiology and atomic physics. In 1961 it got a linear accelerator, which makes sub-atomic particles go wicked fast (for undoubtedly noble purposes). Down the street from USask were indoor soccer's Saskatoon **Accelerators** (2007–10).

[5] NIU was once a normal school that backed **Teachers** or **Profs** then red-shirted **Cardinals**. Early in his long stint as athletic director (1929–54), Chick Evans managed **Evansmen** before serving on the committee that replaced them with **Huskies** in 1940.

[6] References to Puget Sound's climate include *King* County's Seattle **Reign** (as in "rain," 1996–98 ABL and 2013-founded NWSL), the North Seattle College **Storm**, and the WNBA Seattle **Storm** (whose mascot—Doppler—refers to a storm-tracking radar).

UW's pup mascot is Dubs, from the "Dub" shorthand for the *W* in school call letters. (For example, George Washington U. is commonly "G-Dub.") UW's Tacoma campus has its own Hendrix Husky mascot, named for Seattle-born guitar god Jimi.

Despite a location and climate that made UW's **Sun Dodgers** appropriate, a new Yakima arena was called the SunDome when it opened in 1990 with basketball tenants called Yakima **Sun Kings**. They were purchased by the Yakama Nation in 2005 and respelled as *Yakama* **Sun Kings** to reflect the native pronunciation. A few miles from the Yakama Reservation is Yakima Valley Community College. After fifty years as **Indians**, athletes became **Yaks** in 1998.

[7] Jacque Cottrell (HBU athletic media relations dir.), email to the author, 28 March 2005.

[8] Refer to the extensive etymology for *penguin* by Katrin Their, "Of Picts and Penguins: Celtic Languages in the New Edition of the *Oxford English Dictionary*," which appears in Hildegard L.C. Tristam, ed., *The Celtic Languages in Contact* (Potsdam U. Press, 2007): 254–257.

Chapter 59 Notes

[1] Players had often received game-to-game pay, but the **Stockings** were the first to be openly

contracted for a season. It's hard to imagine that the Washington **Nationals** recently past were anything but salaried; they just weren't up front about it. The 1867 **Nats** were the first team to tour west of the Alleghenies. They were sort of on the federal dime, seeing as the good players were Treasury Department employees without any apparent duties. See Benjamin G. Rader, *Baseball: A History of America's Game* (Urbana: U. Illinois Press, 1992): 27.

[2] The **Orioles'** Harry Vonderhorst was the *Son* in Baltimore's Vonderhorst & Son brewery; St. Louis salooner Chris Von Der Ahe owned the **Browns**; Billy Sharsig was the theater agent with brewery interests who ran Philly's **Athletics**; the Kent Malting Company had hooks in the Louisville **Eclipse**. See James Quirk and Rodney D. Fort, *Pay Dirt: The Business of Professional Team Sports* (Princeton, N.J.: Princeton U. Press, 1992): 304.

[3] NLers from Worcester, Massachusetts (1880–82) are listed as **Ruby Legs, Brown Stockings, Brownies**, or even **No-Names**. But Bill Ballou tells us they were only **Worcesters** in local press accounts from that era (email to the author, 24 Jan. 2012). Bill would know, having spent three decades researching and covering sports for the *Worcester Telegram & Gazette*.

[4] Peter Golenbock, *Wrigleyville* (New York: St. Martin's Press, 1996): 80, 99. "Orphans" was often applied to abandoned players. Other baseball teams in the 1945 AAGBL refused to pay travel expenses to play the poor-drawing Minneapolis **Millerettes**, so the Minnesotans finished their only season as road "**Orphans.**" See Barbara Gregorich, *Women at Play: The Story of Women in Baseball* (Orlando: Harcourt Brace, 1993): 111.

[5] John P. Rossi says increased patriotism after the Spanish-American War moved Ban Johnson to rename his Western League "the American League, switching his focus to a national one." See Rossi, *The National Game* (Chicago: Ivan R. Dee, 2000): 60.

[6] The 1899–1901 **Orphans/Cubs** were also **Spuds**, but some Chicagoans wanted a name that was "indicative of 'bear-like strength and a playful disposition.'" The idea may originally have come from Charles Sensabaugh, editor of the *Chicago Daily News*. During the 1900 season Sensabaugh was writing a headline into which neither **Orphans** nor **Spuds** would fit. He substituted **Cubs**" [emphasis added], according to Golenbock, *Wrigleyville*, 99.

[7] New England's Puritans didn't work on the Sabbath, so Saturday's bean supper stayed on the dying coals throughout Sunday, making Boston "Beantown." Baseball historian Bill Nowlin says Boston's early baseballers were never **Pilgrims, Plymouth Rocks, Puritans**, or **Beaneaters**. Despite those names appearing in loads of otherwise well-vetted accounts, Nowlin's exhaustive examination of news stories reveals only casual usage. The **Americans'** other nicknames included "**Somersets**" (owner Charles Somers) and "**Collinsmen**" (manager Jimmy Collins), while the **Nationals** could be offhand "**Doves** or "**Rustlers**" when owned by the Dovey brothers (1907–10) or William H. Russell (1911). See Nowlin, "The Boston **Pilgrims** Never Existed," *The National Pastime*, no. 23 (Cleveland: Soc. for American Baseball Research, 2003): 71–76. Also see Glenn Stout and Richard A. Johnson, *Red Sox Century* (Boston: Houghton Mifflin, 2004): 14. That Boston's boys were never **Pilgrims** is ironic because the Puritans of 1620 weren't even "Pilgrims" until a similarly perfunctory remark from William Bradford's account of Plymouth Plantation was given undue emphasis by historians and churchmen two centuries later. There are, however, Boston **Pilgrims** on other shores; Boston United F.C.—the "**Pilgrims**"—represent England's Lincolnshire, a Puritan stronghold in which a few of the most influential Mayflower passengers had family roots.

[8] The founder of Nyack College was Albert B. Simpson, a Canadian-born evangelist with a global vision. In fact, his namesake bible school was founded in 1921 at Seattle to train missionaries for China. It moved to California, first to San Francisco in 1955 and then to Redding in 1989, where teams were **Vanguards**. In 2004, Simpson U.'s red-white-and-black athletes became **Red Hawks**.

[9] On Quebec Province's western edge, the city of Val-d'Or (valley of gold) popped up in the 1920s. Since 1993 the town has hosted junior hockey's Val-d'Or *Foreurs* (drillers).

[10] Jonathan Greenan (UO communications officer of sports services), email to the author, 2 Feb. 2004. "Gee-gee" is British childspeak for a fast horse (from the command "Gee!" … "Go!"), so the **Gee-Gee's** mascot is an equine.

[11] In 1924 the independent **Maroons** joined the new Anthracite League, a challenge circuit in northeastern Pennsylvania mining towns in which a need to move anthracite coal spurred a steam engine history that justifies the 2013-named Scranton/Wilkes-Barre **Railriders**.

[12] "The Doane College Logo," *Doane Magazine* (spring 2006): inside front cover.

[13] "What is a Maroon," *Roanoke Softball* (2008): 21. In 2009 the **Maroons** were joined by a "maroon-tailed"—as opposed to red-tailed—hawk named Rooney.

Chapter 60 Notes

[1] K.C.'s team in the new-for-2013 NWSL also received a standard Euro-moniker: **F. C. Kansas City**. As for **Sporting**, they'd been the Kansas City **Wiz** (1996) and **Wizards** (1997–2010). *The Wonderful Wizard of Oz* (L. Frank Baum's book about a Kansas farmgirl's dream) was a sensation after its 1900 publication, as were stage and screen versions. Hockey's Topeka **Scarecrows** (1999–2003) were Kansas minor leaguers named for one Yellow Brick Roadie.

[2] A 2006 promotional and marketing agreement between **Real** Salt Lake and **Real** Madrid retroactively legitimized the MLS squad's name. The next year, the MLS's other Rocky Mountain club, the Colorado **Rapids**, partnered with London's famous Arsenal F.C. (the **Gunners**), a side composed of workers from the Royal Armory in 1866.

[3] The stripes (*rayas*) on *Chivas* jerseys were copied from F.C. Bruges, the favorite side of their Belgian-born founder.

[4] Edith Lesley founded her all-female normal school in 1909. She returned from Germany in 1930 with a lantern-wielding elf statue that would be the mascot for teams sometimes called **Elves**, replaced by alliterative **Lynx** in a 1990 student vote. (Lesley went coed in 2005.)

Chapter 61 Notes

[1] Late-century Pittsburgh **Alleghenies** represented Allegheny City on the north side of the Allegheny-Monongahela confluence. It became part of Pittsburgh in 1907. A.C.'s PL **Burgers** put a German spin on "Metropolitans." Many German arrivals put -*burgh* and -*burg* settlements all over North America. When an 1891 federal report standardized those spellings, the city lost its *h*. "Pittsburgers" cried out and got their silent letter back in 1911. The burg's NHL **Penguins** have a mascot named Iceburgh (not Iceberg).

The Allegheny **Athletic Association** (est. 1890) was Pittsburgh's first semi-pro football side then the first fully pro gridiron team anywhere for a two-game season in 1896, beating both the **D.C.A.C.** (Duquesne Country and Athletic Club) and Pittsburgh **A.C.** (run by the baseball **Pirates**' owner Barney Dreyfuss). See "The Cradle of Professionalism," a chapter in Robert W. Peterson's *Pigskin: The Early Years of Pro Football* (New York: Oxford U. Press, 1997).

[2] Ray Schmidt, "The Elmhurst Bluejays," *College Football Historical Society Newsletter* (2005 vol. XVIII, no. IV): 14.

Chapter 62 Notes

[1] Newton Heath F.C. became Manchester **United** Football Club in 1902. This was no blending of independents; the new owners just preferred "**United**." (Newcastle **United**, on the other hand, did result from the 1892 confederation of Newcastle's **East End** and **West End** sides.) At the same time, Manchester swapped green and gold for red and white, which in the 1960s resulted in the "official" name that's rarely used: **Red Devils**. Fans of pro rugby's Salford **Reds** or **Red Devils** (est. 1873) in Manchester's Salford borough accuse Man U of having stolen their colors and name, occasionally calling theirs the *Original* Red Devils.

[2] We concede that *O* and *A* on the 1901 American League uniforms in Baltimore and Philadelphia stood for "**Orioles**" and "**Athletics**." (The *P* worn by the **A's** NL neighbors could suggest

either "Philadelphia" or "**Phillies**.") You can view year-by-year MLB uniforms at "Dressed to the Nines," posted online by baseball's Hall of Fame (baseballhall.org) and based on Marc Okkonen's book *Baseball Uniforms of the 20th Century* (New York: Sterling, 1991).

[3] D&E's *Senator* newspaper first appeared in 1922, but strong teams under Coach Cam Henderson were **Scarlet Hurricanes** the next year. Jennings Randolph, the athletic director who'd hired Henderson, was elected to the U.S. Senate in 1932, three years before D&E jocks became **Senators**, making Mr. Randolph an unnamed co-inspirator for the nick.

[4] Bob Stoner (LU asst. AD for sports media), email to the author, 17 July 2012.

Chapter 63 Notes

[1] See Barbara Gregorich, *Women at Play: The Story of Women in Baseball* (Orlando: Harcourt Brace, 1993): 4, 5, 12.

[2] The few words in "Title IX" didn't explicitly address sports: "No person in the United States shall, on the basis of sex, be excluded from participation in, be denied the benefits of, or be subjected to discrimination under any education program or activity receiving federal financial assistance," but athletic participation is the bill's most publicly visible face.

[3] Jason Brennan (Hood sports info. dir.), email to the author, 19 May 2005. See Alison Walker and Bridgette Harwood, "History of Hood Athletics," *Hood Magazine* (winter, 2004/05): 16.

[4] Nina Lentini, "Sands of Time Obscure Origin of CC Camels," *Source*, 22 Nov. 1999: 4. Also see Peggy Ford and Catherine Adams Phinizy, "How Did the Camel Become the School Mascot?" www.conncoll.edu/athletics/camels (accessed 9 Aug. 2010).

[5] *Winthrop University: Treasures & Traditions* (Rock Hill, S.C.: WU Office of Alumni Relations 2004): 11.

[6] A correspondence (23 Nov. 1935) from Dr. Duke confirms the "**Schoolma'ams**" name in George Earlie Shankle, *American Nicknames: Their Origin and Significance* (New York: H.W. Wilson, 1955): 502.

[7] D. Stanley Eitzen, *Fair and Foul: Beyond the Myths and Paradoxes of Sport* (Lanham, Md.: Rowan & Littlefield, 2009): 52.

[8] Michael Leo Donovan, *The Name Game: Football, Baseball, Hockey & Basketball: How Your Favorite Sports Teams Were Named* (Whitby, Ont.: McGraw-Hill Ryerson, 1997): 176. Don't confuse Saint Mary's College or St. Mary's U. with the University of Saint Mary (Leavenworth, Kan.), where the bell tower atop Saint Mary Hall inspires **Spires**.

[9] "Women Rule!" *The Calvin Spark* (summer 2002), www.calvin.edu/publications/spark/ summer02/women (accessed 5 April 2010). The Preston **Rivulettes** dominated women's ice hockey in the decade before World War II. (Preston was brought into Ontario's new city of Cambridge in 1973.) In this case, *rivulet* already means "small stream," but the name was further diminished by the -*ette* convention.

[10] Barbara Gregorich says the first pro female baseballers were **Blonds** and **Brunettes**, established at Springfield, Illinois in 1876. They played poorly as barnstormers, but by the 1880s "the public had tired of [the] farce." See Gregorich, *Women at Play*: 4. The same source (p. 53) lists the hairstyle-inspired name of the Philadelphia **Bobbies**. The short "bob" cut for women was popular during the years they played (1922–31).

[11] Archival searches reveal past instances of Florida A&M **Rattlerettes**, South Dakota Tech **(Hard) Rockerettes**, University of Science and Arts of Oklahoma **Droverettes**, and North Carolina A&T **Aggiettes**. The bucket-shooting women that corresponded to the Seton Hall **Pirates** were **Bucettes** (1973–85), from *buccaneers*. See "Celebrating 150 Years: Pirate Pride Begins," *Seton Hall Magazine* (winter 2006).

[12] Without the modifier "giant," *panda* refers only to the red, or "lesser," panda (*Ailuridae fulgens*), which is indeed a raccoon relative. Therefore, **Pandas** that are represented by black-

and-white mascots that are not prefixed with "Giant" are taxonomically in error.

[13] The Pioneer Valley is named for the coastal Puritans who went there for better farmland in the mid-1600s. The USL's (male) Western Mass **Pioneers** play in the valley. Their **Lady Pioneers** draw fans and talent from Smith and the area's other women's colleges.

Another female academy, Vassar College, championed sports. A decade of intramural play resulted in the first organized women's baseball team, the 1876 Vassar **Resolutes**. That was already a fairly popular moniker for nineteenth-century ballclubs as indicated by two squads in Boston—one black and one white—both of whom were **Resolute**. The white team had to change its name after losing an 1870 game against the like-named neighbors, having resolved that the winners would remain **Resolutes**. (See Michael E. Lomax, *Black Baseball Entrepreneurs* [Syracuse: Syracuse U. Press, 2003]: 29 and George B. Kirsch, *Baseball in Blue and Gray* [Princeton, N.J.: Princeton U. Press, 2003]: 127.)

Even ignoring the **Resolutes**, other adjectives were popular early nicknames. The 1867 NA season saw multiple instances each of **Active**, **Alert**, and **Athletic** clubs … adjectives all, and we didn't even get to *B* yet. (For hundreds of NA teams and records, see Marshall D. Wright, *The National Association of Base Ball Players* [Jefferson, N.C.: McFarland, 2000].) Some historians suggest that these urgent adjectives (along with derived nouns like "**Excelsior**" and "**Quicksteps**") might have been from fire companies that often fielded teams. Those who argue that Cincinnati's **Bengals** are the only pros with an adjective for a moniker are ignoring plenty of **Athletics**, **Browns**, **Colonials**, or **Xtreme**; once players are **Royals** or **Nationals**, those words are nouns even if their previous history is exclusively that of an adjective.

[14] Pamela Grundy and Susan Shackelford, *Shattering the Glass: The Dazzling History of Women's Basketball* (New York: New Press, 2005): 74.

[15] For most of the 1930s, perennial ATA tennis champion Ora Washington was a **Tribune**. Their rivals were often Chicago's **Roamer Girls** (or "**Roamers**" or "**Roma**"), assembled in 1921 by track star and *Chicago Bee* sports editor Sol Butler. The **Roamers** were also led by a multiple-year winner of the ATA tennis singles title, Isadore Channels (a graduate of Wendell Phillips High, as were many Harlem **Globetrotters**). The **Roamers**' gym was at the Grace Presbyterian Church's Roamer Athletic Club. See www.blackfives.org (Claude Johnson, ed.), a great resource for black hoop history. See also, Bijan C. Bayne, *Sky Kings: Black Pioneers of Professional Basketball* (New York: Franklin Watts, 1997): 24.

[16] Doyle's players were originally Cassville **Red Heads**, taking the "All American" prefix after picking up a couple of AAU All Americans. They had some famous players (including Hazel Walker) and were so popular that Olson often had spin-off teams traveling simultaneously as **Famous Red Heads** or Ozark **Hillbillies**.

[17] In a way, the AAGPL mirrored a wartime society in which women transitioned to jobs vacated by men. The embodiment of this new archetype was "Rosie the Riveter," celebrated in a 1942 Kay Kyser song and subsequently in famous paintings by Norman Rockwell and J. Howard Miller. A women's pro football team in Kenosha secured themselves to Rosie's legacy as Wisconsin **Riveters** (2002). Nashville's Vultee Aircraft employed more women than any other plant during the war. Workers built the Vengeance dive bomber and played for the Vultee Aircraft **Bomberettes**, dominating AAU competition in the late war years.

[18] Casey Miller, *The Handbook of Nonsexist Writing* (New York: Harper & Row, 1988): 72.

[19] The NBA **Hornets** went to New Orleans in 2002 and left the WNBA **Sting** in Charlotte. The **Sting** were absorbed by the new Charlotte **Bobcats** in 2003 and folded after 2006.

[20] Unmoored from their **Laker** partners by name, the Los Angeles **Sparks** hoped that "sparks would fly" in the new league. (See Kelly Whiteside, *WNBA: A Celebration* [New York: HarperHorizon, 1998]: 61.) The other charter WNBA franchises not named in tandem were the Cleveland **Rockers-Cavaliers** and the New York **Liberty-Knicks**. An ABA (II) team tried to steal the spotlight from the NBA's **Suns** as the Phoenix **Eclipse**, but no one looks at an eclipse

and they faded to black after one season (2001/02). You might think the ABA Utah **Stars** saluted the clear night sky over Utah prairies, but they were the relocated Los Angeles **Stars** (1968–70), a name from Hollywood actors later used in the 2000/01 ABA season. Also referring to greater L.A.'s movie industry were Hollywood **Stars** in baseball's Pacific Coast League (1926–35, 1938–57) and another (1936–38) in the California Pro Football League. The PCL **Stars** were co-owned by folks like Gracie Allen, Gary Cooper, Cecil B. DeMille, Barbara Stanwyck, Bing Crosby, and Gene Autry (the cowboy star who'd later own the California **Angels**), a celebrity salad fronted by Brown Derby restaurateur Bob Cobb. Soccer *stars* play for the MLS Los Angeles **Galaxy** (est. 1995). Universal Studios sponsored the AAU Hollywood **Universals**, who won hoop's first official Olympic gold medal in 1936.

[21] Of the lower forty-eight, only Minnesota still has native timber wolves. It also has the NBA Minnesota **Timberwolves** and the Oak Hills Christian College **Wolfpack** (Bemidji).

[22] The WNBA's women weren't the first associated with local men through wordplay. A buck is a vigorous adult male deer or antelope; a doe is the corresponding female of same. So the NBA Milwaukee **Bucks** (est. 1968) shared an arena with WBL Milwaukee **Does** (1978–80).

[23] Jason Behenna (Centenary's asst. sports info. dir.), email to the author, 1 Dec. 2003. It's not known if Centenary's past **Ironsides** owe anything to the Confederate ironclad warships and subs that were built or based at Shreveport's Red River docks during the Civil War.

Don't confuse Centenary College of Louisiana with Centenary College "of New Jersey" (Hackettstown); the latter's **Cyclones** are alliterative only.

[24] Edgar Rice Burroughs wrote twenty-plus popular *Tarzan* novels after 1912. Students at U. Arkansas–Fort Smith elected to have **Lions** in the late 1920s. Their maned mascot is *Numa*, which means "male lion" only in Burroughsian ape-speak.

[25] Pomona College athletes are former **Huns**. A much-repeated story says a newspaper headline accidentally printed "**Hens**," effecting a quick evolution to "**Sagehens**." That would be a convenient mistake because it occurred during the Great War with Germany. The demonization of Germans as "Huns" was their own doing. In the Boxer Rebellion of 1900, the Kaiser told his troops to instill the same kind of fear in Chinese nationalists that the Huns of old had spread across Europe.

Chapter 64 Notes

[1] Plentiful bears—and streams, mountains, forests, and other wildlife—give Arkansas another nickname, "The Natural State." The Texas League's Northwest Arkansas **Naturals** in Springdale were the Wichita **Wranglers** through 2007. TriStar's 1984 baseball movie *The Natural* associates "natural" with the national pastime. In fact, some scenes were shot on the diamond of the Buffalo **Bisons,** then the property of the **Naturals**' future owner.

[2] A movie that's not bad inspired different hockey pros. Universal's *Slap Shot* (1977) was about minor league Charlestown **Chiefs** in a fictional Pennsylvania steel town. The foulmouthed **Chiefs** were send-ups of the real (equally alliterative) Johnstown **Jets** (1950–77). Indeed, some real **Jets** played movie characters similar to themselves.

When Johnstown got a new team in 1988, fans voted to make them **Chiefs**. In 2010 they moved near South Carolina's auto plants as Greenville **Road Warriors**. New-for-2012 juniors were expected to use one of Johnstown's former monikers, but "**Chiefs**" remained a trademark of the **Road Warriors**, and by then their league had other **Jets** in Wisconsin (the 2009-named Janesville **Jets**). They settled for "Johnstown **Tomahawks**" and an Indian chief emblem.

[3] Brian Burnes, Dan Viets, and Robert W. Butler, *Walt Disney's Missouri* (Kansas City: Kansas City Star Books, 2002): 162.

[4] Mike Wojciechowski (Milwaukee **Admirals** v.p. of business development), email to the author, 8 Jan. 2004. The **Admirals** joined the IHL (1977–2001) then the AHL.

[5] Sandra and Susan Steen, *Take It to the Hoop: 100 Years of Women's Basketball* (Brookfield,

Conn.: Twenty-First Century Books, 2003): 59–60. See also Pamela Grundy and Susan Shackelford, *Shattering the Glass: The Dazzling History of Women's Basketball* (New York: New Press, 2005): 96. (The Hutchersons still provide airline service to Wayland Baptist's **Queens**.)

The **Flying Queens** of the 1950s scored 131 consecutive victories, the most ever for a college team, including wins against AAU squads. The streak was ended by the women with the most consecutive AAU crowns, Nashville Business College. The **"Nabucos"** won all national titles from 1962 to '69, but it wasn't a "college team"; NBC simply sponsored them, as evinced by **Nabuco** center Nera White, who was an AAU All American *fifteen* times. (Grundy and Shackelford, 101.) NBC came to dominance after beating Texas's Galveston **ANICOS** (backed by the American National Insurance Co.) in the 1940 AAU tournament.

[6] Valerie Stephenson (Dawson athletic dept.), email to the author, 15 Oct. 2004. The Montreal **Jazz** entered the new National Basketball League of Canada in 2012, saluting summer's *Festival International de Jazz de Montréal* (est. 1967).

[7] Andrew Zimbalist, *Baseball and Billions* (New York: Basic Books, 1992): 33. See also James Quirk and Rodney Fort, *Pay Dirt: The Business of Professional Team Sports* (Princeton, N.J.: Princeton U. Press, 1992): 408. David B. Biesel asserts that U. Toronto's **Varsity Blues** opposed Labatt's initial name for Toronto's expansion club: **Blues**. (Biesel, *Can You Name That Team?* [Lanham, Md.: Scarecrow, 2002]: 67.) In fact, UT, the CFL **Argonauts**, and NHL **Maple Leafs** were wearing the blue from the city flag long before the **Blue Jays** arrived.

[8] For beating American Bill Tilden in a 1927 Davis Cup match, Frenchman René Lacoste got a crocodile-skin suitcase from his coach. Lacoste—thereafter *le Crocodile*—won seven Grand Slam singles titles but is better known for contributions to fashion. He eschewed traditional long-sleeved tennis attire to favor polo shirts. Embroidered crocs appeared on his shirts in 1930, which was probably the first time a designer emblem became its own fashion statement.

[9] Ryan Eigenbrode (NDMU asst. athletic dir.), email to the author, 23 June 2005.

[10] Deborah Reardon (PMC ref. lib.), email to the author, 4 Aug. 2010.

Chapter 65 Notes

[1] Huntington U., "I Am the Forester: Meet Norm," www.huntington.edu/norm-the-forester (accessed 2 Jan. 2014).

[2] Many of Dayton's aeronautically themed teams never got off the ground. The city usually had an ad hoc squad in Chicago's World Professional Basketball Tournament in the war years, including the 1943 Dayton **Dive Bombers** (who eliminated the defending Harlem **Globetrotters**) and the '44 Dayton **Aviators**. Indoor football's new Dayton **Warbirds** didn't complete their 2005 schedule, and the WHA Dayton **Aeros** never took the ice at all, moving to Texas where the space industry made them *Houston* **Aeros** (1972–78). Minor league hockey's Dayton **Jets** (1985–87) and **Bombers** (1991–2010) were relative dynasties.

[3] Drew Brown (Mercy's assoc. athletic dir.) and Kevin T. McGinniss (Mercy's former athletic dir.), respective emails to the author, 15 May 2007 and 25 Dec. 2008.

[4] Paterson's team owed something to **Whirlwinds** of earlier decades who *blew* through on barnstorming tours. New York's **Whirlwinds** (one of the mostly Jewish powerhouses of the post–World War I era) were set up by Madison Square Garden's Tex Rickard to compete against the **Original Celtics**. Boston **Whirlwinds** (1925/26 ABL) later served as the Harlem **Globetrotters'** traveling opponents.

[5] Boeing has a long history of bomber production. The favorite romantic models were the B-17, B-29, and B-52. **Bombers** (along with **Flyers** and **Jets**) are recurring minor league and school teams near Seattle.

[6] Heat and flies verified that this was just the place to play indoors. In fact, greater Houston's independent baseball Sugar Land **Skeeters** [2012–] go by the colloquial name for mosquitoes.

Independent baseball's Lubbock **Crickets** (1995–1998) were named not for Texas insects but for locally born bandmates of Lubbock native Buddy Holly. No Crickets were aboard when the 22-year-old Holly and fellow rock-and-roll pioneers Ritchie Valens and J.P. "Big Bopper" Richardson died when their small plane crashed in February 1959.

Chapter 66 Notes

[1] Roy Blount Jr., "Everyone is Helpless and in Awe," *Sports Illustrated* (17 June 1974): 73–74.

[2] See Larry Massie, "Wolverines in Michigan," *The Chronicle & Newsletter* (spring 2004). Also see David Runk (Associated Press), "Michigan Wolverine Sighting First in Two Centuries," *Lawrence Journal-World*, 26 Feb. 2004: 10A.

[3] Whichever etymology you believe, Michiganians were called land-hungry wolverines by Ohioans from at least the time of the Toledo War (1835–36). That was a hot-tempered but battleless row over the "Toledo Strip," a slice of northernmost (modern) Ohio that the Northwest Ordinance of 1787 had inadvertently left up for grabs.

[4] Going 7-2-1 in their only season, the **Wolverines** own the NFL's highest all-time winning percentage. New York **Giants** owner Tim Mara bought Detroit's **Wolverines** just to fold them and make Benny Friedman a **Giant**, thereby enabling "the drawing appeal of a Jewish football star in New York," according to James Quirk and Rodney Fort, *Pay Dirt: The Business of Professional Team Sports* (Princeton, N.J.: Princeton U. Press, 1992): 35.

[5] UMD's **Terrapins** have a mascot named Testudo, who's named for the turtle superfamily *Testudinidae* to which the diamondback belongs. Until 1933 the former Maryland Agricultural College fielded **Aggies**, **Farmers**, or **Old Liners**. The last owes to George Washington, who'd called his combined Maryland, Pennsylvania, and Delaware regiments his reliable "old line" after the 1776 Battle of Long Island. Maryland officers in the post-war era reapplied the compliment to their own brave troops, effecting the "Old Line State." See Ryan Polk, "The Origin of the Old Line State," (Annapolis: Maryland State Archives, 2005): http://aomol.msa.maryland.gov/html/oldline.html (accessed 5 Aug. 2014).

[6] **Gator**-isms: [1] UF's alligator mascots are Albert and Alberta, after Dr. Albert Murphree, the influential UF president when "**Gators**" was adopted in 1911. [2] In the mid-1960s, UF developed Gatorade to hydrate footballers. [3] Also in Gainesville—"Gator Nation"—is Gainesville Raceway, which hosts spring's Gatornationals, a premier drag racing event. [4] The NASL Miami **Gatos** (1972) were Spanish "cats," only one letter removed from **Gators**.

[7] Kevin M. McCarthy, *Alligator Tales* (Sarasota: Pineapple Press, 1998): 167. Don't confuse SJC's **Gators** with the club-level **Gators** at U. Houston–Downtown (twenty miles away). There are no **Alligators** in major sports, while **Gators** abound. Students at Allegheny College (Meadville, Pa.) published a 1925 humor magazine called the *Allegheny Alligator*, "purely and simply because of the 99.44% alliterative value." (See Bill Salyer, ed., *Allegheny College Softball Media Guide* [2008]: 8.) AC teams were soon **Gators**, having previously been **Methodists**, **Hilltoppers**, and **Blue and Gold**. Even earlier teams were **Timothians** and **Sons of Timothy** after school founder Rev. Timothy Alden. (See Jonathan E. Helmreich, *Eternal Hope: The Life of Timothy Alden, Jr.* [Cranbury, N.J.: Cornwall Books, 2001]: 227.) San Francisco State U. fielded **Golden Gaters** after 1931, being five miles from the famous bridge. A vowel swap made them **Golden Gators** in the 1940s, now just **Gators**. (San Francisco **Golden Gaters** played in the WTT from [1974–78] without reptilian mascots.)

Double-A Norwich **Navigators** (1995–2005) indicated proximity to both the Connecticut coast and U.S. Coast Guard Academy. Their mascot (Gator) was a reptile. The **Navigators** were later Connecticut **Defenders** (2006–09), celebrating ship- and sub-building along that coast. In fact, the *Seawolf* class of subs built or based thereabouts gave names to Arena Football's New England **Sea Wolves** (1999–2001, Hartford) and the AHL's Hartford **Wolfpack** (1997–2010). The '**Pack** had been the NHL Hartford **Whalers'** farm club (as Binghamton **Whalers**) from 1980 to '90. The **Whalers'** former owner returned in a marketing capacity in the midst of the 2010/11 season and made them the Connecticut **Whale**, but they were back to the **Wolf Pack** (two words) for the 2013/14 season.

   The first bilingual college in the U.S., Hostos Community College, educated Hispanics in the Bronx after 1970. Its **Caimans** refer to the smallish cousin in the alligatorid crocodilian subfamily *Caimaninae*, found in Central and South America.

[8]   *This is Graceland: 2004 Football* (Lamoni, Iowa: Graceland U., 2004): 83.

[9]   Cathy Kuehner (SU public relations asst.), email to the author, 9 Oct. 2003.

Chapter 67 Notes

[1]   Bill Burk (JCC athletic dir.), email to the author, 28 Nov. 2003.

[2]   Jacksonville U., "About JU: Timeline," www.ju.edu/aboutju/Pages/Timeline.aspx (accessed 3 Jan. 2013).

Chapter 68 Notes

[1]   BU's terrier is *Rhett* because scarlet is the school color and Rhett Butler was the love interest of Scarlet O'Hara in Margaret Mitchell's novel *Gone With the Wind*. "**Terriers**" was adopted in 1922, which BU calls Rhett's birth year, but Mitchell's book wasn't published until 1936.

   Being crossbred from bull terriers and English bulldogs, Bostons are sometimes "olde Boston bulldogges," explaining the 1929 NFL Boston **Bulldogs**. Boston's 1974 WFL **Bulldogs** became **Bulls**. ("Boston bull" is yet another term for the bulldog, but this team had bovine symbols.) Then—before the season even started—they were New York **Stars**. Without a stable stadium deal, they were Charlotte (N.C.) **Hornets** by mid-season.

   As for "olde Boston bulldogge," post-colonial Bostonians are in on the joke as far as painfully self-aware Old English-isms go. Fans from coast to coast are self-declared citizens of **Red Sox** Nation, but a more local term describes the Olde Towne Team. As Puritans set out for the New England frontiers, they continued to call Boston the "old town." The rules of the Massachusetts Game (the New England version of baseball that was eventually absorbed by New York's Knickerbocker rules) were derived from an even earlier game called town-ball, so an old-timey Boston club would in fact have been a *town* team.

[2]   Some sources say Wofford owes its **Terriers** to a Boston that ran from the stands to interfere with an opposing baserunner in 1909. That's contradicted by Henry N. Snyder, the longtime school president (1902–42) whose correspondence (20 Nov. 1935) reports that no backstory is known for the nickname dating to 1915. See George Earlie Shankle, *American Nicknames: Their Origin and Significance* (New York: H.W. Wilson, 1937): 516. Wofford publications did present vague dog mascots before 1915.

[3]   David Gansell (SFC sports info. dir.), email to the author, 21 May 2010.

Chapter 69 Notes

[1]   Augusta State U. Alumni Assn., "Why the Jaguars," http://www.aug.edu/public_relations/April02/col3.html (accessed 10 Dec. 2012).

[2]   See Diana Perrer, "IUPUI Hopes New Mascot Snares Some Attention," *Indianapolis Star*, 27 Aug. 1998, quoted by Ralph D. Gray, *IUPUI: The Making of an Urban University* (Bloomington: Indiana U. Press, 2003): 195.

[3]   Charles J. Schuttrow, *Saint Joseph's College 1965 Football Brochure* (Rensselaer, Ind.: St. Joseph's Coll., 1965): 3. Schuttrow says the **Cardinals** are former **Reps**, as in SJC *representatives*. (Clark Teuscher [SJC sports info. dir.], assisting email to the author, 14 Feb. 2005.)

[4]   George B. Goodrich, ed., *The Centennial History of the Town of Dryden* (Dryden, N.Y.: Dryden Herald Steam Printing House, 1898): 38.

[5]   Those are just the four-years. At least six California community colleges keep **Cougars**: Lassen Coll. (Susanville), Los Angeles Southwest Coll., Coll. of Alameda, Cuesta Coll., Coll.

of the Canyons (Santa Clarita), and Taft Coll.

[6] The Carolina **Panthers** followed the ABA Carolina **Cougars** (1969–74). They had home arenas in four North Carolina cities (Charlotte, Greensboro, Raleigh, and Winston-Salem).

[7] Ben Lewellyn and Peter Starr, *Panthers on the Gridiron* (Birmingham: Birmingham-Southern Coll., 2007) as excerpted in BSC's *'Southern* magazine (summer 2007): 33. As for Spring Hill College, no one can explain its **Badgers**. Fires and hurricanes have badgered the building at SHC's Mobile campus that keeps such records. Over the Mississippi line at Rust College, a 1940 fire destroyed the admin building and wiped out records that might have explained the Holly Springs school's **Bearcats**. And don't confuse Rust's **Bearcats** with the **Bears** from Shaw University (Raleigh, N.C.), even though Rust was also a "Shaw University" until the name changed in 1915, possibly to avoid confusion with Raleigh's Shaw. (Those HBCUs with **Bears** and **Bearcats** have different eponymous Mr. Shaws.)

[8] Don Horine, "PBCC Adopts Dreher Park Panther as Mascot," *Palm Beach Post*, 30 Dec. 1990: 5B. The PBCC **Pacers** were named in 1965 for the pacer horses that winter at nearby Pompano Park. "**Rebels**" was dropped when the institution integrated in 1965. See Ernestine Williams, "PBCC Considers Change of Pacers," *Palm Beach Post*, 18 Nov. 1989: 1B. (Patricia Alvarez [PBSC lib.], assisting email to the author, 9 June 2010.)

Chapter 70 Notes

[1] The arrival of the new **Jets** pushed the AHL Manitoba **Moose** to Newfoundland as St. John's **IceCaps**, but their Mick E. Moose mascot stayed behind with the pros.

[2] Sticklers for timelines should note that the **Orioles** (I) spent some of 1890 in a minor league after a conflict with the AA. They rejoined in mid-season, replacing Brooklyn's **Gladiators** (for whom no naming backstory survives).

[3] The **Oriole's** "Iron Man"—Cal Ripken, Jr.—appeared in 2,632 straight games and was later an owner of the Aberdeen [Md.] **IronBirds** (2002–), whose jet fighter insignia references the Aberdeen Proving Ground. The **I-Birds** followed the Atlantic League's military-themed Aberdeen **Arsenal** (2000), and there are junior hockey Aberdeen **Wings** (est. 2010).

[4] Karen Zoller (NDC's Fritzsche Library dir.), email to the author, 2 Feb. 2005. Coincidentally, the city had arbitrarily named minor league hockey Cleveland **Falcons** from 1934 to '37.

[5] Up the coast from Oxnard were the Santa Barbara **Condors**, who didn't finish their only ASL season (1977). Perpetual world champion contenders in the sport of ultimate have been catching updrafts with flying discs as Santa Barbara **Condors** since the mid-1970s. Southern California's Chumash people put condors into art and legend, believing the all-white bird got charred black after flying too near a campfire. With overcrowded Chumash villages on the Channel Islands, the earth goddess Hutash crafted a rainbow bridge to the mainland. Hutash turned the Chumash who fell to the sea into dolphins, making those creatures revered brothers and sisters. After California State University–Channel Islands (Camarillo) opened in 2002, administrators granted the wish of Chumash descendents to take up a dolphin mascot. Tight budgets have resulted in no sporting **Dolphins** for now, but CSUCI is an hour upcoast from senior rubgy's Santa Monica **Dolphins**.

[6] "Athletics: Mascot and Colors," *College of DuPage Catalog 2007–2009*: 59. Even though Metro State's **Roadrunners** are not as downtown as they used to be, they share the Auraria campus with the teamless Community College of Denver, which maintains the *metro-* theme through a CityHawk mascot.

[7] Tracey Reavis, "The Nicknames," in Jan Hubbard, ed., *The Official NBA Encyclopedia, Third Edition* (New York: Doubleday, 2000): 97.

[8] Deborah Noland, *The Legacy of Plywood U: A History of State Fair Community College* (Sedalia, Mo.: State Fair Comm. Coll., 2002): 49.

[9] David J. Elrod, "Superbird: Coach Ottinger & His Roadrunners," *Dalton State Magazine*

(spring 2010): 16.

[10] Matthew Molzan, ed., "The Chanticleer and the English Department," *The Word* (spring 2008): 7. We don't know why Coastal Carolinians were **Trojans** until 1963, but one wonders if the two-year school in the University of South Carolina system had simply appropriated the identity from the University of Southern California—a different USC.

[11] David Kingsley, ed., "120 Years of Trinity Football," *Trinity Football Program/Media Guide* (Elmont, N.Y.: University Sports Publications, 2006): 42.

[12] U. Delaware's colors are from the blue-and-gold flag of Sweden (whose national soccer team is *Blågult*, "blue-gold"). The first permanent white settlement in today's Delaware was Fort Christina (now Wilmington) in the New Sweden colony. "**Blue Hens**" could have been advanced by the blue-and-gold football uniforms that appeared in 1889. The blue hen chicken became the state bird in 1939, and UD's fowl mascot is YoUDee.

Chapter 71 Notes

[1] *Futball's* NPSL-USL San Jose **Frogs** F.C. (2006–08) were owned by Hartmut Esslinger of Frog Design, who gave iconic style to the 1981 Macintosh computer from a legendary Silicon Valley firm, Apple. The MLS San Jose **Clash** (1995–99) had a meaningless name, but they did have a cybernetic scorpion that was in line with the area's tech industry. The **Clash** became San Jose **Earthquakes** in 2000, with a new emblem from the California shop of designer Terry Smith. Smith's cool trademarks already included emblems for the San Jose **CyberRays** and Long Beach **Stingrays** and the tech-sounding San Jose **Lasers** (1996–98) of the women's ABL, but he's most famous for the original San Jose **Shark**.

[2] Jim Austin (Landmark Coll. athletic dir.), email to the author, 10 Feb. 2005.

[3] Pat Mrozowski (Brescia U. athletic dir.), email to the author, 24 Aug. 2010.

[4] "Northwest Traditions: Bearcats," *2010–2011 Student Handbook* (Northwest Missouri State U.): 17. Another state normal, Missouri State U., had already hosted **Bears** for a decade when NMSU adopted "**Bearcats**."

[5] "The Drury Student-Athlete Tradition," *Drury Magazine* (winter 2001), reproduced at www. drury.edu/multinl/story.cfm?ID=1667&NLID=125 (accessed 1 Jan. 2014).

[6] There's been no brown in the **Bruins**' black-and-gold uniforms since 1937, which—owing to both etymology and franchise history—is kind of weird. **Bruins** owner Charles Adams was also the majority partner in baseball's Boston **Braves** from 1935 to 1941. He died in '47, but the **Bruins**-affiliated AHLers were Boston **Braves** (1971–74) in remembrance.

Boston's "Hub of the Universe" nickname is from Oliver Wendell Holmes's 1858 remark about attitudes within the state house: "the hub of the solar system." So stop wondering why a *B* on a spoked wheel represents **Bruins** in the "Hub of Hockey."

Chapter 72 Notes

[1] Some places are particularly prone to alliterative appellations. The Massachusetts capital has seen NL Boston **Braves** (1912–52), NHL **Bruins** (est. 1924), AFL **Bulldogs** (1926), NFL **Bulldogs** (1929), ASL **Bears** (1931–32), AHL **Braves** (1971–74), WFL **Bulls** (1974), NLL **Bolts** (1975), USFL **Breakers** (1983), MISL **Blazers** (1992–97), USL **Bulldogs** (1999–2001), WUSA **Breakers** (2001–03), WPS/WPSL/NWSL **Breakers** (est. 2009), and NLL **Blazers** (2009–11). The NL **Braves** were even **Bees** from 1936 to 1940 and "Bs" remains local shorthand for "**Bruins**." Philadelphia fans have followed the **Fury** (NASL, 1978–80), **Phantoms** (AHL, 1996–2009), **Phillies** (NL), **Flyers** (NHL), **Freedom** (WTT), and **Fusion** (ABA, 2005).

Four-year schools with nicks owing mostly to alliteration (otherwise absent herein) include **Bruins** at Bellevue [Neb.] U. and Bob Jones U. (Greenville, S.C.), **Cougars** at Caldwell [N.J.] U. and Cleary U. (Howell, Mich.), **Grizzlies** at Georgia Gwinnett Coll., **Gophers** at Goucher Coll. (Baltimore), **Lightning** at Lehman Coll. (New York), **Mavericks** at Medaille Coll.

(Buffalo, N.Y.), **Pirates** at Park U. (Parkville, Mo.), **Raiders** at Rivier U. (Nashua, N.H.), **Sharks** at Simmons Coll. (Boston), **Stars** at Stephens Coll. (Columbia, Mo.), **Terriers** at Thomas Coll. (Waterville, Maine), **Warriors** at Webber International U. (Babson Park, Fla.), and **Wildcats** of Wilmington U. (New Castle, Del.). Alliterative **Panthers** represent U. of Prince Edward Island (Charlottetown), Principia Coll. (Elsah, Ill.), and SUNY Purchase.

Falcons is a popular *F*-word among collegians. Find **Falcons** at Fanshawe Coll. (London, Ont.), Fisher Coll. (Boston), Fitchburg [Mass.] State U., Florida Coll. (Temple Terrace), Folsom Lake Coll. (Folsom, Calif.), and Friends U. (Kan.). There are **Fighting Falcons** at Fairmont [W.Va.] State U. and **Golden Falcons** at Felician Coll. (Lodi, N.J.). A consonant digraph (*ph-*) supports alliteration for Pfeiffer U.'s **Falcons** (Misenheimer, N.C.).

Also susceptible to alliteration are **Griffins** at Gwynedd Mercy [Pa.] U. and Grossmont Coll. (El Cajon, Calif.). The AHL has Grand Rapids **Griffins** (est. 1996), and classically spelled **Gryphons** represent Ontario's U. of Guelph. Find **Hawks** at Harper Coll. (Palatine, Ill.), Hartwick Coll. (Oneonta, N.Y.), Hilbert Coll. (Hamburg, N.Y.), Holy Names U. (Oakland, Calif.), Humber Coll. (Toronto), Hunter Coll. (New York City), Huntingdon Coll. (Montgomery, Ala.) and Howard Coll. (Big Spring, Texas, which once had female **Hawk Queens**). The University of Hartford's alliterative **Hawks** date to 1947, when it was still Hillyer College.

[2]   Beloit Coll., "Buccaneers Is New Title of Beloit Teams," *Round Table* (4 March 1949): 1. (Fred Burwell [BC archives], assisting email to the author, 29 Jan. 2005.)

[3]   Communication (26 Nov. 1935) from Paul W. Star (Concordia athletic dir.) in George Earlie Shankle, *American Nicknames: Their Origin and Significance* (New York: H.W. Wilson, 1937): 128.

[4]   James Jolly (Coker Coll. marketing/communications dir.), email to the author, 31 Jan. 2005.

[5]   Virginia Intermont College athletes in Bristol became **Cobras** in the late 1970s because one athlete could shape her forearm into a snake, instilling passion in teammates. (See "Milestones," *Intermont* [winter 2009]: 19.) In Intermont's pre-**Cobras** era, we could find only **Blue Problems** (as in problems for opponents) and **White Solutions** (who could "solve any problem"). Both date to 1935 and are reported with a straight face by someone identified only as Intermont's director of physical education. His or her communication (13 Nov. 1935) is cited in Shankle, *American Nicknames* (1937): 554.

[6]   Dean Coll., "Our History," https://www.dean.edu/about/OurHistory.cfm (accessed 7 Aug. 2013).

[7]   June Stephens, ed., "Cuesta Through the Years," *Cuesta College News*, spring 2009: 4.

[8]   Ron Smith, "Westmont Warrior Turns Sixty" (4 Sep. 2007), www.westmont.edu/_sports/static/mascot_history.html (accessed 2 Jan. 2011).

[9]   East coast kids at Tulsa's Oral Roberts University saw New York's **Titans** become **Jets** and voted in 1965 to assign the former title to their Christian athletes. In 1993, ORU's navy-and-gold **Titans** became **Golden Eagles**. See "ORU Athletic Tradition," *Baseball Media Guide* (2009): 5. "New York **Titans**" was revived for an NLL side from 2007 to '09.

[10]   The latter **Jets** adopted the colors and roundel of the Royal Canadian Air Force because the Peg's huge air base provides command and control for global RCAF operations. (The emblem mirrored the uniforms of Ottawa's **RCAF Flyers**, a successful hockey squad of military men in the 1940s.) The **Jets-Coyotes** and **Thrashers-Jets** are different franchises.

Chapter 73 Notes

[1]   Walter O'Malley bought the PCL Los Angeles **Angels** from Chicago **Cubs** owner Philip Wrigley in 1957 to get his **Dodgers** the territorial rights to L.A. When the **Dodgers** arrived in 1958, the legendary PCL **Angels** moved up to Washington State as Spokane **Indians**.

[2]   Refer also to baseball's Southern Maryland **Blue Crabs** (est. 2008). Atlantic blue crabs are in estuaries from New England to Brazil and therefore plentiful along the Jersey coast, as

evinced by baseball's 2001-named Lakewood **BlueClaws**.

[3] Donald M. Fiser, "Lester Harrison and the Rochester Royals," in Steven A. Riess, ed., *Sports and the American Jew* (Syracuse: Syracuse U. Press, 1998): 211. The Rochesterians were co-sponsored by the Eber Brothers brewery. They were **Seagrams** for a while, but newspapers were reluctant to run liquor ads, so they evolved into **Seagrams-Ebers**, **Ebers**, then **Royals**. See Robert W. Peterson, *Cages to Jump Shots* (New York: Oxford U. Press, 1990): 138.

[4] Cincinnati was a bustling Ohio River port and pork processing center on the back side of the Appalachians. Its "Queen City" nickname might have fallen by the wayside if Henry Wadsworth Longfellow hadn't written "Catawba Wine" in 1854, a poem that praised a bottle from the "Queen of the West." Thanks to Longfellow, Cincy history is dotted with **Monarchs**, **Kings**, and **Royals**. The same poem describes the city thus: "So this crystal hive/Is all alive/With a swarming and buzzing and humming." From there, we can demystify the Queen City's assonant Cincinnati **Stingers** (WHA, 1975–79) and their queen bee symbol.

In 1845 a Cincinnati paper called Dayton the "gem" of Ohio's interior, giving the Gem City several Dayton **Gems** in minor league hockey (1964–77, 1979/80, 2009–12).

[5] Ignoring the costly method of lead casting, defect-free buckshot is made at shot towers. Dropped from on high, molten lead forms spheres in free fall and splashes down in a pool to cool and harden into quality shot. Baltimore's 234-foot Phoenix Shot Tower was the tallest masonry building in the U.S. after 1828. In 1881, D.C.'s Washington Monument passed it on the way to 555 feet. It opened in 1885, one year after the UA Baltimore **Monumentals** (1884) reminded Washingtonians that the nation's first Washington Monument had been finished at Baltimore in 1829. (Both Washington Monuments were by architect Robert Mills.)

[6] The MAAA-sponsored **Winged Wheelers** won the first Stanley Cup challenge in 1893, with more in '94 and '95. **Winged Wheelers** (1881–1935) also occupy the early history of the CFL's (first) Montreal **Alouettes**. James Norris and sons Bruce and James (who brought the Chicago **Blackhawks** to the family portfolio in 1952) are all Hall of Fame "builders."

[7] James Quirk and Rodney Fort, *Pay Dirt: The Business of Professional Team Sports* (Princeton, N.J.: Princeton U. Press, 1992): 37.

[8] Leonard Koppett, *24 Seconds to Shoot: An Informal History of the National Basketball Association* (New York: Macmillan, 1968): 18. The **Red Wings'** farm club was the Kalamazoo **Wings** (1974–95). They joined the Minnesota **North Stars** organization as Michigan **K-Wings** (1995–2000). The BAA evolved into the very successful NBA, and one Norris son took an expansionist view of pro leagues. Bruce Norris's idea to put NHL-caliber hockey in European arenas never caught on, but his London **Lions** (1973/74) barnstormed Europe wearing a winged lion emblem that associated them with the **Red Wings**. Bruce then started the first pro LAX league, the 1968-only National Lacrosse Association, in which his Detroit **Olympics** (named for the family's Olympia) were a key franchise. (Minor league hockey's Detroit **Olympics** had already used the Olympia from 1927 to 1936.)

[9] Gloria Averbuch (marketing/communications dir., Sky Blue Soccer, Somerset, N.J.), email to the author, 25 Feb. 2010.

[10] Hampshire Coll. Archives, "The Hampshire College Frog," https://www.hampshire.edu/library/the-hampshire-college-frog (accessed 5 Aug. 2014)

[11] Communication (20 Nov. 1935) from W.J. Griffith (Salem Coll. publicity dir.) in George Earlie Shankle, *American Nicknames: Their Origin and Significance* (New York: H.W. Wilson, 1937): 465.

[12] The remaining *home* games for the 1952 **Texans** were at Hershey, Pennsylvania and Akron, Ohio. (Whether the Dallas **Texans** represented a new franchise or one that inherited the New York **Yanks'** charter isn't clear.)

About the Author

Glenn Pierce is a career technical and freelance writer with respective degrees in English and journalism from the University of Massachusetts Amherst (**Minutemen**, **Minutewomen**) and Northern Essex Community College (**Knights**). He lives near Boston without a wife or children or dogs or cats or any of that business (although he likes dogs very much). Owing to ambitious tennis and rollerhockey schedules, this is his first book.